This book deals with international law in Antarctica and the Arctic. It reviews how each region is managed by the individual legal regimes, and how the specific international laws developed to deal with unique polar conditions have contributed to the development of international law. It considers relevant aspects of the international law of the sea, international environmental law, and resource management law as applied in the polar regions. Consideration is also given to how international relations regime theory provides a framework for understanding the development of the polar legal regimes, and how polar international relations will impact on future legal developments. The conclusion assesses the impact of the polar regions upon the development of international law.

The polar regions and the development of international law

CAMBRIDGE STUDIES IN INTERNATIONAL AND COMPARATIVE LAW

This series (established in 1946 by Professors Gutteridge, Hersch Lauterpacht and McNair) is a forum for studies of high quality in the fields of public and private international law and comparative law. Although these are distinct legal sub-disciplines, developments since 1946 confirm their interrelationship.

Comparative law is increasingly used as a tool in the making of law at national, regional and international levels. Private international law is increasingly affected by international conventions, and the issues faced by classical conflicts rules are increasingly dealt with by substantive harmonisation of law under international auspices. Mixed international arbitrations, especially those involving state economic activity, raise mixed questions of public and private international law. In many fields (such as the protection of human rights and democratic standards, investment guarantees and international criminal law) international and national systems interact. National constitutional arrangements relating to 'foreign affairs' and to the implementation of international norms are a focus of attention.

Professor Sir Robert Jennings edited the series from 1981. Following his retirement as General Editor, an editorial board has been created and Cambridge University Press has recommitted itself to the series, affirming its broad scope.

The Board welcomes works of a theoretical or interdisciplinary character, and those focusing on new approaches to international or comparative law or conflicts of law. Studies of particular institutions or problems are equally welcome, as are translations of the best work published in other languages.

The polar regions and the development of international law

Donald R. Rothwell
University of Sydney

CAMBRIDGE
UNIVERSITY PRESS

Published by the Press Syndicate of the University of Cambridge
The Pitt Building, Trumpington Street, Cambridge CB2 1RP
40 West 20th Street, New York, NY 10011-4211, USA
10 Stamford Road, Oakleigh, Melbourne 3166, Australia

First published 1996

Printed in Great Britain at the University Press, Cambridge

A catalogue record for this book is available from the British Library

Library of Congress cataloguing in publication data

Rothwell, Donald, 1959–
The polar regions and the development of international law
p. cm.
Includes bibliographical references and index.
ISBN 0 521 56182 5 (hc)
1. Polar regions – International status.
JX4084.P65R68 1996
341.2'9 – dc20 95–50952 CIP

ISBN 0 521 56182 5 hardback

VN

Contents

Figures

Tables

Preface

The polar regions have always occupied a unique place in international law. During early expeditions to the poles various territorial claims were made which raised difficulties for the application of traditional principles of territorial sovereignty. The adoption of the 1959 Antarctic Treaty sought to 'freeze' territorial sovereignty for the Treaty's duration. In the Arctic there have been continuing disputes over maritime boundaries and claims based on geographic sectors. More recently, both polar regions have been dominated by concerns over resource management and environmental protection. In Antarctica the debate over whether mining should take place resulted in the rejection of a negotiated Convention and its replacement with a Protocol to the Antarctic Treaty prohibiting mining and implementing new Antarctic environmental protection standards. The eight Arctic states have also recently entered into an arrangement to deal with existing and emerging environmental problems.

These examples demonstrate that general principles of international law and existing international law regimes have been considered inadequate for the polar regions and that instead states with interests in the region have developed their own responses to these legal issues. The polar regions may not in this regard seem any more different from other regions of the world where special legal regimes have been adopted. Discrete areas in need of international regulation have also been subject to international law regimes. What is different in the polar regions is their size compared to other regions, the unique problems they face, the interest of the whole international community in their management and resource potential, and the means that have been adopted to deal with management problems.

This work does not seek to undertake a comparative analysis of the legal regimes of the polar regions. While some comparison will be inevitable, the major goal will be to discuss how the legal regimes which exist in the polar regions deal with similar issues and in doing so make an important contribution to international law. Perhaps the most important contribution they make to an appreciation of international law is that they demonstrate the effectiveness of regional management of international problems. The Antarctic Treaty partly grew out of a recognition that traditional principles of state sovereignty were inappropriate and increasingly Arctic states are also coming to the same recognition. The polar regions therefore present interesting contrasts to other traditional management mechanisms which the international system has relied upon. As such the polar regions are important prototypes for regional management in a world which is increasingly becoming concerned about the effectiveness of global management regimes at all levels.

The work is divided into four parts. Part I reviews the international law and international relations framework in the polar regions (chapter 1) before assessing the environment and resources of the polar regions (chapter 2). Part II reviews the legal regimes in place in the two polar regions. In the case of Antarctica (chapters 3 and 4), attention is given to the Antarctic Treaty System and the legal mechanisms which have been adopted to deal with ongoing problems in Antarctic management which have emerged subsequently to the negotiation of the Antarctic Treaty. For the Arctic (chapters 5 and 6), the existing legal regime is reviewed, with emphasis placed upon various mechanisms adopted under the law of the sea. The developments towards a more integrated Arctic legal regime are also assessed with emphasis given to the Arctic Environmental Protection Strategy and proposals for an Arctic Council.

Part III is a consideration of four discrete areas in which the polar regions demonstrate their unique contributions to the development of international law. The law of the sea (chapter 7), management of resources (chapter 8), international environmental law (chapter 9) and international relations regime theory (chapter 10) have been selected for consideration. In each one of these areas, the polar regions have contributed to a greater understanding of certain international law issues and also demonstrated how they have contributed to certain aspects of international law. To ensure a balanced approach, only areas common to both polar regions have been selected. As a result, specific issues which only arise in one polar region and have no comparable application in the other are not addressed in this study. Accordingly, the right to self-determination of Arctic indigenous peoples is not considered as there is no equivalent issue in the Antarctic. An emphasis is also placed upon polar responses to management and resources issues rather than global mechanisms. The efforts of the International Whaling Commission to regulate whaling globally are therefore not considered in any detail.

Part IV concludes the work (chapter 11) with a consideration of the relationship between the polar regions and international law. It will be demonstrated that the polar regions have made a significant contribution to the development of international law. How international law has been applied, and the mechanisms which have been adopted to deal with management problems in the polar regions demonstrate the unique contributions which the polar regions have made to a greater understanding of how international law operates and its relationship with questions of international cooperation.

The law is stated at 1 January 1995.

Acknowledgments

In a work of this length it is impossible for the author to take all the credit. Numerous individuals and institutions have assisted in various ways and their contributions should be acknowledged. This work originally was created as a doctoral thesis at the University of Sydney, where I was privileged to be guided by two outstanding international lawyers. Professor James Crawford, then Dean of the University of Sydney and now of Jesus College, Cambridge, guided me throughout the writing of the whole thesis. He was always available for consultation, and despite the physical distances and considerable demands upon his own time, was always willing to discuss my progress and read drafts. In his current capacity as Editor of the Cambridge Studies in International and Comparative Law series, he has continued to have an active interest in this work. Professor Ivan Shearer, Challis Professor of International Law at the University of Sydney, became involved as a thesis supervisor upon taking up his position in 1993 and had the burden of reading the whole thesis while also seeing me through to completion and submission. I am much indebted to both these gentlemen who not only supervised my work, but also provided tremendous collegiate encouragement and support.

Thanks must go to a number of other individuals who also assisted in reading various chapters at different stages. Bill Bush, Nigel Bankes, Dr John Heap, Dr Richard Herr, Dr Jim Keeley and David VanderZwaag all assisted in this manner and their insightful comments on areas within their expertise were most helpful. Stuart Kaye collaborated with me on a number of independent works which assisted to formulate ideas on various aspects of this work, while Dr Sanjay Chaturvedi contributed through various interdisciplinary discussions on geopolitical and legal polar issues. The figures were prepared with the assistance of Peter Johnson, Cartographer, Department of Geography, University of Sydney. John Robertson acted as a research assistant during the final preparation of the book and his attention to detail was most appreciated.

Without library resources it would have been impossible to undertake much of this work. Principal thanks must go to Margaret McAleese and her staff at the Law Library, Faculty of Law, University of Sydney for providing a suitable home base. The staff at the Scott Polar Research Institute library (University of Cambridge) were also particularly helpful, with special thanks for the interest and support shown by William Mills, Shirley Sawtell and Bob Headland. In addition thanks must also go to the librarians and staff at the Canadian Circumpolar Institute (University of Alberta), Weir Memorial Law Library (University of Alberta) and the Canadian National Library and Archives (Ottawa).

I also received assistance from various government officials. Jean Page, Andrew Jackson and their colleagues at the Department of Foreign Affairs and Trade, Canberra, assisted by providing copies of difficult to obtain Antarctic Treaty documents and providing an update on Treaty developments. In Canada, various officials of the Department of External Affairs and the Department of Indian and Northern Affairs were helpful in providing copies of relevant documents and also making themselves available for personal interview. Thanks must also be extended to Professor Milton Freeman (University of Alberta), Dr Terry Fenge (Canadian Arctic Resources Committee), the Inuit Circumpolar Conference, Professor Donat Pharand (University of Ottawa) and Dr Ian Stirling (Canadian Wildlife Service) for providing difficult to obtain Arctic research materials.

Funding for travel during the writing of the thesis and this book was provided by the University of Sydney, Law Foundation of New South Wales Scholarship Support Fund, Australian Antarctic Foundation, and the Institute of Antarctic and Southern Ocean Studies. During these travels I was able to conduct research at a number of institutions. Thanks go to Dr John Heap, Scott Polar Research Institute, Cambridge, for sponsoring my visit as a Visiting Scholar, and Professor Tim Christian, Dean of the Faculty of Law, University of Alberta, for arranging my stay in Edmonton as a Visiting Professor. Thanks also must go to Mike Robinson (Arctic Institute of North America, University of Calgary) and Professor Don McRae (Faculty of Law, University of Ottawa) for hosting shorter visits. Appreciation is also extended to the staff at Cambridge University Press for their assistance in finalising the publication of this book.

A work of this magnitude could not have been completed without the support of my family. My parents, Paula and Bob, and Canadian family, Joan and George, provided great moral support and encouragement. Finally, Beth endured the whole process and read and commented on much of the work. Her constant support and companionship was essential to completing this project.

While I am indebted to all of the people and institutions noted above, this work remains my own product and I take all responsibility for errors and omissions.

Table of international and domestic arbitrations, cases and judgments

Table of conventions, treaties and other international instruments

1763 Definitive Treaty of Peace between France, Great Britain and Spain, done in Paris, 10 February 1763, 42 ConTS 279

1825 Convention between Great Britain and Russia concerning the Limits of their Respective Possessions on the North-West Coast of America and the Navigation of the Pacific Ocean, done in St Petersburg, 16 February 1825, 75 ConTS 95

1867 Convention ceding Alaska between Russia and the United States, done in Washington, 30 March 1867, in force 20 June 1867, 134 ConTS 331

1893 Exchange of Notes between Great Britain and Russia for the Protection of Russian Sealing Interests in the North Pacific during the Year 1893, done in St Petersburg on 12, 22 and 30 May 1893, 178 ConTS 451

1911 Treaty between Great Britain and the United States for the Protection of Fur Seals, done in Washington, 7 February 1911, in force 7 July 1911, 213 ConTS 73

Convention between Great Britain, Japan, Russia and the United States respecting Measures for the Preservation and Protection of Fur Seals in the North Pacific Ocean, done in Washington, 7 July 1911, in force 15 December 1911, 214 ConTS 80

1916 Convention between Great Britain and the United States for the Protection of Migratory Birds, done in Washington, 16 August 1916, in force 7 December 1916, 221 ConTS 408

1920 Treaty concerning the Archipelago of Spitsbergen, done in Paris, 9 February 1920, in force 14 August 1925, 2 LNTS 8

1942 USA–Canada Exchange of Notes constituting a Provisional Agreement relating to Fur Seals, done in Washington, 8 and 19 December 1942, in force 30 May 1944, 26 UNTS 363

1946 International Convention for the Regulation of Whaling, done in Washington, 2 December 1946, in force 10 November 1948, 161 UNTS 74

1953 Convention between the United States of America and Canada for the Preservation of the Halibut Fishery of the Northern Pacific Ocean and Bering Sea, done in Ottawa, 2 March 1953, in force 28 October 1953, 222 UNTS 77

1954 International Convention for the Prevention of Pollution of the Sea by Oil, done in London, 12 May 1954, in force 26 July 1958, 327 UNTS 3

1957 Interim Convention between the United States of America, Canada, Japan and Union of Soviet Socialist Republics on the Conservation of North Pacific Fur Seals, done in Washington, 9 February 1957, in force 14 October 1957, 314 UNTS 105

Agreement between the Royal Norwegian Government and the Government of the Union of the Soviet Socialist Republics concerning the Sea Frontier between Norway and the USSR in the Varangerfjord, done in Oslo, 15 February 1957, in force 24 April 1957, 312 UNTS 322

Agreement between the Government of Norway and the Government of the Union of Soviet Socialist Republics on Measures for Regulating the Catch and Conserving Stocks of Seals in the Northeastern Part of the Atlantic Ocean, done in Oslo, 22 November 1957, in force 27 June 1958, 309 UNTS 269

Descriptive Protocol relating to the Sea Frontier between Norway and the Union of the Soviet Socialist Republics in the Varangerfjord, demarcated in 1957, done in Moscow, 29 November 1957, in force 17 March 1958, 312 UNTS 326

1958 Convention on Fishing and Conservation of the Living Resources of the High Seas, done in Geneva, 29 April 1958, in force 20 March 1966, 559 UNTS 285

Convention on the Continental Shelf, done in Geneva, 29 April 1958, in force 10 June 1964, 499 UNTS 311

Convention on the High Seas, done in Geneva, 29 April 1958, in force 30 September 1962, 450 UNTS 82

Convention on the Territorial Sea and Contiguous Zone, done in Geneva, 29 April 1958, in force 10 September 1964, 516 UNTS 205

1959 The Antarctic Treaty, done in Washington, 1 December 1959, in force 23 June 1961, 402 UNTS 71

1963 Treaty Banning Nuclear Weapon Tests in the Atmosphere, in Outer Space and under Water, done in Moscow, 5 August 1963, in force 10 October 1963, 480 UNTS 43

Protocol Amending the Interim Convention between the USA, Canada, Japan and the USSR on the Conservation of North Pacific Fur Seals, 8 October 1963, in force 10 April 1964, 494 UNTS 303

1966 International Covenant on Civil and Political Rights, done in New York, 19 December 1966, in force 23 March 1976, 999 UNTS 171

1969 Vienna Convention on the Law of Treaties, done in Vienna, 23 May 1969, in force 27 January 1980, 1155 UNTS 331

Agreement extending the Interim Convention on the Conservation of North Pacific Fur Seals of 9 February 1957 , in force 3 September 1969, TIAS 6774

1971 Agreement between the Government of Canada and the Government of Norway on Sealing and Conservation of the Seal Stocks in the Northwest Atlantic, done in Ottawa, 15 July 1971, in force 22 December 1971, [1971] CTS 49

1972 Convention on the Conservation of Antarctic Seals, done in London, 1 June 1972, in force 11 March 1978, (1972) 11 ILM 251

Stockholm Declaration on the Human Environment, done in Stockholm, 16 June 1972, (1972) 11 ILM 1, 416

Convention Concerning the Protection of the World Cultural and Natural Heritage, done in Paris, 16 November 1972, in force 17 December 1975, 1037 UNTS 151

Convention for the Prevention of Marine Pollution by Dumping from Ships and Aircraft, done in Oslo, 15 February 1972, in force 7 April 1974, 932 UNTS 3

Convention on the Prevention of Marine Pollution by Dumping of Wastes and other Matter, done in London, Mexico City, Moscow and Washington, 29 December 1972, in force 30 August 1975, 1046 UNTS 120

1973 Convention on International Trade in Endangered Species of Wild Fauna and Flora, done in Washington, 3 March 1973, in force 1 July 1975, 993 UNTS 243

International Convention for the Prevention of Pollution from

Ships, done in London, 2 November 1973, in force 2 October 1983, (1973) 12 ILM 1,319, as amended by the 1978 Protocol, (1978) 17 ILM 546

Canada, Denmark, Norway, USSR – Agreement on the Conservation of Polar Bears, done in Oslo, 15 November 1973, in force 26 May 1976, (1974) 13 ILM 13

Agreement between the Government of Canada and the Government of the Kingdom of Denmark relating to the Delimitation of the Continental Shelf between Greenland and Canada, done in Ottawa, 17 December 1973, in force 13 March 1974, [1974] CTS 9

1974 Convention on the Protection of the Environment between Denmark, Finland, Norway and Sweden, done in Stockholm, 19 February 1974, in force 5 October 1976, 1092 UNTS 279

Convention for the Prevention of Marine Pollution from Land-Based Sources, done in Paris, 21 February 1974, in force 5 May 1978, (1974) 13 ILM 352

1975 Convention on Wetlands of International Importance Especially as Waterfowl Habitat, done in Ramsar, 2 February 1971, in force 21 December 1975, 996 UNTS 245

1976 Protocol Amending the Interim Convention between the United States of America, Canada, Japan, and Denmark on the Conservation of North Pacific Fur Seals of February 9, 1957, 7 May 1976, in force 12 October 1976, TIAS 8, 368

Agreement between the Government of the Kingdom of Norway and the Government of the Union of Soviet Socialist Republics on Mutual Fishing Relations, done in Moscow, 15 October 1976, reprinted in Robin Churchill, Myron Nordquist and S. Houston Lay (eds.) *New Directions in the Law of the Sea* (vol. V) (Dobbs Ferry, NY, 1977) 348

Convention on the Prohibition of Military or any other Hostile Use of Environmental Modification Techniques, done in New York, 22 December 1976, in force 5 October 1978, (1977) 16 ILM 88

1978 Agreement on an Interim Practical Agreement for Fishing in an Adjoining Area in the Barents Sea between Norway and the USSR, done on 11 January 1978, [1978] *Overenskomster med fremmede Stater* 436

Protocol of 1978 Relating to the International Convention for the Prevention of Pollution from Ships, done in London, 1

June 1978, (1978) 17 ILM 546

UNEP Principles of Conduct in the Field of the Environment for the Guidance of States in the Conservation and Harmonious Utilization of Natural Resources Shared by Two or More States, done in Nairobi, 19 May 1978, (1979) 17 ILM 1,097

1979 Convention on the Physical Protection of Nuclear Material, done in Vienna, 26 October 1979, in force 8 February 1987, (1979) 18 ILM 1,422

Convention on the Conservation of Migratory Species of Wild Animals, done in Bonn, 23 June 1979, in force 1 November 1983, (1980) 19 ILM 15

Convention on Long-Range Transboundary Air Pollution, done in Geneva, 13 November 1979, in force 16 March 1983, (1979) 18 ILM 1,442

1980 Convention on the Conservation of Antarctic Marine Living Resources, done in Canberra, 20 May 1980, in force 7 April 1982, (1980) 19 ILM 841

Protocol Amending the Interim Convention between the USA, Canada, Japan and the USSR on the Conservation of North Pacific Fur Seals, 14 October 1980, TIAS 10,020

Agreement between Iceland and Norway in Continental Shelf Area Between Iceland and Jan Mayen, 28 May 1980, (1982) 62 ILR 108

1982 United Nations Convention on the Law of the Sea, done in Montego Bay, Jamaica, 10 December 1982, in force 16 November 1994, (1982) 21 ILM 1,261

World Charter for Nature, UNGA Res. 37/7, adopted 9 November 1982, reprinted in (1983) 22 ILM 455

1983 Agreement Between the Government of Canada and the Government of the Kingdom of Denmark for Cooperation Relating to the Marine Environment, done in Copenhagen, 26 August 1983, in force same day, [1983] CTS 19

1984 Protocol to the 1979 Convention on Long-Range Transboundary Air Pollution on Long-Term Financing of the Cooperative Programme for Monitoring and Evaluation of the Long-Range Transmission of Air Pollutants in Europe (EMEP), done in Geneva, 28 September 1984, in force 24 January 1988, (1988) 27 ILM 701

1985 Vienna Convention for the Protection of the Ozone Layer, done in Vienna, 22 March 1985, in force 22 September 1988, (1987) 26 ILM 1,529

Protocol to the 1979 Convention on Long-Range Transboundary Air Pollution on the Reduction of Sulphur Emissions or their Transboundary Fluxes by at least 30 per cent, done at Helsinki, 8 July 1985, in force 2 September 1987, (1988) 27 ILM 707

1986 Convention on Assistance in the Case of a Nuclear Accident or Radiological Emergency, done in Vienna, 26 September 1986, in force 26 February 1987, (1986) 25 ILM 1,377

Convention on Early Notification of a Nuclear Accident, done in Vienna, 26 September 1986, in force 27 October 1986, (1986) 25 ILM 1,370

Protocol to the 1979 Convention on Long-Range Transboundary Air Pollution Concerning the Control of Emissions of Nitrogen Oxides or their Transboundary Fluxes, done at Sofia, 31 October 1986, in force 1 February 1991, (1989) 28 ILM 212

1987 Montreal Protocol on Substances that Deplete the Ozone Layer, done in Montreal, 16 September 1987, in force 1 January 1989, (1987) 26 ILM 1,541

Agreement Between the Government of Canada and the Government of the United States of America on the Conservation of the Porcupine Caribou Herd, done in Ottawa, 17 July 1987, in force same day, [1987] CTS 31

1988 Agreement between the Government of Canada and the Government of the United States of America on Arctic Cooperation, done in Ottawa, 11 January 1988, in force same day, [1988] CTS 29

Polar Bear Management in the Southern Beaufort Sea. An Agreement Between Inuvialuit Game Council, Inuvik, NWT, Canada and North Slope Borough Fish and Game Management Committee, Barrow, Alaska, USA, done on 29 January 1988 at Inuvik, NWT, Canada, reprinted in Ian Stirling, *Polar Bears* (Ann Arbor, 1988) 212.

Agreement between the Government of the United States of America and the Government of the Union of Soviet Socialist Republics on Mutual Fisheries Relations, done in Moscow, 31 May 1988, in force 28 October 1988, TIAS 11,442

Convention on the Regulation of Antarctic Mineral Resource

Activities, done in Wellington, 2 June 1988, not yet in force, (1988) 27 ILM 868

1989 Hague Declaration on the Environment, done in The Hague, 11 March 1989, (1989) 28 ILM 1,308

Basle Convention on the Control of Transboundary Movements of Hazardous Wastes and their Disposal, done at Basle, 22 March 1989, in force 5 May 1992, (1989) 28 ILM 657

Agreement between the Government of Canada and the Government of the Union of Soviet Socialist Republics on Cooperation in the Arctic and the North, done in Moscow, 20 November 1989, in force same day, [1989] CTS 21

1990 Agreement between the United States of America and the Union of Soviet Socialist Republics on the Maritime Boundary, done in Washington, 1 June 1990, (1990) 29 ILM 941

International Convention on Oil Pollution Preparedness, Response and Co-operation, done in London, 30 November 1990, not yet in force, (1991) 30 ILM 733

Bergen ECE Ministerial Declaration on Sustainable Development, done in Bergen, 15 May 1990, reprinted in Harold Hohmann (ed.), *Basic Documents in International Environmental Law* (Vol. I) (Graham & Trotman: London, 1992) 558

1991 Convention on Environmental Impact Assessment in a Transboundary Context, done in Espoo, 25 February 1991, not yet in force, (1991) 30 ILM 800

Arctic Environmental Protection Strategy, done in Rovaniemi, 14 June 1991, (1991) 30 ILM 1,624

Protocol on Environmental Protection to the Antarctic Treaty, done in Madrid, 4 October 1991, not yet in force, (1991) 30 ILM 1,455

Protocol to the 1979 Convention on Long-Range Transboundary Air Pollution Concerning the Control of Emissions of Volatile Organic Compounds or their Transboundary Fluxes, done in Geneva, 18 November 1991, not yet in force, (1992) 31 ILM 568

1992 Framework Convention on Climate Change, done at New York, 9 May 1992, in force 21 March 1994, (1992) 31 ILM 849

Convention on Biological Diversity, done at Rio de Janeiro, 5 June 1992, in force 29 December 1993, (1992) 31 ILM 818

The Rio Declaration on Environment and Development, done at Rio de Janeiro, 14 June 1992, (1992) 31 ILM 874

Agreement between the Government of Canada and the

Government of the Russian Federation on Cooperation in the Arctic and the North (with Annex), done in Ottawa, 19 June 1992, in force same day, [1992] CTS 18

Convention for the Protection of the Marine Environment of the North-East Atlantic, done in Paris, 22 September 1992, not yet in force, (1993) 32 ILM 1,069

1993 The Nuuk Declaration on Environment and Development in the Arctic, done in Nuuk, 16 September 1993

1994 Convention on the Conservation and Management of Pollock Resources in the Central Bering Sea Area, done in Washington, 16 June 1994, not yet in force, (1994) 34 ILM 67

Agreement Relating to the Implementation of Part XI of the United Nations Convention on the Law of the Sea of 10 December 1982, done in New York, 28 July 1994, (1994) 33 ILM 1,309

Protocol to the 1979 Convention on Long-Range Transboundary Air Pollution on Further Reduction of Sulphur Emissions, done in Oslo, 14 June 1994, (1994) 33 ILM 1,540

Abbreviations

AAT	Australian Antarctic Territory
AEPS	Arctic Environmental Protection Strategy
AJIL	American Journal of International Law
ASOLPO Paper	*Antarctic and Southern Ocean Law and Policy Occasional Paper*
ATCM	Antarctic Treaty Consultative Meeting
ATCP	Antarctic Treaty Consultative Party
ATS	Antarctic Treaty System
AYIL	Australian Yearbook of International Law
Bush	Bush, W. M. *Antarctica and International Law: A Collection of Inter-State Documents* (4 vols. and binder). Oceana: London. vol. I/II – 1982; vol. III/IV 1988; binder – 1990
BYIL	British Yearbook of International Law
CalWILJ	California Western International Law Journal
CanBR	Canadian Bar Review
Case WRJIL	Case Western Reserve Journal of International Law
CCAMLR	Convention on the Conservation of Antarctic Marine Living Resources
CCAS	Convention on the Conservation of Antarctic Seals
ConTS	Consolidated Treaty Series
Cornell ILJ	Cornell International Law Journal
CRAMRA	Convention on the Regulation of Antarctic Mineral Resource Activities
CTS	Canada Treaty Series
CYIL	Canadian Yearbook of International Law
DalLJ	Dalhousie Law Journal
EEZ	Exclusive Economic Zone

Handbook	*Handbook of the Antarctic Treaty System.* (8th) (2 vols.). US Department of State: Washington. 1994
IASC	International Arctic Science Committee
ICC	Inuit Circumpolar Conference
ICJ Reports	International Court of Justice Reports
ICLQ	International and Comparative Law Quarterly
IGY	International Geophysical Year
IJECL	International Journal of Estuarine and Coastal Law
ILM	International Legal Materials
ILR	International Law Reports
IntJ	International Journal
IntOrg	International Organization
IUCN	International Union for the Conservation of Nature and Natural Resources (The World Conservation Union)
IWC	International Whaling Commission
JMLC	Journal of Maritime Law and Commerce
LNTS	League of Nations Treaty Series
MARPOL	1973/1978 International Convention for the Prevention of Pollution by Ships
MPA	Multiple-Use Planning Area
MULR	Melbourne University Law Review
NatResJ	Natural Resources Journal
Nordic JIL	Nordic Journal of International Law
NSR	Northern Sea Route
ODIL	Ocean Development and International Law
Ottawa LR	Ottawa Law Review
PCIJ Reports	Permanent Court of International Justice Reports
ProcAmSocIL	Proceedings of the American Society of International Law
ReDC	Recueil Des Cours
RIAA	Reports of International Arbitral Awards
SC	Statutes of Canada
SCAR	Scientific Committee on Antarctic Research
SPA	Specially Protected Area
SRA	Specially Reserved Area
SSSI	Site of Special Scientific Interest
Stanford JIL	Stanford Journal of International Law
TexILJ	Texas International Law Journal
TIAS	Treaties and other International Acts Series

U Miami LR	University of Miami Law Review
UBCLR	University of British Columbia Law Review
UNCLOS	United Nations Convention on the Law of the Sea
UNTS	United Nations Treaty Series
VaJIL	Virginia Journal of International Law
YIEL	Yearbook of International Environmental Law
YILC	Yearbook of the International Law Commission

Part I

Introduction to the polar regions

1 Introduction

The polar regions and the development of international law

The polar regions have occupied a distinctive place in international law for much of the twentieth century. A number of factors have contributed to this situation. States have encountered difficulty in effectively asserting polar territorial claims. Traditional modes of acquisition of territory, occupation and administration, proved difficult to apply in remote regions suffering from a harsh polar environment. The abundance of natural resources in polar waters raised issues concerning the sovereign rights of coastal states, freedoms of the high seas and resource management. International interest in the need to protect the environment, especially fragile ecosystems such as those in the polar regions, also contributed to increased attention being given to the polar regions. In response both unilateral and multilateral legal initiatives have been relied upon in the polar regions to deal with these questions. There has also been an emphasis upon the adoption of regional management mechanisms and a rejection of state sovereignty or global management approaches. In all these issues, international law has had a role to play.

This study will focus on the polar regions and how, through distinctive responses to unique polar problems, a contribution has been made to the development of international law. The study is based on the premise that the Antarctic and Arctic are separate but similar regions, which, through a combination of geography, environment and political factors, have certain common elements which make them distinctive from other regions and which require specific responses to international legal issues. The polar regions are, however, not identical and there are some very significant differences. Antarctica is a continent surrounded by ocean while the Arctic is an ocean surrounded by continents. The Arctic also has its own indigenous peoples who are seeking greater self-determination within their existing states or as separate states. The Arctic has also been subject in parts to substantial industrial development. Antarctica has a distinctive regional legal regime based on international law developed by states with Antarctic interests. The legal regime of the Arctic, on the other hand, is substantially based on either global international law conventions and norms, or the individual legal systems of the Arctic states. Despite these important distinctions, the polar regions have made important contributions to the development of international law. They represent examples of areas in which international law has been actively applied and adapted to meet special conditions. Given the difficulties which are sometimes encountered in effectively implementing international law at either the global or regional level, the polar regions then represent important case studies for an understanding of the development and application of international law.

This chapter essentially seeks to provide a framework for understanding the important legal issues that will be considered in later chapters. However, it is impossible to understand the legal developments that have occurred in the polar regions without also considering the impact of international relations. Accordingly, a brief review will be undertaken of international relations theory in order to provide a framework for a more detailed consideration of the interaction of international law and international relations in chapter 10.

The international law framework

During early expeditions to the Arctic and Antarctic various territorial claims were made. These raised questions as to how traditional principles of territorial sovereignty could be applied in areas remote from the metropolitan power and where there was no immediate intent to colonise as distinct from acquire.[1] In the Arctic, some states asserted claims on the basis of 'polar sectors' which ran to the North Pole. While sector claims were asserted for administrative convenience, they were also symbolic and allowed for a comparatively

[1] See James Brown Scott, 'Arctic Exploration and International Law' (1909) 3 AJIL 928–41; A. R. Clute, 'The Ownership of the North Pole' (1927) 5 CanBR 19–26; Gustav Smedal, *Acquisition of Sovereignty over Polar Areas* (Oslo, 1931); T. E. M. McKitterick, 'The Validity of Territorial and Other Claims in Polar Regions' (1939) 21 (I & IV) (3rd Ser.) *Journal of Comparative Legislation and International Law* 89–97.

uncontested territorial division of parts of the Arctic.[2] Sector claims based partly on discovery were also made in Antarctica. However, some of the claims overlapped and all of the seven territorial claimants encountered difficulties in effectively exercising sovereignty. As if to acknowledge the difficulty of this problem, the 1959 Antarctic Treaty[3] sought to 'freeze' territorial sovereignty for the Treaty's duration.

These problems regarding the effective assertion of territorial sovereignty at both the North and South Pole have intrigued scholars since the beginning of the twentieth century.[4] In Antarctica this has been fuelled by neither the United States nor Russia (the former USSR) asserting any territorial claims despite their long standing interest in and presence on the continent.[5] The issue is further complicated by the fact that the claims of Argentina, Chile and the UK partially overlap. In addition, there is one sector in Antarctica which remains unclaimed. Apart from the deep sea bed, this is the only area on earth not yet the subject of state sovereignty claims. In the Arctic, territorial claims to most Arctic lands have now been settled. Nevertheless, because of the significance of the Arctic Ocean to the region and its near permanent ice cover, questions have been raised as to whether the Arctic Ocean is subject to claim in much the same way land is.

More recently, international law in the polar regions has been tested by concerns over resource management and environmental protection. In Antarctica, a debate existed over whether mining should be allowed. Throughout the 1980s much effort was expended as interested states negotiated a convention to regulate Antarctic mineral resource activities. This process was finally concluded in 1988 when agreement was reached on the final terms of the Convention on the Regulation of Antarctic Mineral Resource Activities (CRAMRA).[6] However, CRAMRA remained controversial because its fundamental

[2] See Smedal, *Acquisition of Sovereignty* at 54–76. Arctic sector claims are still important for some maritime claims in the region; for a general review see Susan J. Rolston and Ted L. McDorman, 'Maritime Boundary Making in the Arctic Regions' in Douglas M. Johnston and Phillip M. Saunders (eds.), *Ocean Boundary Making: Regional Issues and Developments* (London, 1988) 16–73. [3] 402 UNTS 71, Art. IV.

[4] See the discussion and references thereat in Sir Robert Jennings and Sir Arthur Watts, *Oppenheim's International Law* (9th, vol. I: Pts 2–4) (Harlow, 1992) 692–3.

[5] This is not to suggest that neither the United States nor Russia (especially their nationals) have not from time to time sought to assert territorial claims in Antarctica. See F. M. Auburn, *Antarctic Law and Politics* (London, 1982) 61–81. [6] (1988) 27 ILM 859.

premise was that Antarctica was a region where mining could occur despite being particularly sensitive to environmental impact. In the Arctic, unilateral resource exploitation had taken place in conformity with the right of Arctic states to exploit their own natural resources. This resulted in scarce resources being overexploited. In the case of living resources, some species were threatened, impacting upon the subsistence culture of Arctic indigenous peoples.[7] By the conclusion of the 1980s the polar regions were increasingly considered by a variety of groups as being ripe for stronger measures dealing with environmental protection at both the national and international level. This culminated in 1991 with the negotiation of two important instruments.

In the case of Antarctica, a Protocol on Environmental Protection to the Antarctic Treaty (Protocol) was adopted.[8] The purpose of the Protocol is to implement measures designed to achieve the comprehensive protection of the Antarctic environment. The Protocol overrode CRAMRA as it prohibited mining activities from taking place in Antarctica.[9] It adds to the growing elaboration of the Antarctic Treaty System (ATS) which includes two further international Conventions and over 200 Recommendations made at Antarctic Treaty Meetings. In the case of the Arctic, a very different process was chosen. Following discussions which began in 1989, the Arctic states adopted in 1991 at Rovaniemi, Finland, the 'Arctic Environmental Protection Strategy' (AEPS).[10] The AEPS contains a series of multilateral obligations and seeks to enhance cooperation amongst Arctic states in order to more effectively protect the environment. As there exists no formal multilateral legal framework in the Arctic, the AEPS does not have an existing legal regime to ensure its implementation. However, the AEPS demonstrates the growing concern amongst Arctic nations for the need to implement measures to protect the Arctic environment. It represents further evidence of the gradual move towards the development of a more comprehensive Arctic legal regime.

This review of some of the legal issues confronting the polar regions demonstrates the difficulty in applying some fundamental concepts of international law to them. Recognising territorial sovereignty is difficult where states find it impossible to demonstrate effective administrative control due to the vastness of the region, harsh

[7] In regard to Arctic resource conflicts see generally Oran R. Young, *Arctic Politics* (Dartmouth, NH, 1992) 104–25. [8] (1991) 30 ILM 1,455 (hereafter Protocol).
[9] Protocol, Art. 7. [10] (1991) 30 ILM 1,624 (hereafter AEPS).

environmental conditions and absence of settled populations. The adoption of the frozen sovereignty approach to deal with Antarctic territorial claims is a particular response to this problem. Likewise, sector claims, which, while highly doubtful, are nevertheless tolerated. The management mechanisms which have been adopted in the polar regions have also been unique. A genuine attempt has been made to adopt an ecosystem approach towards environmental management while dealing with emerging environmental problems prior to a crisis being reached. By adopting these and other approaches to polar problems, the polar states have demonstrated the inadequacies of general international law principles and more specialised areas such as the law of the sea when applied to the polar regions. This is not to suggest that the polar regions are in some way immune or exempt from general developments in international law. As will be demonstrated in later chapters, the polar regions have been impacted upon by a number of significant international instruments and customary international law.[11]

The polar regions, through the practice of states in the Arctic and Antarctic, have also made a contribution to the development of international law in that they demonstrate the effectiveness of regional management of international problems. The Antarctic Treaty is the prime example of this approach. The Treaty sought to deal with questions of sovereignty, scientific research and the militarisation of the continent. With these issues seemingly resolved for the Treaty's duration, the Treaty parties sought to build upon the initial Treaty framework through additional measures dealing with existing and emerging issues. The result has been the ATS, which remains the only international legal regime that has managed the affairs of a whole continent and its region. In the Arctic, unilateral state action was initially favoured by Arctic states to deal with Arctic regional problems. There were exceptions to this though, such as the 1911 Convention for the Preservation and Protection of Fur Seals[12] and the 1920 Treaty concerning the Archipelago of Spitsbergen (Svalbard).[13] After World War II the region was at the frontline of the Cold War and military and national security issues impacted upon the ability of Arctic states to engage in Arctic-wide cooperative efforts. This began to change in the 1970s with the development of a number of bilateral

[11] See generally Jonathan I. Charney, 'The Antarctic System and Customary International Law' in Francesco Francioni and Tullio Scovazzi (eds.), *International Law for Antarctica* (Milan, 1987) 55–99. [12] (1911) 214 ConTS 80. [13] 2 LNTS 8.

and multilateral initiatives between Arctic states, primarily in areas of resource management and environmental protection. The development of new principles regarding the law of the sea also forced Arctic states to consider sovereignty questions once again as it became necessary to declare new maritime claims and delimit maritime boundaries. New technology also opened up the Arctic to the prospect of greater mineral resource development and international navigation through ice-clogged waters. All of these changes raised international issues which required cooperative responses. By the conclusion of the 1980s the Arctic states were beginning to adopt similar approaches to those taken in Antarctica. The AEPS was concluded in 1991 and there has also recently been discussion over the need for an 'Arctic Council'.[14]

In response to the unique characteristics of the polar regions, states have adopted distinctive international law responses. Many of these responses have important implications for an understanding of broader international law principles. As Sir Arthur Watts has noted with respect to Antarctica:

> Many propositions of international law stand exposed with particular clarity in the context of Antarctica, many views can be tested (perhaps to destruction) by reference to its special characteristics, the meaning of many rules of international law can be clarified by having to be applied there in unusual circumstances, and many emerging trends in the development of international law can be illustrated, and perhaps reinforced, by what has been happening there.[15]

While the international law issues in the Arctic are not identical to those in Antarctica, this comment is still valid for the Arctic.

The polar regions also present interesting contrasts to other traditional management mechanisms within the international system. Adopting a regional approach to the polar regions may not seem any different from the situation in other regions of the world where special legal regimes have been adopted to deal with marine pollution, trade and transportation. Discrete areas in need of international regulation have also been subject to international legal regimes. What is different in the polar regions is their size compared to other regions, the unique problems they face, the interest of the whole international community in their management and resource potential, and the

[14] See the discussion in chapter 6.

[15] Sir Arthur Watts, *International Law and the Antarctic Treaty System* (Cambridge, 1992) 2.

means that have been adopted to deal with these problems. As such the polar regions are important prototypes for regional management in a world which is increasingly becoming concerned about the effectiveness of global management regimes at all levels.

Finally, it should be noted that the global community has increasingly expressed a concern over how the polar regions are managed. This has partly been due to increased interest in wilderness areas and the need to protect ecosystems, but also because of the important scientific work carried out in the polar regions. There is also a greater appreciation that with their position at the extremities of the earth and their fragile ecosystems the polar regions are important indicators of the impacts of global climate change.[16] The development of management options such as the 'common heritage' concept for areas of global commons has also increased international interest in the polar regions.[17] At the conclusion of the twentieth century it could be argued that the polar regions have a greater international significance than at any other time in history.[18]

The international relations framework

During the past twenty years studies concerning regimes dominated international relations literature.[19] The main interest amongst political scientists was how regime theory could be used to explain

[16] See Scientific Committee on Antarctic Research, *The Role of Antarctica in Global Climate Change* (Cambridge, 1989).

[17] This has especially been the case in regard to whether Antarctica should be considered part of the 'common heritage of mankind' and if the United Nations rather than the ATS is the more suitable body to administer the region: see Zou Keyuan, 'The Common Heritage of Mankind and the Antarctic Treaty System' (1991) 38 *Netherlands International Law Review* 173–98.

[18] This point has often been made by Oran Young, who argued throughout much of the 1980s that the world had entered the 'Age of the Arctic': see Oran R. Young, 'The Age of the Arctic' (1985–86) 61 *Foreign Policy* 160–79; Oran R. Young, *The Arctic in World Affairs* (Seattle, 1989). Similar bi-polar arguments have been made by Peter Beck: see P. J. Beck, 'Entering the Age of Polar Regions: The Arctic and Antarctic are No Longer Poles Apart' (1989) 18(1) AMBIO 92–4.

[19] The main forum for debate has been the journal *International Organization*: see F. Kratochwil and J. G. Ruggie, 'International Organization: A State of the Art on an Art of the State' (1986) 40 IntOrg 753 at 759–63 where the rise in regime literature during the 1970s is discussed. A good example of the literature is also to be found in Stephen D. Krasner (ed.), *International Regimes* (Ithaca, NY, 1983). For an international law perspective on the developments in international relations theory, see Kenneth W. Abbott, 'Modern International Relations Theory: A Prospectus for International Lawyers' (1989) 14 *Yale Journal of International Law* 335–411.

international cooperative behaviour.[20] After a growth in the number of international organisations in the post-war United Nations era, the 1970s presented an opportunity to reflect upon these developments and to gain a greater understanding as to how these organisations were created, and how they operated and responded to changing conditions. It was at this time that some political scientists began to turn to regime theory as a means to explain these developments and answer some of these questions.[21] A theory dealing with international regimes also allowed for a greater understanding of new initiatives in international cooperation.[22] This early work was expanded on to such a degree that regime theory became a major area of study within international relations theory.[23]

Political scientists have already considered the application of regime theory in the polar regions.[24] This contrasts with the work of international lawyers, who, while having considered the legal regime of the polar regions,[25] have given little attention to regime theory.

[20] See Jan Q. Th. Rood, 'The Functioning of Regimes in an Interdependent World' in James N. Rosenau and Hylke Tromp (eds.), *Interdependence and Conflict in World Politics* (Aldershot, UK, 1989) 61–82.

[21] See J. C. Ruggie, 'International Responses to Technology: Concepts and Trends' (1975) 29 IntOrg 557–83; E. B. Haas, 'On Systems and International Regimes' (1974–1975) 27 *World Politics* 147–74.

[22] Regime analysis is still being applied to developing areas of institutional cooperation: see Peter H. Sand, 'International Cooperation: The Environmental Experience' in Jessica Tuchman Matthews (ed.), *Preserving the Global Environment* (New York, 1991) 236–79.

[23] An example would be the work of Keohane: see Robert O. Keohane, *After Hegemony* (Princeton, NJ, 1984) 49–132. See also, Ernst B. Haas, 'Words Can Hurt You; or, Who Said What to Whom About Regimes' in Stephen D. Krasner (ed.), *International Regimes* (Ithaca, NY, 1983) 23 at 24 who noted that since the early 1970s regime theory has developed into:

> a way of understanding the interactions of homo politicus with nature and with culture. It rests on the supposition that our collective understanding of our political choices increasingly depends on how we think about nature and culture. The study of regimes illustrates the range of past and future choices about international collaboration in the context of changing self-understanding.

[24] In the case of the Arctic, see Elizabeth Young, 'The Arctic: Prospects for an International Regime' in R. B. Byers and Michael Slack (eds.), *Strategy and the Arctic* (Toronto, 1986) 105–16; Gail Osherenko and Oran R. Young, *The Age of the Arctic* (Cambridge, 1989) 240–68; Oran R. Young and Gail Osherenko (eds.), *Polar Politics* (Ithaca, NY, 1993). In the case of Antarctica, see M. J. Peterson, *Managing the Frozen South* (Berkeley, CA, 1988); J. S. Dryzek, M. L. Clark and G. McKenzie, 'Subject and System in International Interaction' (1989) 43 IntOrg 475–503 for an application of 'Q methodology' to the Antarctic Treaty System.

[25] In relation to the Antarctic, see for example the following: Gillian D. Triggs (ed.), *The*

However, despite the widely differing approaches, there has recently been an increased interchange between international relations theory and international law. Sufficient respect has been gained for international relations theory that 'many international lawyers have concluded that regime theory can contribute to international law as well as international relations'.[26] Regime theory does indeed have something to offer international lawyers and this is especially the case with the polar regions. To gain an overall understanding of regime theory it is first necessary to consider a number of theoretical issues – what constitutes a regime, what factors are required for regime formation, the impact that the formative process can have on regime structure, the conditions that are necessary for a regime to be effective and how regimes respond to change. Only after a consideration of these various questions is it possible to gain an understanding of regime dynamics.[27]

Regime definition[28]

In approaching the study of regimes, it is first necessary to understand what a regime actually is. When regime studies emerged in the early 1970s, this was a major area of debate. Two of the early contributors were Ruggie and Haas. Ruggie described a regime as 'a set of mutual expectations, rules and regulations, plans and organizational energies and financial commitments, which have been accepted by a group of states'.[29] Haas noted that regimes were 'collective arrangements among nations designed to create or more effectively use scientific or

Antarctic Treaty Regime (Cambridge, 1987); Christopher C. Joyner and Sudhir K. Chopra (eds.), *The Antarctic Legal Regime* (Dordrecht, 1988). In the case of the Arctic, see Barnaby J. Feder, 'A Legal Regime for the Arctic' (1976–8) *Ecology Law Quarterly* 785–829; J. Enno Harders, 'In Quest of an Arctic Legal Regime' (1987) 11 *Marine Policy* 285–98; 'Legal Regimes of the Arctic' (1988) 82 ProcAmSocIL 315–34.

26 Anne-Marie Slaughter, 'Book Review: *Regime Theory and International Relations*' (1995) 89 AJIL 454–6 at 454. On the potential for greater interchange between the disciplines of international law and international relations theory see the papers and discussion which took place at the 1992 meeting of the American Society of International Law: 'International Law and International Relations Theory: Building Bridges' (1992) 86 ProcAmSocIL 167–87.

27 Peterson, *Managing the Frozen South* at 9.

28 Despite nearly twenty years of accumulated literature on regime theory there is still debate as to what regimes are: see Stephan Haggard and Beth A. Simmons, 'Theories of International Regimes' (1987) 41 IntOrg 491–517; Mark W. Zacher 'Toward a Theory of International Regimes' (1990) 44 *Journal of International Affairs* 139–57.

29 Ruggie, 'International Responses' at 570. For a later assessment of some of the problems associated with regime definition see Kratochwil and Ruggie, 'International Organization'.

technological capabilities'.[30] Since that time Haas has widened the scope of his definition describing a regime as:

a set of principles, explicit or implicit, norms, rules and decision-making procedures around which the expectations of actors converge in order to coordinate actors' behaviour with respect to an issue of concern to them all.[31]

Since the original development of the theory by Ruggie and Haas others have also made a contribution to the regime definition debate. In the first major volume collecting works on regime theory, Krasner set the following definition for his contributors:

Regimes can be defined as sets of implicit or explicit principles, norms, rules and decision-making procedures around which actors' expectations converge in a given area of international relations. Principles are beliefs of fact, causation and rectitude. Norms are standards of behaviour defined in terms of rights and obligations. Rules are specific prescriptions or proscriptions for action. Decision-making procedures are prevailing practices for making and implementing collective choice.[32]

While regime definitions by scholars such as Haas have evolved over time, Young has tended to be more consistent in his approach to regime definition. According to Young: 'Regimes are social institutions governing the actions of those interested in specifiable activities. As such, they are recognized patterns of practice around which expectations converge.'[33] Without the need for Krasner's principles, norms and rules, Young's approach is more wide-ranging. Young also distinguishes between domestic and international regimes, noting that the latter can take place outside the jurisdictional boundaries of sovereign states, that they cut across all international boundaries and

[30] Haas, 'On Systems' at 147. A later definition used by Haas was that regimes were 'norms, rules and procedures agreed to in order to regulate an issue area': see Ernst B. Haas, 'Why Collaborate? Issue-Linkage and International Regimes' (1979–80) 32 *World Politics* 357 at 358.

[31] Ernst B. Haas, 'Regime Decay: Conflict Management and International Organizations, 1945–1981' (1983) 37 IntOrg 189 at 192 where 'principles' were considered beliefs of fact, causation and rectitude; 'norms' were standards of behaviour defined in terms of rights and obligations; 'rules' were specific prescriptions and prohibitions with respect to actors' behaviour; and 'procedures' were prevailing practices for making and implementing collective choices.

[32] Stephen D. Krasner, 'Structural Causes and Regime Consequences: Regimes as Intervening Variables' in Stephen D. Krasner (ed.), *International Regimes* (Ithaca, NY, 1983) 1 at 2.

[33] Oran R. Young, 'International Regimes: Problems of Concept Formation' (1979–1980) 32 *World Politics* 331 at 332.

involve actions which have a direct impact on two or more members of the international community.[34]

Another leading scholar of regime theory has been Keohane.[35] He believes that the Krasner definition is a useful starting-point, but because of certain ambiguities he has further expanded upon it.[36] Keohane sees norms as being standards of behaviour, irrespective of whether they are adopted on the grounds of self-interest or otherwise.[37] Having adopted this variation, Keohane expands on some of the distinctive features of a regime. He has argued:

> The principles of regimes define, in general, the purposes that their members are expected to pursue. Norms contain somewhat clearer injunctions to members about legitimate and illegitimate behaviour, still defining responsibilities and obligations in relatively general terms. The rules of a regime are difficult to distinguish from its norms; at the margin, they merge into one another. Rules are, however, more specific: they indicate in more detail the specific rights and obligations of members. Rules can be altered more easily than principles or norms, since there may be more than one set of rules that can attain a given set of purposes. Finally, at the same level of specificity as rules, but referring to procedures rather than substances, the decision-making procedures of regimes provide ways of implementing their principles and altering their rules.[38]

The Keohane approach to regimes also places emphasis on the need for some enforcement procedures by way of 'injunctions'.[39] Keohane believes that injunctions, which are politically consequential but specific enough to allow for the identification of violations, are the essence of international regimes.[40]

The above review demonstrates that while there has been spirited debate amongst various commentators on the question of regime definition, some common features have emerged. Regimes are certainly founded on principles and norms which attract various international actors, though principally states. Regimes create either formal or informal international institutions that deal with identifiable issue

[34] *Ibid.* at 333; for later examples of how Young views this approach, see Oran R. Young, 'International Regimes: Toward a New Theory of Institutions' (1986) 39 *World Politics* 104 at 105–8; Oran R. Young, *International Cooperation* (Ithaca, NY, 1989) 12–23.

[35] For an early work by Keohane which touched on regime issues, see Robert O. Keohane and Joseph S. Nye, *Power and Interdependence: World Politics in Transition* (Boston, 1977).

[36] Keohane, *After Hegemony* at 57.

[37] *Ibid.*

[38] *Ibid.* at 58.

[39] *Ibid.* at 59.

[40] *Ibid.* For a more recent analysis of the study of regimes by Keohane see Robert O. Keohane, 'International Institutions: Two Approaches' (1988) 32 *International Studies Quarterly* 379–96.

areas. These common features of regimes are best identified in the Krasner definition which has gradually won greater acceptance amongst regime theorists.[41] International regimes are therefore principles, norms, rules, and decision-making procedures around which actor expectations converge in a given issue-area.[42]

Regime creation: the need for an issue area

For a regime to come into existence it is accepted by all regime theorists that an 'issue area' is required around which states and international actors converge. The issue area is then the catalyst for regime formation. Recognising the importance of issue areas, two further questions arise: how are they identified and how dense must they be before states will converge to form a regime? The commentators have all addressed various aspects of these two questions. Haas links the creation of an issue area with the notion of interdependence. He argues that international issue areas will arise when states begin to question the terms of their interdependence. An issue area will only completely emerge, however, once stronger states begin to pay attention to the questions which have been raised.[43] Through this process 'Issues become visible, acquire names and places on agendas, elicit studies, and emerge as recurrent topics of discussion in national parliaments and interest groups. The attempt to resolve the issue forces the parties to examine the terms of their mutual dependence.'[44] States and other international actors may decide that they have sufficient mutual interest in the issue area to converge and form a regime.

Keohane regards the scope of an international regime as generally corresponding to the boundaries of given issue areas. This is because regimes are established to deal with problems which states see as being so closely linked that they should be dealt with together.[45] Issue areas are therefore:

> sets of issues that are in fact dealt with in common negotiations and by the same, or closely coordinated bureaucracies, as opposed to issues that are dealt

[41] See Jack Donnelly, 'International Human Rights: A Regime Analysis' (1986) 40 IntOrg 599 at 599–600; Volker Rittberger (ed.), *International Regimes in East–West Politics* (London, 1990) 2–3; Martin List and Volker Rittberger, 'Regime Theory and International Environmental Management' in Andrew Hurrell and Benedict Kingsbury (eds.), *The International Politics of the Environment* (Oxford, 1992) 85 at 89; *cf.* Young, 'International Regimes' at 106.

[42] Krasner, 'Structural Causes' at 1. Actors not only include states as part of the international system, but can also be international organisations and non-governmental organisations (NGOs).

[43] Haas, 'Why Collaborate?' at 362–3 [44] *Ibid.* [45] Keohane, *After Hegemony* at 61.

with separately and in uncoordinated fashion. Since issue areas depend on the actor's perceptions and behaviour rather than on inherent qualities of the subject-matters, their boundaries change gradually over time.[46]

Both Haas and Ruggie have also noted that before an issue area reaches the stage where it is attractive to international actors, two prerequisites are necessary: knowledge and politicisation. The first is described as:

> the sum of technical information and of theories about that information which commands sufficient consensus at a given time among international actors to serve as a guide to public policy designed to achieve some social goal. Knowledge incorporates scientific notions relating to social goals.[47]

Once the necessary knowledge has been gathered around a certain issue area, Ruggie argues that politicisation has to take place. This 'results in the recognition that a collective situation exists. The intensity of politicisation and the sense of importance and urgency an issue is accorded, and the manner in which that issue will be dealt with also depend on what sort of collective situation exists.'[48] For a regime to be created it is important that an issue area exist. However, until these further steps have occurred it may not be possible for states to converge and create a regime in their mutual interest.[49]

Regime creation: methods of formation

Once an issue area has attracted actors who perceive that their common interests will be enhanced by some form of understanding or agreement, the necessary conditions for regime formation can be said to exist. The next step in this process is actual regime formation.[50] This is a complex process which has many variables.[51] Feld, Jordan and Hurwitz have identified three methods of regime formation.[52] The first is by a 'contractarian track'[53] in which the actors meet together for the purpose of negotiating a contract or convention that sets the framework within which the regime is to operate.[54]

46 *Ibid.*

47 Haas, 'Why Collaborate?' at 367.

48 Ruggie, 'International Responses' at 561.

49 For a further analysis of why regimes form at this stage of the process, rather than a state of anarchy remaining, see List and Rittberger, 'Regime Theory' at 91–8.

50 *Ibid.* at 90 describe this as being a process which includes 'both the initiation of the regime, for example through international negotiations ending up in an international agreement, and its implementation through norm and rule-guided action by the participating states'.

51 Haas, 'Why Collaborate?' at 371.

52 See also the analysis of regime formation given by Young, *International Cooperation* at 84–5.

53 W. J. Feld, R. S. Jordan and L. Hurwitz, *International Organizations – A Comparative Approach* (New York, 1983) at 260.

54 An example would be international conventions which seek to codify the law, e.g.,

The second method is the 'evolutionary approach' in which regimes evolve over time. Rules that were originally temporary take on a customary character during this process, or evolve through unilateral action which result in *de facto* or *de jure* regime recognition.[55] The third method is known as the 'piecemeal process' which occurs when the actors reach agreement on certain points in a defined issue area but are unable to obtain a comprehensive consensus. In this case the participants hope that the necessary consensus may be obtained at a later stage by an expansion of the issue area or the policy space becoming closer.[56]

Traditionally, regime theorists have also placed great importance on the need for a hegemonic power to exist if a regime is to form.[57] Regimes that are created through the intervention of a hegemonic power are inevitably influenced by that power during their life.[58] There is also, however, the potential for blocs of actors to be influential. In addition, Young has argued that 'negotiations among self-interested parties as a means of dealing with collective-action problems' can also be decisive.[59] This approach suggests that in some instances, the power of the issue area will be of such importance that

the United Nations Convention on the Law of the Sea, (1982) 21 ILM, 1,261 (UNCLOS).

55 Feld, Jordan and Hurwitz, *International Organizations* n 53 at 260. An example of this type of approach would be the development of the continental shelf regime following the 1945 Truman Declaration, Proclamation No. 2,667, XIII (No. 327) 30 September 1945, *Department of State Bulletin* 485, which eventually resulted in the development of the Convention on the Continental Shelf, 499 UNTS 311.

56 Feld, Jordan and Hurwitz, *International Organizations* at 260. An example of this type of formation would be debate over the breadth of the territorial sea. This was a matter that remained unresolved following the adoption in 1958 of the Convention on the Territorial Sea and Contiguous Zone, 516 UNTS 205, and was also not resolved at the Second UN Conference on the Law of the Sea in 1960. The matter was finally resolved in UNCLOS, Art. 3 which provided for a twelve nautical mile limit of the territorial sea.

57 See e.g., Oran R. Young, 'Political Leadership and Regime Formation: On the Development of Institutions in International Society' (1991) 45 IntOrg 281–308. Gail Osherenko and Oran R. Young, 'The Formation of International Regimes: Hypotheses and Cases' in Young and Osherenko, *Polar Politics* at 9 note that this bias can be partly explained by regime theory being initially applied in cases concerning the rise of international trade and monetary arrangements in the post-World War II era when the United States was a hegemonic power.

58 Keohane, *After Hegemony* at 72 notes: 'To strengthen their bargaining positions, powerful actors impose constraints on weaker ones prior to the formation of a new regime, or may threaten adverse results if the weaker countries refuse to go along with the hegemonic scheme.'

59 Oran R. Young, 'The Politics of International Regime Formation: Managing Natural Resources and the Environment' (1989) 43 IntOrg 349 at 359.

state actors will be drawn towards it because they all uniformly believe that the issue area requires some form of regulation. Individual self-interest does play a part, but global or community concerns also influence state behaviour.[60]

Conditions for effective regimes

Once a regime has been created, the interest of regime theorists turns to the conditions required for an effective regime.[61] A principal feature of effective regimes is the ability of the regime to enforce or impose its decisions upon its members and at the same time to obtain a degree of acceptance from those who are outside of the regime.[62] If these basic goals of implementation and acceptance cannot be achieved the regime will lose its degree of effectiveness and this will eventually result in either regime change or the disintegration of the regime. The regime-formation process will have an important impact on the eventual effectiveness of the regime. The actor, or groups of actors, which dominate during regime formation can have great influence on the shape of the regime and how it eventually operates.[63]

Regime effectiveness then depends very much on regime dynamics. States which are drawn to the regime will have a number of incentives to comply with the regime and this contributes, at least initially, to a high degree of regime effectiveness. Because interdependence amongst states on many issue areas is so strong, reluctant

[60] See *ibid.* at 366–74, where Young notes that increasing global concern over environmental issues has played a crucial role in reducing the importance of hegemonic states in regime formation.

[61] See generally Arild Underdal, 'The Concept of Regime "Effectiveness"' (1992) 27 *Cooperation and Conflict* 227–40. Also see Arthur D. Stein, 'Coordination and Collaboration: Regimes in an Anarchic World' in Krasner *International Regimes* at 125 in regard to the effectiveness of regimes due to 'common aversions'.

[62] Haas, 'Regime Decay' at 193, argues that the concept of regime effectiveness:

> consists of the ability of member states to use the notions enshrined in principles, norms, rules and procedures to moderate successfully the conflicts referred to the organizations; it also involves the ability to persuade members to refer the bulk of their disputes to the organizations instead of seeking unilateral or bilateral solutions. The coherence of a regime consists of the mutual complementarity of its principles, norms, rules and procedures – the support these components give one another.

[63] Haas assessed these factors by considering the participants during regime formation, the approach adopted by the participants, whether any clashes occurred between different factions, and the future of the regime based on the outcome of the 'conference' which resulted in the creation of the regime: Haas, 'Why Collaborate?' at 396.

states may accept certain regimes because of the benefits that may flow through to other areas of interdependence. Duffield argues that this behaviour contributes directly to the achievement of a common purpose in the regime.[64] It may also have an additional benefit in that 'by providing evidence of a state's willingness to compromise and to exercise self-restraint, it may reinforce the tendency – or overcome the reluctance – on the part of other states to comply as well, resulting in even greater benefits both immediately and in the future'.[65] Regime effectiveness can then in some instances be a direct result of the simple desire by states to enter into and comply with arrangements with like-minded states. This is especially the case with multilateral regimes, because they can reduce 'transaction costs' and be the 'least expensive route to a high degree of cost certainty'.[66] Multilateral regimes not only attract a greater number of states, but also, due to the importance of the issue area and the advantages in a multilateral regime, ensure greater adherence to its rules and norms.

Regime change

Once a regime is operational the greatest test that it will face is the pressure for change. This may be a result of either external or internal pressures that raise questions about the issue area not contemplated at the time of formation, or set aside as being too difficult to resolve. Regime change may also be forced by technological, economic, societal and political developments.[67] The effect of regime change can be amendment, modification, replacement or disintegration.[68] How a regime deals with pressure for change will dictate whether it fails and disintegrates or adapts and continues on. While regime theorists have adopted a variety of approaches towards understanding and explaining regime change,[69] there is consensus that all regimes eventually face this pressure and that in most cases it represents the greatest test for the regime.

It is difficult to prescribe a set of common factors that regimes face

[64] John Duffield, 'International Regimes and Alliance Behaviour: Explaining NATO Conventional Force Levels' (1992) 46 IntOrg 819 at 836.

[65] *Ibid.* [66] Zacher, 'Toward a Theory' at 148.

[67] Abram Chayes and Antonia H. Chayes, 'Adjustment and Compliance Processes in International Regulatory Regimes' in Matthews, *Preserving the Global Environment* at 281.

[68] Peterson, *Managing the Frozen South* at 175–7.

[69] Haggard and Simmons, 'Theories' at 498–513.

during regime change as the specific institutional structure adopted by each regime will influence this process.[70] Regimes which contain internal contradictions face perhaps the greatest difficulty in coping with regime change when a fundamental principle of the regime is being challenged.[71] More often though regimes are challenged by external forces. The most recurring examples of regime change arise because of changes in technology.[72] In these cases, unless the regime is able radically to adapt to the change it may disintegrate purely because it has become an anachronism. Other types of regime change may occur because of changes in related regimes or because of the changing policy interests of a hegemon.

Regime theory can only offer explanations to regime change based on after-the-event analysis. However, it has been possible over time to predict that certain types of regimes may be better able to cope with change than others. The salience of the issue area can in these cases be a decisive factor. If states believe that their best interests are served by a multilateral regime dealing with the common problems they face, change is more likely to be accepted than if the issue area is no longer salient.

Regime theory and the polar regions

As political developments have shaped the legal regimes that exist in Antarctica and the Arctic it is useful to give some consideration to why states have sought to cooperate and what impacts these factors will have on the development and future of the polar legal regimes. International relations regime theory offers an understanding of how international law develops around certain issue areas, why the legal regime may succeed or fail and what factors have to be taken into account when there is a need to revise or amend the legal regime. In chapter 10, a detailed analysis will be undertaken of how regime theory can be applied to developments in the polar regions and what benefits international law can gain from such an approach.

[70] One suggested list is found in Peterson, *Managing the Frozen South* at 143–4.

[71] Young, *International Cooperation* at 96–7 gives the example of the pressures regimes based on the principle of unrestricted common property for marine fisheries face when the resource becomes depleted.

[72] *Ibid.* at 99 referring to the growth in new fishing techniques which undermined common-property high-seas fishing regimes.

Conclusion

The polar regions have presented international law with a number of unique problems. In some instances international law has responded to the challenge while in other instances states with polar interests have developed specific responses. Through these developments, a distinctive legal regime has emerged. The international relations amongst polar states has also provided a backdrop against which these international law developments have taken place. A greater appreciation of why and how states cooperate to form regimes which may rely upon international law will result in a greater appreciation of how international law ultimately operates. These are the questions that will be addressed in subsequent chapters.

2 The environment and resources of the polar regions

In the previous chapter it was emphasised that the polar regions provide some unique examples of how international law operates. These unique features of polar international law have in many cases been a response to the polar regions themselves. Many legal principles developed in more temperate lands have not been suited to the polar environment. In addition, the polar regions have many special resource characteristics that are not reproduced elsewhere. The ecosystem is so fragile, that substantial resource exploitation of either living or non-living resources could cause devastating environmental impact. These issues will be explored in this chapter so as to gain a fuller appreciation of the environment and resources of the polar regions.

The boundaries of the polar regions

While the polar regions can generally be defined as being those areas within the Arctic and Antarctic Circles,[1] this definition is not adequate for this study. A purely geographic approach such as this, while convenient from the perspective of providing certainty, has a number of deficiencies.[2] For example, neither Greenland nor the full Antarctic continent fall within the Arctic and Antarctic Circles respectively. If such traditional definitions of the polar regions are deemed unsuitable, others are available. However, as Stonehouse has noted, there is

[1] Bernard Stonehouse, *Polar Ecology* (Glasgow, 1989) 3 defines the polar circles as being 'parallels of latitude approximately 66°32′ from the equator and 23°28′ from the poles, defined by the angle between the axis of rotation of the earth and the ecliptic, or plane of earth's orbit about the sun'.

[2] See Bernard Stonehouse, *North Pole South Pole* (Toronto, 1990) 15.

no general agreement on the boundaries of the polar regions.[3] Both natural scientists, political scientists, geographers and lawyers have all adopted a variety of approaches.[4] It is therefore important to determine boundaries which are both easily recognisable and applicable to the regions being studied.

Antarctica

In the case of Antarctica, the commonly accepted legal definition is the area to which the Antarctic Treaty applies. Under Article VI the Treaty extends to the area south of 60°S. This area includes within it the complete Antarctic continent and much of what is known as the Southern Ocean. It also includes many sub-Antarctic islands, especially those which cluster around the Antarctic Peninsula. However, some major islands such as South Georgia and Kerguelen are not included within this area. Importantly, a boundary extending to 60°S does not include any other continent: the most southern tip of South America extends to 55°S at Tierra del Fuego where the Drake Passage creates a natural barrier to Antarctica.

While a boundary set at 60°S was undoubtedly convenient for administrative purposes when the Treaty was negotiated it has not proven to be as adequate when defining the extent of the Antarctic marine environment. Accordingly, the 1980 Convention on the Conservation of Antarctic Marine Living Resources (CCAMLR) adopted a boundary which while respecting the limits of the Antarctic Treaty extends further north to the 'Antarctic convergence'.[5] The Antarctic convergence marks the boundary between cold Antarctic surface water and warmer sub-antarctic water. It represents a major marine ecological boundary which distinguishes the Antarctic ecosystem from those to the north.[6] CCAMLR defines the outer limits of the area of the Convention's application by way of a set of coordinates that approximates the outer limits of the convergence. As a result of the increasing importance that has been placed by the ATS upon the

[3] Stonehouse, *Polar Ecology* at 1.

[4] For further discussion see *ibid.* at 1–11 where Stonehouse refers to the possibility of determining boundaries on the basis of parallels of latitude, climatic boundaries, the treeline and maritime boundaries. See also the discussion in David Sugden, *Arctic and Antarctic* (Oxford, 1982) 17–20; Euan C. Young, 'Ecology and Conservation of the Polar Regions' (1989) 18 AMBIO (1) 23 at 23–25.

[5] (1980) 19 ILM 841, Art. I.

[6] Young, 'Ecology and Conservation' at 23.

protection of the environment it is therefore appropriate to adopt the northern boundary of CCAMLR as the outer limits of Antarctica for the purposes of this study.[7] It should be noted that the 1991 Protocol on Environmental Protection to the Antarctic Treaty, while having 60°S as the northern limit to its area of operation,[8] makes extensive reference to the need to protect the 'Antarctic environment and dependent and associated ecosystems'.[9] While this approach seems to be consistent with that adopted in CCAMLR, no definition is provided as to how much further north of the 60°S limit this may extend the operation of the Protocol.[10] It is therefore important to note that while for the purposes of this study Antarctica will be considered to be the area within the limits of CCAMLR, the Protocol may apply further north.[11]

The Arctic

In the Arctic, the central focus of the region is the Arctic Ocean. However, a number of continental and other land masses surrounding it have lands that could be characterised as polar. This makes it difficult to define the exact southern limit of the Arctic as a region. If climate is considered to be a distinguishing feature of the polar regions, then there is some attraction in relying upon a boundary based on climatic conditions. To that end the 10°C summer isotherm line is referred to as being the most appropriate boundary between Arctic and sub-Arctic lands.[12] Another much relied upon natural boundary is the 'treeline'. This is an area delimited by the northernmost limits at which trees grow.[13] Beyond the treeline tundra predominates. A boundary based on the treeline has the advantage of being relatively easy to determine and also, similarly to the Antarctic convergence has an impact on the distribution of fauna and flora.[14]

[7] See Figure 1, p. 24.

[8] (1991) 30 ILM 1,455, Art. 1 & 3 (hereafter Protocol).

[9] Protocol, Art. 3.

[10] For comment see Donald R. Rothwell, 'The Madrid Protocol and its Relationship with the Antarctic Treaty System' (1992) 5 *ASOLPO Paper* 3–4.

[11] Until such time as the Protocol is actively implemented it will be impossible to ascertain whether in practice the Protocol will extend further north of 60°S or beyond the CCAMLR boundary.

[12] Stonehouse, *North Pole South Pole* at 15 who notes that this is a line which joins all points where the mean temperature of the warmest month is 10°C.

[13] *Ibid.* at 9.

[14] Sugden, *Arctic and Antarctic* at 17.

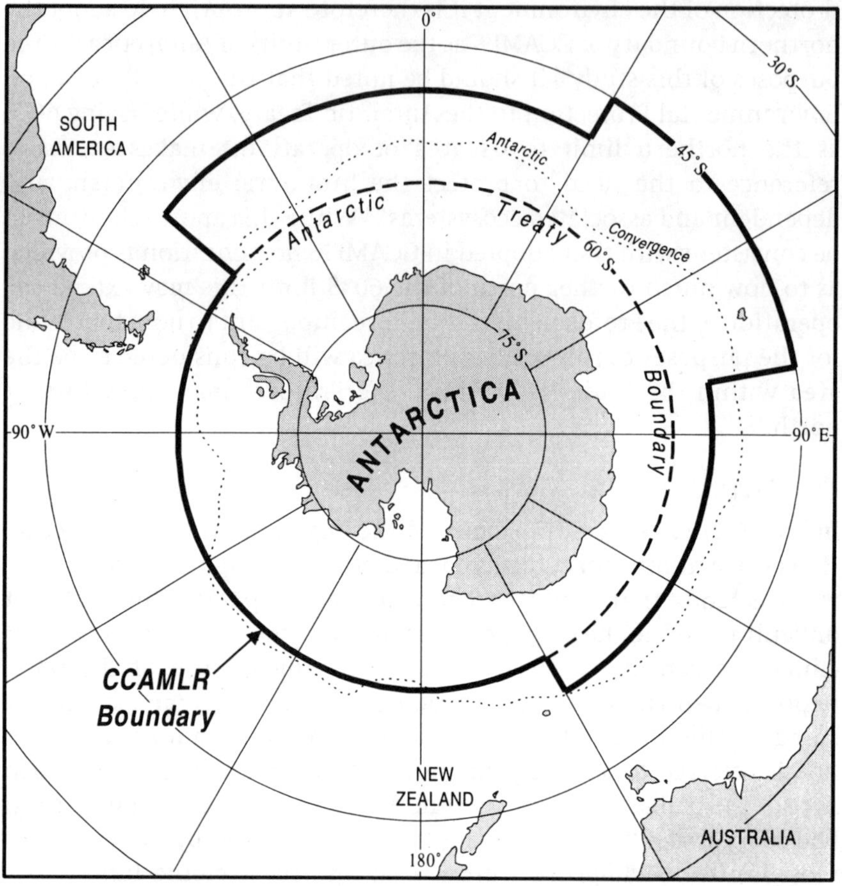

Figure 1 The limits of the Antarctic Treaty, the Convention on the Conservation of Antarctic Marine Living Resources (CCAMLR) and the Antarctic convergence

Unfortunately, Arctic boundaries based on either the 10 °C isotherm or the treeline are subject to considerable variation and make it difficult to determine precisely their limits. Accordingly, the boundary which will be adopted for the purposes of this study as the southern limit of the Arctic is 60 °N. This area includes all of the major maritime areas of the region: the Arctic Ocean, Bering Sea, Beaufort Sea, Barents Sea, Chukchi Sea, Kara Sea, Laptev Sea and Norwegian Sea. It also includes the island groups of Greenland, Iceland, Jan Mayen, Svalbard, Franz Joseph Land, Novaya Zemlya, Severnaya Zemlya, New

Siberian Islands and Wrangel Island plus the area collectively described in this study as the 'Canadian Arctic Archipelago'.[15] Finland and Iceland wholly fall within this boundary as do extensive portions of Norway, Sweden, and the Russian far north including Siberia. The US state of Alaska is also included, with the exception of the Panhandle area and the Aleutian Islands. In Canada, areas of the Yukon, Northwest Territories, Quebec and Newfoundland (Labrador) are north of 60° N. This boundary, while seemingly determined purely on the basis of convenience, does approximate to much of the area included within either a 10° C isotherm or a treeline definition of the Arctic. As a result, for the purposes of this study those states which either completely or partly fall within the Arctic region are Canada, Denmark (Greenland), Finland, Iceland, Norway, Russia, Sweden and the USA.[16]

The polar environment

Climate

The polar regions are dominated by an extreme climate. Freezing temperatures prevail during the winter months. In addition days are extremely short with the sun not rising above the horizon for many weeks during the middle of winter. While polar regions experience long daylight hours during summer, temperatures still remain low.[17] There is a much greater temperature variation, however, in the Arctic where temperatures can differ substantially between summer and winter,[18] with even 0° C having been recorded at the North Pole.[19] The Antarctic is colder with little substantial temperature variation between seasons. Sugden notes that mean July temperatures at the centre of the ice sheet can be -70° C while along the coast it is -25° C.

[15] For the purposes of this study the Canadian Arctic Archipelago is made up of all those islands considered to be Canadian territory which fall north of mainland Canada between the boundaries of the Yukon and the Northwest Territories in the west and Quebec and Labrador in the east, the limits of which extend from Bankes Island in the west along the outer edges of the Queen Elizabeth Islands to Ellesmere Island and then south to Baffin Island.

[16] See Figure 2, p. 28

[17] Marine Resources Project (University of Manchester), *Marine Resources of the Polar Regions: Scientific and Technological Priorities* (Manchester, 1986) 21.

[18] Stonehouse, *Polar Ecology* at 37 lists temperature ranges of as much as 60°C between winter and summer in some areas.

[19] Sugden, *Arctic and Antarctic* at 49.

During the summer the temperatures in the same areas are between -40°C and -2°C.[20] One factor which has a substantial impact on temperature in the polar regions is wind and this is especially prevalent in Antarctica where katabatic winds form as a result of cold air flowing downhill along the ice sheet.[21]

Precipitation in the polar regions is light and they can properly be characterised as arid.[22] This is especially the case in parts of east Antarctica where precipitation in the form of snow can amount to less than 50mm annually.[23] Much of Antarctica is therefore a desert. Arctic precipitation is higher, though still light by global standards. Most precipitation falls during late summer and autumn in the form of snow. Arctic weather is also characterised as being foggy and damp, which makes it very difficult for navigation.[24]

Ice

A unique feature of the polar oceans is that for much of the year they are ice-covered. This raises for consideration questions concerning the status of ice not dealt with under general principles of international law or the law of the sea.[25] To understand further some of these issues it is necessary to have some knowledge of the various categories of ice found in the polar regions.

Ice can generally be divided into two main categories: continental and sea ice. Continental ice has three types: ice sheets, glacial ice and ice shelves.[26] Ice sheets are found in both Antarctica and in Greenland.[27] The Antarctic ice sheet covers more than 98 per cent of the continent. It can best be described as a continental glacier with the centre continually producing more ice which slowly moves out towards the coast. In comparison, the Greenland ice sheet is subcontinental in size and covers about 80 per cent of the island.[28] Glacial

20 *Ibid*; Stonehouse, *Polar Ecology* at 52–6.

21 Louise Crossley, *Explore Antarctica* (Cambridge, 1995) 20. The explorer, Douglas Mawson, described one part of Antarctica as 'The Home of the Blizzard': Douglas Mawson, *The Home of the Blizzard: Being the Story of the Australasian Antarctic Expedition, 1911–1914* (2 vols.) (New York, 1915 rep. 1969).

22 Sugden, *Arctic and Antarctic* at 54.

23 *Ibid.*

24 *Ibid.* at 54–5; Marine Resources Project, at 23.

25 See chapter 7.

26 C. C. Joyner, 'Ice-Covered Regions in International Law' (1991) 31 NatResJ 213 at 220.

27 T. Armstrong, B. Roberts and C. Swithinbank, *Illustrated Glossary of Snow and Ice* (2nd) (Cambridge, 1973) 26 describe an ice sheet as: 'A mass of ice and snow of considerable thickness and large area. Ice sheets may be resting on rock or floating.'

28 Joyner, 'Ice-Covered Regions' at 220.

ice, in the form of smaller 'frozen rivers' of ice which are found in a variety of mountain areas throughout the world, is also found in the polar regions. Ice shelves are thick bodies of ice which at the coastal edge extend out over the water so as to float atop the water or ground themselves on the seabed.[29] More than one-third of Antarctica's coastline is covered with ice shelves.[30] At one time there were a great number of ice shelves in the Arctic but their number has gradually diminished. Arctic ice shelves are now only known to exist off the coast of Canada's Ellesmere Island.[31]

In addition to continental ice, various types of sea ice are also found in the polar regions. Three types are most common: pack ice, fast ice and icebergs.[32] Pack ice usually takes the form of large bodies of frozen sea.[33] It differs between the two polar regions because of the geographical characteristics of each. In the Arctic, pack ice is relatively stable and because of ocean currents swirls about the North Pole and portions of the Arctic Ocean. In Antarctica, pack ice is also present for much of the year but expands considerably during the winter.[34] Fast ice is characteristically attached to land and is frozen seawater which clings to the shores of rocks, inlets and bays.[35] Though subject to seasonal variations, this ice can be relatively permanent and has been

[29] Armstrong, Roberts and Swithinbank, *Illustrated Glossary* at 26, describe an ice shelf as: 'A floating ice sheet of considerable thickness attached to a coast. Ice shelves are usually of great horizontal extent and have a level or gently undulating surface. They are nourished by the accumulation of snow and often by the seaward extension of land glaciers. Limited areas may be aground.'

[30] Christopher C. Joyner, *Antarctica and the Law of the Sea* (Dordrecht, 1992) 198; this accounts for about 10 per cent of the total area of the continent. For a list of Antarctic ice shelves, see J. R. V. Prescott, 'Boundaries in Antarctica' in Stuart Harris (ed.) *Australia's Antarctic Policy Options* (Canberra, 1984) 83 at 94.

[31] Joyner, 'Ice-Covered Regions' at 225; Erik Franckx, *Maritime Claims in the Arctic* (Dordrecht, 1993) 20–1. For a more detailed discussion of Arctic ice shelves, see D. Pharand, *The Law of the Sea of the Arctic with Special Reference to Canada* (Ottawa, 1973) 182–7.

[32] For a review of other types of ice found in polar regions see Armstrong, Roberts and Swithinbank, *Illustrated Glossary*.

[33] *Ibid.* at 31, where pack ice is defined as: 'Any area of sea, river or lake ice other than fast ice, no matter what form it takes or how it is disposed.'

[34] The winter ice pack in the Southern Ocean can expand to encompass an area exceeding 20 million km^2: see Joyner, *Antarctica and the Law of the Sea* at 197; G. J. Mangone, 'The Legal Status of Ice in International Law' in Rudiger Wolfrum (ed.), *Antarctic Challenge III* (Berlin, 1988) 371 at 372.

[35] Armstrong, Roberts and Swithinbank, *Illustrated Glossary* at 14 define fast ice as: 'Sea ice which remains fast along the coast, where it is attached to the shore, to an ice wall, to an ice front, or over shoals, or between grounded icebergs. Fast ice may extend a few m or several hundred km from the shore.'

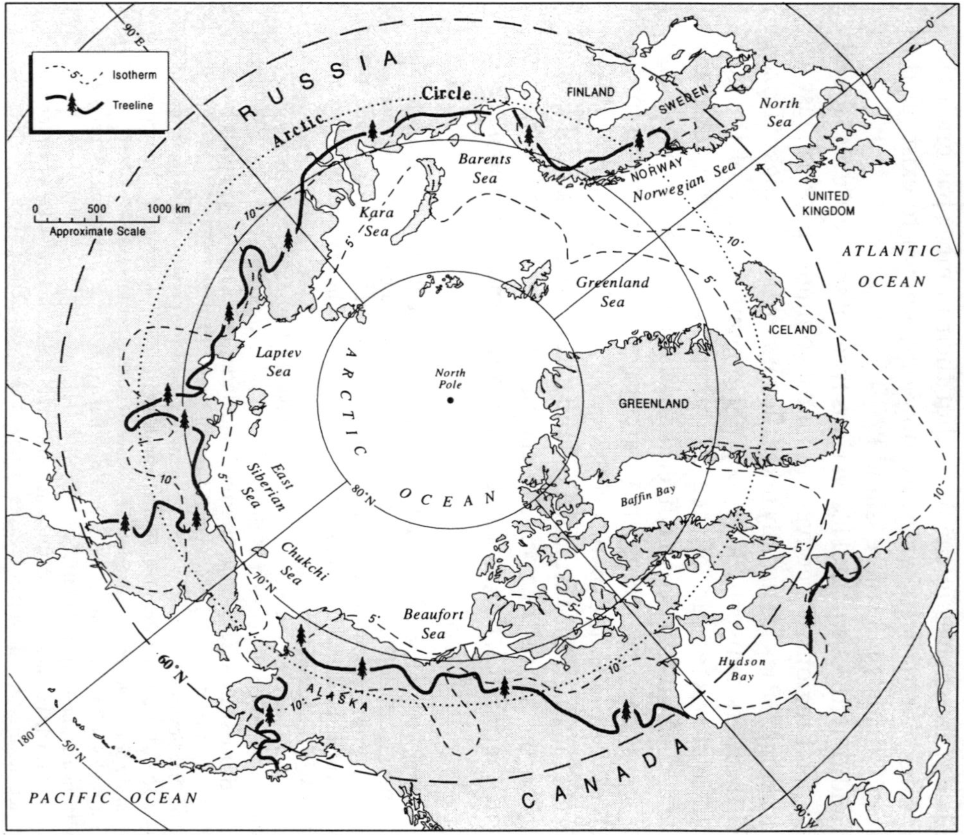

Figure 2 The Arctic region showing the Arctic Circle, the 5° and 10° isotherm line, the treeline and 60° North

used in the Arctic for various activities by indigenous peoples.[36] Icebergs are formed through ice shelves calving.[37] Because there are a greater number of ice shelves in Antarctica, icebergs are more common in the Southern Ocean. The size of icebergs can vary widely with some of enormous proportions having been reported.[38]

Ecosystems

The ecosystems of the polar regions are complex.[39] This is partly a result of the very short summer season, lack of daylight during the winter and the impact of ocean areas. Despite these features, polar ecosystems are diverse. Terrestrial animals are widespread in the Arctic as a result of land areas being connected to extensive continental land masses that are within more temperate areas. These animals range from the polar bear to small mammals such as lemmings and hares. In Antarctica there are no terrestrial animals. Rather, bird and marine life dominate with large populations of penguins and seals found around the coastline of the continent and sub-Antarctic islands. While there are no penguins in the Arctic, the bird life is more diverse and extensive with large migrations annually taking place to and from the Arctic areas of North America and Asia (Siberia). The marine life in polar regions is extensive. Whales and other cetaceans exist in the polar oceans and seas, though not to the extent they were found previously due to extensive whaling operations in the nineteenth and early twentieth centuries. Euan Young has noted that: 'The most surprising feature of polar life is not that it lacks great diversity but that it exists at all.'[40] The comment is especially apt for plants in the polar regions. In Antarctica there is virtually no flora apart from some mosses and lichens. The Arctic has a more extensive collection of plants, some of which are capable of spectacular blooms during spring and summer. Consistent with the Arctic's southern limit often based

[36] Mangone, 'Legal Status' at 373.

[37] This is a process whereby large portions of the ice shelf break off into the surrounding seas, forming icebergs. Armstrong, Roberts and Swithinbank, *Illustrated Glossary* at 20 define an iceberg as a 'Large mass of floating or stranded ice greatly varying in shape, more than 5m above sea level which has broken away from a glacier'.

[38] Joyner has described some icebergs as being as large as Luxembourg or the US state of Connecticut: see Joyner, 'Ice-Covered Regions' at 229. For more details on the size of some icebergs see C. Swithinbank, P. McClain and P. Little, 'Drift Tracks of Antarctic Icebergs' (1977) 18 *Polar Record* 495–501.

[39] See generally Stonehouse, *North Pole South Pole* at 87–105.

[40] Young, 'Ecology and Conservation' at 27.

on the northern reach of the treeline, there are no significant trees or forests found in much of the Arctic.

Environmental impact

An issue of emerging concern throughout the twentieth century has been environmental impact in the polar regions. As Stonehouse has noted: 'Human impact upon polar ecosystems can be devastating.'[41] While not all environmental impact in the polar regions is the same, Antarctica and the Arctic share common characteristics in their ecosystems which make them both vulnerable. The principal reason for this is the fragility of the ecosystem. An activity which may be sustainable in temperate or tropical regions is more difficult to sustain where the ecosystem is continually under threat because of the harshness of the environment. In the Arctic, there is also the additional issue of environmental impact caused by industrial development and the impact this has upon indigenous peoples.[42]

Osherenko and Young noted six reasons why the Arctic environment is particularly susceptible to disturbance by humans. They are:

1. Low temperatures retard the decomposition of natural and man-made substances and the breakdown of pollutants.
2. Regeneration is a protracted process because of the short growing season.
3. Large concentrations of animal populations heighten vulnerability to catastrophes.
4. Marine areas are particularly important in comparison to other regions of the globe.
5. Climatic conditions are likely to produce a more pronounced CO_2 induced warming trend than in temperate regions.
6. Severe weather and ice dynamics make environmental protection and clean-up extremely difficult.[43]

These factors have resulted in an increased awareness of the impact of both local and transboundary activities in the polar regions in recent years.[44]

[41] Stonehouse, *North Pole South Pole* at 193. See also W. Nigel Bonner, 'Environmental Assessment in the Antarctic' (1989) 18(1) AMBIO 83 at 83; Young, 'Ecology and Conservation' at 32–3.

[42] See e.g., Rick Riewe, 'The Demise of the Great White North: Environmental Impacts on the Circumpolar Aboriginal Peoples' (1992) 18 (4) *Information North* 1–7.

[43] Gail Osherenko and Oran R. Young, *The Age of the Arctic* (Cambridge, 1989) 111–17. Similar assessments can be made about Antarctica.

[44] See Ian Stirling and Wendy Calvert, 'Environmental Threats to Marine Mammals in the Canadian Arctic' (1983) 21 *Polar Record* 433–49; Martin W. Holdgate, 'The Use and

In the Arctic, there has been substantial environmental impact as a result of marine and land-based resource development. The heavy exploitation of whales, seals and some fish species has not only affected the stocks, but also the availability of these species for traditional hunting and other purposes by local indigenous peoples. Locally originating land-based environmental impact in the Arctic has principally resulted from non-living resource development and other industrial activities. During the Soviet era there was substantial exploitation of northern resources for oil, gas, timber and other minerals. This has particularly been the case with some mining and industrial sites in Siberia.[45] It is also known that the USSR dumped radioactive waste in waters off its north coast in the Barents Sea.[46] The problem was highlighted in 1994 by the rupturing of an oil pipeline in Russia's Komi republic, about 1,600km north of Moscow, which spilled a considerable quantity of oil onto Arctic tundra.[47] The effects of the spill were exacerbated due to the inability of the Russian authorities to respond quickly to the spill prior to the onset of winter.[48] Environmental groups have also raised concerns over some mining sites in Alaska and northern Canada.[49] Because of the unique noise environment created by ice, Arctic marine environments are also particularly susceptible to the impact of noise created by humans. This was singled out in the 1991 Arctic Environ-

Abuse of Polar Environmental Resources' (1984) 22 *Polar Record* 25–48. In response to the recognition of these impacts, see W. S. Benninghoff and W. N. Bonner, *Man's Impact on the Antarctic Environment* (Cambridge, 1985).

45 See generally Henrik Osterholm, 'Environmental Aspects on the Future of the Barents Seas Region' in Jan Ake Dellenbrant and Mats-Olav Olsson (eds.), *The Barents Region* (Umea, Sweden, 1994) 156–63; Armin Rosencranz and Antony Scott, 'Siberia, Environmentalism, and Problems of Environmental Protection' (1991) 14 *Hastings International and Comparative Law Quarterly* 929–47. For more specific reviews of environmental impact in these regions see Z. I. Mokrousova *et al.*, 'Environmental Pollution and Radiation Circumstances in the Russian Federation in November of 1992' (1993) No. 2 *Russian Meteorology and Hydrology* 99–100; A. M. Ovanesyants *et al.*, 'Natural Environment Pollution from Oil and Gas Production and Refinery Industry' (1991) No. 8 *Russian Meteorology and Hydrology* 96–7.

46 See Peter Jones, 'Russia's Nuclear Dumping Legacy' (1993) 26(5) *Marine Pollution Bulletin* 231–2; Thomas Ries, 'The Nordic Region and Post-Soviet Radioactive Pollution' (1993) 5(9) *Jane's Intelligence Review* 398–400.

47 See Matthew J. Sagers, 'Oil Spill in Russian Arctic' (1994) 18 *Polar Geography and Geology* 95 at 95, who notes that estimates of the spill ranged from 270,000 tons to 14,000 tons.

48 See Stephanie Pain and Kurt Kleiner, 'Frustrated West Watches as Arctic Oil Spill Grows' 5 November 1994, No. 1950, *New Scientist* 8.

49 See generally Osherenko and Young, *The Age of the Arctic* at 129–132.

mental Protection Strategy as being a major Arctic environmental problem.[50]

In Antarctica, local environmental impact has not been as substantial, principally due to a lack of major resource-based industries. The exception to this has been nineteenth-century commercial whaling and sealing, which, similarly to the Arctic experience, had a substantial environmental impact.[51] More recently, grave concerns were expressed over the potential impact upon the Antarctic marine ecosystem from the development of a substantial Southern Ocean fishing industry. The particular focus of this concern was the overexploitation of krill, a small crustacean which plays a pivotal role in the Antarctic food chain.[52] A further impact upon the marine environment has been pollution resulting from normal operating activities of vessels in the Southern Ocean, and also shipwrecks.[53] Land-based local environmental impact in Antarctica has resulted from activities associated with the operation of scientific bases. The further construction and expansion of scientific bases, the accumulation of waste from such bases as a result of construction and daily activities, and even some forms of scientific research have had an environmental impact.[54]

[50] (1991) 30 ILM 1,624 (hereafter AEPS), para 3.4 at 1,640–1, where it is noted:

> Human activities create noise types and levels, which may disturb marine mammals, or mask the 'natural' sounds of importance to those mammals. Some types of noise may affect fish as well as marine mammals. There are a number of serious gaps in our knowledge of the effects of underwater noise on marine mammals, including the inability to assess the effect of repeated noise exposure on stocks. There is considerable evidence that most types of disturbance do not cause mortality. However, some noisy activities, including low level overflights by aircraft, near seals and walrus at haul out sites can cause mortality through stampedes or abandonment.

[51] J. A. Gulland, 'The Management Regime for Living Resources' in Christopher C. Joyner and Sudhir K. Chopra (eds.), *The Antarctic Legal Regime* (Dordrecht, 1988) 219 at 221.

[52] *Ibid.* at 220, where Gulland noted with respect to the importance of krill to the Antarctic ecosystem that Antarctic 'resources differ from those in most other parts of the world in terms of the short food chain from primary production to the top predators (in this case killer whales), the small number of species involved, and the degree to which the dynamics of the whole system are governed by a single species – the krill'.

[53] One recent example was the loss of the *Bahia Paraiso*: see 'Argentine Ship Sinks Near Palmer Station' (1989) 24(2) *Antarctic Journal of the United States* 3–7.

[54] See generally Environmental Defense Fund, *Securing Environmental Protection in Antarctica* (Washington, 1989) 10–11. The best-known example of environmental impact resulting from a construction project was the building of an airstrip at the French base at Pointe Geologie in Adelie Land: see generally James N. Barnes, 'Legal Aspects of Environmental Protection in Antarctica' in Joyner and Chopra, *The Antarctic Legal Regime*, at 258–9.

As the IUCN–World Conservation Union noted in 1991: 'The impacts, while localized, have been considerable, and in some regrettable cases wildlife has been displaced and protected areas have been damaged.'[55] Environmental impact from tourism has also become a concern.[56] While this activity is still limited to only a few areas of the continent, repeated use of a few sites for tourist visits can cause extensive damage. With Antarctic tourism on the rise, the environmental impact resulting from these activities is an issue of growing concern.[57] Antarctica, just like the Arctic, is also particularly susceptible to the effects of noise and overflights by aircraft which can result in severe disturbance to breeding colonies of penguins or other sea-birds. This form of impact also extends to the use of explosives, for geophysical seismic investigations, or electrical generators.[58]

The polar regions have also been subject to the effects of transboundary pollution.[59] There has long been a recognition of the phenomenon of 'Arctic haze' and the need for transboundary pollutants affecting air quality in the Arctic to be regulated.[60] This concern has grown into fears over the depletion of the ozone layer above the poles and the impact this will have not only on the polar regions but the whole globe.[61] The state of transboundary environmental impact in the Arctic was highlighted in the negotiations leading up to the conclusion of the AEPS. Of the six environmental problems identified

55 IUCN–The World Conservation Union, *A Strategy for Antarctic Conservation* (Gland, Switzerland, 1991) 20.

56 Environmental Defense Fund, *Securing Environmental Protection* at 12. See also the testimony of Bruce Manheim Jr, before United States of America, House of Representatives, *Hearing before the Subcommittee on Fisheries and Wildlife Conservation and the Environment, Oceanography and Great Lakes, Coast Guard and Navigation of the Committee on Merchant Marine and Fisheries* (101st Congress, 2nd Session, 26 June 1990) 119–24.

57 On the prospects for further tourism development in Antarctica see Richard Herr, 'Antarctic Tourism: Australia, Regulation and the Industry' in John Handmer and Martijn Wilder (eds.), *Towards a Conservation Strategy for the Australian Antarctic Territory* (Canberra, 1993) 91–107.

58 IUCN–The World Conservation Union, *A Strategy for Antarctic Conservation* at 21.

59 Recent evidence suggests that Greenland was subject to transboundary pollution from European lead and silver smelting conducted between 1000BC and 1500AD, see Sungmin Hong *et al.*, 'Greenland Ice Evidence of Hemispheric Lead Pollution Two Millennia Ago by Greek and Roman Civilizations' (1994) 265 (5180) *Science* 1,841–3.

60 Jost Heintzenberg, 'Arctic Haze: Air Pollution in Polar Regions' (1989) 18 AMBIO 50–5; Osherenko and Young, *The Age of the Arctic* at 123–5.

61 See J. Barrie Maxwell and Leonard A. Barrie, 'Atmospheric and Climatic Change in the Arctic and Antarctic' (1989) 18 AMBIO 42–9. One particular area of concern here is that a substantial melting of the polar ice caps would result in sea-level rise which would impact upon many low-lying coastal and island communities.

as being Arctic-wide, five were of a transboundary nature: persistent organic contaminants, oil pollution, heavy metals, radioactivity and acidification.[62] One of the goals of the AEPS process is to study constantly the environmental impact of these pollutants through the 'Arctic Monitoring and Assessment Program'.[63] Despite the remoteness of Antarctica from large northern industrialised societies, the region has not been immune from transboundary environmental impact. Depletion of stratospheric ozone has been most pronounced over Antarctica and the Southern Ocean.[64] In addition, Antarctica is particularly vulnerable to the effects of global warming. One potential impact would be increased melting of the ice shelves, which would result in a global rise in sea levels.[65]

Polar topography

The Antarctic region is dominated by the Antarctic continent and the Southern Ocean. The Antarctic continent is the fifth largest and covers an area of approximately 14 million km^2, representing one-tenth of the earth's total land surface.[66] The continent is unique because of the polar ice sheet which permanently covers 98 per cent of the land surface. The ice has a mean thickness of 1,880m and in places reaches 4,000m thick.[67] Another feature is the presence of substantial ice shelves which project out from the coastline. The two largest are the Ross and the Ronne. A consequence of the ice sheet is that the true bedrock surface of the continent is depressed. If the ice were to be removed, isostatic readjustment would occur with up to 1,000m of uplift resulting in some areas.[68] With the continent estimated to contain 30.11 million km^3 of ice it is therefore understandable that it

[62] AEPS, paras. 3.1–3.6 at 1,635–43.

[63] AEPS, para. 6 at 1,655–9.

[64] IUCN–The World Conservation Union, *A Strategy for Antarctic Conservation* at 21.

[65] See Sharon Begley *et al.*, 'Ice Cubes for Penguins' 116 (5964) (4 April 1995) *The Bulletin* 64, where existing evidence of the melting of ice shelves is discussed. On the issue of sea-level rise, see Crossley, *Explore Antarctica* at 98–107, who notes at 107 that: 'The combination of ocean expansion with a reduction in sea ice, possibly some melting of ice shelves and a small positive mass balance of the Antarctic ice sheet, could cause a rise in sea level of up to 40cm by 2030. This would be sufficient to inundate many coral atolls in the Pacific and Indian Oceans, and low-lying countries like Bangladesh.'

[66] Stonehouse, *Polar Ecology* at 19; Marine Resources Project, *Marine Resources* at 25.

[67] Stonehouse, *Polar Ecology* at 19.

[68] D. J. Drewry, 'The Antarctic Physical Environment' in Gillian D. Triggs (ed.), *The Antarctic Treaty Regime* (Cambridge, 1987) 6 at 8–9.

has been commented that: 'Ice is probably the most individual characteristic of Antarctica.'[69] Because of the continual process of calving along the ice shelves, some of the continent's ice eventually finds its way into the Southern Ocean as tabular icebergs. Antarctic and sub-Antarctic islands are not as ice-covered as the continent, though glaciers are found on some. Many are volcanic and are of a relatively recent origin. Most are found in the vicinity of the Antarctic Peninsula and the Drake Passage area.[70]

The Southern Ocean has been estimated at being 37.5 million km^2 in size.[71] However, these estimates vary because its exact limits are difficult to define. Some maps and charts do not even acknowledge the existence of the Southern Ocean. Rather, they indicate that the Atlantic, Pacific and Indian Oceans extend as far south as Antarctica. This ignores the close relationship between the Southern Ocean and the Antarctic continent.[72] While ice is a dominant feature of the Arctic Ocean, it is even more so in the Southern Ocean. A fringe of pack ice surrounds the continent even during summer. By early spring, pack ice in the Southern Ocean grows to about 20 million km^2.[73] The effect of this is that the total area of the continental land mass and pack ice doubles during winter. Because the Southern Ocean is relatively open to the effects of ocean currents and prevailing winds, both pack ice and icebergs have a large area within which they can disperse. In total, 85 per cent of Antarctic pack ice melts each summer.[74]

The Arctic region is dominated by the Arctic Ocean and smaller seas which fringe it. The Arctic Ocean has an area between 9.5 and 10 million km^2 which represents about 2.6 per cent of the total oceanic surface.[75] An important characteristic of the Arctic Ocean is that it is predominantly semi-enclosed with the only major outlets being Bering Strait into the North Pacific Ocean and Fram Strait into the North Atlantic. Because of this characteristic, some commentators refer to the Arctic as being a 'Polar Mediterranean'.[76] A major feature

69 *Ibid.* at 15. 70 Stonehouse, *Polar Ecology* at 21–2. 71 *Ibid.* at 126.

72 The exact northern limits of the Southern Ocean are debatable. However, this is not significant for this study as the northern boundary of the region which has been adopted depends on the CCAMLR definition and not the northern limits of the Southern Ocean.

73 Drewry, 'The Antarctic Physical Environment' at 20.

74 Marine Resources Project, *Marine Resources* at 27.

75 Stonehouse, *Polar Ecology* at 17; Louis Rey, 'The Arctic Ocean: A "Polar Mediterranean"' in Louis Rey (ed.), *The Arctic Ocean* (London, 1982) 3 at 31.

76 Rey, *The Arctic Ocean* at 38; Bo Johnson Theutenberg, 'The Arctic Law of the Sea' (1983) 52 Nordic JIL 3 at 3.

of the Arctic Ocean is the permanent ice-cover. This ice, which is in most cases very old sea ice frozen into massive packs, not only permanently covers the North Pole but also reaches to the coastlines of some of the far northern islands in the Arctic such as the Canadian Arctic Archipelago and northern Greenland. At its annual maximum during winter the pack ice reaches 10 million km^2, which constitutes about 30 per cent of the world's sea ice.[77] The Arctic pack ice slowly circulates around the North Pole. During the summer thaw, some finds its way south through natural exit-points into more open and warmer waters. This especially occurs in Fram Strait and to a lesser extent in the Bering and Davis Straits.[78] The result is that many of the smaller seas which fringe the Arctic Ocean, such as the Kara, Barents, Beaufort, Bering and Laptev Sea, are ice-clogged even during the summer months.

The land area of the Arctic region can best be described as tundra and polar deserts.[79] There is great variation, however, in the land surface. Much of Greenland is covered by an ice sheet which rises to 3,230m and is sustained by a heavy snowfall. There are also ice sheets on some islands in the Canadian Arctic Archipelago, Svalbard and Novaya Zemlaya.[80] Glaciers are also to be found throughout much of the Arctic, especially in Alaska. Land areas which are at the southern limits of the Arctic region are primarily ice free, though snow-covered for much of the year. It has been estimated that the ratio of tundra to ice in the Arctic is 5.5 million km^2 to 2.1 million km^2.[81]

Polar resources

Marine living resources have been the principal Antarctic resource subject to exploitation.[82] For many years these resources went unexploited because their existence was unknown and vessels had been unable to penetrate the pack ice. This changed during Captain James

[77] Rey, *The Arctic Ocean* at 34; see also Stonehouse, *Polar Ecology* at 129.

[78] Rey, *The Arctic Ocean* at 38 notes that there is a yearly release into the Atlantic and Bering Sea of close to 3,500 km^3, nearly 1 million megatonnes, of ice. See also Stonehouse, *Polar Ecology* at 131.

[79] Young, 'Ecology and Conservation' at 24.

[80] Stonehouse, *Polar Ecology* at 16.

[81] Young, 'Ecology and Conservation' at 24.

[82] See George A. Knox, 'The Living Resources of the Southern Ocean: A Scientific Overview' in Francisco Orrego Vicuna (ed.), *Antarctic Resources Policy* (Cambridge, 1983) 21–60.

Cook's circumnavigation of the continent in 1772–75 when he not only succeeded in sailing into and through the pack ice (though never so far as actually to sight the continent) but also sighted abundant numbers of seals on sub-Antarctic islands.[83] This proved the catalyst for an influx of sealers eager to exploit the newly discovered resource and it was not long before whalers followed. As a result, Antarctic seal and whale stocks were placed under considerable pressure during the nineteenth century. It is only recently, through a combination of international management and declining commercial interest in the resource during the latter part of the twentieth century that stocks have begun to recover.[84] The southern fur seal and the southern elephant seal were the most exploited of the seal species, while blue, fin, sei and recently minke whales have all been subject to heavy exploitation.[85] Commercial exploitation of penguins also occurred on some sub-Antarctic islands in the nineteenth and early twentieth centuries but ceased prior to World War II.[86]

The fish stocks of the Southern Ocean are limited, being largely found in areas surrounding the continental shelves of the Antarctic Peninsula and sub-Antarctic islands.[87] While there is evidence that attempts to exploit the Southern Ocean fishery began as far back as 1904 in and around South Georgia, scientific research into the potential of such a fishery did not seriously begin until the 1950s.[88] The USSR and other communist countries began commercial fishing activities throughout parts of the Southern Ocean in the 1960s. These activities extended into the 1970s, but peaked by the end of the 1970s and have not returned to those levels.[89] One commentator has noted that the 'productivity of the fish stocks probably is not high enough to enable high-sustained catches to be taken' in the Southern Ocean.[90]

83 Deborah Shapley, *The Seventh Continent* (Washington, 1985) 7.

84 See Gulland, 'The Management Regime' at 221–2.

85 Knox, 'The Living Resources' at 37, 40–2.

86 Graham Chittleborough, 'Nature, Extent and Management of Antarctic Living Resources' in Stuart Harris (ed.), *Australia's Antarctic Policy Options* (Cambridge, 1984) 135 at 143.

87 Gulland, 'The Management Regime' at 222.

88 J.-C. Hureau and W. Slosarczyk, 'Exploitation and Conservation of Antarctic Fishes and Recent Ichthyological Research in the Southern Ocean' in O. Gon and P. C. Heemstra (eds.), *Fishes of the Southern Ocean* (Grahamstown, South Africa, 1990) 52 at 52.

89 *Ibid.* at 53–6; Dietrich Sahrhage, 'Present Knowledge of Living Marine Resources in the Antarctic, Possibilities for their Exploitation and Scientific Perspectives' in Rudiger Wolfrum (ed.), *Antarctic Challenge* (Berlin, 1984) 67 at 76–7.

90 Gulland, 'The Management Regime' at 222. For a further review of fish stocks in the Southern Ocean, see Inigo Everson, 'Antarctic Fisheries' (1978) 19 *Polar Record* 233–51.

This situation does not apply to krill, which are found in abundant quantities. It has proven difficult to assess accurately the size of krill stocks because of a lack of scientific knowledge about the species.[91] This has in turn made it difficult to assess the potential impact of krill exploitation upon the Antarctic marine ecosystem. While krill catches were reported as far back as 1964, significant commercial exploitation did not commence until 1976.[92] Today, management of krill exploitation is dealt with under CCAMLR.

A substantial number of mineral resources have also been discovered in the Antarctic.[93] These discoveries have been made as a result of both scientific and commercial exploration. Mineral deposits on the continent include iron, titanium, uranium, tin, coal, copper, zinc, lead and silver.[94] Considerable efforts have also been expended in the search for oil and gas in the Southern Ocean. Some important discoveries were made in the 1970s and it is now known that varying reserves lie scattered throughout parts of the Southern Ocean.[95] While there is some debate amongst scientists as to the actual minerals potential of the region, it does seem widely accepted that few of these resources have any current commercial value.[96]

Arctic living resources have always been subject to exploitation by man because indigenous peoples in the Arctic relied upon such resources for subsistence. A variety of species of whales, seals, fish, and birds plus polar bears and caribou/reindeer were subject to subsistence hunting by Arctic indigenous peoples. While traditional hunting activities still take place, there is today a much greater reliance

[91] See the varying figures noted in Knox, 'The Living Resources' at 32.

[92] *Ibid.* at 33.

[93] For reviews see Robert William *et al.*, 'The Mineral Resource Potential of Antarctica: Geological Realities' in Grahame Cook (ed.), *The Future of Antarctica: Exploitation Versus Preservation* (Manchester, 1990) 25–43; Franz Tessensohn, 'Present Knowledge of Non-Living Resources in the Antarctic, Possibilities for their Exploitation and Scientific Perspectives' in Rudiger Wolfrum (ed.), *Antarctic Challenge* (Berlin, 1984), 189–210.

[94] Tore Gjelsvik, 'The Mineral Resources of Antarctica: Progress in Their Identification' in Francisco Orrego Vicuna (ed.), *Antarctic Resources Policy* (Cambridge, 1983) 61 at 62.

[95] *Ibid.* at 63–4.

[96] See Geoffrey Larminie, 'The Mineral Potential of Antarctica: The State of the Art' in Arnfinn Jorgensen-Dahl and Willy Ostreng (eds.), *The Antarctic Treaty System in World Politics* (London, 1991) 79–93 who at 91 noted:

> In conclusion, what then is the energy and mineral resource potential of Antarctica? The answer is 'don't know, but probably poor', and if anything were discovered, as of now the economics of development are prohibitive and likely to remain so for at least another 20 years.

upon food imported from the south and communities which solely rely upon the hunting of such resources are in decline.[97] Commercial resource exploitation first occurred in the Arctic during the nineteenth century when seals and whales were extensively hunted with commercial fishing of coldwater fish species also occurring. This emphasis upon the commercial exploitation of Arctic marine living resources has continued in the twentieth century with some states such as Iceland having a resource-dependent economy. While commercial whaling has been curbed due to a combination of scarcity of the resource and international regulation, substantial exploitation of other Arctic fisheries continues. A similar position exists with some species of seals.[98] One result of the extensive commercial exploitation of Arctic marine living resources has been the impact upon the traditional subsistence hunt. As a result the Arctic has witnessed a number of major resource conflicts throughout the past two centuries.[99]

Non-living resources in the Arctic have only been subject to extensive exploitation during the twentieth century.[100] This is partly a result of the increase in demand for some resources and the development of techniques allowing for resource exploration in the polar regions. The most prominent non-living resource discoveries have been in oil and gas. Large reserves are known to exist both onshore and offshore the Canadian and Russian Arctic (Siberia) and Alaska. There are also potential reserves in the Kara, Barents and Norwegian Sea.[101] Apart from oil and gas, there are also large reserves of coal in parts of Siberia and Svalbard.

Polar peoples

One of the major contrasts between the two polar regions is that Antarctica has no indigenous population. The most southerly dwell-

[97] Stonehouse, *Polar Ecology* at 188–9.

[98] *Ibid.* at 144.

[99] See generally Holdgate, 'The Use and Abuse'. For a specific discussion of this issue as it affects indigenous peoples see Ray Gambell, 'Bowhead Whales and Alaskan Eskimos: A Problem of Survival' (1983) 21 *Polar Record* 467–73.

[100] See P. Miles and N. J. R. Wright, 'An Outline of Mineral Extraction in the Arctic' (1978) 19 *Polar Record* 11–38.

[101] See James W. Clarke, 'Oil and Gas Resources in the Offshore Soviet Arctic' in Lawson W. Brigham (ed.), *The Soviet Maritime Arctic* (London, 1991) 108–22; Oran R. Young, *Arctic Politics* (Dartmouth, NH, 1992) 105; Franckx, *Maritime Claims* at 28–31.

ing indigenous peoples inhabit the far southern tip of South America in Tierra del Fuego. Nevertheless there has been an active human interest in Antarctica since the nineteenth century following the discovery of substantial whale and seal stocks. However, with the exception of temporary settlements and small whaling stations established on some sub-Antarctic islands, there were no attempts to colonise either the continent or Antarctic and sub-Antarctic islands. The development of scientific programmes for exploration and research in Antarctica eventually resulted in the establishment of scientific stations which can provide year round or summer-only accommodation. There are now thirty-seven permanent bases administered by seventeen states, with another four on sub-Antarctic islands. The winter population is about 1,000 people, with approximately 4,000 staying during the summer. The largest scientific station is the US base at McMurdo on Ross Island which accommodates between 300–1,200 people depending on seasons. Crossley has estimated that there is one person per 14,000km^2 on the continent.[102]

The Arctic has been inhabited by several different groups of peoples. Some have been nomadic travellers, while others are indigenous. Arctic indigenous peoples include the Inuit or Eskimos who inhabit parts of Alaska, northern Canada and Greenland.[103] These people traditionally lived a pure subsistence culture which revolved around survival in the harsh Arctic climate. Because of the abundance of food to be found around coastal areas and the ice edge, they traditionally lived near open water.[104] The Inuit developed a particular culture that depended on the exploitation of animals found on sea ice. As a result, rights over and the ability to use sea ice for traditional purposes have great significance for these peoples.[105] Other Arctic indigenous peoples include the Saami (formerly known as Lapps), the Nenet, the Yakut and the Chukchi. These groups are mainly spread across northern Scandinavia and Siberia. They share a common ancestry with the Inuit; however, they have developed a way of life which is more land-based.[106] Some parts of the Arctic do not have an indigenous population. Svalbard is an example. It was

[102] Crossley, *Explore Antarctica* at 43; Stonehouse, *Polar Ecology* at 189–91.

[103] Stonehouse, *North Pole South Pole* at 19.

[104] Stonehouse, *Polar Ecology* at 185–7.

[105] See the collection of essays in *Sikumiut 'The People who Use the Sea Ice'* (Ottawa, 1984). For a legal perspective of this issue, see David VanderZwaag and Donat Pharand, 'Inuit and the Ice: Implications for Canadian Arctic Waters' (1983) 21 CYIL 53–84.

[106] Stonehouse, *Polar Ecology* at 187.

colonised by peoples from what is now Norway and Russia. Similarly, Iceland was founded by Norse settlers. Because of resource development activities, the polar regions have also attracted settlers from the south so that in Alaska, Canada and Russia there has been substantial 'colonisation' of Arctic lands by peoples from southern parts of those countries.

Indigenous peoples in the Arctic have increasingly become concerned about protection of their native cultures and the impact of development upon their environment. Commencing in the 1960s the Inuit have become politically organised with representative groups existing in Alaska, Canada and Greenland.[107] The Inuit Circumpolar Conference (ICC) has been an outgrowth of this development and has significantly increased the political voice of the Inuit.[108] In 1992, the ICC met with a delegation from the former USSR, participating for the first time. Other groups which represent Arctic indigenous peoples are the Nordic Saami Council and the Association of Small Peoples of the North. The growth in international recognition of the rights of indigenous peoples to some form of self-determination and access to traditional resources has posed new challenges for Arctic states.[109] One response has been to arrive at extensive land-claim settlements, thereby conferring partial autonomy over land and resources back to native peoples. The most recent example of this process was the decision in 1992 by Canada to grant self-government and extensive land rights to the Inuit and Dene peoples of the Northwest Territories.[110] Another response has been to involve the ICC in negotiations for the creation of various multilateral and bilateral Arctic regimes such as the AEPS.[111] The reconciliation of native claims and the

[107] G. Luton, 'Strategic Issues in the Arctic Region' (1986) 6 *Ocean Yearbook* 399 at 408–10.

[108] The ICC held its first meeting in 1977 in Barrow, Alaska: see Sue C. Wrenn, 'First Inuit Circumpolar Conference, 1977' (1978) 19 *Polar Record* 64–6. For an example of the input the ICC has had into the Arctic policy development process, see Inuit Circumpolar Conference, *Principles and Elements for a Comprehensive Arctic Policy* (Montreal, 1992).

[109] See generally Osherenko and Young, *The Age of the Arctic* at 72–109; Frederik Harhoff, 'Constitutional and International Legal Aspects of Aboriginal Peoples' (1988) 3 Nordic JIL 289–94; Vadim Fotinov, 'United Northern Emirates: The Future of the Former Soviet Union?' (1991) 2(3) *Arctic Circle* 10–11.

[110] L. J. MacLachlan, 'Comprehensive Aboriginal Claims in the N. W. T.' (1992) 18(1) *Information North* 1–7.

[111] AEPS, para. 10 at 1,668. For a review of the role played by the ICC and other groups in the negotiation of the AEPS see Monica Tennberg, 'The Rovaniemi Process and New International Actors' (paper presented at the First International Congress of Arctic Social Sciences, Université Laval, Ste-Foy, Quebec, 1992).

conferring of economic and social rights upon Arctic indigenous peoples is only part of the self-determination process and more will need to be achieved across the Arctic before the process is complete and all Arctic peoples have a voice in Arctic issues.[112] The development of Arctic management regimes and increased international cooperation will be a part of that process.

Common polar issues

The Arctic and Antarctic have a number of important common issue areas which provide a genuine link between the two regions. These common issue areas demonstrate that while some commentators believe that the two polar regions are 'poles apart' from both a scientific and legal political perspective,[113] there is still much to be gained from considering the two regions side by side. The existence of the common issue areas has often been overlooked; bi-polar comparisons having been considered inappropriate due to the great physical differences between the two regions. This is not the case, however, when the regions are compared from the perspective of their polar environments, their importance to science, and their similar histories of inter-state rivalry and diplomatic conflict. These common issue areas are also major driving forces behind the development of legal and political mechanisms in both regions. Four common issue areas have been identified: science, territorial sovereignty, national security and environment.

Both polar regions are significant because of the scientific research

[112] Rhoda Innusuk, 'The Circumpolar Challenge' (1988) 3 Nordic JIL 348–52.

[113] See Jim Flegg, Eric Hosking and David Hosking, *Poles Apart* (London, 1990) 10 where it is argued:

> Despite the similarities evident in their spectacularly beautiful scenery, in their savagely harsh climate, and more recently in the epic stories of their exploitation by man, the Arctic and the Antarctic are amazingly different in a great many respects – quite literally, poles apart.

Osherenko and Young, *The Age of the Arctic* at 244 have argued from a political science perspective that:

> simplistic comparisons between the Arctic and Antarctic do more to confuse the analysis of prospects for international cooperation in the Arctic region than to shed light on this topic. The simple fact that interested parties have achieved considerable success in establishing an international regime for one polar region does not entitle us to conclude that the other polar region is ripe for success in these terms.

that emanates from them. Antarctica is often called a 'continent of science'; a reflection of the fact that the predominant activity and 'export' is science.[114] The potential to conduct scientific research in Antarctica was one reason which initially attracted national expeditions to the region. This tradition began with Cook's circumnavigation of 1772–5, when seawater temperature observations were made, and it has continued into the twentieth century.[115] One important catalyst for the negotiation of the Antarctic Treaty was the international cooperation which resulted from the 1957–8 International Geophysical Year (IGY). All of the twelve states invited to participate at the 1959 Washington Conference to consider the negotiation of an Antarctic Treaty were IGY participants in Antarctica. The importance of science in Antarctica was subsequently recognised in the Antarctic Treaty. It is a prerequisite for any acceding state becoming a Consultative Party.[116] As a result, it has been noted that: 'Antarctic science is the key to international credibility both for a nation within the ATS and for the Antarctic Treaty System within the broader international community of nations.'[117]

In the Arctic, science has not played as significant a role. This is partly a reflection of the difficulty in conducting scientific research in a region dominated by maritime areas which are ice-clogged for much of the year. The IGY did not create a substantial impetus for greater cooperative scientific research in the Arctic.[118] Nevertheless, a number

[114] R. M. Laws, 'Scientific opportunities in the Antarctic' in Gillian D. Triggs (ed.), *The Antarctic Treaty Regime* (Cambridge, 1987) 28–48. For a comment on this perception that Antarctica is a 'continent of science' see Willy Ostreng, 'Polar Science and Politics: Close Twins or Opposite Poles in International Cooperation?' in Steinar Andresen and Willy Ostreng (eds.), *International Resource Management* (London, 1989) 88 at 90–9; Bruce Davis, 'Science and Politics in Antarctic and Southern Oceans Policy: A Critical Assessment' in R. A. Herr, H. R. Hall and M. G. Haward (eds.), *Antarctica's Future* (Hobart, 1990) 39–45.

[115] See Robert H. Rutford, 'Summary of Science in Antarctica Prior to and Including the International Geophysical Year' in *Antarctic Treaty System* (Washington, 1986) 87–101.

[116] See Antarctic Treaty, Arts. II, III, IX(2). For an assessment of how a determination is made as to whether the necessary interest in Antarctic science has been demonstrated, see Patrick G. Quilty, 'Antarctica as a Continent for Science' in R. A. Herr, H. R. Hall and M. G. Haward (eds.), *Antarctica's Future* (Hobart, 1990) 29 at 30.

[117] Quilty, 'Antarctica as a Continent for Science' at 29. For a view of the role of science within the ATS, see E. Fred Roots, 'The Role of Science in the Antarctic Treaty System' in *Antarctic Treaty System* (Washington, 1986) 169–84.

[118] Osherenko and Young, *The Age of the Arctic* at 257 comment that the 1882–3 International Polar Year was the high point of international scientific cooperation in the Arctic!

of large national scientific programmes have been conducted in the region[119] and increasingly there have been bilateral scientific research exchanges and projects developed between Arctic states.[120] The International Arctic Science Committee (IASC), formed in 1990,[121] may also provide greater impetus for enhanced international cooperation in Arctic science. In conjunction with the Scientific Committee on Antarctic Research (SCAR), which plays a role in the ATS, these scientific bodies demonstrate the scientific importance of the polar regions.[122]

In both regions territorial sovereignty has also been a significant issue. In Antarctica concern over unsettled sovereignty claims was a catalyst for the negotiation of the Antarctic Treaty.[123] Because of the nature of the region, the sovereignty concerns have been predominantly terrestrial, though occasionally maritime issues do arise. In the Arctic the reverse is true with maritime boundary issues predominating, especially with the growth of offshore areas subject to national jurisdiction.[124] However, given the potential mineral and other resource potential of both regions, sovereignty questions should not be seen in terms of traditional disputes over land for peoples but rather in economic terms. In these circumstances, though the sovereignty issues differ, the economic issues which are at stake are very similar.

[119] For a review of the output of such research see the papers published in the journals: *Arctic Research of the United States* (published by the US National Science Foundation) and *Arctic* (journal of the Arctic Institute of North America).

[120] See Agreement Between the Government of Canada and the Government of the Union of Soviet Socialist Republics on Cooperation in the Arctic and the North, [1989] CTS 21. For a review of Canadian–USSR scientific exchanges see Walter Slipchenko, 'Canada–USSR Arctic Science Exchange Programme: An Historical Perspective of Arctic Cooperation' in Lawson W. Brigham (ed.), *The Soviet Maritime Arctic* (London, 1991) 235–57.

[121] See International Arctic Science Committee, *Founding Articles for an International Arctic Science Committee* (Ottawa, 1990).

[122] For discussion of these two bodies see Carlos Rinaldi, 'SCAR in the ATS: Conflict or Harmony?' in Arnfinn Jorgensen-Dahl and Willy Ostreng (eds.), *The Antarctic Treaty System in World Politics* (London, 1991) 153–60; Franckx, *Maritime Claims* at 248–61. Because of its importance, science also has a political influence in both regions: see Aant Elzinga and Ingemar Bohlin, 'The Politics of Science in Polar Regions' (1989) 18(1) AMBIO 71–6.

[123] Christopher D. Beeby, 'The Antarctic Treaty System: Goals, Performance and Impact' in Arnfinn Jorgensen-Dahl and Willy Ostreng (eds.), *The Antarctic Treaty System in World Politics* (London, 1991) 4 at 5–7.

[124] D. M. Johnston (ed.), *Arctic Ocean Issues in the 1980's* (Honolulu, 1982) 18–23; Susan J. Rolston and Ted L. McDorman, 'Maritime Boundary Making in the Arctic Regions' in Douglas M. Johnston and Phillip M. Saunders (eds.), *Ocean Boundary Making* (London, 1988) 16–73.

In both regions national security is also an issue.[125] In Antarctica the overlapping territorial claims to the Antarctic Peninsula by the UK, Argentina and Chile have a long history which, especially for the two South American states, has great significance for national security. The UK–Argentina dispute over the Falkland (Malvinas) Islands is closely linked to the Antarctic claims of both states.[126] In addition, the need to resolve concerns over the potential militarisation of Antarctica during a time when the Cold War was at its height was another factor which influenced states to negotiate the Antarctic Treaty. The Treaty sought to diffuse these concerns by declaring that the continent was to be used only for 'peaceful purposes' and prohibiting military establishments (Article I) while also prohibiting nuclear explosions (Article V). Since the conclusion of World War II and the outbreak of the Cold War the Arctic has been a region in which national security and strategic issues have been given high priority.[127] This has primarily been a consequence of the development of nuclear weapons and the proximity of the US and the USSR to each other. The Cold War had the effect of placing most of the Arctic states in the middle of any possible outbreak of military hostilities between the superpowers and this contributed to a further raising of national security concerns in the region. The capacity of nuclear-powered submarines to navigate under the Arctic ice also made the Arctic Ocean a significant region for naval activity.[128] Many initiatives to develop greater cooperation in the Arctic have revolved around the need to confront these national security concerns.[129]

Antarctic resource management has been an issue which has confronted the Antarctic Treaty parties for the past twenty years. The issue has increasingly become one of seeking to sustain resource development while also protecting the environment. In the case of marine living resources, this was seen as a compromise which could be achieved and successfully managed though ultimately in the case of

125 R. Purver, 'Security and Arms Control at the Poles' (1984) 39 IntJ 888–910.

126 C. H. M. Waldock, 'Disputed Sovereignty in the Falkland Islands Dependencies' (1948) 25 BYIL 311–53.

127 Osherenko and Young, *The Age of the Arctic* at 17–44; Luton, 'Strategic Issues' at 399–416.

128 Oran R. Young, 'The Age of the Arctic' (1986) 29(1) *Oceanus* 9–17.

129 See, for example, Canadian Institute of International Affairs, *The North and Canada's International Relations* (Report of a Working Group of the National Capital Branch) (Ottawa, 1988) and the essays in Kari Mottola (ed.), *The Arctic Challenge* (Boulder, CO, 1988).

minerals such a compromise was impossible. Resource management is also a major issue in the Arctic where mineral resource exploitation has long been occurring. The Arctic states have not been as concerned about the environmental impact on their mineral resource activities as the Antarctic states. Nevertheless, resource management remains an issue especially in regard to maritime claims which may prove decisive in gaining access to certain resources.[130]

Polar environmental protection is a relatively recent issue. However, with the growth of a vocal environmental movement and an ever-increasing worldwide concern about the protection of the global environment, polar environmental issues have become of prime significance. They are not dealt with in any detail in the Antarctic Treaty itself, but the ATS has increasingly become environmentally focused. All of the major additional legal instruments adopted since the Treaty entered into force have dealt in some form with environmental protection – though none has been as comprehensive as the 1991 Protocol. In the Arctic there has been a growing movement towards greater environmental protection. The AEPS is an outgrowth of these concerns and a realisation that all Arctic states must jointly and cooperatively deal with environmental issues if the Arctic is not to become permanently damaged.

Conclusion

This study concentrates on the common features of the polar regions and assesses how the distinctive international law responses that have been adopted by polar states have contributed to the development of international law. This is not to suggest that the polar regions are identical nor that the legal issues that arise in each region are exactly the same. While both Antarctica and the Arctic share many common polar characteristics, they differ substantially from each other in one major respect. Antarctica is a continent which is surrounded by the Southern Ocean while the Arctic is predominantly characterised as a region based around an ocean surrounded by continents. This important distinction has inevitably impacted on the international law developments that have occurred in both regions. In the case of Antarctica, much of the international law in the region has developed

130 See the examples discussed in Willy Ostreng, 'Delimitation Arrangements in Arctic Seas: Cases of Precedence or Securing of Strategic/Economic Interests?' (1986) 10 *Marine Policy* 132–54.

around the question of sovereignty not only to the continent but also to offshore maritime areas. In the case of the Arctic, the law of the sea has played an important role but also important have been bilateral and other regional initiatives to deal with common problems. The question of sovereignty has also been dealt with differently in Antarctica than in the Arctic and this has had a continuing impact on how the ATS developed. The Arctic has been subject to much more extensive industrial development than Antarctica,[131] resulting in substantial industrial environmental impact. Finally, the Arctic has indigenous peoples while Antarctica does not. As a result, Arctic initiatives towards greater regional cooperation are increasingly based on the premise that Arctic indigenous peoples have a legitimate role to play in that process. There is also the dynamic of self-determination being granted to some groups of Arctic indigenous peoples and the impact this is having on the policies of Arctic states.

From a legal perspective, some of these distinctions are more important than others. It is perhaps because of the physical differences between the two regions, and the way in which sovereignty has been dealt with, that Antarctica has a legal regime based more on a single treaty than the Arctic. The growing recognition of the rights of indigenous peoples in the Arctic also has consequences for environmental and resource management in the Arctic that are not duplicated in Antarctica. Despite these distinctions, the polar regions still share many common features and together they have been able to make a contribution to the development of international law. It is these common polar issue areas that are the subject of this study.

[131] See Gennady Luzin, 'Mega Projects and the Environment: The Use of Natural Resources in the Arctic' in Heikki Jussila *et al.* (eds.), *Shifts in Systems at the Top of Europe* (Stockholm, 1993) 89–97.

Part II

The legal regimes of the polar regions

3 The Antarctic Treaty

The Antarctic Treaty[1] is the basis of the legal regime in Antarctica. It was negotiated in 1959 with the intention of resolving Antarctic sovereignty disputes, demilitarising the continent and allowing peaceful and cooperative scientific research to continue and flourish. During its more than thirty years of operation the Treaty has provided the foundation for the development of a sophisticated legal regime – commonly known as the Antarctic Treaty System (ATS). In this chapter, the focus will be on the Antarctic Treaty – its negotiation, implementation and interpretation. Chapter 4 will concentrate on the ATS. Because of the unique status of territorial claims in Antarctica and how the Treaty dealt with Antarctic sovereignty, it is appropriate to begin with a review of the Antarctic territorial claims.

The territorial claims

Discovery and exploration

To gain a proper understanding of Antarctica and the Antarctic Treaty it is useful to be aware of the background to the exploration and opening of the continent to territorial claims.[2] Antarctica was truly the last unknown continent. When the existence and full extent of the Australian continent was confirmed in the late eighteenth century, Antarctica was still unknown. Captain James Cook is still regarded as being primarily responsible for laying the foundation for the eventual

[1] 402 UNTS 71.

[2] There are numerous references on this topic, many written by the expeditioners themselves. For an historical background, see E. W. Hunter Christie, *The Antarctic Problem* (London, 1951); Philip W. Quigg, *A Pole Apart* (New York, 1983) 5–38; Deborah Shapley, *The Seventh Continent* (Washington, 1985) 1–88.

discovery of the southern continent. Cook had been responsible in 1770 for discovering the east coast of Australia and claiming it on behalf of Britain. However, he was not content that this voyage had conclusively established the existence of the 'Great Southern Land' which had often been spoken of. From 1772 Cook spent three summers searching the Southern Ocean for Antarctica. His voyage became the first circumnavigation of the continent and while he never sighted the mainland, the 'ice barrier' always blocking his route, his observations and discovery of various sub-Antarctic islands convinced others that there remained a land beyond the ice. Cook's reports of large seal colonies sparked an era of commercial activity in the Southern Ocean. In the early nineteenth century sealers, and whalers who followed, played an important part in opening up the region for further exploration and exploitation.[3]

The first confirmed sightings of the Antarctic continent occurred in the 1820s with Bransfield (Britain), Palmer (United States) and Bellingshausen (Russia) all being credited with having sighted the mainland on various voyages. There is still dispute though over who was the first.[4] While this debate is primarily of historical interest, it does demonstrate that even at this early stage of European interest in Antarctica the potential existed for dispute to arise over the discovery of territory and new lands. Further discoveries were made in the 1830s by Weddell, Briscoe, Kemp and Balleny. All were sealers operating in the Southern Ocean but who in the course of their activities discovered and sighted additional areas of the mainland and various islands. The effect of these voyages and discoveries was to stimulate the interest of European governments and scientific organisations with the result that further full-scale scientific voyages of discovery were planned for the Antarctic.[5]

Apart from the sealers and whalers, most expeditions to Antarctica during the early to middle of the nineteenth century were voyages of discovery only. It was rare for proclamations of territorial claims to be made at that time. In many cases, just battling through the ice and surviving the polar conditions was considered a sufficient reward for the effort. Many of the expeditions also took the opportunity to name their discoveries but this was usually accomplished from on board a vessel: achieving a landing on the continent was in most places impossible at that time. During the 1840s Wilkes (United States),

[3] Quigg, *A Pole Apart* at 8–9; Shapley, *The Seventh Continent* at 7–8.

[4] Shapley, *The Seventh Continent* at 23–7.

[5] Quigg, *A Pole Apart* at 16–17.

D'Urville (France) and Ross (Britain) discovered and named further areas of the continent. These voyages in particular began a trend towards Antarctic expeditions directed not only to discovery but also towards the formal taking of possession of discovered lands, especially islands which could actually be landed on and have the flag planted.[6]

Despite the advances in knowledge and understanding of the Southern Ocean and the Antarctic continent, interest in Antarctica waned during the remainder of the nineteenth century as European powers became more interested in Arctic exploration. Uncontrolled exploitation of both seals and whales also resulted in stocks being depleted and commercial interest in the region diminished. The beginning of the twentieth century, however, saw the commencement of the 'Heroic Era' of Antarctic exploration. There was unprecedented interest in the continent for both scientific and national reasons. Numerous expeditions ventured to Antarctica. For the first time the continent was actually occupied. Wintering quarters were established in an effort to make best use of the short summer season. Expeditions from Belgium, Germany and Sweden all set out for Antarctica; however, it was the British 'Discovery Expedition' led by Scott which was the most extensive and successful. Scott's 1901–4 expedition paved the way for a later British expedition by Shackleton in 1907–9. A major aim of both expeditions was to reach the geographic South Pole. The Pole was eventually reached in 1911 by Norway's Amundsen, to be followed by Scott a month later in January 1912.[7] While the 'race' for the Pole was a contributing factor to the expeditions, there was also a genuine scientific interest in the continent which at times blended

[6] See 'Account of Sir James Clark Ross taking Possession of Cockburn Island and Contiguous Lands (6 January 1843)' reprinted in Bush (vol. III), 225; see *ibid.* at 221–4 for a discussion concerning Cook's taking possession of South Georgia Island in 1775, and other British explorers who also claimed possession of various islands sighted and landed on during their voyages.

[7] See Trevor Hatherton, 'Antarctica Prior to the Antarctic Treaty – A Historical Perspective' in *Antarctic Treaty System* (Washington, 1986) 15 at 26–8, where it is noted with respect to the reaching of the Pole by Amundsen and Scott, that:

> From the beginning of the great Age of Discovery in the late 1400s it had taken a century to put Europeans as far as 60°S latitude. It took a further 300 years to breach the pack ice to the continent proper but only a decade to cross the last 12° when the first parties travelled by land. It is a matter of reflection that, in spite of eccentricities of civilizations and demography, the two poles, having otherwise geographically opposed characteristics, were reached for the first time by humans almost simultaneously.

The North Pole had first been reached on 6 April 1909 by Peary (United States).

with the goal of discovery. Consequently, the reaching of the Pole did not diminish interest in the continent, and national expeditions continued to be sponsored by various countries including Australia, Great Britain, Japan, New Zealand and the United States. Unlike previous expeditions, however, the expeditions of the early twentieth century were dominated by the desire to discover new lands on behalf of the sponsoring sovereign. Proclamations of discovery and the annexation of discovered and explored lands became a central feature of 'scientific expeditions'.

Assertion of claims

From the early 1900s till 1950 a series of claims were made by seven states: Argentina, Australia, Chile, France, New Zealand, Norway and the United Kingdom.[8] These claims still remain in place. The claims of Argentina, Chile and the United Kingdom overlap in the region known as the Antarctic Peninsula. One area of Antarctica, comprising Ellsworth Land and Marie Byrd Land, remains unclaimed. It remains the only unclaimed area of land on earth.

The UK has the longest standing claim in Antarctica, the basis of which rests upon its disputed ownership of the Falkland Islands, Cook's proclamation of sovereignty over the island of South Georgia and various acts of discovery. Acting on these various claims, the limits of the 'Falkland Islands and their Dependencies' were outlined in Letters Patent of 21 July 1908.[9] The definition of the boundaries of the Dependencies was amended in 1917 and later confirmed in 1948.[10]

[8] See Figure 3, p. 56. There exists an extensive literature on the bases, extent and validity of the territorial claims in Antarctica: see e.g. Thomas Willing Balch, 'The Arctic and Antarctic Regions and the Law of Nations' (1910) 4 AJIL 265–75; Philip C. Jessup, 'Sovereignty in Antarctica' (1947) 41 AJIL 117–19; C. H. M. Waldock, 'Disputed Sovereignty in the Falkland Islands Dependencies' (1948) 25 BYIL 311–53; Peter A. Toma, 'Soviet Attitude Towards the Acquisition of Territorial Sovereignty in the Antarctic' (1956) 50 AJIL 611–26; J. R. V. Prescott, 'Boundaries in Antarctica' in Stuart Harris (ed.), *Australia's Antarctic Policy Options*, (Canberra, 1984) 83–111; Gillian D. Triggs, *International Law and Australian Sovereignty in Antarctica* (Sydney, 1986) 82–101, 312–24.

[9] 'Letters Patent Providing for the Government of the Falkland (Malvinas) Islands Dependencies (21 July 1908)' reprinted in Bush (vol. III), 251–2.

[10] 'Letters Patent Providing for the Further Definition and Administration of the Falkland (Malvinas) Islands Dependencies (28 March 1917)' reprinted in Bush (vol. III), 264–5; 'The Falkland Islands Letters Patent, 1948, Dated December 13, 1948, Passed under the Great Seal of the Realm Constituting the Office of Governor and Commander-in-Chief of the Colony of the Falkland Islands, and Making Provision for the Government Thereof (13 December 1948)' reprinted in Bush (vol. III), 305–8.

Finally, the 'British Antarctic Territory' was created in 1962 by dividing the Antarctic portion of what is now the UK claim from the Falkland Islands' claim at 60°S.[11]

Both the Australian and New Zealand claims have their basis in acts of discovery and proclamations made on behalf of Britain, together with later discoveries and proclamations made on behalf of each country. Following World War I, Australia, encouraged by the desire of Britain to ensure that its claims to Antarctica were respected, independently began to take steps towards making a claim to a portion of the continent. The Australian explorer, Douglas Mawson, who commanded the first Australian Antarctic Expedition in 1911–14, was particularly responsible for making Australian Antarctic claims. These claims were based upon acts of discovery and the sighting and charting of large tracts of the Antarctic coastline and inland areas.[12]

Early in the 1920s Britain began to explore which legal mechanism could be relied upon for handing over the administration of certain of its Antarctic territories to New Zealand.[13] This was achieved in 1923 by an Order in Council made under the Imperial British Settlements Act 1887 which created the Ross Dependency and transferred 'all the powers and authorities' over the area to the New Zealand Governor-General.[14] Following this decision concern was expressed as to the uncertain legal status of any potential Australian claims to the continent. This matter was considered in some detail at the 1926 Imperial Conference when a report by the 'Committee on British Policy in the Antarctic' was presented.[15] The report highlighted the need to ensure the effective assertion of sovereignty over areas of 'British domination' in Antarctica. Thereafter, Australia

[11] See 'The British Antarctic Territory Order, 1962 (26 February 1962)' reprinted in Bush (vol. III), 370–3.

[12] Gillian Triggs, 'Australian Sovereignty in Antarctica: Part II' (1982) 13 MULR 302 at 304–5.

[13] 'Colonial Office Request to the Law Officers of the Crown for an Opinion Concerning British Sovereignty over the Ross Sea Coasts and their Hinterland (27 November 1922)' and 'Opinion of the Law Officers of the Crown Concerning British Sovereignty over the Ross Sea Coasts and their Hinterland (3 January 1923)', reprinted in Bush (vol. III), 40–3.

[14] 'Order in Council under the British Settlements Act, 1887 (50 & 51 Vict. c. 54), providing for the Government of the Ross Dependency (30 July 1923)' reprinted in Bush (vol. III), 44. For further details on the Ross Dependency see F. M. Auburn, *The Ross Dependency* (The Hague, 1972).

[15] 'Report of the Committee Appointed by the Imperial Conference 1926 to Consider British Policy in the Antarctic (19 November 1926)', reprinted in Bush (vol. II), 100–4.

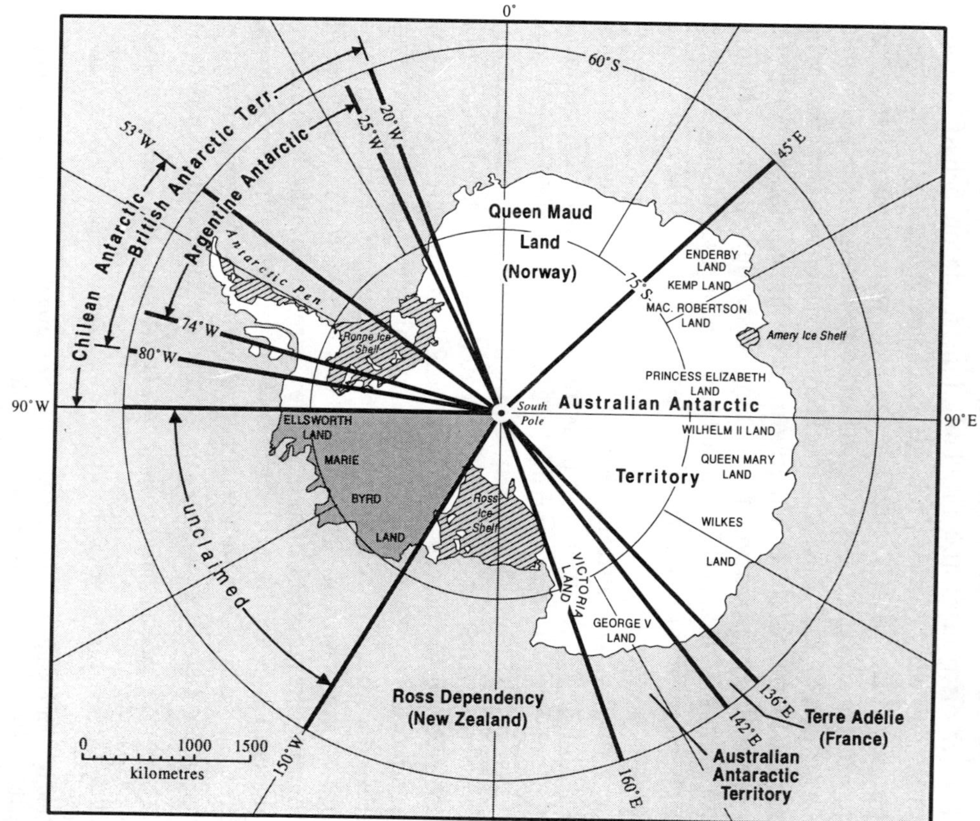

Derived from: *The Natural Resources of the Australian Antarctic Territory.*

Figure 3 The boundaries of Antarctic territorial claims

began to take a more active interest in asserting an Antarctic claim. Mawson was requested to return to the continent to lead the 'British, Australian and New Zealand Antarctic Expedition' (BANZARE) of 1929–31 and to take every opportunity to 'plant the British flag' and read the appropriate proclamation of annexation of territory.[16] Extensive claims were made by Mawson during this expedition. The first effort to assert full legal title over what is now the Australian Antarctic Territory (AAT) came with an Order in Council of the British Government on 7 February 1933 which asserted British sovereign rights over the AAT and placed it under the administration of the Commonwealth of Australia. This order was adopted in Australia by the Australian Antarctic Territory Acceptance Act 1933 (Australia).[17]

The proclamation of the AAT intentionally avoided any claim to the area known as Adelie Land. There had been ongoing correspondence between Britain and France for twenty years over the status and extent of any French claim to the Antarctic mainland. No doubt in response to the formal proclamation of the AAT, France in a Note to the United Kingdom of 24 October 1933 outlined the extent of its claim to Adelie Land.[18] The limits of Adelie Land as proposed in the Note were rejected by Britain in 1934,[19] but after further correspondence the limits and boundary of the French claim were finally settled in 1938.[20]

Norway's first formal claim in Antarctica was over Bouvet Island in 1928. However, in 1929 Norway reminded the United States that following the discoveries and claims made by Amundsen on his journey to the South Pole it had a 'valid basis for a claim of priority to acquire such territories whenever the requirements of international law as to effective occupation of a new territory shall have been fulfilled'.[21] Following extensive German activity in Antarctica in the late 1930s, Norway formally sought to bring part of the

16 See Triggs, *Australian Sovereignty* at 107–8.

17 Although the Act received the royal assent and commenced on 13 June 1933, the necessary Order in Council to implement the Act was not made till 24 August 1936. For comment see Bush (vol. II), 147–9.

18 'French Note to the United Kingdom Proposing 136°E and 147°E Longitude as the Limits of Adelie Land (24 October 1933)', reprinted in Bush (vol. II), 498–9.

19 'British Note to France Proposing 136 1/2°E and 142°E Longitude as the Limits of Adelie Land (13 April 1934)' reprinted in Bush (vol. III), 499.

20 'Decree Defining the Limits of Adelie Land (1 April 1938)', reprinted in Bush (vol. II), 505–6.

21 'Norwegian Note to the United States Concerning Norwegian Grounds for a Claim to Priority over the Areas Claimed or Discovered during Amundsen's Antarctic Expedition (15 April 1929)', reprinted in Bush (vol. III), 124–5.

continent under its control in 1939. However, the proclamation only explicitly referred to the 'land lying within this coast and the environing sea'.[22] This has resulted in uncertainty as to the true extent of the Norwegian claim because it is not based on a traditional sector. However, there is sufficient evidence to suggest that Norway intentionally sought to leave open the possibility of asserting a claim over not only the Antarctic coast but also inland areas first discovered by Amundsen.[23]

Argentina and Chile engaged in considerable correspondence during the first half of the twentieth century over the extent of their respective claims to Antarctica. These claims were also complicated because they each overlapped with those made by the United Kingdom. Chile proclaimed the limits of its claim to the Chilean Antarctic Territory in a Decree of 6 November 1940 which took in a sector between 53°W and 90°W.[24] Argentina responded immediately to this claim, contesting its validity and asserting the potential strength of an Argentinian claim to the same area.[25] In October 1941 Argentina sought to make the extent of its claim more certain by publishing maps through the Instituto Geografico Militar which showed the extent of the claim as lying between 25°W and 75°W.[26] The Argentinian claim went through a series of redefinitions following its initial assertion. The most recent was in 1957 when the 'National Territory of Tierra Del Fuego, Antarctica and Islands of the South Atlantic' was proclaimed within a sector from 25°W to 74°W south of 60°S.[27]

[22] 'Royal Proclamation Defining the Area of Norwegian Sovereignty in Antarctica (14 January 1939)', reprinted in Bush (vol. III), 149; *cf.* note 21 above where specific reference was made to possible Norwegian interest in 'territory immediately circumjacent to the South Pole' and 'territories on both sides of Captain Amundsen's route to the South Pole south of Edward VII's Land and including i.a. Queen Maud's Range'.

[23] Prescott, 'Boundaries in Antarctica' at 90; F. M. Auburn, *Antarctic Law and Politics* (London, 1982) 29–30; Bush (vol. III), 148.

[24] 'Decree No. 1,747 Declaring the Limits of the Chilean Antarctic Territory (6 November 1940)', reprinted in Bush (vol. II), 310–11.

[25] 'Argentine Note to Chile in Response to the Notification of Chilean Claims to Antarctica (12 November 1940)', reprinted in Bush (vol. I), 606–9.

[26] 'Chilean Memorandum to Argentina Reserving Chilean Rights with Regard to an Argentine Map Showing Territory Claimed by Chile as Belonging to Argentina (3 March 1942)', reprinted in Bush (vol. I), 610; Prescott, 'Boundaries in Antarctica' at 91.

[27] 'Decree-Law No. 2,191 Re-establishing the National Territory of Tierra Del Fuego, Antarctica and Islands of the South Atlantic (28 February 1957)', reprinted in Bush (vol. II), 15–26.

Validity of the territorial claims and the acquisition of territory in international law

While it is not the intent of this work to consider in detail the legal validity of the seven Antarctic claims,[28] it is worthwhile to consider the general position with respect to the acquisition of sovereignty, and in particular the issues which arise in polar regions. It is generally recognised that there are five traditional methods of acquiring sovereignty over territory. They are: occupation, annexation, accretion, prescription and cession.[29] In the case of Antarctica, many of the claims are based on original acts of discovery. However, as was held in the *Island of Palmas Arbitration*,[30] states whose basis of claim is discovery have only an inchoate title which must be perfected by later acts demonstrating an actual intent to exercise sovereignty over the discovered lands. In that case, the Netherlands succeeded in having its claim over the island recognised because it was able to demonstrate a better title to the island due to its continuing assertion of sovereignty over time despite claims made by the United States based on discovery.[31] Therefore, a claim of sovereignty based on an act of discovery followed by an act of proclamation is insufficient to prove sovereign title over discovered territories. There must be an actual and continuing intent to exercise sovereignty over a period of time.[32] This element was emphasised in the *Eastern Greenland Case*, where the Permanent Court of International Justice noted that:

[28] There is a very extensive literature on this subject: see generally Green Haywood Hackworth, *Digest of International Law* (vol. I) (Washington, 1940) 449–76; Charles Cheney Hyde, 'Acquisition of Sovereignty over Polar Areas' (1933–1934) 19 *Iowa Law Review* 286–94; D. P. O'Connell, *International Law* (vol. 1) (London, 1970) 450–3; Emilio J. Sahurie, *The International Law of Antarctica* (New Haven, CT, 1992) 193–350. On the status of the Australian claim see generally Triggs, *Australian Sovereignty*; on the New Zealand claim, see Ivor L. M. Richardson, 'New Zealand's Claims in the Antarctic' (1957) 33 *New Zealand Law Journal* 38–42; on the claims to the Antarctic Peninsula by Argentina, Chile and the UK see Robert D. Hayton, 'The "American" Antarctic' (1956) 50 AJIL 583–610.

[29] I. A. Shearer, *Starke's International Law* (11th) (London, 1994) 145; I. Brownlie, *Principles of Public International Law* (4th) (Oxford, 1990) 131; Sir Robert Jennings and Sir Arthur Watts, *Oppenheim's International Law* (9th, vol. I: Pts 2–4) (Harlow, UK, 1992) 679 (who substitute subjugation for annexation); O'Connell, *International Law* at 408–43 also deals with historic rights and *Debellatio*.

[30] *The Netherlands* v. *United States of America* (4 April 1928), 2 RIAA 829.

[31] *Ibid.* at 845–6, 857, 864–6.

[32] See the *Clipperton Island Arbitration* (*France* v. *Mexico*), 2 RIAA 1105; and generally on these issues Brownlie, *Principles* at 140–5; Shearer, *International Law* at 147–51.

a claim to sovereignty based not upon some particular act or title such as a treaty of cession but merely upon continued display of authority, involves two elements each of which must be shown to exist: the intention and will to act as sovereign, and some actual exercise or display of such authority.[33]

The standard required is often described as being one of 'effective occupation'.

Is it possible though effectively to occupy a polar region which is physically separated from the metropolitan power by a great distance and is not suitable for colonising? Judge Huber noted in the *Island of Palmas Arbitration* that:

Manifestations of territorial sovereignty assume, it is true, different forms, according to conditions of time and place. Although continuous in principle, sovereignty cannot be exercised in fact at every moment on every point of a territory. The intermittence and discontinuity compatible with the maintenance of the right necessarily differ according as inhabited or uninhabited regions are involved.[34]

In the *Eastern Greenland Case* reference was expressly made to the difficulty of fulfilling the requirements of effective occupation in polar regions. It was noted that:

It is impossible to read the records of the decisions in cases as to territorial sovereignty without observing that in many cases the tribunal has been satisfied with very little in the way of the actual exercise of sovereign rights, provided that the other State could not make out a superior claim. This is particularly true in the case of claims to sovereignty over areas in thinly populated or unsettled countries.[35]

In light of these pronouncements, Brownlie has described the standard required to establish 'effective occupation' as one which emphasises 'state activity, and especially acts of administration', noting that occupation does not necessarily signify actual settlement.[36] It would

[33] *Legal Status of Eastern Greenland (Norway* v. *Denmark)* (1933) PCIJ Reports, Ser. A/B, No. 53, 45–6. [34] 2 RIAA 840.

[35] (1933) PCIJ Rep, Ser. A/B, No. 53, 46. O'Connell, *International Law* at 412 commented on the decision that 'Considering the arctic and inaccessible character of the uncolonised parts of Greenland the display of Danish authority during the relevant period had been sufficient to support a claim to sovereignty.'

[36] Brownlie, *Principles* at 138; *cf.* Jennings and Watts, *International Law* at 688 who note: 'Occupation thus effected is real occupation, and, in contradistinction to fictitious occupation, is named effective occupation. Possession and administration are the two essential facts that constitute an effective occupation.' Also see O'Connell, *International Law* at 413, who notes 'actual settlement of territory is no more than evidence of the facts of possession, which, depending on the circumstances, may be satisfactorily established in the absence of habitation of any sort'.

seem then that on this basis there would be no need for a state wishing to substantiate its Antarctic claims to engage in the building of towns and villages or to send colonising settlers from its metropolitan population.

While commentators have certainly agreed that the strict standard applied to more temperate lands is not appropriate for Antarctica,[37] they have not altogether dismissed the need for some of the incidents of effective occupation to be made out. Castles argues that the cases on the topic emphasise the importance of the creation of a system of laws in the territory claimed and activities demonstrating a clear intention to keep the territory under administrative control.[38] In their attempts to establish and support the continuation of their territorial claims, most of the seven claimants have relied upon a variety of administrative and legislative acts,[39] in conjunction with 'occupation' of various scientific bases and sites plus continued exploration and scientific research. Given the uncertain status of their claims the response of the seven claimants has to date been one of pragmatism.

A significant feature of the Antarctic claims is that they are based on a 'sector'.[40] The claims commence at points on the Antarctic coast and converge along degrees of longitude to the geographic South Pole. Sector claims have some precedent in the Arctic and are thought to be based on principles such as contiguity, 'hinterland' or the 'spheres of influence' doctrine.[41] The effect of sector claims in the polar regions is

[37] Auburn, *Antarctic Law* at 13: 'There is a clear trend towards a lenient standard for sparsely populated regions'; Triggs, *Australian Sovereignty* at 82: 'The doctrine of effective occupation has been reduced to a highly flexible and relative concept in remote and uninhabited areas by the decisions of international tribunals'; Philip C. Jessup and Howard J. Taubenfeld, *Controls for Outer Space and the Antarctic Analogy* (New York, 1959) 141: 'Obviously, the need for "effective occupation" is tempered by the difficulties of settlement in polar regions, and less exacting standards have been held applicable.'

[38] A. C. Castles, 'The International Status of the Australian Antarctic Territory' in D. P. O'Connell (ed.), *International Law in Australia* (1966) 341 at 355.

[39] Most of the Antarctic claimants have enacted a range of legislative instruments dealing with their Antarctic territories and also giving effect to various provisions of the Antarctic Treaty System. Other sovereignty-related activities have included the issuing of postage stamps and the appointment of a postmaster, the appointment of officers to enforce laws and conduct coronial enquiries, visits by politicians, naming of bases as towns, wedding ceremonies and childbirth.

[40] The exception is Norway, whose claim extends inland from the coastline to an indeterminate point.

[41] Jennings and Watts, *International Law* at 693; O'Connell, *International Law* at 449. For a further discussion see Gustav Smedal, *Acquisition of Sovereignty over Polar Areas* (Oslo, 1931) 54–76; Oscar Svarlien, 'The Sector Principle in Law and Practice' (1960) 10 *Polar Record* 248–63.

that states can assert claims along lines of latitude that run directly to the Pole, thereby dividing up the region. In the Arctic, sector claims are based on the geographical proximity of the claimant state,[42] and have been relied upon throughout the twentieth century by Canada and Russia as one basis for their Arctic territorial and maritime claims. However, the validity of this principle has never been tested and many commentators do not accept the sector theory as a separate rule of international law.[43] In Antarctica, the geographical circumstances differ considerably from those in the Arctic and only Argentina and Chile would seem to have any reasonable basis upon which to assert sector claims.[44] While there has been much academic speculation about the validity of Antarctic sector claims,[45] it would seem that in many instances Antarctic claims are based upon sectors more for administrative convenience than because of actual reliance upon the principle. There is very little documentary evidence to suggest that any claimant has actually sought to rely upon the principle to justify its claim. Castles has said of the Antarctic sector claims:

> The fact that some claims . . . are delineated then in the form of 'sectors' would seem to add nothing of substance to support claims to sovereignty within these areas. The sectors merely define the limits of the territory to which these countries lay claim and insofar as systems of law and other acts have been carried out expressing an intention to control these sectors, the areas contained within these regions may arguably be said to be vested in the form of an inchoate title in the claimant States, awaiting perfection of title by the extension of State authority in the form of occupation.[46]

It is not possible, nor necessary, in the context of this work to make definitive determinations as to the status of the seven Antarctic territorial claims. Nevertheless, the existing claims, grounded upon acts of discovery, occupation, and administration, are based on recognised principles of international law. This is not to suggest that each claim has exactly the same merits. There have been some substantial variations in practices by the claimants in regard to

[42] Jennings and Watts, *International Law* at 693.

[43] Brownlie, *Principles* at 151; Shearer, *International Law* at 149–50; Jennings and Watts, *International Law* at 693; Donat Pharand, *Canada's Arctic Waters in International Law* (Cambridge, 1988) 79; Auburn, *Antarctic Law* at 31 who notes: 'The sector theory is an Aunt Sally of international law, more of a political than a legal principle.'

[44] Auburn, *Antarctic Law* at 23–4.

[45] *Ibid.*; see also Triggs, *International Law* 89–95; O'Connell, *International Law* at 451; J. S. Reeves, 'Antarctic Sectors' (1939) 33 AJIL 519–21.

[46] Castles, 'International Status' at 357.

claimed territories both prior to and after entry into force of the Antarctic Treaty. The claims of Argentina, Chile and the UK overlap and if there were ever a need to judge the validity of each claim the principles discussed above would become important. As for the other four claims, no competing claims have yet been made to those areas. The historic interests and long-standing Antarctic activities of both the United States and Russia could form the basis for extensive claims to parts of the continent. If such claims were to be made by these two states, then questions would arise concerning the interpretation of the Antarctic Treaty. At present, however, it would seem that the seven territorial claimants have a substantial basis on which to support at least part of their Antarctic territorial claims. Whether, through the limitations placed upon assertions of sovereignty by the Antarctic Treaty, combined with the substantial Antarctic activities conducted by other states on the continent, these claims would be upheld if ever challenged is at present difficult to determine.[47]

The Cold War

Because of the perception that there was little of economic value to be found in Antarctica (apart from perhaps the marine living resources of the Southern Ocean), up till World War II there had been no great international interest in the continent except from scientists and states keen to assert claims. The sudden arrival of a German expedition in 1938–9,[48] however, demonstrated that despite its remoteness Antarctica was seen as having strategic, and perhaps military, importance. The geopolitical importance of Antarctica was further highlighted following World War II when both the United States and the Soviet Union began to engage in a range of Antarctic activities.

In the immediate post-war years (by which time all of the seven territorial claims had been asserted) the United States played a very active role in Antarctic affairs. It had the largest contingent of scientific personnel on the continent, supported by a large research-

[47] For a discussion of how Australia's claim to the AAT may have been affected in this way, see Triggs, *International Law* at 322.

[48] 'Report of the Discoveries and Claims made by the German Antarctic Expedition of 1938–1939 (11 April 1939)' reprinted in Bush (vol. III), 2–4. This expedition is credited with being the catalyst for the 1939 Norwegian claim: see the German response to that claim, 'German Note to Norway Reserving the Position of the German Government with regard to the Norwegian Claim in Antarctica (23 January 1939)', reprinted in Bush (vol. III), 151–2.

funding infrastructure that was probably more extensive than all of the seven claimants combined. The American military also had an interest in Antarctica. It was seen as a potential proving and training ground for the United States in the event of military activities occurring in the Arctic or Siberia.[49] While the onset of the Cold War had certainly influenced the level of United States involvement in Antarctica, it remained reticent about making any territorial claim. As Auburn has asked: 'Why did the nation having the most extensive record of Antarctic activities not make a claim?'[50] There is evidence to suggest that conflicting views existed within the Department of State over which policy should be adopted.[51] However, despite Lincoln Ellsworth making a series of claims in 1935 and 1939, and the Byrd expedition from 1939–41 being officially supported by the Government, no claims made on behalf of the United States were ever recognised by the Government.[52]

Notwithstanding the unusual attitude of the United States towards territorial claims, it was active on the diplomatic front in an effort to help solve the emerging problem of overlapping and contested Antarctic sovereignty claims. In the immediate post-war years tensions mounted between Argentina, Chile and the United Kingdom over their claims to the Antarctic Peninsula.[53] In response, the United States suggested in June 1948 that a moratorium be placed on all claims, and that consideration be given to the continent being administered under a United Nations Trusteeship.[54] This was followed by a proposal for a condominium.[55] Argentina and the United

[49] Auburn, *Antarctic Law* at 94. [50] *Ibid.* at 61.

[51] *Ibid.* at 64 where it is noted: 'In essence the State Department was unable to make up its mind.'

[52] See 'Account of Claim made by Lincoln Ellsworth on behalf of the United States (23 November 1935)', reprinted in Bush (vol. III), 435–6; 'Record of Claim Dropped from an Aeroplane by Lincoln Ellsworth over the American Highlands (11 January 1939)', reprinted in Bush (vol. III), 442–3. Nevertheless, numerous commentators have written about the 'American Antarctic': see Quigg, *A Pole Apart* at 126–33; Reeves, 'Antarctic Sectors' at 520–1; Hayton, 'The "American Antarctic"'; Todd Jay Parriott, 'Territorial Claims in Antarctica: Will the United States Be Left Out in the Cold?' (1986) 22 Stanford JIL 67–121.

[53] This eventually resulted in the UK seeking to have the dispute determined by the International Court of Justice: see *Antarctica Cases* (*UK* v. *Argentina*, *UK* v. *Chile*) [1956] ICJ Pleadings. However, the case never reached the merits stage because of problems with the Court's jurisdiction. See also Hunter Christie, *Antarctic Problem* at 239–85.

[54] 'United Nations Draft Agreement for placing Antarctica under a United Nations Trusteeship (June 1948)' reprinted in Bush (vol. III), 461–3.

[55] 'United States Draft Agreement Providing for a Condominium over Antarctica (July 1948)', reprinted in Bush (vol. III), 464–5.

Kingdom were opposed to any solution which could result in their losing territorial sovereignty; by contrast, Chile took the proposal further in the 'Escudaro Declaration' which suggested that sovereignty claims be held in abeyance for five years during which time scientific cooperation would be encouraged.[56] Eventually, all of these various proposals were unacceptable because of a rejection by most of the claimants of any form of settlement which would result in the internationalisation of their existing claims.[57]

An important consequence of the United States initiative was that it awakened the interest of the Soviet Union in Antarctica. Despite the role played by the explorer Bellingshausen in the early discovery of the continent, Russia and subsequently the Soviet Union had not taken an active interest in Antarctic affairs. However, at a meeting of the Geographical Society of the USSR in 1949 it was declared that the Soviet Union had an 'indisputable right' to 'participate in the solution of the problems of the Antarctic' and that:

> No attempt to solve the problem of a regime for the Antarctic without participation of the Soviet Union can find any justification. The problems of the Antarctic must be solved primarily by those states that have the historical right to participate in this solution.[58]

This was followed soon thereafter by a formal government statement making clear its views that any settlement of Antarctic issues should involve the Soviet Union.[59] Despite some efforts to refute any right of the Soviet Union to participate in Antarctic affairs, and especially any Soviet right to assert a territorial claim,[60] the consequence of these events was that the Soviet Union was now irretrievably involved in the development of any multilateral Antarctic policy. Soviet interest in the history of Antarctic discovery and future directions for the continent was supplemented in 1956 by the establishment of the first

[56] 'Chilean Statement Concerning the United States' Proposals to Internationalise Antarctica (28 October 1948)', reprinted in Bush (vol. II) 385–6; J. F. Lovering and J. R. V. Prescott, *Last of Lands . . . Antarctica* (Carlton, Victoria, 1979) 153.

[57] J. Hanessian, 'The Antarctic Treaty 1959' (1960) 9 ICLQ 436 at 436–48; Robert D. Hayton, 'The Antarctic Settlement of 1959' (1960) 54 AJIL 349 at 352.

[58] 'Resolution Concerning Antarctica Adopted by the All-Soviet (or All-Union) Geographical Society (10 February 1949)' reprinted in Bush (vol. III), 207.

[59] 'Soviet Memorandum on the Participation of the Soviet Union in any International Settlement concerning Antarctica (7–8 June 1950)', reprinted in Bush (vol. III), 208–9. For discussion on the Soviet action see Boleslaw A. Boczek, 'The Soviet Union and the Antarctic Regime' (1984) 78 AJIL 834 at 835–7.

[60] See Hanessian, 'The Antarctic Treaty' at 446–7; Boczek, 'Soviet Union' at 837.

Soviet scientific station, Mirnyy, within the AAT.[61] This was followed in 1957 by the establishment of Vostok station, also within the AAT.[62]

The enthusiastic participation by the Soviet Union in the 1957–58 International Geophysical Year (IGY), during which time seven Soviet scientific bases were eventually established in the AAT, demonstrated the Soviet intention to play a very active role in Antarctic affairs.[63] This activity, in conjunction with the 1957 launch of the Sputnik satellite by the Soviet Union, further convinced some Antarctic states of the seriousness of the Soviet scientific challenge. The presence of the two superpowers on the continent during the height of the Cold War demonstrated the strategic importance of Antarctica at this time. In light of all these developments, it was seen that a treaty which renounced military activities in Antarctica and sought to resolve the problems of Antarctic sovereignty was important if the continent was to remain free of the Cold War and maintain its role as a scientific laboratory.[64]

The International Geophysical Year

During the immediate post-war era and throughout the 1950s, Antarctica was increasingly becoming a continent dominated by science. This was a continuation of the long-held scientific interest in the continent. Even on the voyages of discovery to Antarctica by Cook and the expeditions by Scott and Shackleton, science was a key motivator. Science had become the principal reason for man remaining in Antarctica and was seen by some to represent the only 'export' from the continent.[65] Scientists relished the opportunity to carry out their work in what was considered a pristine environment which allowed for the conduct of traditional and polar science.

61 J. Hanessian, 'Antarctica: Current National Interests and Legal Realities' (1958) 52 ProcAmSocIL 145 at 157–8; Boczek, 'Soviet Union' at 838.

62 As a result of these activities by the Soviet Union within the AAT, Australia became concerned that its sovereignty was being contested and its claim was under threat: see Hayton, 'Antarctic Settlement' at 353; L. F. E. Goldie, 'International Relations in Antarctica' (1958) 30 *Australian Quarterly* 7 at 19, 23.

63 Hanessian, 'Current National Interests' at 157–8. For Soviet views on sovereignty in Antarctica and possible options for the settlement of these and other issues, see Toma, 'Soviet Attitude'.

64 Shapley, *The Seventh Continent* at 90.

65 For an assessment on scientific research opportunities, see R. M. Laws, 'Scientific Opportunities in the Antarctic' in Gillian D. Triggs (ed.), *The Antarctic Treaty Regime* (Cambridge, 1987) 28–48.

Two major developments based around this research activity occurred in the late 1950s. The first was the establishment by the International Council for Scientific Unions of the 'Special Committee on Antarctic Research' (SCAR).[66] Subsequently renamed the 'Scientific Committee on Antarctic Research', SCAR has played a valuable and continuing role in the coordination and publication of Antarctic research.[67] The second development was the IGY, held between 1957–58. The IGY was a concept which was developed from two previous 'Polar Years' in which substantial coordinated research was conducted by various countries in the polar regions.[68] The Third Polar Year became the IGY, with twelve nations participating and forty-eight new scientific stations being established on the continent (in addition to the existing seven stations). During the year substantial advances in polar science were made and the continent was crossed for the first time.[69] The effect of the IGY was to demonstrate the importance of Antarctic science and the virtue of international cooperation between Antarctic scientists and the countries operating on the continent.

Against the background of the United States-sponsored proposal in the late 1940s for internationalisation of Antarctica and the continuing debate on this topic,[70] scientists and diplomats saw that an opportunity existed during the IGY process for formal negotiations concerning the future of Antarctica to commence. From this process, it was hoped that a legal regime could be developed which would encapsulate many of the scientific and cooperative goals of the IGY, and which would also deal with the underlying political concerns of the claimant states. In October 1959, after informal discussion amongst interested states, the United States invited a number of states to a Conference dealing with Antarctica. Six weeks later on 1

[66] Hanessian, 'Current National Interests' at 149.

[67] See James H. Zumberge, 'The Antarctic Treaty as a Scientific Mechanism – The Scientific Committee on Antarctic Research and the Antarctic Treaty System' in *Antarctic Treaty System* (Washington, 1986) 153–68.

[68] The First International Polar Year was held in 1882–3 in which twelve nations participated and fourteen stations were involved, two of which were located in the southern hemisphere at South Georgia and Cape Horn; the Second International Polar Year was held between 1932–3 and while forty-four countries participated no mainland Antarctic station was established: see Robert H. Rutford, 'Summary of Science in Antarctica Prior to and Including the International Geophysical Year' in *Antarctic Treaty System* (Washington, 1986) 87 at 98–9.

[69] Rutford, 'Summary of Science' at 99; see also W. Sullivan, 'The International Geophysical Year' (1959) 521 *International Conciliation* 259–336.

[70] This is best considered in Hanessian, 'Antarctic Treaty' at 436–55.

December 1959, the Conference concluded with the signing of the Antarctic Treaty.

The 1959 Antarctic Conference

It has already been noted that concerns over sovereignty, the future of scientific research, and continental security in the midst of the Cold War were major factors leading to the Conference on Antarctica. However, other factors also played a role in this process. They were:

(a) the expression of interest by some of the Antarctic states in the internationalisation of the continent through the United Nations – in particular the support of New Zealand Prime Minister, Walter Nash, for Antarctica being placed under United Nations trusteeship;[71]
(b) agreement amongst Australia, New Zealand and the UK that any international settlement dealing with Antarctica should be based on the free development of science and that the continent should not be used for military purposes;[72]
(c) the interest which was expressed in Antarctica by states which at that time had no record of activity in the continent; in particular, India suggested at the United Nations that the 'Question of Antarctica' be placed on the General Assembly's agenda; and[73]
(d) a so-called 'Gentlemen's Agreement' reached amongst the seven territorial claimants to abandon political debate and activity relating to contested territorial claims for the duration of the IGY.[74]

These developments indicated that there was the potential to reach a settlement on some of the outstanding issues concerning Antarctica. This initial promise was confirmed during a series of informal discussions which took place in February and March 1958 amongst states with an interest in Antarctic affairs. At that time, the United States put forward a proposal for the development of an Antarctic regime based upon the following principles:

(a) free access to Antarctica by all nations interested in carrying out scientific research;

[71] See 'New Zealand Statement at the Conference on Antarctica in Washington that it was Prepared to Consider the Relinquishment of National Rights and Claims to Antarctica (15 October 1959)' reprinted in Bush (vol. III), 77–8.

[72] Hanessian, 'Antarctic Treaty' at 452–5.

[73] U. N. Doc. A/3852, 15 July 1958. Brazil, Uruguay and Peru had also begun to consider whether they could assert Antarctic sovereignty claims: see Hayton, 'Antarctic Settlement' at 352; Hanessian, 'Antarctic Treaty' at 451–2.

[74] See Hanessian, 'Antarctic Treaty' at 449, 455; Triggs, *Australian Sovereignty* at 134–6.

(b) the growth of scientific cooperation and exchange of information and data among participating nations;
(c) the use of Antarctica for peaceful purposes only;
(d) non-militarisation of the area;
(e) guaranteed rights of unilateral access and inspection by all participating parties to all parts of Antarctica;
(f) the freezing of the legal status, so that no one state need renounce any claims or rights currently held; and
(g) the creation of an administrative unit in which all participating states would have an equal footing.[75]

It was following these negotiations that United States President Eisenhower issued an invitation in May 1958 to eleven other states[76] to attend a Conference to discuss the future of Antarctica. All the states invited were either those which had made territorial claims, or had during the course of the IGY demonstrated a substantial interest in Antarctic affairs.

The invitation was accepted by all invitees and the United States announced that an informal working group would be created to prepare for the Conference.[77] Sixty preparatory meetings were held from June 1958 until the commencement of the Conference in October 1959. The meetings were instrumental in resolving many of the most disputed issues over the future management of Antarctica. These were:

(a) territorial sovereignty and unresolved claims;
(b) the reluctance of some nations to accept any proviso for an international administrative body such as the United Nations;
(c) the opposition by several states to the principle of demilitarisation with its corollaries of inspection and control;
(d) that Antarctica be subject to peaceful and scientific uses only;
(e) the actual zone of application of the treaty;
(f) the question of whether provisions to cover economic exploitation should be included in the treaty;
(g) membership of the treaty; and
(h) the administration of any negotiated treaty.[78]

[75] Hanessian, 'Antarctic Treaty' at 456.

[76] The invitees were Argentina, Australia, Belgium, Chile, France, Japan, New Zealand, Norway, South Africa, the United Kingdom and the Soviet Union, which, with the United States, were all present at the Antarctic Conference.

[77] For a comprehensive review see Peter J. Beck, 'Preparatory Meetings for the Antarctic Treaty 1958–59' (1985) 22 *Polar Record* 653–64.

[78] *Ibid.*; Hanessian, 'Antarctic Treaty' at 461.

In November 1958 the United States Chairman of the Meetings produced a series of informal working papers containing in effect a draft treaty, which formed the basis for the discussions at the Washington Conference a year later.[79]

The Antarctic Conference eventually convened in Washington in October 1959. The United States hosted and chaired the Conference, with delegations from Argentina, Australia, Belgium, Chile, France, Japan, New Zealand, Norway, South Africa, the Soviet Union and the United Kingdom attending. In their opening statements the Conference delegates each presented their individual national policy positions towards Antarctica and the forthcoming negotiations. Despite the potential for differing national policies to create dissension, there was substantial agreement that the negotiations would eventuate in an accord for Antarctica which would result in the continent being used only for peaceful purposes, free of political conflict, and open for the conduct of scientific investigations.[80]

With so much common ground amongst the national delegations, and the work of the Preparatory Meetings proving an invaluable collection of working papers as a basis, work proceeded swiftly. Two main committees were created to deal with the Conference agenda: Committee I on scientific matters, and Committee II on political and legal subjects.[81] As was the practice at the Preparatory Meetings, apart from the opening statements the Conference proceeded in closed session. The major areas of contention that emerged were the area of the Treaty's application, matters of jurisdiction and the settlement of disputes, and provisions governing accession to the Treaty.[82] However, these did not prove to be major obstacles and six weeks after the

[79] Beck, 'Preparatory Meetings' at 662. Confirmation on the progress made at these meetings is also found in 'Chilean Report of the Proceedings During 1959 of the Preparatory Working Group for the Conference on Antarctica (1959)', reprinted in Bush (vol. I), 29–30.

[80] See e.g. The Conference on Antarctica: Doc. No. 4 (Welcoming Statement, Mr Christian Herter, US Secretary of State) 15 October 1959; Doc. No. 5 (Opening Statement, South African Delegation) 15 October 1959; Doc. No. 6 (Opening Statement, New Zealand Delegation) 15 October 1959; Doc. No. 7 (Opening Statement, Japanese Delegation) 15 October 1959. For reproduction and discussion of these statements see Hanessian, 'Antarctic Treaty' at 464–6; Hayton, 'Antarctic Settlement' at 355–7.

[81] Hanessian, 'Antarctic Treaty' at 466; Hayton, 'Antarctic Settlement' at 358. Further committees dealing with credentials, drafting and style were also created.

[82] Hanessian, 'Antarctic Treaty' at 467. For an historical perspective of the Conference, see Oscar Pinochet de la Barra, 'Reminiscences of the 1959 Antarctic Treaty Conference' (1992) 27(2) *Antarctic Journal of the United States* 9–11.

Conference began it concluded on 1 December with the signing by all twelve participants of the Antarctic Treaty. The Treaty was ratified without undue delay and all of the twelve Conference participants became original parties.[83] Poland acceded to the Treaty prior to its entry into force, so that upon the simultaneous ratification of the treaty by Argentina, Australia and Chile on 23 June 1961 the Treaty entered into force with thirteen parties.

The Antarctic Treaty

Compared to the very extensive international legal instruments negotiated in the 1990s, the Antarctic Treaty seems a very straightforward document. Comprising only fourteen articles it combines some very basic measures dealing with demilitarisation and conduct of science with some very sophisticated provisions dealing with sovereignty and Treaty review. The Treaty focuses on the critical issues of Antarctica's management and future as identified by the Antarctic states in the 1950s. Provisions dealing with demilitarisation, the importance of science, and the resolution of sovereignty claims in particular stand out. The significance of these issues is noted in the Treaty's Preamble. It emphasises several aspirations which are embodied in the text of the Treaty: that the continent be used for peaceful purposes and not become the scene or object of international discord, that the spirit of scientific cooperation which developed during the IGY should continue and that the Treaty should be in harmony with the principles of the United Nations.

Demilitarisation and peaceful purposes

A major goal at the Antarctic Conference was to demilitarise Antarctica and to provide that the continent should be used only for peaceful purposes. Article I implements this objective, providing that: 'Antarctica shall be used for peaceful purposes only.' While not defining 'peaceful purposes', the second sentence of the Article prohibits the

[83] The greatest difficulty that existed during the interim period between signature and ratification occurred in the United States where some opposition was expressed in the Senate over the failure of the United States to assert a sovereignty claim prior to the entry into force of the Treaty: see 'The Antarctic Treaty, Hearing before the Committee on Foreign Relations', Ex. B, 86th Congress, 2nd Session (14 June 1960); 'The Antarctic Treaty, Report from the Senate Committee on Foreign Relations', Ex. Rep. 10, 86th Congress, 2nd Session (23 June 1960), reprinted in Bush (vol. III), 479–80.

conduct of military activities in Antarctica.[84] Consequently, no military bases or fortifications were to be established, and military manoeuvres or the testing of weapons were prohibited. An exception arises where military personnel or equipment are used for scientific research or other peaceful purposes.[85] This provision has been successfully enforced throughout the duration of the Treaty. No armed conflict has occurred within the Treaty area. Article I was honoured during the 1982 Falklands War between two Treaty parties – Argentina and the UK – at which time a particular effort was made to ensure that no military, particularly naval, activities occurred south of 60° S.[86] The failure of the Treaty to define 'peaceful purposes' does, however, leave open the issue of whether military-related research can legitimately be conducted in Antarctica. While there is no clear evidence of such research having been conducted since 1959, the number of legitimate military personnel working in Antarctica under Article I(2) has occasionally raised the issue of whether all Antarctic research is dedicated to peaceful purposes.[87]

The demilitarisation of the continent is completed by Article V which prohibits nuclear explosions and the disposal of radioactive waste. This provision was resisted by the United States and the Soviet Union, and was only accepted on the basis that Article V(2) made provision for the application of certain international instruments dealing with the use of nuclear energy and the disposal of nuclear waste.[88] However, Article V(2) only provides for the application of international agreements that all Antarctic contracting parties eligible to attend Antarctic Treaty meetings have become parties to. While Antarctica has been kept free of nuclear weapons, it has not

[84] Hanessian, 'Antarctic Treaty' at 468; *cf.* Auburn, *Antarctic Law* at 97.

[85] Art. I(2). This exception is an acknowledgment that the scientific activities of most Antarctic parties could not be mounted without some military assistance. The Antarctic scientific programmes of some states are actually directed by branches of the military: see Auburn, *Antarctic Law* at 95–6. This provision was included in response to concerns raised by Chile and the United States: see *ibid.* at 95; Bush (vol. I), 52.

[86] For a review of the relationship between the Falklands War and Antarctic issues see D. W. Greig, 'Sovereignty and the Falkland Islands Crisis' (1983) 8 AYIL 20–70; Robert Fox, *Antarctica and the South Atlantic* (London, 1985).

[87] Auburn, *Antarctic Law* at 95–7 where at 97 it is argued:

> 'Peaceful purposes' should be naturally construed. To argue that it should include all activity not clearly identified as military has little justification in the Treaty text and goes against the linking of peaceful purposes and the prevention of international discord.

[88] Bush (vol. I), 63.

been nuclear free. Between 1962–72, the United States operated a nuclear power plant at its McMurdo Station. While nothing in the Treaty prohibited such an activity, it seemed to be in conflict with the 'spirit' of a nuclear-free Antarctica.[89] In partial recognition of this gap in the wording of Article V, the Antarctic Treaty Consultative Parties (ATCPs) agreed at Antarctic Treaty Consultative Meeting (ATCM) I (1961) to the exchange of information on the use of nuclear equipment within the Treaty area.[90] There has also been interest expressed at ATCMs over the use of radio isotopes.[91] Nevertheless, as the operation of the United States nuclear power station demonstrated, there is considerable scope within the Treaty for individual parties to adopt their own practices in regard to non-military-type nuclear materials in Antarctica.[92]

Scientific research

Science was the other key element in the Treaty's implementation and to further this goal Article II attempts to promote the continuation of the 'freedom of scientific investigation' which occurred during the IGY. The continuation of such scientific research is encouraged, subject to the provisions of the Treaty. In furtherance of this ideal of Antarctica being a 'continent of science', Article III seeks to provide for ways in which international scientific cooperation can continue. Under this provision the parties to the Treaty agree to support the exchange of information on specific programmes so as to permit economy and efficiency of operations, the exchange of scientific personnel between expeditions and stations and the exchange and free availability of scientific observations and results.[93] These provisions are further supported by measures in Article VII dealing with

[89] Prior to the establishment of the McMurdo Power Station, there had already been some degree of opposition within the United States over the ban on nuclear explosions and radioactive waste provided for in Art. V: see 'Senate Report on Grounds for Opposing Ratification of the Antarctic Treaty (1960)', reprinted in Bush (vol. III), 480.

[90] Recommendation I-XIII: 'Exchange of Information on Nuclear Equipment and Techniques'.

[91] Recommendation VI-5; VI-6; VIII-6; VIII-11.

[92] Norway adopted legislation in 1960 (later amended in 1972) to outlaw the use or possession of a nuclear reactor, nuclear fuel or radioactive products, or otherwise use nuclear energy in Antarctica: see Bush (vol. III), 171–4.

[93] Art. III(1); see P. Quilty, 'Cooperation in Antarctica in Scientific and Logistic Matters: Status and Means of Improvement' in Rudiger Wolfrum (ed.), *Antarctic Challenge III* (Berlin, 1988) 65–77.

inspection and exchange of other information. Encouragement is also given to the establishment of working relations with United Nations agencies and organisations with scientific or technical interests in the Antarctic.[94]

The Treaty has assisted in Antarctica continuing to be a 'continent of science' since the end of the IGY. The 'freedom of scientific investigation' provided for in Article II has been interpreted by the United States as being the right of 'free access to all of Antarctica',[95] and the proliferation of scientific bases and stations since 1959 demonstrates that no part of the continent has been sealed off from scientific research. The United States Amundsen–Scott base at the South Pole straddles all of the territorial claims which converge at that point. The only real limitations imposed upon scientific research have been those adopted under the Treaty. Various recommendations and provisions of some other ATS instruments have dealt with the conduct of scientific research.[96]

The Scientific Committee on Antarctic Research (SCAR) has been the major body responsible for coordinating cooperative scientific research and exchange of scientific information (Article III).[97] The exchange of scientific personnel provided for under the Treaty has continued in the tradition of the IGY.[98] There have been numerous examples of scientists from non-Antarctic Treaty states visiting Antarctic scientific stations and bases and in some instances it has been through the support and assistance given by an ATCP that acceding states have been able to gain the scientific expertise to enable them to apply successfully for ATCP status. While SCAR has operated as the *de*

[94] Art. III(2); the World Meteorological Agency, International Telecommunications Union and UN Environment Programme have all taken an active interest in Antarctic science.

[95] 'Senate Report on Grounds for Opposing Ratification of the Antarctic Treaty (1960)', reprinted in Bush (vol. III), 479–80.

[96] See Recommendations VI-5 (The Use of Radio-Isotopes in the Antarctic); X-4 (Man's Impact on the Antarctic Environment: Collection of Geological Specimens); XIII-4 (Man's Impact on the Antarctic Environment: Code of Conduct for Antarctic Expeditions and Station Activities: Waste Disposal); for discussion see Frank Wong and Felicity Newman, 'Restrictions to Freedom of Scientific Research through Environmental Protection' in Rudiger Wolfrum (ed.), *Antarctic Challenge II* (Berlin, 1986) 103–9.

[97] Recommendation I-I (Exchange on Information on Scientific Programmes); see Zumberge, 'Antarctic Treaty'.

[98] The matter was considered of such importance that it was the subject of a Recommendation at ATCM I (1961); see Recommendation I-II (Exchange of Scientific Personnel).

facto science secretariat under the Treaty, various other international organisations and bodies have been involved in Antarctic scientific research, as was envisaged under Article III(2).[99]

Despite the Treaty's provisions dealing with the exchange of scientific information resulting from Antarctic research, concerns have occasionally been expressed over some parties not being as forthcoming in exchanging details concerning the results of their scientific research.[100] This matter has also been extensively addressed by a large number of ATCM Recommendations.[101] Nevertheless, in recent times there has been a considerable public release of scientific data gathered from Antarctic research, especially in regard to the depletion of the ozone layer. From this experience it would seem that the results of scientific research, subject only to potential concerns over the politically sensitive nature of some research, is as freely exchanged in Antarctic fora as in other scientific fora.

Sovereignty

The difficult question of sovereignty in Antarctica is dealt with in Article IV. There are two parts to the Article. The first provides:

1 Nothing contained in the present Treaty shall be interpreted as:
  a. a renunciation by any Contracting Party of previously asserted rights of or claims to territorial sovereignty in Antarctica;
  b. a renunciation or diminution by any Contracting Party of any basis of claim to territorial sovereignty in Antarctica which it may have whether as a result of its activities or those of its nationals in Antarctica, or otherwise;
  c. prejudicing the position of any Contracting Party as regards its recognition or non-recognition of any other State's right of or basis of claim to territorial sovereignty in Antarctica.

Article IV(1) seeks to deal with the position concerning the existing territorial claims, and potential claims that could be made in Antarctica. It seeks to deal with the interests of a variety of states. These include the seven territorial claimants, those territorial claimants who may be in dispute with other claimants over the validity of their

[99] In particular the World Meteorological Organization and International Telecommunications Union have played an active role, as has the United Nations Environment Programme: see Bush (vol. I), 56.

[100] Patrizia De Cesari, 'The Regime of Scientific Research' in Francesco Francioni and Tullio Scovazzi (eds.), *International Law for Antarctica* (Milan, 1987) 247 at 255–6.

[101] See Recommendations II-I, II-8; IV-27; VI-2; VI-3; VI-6; VI-12; VI-13; VII-7.

claims,[102] and states such as the United States and the Soviet Union who may wish to assert a territorial claim in the future. The formula provided in Article IV(1) is such that all the principal parties in Antarctic affairs could come together under the control of a single regime without compromising their position on the status of sovereignty claims, or potential sovereignty claims.

Article IV(2) addresses the issue of the continuing impact of the Treaty upon sovereignty claims throughout the duration of the Treaty. It provides:

> 2. No acts or activities taking place while the present Treaty is in force shall constitute a basis for asserting, supporting or denying a claim to territorial sovereignty in Antarctica or create any rights of sovereignty in Antarctica. No new claim, or enlargement of an existing claim, to territorial sovereignty in Antarctica shall be asserted while the present Treaty is in force.

Article IV(2) deals with two situations. The first is the enhancement of an existing sovereignty claim based on traditional concepts of perfection of an inchoate title to territory. The second, as provided for in the second sentence of Article IV(2), is an outright prohibition on the assertion of new claims or the enlargement of existing claims while the Treaty is in force. The effect of Article IV(2) is that all claims, bases of claims, or potential claims were suspended as of 23 June 1961 and that nothing which occurs while the Treaty is in force will affect the pre-existing position of all the interested parties – both claimants potential claimants, and non-claimants. As a result, the boundaries of existing territorial claims in Antarctica remain in place for the duration of the Treaty.

Article IV therefore sought to take into account the positions of each of the various parties which had an interest in Antarctica at the time of the Treaty's negotiation. It can be interpreted as follows:

1. The Treaty is not to be taken as a renunciation of existing claims to territorial sovereignty by any party.
2. The Treaty is not to be taken as a renunciation or diminution of any basis of claim to territorial sovereignty which any party may have.
3. The Treaty does not prejudice the position of any party as regards its recognition or non-recognition of any other party's right of or claim to territorial sovereignty in Antarctica.

[102] Art. IV(1)(c) particularly applies to the mutual non-recognition by Argentina, Chile and the UK of their claims.

By entering into the Treaty no claimant state can be considered to have prejudiced its position, while other potential claimant states such as the United States also do not prejudice their position by entering into the Treaty.

Article IV has been described as the 'cornerstone of the Antarctic Treaty'.[103] In the words of the New Zealand diplomat, Christopher Beeby, Article IV 'represented, and it still represents, that Antarctica will remain peaceful and stable – will not become, in the words of the Treaty, "the scene or object of international discord".'[104] Yet, while Article IV has been rightly seen as one of the most important factors in the stability of the Treaty, it has also provoked a substantial legal debate. It has been argued that the wording of Article IV(1) is such that it can 'mean all things to all states'.[105] While Article IV may create legal uncertainty, it provided a diplomatic resolution to concerns over Antarctic sovereignty. As noted by Sir Arthur Watts, then Legal Adviser to the UK Foreign and Commonwealth Office:

> Despite a few areas of uncertainty in the scope and interpretation of Article IV of the Antarctic Treaty, it is still a remarkably comprehensive provision, covering a uniquely complicated situation. What is more, it works in practice.[106]

While Article IV has been successful in removing the question of sovereignty from the Antarctic agenda for the duration of the Treaty,[107] it has not resolved the question of Antarctic sovereignty. This fact is often overlooked. John Heap, a member of numerous UK delegations to Antarctic Treaty meetings, once issued a reminder that 'The Antarctic Treaty did not, as is frequently asserted, solve the Antarctic territorial question. It provided only for a *modus vivendi* as

[103] R. Trolle-Anderson, 'The Antarctic Scene: Legal and Political Facts' in Gillian D. Triggs (ed.), *The Antarctic Treaty Regime* (Cambridge, 1987) 57 at 59.

[104] Christopher Beeby, 'The Antarctic Treaty System as a Resource Management Mechanism: Nonliving Resources' in *Antarctic Treaty System* (Washington, 1986) 269 at 270.

[105] Gillian D. Triggs, 'The Antarctic Treaty Regime: A Workable Compromise or a "Purgatory of Ambiguity"?' (1985) 17 Case WRJIL 195 at 201; Auburn, *Antarctic Law* at 104 notes that: 'Article IV was deliberately drafted to enable States with conflicting interests to adopt differing views as to its meaning.'

[106] Arthur D. Watts, 'The Antarctic Treaty as a Conflict Resolution Mechanism' in *Antarctic Treaty System* (Washington, 1986) 65 at 69.

[107] Sir Arthur Watts, *International Law and the Antarctic Treaty System* (Cambridge, 1992) 124–5.

between the players.'[108] The seven Antarctic territorial claims still exist and the two next best-placed claimants, the United States and Russia, remain well positioned to assert a territorial claim if they so choose. While respecting the terms of the Treaty as far as asserting new claims and exercising jurisdiction (Article VIII), some of the territorial claimants have made little or no effort to reduce their activities within their claimed sectors. The reality is that territorial sovereignty, and the maintenance and continued assertion of that sovereignty, is just as live an issue today as it was in the 1950s. A number of incidents during the past decade serve to demonstrate this point.[109]

One example arose during the negotiations in the 1980s for an Antarctic mineral regime. During the negotiations it was never contemplated that mining activity would take place without the involvement of the party which asserted a territorial claim over the site or area subject to exploration or exploitation. Article 9 of the Convention on the Regulation of Antarctic Mineral Resource Activities (CRAMRA)[110] made it clear that the legal positions established under the Antarctic Treaty with respect to territorial sovereignty remained in place under the Convention. This was also reflected in the decision-making mechanisms of CRAMRA which established a Regulatory Committee to consider applications and issue permits for the exploration and development of Antarctic mineral resources.[111] Membership of the Committee was to be made up by the United States and the Soviet Union[112] and also 'the member, if any, or if there are more than one, those members . . . which assert rights or claims in the identified area'.[113] Consequently, claimant states would always be represented and could participate in the decision-making process of the Committee concerning potential and actual minerals activities within their claimed Antarctic territory. These CRAMRA provisions reflected the continuing importance of the territorial claimants in the ATS.

Similar concerns over the status of Antarctic territorial claims arose

[108] J. A. Heap, 'Antarctic Sovereignty: A Source of Stress?' in R. A. Herr, H. R. Hall and M. G. Haward (eds.), *Antarctica's Future* (Hobart, 1990) 181 at 184.

[109] An ongoing issue concerning the effect of Art. IV is the consequence it has for the declaration of maritime zones around Antarctica; this question will be considered in detail in chapter 7.

[110] (1988) 27 ILM 868 (hereinafter CRAMRA).

[111] CRAMRA, Art. 31.

[112] CRAMRA, Art. 29(2)(b), which in effect acknowledges the United States and the Soviet Union by referring to them as the 'two members of the Commission . . . which assert a basis of claim in Antarctica'.

[113] CRAMRA, Art. 29(2)(a).

during the debate over whether a comprehensive environmental protection regime should be adopted. At this time the suggestion was made that Antarctica be designated a 'World Park'.[114] This was an issue that had arisen previously. At ATCM VIII (1975) New Zealand had raised for consideration Antarctica's potential designation as a 'World Park'. At that time the proposal received little support because New Zealand suggested that the consequence of such a designation would be the 'internationalisation' of Antarctica under the auspices of the United Nations. This would have resulted in claimant states being required to renounce their territorial claims.[115] When this issue resurfaced in 1989 a deliberate attempt was made to adopt a different nomenclature such as 'Antarctic Wilderness Reserve' or 'nature reserve, land of science'.[116] This was done to ensure that no confusion existed over whether the proposals being made at the time for a comprehensive Antarctic environmental protection regime would involve the 'internationalisation' of Antarctica. At no time during the two years that Australia and France pursued this question at either a bilateral level or at Antarctic fora was any suggestion made that the Antarctic Treaty would not be the foundation for the implementation of such an environmental regime. By adopting this approach, the question of Antarctic sovereignty did not become an issue amongst the ATCPs.[117]

The intent, interpretation and potential application of Article IV has been and remains a source of great debate.[118] While there is no denying that Article IV does create the potential for legal uncertainty, the provision represents a political compromise which helped to stabilise the competing political interests of the parties. Shapley

[114] For the argument presented by the conservation movement on this issue see Geoff Mosley, *Antarctica* (Hawthorn, Victoria, 1986).

[115] B. E. Talboys, 'New Zealand and the Antarctic Treaty' (1978) 28/3/4 *New Zealand Foreign Affairs Review* 29 at 33.

[116] See 'Franco-Australian Draft Working Paper on Possible Components for a Comprehensive Convention for the Preservation of Antarctica' (XV ATCM/Working Paper/3) reprinted in *Final Report of the Fifteenth Antarctic Treaty Consultative Meeting* (Paris, 9–20 October 1989) 209; M. Cockburn, 'Hawke Ties a Diplomacy Knot with Rocard' 21 June 1989, *The Sydney Morning Herald* 9; A. Darby, 'Aust Wants Antarctic "Reserve"' 30 September 1989, *The Sydney Morning Herald* 7.

[117] See R. J. Hawke, 'Government Plan for the Environment' (1989) 60 *Australian Foreign Affairs and Trade* 333 at 335; M. Rocard, 'Opening Address to the Fifteenth Antarctic Treaty Consultative Meeting', reprinted in *Final Report of the Fifteenth Antarctic Treaty Consultative Meeting* (Paris, 9–20 October 1989) 113–18.

[118] See e.g. Auburn, *Antarctic Law* at 104–10; Triggs, *International Law* at 137–50; Bush (vol. I), 56–63; D. W. Grieg, 'Territorial Sovereignty and the Status of Antarctica' (1978) 33 *Australian Outlook* 117–29; Watts, *International Law* at 124–40.

contends that 'Article IV is the treaty's linchpin. In effect it was an admission that the problem preoccupying them for three decades was insoluble.'[119] Despite all of the 'sovereign activity' that takes place in Antarctica, the application of Article IV is still respected. Irrespective of the legal unreality created by Article IV it obviously is seen by all the parties as vital to the Treaty's continued success.

Area of application

Article VI defines the zone of application of the Treaty as being the area south of 60° South latitude, including all ice shelves. Specifically it provides:

> The provisions of the present Treaty shall apply to the area south of 60° South Latitude, including all ice shelves, but nothing in the present Treaty shall prejudice or in any way affect the rights, or the exercise of the rights, of any State under international law with regard to the high seas within that area.

This provision was subject to considerable disagreement at the Washington Conference, especially in regard to those islands of the Southern Ocean which fell within the Treaty area.[120] The effect of the limitation of application of the Treaty to an area no further north than 60° S is that the South Shetland Islands – jointly claimed by Argentina, Chile and the UK – and the South Orkneys – claimed by Argentina and the UK – and Peter I Island and the Balleny Islands fall within the area of application. However, some major sub-Antarctic islands are excluded. These include the Falkland Islands, the South Sandwich Islands, South Georgia, Prince Edward Island, Kerguelen, Marion Island, Macquarie Island, Heard and McDonald Island, Campbell Island, Bouvet Island, Gough Island and Crozet Island.[121] Article VI should not, however, be taken as being a definition of what is 'Antarctica' or the 'Antarctic'. No agreement could be reached on this question at the 1959 Conference.[122]

Article VI importantly includes ice shelves within the area of application, but makes an exception in the case of the high seas. Given the prevalence and enormous size of Antarctic ice shelves, it was important for some effort to be made to recognise specifically the

[119] Shapley, *The Seventh Continent* at 92; see also Trolle-Anderson, 'Antarctic Scene' at 59; *cf.* Lee Kimball, 'Whither Antarctica?' (1985) 11(3) *International Studies Notes* 16 at 17.

[120] Hanessian, 'Antarctic Treaty' at 471–2.

[121] All these sub-Antarctic islands north of 60° S are claimed by either an Antarctic territorial claimant or South Africa.

[122] Hanessian, 'Antarctic Treaty' at 472. See the discussion of this issue in chapter 2.

application of the Treaty to formations which cannot easily be classified as either land or water.[123] The inclusion of ice shelves in Article VI recognises the *sui generis* character of the ice formations and seeks to overcome any potential problem in Treaty application which could have arisen. The apparent intent to exclude the application of the Treaty from interfering with high seas rights within the area up to 60°S reflected a divergence of views at the 1959 Conference. One participant at the Conference later stated that 'we drafted that provision so as to leave indefinite the question of what was the high seas'.[124] This uncertainty created difficulties when questions arose as to the extent of the Treaty's application after its entry into force. Particular issues of significance have been the status of the seas which lie under the ice shelves, the extent of the Treaty's application to the Southern Ocean, and the effect of the Article VI attempt at saving high seas rights within the Treaty area.[125]

While Article VI specifically applies the Treaty to Antarctic ice shelves, the status of the seawater under the ice shelves remains unclear. In the case of the two largest ice shelves – the Ross and the Ronne – there are substantial bodies of water directly beneath the ice which are navigable by submarine.[126] As the Treaty supposedly does not prejudice existing high seas rights, if such an activity were to occur, could high seas freedom of navigation be claimed despite the ice shelf being within a claimed territorial sector? While no incident has yet occurred that directly raises this issue, it does illustrate the uncertainty of whether the Treaty was intended to apply to the high seas and also the status of certain bodies of water adjacent to and surrounding the continent.

There has during the term of the Antarctic Treaty been considerable discussion as to whether the Treaty only applies to land and ice south

[123] Art. VI does not provide a definition of ice shelves, but see Bush (vol. I), 65 where it is reported that Japan has interpreted ice shelves to mean 'all the zones more or less permanently covered by ice, including the airspace above and the waters below such zones', while the United States described ice shelves as 'thick portions of ice attached to the land and extending seaward'.

[124] Statement by Mr Herman Phelger (legal adviser of the Department of State and head of the United States delegation at the Washington Conference), 'Evidence Before the United States' Senate Concerning the Scope of the Antarctic Treaty (14 June 1960)', reprinted in Bush (vol. I), 114.

[125] For a general review of some of these issues see Christopher C. Joyner, *Antarctica and the Law of the Sea* (Dordrecht, 1992).

[126] See F. C. Alexander, 'Legal Aspects: Exploitation of Antarctic Resources' (1978–1979) 33 U Miami LR 371 at 384–97.

of 60°S or whether it has an extended application so as to impact upon the Southern Ocean. There is some evidence that the Treaty was intended to apply to certain high seas activities. Article I prohibits the conduct of military manoeuvres. This is an activity which can be conducted on both land and sea. Recommendations can be made dealing with the 'preservation and conservation of living resources in Antarctica'.[127] As most living resources in Antarctica are found in the Southern Ocean, and since there is nothing in this provision which limits its application to only terrestrial living resources, it is reasonable to assume that the Treaty was intended to apply to certain high seas activities. Despite the inference that the Southern Ocean was intended to be affected by the Treaty, practice during the first decade of its operation suggested a division of opinion amongst the parties.[128] A more generous interpretation began to be adopted towards the end of the 1960s. Recommendation V-3 in 1968 dealt specifically with the Southern Ocean. While strictly not negotiated within the framework of the Antarctic Treaty, the 1972 Convention for the Conservation of Antarctic Seals (CCAS)[129] dealt with the conservation of seals and declared certain sea regions to be specially protected. This approach has been confirmed through the adoption of subsequent Recommendations dealing with marine pollution and navigation in Antarctic waters,[130] and perhaps most significantly through the 1980 Convention on the Conservation of Antarctic Marine Living Resources (CCAMLR).[131] To ensure the practical operation of Article IV of the Treaty, the Southern Ocean also needs to be caught by the Treaty's provisions. If the Treaty only applied to the Antarctic continent and ice shelves plus islands south of 60°S, the impact of Article IV on sovereignty claims would be limited given the developments in the law of the sea allowing coastal states to make extensive offshore maritime claims.[132] If the Treaty was therefore to resolve completely

[127] Art. IX(1)(f). [128] Auburn, *Antarctic Law* at 130–2.

[129] (1972) 11 ILM 251. See also Report and Recommendations of the Sixth Antarctic Treaty Consultative Meeting (Tokyo, 19–31 October 1970) reprinted in Bush (vol. I), 225 at 227, para. 10 where it was noted that negotiation of CCAS had to be held outside the framework of the Antarctic Treaty System because 'the conservation of seals in the sea does not fall within the scope of the latter'.

[130] See Recommendations XV-4 (Human Impact on the Antarctic Environment: Prevention, Control and Response to Marine Pollution); XV-19 (Cooperation in Hydrographic Charting of Antarctic Waters).

[131] (1980) 19 ILM 841.

[132] Triggs, *International Law* at 158; see also C. C. Joyner, 'The Exclusive Economic Zone and Antarctica' (1981) 21 VaJIL 691–725.

Antarctic sovereignty issues it was necessary not only for land areas and ice to be covered but also the surrounding Southern Ocean.

The final aspect of Article VI to note is that it seems to imply that there is a high seas saving of rights for all states, both Treaty parties and third parties, within the region. This raises the problem of the relationship between the Antarctic regime and the law of the sea, especially in regard to fishing. However, this purported saving of high seas rights under Article VI has been diminished by various Recommendations, CCAS and CCAMLR which have all purported to derogate from traditional high seas rights, in particular the freedom of fishing.

Enforcement and inspection

As with any international legal regime, enforcement of the Antarctic Treaty represented a problem. The principal response was the establishment in Article VII of procedures for self-policing of the Antarctic Treaty by those Treaty parties qualified to attend and participate at the Antarctic Treaty meetings established under Article IX.[133] Article VII(1) provided Treaty parties with the ability to designate observers who may carry out inspections within and outside the Antarctic Treaty area. All areas of Antarctica are potentially subject to inspection, including all stations and their installations and equipment.[134] The inspection system is further extended by allowing inspections of all ships and aircraft 'at points of discharging or embarking cargoes or personnel in Antarctica'.[135] The observers who carry out inspections are to be nationals of the Treaty party which so designates them; their names being communicated to other Treaty parties who also have the right to designate observers.[136]

Article VII(5) also formalises procedures for the exchange of information between all contracting parties, irrespective of whether they are eligible to attend Antarctic Treaty meetings. Under this provision, advance notice is to be given of all expeditions to and within Antarctica by ships or nationals of the contracting party, all stations in Antarctica occupied by nationals of the contracting party, and all military personnel or equipment introduced into Antarctica under the provisions of Article I(2). As all areas of Antarctica are open to inspection under Article VII, all scientific research, and especially activities conducted at scientific stations, is capable of being subject to

133 Art. VII(1) applies to those Treaty parties now known as 'Antarctic Treaty Consultative Parties'; however, the Article has general application to all Treaty parties. 134 Art. VII(3). 135 Art. VII(3). 136 Art. VII(1).

periodic scrutiny by designated observers. The requirement of advance notice under Article VII(5) of scientific expeditions and maintenance of scientific stations was a further indication of a desire amongst the Treaty parties that scientific activities and the development of stations not be unchecked.

These procedures allowing for inspections to be conducted by designated observers were initially considered an essential aspect of the Treaty's successful implementation.[137] However, during the first ten years of the Treaty's operation very few inspections were carried out, and those that were rarely seemed to have any real impact in assessing whether the objectives of the Treaty were being promoted, or whether Recommendations were being adhered to.[138] As Auburn has noted :

> Inspection has, in practice, not proved to be as effective in policing the Treaty as it might have been. This is of special importance for a regime lacking any practical enforcement methods.[139]

In recent years, inspections have been conducted more frequently.[140]

Between ATCM XV (1989) and ATCM XIX (1995) a total of seventy-one inspections had been reported by ATCPs. This indicates an increased awareness of the importance of conducting inspections amongst ATCPs. As was noted at ATCM XIV (1987): 'inspection reports may identify and bring to the attention of Contracting Parties, emerging problems requiring correction or improvement, problems which otherwise could result in, for example, damage to the Antarctic environment or conflicts of use'.[141] However, some parties are still concerned with the operation of the inspection system,[142] and this is

137 The United States in particular supported the active use of inspections; see Bush (vol. I), 70–1.

138 See the criticisms of Auburn, *Antarctic Law* at 111–15; and Triggs, *International Law* at 157.

139 F. M. Auburn, 'Aspects of the Antarctic Treaty System' (1988) 26 *Archiv des Völkerrechts* 203 at 205.

140 See Final Report (ATCM XV), note 116 above at p. 35, para. 172 noting inspection reports had been submitted to ATCM XV (1989) by the United States, the Soviet Union, Australia, the United Kingdom, New Zealand and Chile; between ATCM XV (1989) and ATCM XVI (1991) eleven ATCPs had conducted inspections at a total of forty-five stations: *Final Report of the Sixteenth Antarctic Treaty Consultative Meeting* (Bonn, 7–18 October 1991) Annex E, 317–20.

141 *Final Report of the Fourteenth Antarctic Treaty Consultative Meeting* (Rio de Janeiro, 5–16 October 1987) 62, para. 153.

142 At ATCM XIV (1987) Australia, Chile and the United States all delivered working papers dealing with this question: see *ibid.* at 62–6, paras. 153–9.

an indicator that difficulties still remain. Nevertheless, its importance and value to the Treaty is appreciated. The United States has noted that the wide availability of inspection reports contributed to 'accurate and complete information about the Antarctic Treaty System and to maintaining the confidence of parties to the Antarctic Treaty, and others asserting an interest in Antarctica, that the objectives of the Antarctic Treaty, its provisions, and Recommendations adopted pursuant to it, are being fully implemented and enforced'.[143] Despite the value attached to the inspection system, its effectiveness must be questioned. There have been few reported violations of the Treaty flowing from a 'Treaty-administered' inspection.[144] This is to be contrasted with the alleged violations of the Treaty reported by non-governmental organisations such as Greenpeace International, who have carried out their own private inspections of various scientific stations and bases.[145]

Control of nationals

Article VIII attempts to deal with jurisdiction over nationals,[146] a difficult problem given the Treaty's non-recognition of sovereignty on the continent.[147] This provision applies to designated observers under

143 *Ibid.* at 64, para. 155.

144 Auburn, 'Aspects' at 205 refers to one reported violation being uncovered by a United States inspection team in 1985: no reference is made to what sanction or action was taken following this report.

145 The best-documented reported infringement of the Treaty and its associated provisions was the construction during the 1980s by France of an airstrip in the Pointe Geologie area, within their claimed sector. However, questions as to the environmental impact of this construction were mainly raised by non-governmental environmental organisations such as Greenpeace. This was despite the fact that the area had been subject to inspections by both the United States and Australia. See Auburn, 'Aspects' at 206–7; Christopher C. Joyner, 'Protection of the Antarctic Environment: Rethinking the Problems and Prospects' (1986) 19 Cornell ILJ 259 at 268–70.

146 This work does not consider in detail questions concerning the exercise of jurisdiction in Antarctica over nationals either within or beyond territorial limits; for more detailed consideration see Justin W. Williams, 'Legal Implications: Jurisdiction' in Gerald S. Schatz (ed.), *Science, Technology and Sovereignty in the Polar Regions* (Lexington, MA, 1974) 49–55; B. M. Carl, 'The Need for a Private International Law Regime in Antarctica', in C. C. Joyner and S. H. Chopra (eds.), *The Antarctic Legal Regime* (Dordrecht, 1988) 65–95.

147 There are numerous 'gaps' in the jurisdictional coverage envisaged by Art. VIII, partly as a consequence of it not being drafted so as to cover all jurisdictional questions that could arise with respect to the application of state laws in Antarctica; some of these problems were highlighted during the ratification hearings of the Antarctic Treaty before the United States Senate: see Bush (vol. I), 112–13.

Article VII(1), scientific personnel exchanged under Article III and members of staff accompanying such persons. The state party of which these persons are nationals may exercise jurisdiction over their activities wherever they may be in Antarctica. Article VIII does not prejudice the position of the contracting parties with respect to 'jurisdiction over all other persons in Antarctica.'[148] However, Article VIII does not conclusively affirm the right of claimant states to assert territorial jurisdiction against nationals of non-Treaty parties. This is important, as the exercise of such jurisdiction could raise issues under Article IV. This problem with the extent of Article VIII was recognised during the Treaty negotiations and provision was made in Article IX(1)(e) for questions concerning the exercise of jurisdiction to be considered by the Treaty parties at Treaty Meetings.[149] Article VIII(2) provides that in the case of dispute over the exercise of jurisdiction over personnel, the parties shall consult together with a view to reaching a mutually acceptable solution. At ATCM XVIII (1994), Uruguay presented a working paper dealing with questions relating to the exercise of jurisdiction in Antarctica. It was recognised by the ATCPs that the Antarctic Treaty deliberately left open some questions dealing with jurisdiction. However, it was a matter that required more detailed consideration. The issue has been placed on the agenda for a forthcoming ATCM.[150]

Parties

Article IX creates a distinction between various parties to the Treaty based on eligibility to attend ATCMs. There are three different types of state parties to the Antarctic Treaty. The original twelve which attended the Antarctic Conference are eligible to attend ATCMs under Article IX(1). States which have acceded to the Treaty[151] and have met the criteria under Article IX(2) are also able to participate at ATCMs. Finally, there are those states which have acceded to the Treaty but

[148] Art. VIII(1).

[149] Questions relating to the exercise of jurisdiction in the Antarctic have been considered at recent ATCM meetings: see *Final Report of the Eighteenth Antarctic Treaty Consultative Meeting* (Kyoto, 11–22 April 1994) para. 22–3.

[150] *Final Report of the Eighteenth Antarctic Treaty Consultative Meeting* (Kyoto, 11–22 April 1994) 27, para. 122–3.

[151] Art. XIII(1), which provides that the Treaty 'shall be open for accession by any State which is a member of the United Nations, or by any other State which may be invited to accede to the Treaty with the consent of all the Contracting Parties whose representatives are entitled to participate in the meetings provided for under Article IX of the Treaty'.

which have yet to meet the requirements of Article IX(2).[152] Those states eligible to attend under Article IX are commonly known as Antarctic Treaty Consultative Parties (ATCPs). Those which are not are known as Non-Consultative Parties. The ATCPs are divided into two groups. The first is made up by the twelve original parties which attended the Antarctic Conference and are named in the Preamble.[153] Article IX(1) confers a continuing right on these states to attend ATCMs. The second group of ATCPs is comprised of states which acceded to the Treaty and have met the requirements of Article IX(2) by demonstrating their 'interest in Antarctica by conducting substantial scientific research activity there, such as the establishment of a scientific station or the despatch of a scientific expedition'. Once an acceding state has been declared to meet this standard, they become eligible to attend ATCMs and participate in the making of Recommendations.[154]

At present there are fourteen Treaty parties which have met the requirements of Article IX(2).[155] In addition to the twelve original parties, this makes a total of twenty-six parties which are eligible to attend ATCMs. Fifteen ATCPs have been admitted since the Treaty entered into force. These are Poland (1977), the Federal Republic of Germany (1981), India and Brazil (1983), China and Uruguay (1985), Italy and the German Democratic Republic (1987), Spain and Sweden (1988), Finland, the Republic of Korea and Peru (1989) and the Netherlands and Ecuador (1990). Following the reunification of Germany in 1990 there is one less admitted ATCP.

One of the most contentious issues which has arisen with respect to the admission of new ATCPs is the criteria used to make a determination under Article IX(2).[156] States seeking ATCP status must be able to demonstrate a substantial scientific research interest in Antarctica. The criteria are neither specific nor exhaustive, and it is possible for

152 See Table 1 for full details of contracting parties (pp. 88–9).

153 This group does not include Poland, which while an original party to the Treaty upon its entry into force, did not participate at the Washington Conference but rather acceded to the Treaty on 8 June 1961, fifteen days prior to its entry into force.

154 ATCPs are also allowed to designate observers to participate in inspections as per Art. VII.

155 Both the Federal Republic of Germany and the German Democratic Republic met the requirements of Art. IX(2) during their time as two separate states; following their reunification there is now one less ATCP. Therefore, since the entry into force of the Treaty seventeen parties have been granted ATCP status.

156 For a recent review of this issue see Serge Pannatier, 'Acquisition of Consultative Status under the Antarctic Treaty' (1994) 30 *Polar Record* 123–9.

Table 1 *Contracting parties to the Antarctic Treaty*
This table lists in chronological order the dates of ratification by the original parties of the Antarctic Treaty, or dates of accession by other parties. ATCP status is also shown, with the date that status was conferred indicated for acceding states.

	State	Date	Status
1	United Kingdom*	31/05/1960	OS/CP
2	South Africa	21/06/1960	OS/CP
3	Belgium	26/07/1960	OS/CP
4	Japan	04/08/1960	OS/CP
5	United States of America	18/08/1960	OS/CP
6	Norway*	24/08/1960	OS/CP
7	France*	16/09/1960	OS/CP
8	New Zealand*	01/11/1960	OS/CP
9	Russia[a]	02/11/1960	OS/CP
10	Poland	08/06/1961	AS/CP(29/07/1977)
11	Argentina*	23/06/1961	OS/CP
12	Australia*	23/06/1961	OS/CP
13	Chile*	23/06/1961	OS/CP
14	Czech Republic[b]	01/01/1993	SS
15	Slovak Republic[b]	01/01/1993	SS
16	Denmark	20/05/1965	AS
17	Netherlands	30/03/1967	AS/CP(19/11/1990)
18	Romania	15/09/1971	AS
19	Germany[c]	19/11/1974	AS/CP(03/03/1981)
20	Brazil	16/05/1975	AS/CP(12/09/1983)
21	Bulgaria	11/09/1978	AS
22	Uruguay	11/01/1980	AS/CP(07/10/1985)
23	Papua New Guinea	16/03/1981	AS
24	Italy	18/03/1981	AS/CP(05/10/1987)
25	Peru	10/04/1981	AS/CP(09/10/1989)
26	Spain	31/03/1982	AS/CP(21/09/1988)
27	China	08/06/1983	AS/CP(07/10/1985)
28	India	19/08/1983	AS/CP(12/09/1983)
29	Hungary	27/01/1984	AS
30	Sweden	24/04/1984	AS/CP(21/09/1988)
31	Finland	15/05/1984	AS/CP(09/10/1989)
32	Cuba	16/08/1984	AS
33	Republic of Korea	28/11/1986	AS/CP(09/10/1989)
34	Greece	08/01/1987	AS
35	Democratic People's Republic of Korea	21/01/1987	AS
36	Austria	25/08/1987	AS
37	Ecuador	15/09/1987	AS/CP(19/11/1990)

Table 1 *(continued)*

38	Canada	04/05/1988	AS
39	Colombia	31/01/1989	AS
40	Switzerland	15/11/1990	AS
41	Guatemala	31/07/1991	AS
42	Ukraine[d]	28/10/1992	SS

KEY: OS = Original Signatory, CP = Consultative Party, AS = Acceding State, SS = Succeeding State

* Claimant state

[a] Russia succeeded to the obligations of the former USSR on 21/12/1991.

[b] The Czech Republic and the Slovak Republic succeeded to the obligations of the former Czechoslovakia on 01/01/1993.

[c] Both the former German Democratic Republic and the Federal Republic of Germany acceded to the Antarctic Treaty (19/11/1974, 05/02/1979) and both were granted ATCP status (05/10/1987, 03/03/1981). The new German state succeeded to these obligations upon reunification on 02/10/1990.

[d] Ukraine succeeded to the obligations of the former USSR under the Treaty on 28/10/1992.

other practices to be relied upon to support admission.[157] Initially, the view was taken that at a minimum a scientific base had to be established for a party to be entitled to ATCP status.[158] This approach was a rather restrictive interpretation of Article IX, as demonstrated by the fact that it took Poland sixteen years to be accepted as an ATCP despite having an active scientific programme in Antarctica for much of that time.[159] Since then the procedures for admission of ATCPs have been reviewed and it would seem that the threshold required under Article IX(2) has been lowered. The result has been that since 1983 thirteen states have been granted ATCP status. In some instances, states have been granted ATCP status very quickly.[160]

Despite this change in attitude towards the admission of new Consultative Parties, the requirements of Article IX(2) impose a heavy financial burden. This has helped to fuel criticism that the Treaty operates as a 'club' for the states that were original signatories, or those which have the economic and scientific capacity to mount

[157] For a discussion of some of the factors considered when assessing an ATCP application, see *ibid.* at 126–7; Patrick G. Quilty, 'Antarctica as a Continent for Science' in R. A. Herr, H. R. Hall and M. G. Haward (eds.), *Antarctica's Future* (Hobart, 1990) 29 at 30. [158] Auburn, 'Aspects' at 209.

[159] See F. M. Auburn, 'Consultative Status under the Antarctic Treaty' (1979) 28 ICLQ 514–22.

[160] In 1983, India, which acceded to the Treaty on 19 August 1983, had its application for ATCP status accepted on 12 September. See Auburn, 'Aspects' at 209 who suggests that India may have been assured of its ATCP status prior to acceding to the Treaty.

credible Antarctic scientific research programmes.[161] One response has been to share or reactivate abandoned scientific research stations. This not only minimises infrastructure costs for new Treaty parties but also assists in decreasing the environmental impact involved in building and maintaining scientific stations. While this initiative has helped to reduce some of the costs associated with conducting Antarctic science for new Treaty parties, it is important to note that Article IX(2) requires a continuing interest and commitment to Antarctic research. Consequently, states seeking ATCP status must ensure that they not only reach the standard required for admission under Article IX(2) but also ensure they are capable of maintaining it.[162] This is to be contrasted with the somewhat privileged position of the original signatories, who are guaranteed their positions in Article IX(1) irrespective of their current Antarctic research programmes.[163]

The final category of parties to the Treaty are those states which have acceded to the Treaty but which have yet to meet the criteria set down in Article IX(2). While these states are bound by most provisions which affect contracting parties, they are unable to participate in the taking of decisions at ATCMs or in some of the Treaty's modification and amendment processes. Because these Treaty parties are ineligible to participate in the Recommendation-making process they have become known as 'Non-Consultative Parties'. There are currently sixteen Non-Consultative Parties to the Antarctic Treaty.[164] Under the terms of the Treaty no provision is made for the participation of these states at ATCMs and there is little benefit that such a state gains from the Treaty under its original terms.[165] During debates in the United

[161] Gillian D. Triggs, 'The Antarctic Treaty System: Some Jurisdictional Problems' in Gillian D. Triggs (ed.), *The Antarctic Treaty Regime* (Cambridge, 1987) 88 at 95. For a discussion of the Brazilian and Indian perspectives on their application for and admission as ATCPs, see L. F. Macedo de Soares Guimaraes, 'The Antarctic Treaty System from the Perspective of a New Consultative Party' in *Antarctic Treaty System* (Washington, 1986) 337–44; and S. Z. Qasim and H. P. Rajan, 'The Antarctic Treaty System from the Perspective of a New Member' in *Antarctic Treaty System* (Washington, 1986) 345–74.

[162] Triggs has suggested that Art. IX(2) be amended by deleting the words after 'demonstrates its interest in Antarctica': see Triggs, 'Antarctic Treaty System' at 97.

[163] See Bush (vol. I), 83 where the position of Belgium and Norway is discussed.

[164] These are the Czech Republic, Slovak Republic, Denmark, Romania, Bulgaria, Papua New Guinea, Hungary, Cuba, Greece, the Democratic People's Republic of Korea, Austria, Canada, Colombia, Switzerland, Guatemala and the Ukraine.

[165] For the view of a Non-Consultative Party see Peter Bruckner, 'The Antarctic Treaty System from the Perspective of a Non-Consultative Party to the Antarctic Treaty' in *Antarctic Treaty System* (Washington, 1986) 315–35.

Nations throughout the 1980s on the subject of Antarctica and the operation of the Treaty System, attention was drawn to the division which existed between ATCPs and Non-Consultative Parties. It was argued that because Non-Consultative Parties were ineligible to attend ATCMs, the Treaty had little attraction for states wishing to accede, unless they were prepared to mount a substantial Antarctic research programme to become eligible for ATCP status. In response to these criticisms, Non-Consultative Parties were invited to attend as observers at ATCM XII (1983) and ATCM XIII (1985).[166] Subsequently, Recommendation XIII-15 was adopted: it provides that the host country of future Consultative Meetings may invite Non-Consultative Parties to appoint representatives to attend the Meeting. This provision has resulted in broadening participation at ATCMs, and also given the Non-Consultative Parties a greater participatory role in the Treaty system. Under revised Rules of Procedure for ATCMs adopted at ATCM XVII (1992) it is now possible for an invited Non-Consultative Party to attend all plenary and other sessions of an ATCM, by invitation address the Meeting, and also submit documents for distribution at the Meeting.[167] Despite this enhanced role for Non-Consultative Parties, there still remains no obligation upon the host states to issue an invitation to attend the ATCM.

Meetings

Article IX establishes the procedure under which Antarctic Treaty Consultative Meetings (ATCMs) are held.[168] The first meeting was scheduled for Canberra, two months after the Treaty entered into force. Thereafter, meetings were to be held at 'suitable intervals and places'.[169] The Treaty envisaged that at each ATCM there would be an exchange of information and consultation on matters of common interest. The most important aspect of these meetings, however, was for the parties to engage in 'formulating and considering, and recommending to their Governments, measures in furtherance of the principles and objectives of the Treaty'.[170] The effect of these provisions is that at ATCMs Recommendations can be made by the participants to their governments on measures which further the principles and objectives of the Treaty. These Recommendations may include measures regarding:

[166] *Handbook* (Pt 1), 32. [167] ATCM XVII (1992), note 149 above at 425.

[168] This term was accepted by the Rules of Procedure adopted prior to ATCM I (1961), reprinted in Bush (vol. I), 116. [169] Art. IX(1) [170] Art. IX(1).

(a) use of Antarctica for peaceful purposes only;
(b) facilitation of scientific research in Antarctica;
(c) facilitation of international scientific cooperation in Antarctica;
(d) facilitation of the exercise of the rights of inspection;
(e) questions relating to the exercise of jurisdiction in Antarctica; and
(f) preservation and conservation of living resources in Antarctica.[171]

Recommendations agreed upon at an ATCM only become effective after they have been approved by all of the contracting parties eligible to attend the ATCM.[172] The Treaty is silent as to the status of Recommendations as against acceding states. The Treaty further provided that while ATCMs had the ability to discuss and implement various measures on certain stated topics, the day-to-day operation of the Treaty after its entry into force was not dependent on the existence of these Recommendations. This is supported by Article IX(5) which provides, as an interim measure, that any or all of the rights conferred under the Treaty could be exercised from the date of its entry into force irrespective of the existence of Recommendations being adopted at an ATCM. While ATCMs were designed to implement new Antarctic policy by way of Recommendations, there was also an intent that the Meetings serve as a clearing house for the exchange of information gathered under the various processes allowed for by the Treaty. In particular, reports from observers designated under Article VII were to be distributed to the representatives of the contracting parties attending ATCMs.[173] In addition to the ATCPs, from time to time various international organisations and NGOs are invited to attend ATCMs as observers. The numbers of groups invited to attend in this capacity has expanded considerably at recent Meetings.[174] Both SCAR and the Commission for the Conservation of Antarctic Marine Living Resources attend ATCMs as observers in accordance with Recommendation XIII-2.

[171] Art. IX(1) [172] Art. IX(4) [173] Art. IX(3).

[174] At ATCM XVI (1991) and ATCM XVII (1992) the following groups attended in an observer capacity : the Antarctic and Southern Ocean Coalition (ASOC), the Intergovernmental Oceanographic Commission (IOC), the International Civil Aviation Organisation (ICAO), the International Hydrographic Organisation (IHO), the International Maritime Organisation (IMO), the International Union for the Conservation of Nature and Natural Resources (IUCN), the United Nations Environment Program (UNEP), the World Meteorological Organization (WMO), and the World Tourism Organisation (WTO). See *Final Report of the Sixteenth Antarctic Treaty Consultative Meeting* at 4–5, para. 5; *Final Report of the Seventeenth Antarctic Treaty Consultative Meeting* at 8–9, para 6.

Meeting frequency and procedure

As envisaged in Article IX(1), the first Antarctic Treaty Meeting was held in Canberra in 1961. Further Meetings were held in Buenos Aires (1962), Brussels (1964), Santiago (1966), Paris (1968), Tokyo (1970) and Wellington (1972). Thereafter, there was a delay of two and half years till the next meeting in Oslo in 1975. Meetings were then held every second year till ATCM XVI (1991). Since then Meetings have been held annually except for an eighteen-month gap between ATCM XVII (1992) and ATCM XVIII (1994).[175] There is no requirement that ATCMs be held at any specified time, only that Meetings be held 'at suitable intervals'. One important consequence of the adoption of the 1991 Protocol on Environmental Protection to the Antarctic Treaty (Protocol)[176] has been the decision to hold ATCMs on an annual basis and this has been implemented since ATCM XVIII (1994).

Special ATCMs have also occasionally been held since 1977. These Meetings are arranged on an *ad hoc* basis and have primarily been relied upon as a means for considering applications by states for ATCP status, or for considering at a forum outside of the regular ATCMs special issues which had arisen for consideration within the ATS. The use of Special ATCMs was a feature in the negotiation of the Antarctic minerals regime throughout the 1980s.[177] The Special ATCM IV convened initially in 1982 and did not conclude until 1988, during which time twelve separate sessions had been held in Wellington, Bonn, Washington, Tokyo, Rio de Janeiro, Paris, Hobart and Montevideo. An unusual aspect of these Meetings was that the chairman of the first Meeting in Wellington, Christopher Beeby, retained that position throughout in order to maintain continuity during the mineral negotiations. Special ATCM XI, which met in Vina del Mar, Chile during November and December 1990 and Madrid during April and June 1991, was used as the forum for negotiating the Protocol.

In preparation for the holding of ATCMs, it became the practice to hold Preparatory Meetings where the host state for the forthcoming ATCM would seek to set the Meeting agenda and various parties would present position papers on matters for discussion. The advantage of this process was that once the scheduled ATCM was eventually

175 See Table 2 for full details of meetings conducted under the Antarctic Treaty (p. 94).
176 (1991) 30 ILM 1,455 (hereinafter Protocol).
177 See Arthur D. Watts, 'Lessons to be Learned from the Mineral Resources Negotiations' in Rudiger Wolfrum (ed.), *Antarctic Challenge III* (Berlin, 1988) 319–31.

Table 2 *Meetings conducted under the Antarctic Treaty*

Antarctic Treaty Consultative Meetings			
I		10–24 July 1961	Canberra
II		18–28 July 1962	Buenos Aires
III		2–13 June 1964	Brussels
IV		3–18 November 1966	Santiago
V		18–29 November 1968	Paris
VI		19–31 October 1970	Tokyo
VII		30 October–10 November 1972	Wellington
VIII		9–20 June 1975	Oslo
IX		19 September–7 October 1977	London
X		17 September–5 October 1979	Washington
XI		23 June–7 July 1981	Buenos Aires
XII		13–27 September 1983	Canberra
XIII		8–18 October 1985	Brussels
XIV		5–16 October 1987	Rio de Janeiro
XV		9–20 October 1989	Paris
XVI		7–18 October 1991	Bonn
XVII		11–20 November 1992	Venice
XVIII		11–22 April 1994	Kyoto
XIX		8–19 May 1995	Seoul
Special Antarctic Treaty Consultative Meetings			
I		25, 27, 29 July 1977	London
II	1	27 February–10 March 1978	Canberra
	2	17–28 July 1978	Buenos Aires
	3	5–6 May 1980	Canberra
III		3 March 1981	Buenos Aires
IV	1	14–25 June 1982	Wellington
	2	17–28 January 1983	Wellington
	3	11–22 July 1983	Bonn
	4	18–27 January 1984	Washington
	5	23–31 May 1984	Tokyo
	6	26 February–8 March 1985	Rio de Janeiro
	7	23 September–4 October 1985	Paris
	8	14–25 April 1986	Hobart
	9	27 October–12 November 1986	Tokyo
	10	11–20 May 1987	Montevideo
	11	18–29 January 1988	Wellington
	12	2 May–2 June 1988	Wellington
V		12 September 1983	Canberra
VI		7 October 1985	Brussels
VII		5 October 1987	Rio de Janeiro
VIII		20–21 September 1988	Paris
IX		9 October 1989	Paris
X		19 November 1990	Vina del Mar
XI	1	19 November–6 December 1990	Vina del Mar
	2	22–30 April, 17–22 June and 3–4 October 1991	Madrid

convened the agenda would have been set and most of the participants would have been aware of the major issues to be discussed. This was seen to facilitate the decision-making process when Recommendations were under consideration.[178] Following the recent decision to hold ATCMs annually, Preparatory Meetings have, however, been dispensed with.

Apart from ATCM I (1961) in Canberra, the Treaty did not specify where ATCMs were to be held. The practice which evolved is for the Meetings to rotate amongst the ATCPs in alphabetical order (English language) of their names. However, there have been occasions when this practice has not been followed. In 1977 South Africa declined to host a Meeting. The Soviet Union has similarly declined to host an ATCM. As from ATCM XII (1983) some states have hosted their second Meeting and concerns have been raised over the financial burden this places upon some ATCPs.[179] However, as there are now twenty-six ATCPs there are a greater number of parties eligible to host Meetings. Nevertheless, this burden is increased when the need for Preparatory Meetings and Special ATCMs is taken into account, plus the obligation upon the host to publish and distribute Meeting documents. The question of cost-sharing as a consequence of the burdens of hosting ATCMs arose for consideration at both ATCM XIII (1985) and ATCM XIV (1987).[180] This has resulted in renewed support amongst some ATCPs for the creation of a Secretariat. However, it is uncertain whether if such a body were created ATCMs would in the future be held at the Secretariat Headquarters or whether the rotational system would remain in place.[181]

While the main order of business at each ATCM is discussion and agreement on Recommendations, Article IX(1) recognises the importance of an ATCM for facilitating the exchange of information and providing a forum where consultations can occur. However, apart from these general guidelines plus the requirement that reports from Antarctic Treaty inspections also be presented at ATCMs,[182] no specific

[178] For a review of the conduct of Preparatory Meetings see Truls Hanevold, 'The Antarctic Treaty Consultative Meetings – Form and Procedure' (1971) 5 *Cooperation and Conflict* 183 at 189–93.

[179] There are no provisions in the Antarctic Treaty which require ATCPs to make financial contributions in association with their membership.

[180] *Handbook* (Pt 1), 29.

[181] Under CCAMLR, Hobart is the designated site for the Commission on the Conservation of Antarctic Marine Living Resources, CCAMLR, Art. XIII. All meetings of the Secretariat are held in Hobart.

[182] Art. IX(3).

procedures are established in the Treaty for the conduct of Meetings. Rules of procedure were established at ATCM I (1961), and these have been followed, subject to some amendments, since.[183] The rules provide for both open plenary and closed sessions, with all parties strongly encouraged to submit for consideration working documents, proposals and draft Recommendations in advance.[184] Unless otherwise determined, only the opening session is held in public. This has led to the criticism that ATCMs are closed affairs and that ATCPs are not prepared to open themselves to public scrutiny. A further matter of concern related to the lack of public access granted to ATS documents generated at ATCMs. It was only during the 1980s, once again partly in response to criticism that was levelled in the United Nations, that Treaty documents became more freely available.[185] A report of each ATCM is now prepared by the host and published in the official Treaty languages. These reports contain the 'Final Report' of the Meeting, a list of Recommendations and any additional declarations which may have been made, together with accompanying documents such as reports on the operation of various ATS bodies and various Working Papers circulated at the Meeting. A *Handbook of the Antarctic Treaty System* has also been published by the Consultative Parties.

Recommendations

As provided for under Article IX(1), Recommendations adopted at ATCMs may deal with any of the specific matters listed in that Article, or further the principles and objectives of the Treaty. Recommendations have been made at every ATCM and cover a wide range of topics. Following ATCM XVIII (1994), 204 Recommendations had been adopted. The procedure is for proposed Recommendations (which have frequently been developed from various working papers or in Preparatory Meetings) to be debated and eventually adopted by consensus.[186] Article IX(4) provides that Recommendations 'become effective when approved by all the Contracting Parties whose representatives were entitled to participate in the meetings held to consider those measures'. Hence, something akin to a Treaty ratifica-

[183] See 'Rules of Procedure of Antarctic Treaty Consultative Meetings', in *Handbook* (Pt 1), 271. The original 1961 rules were subject to revision in 1983 and 1987.

[184] Bush (vol. I), 86; Hanevold, 'Antarctic Treaty Consultative Meetings' at 193–8.

[185] See *Handbook* (Pt 1), 60. Documents from ATCMs which were previously classified have now gradually been made available to the public also.

[186] Rule 24, Revised Rules of Procedure 1987, reprinted in *Handbook* (Pt 1), 271.

tion process and formal notification to the depositary takes place. In its role as depositary, the United States receives notification of acceptance of Recommendations, advises other Treaty parties of this acceptance and maintains a list on the status of each Recommendation.

Due to the requirements of Article IX(4), long delays have occurred in some Recommendations becoming effective. At times this has partly been a result of the need for Treaty parties to implement legislation to give effect to Recommendations, or to change practices adopted at scientific bases and by national expeditions.[187] In some instances though, the delays in formal acceptance of some Recommendations have been considerable. In 1962 the ATCPs adopted Recommendation II-IX urging themselves to approve Recommendations 'as soon as possible'. However, this has not always been followed.[188] Despite the importance attached to them, there were, for example, substantial delays associated with the 1964 Agreed Measures on the Conservation of Antarctic Fauna and Flora becoming effective.[189]

The question of the legally binding nature of Recommendations is important. Article IX(1) refers to the ATCPs 'recommending to their Governments' certain measures in furtherance of the Treaty, and while this would not seem to indicate that such Recommendations have any legally binding status, the requirement in Article IX(4) of subsequent approval of Recommendations before they become effective indicates that Recommendations are not considered under the Treaty to be merely recommendatory, but legally binding. As Bush has noted, the wording in some Recommendations is such that they can be interpreted as either being mandatory or not, but even if they are considered mandatory are they enforceable in international law?[190] If it is considered that once a Recommendation becomes effective it is an integral part of the Antarctic Treaty, then under the terms of Article X

[187] For example, Australia did not give the Agreed Measures effect within the AAT till 1980 upon adoption of the Antarctic Treaty (Environment Protection) Act 1980 (Australia).

[188] Auburn, *Antarctic Law* at 167 noting that the United States only approved Recommendation III-VII (originally adopted in 1964) in 1979, despite this only being a procedural Recommendation. Auburn has described this problem as 'a serious defect in a system which claims to be the legitimate decision-maker for a whole continent': Auburn, 'Aspects' at 204.

[189] Auburn, *Antarctic Law* at 272–3; Triggs, *International Law* at 163 notes that it took fifteen years for the Agreed Measures to become effective.

[190] Bush (vol. I), 96–7.

the ATCPs are bound to not engage 'in any activity in Antarctica contrary to the principles or purposes of the present Treaty'. While it would seem difficult to accept Bush's suggestion that Recommendations should be accorded individual Treaty status,[191] there can be no denying that some Recommendations, such as the 1964 Agreed Measures, have all of the necessary requirements to be classified as a Treaty.

One indication of the status accorded by the ATCPs to Recommendations is an Explanatory Statement to Recommendation III-VII (1966). The connection made in the Statement between Recommendations being an 'essential part in the overall structure of cooperation established by the Treaty' is a strong indication that the ATCPs believe Recommendations have some legally binding effect. Watts has argued that at the time of their adoption at ATCMs, the measures only take the form of Recommendations which may then be subject to subsequent legal effect after consideration by each ATCP.[192] As a result, merely exhortatory Recommendations may not have any legally binding effect, whereas others which create new regulations for the operation of scientific bases (or other activities in Antarctica) and impose obligations upon ATCPs to implement them by way of national legislation will be legally binding. The legal nature of each Recommendation will therefore vary according to the circumstances of its adoption and the action taken to implement it. As noted by Watts: 'The nature and effect of the measures adopted at Consultative Meetings is not free from legal difficulty, but in practice they have come close to being made in exercise of a quasi-legislative function.'[193]

Of considerable importance to the ATS is the application of the Recommendations to newly admitted ATCPs and also to Non-Consultative Parties. In 1964 newly admitted Consultative Parties were invited by Recommendation III-VII 'to consider accepting' already existing Recommendations.[194] Despite there being no new Consultative Party at that time eligible to consider accepting such Recommendations, the ATCPs again addressed this question in 1966 when in an explanatory statement to accompany Recommendation III-VII they noted:

[191] Bush (vol. I), 97; *cf.* Watts, *International Law* at 26.
[192] Watts, *International Law* at 25.
[193] *Ibid.* at 24.
[194] Belgium had proposed that the Treaty be amended to make acceptance of Recommendations mandatory: Auburn, *Antarctic Law* at 167.

1. In becoming parties to the Antarctic Treaty, states bind themselves to carry out its provisions and to uphold its purposes and principles.
2. Recommendations which become effective in accordance with Article IX of the Treaty are, in terms of that Article, 'measures in furtherance of the principles and objectives of the Treaty'.
3. Approved Recommendations are an essential part of the overall structure of co-operation established by the Treaty.
4. In pursuance of the principles and objectives of the Treaty there should be uniformity of practice in the activity of all parties active in Antarctica.
5. Approved Recommendations are to be viewed in the light of the obligations assumed by Contracting Parties under the Treaty and in particular Article X.[195]

In 1975 the ATCPs once again considered this issue, and Recommendation VIII-8 urged 'the States that have or will become Parties to the Antarctic Treaty to approve the Recommendations adopted at Consultative Meetings'. Poland, which became the first acceding state to be granted Consultative Party status in 1977, accepted all the Recommendations adopted at the first eight ATCMs prior to seeking Consultative Party status.[196] There has been no indication since that time of newly admitted Consultative Parties experiencing difficulty with their applications because they have failed, or do not wish, to adopt already approved Recommendations.[197] While the Consultative Parties have also sought to encourage Non-Consultative Parties to approve existing Recommendations,[198] this is not an offer which has been readily accepted apart from those parties which are seeking Consultative status. No current Non-Consultative Parties have accepted existing Recommendations.

The status of Recommendations has been considered at recent ATCMs. Prompted by the effect that the entry into force of the Protocol will have upon many existing Recommendations dealing with the Antarctic environment, and the need to increase the efficiency and clarity of the decision-making procedures within the ATS, new procedures were agreed upon at ATCM XIX (1995).[199] From ATCM XIX (1995) it was agreed that three categories of decision-making would be adopted. They are:

[195] Explanatory Statement concerning Recommendation III-VIII, reprinted in Bush (vol. I), 195. [196] Auburn, *Antarctic Law* at 169.

[197] For a list of approved Recommendations and their status for each Consultative Party as at 1994, see *Handbook* (Pt 1), 285. [198] See Recommendations III-VII; VIII-8

[199] *Final Report of the Nineteenth Antarctic Treaty Consultative Meeting* (Seoul, 8–19 May 1995), 19, paras. 69–70.

1. Measures: the text of which is intended to be legally binding once it has been approved by all ATCPs and is to be expressed as adopted in conformity with Article IX(4) of the Antarctic Treaty.
2. Decisions: the text of which relates to an internal organisational matter that is operative following adoption at an ATCM.
3. Resolutions: A hortatory text adopted at an ATCM.[200]

These procedures became operative at ATCM XIX, at which both Measures and Decisions were adopted. It seems clear that it is intended that all Measures that are adopted in the future will have the same force intended for Recommendations. One virtue of these new procedures is that ATCPs will have a clearer indication of what legal obligations flow from decision-making at an ATCM. This is to be contrasted with the previous procedures which allowed for Recommendations to deal with some matters that were not suitable for legally binding Treaty obligations. It was made clear at ATCM XIX that these new procedures do not in any way affect the status of previously adopted Recommendations.[201]

Dispute resolution

Resolution of disputes under the Treaty is provided for under Article XI. At the Antarctic Conference there was an attempt to implement compulsory dispute settlement through the International Court of Justice, but this was unsuccessful.[202] Instead, what is provided for is a system which encourages the peaceful settlement of disputes by the parties themselves, with resolution by the International Court of Justice being one of the options open to them. In instances of disputes between the parties as to the application or interpretation of the Treaty, the parties are to consult among themselves so as to solve the problem by reliance upon negotiation, enquiry, mediation, conciliation, arbitration, judicial settlement, or other peaceful means of their own choice.[203] If the dispute cannot be solved, then with the consent of all the disputing parties the matter is to be referred to the International Court of Justice. Failure to reach agreement on having the dispute referred to the Court does not absolve the parties from continuing to seek a peaceful resolution of the matter. Article XI does not seek to distinguish between various types of disputes which may arise under the Treaty, so that accordingly a simple dispute involving the interpretation of an ATCM Recommendation would be subject to

[200] *Ibid.*, Part II, Annex B. [201] *Ibid.*
[202] Auburn, *Antarctic Law* at 138–9. [203] Art. XI(1).

the same dispute resolution processes under Article XI as would be a purported exercise of sovereignty in breach of Article IV.

Amendment

Article XII provides for two types of amendment processes. The first is ordinary amendment or modification occurring during the life of the Treaty. There must be unanimous agreement amongst the ATCPs of the proposed amendment or modification. This must subsequently be followed by unanimous ratification of the proposed change to the Treaty.[204] Non-Consultative Parties are required to ratify the amendment or modification within two years of its entry into force, or they shall under Article XII(1)(b) be deemed to have withdrawn from the Treaty. This procedure reinforces the position of influence granted under the Treaty to the ATCPs and the important distinction which the Treaty creates between Consultative and Non-Consultative Parties.

The second amendment or modification procedure deals with the holding of a Review Conference. Under this mechanism, at the completion of thirty years from the date of entry into force of the Treaty, any ATCP can request a Review Conference. Both Consultative and Non-Consultative Parties are entitled to attend such a Conference.[205] Any amendments or modifications to the Treaty which are accepted by a majority at the Conference, including a majority of the ATCPs, enter into force in the same manner as provided for in Article XII(1).[206] If such modifications or amendments are not ratified within a two-year period, then any party may after that time give notice of its withdrawal from the Treaty. This withdrawal takes effect two years after the receipt of such notice.[207]

The Review Conference mechanism has often been subject to misinterpretation. Article XII(2)(a) does not provide for the expiry of the Treaty at the end of the thirty year period. Rather, it provides for a mechanism in which the complete Treaty can be subject to review after the expiration of thirty years. Nothing in the Treaty indicates that it was only intended to operate for a defined term.[208] Nevertheless, the prospect does exist that if modifications or amendments agreed to at a Review Conference do not enter into effect after two

204 Art. XII(1)(a). 205 Art. XII(2)(a). 206 Art. XII(2)(b).

207 Art. XII(2)(c); for a discussion of the effect of Art. XII see S. K. N. Blay, R. W. Piotrowicz and B. M. Tsamenyi, 'Antarctica after 1991: The Legal and Policy Options' (1989) 2 *ASOLPO Paper* 3–5

208 Auburn, *Antarctic Law* at 143 noted that proposals at the Antarctic Conference for the term of operation of the Treaty ranged from ten years to an indefinite period.

years, any party may announce its intention to withdraw from the Treaty. It is possible, therefore, that if at a Review Conference substantial disagreement existed amongst Treaty parties over a proposed modification, then disaffected state parties could choose withdrawal from the Treaty as an option. While it is difficult to predict the potential impact of such action, it does raise the issue of whether the Treaty could be terminated as a result of falling membership. The Treaty, however, does not specifically address the question of its own termination.[209] Neither is provision made for the withdrawal of a party from the Treaty under the accepted rules of international law.[210]

Despite the considerable developments that have taken place with the Antarctic Treaty, until 1991 there had been no serious effort to amend or modify the Treaty. The Protocol is the first formal addition to the Treaty other than Recommendations. CCAS, CCAMLR and CRAMRA were all separate legal instruments. The formal relationship between the Treaty and Protocol is unusual. Article 4 of the Protocol provides that it 'shall supplement the Antarctic Treaty and shall neither modify or amend that Treaty'. This choice of wording is curious. Article XII(1a) of the Treaty refers to the Treaty being 'modified or amended'. With the Protocol described as supplementing the Treaty, there seems to be an indication that the primacy of the Antarctic Treaty remains. This may be a reflection of the fact that none of the provisions of the Treaty were actually amended or modified by the Protocol. Rather, the Protocol extends the operation of the Treaty and gives it an additional focus dealing with Antarctic environmental protection.

If this characterisation of the Protocol is correct, it would seem that the careful choice of words adopted in the Protocol was an attempt by the ATCPs to circumvent the amendment and modification procedure found in Article XII(1) of the Treaty. This may have resulted from a concern amongst the ATCPs that the combination in the Protocol of a prohibition on Antarctic minerals activities and comprehensive environmental protection provisions, measures which would require implementation by way of domestic legislation for most ATCPs, could have created political difficulties for some Treaty parties. By using

[209] *Ibid.* at 145.

[210] Such rules exist under both custom and in the Vienna Convention on the Law of Treaties, 1155 UNTS 331 (hereinafter VCLT). However, because of the technical provisions for the application of the Convention it would not apply directly to the Antarctic Treaty. Nevertheless, some provisions of the Convention are considered to reflect customary international law and may apply by their own force: see Arts. 54, 56, 62, 65 and 67.

language which indicates that neither an Article XII(1) modification nor amendment were attempted, the ATCPs could ensure that if some Non-Consultative Parties do not eventually ratify the Protocol then the opportunity for them to withdraw from the Treaty under Article XII(1b) will not exist. However, this assumes that the Protocol could be added by a means other than that which exists under the Treaty. Under international law, modification or addition to a Treaty is only acceptable if all the Treaty parties participate.[211] The only exception to this is where the Treaty so provides. This Antarctic Treaty does so provide in Article XII. As the Protocol was negotiated through the institutions of the ATS at a Special ATCM, and only enters into force once accepted by all the ATCPs, the conclusion must be then that the procedure under Article XII(1) was utilised in this instance.

Despite the expectation that a Review Conference could be called in 1991, this did not eventuate. Nevertheless, a Review Conference can be called at any time after the expiration of the thirty year period. It is therefore possible, that an ATCP could call a Review Conference at any time. Following the negotiation of the Protocol in 1991, it seems that the prospects for the holding of a Review Conference in the immediate future are slim. However, if substantial delays occur with the implementation of the Protocol, one consequence may be that a disillusioned ATCP may seek to have the status and future of the Treaty reviewed at such a Conference.

Third parties

The Antarctic Treaty makes little reference to third parties. However, because there were so few states initially involved in the Treaty's negotiation it was recognised that the relationship between third parties and the Treaty may be important. This was especially a concern in regard to the Treaty's position regarding territorial claims. Article X seeks to deal with the question of third parties and the Antarctic Treaty. It provides that the parties agree to exert appropriate efforts consistent with the Charter of the United Nations to the end that 'no one engages in any activity in Antarctica contrary to the principles or purposes' of the Treaty.[212] The effect of this Article is uncertain and

[211] VCLT, Arts. 39–41.

[212] This provision is supported by Art. 2(6) of the United Nations Charter which provides that: 'The Organization shall ensure that states which are not Members of the United Nations act in accordance with these Principles in so far as they may be necessary for the maintenance of international peace and security.'

there has been no instance to date in which a Treaty party has sought to rely upon it in relation to activities conducted by third parties.[213]

The relationship between the Treaty and third parties has been a matter of increasing significance in recent years.[214] There are two aspects to this interrelationship: the role of third parties, mostly international and non-governmental organisations, in the functioning of the Antarctic Treaty through its formal institutions; and the role of third parties who have criticised and challenged the legitimacy of the ATS as being the appropriate regime for Antarctica.

As to the first of these relationships, the importance of SCAR to the ATS has already been noted. That the relationship between SCAR and the Treaty was institutionalised at ATCM I (1961) shows the immediate significance that was attached by the ATCPs to developing good and continuing relationships with SCAR.[215] That there was no provision for the creation of a permanent secretariat to support the Antarctic Treaty has made the relationship with SCAR even more important given that in effect it has filled that role in regard to Antarctic science – an activity it has conducted within the parameters of the Treaty.[216] The Antarctic Treaty also envisaged an active relationship with the United Nations. Article III(2) in particular encouraged cooperative working relationships with various UN agencies. This, too, was a matter considered at ATCM I (1961) and strong relationships have developed between the ATS and the UN's specialised agencies.[217] The strength of

[213] One of the difficulties in interpreting Art. X is that to date there has never been an occasion in which it has been relied upon. For discussion, see Stefan Brunner, 'Article 10 of the Antarctic Treaty Revisited' in Francesco Francioni and Tullio Scovazzi (eds.), *International Law for Antarctica* (Milan, 1987) 27–51. For a general review of the question of states as third parties to treaties, see Christine Chinkin, *Third Parties in International Law* (Oxford, 1993) 25–144; see also the discussion in chapter 11.

[214] This discussion will not consider the question of the legal or binding effect of the Treaty upon third parties; that and the related issues of whether the ATS can be characterised as an 'objective regime' are considered in chapter 11.

[215] Recommendations I-I, I-IV.

[216] Auburn, *Antarctic Law* at 171 has noted : 'The diplomacy of Antarctica is conducted at the Consultative Meetings. Science belongs to SCAR.' See also Zumberge, 'Antarctic Treaty'; Carlos Rinaldi, 'SCAR in the ATS: Conflict or Harmony?' in Arnfinn Jorgensen-Dahl and Willy Ostreng (eds.), *The Antarctic Treaty System in World Politics* (London, 1991) 153–60.

[217] See Recommendation I-V; see also Gillian D. Triggs, 'The United Nations in Antarctica? A Watching Brief' in Gillian D. Triggs (ed.), *The Antarctic Treaty Regimes* (Cambridge, 1987) 229 at 231; Richard A. Woolcott, 'The Interaction Between the Antarctic Treaty System and the United Nations System' in *Antarctic Treaty System* (1986) 375 at 379–82.

these is evidenced by the large number of UN bodies and other related specialised agencies which may be invited to attend ATCMs as observers. Another group which have had a continuing and recently very active interest in Antarctic affairs have been non-governmental organisations (NGOs).[218] During the 1980s especially, these groups played a very active role in the debate concerning the negotiation of an Antarctic minerals regime and the need for stronger Antarctic environmental protection. However, while environmental groups such as Greenpeace International and ASOC[219] have had a considerable impact on Antarctic debates, both from a public and also an ATCP perspective, there has been little formal recognition by the ATS of these bodies. Nevertheless, because several states have included representatives from environmental organisations on their national delegations to ATCMs and Special ATCMs, some NGOs have been influential in the development of national policy, and indirectly upon the ATS itself.[220]

The second relationship is that which exists between Antarctic Treaty parties and non-Treaty parties. Since the 1950s, there has been a growing interest in Antarctica by states with no 'polar tradition' or who have not engaged in activities on the continent. But apart from the attempt by India in 1956 to have the question of Antarctica's future debated at the United Nations,[221] this interest by third states did not initially have the potential to threaten the *status quo*. The situation changed in the 1980s when the ATS was subjected to sustained criticism from third states at the United Nations. The catalyst for this attention was the success of the 'Group of 77' at various United Nations fora throughout the 1970s in having the views of developing states incorporated into a variety of international declarations and legal instruments. The most important initiative was

[218] For a review of the role played by non-governmental organisations in Antarctic affairs see Lee Kimball, 'The Role of Non-Governmental Organizations in Antarctic Affairs' in Christopher C. Joyner and Sudhir K. Chopra (eds.), *The Antarctic Legal Regime* (Dordrecht, 1988) 33–63.

[219] The 'Antarctic and Southern Ocean Coalition'. ASOC became very active during the negotiation of CCAMLR and CRAMRA, publishing a bulletin titled 'ECO' which appeared at various CCAMLR Commission Meetings and at the numerous Special ATCMs during the negotiation of CRAMRA.

[220] Both Australia and the United States have included NGO representatives on their Antarctic Treaty delegations.

[221] 'Indian Explanatory Memorandum in Support of its Request for the Inclusion of an Item on Antarctica on the Agenda of the Eleventh Session of the United Nations' General Assembly – 16 October 1956', reprinted in Bush (vol. I), 505.

the recognition granted at the Third United Nations Conference on the Law of the Sea that the deep sea bed constituted part of the 'common heritage of mankind'.[222] When the Conference concluded in 1982, some members of the Group of 77 began to focus their attention on Antarctica. Some suggested that Antarctica also be declared a part of the common heritage.[223] The debate within the United Nations, which began at the same time as negotiations within the ATS concerning an Antarctic minerals regime, was led by Third World states who were not parties to the ATS. They were concerned that the ATCPs were engaged in a process of dividing up the mineral riches of the continent for themselves. Concern was also expressed over the exclusive nature of the ATS. It was alleged that a 'club mentality' existed amongst the ATCPs, and that acceding parties had little active role to play in the Treaty's operation.[224]

The ATCPs responded to the criticism by appointing the then Australian Ambassador to the United Nations, Richard Woolcott, to act as their spokesperson. In the United Nations and elsewhere, Woolcott presented the view of the ATCPs that the Treaty was not closed to newcomers and that accession and active participation in Antarctic affairs by new states was welcomed. In response to the claims that Antarctica be declared a part of the common heritage, it was noted that unlike other regions of the world where this concept had been applied, Antarctica was subject to territorial claims and had also been successfully managed by the Treaty for some time.[225] Nevertheless, in accordance with UN General Assembly Resolution 38/77 the UN Secretary-General undertook a comprehensive study of the ATS be-

[222] United Nations Convention on the Law of the Sea, (1982) 21 ILM 1,261. Art. 136 of the Convention declares that: 'The Area and its resources are the common heritage of mankind', with the 'Area' defined by Art. 1 as 'the sea-bed and ocean floor and subsoil thereof, beyond the limits of national jurisdiction'.

[223] See the speech to the UN General Assembly by the Malaysian Prime Minister, Mahithir bin Mohammad: UN Doc. No. A/37/PV 10 at 17 (37th Session of the General Assembly, 29 September 1982).

[224] For an overview see Peter J. Beck, *The International Politics of Antarctica* (London, 1986) 270–305; and for reviews on the annual UN debate by the same author see 'The United Nations and Antarctica' (1984) 22 *Polar Record* 137–44; 'The United Nations and Antarctica 1986' (1987) 23 *Polar Record* 683–90; 'Another Sterile Annual Ritual? The United Nations and Antarctica 1987' (1988) 24 *Polar Record* 207–12; see also M. Hayashi, 'The Antarctica Question in the United Nations' (1986) 19 Cornell ILJ 275–90.

[225] See generally Woolcott, 'Interaction'; Richard Woolcott, 'The Legitimacy of the United Nations' Challenge to the Antarctic Treaty' in Rudiger Wolfrum (ed.), *Antarctic Challenge III* (Berlin, 1988) 229–52.

tween 1983 and 1985.[226] A number of resolutions were also passed in the UN General Assembly concerning the operation of the Antarctic Treaty, in particular concerning the role of South Africa as a Treaty party. But the ATCPs refused to accept the substantive criticisms that the Treaty was not effectively managing the continent. Their only concession was to allow Non-Consultative Parties to attend ATCMs as observers and to make ATCM documents more publicly available.[227] Towards the end of the decade, the UN debate began to focus more on Antarctic environmental protection than on the potential implementation of a minerals regime.[228] While the UN debate seems to have lost much of its momentum now that the ATCPs have rejected an Antarctic minerals regime, the non-participation in the ATS of a large number of seemingly disaffected states who are not technically bound by the provisions of the Treaty remains an issue.[229]

Conclusion

The Antarctic Treaty grew out of a desire to see Antarctica demilitarised during the height of the Cold War so that scientific research on the continent could be continued in the spirit of cooperation which had developed throughout the 1950s and especially during the IGY. The Treaty reflects the preoccupation that existed with these questions at the time of its negotiation. Another principal catalyst for the Treaty was an attempt to resolve the question of Antarctic sovereignty. That the Treaty did not attempt to solve this question reflected the difficulty of the issue. Nevertheless, the Treaty has been able to deal successfully with the sovereignty question, so much so that the only major 'threat' to the *status quo ante* came during the 1980s with calls for Antarctica to be declared part of the common heritage.

226 Report of the Secretary-General: Study requested under General Assembly Resolution 38/77, *Question of Antarctica* (UN Doc. A/39/583: 31 October 1984). See also Peter J. Beck 'The United Nations' Study on Antarctica, 1984' (1985) 22 *Polar Record* 499–504.

227 See Recommendation XIV-1; also *Handbook* (Pt 1), 33, 67.

228 Peter J. Beck, 'Antarctica, Vina del Mar and the 1990 UN Debate' (1991) 27 *Polar Record* 211–16; Peter J. Beck, 'The United Nations and Antarctica, 1992: Still Searching for that Elusive Convergence of View' (1993) 29 *Polar Record* 313–20; Peter J. Beck, 'The United Nations and Antarctica 1993: Continuing Controversy about the UN's Role in Antarctica' (1994) 30 *Polar Record* 257–64.

229 Pakistan, a non-Treaty party, has sent scientific expeditions to Antarctica. This has raised concerns over whether other third states will begin to engage in Antarctic activities outside of the ATS: see A. Darby, 'Pakistan Looks for a Crack in the Ice' 12 December 1990, *The Sydney Morning Herald*, 4.

During the term of the Treaty's operation, there has also been a considerable growth in the complexity of its operations. Not only has there been a need to facilitate the exchange of information under Treaty provisions, but there has also been a large number of Recommendations adopted, and also a growth in the number of Treaty parties active in Antarctic affairs. As a result of these developments there has been much recent debate over the need to establish an Antarctic secretariat. It is a curiosity that, as Auburn notes, the 'Treaty did not set up even the most minimal form of international organisation'.[230] One consequence is that the host governments of the regular ATCMs have a considerable burden placed upon them to organise the meetings. Another is that difficulty has been experienced in collating the various Recommendations, Reports and debates that have taken place at ATCMs. While a *Handbook of the Antarctic Treaty System* has now been produced, it is by no means as comprehensive as it could be. Finally, because of the lack of a secretariat, and despite the significant role played by SCAR, there is no body created under the Treaty which is responsible for coordinating Antarctic research activity and the public dissemination of that research.[231] The increasing sophistication of international regimes and interrelationship between many which deal with the environment, science and resource management is another factor that is increasingly placing pressure upon the ATS to have an institutional body which can maintain contact with these developing institutions and facilitate better communication amongst the ATCPs.[232]

The need for some institutional infrastructure has been recognised in the legal instruments negotiated in support of the Treaty. CCAMLR created a Commission which is responsible for the on-going regulatory functions of the Convention.[233] The Commission, however, only has a limited mandate regarding the scientific research and monitoring functions which are carried out under the terms of CCAMLR and does

[230] Auburn, *Antarctic Law* at 155, where it is suggested that this was a deliberate response to concerns which had been expressed by Argentina, Australia and Chile about international administration.

[231] While SCAR has a substantial role in this process as far as scientific research is concerned, there is no formal conferral of this role under the Treaty. See for discussion Auburn, *Antarctic Law* at 171–83.

[232] For a comment on the question of a secretariat see L. A. Kimball, 'Antarctica: The Challenges That Lie Ahead' (1989) 18 AMBIO 77 at 81; R. Tucker Scully, 'The Institutional Development of the Antarctic Treaty System: The Question of a Secretariat' in Rudiger Wolfrum (ed.)., *Antarctic Challenge III* (Berlin, 1988) 41–52.

[233] CCAMLR, Art. VII.

not have a wider interest in all Antarctic research. CRAMRA also created a number of institutions designed to participate in a variety of decision-making processes under the Convention. The most important of these was the Antarctic Mineral Resources Commission.[234] It was envisaged that the Commission could establish permanent headquarters in New Zealand and also have a secretariat.[235] A Committee for Environmental Protection is the major institution created by the Protocol;[236] however, no existing provision has been made for the Committee to have a permanent location or secretariat-type function.

There has been some discussion at recent ATCMs concerning the lack of a permanent infrastructure for the Treaty. A working paper on the topic, presented by the United States at ATCM XV (1989), argued that the establishment of such a permanent infrastructure was necessary in order to 'carry on the dynamism' of the ATS.[237] At ATCM XVII (1992) consensus for the first time emerged over the agreed need for a secretariat.[238] Since that time there has been continuing debate amongst the ATCPs on this topic. Italy hosted an informal meeting of the parties to discuss these issues in some more detail during 1993 and this resulted in several reports presented at ATCM XVIII (1994). It was hoped that the debate would have been concluded at ATCM XIX (1995); however, there remains no consensus on the location of a secretariat, though ATCPs are still committed in principle to the concept. The choice of a site for the secretariat could prove to be a major political issue. Argentina and the United States have both formally offered to serve as headquarters for the proposed secretariat.[239]

Notwithstanding the secretariat debate, the Treaty has been a successful framework instrument for the management of Antarctic affairs. However, it is the Treaty system which has grown up from Recommendations and additional international instruments such as CCAS and CCAMLR which has allowed the Treaty to have a much greater impact than its original terms allowed. To understand the Antarctic legal regime it is necessary to look at not only the Treaty but the ATS, and it is to this that attention will turn in chapter 4.

[234] CRAMRA, Art. 18. The other bodies envisaged under CRAMRA were a Scientific, Technical and Environmental Advisory Committee (Art. 23), Special Meeting of Parties (Art. 28) and Antarctic Mineral Resource Regulatory Committee (Art. 29).

[235] CRAMRA, Arts 20 (5) and 33.

[236] Protocol, Art. 11.

[237] *Final Report of the Fifteenth Antarctic Treaty Consultative Meeting* at 10.

[238] *Final Report of the Seventeenth Antarctic Treaty Consultative Meeting* at 21–3, paras. 41–51.

[239] *Ibid.* at 22, para. 44.

4 The Antarctic Treaty System

Why an Antarctic Treaty System?

When the Antarctic Treaty[1] was negotiated in 1959 it was never envisaged that the Treaty would be the only basis for the management of Antarctic affairs. This is evidenced by the failure of the Treaty to deal with resource management issues or Antarctic environmental protection. Article IX provided that at Antarctic Treaty Consultative Meetings (ATCMs) the Antarctic Treaty Consultative Parties (ATCPs) could discuss matters of importance and make Recommendations to deal with those issues. The Treaty was not to remain a lifeless international instrument. It was not intended that Antarctica be only managed on the basis of the principles and international conditions which existed in the 1950s. Rather, the potential existed for an evolving regime that could cope with a variety of Antarctic management issues which the Treaty was unable to deal with or which had not been foreseen at the time of its negotiation.

Despite the decision not to create a secretariat to manage its implementation and operation,[2] through the process of regular ATCMs and the adoption of Recommendations, the Treaty parties had regular opportunities to deal with matters of concern. Through this process and the adoption of supporting conventions, the Antarctic Treaty System (ATS) has emerged. The 1991 Protocol on Environmental Protection to the Antarctic Treaty (Protocol)[3] formally recognised the ATS as comprising:

[1] 402 UNTS 71.

[2] While there seemed to be need at the time for a secretariat to support the Treaty, the decision to not create such a body was deliberate. See F. M. Auburn, *Antarctic Law and Politics* (London, 1982) 155.

[3] (1991) 30 ILM 1,455 (hereinafter Protocol).

. . . the Antarctic Treaty, the measures in effect under that Treaty, its associated separate international instruments in force and the measures in effect under those instruments.[4]

In effect then, the ATS includes the Antarctic Treaty and Recommendations adopted thereunder, the 1972 Convention for the Conservation of Antarctic Seals (CCAS),[5] the 1980 Convention on the Conservation of Antarctic Marine Living Resources (CCAMLR),[6] the 1988 Convention on the Regulation of Antarctic Mineral Resource Activities (CRAMRA),[7] and the Protocol. As defined, the ATS does not include provisions of general international law or other treaties. However, while certain regional and global treaties are not formally recognised as part of the ATS, this has not stopped the ATCPs specifically adopting provisions from those regimes in Antarctica,[8] or maintaining contact with the institutions created under those regimes.[9]

While various Recommendations and the 1964 Agreed Measures for the Conservation of Antarctic Fauna and Flora (Agreed Measures)[10] have played a very significant part in developing the ATS, the separate Conventions such as CCAS and CCAMLR have had the greatest impact. In addition, the formal conclusion of the CRAMRA negotiations proved to be the catalyst for a major reconsideration by the ATCPs over whether they should adopt a minerals regime or a regime which rejected mining and promoted enhanced environmental protection. This resulted in the adoption of the Protocol. Each of these Conventions and the Protocol will be separately discussed in this chapter.

Recommendations: general

Recommendations adopted at ATCMs have been the primary method by which the ATCPs have been able to deal with matters relating to the

[4] Protocol, Art. 1(e). [5] (1972) 11 ILM 251 (hereinafter CCAS).

[6] (1980) 19 ILM 841 (hereinafter CCAMLR). [7] (1988) 27 ILM 868 (hereinafter CRAMRA).

[8] See Protocol, Annex IV, which seeks to implement similar measures to those adopted by the 1973 International Convention for the Prevention of Pollution from Ships, (1973) 12 ILM 1,319, as amended by the 1978 Protocol, (1978) 17 ILM 546.

[9] An example of one global treaty which has particular application in Antarctica is the 1946 International Convention for the Regulation of Whaling, 161 UNTS 74. Art. I(2) applies to 'all waters in which whaling is prosecuted by such factory ships, land stations, and whale catchers', thereby dealing with whaling in the Southern Ocean. The ATS has maintained links with the International Whaling Commission and has a close interest in the regulation of whaling in the waters of the Southern Ocean.

[10] The Agreed Measures are actually found in Recommendation III-VIII adopted at ATCM III (1964), reprinted in Bush (vol. I), 146–69; *Handbook* (Pt 2), 2,048 (hereinafter Agreed Measures).

implementation and operation of the Antarctic Treaty. Article IX (1) lists six subjects that may be dealt with by way of Recommendations. However, the list is not exhaustive and when the 204 Recommendations adopted between ATCM I (1961) and ATCM XVIII (1994) are reviewed it can be seen that some have dealt with matters not specifically listed in Article IX(1).[11]

The Recommendations belong to four broad categories:

(a) *Antarctic operations Recommendations*: dealing with matters relating to facilitating the physical presence of people in Antarctica and assisting the conduct of scientific research, including questions ranging from postal and telecommunications to meteorology and transport;

(b) *environmental Recommendations*: dealing primarily with the 1964 Agreed Measures and the various categories of special areas which are protected thereunder such as Sites of Special Scientific Interest and Specially Protected Areas. There has also been a concentration on other environment-specific issues such as sealing, living resources, minerals, pollution, the disposal of wastes and more recently the adoption of comprehensive measures for the protection of the Antarctic environment;

(c) *science Recommendations*: dealing with either the role of the Scientific Committee on Antarctic Research (SCAR) in Antarctica, the siting of scientific stations, or general logistical questions relating to the successful pursuit of science;

(d) *Treaty Recommendations*: dealing with questions such as the procedure and timing of ATCMs, operational aspects of the Treaty such as inspections, anniversaries, and the application of the Treaty to third parties, new islands and the Southern Ocean.[12]

Since ATCM IV (1966) environmental Recommendations have been the dominant category adopted at ATCMs. Of the 204 Recommendations, 118 (58 per cent) fall into this category. Of the remainder, 41 (20 per cent) can be categorised as Treaty Recommendations, 27 (13 per cent) as Antarctic operations Recommendations and 18 (9 per cent) as science Recommendations. The increasing dominance of environmental Recommendations throughout the life of the Antarctic Treaty demonstrates the continuing concern amongst the ATCPs with environmental questions, and also the inadequacy of the Treaty's original

[11] An example is Recommendation XV-22 (Antarctic Treaty Thirtieth Anniversary Commemorative Stamp Issue).

[12] For another categorisation of these Recommendations see M. W. Holdgate, 'Regulated Development and Conservation of Antarctic Resources' in Gillian D. Triggs (ed.), *The Antarctic Treaty Regime* (Cambridge, 1987) 128 at 132–3.

provisions in dealing with the Antarctic environment. That there have been so few Recommendations dealing specifically with the conduct of Antarctic science also demonstrates that this was an area in which the Treaty did provide for a framework within which Antarctic science could operate. Because of the existing networks created by the International Geophysical Year (IGY) for the conduct of science and the coordinating activities of SCAR, it has therefore not been necessary for the ATCPs to adopt many Recommendations dealing with science despite the Treaty's emphasis on promoting this activity.

Environmental Recommendations: the 1964 Agreed Measures

The increasing attention given to environmental questions at ATCMs has seen the ATS become an environmentally focused regime. It therefore seems appropriate to give some specific attention to those Recommendations which have been adopted to deal with the Antarctic environment. This process commenced with the 1964 Agreed Measures. The Agreed Measures were actually adopted through Recommendation III-VIII at ATCM III (1964) and represent the first comprehensive provisions in the ATS to protect the Antarctic environment. They declare the Antarctic Treaty area to be a 'Special Conservation Area'[13] and seek to bind not only Antarctic Treaty parties but also to impact upon third parties.[14]

Article I provides that the area of application of the Agreed Measures is the same as that of the Antarctic Treaty, with paragraph 2 making specific reference to the saving of high seas rights.[15] As with the debate that occurred with interpreting Article VI of the Antarctic Treaty, initially it was assumed that the Agreed Measures did not apply to the Southern Ocean. This became a major issue of contention given that some Antarctic fauna depend upon the sea for their food.[16] The initial

[13] Bush (vol. I), 146, Preamble.

[14] Agreed Measures, Arts. IV, X and XI. Art. X of the Agreed Measures is in similar terms to Art. X of the Treaty. Art. XI refers to the need for crew members of non-Treaty-flagged vessels to be made aware of the contents of the Agreed Measures.

[15] Agreed Measures, Art. I (2) provides:

> However, nothing in these Agreed Measures shall prejudice or in any way affect the rights, or the exercise of the rights, of any State under international law with regard to the high seas within the Treaty Area, or restrict the implementation of the provisions of the Antarctic Treaty with respect to inspection.

[16] See Gillian Triggs, *International Law and Australian Sovereignty in Antarctica* (Sydney,

practice was not to apply the Agreed Measures to marine areas. But over time, in conjunction with a more liberal approach being taken to Article VI of the Treaty, this has been relaxed. The adoption in 1987 of Recommendation XIV-6, dealing with the classification of Marine Sites of Special Scientific Interest, shows that the limitation on application of the Agreed Measures to marine areas is no longer operative. Nevertheless, since their adoption the Agreed Measures have primarily been applied to the Antarctic continent and ice shelves.

The main focus of the Agreed Measures was to protect Antarctic flora and fauna from the impact of man's increasing activity on the Antarctic continent. To this end Article VI imposed an obligation upon all participating governments to prohibit 'within the Treaty area the killing, wounding, capturing or molesting of any native animal or native bird, or any attempt at any such act, except in accordance with a permit'. Permits could only be issued in instances where they were necessary to provide 'indispensable food' for men or dogs, to provide specimens for scientific study, scientific information, or to provide specimens for museums and other related institutions.[17] In issuing permits, the responsible government was required to take into account the ability of the native mammals or birds being taken to reproduce and maintain the species, the variety of species and the balance of the natural ecological system.[18] The Agreed Measures also prohibited harmful interference with 'the normal living conditions of any native mammal or bird' and listed certain activities which were considered to be such.[19] Certain native mammals and birds were also accorded the status of 'Specially Protected Species' for which permits could only be issued for their taking in limited circumstances.[20]

1986) 182; Auburn, *Antarctic Law* at 270–1; W. M. Bush, 'The Antarctic Treaty System: A Framework for Evolution' in R. A. Herr, H. R. Hall and M. G. Haward (eds.), *Antarctica's Future* (Hobart, 1990) 119 at 131–2.

[17] Agreed Measures, Art. VI(2). [18] Agreed Measures, Art. VI(4).

[19] Agreed Measures, Art. VII, para. 2, which includes as activities constituting harmful interference:

(a) allowing dogs to run free;
(b) flying helicopters or other aircraft in a manner which would unnecessarily disturb bird and seal concentrations;
(c) driving vehicles unnecessarily close to birds and seal concentrations;
(d) use of explosives close to birds and seal concentrations;
(e) discharge of firearms close to bird and seal concentrations; and
(f) any disturbance of bird and seal colonies during the breeding period by persistent attention from persons on foot.

[20] Agreed Measures, Art. VI(5)–(7). Annex A of the Agreed Measures listed fur seals and the Ross seal as 'Specially Protected Species'.

While much of the Agreed Measures dealt with the protection of Antarctic fauna, the protection of Antarctic flora in addition to fauna came under particular protection with the creation of 'Specially Protected Areas' (SPAs).[21] These were to be areas of 'outstanding scientific interest' accorded special protection under the Agreed Measures so as to 'preserve their unique natural ecological system'.[22] In addition to the provisions which applied generally under the Agreed Measures, within an SPA the collection of native plants and the entry of persons was prohibited without a permit, and the driving of any vehicle within the designated area was absolutely prohibited.[23] Permits would only be issued in instances where there was a compelling scientific purpose and when the actions permitted would not jeopardise the natural ecological system in the area.[24] SPAs were initially listed in Annex B of the Agreed Measures; however, it was recognised that there would be a need for further areas to come under protection and to that end provision was made for amendment through 'diplomatic channels'.[25]

Twenty-four areas have been listed as SPAs under the Agreed Measures.[26] The procedure for adoption of SPAs involves acceptance of the designation at an ATCM following a submission put forward by either SCAR or an ATCP. The areas are fully described in Annex B of the Agreed Measures, with maps and coordinates accompanying the designation. From time to time it has also been found necessary to extend the boundaries of existing SPAs and this has also been achieved by way of a Recommendation.[27] At ATCM XV (1989), at a time when there was considerable international interest in the protection of the Antarctic environment, it was agreed to amend the Agreed Measures to provide for the creation of management plans for each SPA.[28] This

[21] Agreed Measures, Art. VIII.

[22] Agreed Measures, Art. VIII(1). Auburn, *Antarctic Law* at 274, has questioned the classification of some original SPAs suggesting that they did not come within the definition and that there may have been politically motivated reasons why certain sites had been designated as such.

[23] Agreed Measures, Art. VIII(2).

[24] Agreed Measures, Art. VIII(3).

[25] Agreed Measures, Art. XIV.

[26] The first fifteen SPAs were designated at ATCM IV (1966). For details on each SPA see *Handbook* (Pt 2), 2,131 and Measure XIX-5 (Antarctic Protected Area System: Specially Protected Areas).

[27] See Recommendation XIII-13 (Specially Protected Area No. 7: Cape Hallett, Victoria Land: Extension of Boundaries).

[28] Recommendation XV-8 (Antarctic Protected Area System: Agreed Measures for the Conservation of Antarctic Flora and Fauna: Amendment to Article VIII). Agreed Measures, Art. XIV provided for their amendment by unanimous agreement of the ATCPs.

was in response to concerns that permits were being too readily issued for access to SPAs, and that once an area had been designated it was not being effectively managed so as to ensure its protection from human impact.[29] The effect of these changes was to require the development of management plans for all the existing SPAs and the inclusion of such plans in all areas which were being designated in the future.[30]

At ATCM VII (1972) concerns were raised that scientific research was being hampered by the designation of certain areas as SPAs and the reluctance of some governments to issue permits for research within those areas despite 'compelling scientific purposes'.[31] As a consequence, at ATCM (1975) Recommendation VIII-3 was adopted which provided for the designation of 'Sites of Special Scientific Interest' (SSSI). The purpose of this additional category was to allow scientific research to be pursued within certain areas set aside for research.[32] Sites were only to be designated when scientific research was proposed or actually being carried out, and when:

(a) there was a demonstrable risk of interference which would jeopardise those scientific investigations; and
(b) the sites were of exceptional scientific interest requiring long-term protection from harmful interference.[33]

Designation as an SSSI is not permanent but is for a specified time, though it is subject to extension following a review by SCAR.[34] Management plans were also required for a site to be designated as an SSSI.[35] The plans not only had to set out details of the site and its particular scientific value, but also provide details on the proposed

[29] For a review of the operation of the SPA system prior to these amendments see Boleslaw A. Boczek, 'Specially Protected Areas as an Instrument for the Conservation of the Antarctic Nature' in Rudiger Wolfrum (ed.), *Antarctic Challenge II* (Berlin, 1986) 65–101.

[30] See Recommendation XV-9 (Antarctic Protected Area System: Development of Improved Descriptions and Management Plans for Specially Protected Areas).

[31] See Recommendation VII-3 (Sites of Special Scientific Interest).

[32] F. M. Auburn, 'The Antarctic Environment' [1981] *Year Book of World Affairs* 248 at 261 describes the adoption of the SSSI as 'a compromise', arguing that: 'Rather than facing the difficult task of bringing the Agreed Measures up to date a new category has been established.'

[33] Recommendation VIII-3, para. 1(a).

[34] At ATCM XIX (1995) it was decided to extend the SSSI designation of twelve sites that were due to expire on 31 December 1995 till 31 December 2000: see *Final Report of the Nineteenth Antarctic Treaty Consultative Meeting* (Seoul, 8–19 May 1995), 26, para. 103.

[35] On the effectiveness of SSSI management plans, see P. L. Keage, P. R. Hay and J. A. Russell, 'Improving Antarctic Management Plans' (1989) 25 *Polar Record* 309–14.

forms of scientific investigation that was to occur.[36] Once designated, the administration of visits to a particular site was a matter for the various institutions responsible for Antarctic scientific expeditions in each Treaty party, and not the territorial claimant within whose claimed area the site lay. Seven SSSIs were originally designated in 1975, and up till ATCM XIX (1995) a total of thirty-four sites have been designated.[37] As already noted, the catalyst for the designation of an SSSI was that an SPA classification was seen as too restrictive for effective scientific research. It is not surprising then that some previously designated SPAs have now become SSSIs.[38] At ATCM XVI (1991) an SSSI was also redesignated. This indicates that on some occasions the interim protection provided for an SSSI may be insufficient, especially once its true value is understood following intensive scientific research.[39] In a further recognition that SSSIs should not be limited to the Antarctic continent, Recommendation XIV-6 (1987) allows for designation and research access to Marine Sites of Special Scientific Interest on much the same grounds as SSSIs. While some existing SSSIs have a marine component to them,[40] the specific recognition of the need for specially designated Marine SSSIs demonstrates that these areas have special needs and require appropriate protection.[41]

Another aspect of environmental Recommendations adopted under the ATS has been those Recommendations dealing with Historic Sites and Monuments. This was a matter which initially came before ATCM I (1961), when Recommendation I-IX called on governments to 'adopt all adequate measures to protect tombs, buildings or objects of historic interest from damage and destruction'. This was the subject of further Recommendations at subsequent ATCMs, when it was proposed that historic monuments be appropriately marked by notices in English,

36 Recommendation VIII-3, para. 1(c).

37 See *Handbook* (Pt 2), 2,184; and Recommendation XVI-2 for a listing of all the sites.

38 See Recommendation XV-7 (Antarctic Protected Area System: Redesignation of Specially Protected Area No. 11, Cape Shirreff, as Site of Special Scientific Interest No. 32).

39 See Recommendation XVI-4 (Antarctic Protected Area System: Specially Protected Areas Re-designation of Site of Special Scientific Interest No. 30, Avian Island, Marguetite Bay, Antarctic Peninsula as Specially Protected Area No. 21).

40 See SSSI No. 28 South Bay, Droumer Island, Palmer Archipelago which was designated because it was subject to a long-term research programme on marine organisms.

41 To date there have been few sites designated as Marine SSSIs: see Recommendation XVI-3 (Antarctic Protected Area System: New Marine Sites of Special Scientific Interest).

French, Spanish and Russian and that a list of such sites be drawn up.[42] Recommendation VII-9 (1972) formally created a list of 'Historic Monuments' and seventy sites have now been included on the list.[43] These sites range from flag masts, cairns, huts used by various explorers and machinery embedded in the snow and ice, to grave sites. Unlike the procedures established to support SPAs and SSSIs there is no protection mechanism under the Treaty, the Agreed Measures or by way of Recommendations for these historic sites. This matter was addressed at ATCM XIV (1987) when concern was raised about the vulnerable condition of the monuments and the risk of damage from human interference.[44] The Meeting urged governments to ensure that 'all necessary steps were taken to ensure the survival of historic monuments and that additional measures to ensure improved protection for historic monuments would also be carefully considered if and when required'.[45] The position remains, however, that there does not exist a comprehensive regime for the protection of such sites under the ATS.

During the 1980s, when debates were occurring within and outside the ATS over the degree of effective environmental protection in Antarctica, the ATCPs responded by implementing new measures to deal with some of these concerns.[46] SCAR was requested, through Recommendation XIII-5 (1985), to prepare a report on the existing mechanisms in the ATS for the protection of certain areas and whether additional categories were necessary. In 1985 SCAR released a report titled 'Man's Impact on the Antarctic Environment'.[47] The main response to the report was the adoption at ATCM XIV (1987) of Recommendation XIV-2, dealing with the implementation of a regime of environmental impact assessment in Antarctica. The Recommendation provided that: 'In the planning process leading to decisions about scientific research programmes and their associated logistic support

[42] See Recommendations V-4 (Historic Monuments), VI-14 (Historic Monuments).

[43] See *Handbook* (Pt 2), 2,253; *Final Report of the Nineteenth Antarctic Treaty Consultative Meeting*, at 27, para. 105–7.

[44] *Final Report of the Fourteenth Antarctic Treaty Consultative Meeting* (Rio de Janeiro, 5–16 October 1987) 59, para. 144.

[45] *Ibid.* at 59, para. 144

[46] Some of the concerns reflected an unease about the effectiveness of the existing measures: see P. L. Keage, *Antarctic Protected Areas* (Hobart, 1986); Lorne Kriwoken and Peter Keage, 'Antarctic Environmental Politics: Protected Areas' in John Handmer (ed.), *Antarctica* (Canberra, 1989) 31–48.

[47] Scientific Committee on Antarctic Research, *Man's Impact on the Antarctic Environment* (Cambridge, 1985).

facilities' those national organisations responsible for Antarctic activities 'evaluate the environmental impact of such activities' in accordance with a series of guidelines elaborated in the Recommendation.[48] On the basis of either an initial or a comprehensive environmental evaluation, decisions were to be made by appropriate national authorities as to whether activities should be allowed to proceed. While this process of environmental impact assessment placed considerable management responsibility upon the state whose nationals were seeking to engage in scientific research activities in Antarctica, there was also a recognition that other 'Parties concerned shall be informed, and be given the opportunity to comment' on the evaluation. This provided a mechanism through which territorial claimants could be part of the process.[49]

In 1989 further measures were taken to enhance the protection of the Antarctic environment by the adoption of two new initiatives. The first was the creation of 'Specially Reserved Areas' (SRAs).[50] This initiative was in recognition of the fact that neither SPAs nor SSSIs adequately protected areas of 'outstanding geological, glaciological, geomorphological, aesthetic, scenic or wilderness value'.[51] Consistent with the modern approach to the protection of specific areas in Antarctica, designated SRAs were also required to have a management plan for their use attached to their site description. Entry into SRAs was prohibited unless in accordance with the management plan, or under a permit issued by an appropriate national authority for a compelling scientific purpose.[52] It is intended that SRAs will eventually include representative examples of major sites of geological, glaciological and geomorphological features and areas of outstanding aesthetic, scenic and wilderness values.

The second measure taken in 1989 to enhance protection of the Antarctic environment was the adoption of Recommendation XV-11, calling for the creation of Multiple-Use Planning Areas (MPAs).[53] MPAs were created through a recognition that some areas of the continent were increasingly subject to multiple use by groups such as scientific expeditions and tourist operators. While such use was legitimate, there was a growing need for coordination in order to minimise

[48] Recommendation XIV-2, para. 1. [49] Recommendation XIV-2, para. 2.

[50] Recommendation XV-10 (Antarctic Protected Area System: Establishment of Specially Reserved Areas (SRAs)).

[51] Recommendation XV-10, para. 1. [52] Recommendation XV-10, para. 4.

[53] Recommendation XV-11 (Antarctic Protected Area System: Establishment of Multiple-Use Planning Areas (MPAs)).

environmental impact. MPAs are to be designated pursuant to a management plan describing the physical site, the current use of the site, and specific management measures for the site.[54] An MPA may also include already designated SPAs, SSSIs, SRAs or Historic Monuments.

Implementation and enforcement of the Agreed Measures and related Recommendations dealing with environmental management are the responsibility of individual Treaty parties. The Agreed Measures require each Treaty party which has adopted the Measures to take appropriate action to implement them.[55] This involves the enactment of appropriate domestic legislation by the Treaty parties and the application of those laws to the acts of their nationals in Antarctica.[56] However, there is the potential for conflicting application of these laws if recognition is not given to acts carried out under a permit issued by another Treaty party.[57] The enforcement of the Agreed Measures has also raised some concerns. Similarly to the Antarctic Treaty, no enforcement provisions are provided for in either the Agreed Measures or accompanying additional environmental Recommendations. Consequently, the only form of enforcement that has existed is the moral sanction resulting from an infringement being discovered during the conduct of an Antarctic Treaty inspection under Article VII of the Treaty. Even when breaches have been documented there has been very little response from the parties concerned or expression of disquiet from other Treaty parties at ATCMs.[58] The best-documented evidence of an apparent breach of the Agreed Measures occurred in the early 1980s, when France commenced construction of an airstrip in the Pointe Geologie area of their claimed sector. The area in which the construction took place was particularly sensitive to environmental impact because of penguin colonies, a fact which had been recognised by the French who had established a research facility in the area to study the birds. However, despite the concerns of environmental groups,[59] and efforts by

[54] Recommendation XV-11, para. 4. [55] Agreed Measures, Art. III.

[56] See Bush (vol. I), 161–2 for a review of some domestic legislation enacted to implement the Agreed Measures. [57] See Auburn, *Antarctic Law* at 272.

[58] See the examples referred to by Auburn, *Antarctic Law* at 276–7; Triggs, *International Law* at 182.

[59] There are numerous reports of penguins being killed by explosions during the construction process and also destruction of their nests and eggs: see James N. Barnes, 'Legal Aspects of Environmental Protection in Antarctica' in Christopher C. Joyner and Sudhir K. Chopra (eds.), *The Antarctic Legal Regime* (Dordrecht, 1988) 241 at

Australia and New Zealand to raise privately with France their concerns over the environmental impact of the project, this apparent breach of the Agreed Measures was allowed to go unsanctioned. This particular incident demonstrated that the Agreed Measures and associated Recommendations are seen by some ATCPs to constitute only a code of practice which is not binding and not subject to sanction for breach.

Convention for the Conservation of Antarctic Seals (CCAS)

During the 1960s there had been various occasions when ATCPs expressed concerns about the potential for commercial sealing activities recommencing in the Southern Ocean. To that end, various disparate measures were taken through Recommendations and the 1964 Agreed Measures to deal with the matter.[60] Because of doubts over the extent of the Antarctic Treaty's reach over what was essentially a high seas freedom, and concerns that sealing activities may be carried out by non-Antarctic Treaty parties, it was recognised at ATCM V (1968) that it would be necessary to negotiate measures outside of the Antarctic Treaty framework if the regulation of sealing was to be a success.[61] The matter was given further consideration at ATCM VI (1970) where it was decided to remove the issue from the Treaty agenda and deal with it at a separate diplomatic Conference.[62] A Conference open to all interested parties convened in London in 1972. However, despite the hope that non-Antarctic Treaty parties would attend the only participants were ATCPs.[63] The Conference lasted for nine days during which time a draft Convention was finalised. The Convention was opened for signature on 1 June 1972 and entered into force in 1978. There are eleven original parties to the Convention,[64]

258–9; Christopher C. Joyner, 'Protection of the Antarctic Environment: Rethinking the Problems and Prospects' (1986) 19 Cornell ILJ 259 at 268–70.

60 As for Recommendations, see III-11 (Pelagic Sealing and the Taking of Fauna on Pack Ice); IV-21 (Interim Guide Lines for the Voluntary Regulation of Antarctic Pelagic Sealing).

61 See Recommendation V-8 (Examination of Draft Convention for the Regulation of Antarctic Pelagic Sealing); also Triggs, *International Law* at 189.

62 See Bush (vol. I), 227.

63 The states which attended the meeting were Argentina, Australia, Belgium, Chile, France, Japan, New Zealand, Norway, South Africa, the USSR, the UK and the USA – none of whom were at that time engaged in commercial sealing in the Southern Ocean.

64 They are Argentina, Australia, Belgium, Chile, France, Japan, Norway, South Africa,

with five other states having been invited to accede.[65] All CCAS parties are also parties to the Antarctic Treaty.

The Convention specifically applies to the seas south of 60°S latitude,[66] though there is some scope for its application to floating sea ice north of that area.[67] The intention was to complement the Agreed Measures, which protect seals on the continent, Antarctic islands and on sea ice. CCAS does not apply to the Antarctic continent or to floating sea ice within the Treaty area. Consequently, its effect is limited to pelagic sealing. Six seal species are dealt with under the Convention[68] with complete protection granted to the Ross, southern elephant and fur seals,[69] while catch limits are set for the crabeater, leopard and Weddell seal.[70] Similar to the provisions of the Antarctic Treaty, each party to the Convention is to exchange information on steps taken to implement the Convention and statistical information of reported catches.[71] In an effort to provide the Convention parties with specialised scientific advice, SCAR is given the role of assessing and reporting on information provided to it by the state parties.[72]

Despite the fact that enforcement is solely a matter for the flag state,[73] CCAS has been a success, though undoubtedly aided by the diminishing interest shown in Antarctic sealing. The procedure established under Article 7 allowing for a regular five-year review of the Convention was not utilised in 1983. However, in 1988, amidst reports that Soviet vessels had begun to engage in extensive sealing activities, the parties met for the first review.[74] Despite these reports, it

Russia, the UK and the USA.

65 The states which have acceded are Poland, Germany, Canada, Brazil and Italy. CCAS, Art. 12 provides that states 'may be invited to accede' to the Convention.

66 CCAS, Art. 1(1): 'The Convention applies to the seas south of 60° South Latitude, in respect of which the Contracting Parties affirm the provisions of Article IV of the Antarctic Treaty.'

67 CCAS, Art. 5(7).

68 CCAS, Art. 1(2); the southern elephant seal, leopard seal, Weddell seal, crabeater seal, Ross seal and southern fur seals.

69 CCAS, Annex, Clause 2; in order to protect the breeding stock, Weddell seals are also completely protected during 1 September to 31 January inclusive.

70 CCAS, Annex, Clause 1.

71 CCAS, Art. 5, Annex, Clause 6.

72 CCAS, Art. 5.

73 CCAS, Arts. 2(2), 5(5).

74 Knowles Kerry, 'Terrestrial Flora and Fauna of the AAT' in John Handmer and Martijn Wilder (eds.), *Towards a Conservation Strategy for the Australian Antarctic Territory* (Canberra, 1993) 53 at 62 notes that the Russian sealing expedition harvested all species, but mostly crabeater seals, in the 1986–87 season with a take of approximately 4,500 seals.

was concluded that there was insufficient evidence to suggest that commercial sealing had been or even would be initiated during the immediate future.[75] Consequently, apart from some minor amendments to the Convention's Annex, few substantive changes were agreed upon at this Meeting.[76] As noted in 1991 by the UK as the CCAS Depositary: 'In the period since the Convention was adopted there has been no commercial sealing in Antarctica, nor is any foreseen.'[77] Consequently, the Convention has been relatively uncontroversial since its entry into force.[78]

Convention on the Conservation of Antarctic Marine Living Resources (CCAMLR)

The Convention on the Conservation of Antarctic Marine Living Resources (CCAMLR) developed as a consequence of a Recommendation made at ATCM VIII (1975). Following a further Recommendation made at ATCM IX (1977),[79] the methods and principles of procedure to establish such a conservation regime in Antarctica were established. A series of meetings amongst the ATCPs followed and in May 1980, a special Conference was convened in Canberra.[80] The Conference successfully concluded later that month and CCAMLR was opened for signature in August 1980. The Convention entered into force on 7 April 1982 after the necessary eighth ratification had been received.[81]

75 Report of the 1988 Meeting to Review the Operation of the Convention for the Conservation of Antarctic Seals, London, 12–16 September, paras. 12, 26, reprinted in *Handbook* (Pt 1), 162.

76 For a review of the Meeting, see Anne Marchal, 'Convention for the Conservation of Antarctic Seals: 1988 Review of Operations' (1989) 25 *Polar Record* 142–3. There was no Review Meeting conducted in 1993.

77 'Report Submitted to the XVIth Antarctic Treaty Consultative Meeting by the Depositary Government of the Convention for the Conservation of Antarctic Seals (United Kingdom) in Accordance with Recommendation XIII-2, Paragraph 2(d)' reprinted in *Final Report of the Sixteenth Antarctic Treaty Consultative Meeting* (Bonn, 7–18 October 1991) 223 at 227 (Annex B of para. 2(d) of the Report).

78 For a further review of CCAS see Bush, 'The Antarctic Treaty System' at 129–35.

79 See Recommendations VIII-10, IX-2.

80 The Conference, which was not designated as a Special ATCM, was presumably held outside of the ATS in an attempt to encourage participation by non-Antarctic Treaty parties who may have been engaging in Southern Ocean fishing activities.

81 For a discussion on the negotiation of CCAMLR see James N. Barnes, 'The Emerging Convention on the Conservation of Antarctic Marine Living Resources: An Attempt to Meet the New Realities of Resource Exploitation in the Southern Ocean' in Jonathan I. Charney (ed.), *The New Nationalism and the Use of Common Spaces* (Totowa, NJ, 1982) 239–88.

There are twenty-nine parties to the Convention,[82] including the European Economic Community.[83]

CCAMLR follows the lead established by CCAS in being a Convention directed specifically to the protection and conservation of a marine resource. However, instead of having a species focus, it concentrates on a marine ecosystem. This follows from the Convention being negotiated as a direct response to concerns over the exploitation of krill. The Antarctic krill fishery began in the late 1950s. However, it was not till the 1970s that the commercial potential for the fishery was realised and catch figures began to increase.[84] There are widely varying estimates of the krill stock in the Southern Ocean, ranging from less than 100 million to 7 billion tons.[85] What is known is that krill form a pivotal link in the Antarctic marine living food chain and that commercial overexploitation of the fishery would have dire consequences for Antarctic marine and bird life. While there were concerns over other potential and already existing Antarctic fisheries at the time of CCAMLR's negotiation, the concerns over krill were the driving force behind the negotiation of the Convention and its rapid implementation.[86]

Area of application

To implement an ecosystem approach in resource management CCAMLR adopted a number of features which make it distinctive from

[82] The contracting state parties are Argentina, Australia, Chile, France, Germany, Japan, New Zealand, South Africa, Russia, the UK, the USA (1982), Belgium, Norway, Poland, Spain, Sweden (1984), India, Republic of Korea, Uruguay (1985), Brazil (1986), Greece (1987), Canada (1988), Finland, Italy, Peru (1989), the Netherlands (1990), Bulgaria (1992) and the Ukraine (1994); the European Economic Community also became a member in 1982.

[83] Specific provision was made in CCAMLR for membership by 'regional economic integration organizations' (Art. XXIX) because under the terms of the European Economic Community some member states have conferred certain powers with respect to fisheries upon the Commission, with the consequence that it was impossible for some Antarctic Treaty parties who became parties to CCAMLR to fulfil all the obligations under the Convention: see Bush (vol. I), 422–3.

[84] Paul Arthur Berkman, 'The Antarctic Marine Ecosystem and Humankind' (1992) 6 *Reviews in Aquatic Science* 295 at 313–14.

[85] *Ibid.* at 312.

[86] David M. Edwards and John A. Heap, 'Convention on the Conservation of Antarctic Marine Living Resources: A Commentary' (1981) 20 *Polar Record* 353 at 354–5; Stephen Nicol, 'CCAMLR and its Approaches to Management of the Krill Fishery' (1991) 27 *Polar Record* 229 at 229; for further background see Matthew Howard, 'The Convention on the Conservation of Antarctic Marine Living Resources: A Five-Year Review' (1989) 38 ICLQ 104 at 108–12.

other component instruments in the ATS. The Convention's area of application extends to:

> Antarctic marine living resources of the area south of 60° South latitude and to the Antarctic marine living resources of the area between that latitude and the Antarctic convergence which form part of the Antarctic marine ecosystem.[87]

The significance in this is that for the first time the ATS recognised the Antarctic convergence and its importance for the purposes of delimiting the maritime area subject to Antarctic influence.[88] CCAMLR does not, however, extend to all activities that take place within that area. Rather it only applies to Antarctic marine living resources. These are defined as 'the populations of fin fish, molluscs, crustaceans and all other species of living organisms, including birds found south of the Antarctic convergence'.[89] It is therefore a Convention specifically dealing with the marine living resources of the Southern Ocean.[90]

By extending the operation of CCAMLR beyond the limits of the Antarctic Treaty and impacting upon the potential sovereign rights of claimant states freely to exploit marine resources in adjacent offshore areas, the Convention raised the issue of Antarctic sovereignty. Article IV deals with this issue by providing that all parties are bound by Articles IV and VI of the Antarctic Treaty in their relations with each other. Accordingly, non-Antarctic Treaty parties which join CCAMLR become bound by those provisions of Article IV of the Treaty which expressly impose limitations on the assertion of territorial claims. However, neither of these provisions of the Antarctic Treaty was intended to apply north of the Antarctic Treaty area. Consequently Article IV(2) of CCAMLR provides:

> Nothing in this Convention and no acts or activities taking place while the present Convention is in force shall:

[87] CCAMLR, Art. I (1).

[88] The 'Antarctic Convergence' is defined in CCAMLR, Art. I(4) as:

> a line joining the following points along parallels of latitude and meridians of longitude:50°S, 0°; 50°S, 30°E; 45°S, 30°E; 45°S, 80°E; 55°S, 150°E; 60°S, 150°E; 60°S, 50°W; 50°S, 50°W; 50°S, 0°.

See J. R. V. Prescott, 'Boundaries in Antarctica' in Stuart Harris (ed.), *Australia's Antarctic Policy Options* (Canberra, 1984) 83 at 105–8.

[89] CCAMLR, Art. I(2).

[90] Edwards and Heap, 'Convention on the Conservation of Antarctic Marine Living Resources' at 354–5.

(a) constitute a basis for asserting, supporting or denying a claim to territorial sovereignty in the Antarctic Treaty area or create any rights of sovereignty in the Antarctic Treaty area;
(b) be interpreted as a renunciation or diminution by any Contracting Party of, or as prejudicing, any right or claim or basis of claim to exercise coastal state jurisdiction under international law within the area to which this Convention applies;
(c) be interpreted as prejudicing the position of any Contracting Party as regards its recognition or non-recognition of any such right, claim or basis of claim;
(d) affect the provision of Article IV, paragraph 2 of the Antarctic Treaty that no new claim, or enlargement of an existing claim, to territorial sovereignty in Antarctica shall be asserted while the Antarctic Treaty is in force.

While this provision bears an obvious similarity to Article IV of the Antarctic Treaty, there are some differences. Though the focus remains on the Antarctic Treaty area south of 60°S, paragraph 2(b) makes specific reference to the Convention not representing a renunciation or diminution by any party of its ability to exercise its rights as a coastal state within the Convention area. Therefore, despite the CCAMLR Convention area extending to the maritime zones of sub-Antarctic islands,[91] those states which possess uncontested territorial sovereignty over those islands do not concede their sovereignty rights by becoming parties to the Convention. However, the Convention also makes allowance for those states which do not recognise any territorial claims in Antarctica or to islands in the Southern Ocean. Accordingly, irrespective of each individual state's approach to Antarctic territorial claims, CCAMLR seeks to maintain the *status quo* as established by the Antarctic Treaty.[92] The mechanism adopted is often referred to as the 'bifocal' approach.[93]

[91] The islands north of 60°S to which CCAMLR applies are Bouvet Island (Norway), Marion and Prince Edward Islands (South Africa), Crozet Islands (France), Kerguelen Islands (France), Heard and McDonald Islands (Australia), Shag Rocks (UK), South Georgia Island (UK) and the South Sandwich Islands (UK), of which Argentina and the UK are in dispute over the sovereignty of the last three; see Bush (vol. I), 405–6.

[92] The basis for CCAMLR, Art. IV can be found in Recommendation IX-2, para. III (Establishment of a Definitive Conservation Regime) in which it is provided: 'the regime should, however, extend north of 60° South latitude where that is necessary for the effective conservation of species of the Antarctic ecosystem, without prejudice to coastal state jurisdiction in that area.'

[93] Edwards and Heap, 'Convention on the Conservation of Antarctic Marine Living Resources' at 360; Auburn, *Antarctic Law* at 221; Triggs, *International Law* at 195 who argues that:

Despite the intent of Article IV, a specific exemption from a strict application of CCAMLR was sought and obtained by France during the negotiation process. In a statement issued at the close of the CCAMLR negotiations in 1980 the Conference chairman noted that measures already in place for the conservation of marine living resources in the waters adjacent to the French-claimed islands of Kerguelen and Crozet would remain in place until modified by France acting within the framework of the Convention.[94] In addition, France retained the power to exclude the waters surrounding the two islands from consideration during deliberations over the implementation of Conservation Measures. If France did not so choose, then any Conservation Measures adopted equally applied to France and would be enforced by France in the waters adjacent to the two islands.[95] These exceptions also apply to the waters adjacent to islands within CCAMLR's area of application over which the existence of state sovereignty is recognised by all CCAMLR parties.[96] While the legal effect of these statements is doubtful (they are neither formally attached to the Convention nor a French reservation),[97] throughout the life of CCAMLR the French position concerning Kerguelen and Crozet has been respected.[98] South

The contrived result achieved by such a dual interpretation creates instability. The success of this 'bifocal' approach assumes that the parties will continue to demonstrate goodwill, and depends upon acceptance of the Convention by third States in the absence of clearly understood and agreed standards of conduct.

94 See 'Final Act of Conference on the Conservation of Antarctic Marine Living Resources, Canberra, 1980', para. I(1), reprinted in *Handbook* (Pt 1) 175; 'Statement of the Chairman of the Conference on the Conservation of Antarctic Marine Living Resources Concerning Application of the Convention Drawn up at the Conference', reprinted in Bush (vol. I), 391–2.

95 'Final Act of the Conference on the Conservation of Antarctic Marine Living Resources, Canberra, 1980' para. I(2), (3), (4).

96 In addition to the French islands of Crozet and Kerguelen, sovereignty is uncontested over the Australian-claimed Heard and McDonald Islands, Norwegian-claimed Bouvet Island and South African-claimed Marion and Prince Edward Islands.

97 Auburn, *Antarctic Law* at 222 describes them as a 'legally redundant and ineffective recital'. For further comment see Bush (vol. I), 392–3.

98 See the exchange which occurred in Commission for the Conservation of Antarctic Marine Living Resources, *Report of the Tenth Meeting of the Commission* (Hobart, Australia: 21 October–1 November 1991) 14–15, paras. 6.3–6.4. Also see Commission for the Conservation of Antarctic Marine Living Resources, *Report of the Eleventh Meeting of the Commission* (Hobart, Australia: 26 October–6 November 1992) 18, paras. 6.8–6.9 where both France and South Africa sought to reserve their positions regarding the application of the newly established 'Scheme of International Scientific Observation' applying in the EEZ waters of Kerguelen and Crozet Islands (France) and the Prince Edward Islands (South Africa).

Africa has also sought to exclude some Conservation Measures from the waters around the Prince Edward Islands.[99]

Operating provisions

Importantly, what CCAMLR seeks to achieve for the living resources of the Southern Ocean is conservation in terms of 'rational use': for the purposes of the Convention that is how the term 'conservation' is interpreted.[100] Article II provides guidelines as to how 'rational use' is to be implemented when harvesting of Antarctic marine living resources takes place. Such activities are to be conducted in accordance with the following principles of conservation:

> (a) prevention of decrease in the size of any harvested population to levels below those which ensure its stable recruitment . . . ;
> (b) maintenance of the ecological relationships between harvested, dependent and related populations of Antarctic marine living resources and the restoration of depleted populations . . . ;
> (c) prevention of changes or minimisation of the risk of changes in the marine ecosystem which are not potentially reversible over two or three decades . . . [101]

Through implementing these objectives to safeguard not only those marine living resources subject to potential harvesting, but also the wider marine and related environment, CCAMLR adopts the 'ecosystem' approach to marine living resource management.[102]

A Commission is established to serve both a secretariat role and adopt and implement the ecosystem approach to marine living resource management. Membership of the Commission is made up of those original parties which adopted the Convention, state parties which have acceded to the Convention and engage in harvesting or

[99] See Commission for the Conservation of Antarctic Marine Living Resources, *Report of the Twelfth Meeting of the Commission* (Hobart, Australia: 25 October–5 November 1993) 26, para. 8.6.

[100] CCAMLR, Art. II(2). For discussion on how such a conservation regime is to be applied see Marinelle Basson and John R. Beddington, 'CCAMLR: The Practical Implications of an Eco-System Approach' in Arnfinn Jorgensen-Dahl and Willy Ostreng (eds.), *The Antarctic Treaty System in World Politics* (London, 1991) 54–69.

[101] CCAMLR, Art. II(3).

[102] Edwards and Heap, 'Convention on the Conservation of Antarctic Marine Living Resources' at 354–5; Boleslaw A. Boczek, 'The Protection of the Antarctic Ecosystem: a Study in International Environmental Law' (1983) 13 ODIL 347 at 375–6; Douglas S. Butterworth, 'Antarctic Marine Ecosystem Management' (1986) 23 *Polar Record* 37 at 38–40; Bo Fernholm and Goran T. Rudback, 'Marine Resource Management for the Antarctic' (1989) 18(1) AMBIO 68–70.

research of Antarctic marine living resources, and regional economic organisations.[103] At present there are twenty-one Commission members.[104] The Commission has assigned to it a variety of roles, including conducting research and gathering data on Antarctic marine living resources, analysis of catch statistics, identification of conservation needs and the implementation of systems of inspection so as to monitor the effect of the Convention.[105] The Commission also has the important responsibility under the Convention of adopting Conservation Measures concerning Antarctic marine living resources.[106] The headquarters of the Commission are located in Hobart, Australia.[107] The Commission is supported by a Scientific Committee,[108] the membership of which is comprised of scientific representatives from the Commission parties.[109] The work of the Commission has also been assisted by three permanent working groups dealing with ecosystem monitoring, fish Stock assessment and krill.[110] From time to time *ad hoc* working groups have also been created to deal with specific matters. Each member state makes contributions to the operating budget of the Commission and Science Committee.[111]

CCAMLR has so far had its most significant impact through the implementation by the Commission of various 'Conservation Measures'. These Measures are in most instances initially formulated in the Scientific Committee and then passed on to the Commission for consideration and adoption at its regular annual meetings.[112] Once

[103] CCAMLR, Art. VII.

[104] The Commission members are: Argentina, Australia, Belgium, Brazil, Chile, the European Economic Community, France, Germany, India, Italy, Japan, Republic of Korea, New Zealand, Norway, Poland, Russia, South Africa, Spain, Sweden, the UK and the USA. Acceding states which are not presently engaging in harvesting or research within the Convention area are invited to attend Commission meetings as observers.

[105] CCAMLR, Art. IX.

[106] CCAMLR, Art. IX(1)(f).

[107] CCAMLR, Art. XIII.

[108] CCAMLR, Art. XIV.

[109] CCAMLR, Art. XIV(2); see also Arts. XV, XVI and XVII.

[110] Nicol, 'CCAMLR and its Approaches to Management' at 230–1.

[111] Art. XIX; for further analysis of these provisions see N. D. Bankes, 'Environmental Protection in Antarctica: A Comment on the Convention on the Conservation of Antarctic Marine Living Resources' (1981) 19 CYIL 303–19; Boczek, 'Protection of the Antarctic Ecosystem' at 374–81.

[112] CCAMLR, Art. XIII(2) makes provision for the holding of annual meetings by the Commission, while other Special Meetings may be convened at the request of one-third of the members or under Art. XXX dealing with amendment to the Convention; the regular annual meetings are now held at the commencement of the Antarctic summer in October/November in order to have conservation measures in place for the forthcoming fishing season and so that accurate data can be available on catches in the immediately previous season.

adopted, Conservation Measures become binding on parties 180 days after notification.[113] Up to and including the Thirteenth Meeting of the Commission in 1994, eighty-seven Conservation Measures had been adopted dealing with such issues as mesh size in trawls, the prohibition and regulation of fishing in certain regions, limiting the catch of certain species, catch reporting systems and closed seasons.[114] Many Conservation Measures, however, are designed to have a seasonal influence as they impose limitations on catch which are subject to annual review.[115]

The enforcement mechanisms of CCAMLR are principally related to the measures taken by the parties. Article XXI imposes obligations upon parties to take appropriate measures within their competence to ensure compliance with Conservation Measures. An inspection system, similar to that established under the Antarctic Treaty, is created under Article XXIV. This allows for boarding and inspection of vessels operating within the Convention area by designated observers and inspectors. Inspection is not limited to the flag state, only enforcement. A 'System of Inspection' was implemented for the first time in the 1989–90 season in furtherance of the provisions of Article XXIV.[116] Twenty-six CCAMLR inspectors were nominated by members of the Commission for the 1992–93 season. However, the actual number of inspections that are carried out remains low.[117] In addition, flag-state prosecution for breach of CCAMLR provisions has also been variable.[118]

[113] CCAMLR, Art. IX(6).

[114] Details on these various Conservation Measures are to be found in the annual Reports of the Commission.

[115] The number of Conservation Measures which have continuing effect is therefore much less than the eighty-seven which have been adopted in total. For example, during the 1992–93 season (when sixty-two Conservation Measures had been adopted), the Commission indicated that thirty Conservation Measures were in force: see Commission for the Conservation of Antarctic Marine Living Resources, *Schedule of Conservation Measures in Force 1992/93* (1992).

[116] Darry Powell, 'Antarctic Marine Living Resources and CCAMLR' in R. A. Herr, H. R. Hall and M. G. Haward (eds.), *Antarctica's Future* (Hobart, 1990) 61 at 67–8.

[117] In 1992–93, only one inspection was reported to the Commission: see Commission for the Conservation of Antarctic Marine Living Resources, *Report of the Twelfth Meeting of the Commission* at 20, para. 6.2; in 1993–94, three inspections were reported: see Commission for the Conservation of Antarctic Marine Living Resources, *Report of the Thirteenth Meeting of the Commission* (Hobart, Australia, 26 October–4 November 1994) 15, para. 5.2.

[118] In 1990 only one violation, by a USSR vessel, was reported to the Commission: Commission for the Conservation of Antarctic Marine Living Resources, *Report of the Ninth Meeting of the Commission* (Hobart, Australia, 22 October–2 November 1990) 33, para. 12.1; while in 1991 three violations by USSR vessels for 'improper maintenance

Ultimately these are matters which rest with the legal system of each Commission member. However, it does add to the underlying suspicion of the quality of enforcement under the Convention.[119] In addition to the inspection system, a 'Scheme of International Scientific Observation' has been implemented.[120] While this scheme is not directed towards enforcement, it does allow the Commission to gain a more direct understanding of some of the issues concerned in implementing Conservation Measures and problems caused through by-catch and incident mortality.

Because the Commission operates on the basis of consensus, adopting Conservation Measures which have a substantial impact upon existing harvesting practices and activities has been difficult to achieve.[121] Although the Commission's membership is dominated by non-fishing members, because of the consensus approach adopted at Commission meetings those members which are currently engaged in Southern Ocean fishing have considerable influence.[122] In addition, because of the delays caused by the Commission's procedures, it has been suggested that CCAMLR has contributed little to the protection of the Antarctic marine ecosystem. Measures have only been adopted 'when the stocks they were designed to protect were in such a depleted state so as to discourage exploitation on economic grounds; or they have been adopted with the knowledge that they will not be effective'.[123] Despite initially concentrating on the protection of finfish stocks,[124] the Commission has been criticised for its failure adequately

of documentation' were reported: see Commission for the Conservation of Antarctic Marine Living Resources, *Report of the Tenth Meeting of the Commission* at 20, para. 8.2. See also Commission for the Conservation of Antarctic Marine Living Resources, *Report of the Eleventh Meeting of the Commission* at 17–18, paras. 6.2–6.5 and 'Report of the Meeting of the Standing Committee on Observation and Inspection (SCOI)' at 89–93.

[119] J. P. Puissochet, 'CCAMLR – A Critical Assessment' in A. Jorgensen-Dahl and W. Ostreng (eds.), *The Antarctic Treaty System in World Politics* (London, 1991) 70 at 75 notes that: 'The system is not very binding.'

[120] Commission for the Conservation of Antarctic Marine Living Resources, *Report of the Eleventh Meeting of the Commission* at 18, para. 6.6–6.12.

[121] J. P. Croxall, I. Everson and D. G. M. Miller, 'Management of the Antarctic Krill Fishery' (1992) 28 *Polar Record* 64 at 64; Nicol, 'CCAMLR and its Approaches to Management' at 235–6.

[122] Croxall *et al.*, 'Management of the Antarctic Krill Fishery' at 66; *cf.* F. Orrego Vicuna, 'The Effectiveness of the Decision-Making Machinery of CCAMLR: An Assessment' in A. Jorgensen-Dahl and W. Ostreng (eds.), *The Antarctic Treaty System in World Politics* (London, 1991) 25–42.

[123] Howard, 'Convention on the Conservation of Antarctic Marine Living Resources' at 131.

[124] Powell, 'Antarctic Marine Living Resources' at 62.

to deal with the threat posed to krill. Nicol has argued that given CCAMLR was primarily negotiated to deal with the threat to krill and that the overexploitation of the stock would impact upon the whole Antarctic marine ecosystem, the Commission was too slow to deal with the issue.[125] This criticism has been answered with the response that developing appropriate management strategies for krill has been difficult because the fishery is unsuited to traditional management techniques.[126] After having the management of krill placed on the working agenda of the Commission in 1990, a decision was made at the 1991 Meeting to adopt a Conservation Measure which limited the total catch of krill to 1.5 million tonnes in any fishing season.[127] However, this limitation only applied to a designated area within the Atlantic sector of the CCAMLR area and not to the whole Southern Ocean.[128] This conservation measure has remained in place for the 1992–93, 1993–94 and 1994–95 seasons.[129] After substantial work, the Scientific Commission is now of the view that a potential yield for krill within Statistical Area 48 (part of the Atlantic sector) is 4.1 million tonnes.[130] The next task for the Commission will be to determine how this potential yield can be allocated by way of catch limits in Conservation Measures.

CCAMLR's record

Since its entry into force, CCAMLR has received mixed reviews. While initially heralded as a milestone for the ATS and a model conservation

125 Nicol, 'CCAMLR and its Approaches to Management' at 236. S. Nicol, 'No Agreement Yet on Krill Fishery' (December 1990) 64 *ANARE News* 6; S. Nicol, 'Management of the Krill Fishery: Was CCAMLR Slow to Act?' (1992) 28 *Polar Record* 155–7.

126 Croxall *et al.*, 'Management of the Antarctic Krill Fishery' at 65; for a discussion on the complexity of devising appropriate management schemes for krill see Butterworth, 'Antarctic Marine Ecosystem Management' at 37–47.

127 See Conservation Measure 32/X, reprinted in Commission for the Conservation of Antarctic Marine Living Resources, *Report of the Tenth Meeting of the Commission* at 29: see also 16–17 for the Commission's discussion on this Measure.

128 It should be noted, however, that CCAMLR total catch statistics have shown that the overwhelming majority of krill catch has during recent seasons come from Statistical Area 48.

129 See Conservation Measure 45/XI, reprinted in Commission for the Conservation of Antarctic Marine Living Resources, *Report of the Eleventh Meeting of the Commission* at 30.

130 Commission for the Conservation of Antarctic Marine Living Resources, *Report of the Thirteenth Meeting of the Commission*, at 25, para. 8.3–8.6. For a further discussion of the state of the krill fishery, see R. R. Makarov *et al.*, 'A Current Assessment of the Antarctic Krill Fishery' (1994) 18 *Polar Geography and Geology* 76–94.

regime[131] there have been doubts over whether the Convention can achieve its goals. Some of the problems which have been identified are the inability to impose catch quotas on third parties due to the continued uncertainty of offshore jurisdiction in Antarctica, non-membership of CCAMLR by principal fishing states, the continuing special status given by CCAMLR to the Antarctic Treaty and ATCPs, and the difficulty in obtaining accurate commercial and scientific data on fish stocks.[132] Problems in obtaining adequate data on fish stocks and catch results have particularly impacted upon the ability of the Scientific Committee to provide the Commission with assessments on the state of various stocks. This in turn impacts upon the Commission's ability to make effective Conservation Measures.[133] Recently, there are indications that the Commission may have reached a turning point. While commentators concede that initially there were difficulties in the relationship between the Commission and the Scientific Committee – one being a political body and the other scientific – the scope of recent Conservation Measures and the efforts now being made to regulate the krill fishery are indicators that the Convention's promise is now beginning to be fulfilled.[134] Given the importance attached to CCAMLR management of krill, the future effectiveness of the regime will be judged against its ability to manage that resource stock.

Convention on the Regulation of Antarctic Mineral Resource Activities (CRAMRA)

As has been shown above, soon after the conclusion of the Antarctic Treaty, concerns were raised about the protection and conservation of Antarctica. The implementation of the 1964 Agreed Measures and CCAS were responses to these concerns. However, CCAS, and later CCAMLR, were also resource regimes in which the ATCPs sought to

[131] Kurt M. Shusterich, 'The Antarctic Treaty System: History, Substance, and Speculation' (1984) 39 IntJ 800 at 811–12; J. G. Gardam, 'Management Regimes for Antarctic Marine Living Resources – An Australian Perspective' (1985) 15 MULR 279 at 290–312.

[132] See Howard, 'Convention on the Conservation of Antarctic Marine Living Resources' generally.

[133] See Convention on the Conservation of Antarctic marine Living Resources, *Report of the Ninth Meeting of the Commission* at 7, paras. 4.3–4.4; *Report of the Tenth Meeting of the Commission* at 7, para. 4.2; Croxall *et al.*, 'Management of the Antarctic Krill Fishery' at 65; Puissochet, 'CCAMLR – A Critical Assessment' at 74–5.

[134] Orrego Vicuna, 'The Effectiveness of the Decision-Making Machinery' at 26–33.

implement legal frameworks for the responsible exploitation of Antarctic resources, though, in some instances this actually resulted in a complete prohibition on exploitation. Throughout much of this time there was also the realisation that Antarctic mineral resource activity was another area of Antarctic activity effectively in a legal vacuum. The issue was not dealt with in the Antarctic Treaty. At the time of its negotiation the commencement of mining activities in Antarctica was a remote possibility. However, with the discovery of certain mineral reserves in the course of scientific research, changing worldwide economic conditions and concerns over the continued availability of petroleum products from traditional suppliers, concerns began to be expressed during the 1970s about the lack of an Antarctic minerals regime and the need for one to be negotiated.[135]

The moratorium and minerals debate: 1977–88

At ATCM IX (1977) there were concerns that an effective minerals regime may not be in place prior to the commencement of commercial mining. This resulted in Recommendation IX-1, which sought to place a moratorium on Antarctic mining during such time as the question was under active consideration at ATCMs.[136] The effect of this Recommendation was to attempt to halt any potential mineral activities until such time as the ATCPs could negotiate and implement a minerals regime.

Following ATCM X (1979) and ATCM XI (1981) agreement was reached on the convening of a Special Consultative Meeting to elaborate a regime on Antarctic mineral resources.[137] The regime was to be based on the following principles:

[135] See Recommendations VII-6 (Antarctic Resources – Effects of Mineral Exploitation); VIII-16 (Antarctic Resources – Effects of Mineral Exploration).

[136] Recommendation IX-1, para. 8 reads:

> They urge their nationals and other States to refrain from all exploration and exploitation of Antarctic mineral resources while making progress towards the timely adoption of an agreed regime concerning Antarctic mineral resource activities. They will thus endeavour to ensure that, pending the timely adoption of agreed solutions pertaining to exploration and exploitation of mineral resources, no activity shall be conducted to explore or exploit such resources. They will keep these matters under continuing examination.

For a discussion of the legal effect of the moratorium see Auburn, *Antarctic Law* at 259–63.

[137] See Recommendation XI-1 (Antarctic Mineral Resources).

(a) the Consultative Parties should continue to play an active and responsible role in dealing with the question of Antarctic mineral resources;
(b) the Antarctic Treaty must be maintained in its entirety;
(c) protection of the unique Antarctic environment and of the dependent ecosystems should be a basic consideration;
(d) the Consultative Parties, in dealing with the question of mineral resources in Antarctica, should not prejudice the interests of all mankind in Antarctica;
(e) the provisions of Article IV of the Antarctic Treaty should not be affected by the regime. It should ensure that the principles embodied in Article IV are safeguarded in application to the area covered by the Antarctic Treaty.[138]

The first session of Special ATCM IV was held in Wellington during June 1982. In total, twelve sessions were held during the course of the next six years at various ATCP cities.[139] The final session met in Wellington from 2 May till 2 June 1988 and concluded with agreement being reached on a convention text. The Convention on the Regulation of Antarctic Mineral Resource Activities (CRAMRA) was eventually opened for signature in Wellington on 25 November 1988.[140]

CRAMRA sought to establish a strict regulatory regime for Antarctic minerals activities relating to prospecting, exploration, exploitation

[138] Recommendation XI-1, para. 5; for an assessment of some of the legal issues which were considered to arise with respect to Antarctic mining see Roland Rich, 'A Minerals Regime for Antarctica' (1982) 31 ICLQ 709–25; Gillian D. Triggs, 'A Minerals Regime for Antarctica: Compromise or Conflict?' (1984) *Australian Mining and Petroleum Law Association Yearbook* 525–54; Auburn, *Antarctic Law* at 263–7.

[139] The dates and locations of the various meetings were as follows:

1. Wellington, 14–25 June 1982
2. Wellington, 17–28 January 1983
3. Bonn, 11–22 July 1983
4. Washington, 18–27 January 1984
5. Tokyo, 23–31 May 1984
6. Rio de Janeiro, 26 February–12 March 1985
7. Paris, 23 September–6 October 1985
8. Hobart, 14–25 April 1986
9. Tokyo, 27 October–12 November 1986
10. Montevideo, 11–20 May 1987
11. Wellington, 18–29 January 1988
12. Wellington, 2 May–2 June 1988.

[140] For comment on the negotiation of the Convention see Arthur D. Watts, 'Lessons to be Learned from the Mineral Resources Negotiations' in Rudiger Wolfrum (ed.), *Antarctic Challenge III* (Berlin, 1988) 319–31; Gillian D. Triggs, 'Negotiation of a Minerals Regime' in Gillian D. Triggs (ed.), *The Antarctic Treaty Regime* (Cambridge, 1987) 182–95.

and development.[141] While based on the assumption that minerals activities would occur at some time in the future, there was a very strong environmental protection component in the Convention, designed to ensure minimal impact upon the Antarctic environment.[142] The Convention was considered an 'integral part of the Antarctic Treaty system'[143] and applied to the Antarctic Treaty area.[144] Given the uncertainty over whether Article VI of the Antarctic Treaty extended to the high seas, and the potential for offshore minerals exploration of oil and gas to occur in the Southern Ocean, it is important to note that CRAMRA was specifically extended to the Southern Ocean. Article 5(2) provided:

> the Parties agree that this Convention shall regulate Antarctic mineral resource activities which take place on the continent of Antarctica and all Antarctic islands, including all ice shelves, south of 60° south latitude and in the seabed and subsoil of adjacent offshore areas up to the deep seabed.

This definition of the extent of CRAMRA's application clearly left room for any law of the sea regime dealing with deep sea bed mining to apply in the Southern Ocean in areas beyond the limits of national jurisdiction.[145]

The rejection of CRAMRA

Article 62 of CRAMRA created a complex mechanism for its entry into force. Sixteen of the ATCPs which participated at the final session of the Special ATCM IV in Wellington had to become parties to the Convention, including all the necessary state parties to make up the various institutions created by the Convention. In addition, these sixteen ATCPs were to be made up of five developing countries and

[141] For a review of the Convention see Lee A. Kimball, *Special Report on the Antarctic Minerals Convention* (Washington, 1988); P. J. Beck, 'Convention on the Regulation of Antarctic Mineral Resource Activities: A Major Addition to the Antarctic Treaty System' (1989) 25 *Polar Record* 19–32; Christopher C. Joyner, 'The Evolving Antarctic Minerals Regime' (1988) 19 ODIL 73–95; A. D. Watts, 'The Convention on the Regulation of Antarctic Mineral Resource Activities, 1988' (1990) 39 ICLQ 169–82; Francisco Orrego Vicuna, *Antarctic Mineral Exploitation* (Cambridge, 1988).

[142] See the provisions contained in CRAMRA, Art. 2.

[143] CRAMRA, Art. 2(1).

[144] CRAMRA, Art. 5.

[145] However, note that CRAMRA, Art. 5(2) also provided that this provision was 'without prejudice to the responsibilities of the Antarctic Treaty Consultative Parties under the Antarctic Treaty and measures pursuant to it'. See also CRAMRA, Art. 5(4) and the discussion in Rudiger Wolfrum, *The Convention on the Regulation of Antarctic Mineral Resource Activities* (Berlin, 1991) 31–4.

eleven developed countries.[146] The effect of the requirements of Article 62 became very important in 1989 when Australia and France declared in May that they would not sign the Convention and instead would campaign for the creation of a 'comprehensive environmental protection' regime for Antarctica. While it was unnecessary for either Australia or France to be original signatories of the Convention during the twelve months it was open for signature,[147] both the Final Act of Special ATCM IV and Article 62[148] made it clear that the Convention was not intended to enter into force without the participation of all seven claimant states.

Following the refusal of Australia and France to sign CRAMRA the future of the Convention came under increasing threat. In Paris at ATCM XV (1989), Australia and France, with the support of the environmental movement (which had long been campaigning for the declaration of Antarctica as a 'world park'), proposed that the ATCPs should seriously consider the negotiation and implementation of a comprehensive environmental protection regime for Antarctica.[149] A central feature of these proposals was that mining activities in Antarctica be prohibited either permanently or for many years. The ATCM concluded with the adoption of two Recommendations. First, Recommendation XV-1 called for a Special ATCM to be convened so as to consider the negotiation of 'the further elaboration, maintenance and effective implementation of a comprehensive system for the protection of the Antarctic environment and its dependent and associated ecosystems'. Second, Recommendation XV-2 provided that a meeting be held in 1990 to consider proposals relating to the further

146 No attempt was made to distinguish between which ATCPs were considered to be either developing or developed countries. For an interpretation of CRAMRA, Art. 62 see S. K. N. Blay and B. M. Tsamenyi, 'The Convention on the Regulation of Antarctic Mineral Resource Activities (CRAMRA): Can a Claimant Veto it?' (1989) 1 *ASOLPO Paper*.

147 CRAMRA, Art. 60 provided that the Convention was open for signature between 25 November 1988 and 25 November 1989.

148 See 'Final Act of the Fourth Special Antarctic Treaty Consultative Meeting on Antarctic Mineral Resources' reprinted in *Handbook* (Pt 1), 201 which provided:

> With respect to Article 62 of the Convention, the Meeting agreed that all of the institutions of the Convention could not be established in respect of every area of Antarctica unless all the States referred to in Article IV(1)(a) and (b) of the Antarctic Treaty and at least four States referred to in paragraph 1(c) of that Article were Parties to the Convention, and that these included at least three developing countries.

149 For a discussion of Australian policy towards CRAMRA see S. K. N. Blay and B. M. Tsamenyi, 'Australia and the Convention for the Regulation of Antarctic Mineral Resource Activities (CRAMRA)' (1990) 26 *Polar Record* 195–202.

development of CRAMRA's liability provisions.[150] While Recommendations XV-1 and XV-2 sought to maintain the fiction that it was still possible to retain CRAMRA while also investigating options for a comprehensive environment protection regime, it eventually became clear that the two were not compatible. Following ATCM XV (1989) political support began gradually to swing behind the adoption of an instrument to provide for comprehensive protection of the Antarctic environment and a simultaneous prohibition on mining. The process was completed with the adoption of the Protocol in 1991 which effectively meant that CRAMRA would never enter into force.

CRAMRA remains ready for ratification or accession and providing all the necessary states become parties there is nothing to stop its entry into force at some future point in time. However, with the Protocol gathering more support from ATCPs as they ratify and adopt measures to implement its terms, the reality is that CRAMRA has been abandoned. The Convention had the potential in 1988 to become the most sophisticated addition to the ATS, providing for the creation of both permanent and *ad hoc* institutions to regulate and monitor Antarctic mineral resource activities.[151] While CRAMRA was often referred to as a 'Minerals Convention' there was a serious attempt made to maintain a balance between the regulation of minerals activities and preserving the Antarctic environment. Christopher Beeby, Chairman of Special ATCM IV and credited with great influence in the development of the Convention, has described it as not incorporating a judgment that mining in Antarctica was acceptable and that it should or would take place, but rather as 'a mechanism for assessing the possible impact on the environment of Antarctic mineral resource activities, determining whether they are acceptable, and, if so, regulating them in detail'.[152] Whether CRAMRA

[150] The particular provision was CRAMRA, Art. 8(7). For some details see Henry C. Burmester, 'Liability for Damage from Antarctic Mineral Resource Activities' (1989) 29 VaJIL 621–60; Rudiger Wolfrum, 'The Unfinished Task: CRAMRA and the Question of Liability' in A. Jorgensen-Dahl and W. Ostreng (eds.), *The Antarctic Treaty System in World Politics* (London, 1991) 120–32. A one-day meeting on this question was held on 29 November 1990 in Vina del Mar, Chile: see 'Report to the XVIth Antarctic Treaty Consultative Meeting on the Meeting held pursuant to Recommendation XV-2', reprinted in Commission for the Conservation of Antarctic Marine Living Resources, *Final Report of the Sixteenth Antarctic Treaty Consultative Meeting* at 256.

[151] These institutions were the Commission, the Advisory Committee, the Secretariat, the Special Meeting of Parties and the Regulatory Committee.

[152] Christopher Beeby, 'The Convention on the Regulation of Antarctic Mineral Resource Activities and its Future', in R. A. Herr, H. R. Hall and M. G. Haward (eds.), *Antarctica's Future* (Hobart, 1990) 47 at 49.

may have been able to achieve these goals is now a matter of speculation.

Protocol on Environmental Protection to the Antarctic Treaty[153]

Negotiation of the Protocol

Compared to other significant instruments negotiated within the ATS, the Protocol came with a rush. From the time that Australia and France announced that they would not sign CRAMRA it only took two years for the Protocol to be negotiated and to replace the contemplated minerals regime. The formal starting point of the Protocol's negotiation came at ATCM XV (1989) when Recommendation XV-1 called upon the ATCPs to:

> undertake as a priority objective the further elaboration, maintenance and effective implementation of a comprehensive system for the protection of the Antarctic environment and its dependent and associated ecosystems aimed at ensuring that human activity does not have adverse impacts on the Antarctic environment or its dependent or associated ecosystems or compromise the scientific, aesthetic or wilderness values of Antarctica.

Following the adoption of this Recommendation debate took place over the merits of CRAMRA and a comprehensive environmental protection regime. There existed a range of views amongst the ATCPs.[154] Japan, the UK and the US very much favoured the retention of CRAMRA as a viable mining regime, while at the same time developing stronger provisions for environmental protection. Australia and France argued that CRAMRA should be discarded, an absolute prohibition placed on mining and comprehensive environmental

[153] For a detailed review of the Protocol see Catherine Redgwell, 'Environmental Protection in Antarctica: The 1991 Protocol' (1994) 43 ICLQ 599–634; S. K. N. Blay, 'New Trends in the Protection of the Antarctic Environment: The 1991 Madrid Protocol' (1992) 86 AJIL 377–99; Francesco Francioni, 'The Madrid Protocol on the Protection of the Antarctic Environment' (1993) 28 TexILJ 47–72; Christopher C. Joyner, 'The 1991 Madrid Environmental Protocol: Rethinking the World Park Status for Antarctica' (1992) 1(3) *Review of European Community and International Environmental Law* 328–39.

[154] This tension can be seen in the papers in Grahame Cook (ed.), *The Future of Antarctica* (Manchester, 1990), by John Heap (UK Foreign and Commonwealth Office), 'The Political Case for the Minerals Convention' 44–52, and John Burgess (Australian Department of Foreign Affairs and Trade), 'Comprehensive Environmental Protection of the Antarctic: New Approaches for New Times' 53–67.

protection measures be negotiated.[155] Ultimately, these various views were put at the sessions of Special ATCM XI.

The first session of Special ATCM XI was held between 19 November and 6 December 1990 in Vina del Mar, Chile. Considerable progress was made at the meeting towards reaching agreement on an environmental regime. However, two issues created division. These were whether Antarctic mineral resource activities were wholly incompatible with the negotiation of a comprehensive environmental protection regime and the form that the negotiated instrument should take. Despite these disagreements, the head of the Norwegian delegation to the Meeting, Rolf Trolle Anderson, was able to draft a single negotiating text by the conclusion of the session.[156] This draft text was the basis for further negotiations at three subsequent sessions of Special ATCM XI held in Madrid, Spain during 1991. Once general agreement was reached on the need to implement a moratorium on Antarctic mineral activities, there was rapid progress in agreeing to the terms of an instrument designed to implement greater environmental protection for Antarctica. The only significant area of disagreement was over how long a mining prohibition should remain in force. Australia and France had always favoured a permanent prohibition on mining. However, as a compromise it was proposed that a fifty-year moratorium be implemented. Attention then shifted to the modification and amendment provisions of the Protocol. In the draft of the Protocol agreed to at the April 1991 session it was possible to amend the provisions of draft Article 6 dealing with a moratorium on mining, but only if there existed in place 'a binding legal regime on Antarctic mineral resource activities'. The modification or amendment to the mining provision also required the ratification of 75 per cent of the

[155] The various positions in this debate can be seen from the working papers which were submitted at ATCM XV by France and Australia (XV ATCM/Working Paper/2 and XV ATCM/Working Paper/3) and the United States (XV ATCM/Working Paper/8), reprinted in *Final Report of the Fifteenth Antarctic Treaty Consultative Meeting* (Paris, 9–20 October 1989) 202–13, 237–42.

[156] For a review of the Vina del Mar Meeting see 'Report Submitted By the Chairman of the XIth Antarctic Treaty Special Consultative Meeting (Vina del Mar)', reprinted in *Final Report of the Sixteenth Antarctic Treaty Consultative Meeting* at 253; 'Antarctic Treaty: Comprehensive Protection for Antarctica' (1991) 12 *Environmental Policy and Law* 11–13; P. J. Beck, 'Antarctica, Vina del Mar and the 1990 UN Debate' (1991) 27 *Polar Record* 211–16; R. Tucker Scully, 'The Eleventh Antarctic Treaty Special Consultative Meeting' (1991) 11 (1) *International Challenges* 77–90; also see the separate remarks by Christopher C. Joyner and William M. Bush, 'The Future of the Antarctic Regime: New Directions' (1991) 85 ProcAmSocIL 461 at 464–75.

ATCPs, including the ratifications of all ATCPs at the time the Protocol was adopted.[157] At the conclusion of this session the intention was to resume for a final drafting session in June 1991 at which time the Protocol would be signed on 23 June, the thirtieth anniversary of the entry into force of the Antarctic Treaty. However, when the ATCPs reconvened in Madrid in June 1991 the United States expressed concerns over the amendment procedures and argued that in effect, because of the requirement of unanimous acceptance by the original ATCPs to the Protocol of any modifications or amendments concerning the minerals prohibition, a permanent prohibition on minerals activities was being implemented.[158] Because of the US view, there was no final agreement reached amongst the ATCPs on the Protocol at the June session. The final version of the Protocol, which was eventually agreed upon and signed in Madrid at the 4 October 1991 session,[159] contained a compromise provision dealing with modification or amendment of the Protocol.[160] This represented the desire of the great majority of ATCPs to ensure that the advances in the negotiation towards some form of permanent prohibition on mining were not lost, and the concerns of the US that the Protocol did not completely foreclose the option of Antarctic mining. The Protocol was eventually adopted by the ATCPs on 4 October 1991.[161] It was opened for signature on the same day and immediately signed by twenty-three of the twenty-six existing ATCPs and seven of the fourteen Non-Consultative Parties.

Protocol supplements the ATS

The Preamble to the Protocol confirms the close relationship between the Protocol and the Antarctic Treaty. There is a reconfirmation of the importance of ensuring that Antarctica is used for peaceful purposes, that it does not become the scene of international discord and that the

157 Art. 24, Protocol to the Antarctic Treaty on Environmental Protection (Draft), XI ATSCM/2/30 (29 April 1991).

158 A. Darby, 'US Threat to Antarctic Mining Ban Treaty', 15 June 1991, *The Sydney Morning Herald*; A. Darby, 'US Puts Antarctic Pact in Doubt', 20 June 1991, *Sydney Morning Herald* 10; 'US Under Fire for Antarctic Indecision', 24 June 1991, *The Canberra Times* 6.

159 This followed a sudden reversal in policy by the US concerning the amending procedures of the Protocol with respect to mining: see L. Taylor, 'US Switches to Support Antarctic Mine Ban', 5 July 1991, *The Australian* 8; G. Austin, 'Bush Comes Around on Antarctic Mining Ban', 5 July 1991, *The Sydney Morning Herald* 5.

160 Protocol, Art. 25(5).

161 This was the date on which the Final Act of the Meeting was also signed.

global and regional importance of Antarctic science remain a primary consideration. The Preamble also recognises the existence of the ATS and the impact of other component parts in the System, such as CCAMLR. The Protocol also provides that it 'shall supplement the Antarctic Treaty and shall neither modify nor amend that Treaty'.[162] With the Protocol described as supplementing the Antarctic Treaty, the continued primacy of the Treaty would seem to be confirmed.

Protocol applies in the Antarctic Treaty area

The Protocol adopts as its area of application the 'Antarctic Treaty area'.[163] This is not surprising as the Protocol is designed to supplement the Treaty. However, given the rather uncertain terminology used in the Treaty with respect to the area of application it is disappointing that the Protocol did not attempt to clarify this problem. By adopting the same area of application as the Treaty a number of important associated ecological regions immediately to the north of the Treaty area are excluded.[164] The adoption of this area of application seems to be in conflict with the 'ecosystem' approach of the Protocol which seeks to protect not only the Antarctic environment but also its 'dependent and associated ecosystems'.[165] If the Protocol was to be truly effective in implementing this goal it would have been more appropriate to adopt the same area of application as CCAMLR. The Protocol would thereby have had a greater impact in ensuring the effective implementation of its measures in the Southern Ocean. What the existing area of application does perhaps confirm is the bias inherent in the Protocol towards protecting the Antarctic continent rather than the greater Antarctic and Southern Ocean area.

Prohibition on mining

The immediate impact of the Protocol is to end the debate over whether a minerals regime should be implemented in Antarctica. Article 7 of the Protocol states: 'Any activity relating to mineral resources, other than scientific research, shall be prohibited.' Such a definitive statement would seem to bring to an end the debate over Antarctic minerals activity for the duration of the Protocol, or until

162 Protocol, Art. 4. 163 Protocol, Art. 1(b).

164 This includes the islands of the South Sandwich Island group, South Georgia, Kerguelen, Marion Island, Macquarie Island, Heard Island, Campbell Island, Bouvet Island, Gough Island and Crozet Island.

165 See Protocol, Art. 3.

such time as Article 7 is amended or reviewed. One potential difficulty, though, may arise because of the exception Article 7 makes for scientific research. Though such research activities would themselves now become subject to other provisions of the Protocol there is the potential, as has been alleged to occur with whaling in the Southern Ocean, for the facade of science to be used to exploit this exception. However, while the experience of the International Whaling Commission and the liberal interpretation by some member states of taking whales for scientific research has created problems,[166] there may not be the same scope for abuse with Antarctic mining. With the implementation of the Protocol, many scientific expeditions which are 'mining for science' will have their activities regulated and monitored. Under these conditions, and given the cost of making mining activity in Antarctica commercially profitable, it is most unlikely that there will be scope for the abuse of this exception.

The Protocol's environmental provisions

Despite the Protocol's significant impact upon mining activities, its principal provisions are those dealing with environmental protection. The parties commit themselves to the goal of 'comprehensive protection of the Antarctic environment and dependent and associated ecosystems' and designate Antarctica as a 'natural reserve, devoted to peace and science'.[167] The level of this commitment is demonstrated in Article 3 where a series of fundamental principles dealing with the Antarctic environment are accepted for the 'planning and conduct of all activities in the Antarctic Treaty area'. The impact of this provision is that all activities in the Antarctic area are to be planned and conducted so as to avoid:

(a) adverse effects on climate or weather patterns;
(b) significant adverse effects on air or water quality;
(c) significant changes in the atmospheric, terrestrial (including aquatic), glacial or marine environments;
(d) detrimental changes in the distribution, abundance or productivity of species or populations of species of fauna and flora;
(e) further jeopardy to endangered or threatened species or populations of such species;
(f) degradation of, or substantial risk to, areas of biological, scientific, historic, aesthetic or wilderness significance.[168]

[166] Sara L. Ellis, 'Japanese Whaling in the Antarctic: Science or Subterfuge?' (1988) 31(2) *Oceanus* 68–9. [167] Protocol, Art. 2. [168] Protocol, Art. 3(2)(b).

To ensure that these goals are met, planning and monitoring mechanisms are to be put in place which will affect the conduct of all existing and future activities within the Antarctic Treaty area.

A major feature of the Protocol is the provision for Environmental Impact Assessment (EIA) procedures to be carried out on all activities undertaken pursuant to 'scientific research programmes, tourism and all other governmental and non-governmental activities' for which notice is required to be given under Article VII of the Antarctic Treaty.[169] The EIA process will classify activities on the basis of whether they have one of three types of impacts upon the Antarctic environment or dependent or associated ecosystems:

(a) less than a minor or transitory impact;
(b) a minor or transitory impact; or
(c) more than a minor or transitory impact.

Consistent with the cooperation which the Antarctic Treaty promotes amongst the ATCPs, the Protocol encourages the parties to cooperate in the planning and conduct of their activities in the Treaty area. Cooperation can take the form of programmes of scientific, technical or educational value, assistance in the preparation of an EIA, the choice of sites for prospective stations, and joint expeditions and the sharing of stations and other facilities.[170]

The Committee for Environmental Protection

The Protocol creates a new organisation for the ATS – the Committee for Environmental Protection. The Committee, which is to be made up of representatives of all parties to the Protocol, has the function of monitoring the implementation of the Protocol and reporting on progress at ATCMs. While not having any power to enforce the Protocol, the Committee is designed as an expert body which is to assist the ATCPs in ensuring the effectiveness of the Protocol. To that end, it can provide advice on the need to update or strengthen the Protocol, the need for additional Annexes, the application and implementation of EIA procedures, means of minimising or mitigating environmental impact of activities in the Antarctic Treaty area, inspection procedures and the collection and evaluation of information relating to environmental protection.[171] Unlike the Commission for the Conservation of Antarctic Marine Living Resources created

[169] Protocol, Art. 8. [170] Protocol, Art. 6. [171] Protocol, Art. 12(1).

under CCAMLR, it is not initially intended to make the Committee a permanent body with its own headquarters and staff. However, there is scope under the terms of the Protocol for measures to be adopted which could provide for the creation of a body with secretariat-type functions if demand warrants.[172] In the interim period between negotiation of the Protocol and its entry into force the ATCPs have taken steps to ensure that ATCMs take into account the role that the Committee will have with respect to Antarctic environmental issues. To that end, a 'Transitional Environmental Working Group' (TEWG) was created prior to ATCM XIX (1995) in order to begin on a preliminary basis the work of the Committee.[173]

The Annexes

A principal feature of the Protocol is the Annexes. These form an integral part of the Protocol. When adopted in October 1991, there were four Annexes. A fifth Annex was quickly added at ATCM XVI (1991). Additional Annexes, or amendments and modifications to Annexes, can be agreed upon from time to time at ATCMs by way of Recommendations.[174] By adopting this procedure whereby Annexes can be added and either modified or amended by way of Recommendations, recognition has been given to the need to have flexibility in the Protocol so that changing demands and new problems can be dealt with speedily.

Of the five Annexes, Annex I is the most significant as it creates the procedure for an EIA. Article 3 of the Annex provides details on the requirements for a comprehensive environmental evaluation of a proposed activity under the EIA process. This will result in a determination being made as to whether the proposed activity may proceed or if the proposal goes before the Committee and the ATCPs. The combined effect of Annexes II and V will be substantially to overhaul the existing ATS measures dealing with the protection of Antarctic fauna and flora and various protected areas. Annex II deals with the conservation of fauna and flora establishing procedures whereby such cannot be taken or interfered with except when a permit has been issued. A feature of this Annex is Article 4 which places limitations on

[172] Protocol, Art. 9 allows for the adoption of additional Annexes. It is possible that such a body could be created by this means, or through a modification or amendment of the Protocol under the terms of Art. 25.

[173] *Final Report of the Nineteenth Antarctic Treaty Consultative Meeting* 11, paras. 41–6.

[174] Protocol, Art. 9.

the introduction of non-native species, parasites and diseases into Antarctica.[175] Annex V, adopted at ATCM XVI (1991), substantially replicates the existing protected areas system that has evolved since the introduction of SPAs and SSSIs. Provision exists for the designation of Antarctic Specially Protected Areas, Antarctic Specially Managed Areas, Historic Sites and Monuments, and the adoption of management plans.[176] All existing sites designated under the previous measures become similarly designated under the Annex, with the exception of SSSIs which along with SPAs are now to be designated as Antarctic Specially Protected Areas.[177]

Annex III, which deals with waste disposal in Antarctica, substantially builds upon the provisions adopted in 1989 under Recommendation XV-3.[178] This Annex, which applies to all activities undertaken in the Treaty area 'pursuant to scientific research programmes, tourism and all other governmental and non-governmental activities'[179] provides that:

> The amount of wastes produced or disposed of in the Antarctic Treaty area shall be reduced as far as practicable so as to minimise impact on the Antarctic environment and to minimise interference with the natural values of Antarctica, with scientific research and with other uses of Antarctica which are consistent with the Antarctic Treaty.[180]

Obligations are imposed to clean up existing and abandoned waste sites, and modify waste disposal practices. To further the implementation of responsible waste disposal practices in Antarctica, each party which conducts activities in the Treaty area is also required to formulate waste management plans.[181]

Annex IV relates to the prevention of marine pollution and, as with Annex III, also builds on a Recommendation which had been adopted in 1989.[182] It applies not only to each Protocol party but also to ships

175 Protocol, Art. 4(2) in particular deals with the removal of dogs such as huskies as from 1 April 1994.

176 Protocol, Annex V, Arts. 3, 4, 5, 8. For a critique of this system see Colin M. Harris, 'Standardisation of Zones Within Specially Protected and Managed Areas under the Antarctic Environmental Protocol' (1994) 30 *Polar Record* 283–6.

177 Protocol, Annex V, Art. 3(3).

178 Recommendation XV-3 (Human Impact on the Antarctic Environment: Waste Disposal).

179 Protocol, Annex III, Art. 1(1).

180 Protocol, Annex III, Art. 1(2).

181 Protocol, Annex III, Art. 8.

182 Recommendation XV-4 (Human Impact on the Antarctic Environment: Prevention, Control and Response to Marine Pollution); the effect of this Recommendation was

entitled to fly its flag and other ships engaged in supporting a party's operations while within the Antarctic Treaty area.[183] The Annex seeks to apply some similar standards to those established by the 1973/1978 International Convention for the Prevention of Pollution from Ships (MARPOL).[184] The discharge of oil and noxious liquid substances is accordingly prohibited unless strict exceptions are met.[185] The disposal of garbage and sewage is also strictly controlled.[186] The Annex also provides in Article 12 for the development amongst the Treaty parties of emergency response plans to combat marine pollution.[187]

Amendment and review

The Protocol adopts the same modification or amendment procedures as those found in Article XII(1) of the Antarctic Treaty. Accordingly, the Article 7 prohibition on mining can only be lifted during the initial period of the Protocol's term by unanimous agreement amongst the ATCPs. However, like the Antarctic Treaty, the Protocol also provides for a Review Conference. Such a Conference may be convened fifty years after entry into force of the Protocol. If any modification or amendment to the Protocol, including Article 7, is proposed at that Conference, it may be adopted on a majority vote of the existing ATCPs, including 75 per cent of the ATCPs which originally adopted the Protocol. Modifications or amendments only enter into force upon ratification by 75 per cent of the ATCPs, including all of the ATCPs which originally adopted the Protocol.

In regard to Article 7, it is provided that the prohibition on Antarctic mineral resource activities cannot be lifted unless there is in place a

to call upon Treaty parties to ensure that their vessels that were engaged in or supporting Antarctic operations complied with the following conventions:

1. 1972 Convention on the Prevention of Marine Pollution by Dumping of Wastes and Other Matter (London Dumping Convention)
2. 1973/1978 International Convention for the Prevention of Pollution from Ships (MARPOL 73/78);
3. 1978 International Convention on Standards of Training, Certifications and Watchkeeping for Seafarers (STCW Convention);
4. 1974 International Convention for the Safety of Life at Sea (SOLAS);
5. 1966 International Convention on Load Lines (Load Lines Convention);
6. 1972 Convention on the International Regulations for Preventing Collisions at Sea (COLREGS).

183 Protocol, Annex IV, Art. 2. 184 See note 8 above.

185 Protocol, Annex IV, Arts. 3 and 4. 186 Protocol, Annex IV, Arts. 5 and 6.

187 This is consistent with Protocol, Art. 15 which calls for the development of a variety of contingency plans to respond to incidents which have the potential to have adverse impacts upon the Antarctic environment.

binding legal regime on Antarctic mineral resources which 'fully safeguards the interests of all States referred to in Article IV of the Antarctic Treaty'.[188] In addition, there is an opting-out clause for those ATCPs which do not agree with any proposed modification or amendment of the Protocol. Like the provisions of Article XII(2) of the Antarctic Treaty, if after three years from agreement being reached any proposed modification or agreement has not entered into force, then any party may give notice of withdrawal which will take effect two years after receipt of such notice by the Depositary.[189] The combined effect of these provisions is that unless there is unanimous agreement on removing the prohibition on Antarctic mining activities prior to expiration of the fifty-year period, the processes associated with the Review Conference mean that the Article 7 prohibition is binding on the ATCPs for at least fifty-five years.

Entry into force

The Protocol will only enter into force upon the deposit of instruments of ratification, acceptance, approval, or accession by all of the ATCPs who had such status on the date the Protocol was accepted.[190] By the time of ATCM XIX (1995), only sixteen of the necessary twenty-six ATCPs had ratified the Protocol.[191] This does not seem to indicate a significant level of commitment to the Protocol in terms of state implementation and acceptance three and a half years since its adoption in October 1991. However, the ratification of some states has been delayed by their desire to have appropriate domestic legislation in place. In order to speed up the ratification process it was agreed at ATCM XIX (1995) that those states which had implemented appropriate domestic legislation to give effect to the terms of the Protocol would make these documents available to those states which had yet to ratify.[192] Despite the delay in entry into force of the Protocol, a number of ATCPs have already implemented domestic legislation

188 Protocol, Art. 25(5)(a).

189 Protocol, Art. 25(5)(b).

190 Protocol, Art. 23. At that time there were twenty-six ATCPs.

191 In order of acceptance the ratifying states are: Spain (1 July 1992), Ecuador (4 January 1993), France (5 February 1993), Peru (8 March 1993), Norway (16 June 1993), Argentina (28 October 1993), Sweden (30 March 1994), Australia (6 April 1994), the Netherlands (14 April 1994), China (2 August 1994), Germany (25 November 1994), New Zealand (22 December 1994), Chile (11 January 1995), Uruguay (11 January 1995), United Kingdom (25 April 1995) and Italy (which announced its ratification during ATCM XIX, 8–19 May 1995)

192 *Final Report of the Nineteenth Antarctic Treaty Consultative Meeting* 11, para. 37.

which gives effect to many Protocol provisions while ATCMs have actively considered a variety of issues relating to the implementation of the Protocol. Discussion has also been taking place over the adoption of an additional Annex dealing with liability. On the basis of these indicators, it does not seem likely that the entry into force of the Protocol will be substantially delayed.

The relationship between the instruments of the Antarctic Treaty System

The ATS has gradually evolved during the past thirty years from the basic Treaty to a very complex set of interrelated provisions comprising the Treaty, Recommendations and supporting Conventions. Recommendations represent minor modifications and extensions of the Treaty regime. Through the development of integrated sets of Recommendations, such as the Agreed Measures and accompanying provisions dealing with protected areas, the Treaty has been able to establish a system of measures designed to further Antarctic environmental protection. However, in regard to other issues, such as seals and marine living resources, the ATS adopted separate but supporting Conventions. While hindsight has shown that the provisions of CCAS could more than likely have effectively been dealt with under the Treaty, the extended area of its operation required CCAMLR to be a separate legal instrument outside of the Treaty. Nevertheless, CCAMLR has a substantial degree of connection with the Treaty. Both claimant states and ATCPs play a significant role in the operation of the Commission established under CCAMLR, which also reports to ATCMs. The role of SCAR in both CCAMLR and under the Treaty is another connecting factor.

Of all the various developments in the ATS, the 1991 Protocol has the potential to have the greatest impact. No part of the existing Antarctic regime will be left untouched. When considering the relationship of the Protocol to other component parts of the ATS it is important to remember Article 4 of the Protocol which provides that it 'shall supplement the Antarctic Treaty and shall neither modify nor amend that Treaty'. That the Protocol does not 'override' the other provisions of the ATS is confirmed in Article 4(2) which provides that it shall not 'derogate from the rights and obligations' of the parties to the Protocol with respect to the other component parts of the ATS. Article 5 further reinforces the notion of an integrated ATS in which the Protocol is just one component part. It provides that the parties to the various instruments in force within the ATS shall continue to consult with each other and avoid interference with the achievement of the principles and objectives of each of those instruments. Nevertheless, given the tremendous impact that the Protocol will potentially have upon the ATS it is difficult to envisage that it will not create individual problems of consistency with some of the existing legal instruments.

Will the Protocol create a more integrated ATS? During the past thirty years the ATS has been able to deal successfully with a range of issues confronting Antarctica. However, the legal instruments adopted were rather disparate so that it became necessary to consult a number of sources in order to ascertain what is the applicable law or regulation. The Protocol will solve some of these problems because of its framework mechanism which allows for the development of various Annexes. Instead of having to bring together the various Recommendations under different headings so as to gain a perspective on the appropriate standards, the combination of the Protocol and its Annexes will result in it being possible to gain a clearer understanding of the environmental provisions that apply in Antarctica. It will also allow for more simplified procedures to be followed that will facilitate updating, improvement and creation of new standards by way of additional Annexes. The ATCPs will also be assisted in this role by the Committee for Environmental Protection, which will to a certain extent take over some of the responsibility which previously rested with SCAR. When the role of the Protocol is considered in this light, however, it is, despite the intention of Article 4 of the Protocol, difficult to accept that it will not amend or modify existing practice within the ATS.

A major effect of the Protocol upon the existing ATS will be to supersede many of the existing provisions of the Agreed Measures and related environmental Recommendations. This is because, as described above, the Protocol creates a new management regime for Antarctic fauna and flora and protected areas. Annexes II and V of the Protocol substantially revise the previous procedures which existed for the protection, designation and maintenance of Antarctic fauna and flora and protected areas. It would seem then that the effect of the Protocol is to sweep aside the Agreed Measures, as adopted in 1964 and subsequently modified, and the protected area system under which

SSSIs, Marine SSSIs and Sites of Historic Interest were designated.[193] Only Specially Reserved Areas and Multiple-Use Planning Areas, both of which had only been adopted at ATCM XV (1989), remain untouched under the Protocol's system of protected fauna, flora, species and areas. The Protocol has a minimal effect upon CCAS as there was no intention to devise catch limits on fisheries, seals or whales. There is a consequential impact, though, which bolsters the efforts of CCAS to conserve Antarctic seals. As was the case with the Agreed Measures, Annex 2 designates Ross and fur seals as 'Specially Protected Species' under which permits can only be issued for their taking when there is a compelling scientific purpose.[194] Seals are also specifically protected from harmful interference under the general provisions dealing with the protection of native fauna and flora. Another consequential impact upon seals will be the efforts made in the Protocol to clear up marine pollution under Annex IV.

Similar to the potential relationship between CCAS and the Protocol, the effect of the Protocol upon CCAMLR will be to create an overall Antarctic environmental framework within which some of the mechanisms established under the Convention may operate. There is the potential, though, for some conflict between CCAMLR and the Protocol. This could particularly be the case with respect to the environmental principles created by Article 3 of the Protocol as they may conflict with CCAMLR principles dealing with resource management. One interpretation of Articles 4 and 5 of the Protocol would suggest that it was not intended to impact upon the operation of CCAMLR. The wider area of operation of CCAMLR, in contrast with the more restricted area of the Protocol's operation within the Antarctic Treaty area, also supports the view that the Protocol was not designed to deal comprehensively with environmental matters in the Southern Ocean. Even so, Article 3 of the Protocol does create a new set of environmental principles upon which all activities in the Antarctic Treaty area are to be conducted, especially activities such as fishing which impact upon the 'Antarctic environment and dependent and associated ecosystems'. Consequently, there are enough specific references in Article 3 to have an impact upon the way in which the Commission

[193] At both ATCM XVI (1991) and ATCM XVII (1992) it was recognised that the Protocol would have the effect of superseding some existing Recommendations. See *Final Report of the Sixteenth Antarctic Treaty Consultative Meeting* at Annex D, 307–15; *Final Report of the Seventeenth Antarctic Treaty Consultative Meeting* (Venice, 11–20 November 1992) 24, para. 54.

[194] Protocol, Annex II, Art. 3(4).

makes its decisions in regard to Conservation Measures and especially allowable catch levels. Examples of this can be found in Article 3(2) of the Protocol which require in the planning and conduct of activities within the Antarctic Treaty area a consideration of:

(a) the limiting of adverse impacts on the Antarctic environment and dependent and associated ecosystems;
(b) means of avoiding significant changes in marine environments; and
(c) avoiding further jeopardy to endangered or threatened species or populations of species.

To further these provisions, Article 3 provides that any planned activities must be based on appropriate information detailing the potential impact of such an activity. The CCAMLR Commission already carries out such research on Antarctic marine living resources.[195] Another environmental principle which is significant for CCAMLR is Article 3(2)(e) which requires monitoring to take place so as to 'facilitate early detection of the possible unforeseen effects of activities carried on both within and outside the Antarctic Treaty area' in regard to the Antarctic environment and dependent and associated ecosystems. This provision complements CCAMLR's role within the Antarctic Treaty area and north to the Antarctic convergence. Therefore, while some provisions of the Protocol seem to reinforce the CCAMLR approach, the potential does exist for the more expansive environmental principles of the Protocol to conflict with decisions being made by the CCAMLR Commission.

Not only is there the potential for conflict between some existing ATS mechanisms, but there also exists a potential for institutional clashes to occur. These could, for example, eventuate between the Committee for Environmental Protection and the Commission for the Conservation of Antarctic Marine Living Resources over the management of krill. This is an area in which the Commission has in the past been criticised because of its failure to implement stringent catch levels for the resource, with concerns being raised over the consequential impact this may have upon the Antarctic marine ecosystem.[196] This is also a matter which directly falls within the ambit of the Protocol. Would it therefore be possible for the Committee for Environmental Protection to report adversely upon the CCAMLR Commission? If it were to do so how would this conflict with the provisions of Article 5 of the Protocol dealing with consultation and

[195] See CCAMLR, Art. IX. [196] Nicol, 'No Agreement'.

cooperation between the various respective institutions of the ATS? Another area of conflict which can arise between CCAMLR and the Protocol is the extended area of application of CCAMLR, thereby resulting in the possibility that different management practices for the marine ecosystem may be adopted beyond the Antarctic Treaty area up to the Antarctic convergence. It is not suggested that radical differences could arise, but there is enough scope for differing practices to emerge so as to create management and enforcement problems. Because of the very principles which it is trying to implement, the Protocol therefore has the potential to clash with existing instruments, and this may create initial problems for the ATS as existing institutions adjust to its impact.

Conclusion

The ATS has been a remarkable example of how international law can provide the foundation for the development of a legal and political regime which can solve immediate problems but also evolve over a period of time to deal with subsequent issues. When the Treaty was negotiated in 1959 there was much tension amongst those states actively engaged in Antarctica over the status of territorial claims, conflicting territorial claims, the presence of the superpowers and the potential for the continent to become the scene of increased military activity. That the Treaty was able to deal with most of these issues, and also effectively to set aside the sovereignty issue, is a great testament not only to its provisions but also the goodwill which existed amongst the initial Treaty parties to make the settlement a success. However, while these were the immediate issues for the Treaty to deal with it was foreseen that there would be a continuing process of developing additional measures to address other issues which emerged during the course of the Treaty's existence. Hence, the adoption of 204 Recommendations at eighteen ATCMs between 1961 and 1994 is further testament to how the Treaty has been able to evolve.

While the complex network of Recommendations dealing with a wide variety of issues is impressive, perhaps the most significant aspect of the ATS has been the formulation of additional separate Conventions and the Protocol. In each case, these additional instruments were negotiated to deal with potential and emerging problems for which no adequate legal regime existed. In most instances, each of these instruments has unique features which represented and still represents significant advancements in resource management and environmental protection. The ATS has also increasingly focused on the protection of the Antarctic environment and while some allowances have been made for resource exploitation in CCAS and CCAMLR, the overall philosophy of the ATCPs is best described as representing the 'precautionary approach' to environmental management. No better example of this exists than CRAMRA. It was negotiated at a time when there were no serious prospects for mineral resource activities taking place. Yet, despite all the effort and innovation invested in CRAMRA, the ATS had the ability to reject the Convention within two years of its conclusion and instead prohibit mining activities while also developing a new regime for comprehensive Antarctic environmental protection.

By adopting innovative approaches to solving sovereignty disputes, rejecting traditional notions of territorial jurisdiction, creating a regime in which emphasis is given to freedom of scientific research, establishing protective measures for the flora and fauna of a whole continent and region, implementing an ecosystem approach to marine living resource management, prohibiting all mining activities in order to protect the environment and implementing a legal system that seeks to protect the dependent and associated environment of the region from the impact of all human activities, the ATS has made substantial contributions to international law. It has been these and other factors that have caused many commentators to praise the ATS for what it has achieved and the model it represents for international cooperation.[197] In subsequent chapters these individual and collective contributions will be further examined.

[197] See as an example Emilio J. Sahurie, *The International Law of Antarctica* (New Haven, CT, 1992) 575; M. J. Peterson, *Managing the Frozen South* (Berkeley, CA, 1988) 194–223; Sergei N. Karev, 'Cooperative Momentum? The Antarctic Treaty System and the Prevention of Conflict' in Arnfinn Jorgensen-Dahl and Willy Ostreng (eds.), *The Antarctic Treaty System in World Politics* (London, 1991) 372–7; Olav Schram Stokke, 'The Relevance of the Antarctic Treaty System as a Model for International Cooperation' in Arnfinn Jorgensen-Dahl and Willy Ostreng (eds.), *The Antarctic Treaty System in World Politics* (London, 1991) 357–71; Philippe Sands, 'The Antarctic Treaty Regime: A Model for International Environmental Law?' in Joe Verhoeven, Philippe Sands and Maxwell Bruce (eds.), *The Antarctic Environment and International Law* (London, 1992) 53–61.

5 International law in the Arctic

As discussed in chapter 2, the Arctic as a region is dominated by maritime areas, especially the Arctic Ocean. Nonetheless, there are significant areas of continental land masses extending into the Arctic from the south. The role of international law in the Arctic has been strongly influenced not only in regard to areas beyond national jurisdiction, but also by the rights of coastal states over navigation and resources. At the same time, however, with the exception of the Svalbard Archipelago, all land areas within the Arctic region fall under the uncontested sovereignty of one of the eight Arctic states. The domestic legal responses of the Arctic states therefore have a major role to play in the Arctic legal regime. Nonetheless, this prevalence of Arctic domestic law has not prevented the development of an identifiable international law regime in the region. Principles of international law dealing with resource management and environmental protection have increasingly impacted on the manner in which Arctic states govern their respective territories. As a consequence, Arctic states have been forced gradually to adopt a range of bilateral and multilateral responses to specific Arctic issues. In other words, a distinctive 'Arctic international law' has begun now to emerge. At the same time, the Arctic has also become subject to an increasing array of global international law mechanisms, both treaty and custom based, which deal with problems such as marine pollution, climate change and biodiversity. Together, these measures constitute what may be termed an 'Arctic legal regime'.[1]

[1] A variety of commentators during the past forty years have referred to the 'Arctic legal regime': see e.g. Barnaby J. Feder, 'A Legal Regime for the Arctic' (1976–8) *Ecology Law Quarterly* 785–829; John Lawrence Hargrove and Nancy J. Kellner, 'The International Legal Regime of the Arctic' in Ira Dyer and Chryssostomos

This chapter will begin with a broad overview of the elements of this regime, before considering in more detail three specific areas: sovereignty, the law of the sea and environmental protection.[2] This will provide the basis for a more detailed consideration in chapter 6 of some recent initiatives in the Arctic which may indicate that the Arctic states are moving towards a more comprehensive and unified regional legal regime.

The legal regime

As matters currently stand, there is no single basis for these various components of international law which have specific and general application in the Arctic. Unlike Antarctica, there is no regional structure which exists to facilitate or promote cooperation and the development of international law amongst the eight Arctic states.[3] However, because of the significance of the Arctic Ocean in the region, the law of the sea has been seen as potentially providing a focus for the development of more comprehensive and integrated legal mechanisms. The 1982 United Nations Convention on the Law of the Sea (UNCLOS)[4] has been a major catalyst in this regard. Some consideration has also been given to whether the Arctic could be classified a 'marine region'.[5] While it is true that law of the sea issues have predominated in bilateral relations and recently been the focus of more regional attention, other global legal regimes are beginning to have an impact upon the region. This is especially so in the case of those dealing with environmental protection. Examples of such international law initiatives include the 1979 Convention on Long-Range Transboundary Air Pollution,[6] the 1985 Vienna Convention for

Chryssostomidis (eds.), *Arctic Technology and Policy* (Washington, 1984) 47–60; 'Legal Regimes of the Arctic' (1988) 82 ProcAmSocIL 315–34; A. L. Kolodkin and M. E. Volosov, 'The Legal Regime of the Soviet Arctic: Major Issues' (1990) 14 *Marine Policy* 158–68.

2 The primary focus will be on international Arctic issues and international responses. While it is recognised that the Arctic legal regime has domestic legal implications for the Arctic states, no detailed consideration will be given to the domestic implementation of the Arctic legal regime by these states.

3 Alan E. Boyle, 'Remarks – Legal Regimes of the Arctic' (1988) 82 ProcAmSocIL 315 at 324.

4 (1982) 21 ILM 1,261 (hereinafter UNCLOS).

5 See J. Enno Harders, 'In Quest of an Arctic Legal Regime' (1987) 11 *Marine Policy* 285–98; David VanderZwaag, John Donihee and Mads Faegteborg, 'Towards Regional Ocean Management in the Arctic: From Co-existence to Cooperation' (1988) 37 *UNB Law Journal* 1–33.

6 (1979) 18 ILM 1,442.

the Protection of the Ozone Layer[7] and the subsequent Montreal Protocol,[8] and the 1992 Convention on Biological Diversity.[9]

Apart from the law of the sea, much of the Arctic legal regime has developed around bilateral agreements between individual Arctic states. These agreements have dealt with a great variety of matters, from original land frontier delimitations to fishery agreements, protection of wildlife, cooperative marine environmental measures, and most recently environmental protection of the marine, atmospheric and terrestrial environment from various types of pollutants.[10] Importantly for the development of a more comprehensive Arctic legal regime, these bilateral agreements show that Arctic states are moving towards greater cooperation on a wide variety of matters, which, as Osherenko and Young have noted, is a 'hopeful sign with respect to the capacity of the Arctic states to cope with the growing array of conflicts that transcend national boundaries'.[11]

A good example of how continuing bilateral discussion and consideration of issues of mutual concern can lead to more sophisticated arrangements is found in the Canada–USSR Arctic Science Exchange Programme. Bilateral discussions concerning Canadian–Soviet scientific exchanges commenced in 1972 at which time efforts were made to identify areas of common interest in Arctic science, research and development. By 1984, these discussions had matured into a formal 'Protocol of Consultation' which has been built upon in later agreements.[12] More recently, Canada and Russia entered into an Agreement on Cooperation in the Arctic and the North.[13] This Agreement seeks to encourage greater cooperation between the two states in matters relating to the Arctic and the North and to that end creates a

[7] (1987) 26 ILM 1,529.

[8] (1987) 26 ILM 1,541, as amended.

[9] (1992) 31 ILM 818.

[10] For some examples see Gail Osherenko and Oran R. Young, *The Age of the Arctic* (1989) 292–5.

[11] *Ibid.* at 295.

[12] See Walter Slipchenko, 'Canada–USSR Arctic Science Exchange Programme: An Historical Perspective of Arctic Cooperation' in Lawson W. Brigham (ed.), *The Soviet Maritime Arctic* (London, 1991) 235–57; Erik Franckx, *Maritime Claims in the Arctic* (Dordrecht, 1993) 254–7. A further example of Canadian–USSR cooperation, which deals with scientific cooperation but also broader issues, is the 1989 Agreement between the Government of Canada and the Government of the Union of Soviet Socialist Republics on Cooperation in the Arctic and the North, [1989] CTS 21.

[13] 1992 Agreement between the Government of Canada and the Government of the Russian Federation on Cooperation in the Arctic and the North (with Annex), [1992] CTS 18.

'Canada–Russia Mixed Commission on Cooperation in the Arctic and the North'. While this particular example of international cooperation could not be characterised as one which imposes substantial legal obligations upon the two parties, it does demonstrate that Arctic states are able to reach cooperative agreements that have a lasting impact on their mutual relations.[14]

A more concrete example of bilateral cooperation between two Arctic states is the 1988 Arctic Cooperation Agreement between Canada and the United States.[15] The Agreement is a curious mix of provisions which seek to support the need for greater Canadian–United States cooperation on certain issues and one which deals with an important difference of international law which had developed between the two states. It seeks to reaffirm the need for Canadian–United States cooperation in the Arctic so as to advance 'their shared interests in Arctic development and security'[16] and acknowledges that importance should be attached by both countries to protection of the unique environment of the Arctic, the well-being of its inhabitants and the uniqueness of ice-covered maritime areas. It is on the issue of ice-breaker navigation, particularly access to and use of the Northwest Passage, that the Agreement seeks to deal with some delicate international law issues which had arisen between Canada and the United States.[17] Both states acknowledge their shared interests in safe and effective icebreaker navigation off their Arctic coasts and the need for increased knowledge on how to protect the Arctic marine environment. To that end, the Agreement specifically provides:

(a) that both states facilitate and develop cooperative measures for navigation by their icebreakers in their respective Arctic waters;
(b) that in accordance with international law both states take advantage of their icebreaker navigation to share research information so as to advance their understanding of the marine environment; and
(c) that navigation by United States icebreakers within waters claimed by Canada to be internal be undertaken with the consent of Canada.[18]

[14] For a consideration of other cooperative agreements entered into on a bilateral basis, see Walter Slipchenko, 'International Arctic Cooperation: A Canadian Dream or a Necessity', in *The Arctic: Choices for Peace and Security* (West Vancouver, 1989) 93–104.

[15] 1988 Agreement between the Government of Canada and the Government of the United States of America on Arctic Cooperation, [1988] CTS 29 (hereinafter 1988 Arctic Cooperation Agreement).

[16] 1988 Arctic Cooperation Agreement, Clause. 2.

[17] This is a matter dealt with in greater detail at pp. 191–6 below.

[18] 1988 Arctic Cooperation Agreement, Clause 3.

In addition, Clause 4 provides that the respective positions of both states with respect to the law of the sea in the Passage and in other maritime areas would not be affected by the Agreement.[19]

The Agreement primarily deals with ice-breaker navigation and operation and their environmental impact. There was no intention to deal with navigation by other vessels through Canadian Arctic waters, excepting Clause 2 which generally states that 'navigation and resource development in the Arctic must not adversely affect the unique environment of the region and the well-being of its inhabitants'. Navigation through the Northwest Passage by vessels similar to the *Manhattan*, the United States-registered oil tanker which crossed the Passage in 1969, is accordingly not covered by the Agreement. That both parties specifically reserved their respective positions on other law of the sea issues affecting the region is a further indication that the Agreement is limited to ice-breakers. By entering into the Agreement then, the United States is not seen to be making any concession towards Canada's claims of sovereignty over the Northwest Passage.[20] The Canadian position that the Passage is not an international strait also remains intact.

This Agreement is an example of the increasing efforts amongst Arctic states to deal with specific bilateral and regional problems. It is, however, perhaps more significant for what it did not deal with rather than what it achieved. It sidestepped a wide range of issues that have been at the core of an ongoing dispute over navigation rights through the Northwest Passage.[21] Although resolving the question of navi-

[19] 1988 Arctic Cooperation Agreement, Clause 4 provides:

> Nothing in this Agreement of cooperative endeavour between Arctic neighbours and friends nor any practice thereunder affects the respective positions of the Governments of the United States and of Canada on the Law of the Sea in this or other maritime areas or their respective positions regarding third parties.

[20] Legally this may be the position; however, politically the Canadian government saw the Agreement as a significant step 'in emphasizing Canada's control over our North': see Statement by the Secretary of State for External Affairs, Joe Clark, in 'Canadian Practice in International Law – Parliamentary Declarations in 1987–1988' (1988) 26 CYIL 350.

[21] For a review of the Agreement see J. Honderich, 'Canada–US Agreement on the Northwest Passage: Compromise or Cop-out?' (1988) 14(4) *Information North* (Newsletter of the Arctic Institute of North America) 1–4; R. G. Purver, 'Aspects of Sovereignty and Security in the Arctic' in D. McRae and G. Munro (eds.), *Canadian Oceans Policy: National Strategies and the New Law of the Sea* (Vancouver, 1989) 165 at 170–3; in regard to ice-breaking operations in the Arctic see Lawson W. Brigham, 'Arctic Icebreakers: US, Canadian, and Soviet' (1986) 29(1) *Oceanus* 47; Franckx, *Maritime Claims* at 261–4.

gation by ice-breakers, more substantial areas of disagreement concerning navigation through the Passage and Canadian Arctic waters remained unresolved.[22] The Agreement is also then an example of how the Arctic legal regime has yet to deal comprehensively with some regional issues.

While bilateral legal initiatives in the Arctic have been in place for a long time, regional legal initiatives are more difficult to identify. One of the earliest examples of any attempt by states to deal with a specific Arctic issue was the 1911 Convention between the United States, Great Britain, Russia and Japan for the Preservation and Protection of Fur Seals.[23] The Convention sought to deal with managing the exploitation of fur seals in the Bering Sea and far North Pacific Ocean and became the basis for a number of subsequent agreements which continued through the twentieth century.[24] Another early example of a regional initiative to deal with an Arctic problem is the 1920 Treaty concerning the Archipelago of Spitsbergen (Svalbard).[25] This Treaty deals with the legal regime and sovereignty of the Svalbard Archipelago, located in a region north of Norway surrounded by the Barents, Norwegian and North Greenland Sea. It is an example of where the resource riches of the region, and the desire to exploit those resources, acted as a catalyst for the resolution of sovereignty issues. The Treaty officially recognised Norway as the territorial sovereign, but all state parties still retained a right of access to the Archipelago's resources. Another important example of a multilateral Arctic initiative is the 1973 Agreement on the Conservation of Polar Bears between Canada, Denmark, Norway, the USSR and the USA.[26] However, until the eight Arctic states negotiated the 1991 Arctic Environmental Protection Strategy (AEPS),[27] there had been few other examples of the Arctic states developing multilateral responses to regional problems.

The Arctic legal regime then is disparate. There is no single legal

[22] The Agreement was put to the test soon after its conclusion when in October 1988 the US Department of State requested that the USCG *Polar Star* be permitted to transit the Northwest Passage. Permission was granted and a Canadian Coast Guard ice-breaker accompanied the *Polar Star* during the transit: see US Note No. 425, 10 October 1988, reprinted in (1989) 28 ILM 144; Canadian response to US Note No. 425, 10 October 1988, reprinted in (1989) 28 ILM 145; B. McAllister, 'US Breaks Diplomatic Ice to Aid Ship' *Washington Post*, 11 October 1988, A1.

[23] 214 ConTS 80; Great Britain signed on behalf of Canada.

[24] Further consideration is given to this Convention in chapter 8.

[25] 2 LNTS 8 (hereinafter Spitsbergen Treaty).

[26] (1974) 13 ILM 13 (hereinafter Polar Bear Agreement).

[27] (1991) 30 ILM 1,624 (hereinafter AEPS).

instrument providing a basis. It primarily focuses on the international law of the sea but also comprises a number of other initiatives – global, regional and bilateral – dealing with a variety of matters. To gain an accurate view of the regime, it is therefore necessary to look at the specific legal measures which apply in the principal issue areas.

Arctic international law

To assess the extent of the Arctic legal regime, three areas have been chosen. They are: Arctic sovereignty, the law of the sea and environmental protection. Each represents areas in which international law has had a substantial influence in Arctic affairs and when combined they form the basis of the existing Arctic legal regime. In some instances, specific responses have been developed to deal with Arctic legal problems. In combination, the principles of customary international law and treaties which apply in each of these three areas provide the starting point for an understanding of the Arctic legal regime.

Arctic sovereignty

Any consideration of the Arctic legal regime inevitably raises questions of sovereignty. Maritime sovereignty particularly is a major issue because of the dominating presence of the Arctic Ocean in the region. In this section, consideration will be given to both territorial and maritime sovereignty by assessing how in some instances sovereignty has been asserted and how sovereignty disputes have been resolved. By and large sovereignty over territorial lands in the Arctic has not been a matter of great dispute. While some islands, such as the Svalbard Archipelago, have been at the centre of some disputes, there has never been military conflict. Arctic maritime boundaries and claims have been much more difficult to settle, principally due to the significant resources which may be involved. Because of the expansion of maritime zones in the past three decades, Arctic maritime boundaries have only become a matter of dispute in recent times, and accordingly some remain to be settled.

Arctic territorial claims

Arctic sovereignty has been a continuing concern ever since Arctic lands, islands and marine areas became the subject of scientific interest and national exploration. In some instances no disputes existed over title to Arctic territories primarily because, through a combination of discovery, effective occupation and assertion of legal title, states were able to assert an unchallenged claim to Arctic lands. In other instances, such as the 1867 cession of Alaska to the United States by Russia,[28] title was acquired in an uncontroversial way. In fact, there has been very little dispute over the title to Arctic lands which are part of either the North American or Asian–European continents. The disputes which have occurred have instead been over islands and the maritime areas of the large Arctic Ocean. These disputes were in part a consequence of the region being subject to various claims of discovery by explorers from a variety states[29] and also the perceived resource potential of many areas of the Arctic. The islands of the Svalbard Archipelago, and the variety of claims made to them over the past 400 years, are a good example.

Exploration of the Arctic in the eighteenth and nineteenth centuries fuelled these disputes as explorers from Great Britain, the United States, Russia and Scandinavia all sought out new Arctic lands. The search for a Northwest Passage around the top of the North American continent also resulted in many of the islands which now make up the Canadian Arctic Archipelago being first discovered. The race for the North Pole also assisted in a greater appreciation being gained of the extent of the Arctic Ocean and the islands scattered throughout.[30] The eventual reaching of the Pole in 1909 and the claims by both Peary and Cook to have been the first to do so also demonstrated the tremendous degree of rivalry which existed in Arctic exploration and the national prestige associated with such a discovery. Given that both men were American their achievement was considered by some to confer a claim by the United States on the Pole itself.[31] The United States did not

[28] 1867 Convention Ceding Alaska between Russia and the United States, 134 ConTS 331.

[29] T. A. Taracouzio, *The Soviet Union and International Law* (repr. 1972) 56–7 notes that the Soviet response to these problems was to adopt a different approach to the doctrine of discovery and to argue that 'irrespective of the nationality of the discoverers or explorers, sovereignty to lands discovered automatically vests with the state within whose sphere or sector of "terrestrial gravitation" the land is found'. This principle is similar to the 'sector theory'.

[30] See generally Pierre Berton, *The Arctic Grail: The Quest for the Northwest Passage and the North Pole 1818–1909* (New York, 1988).

[31] The discovery of the North Pole and the legal consequences which resulted from the event generated some legal debate at the time: see James Brown Scott, 'Arctic Exploration and International Law' (1909) 3 AJIL 928–41; Thomas Willing Balch, 'The Arctic and Antarctic Regions and the Law of Nations' (1910) 4 AJIL 265–75.

eventually assert any claim over the North Pole, which is not surprising given that at the time there was no precedent for claims to maritime areas so distant from the littoral state, or for claims over ice not physically connected to a continent.[32] Most Arctic territorial disputes were based on traditional claims and counter-claims such as who had discovered which island, whether a claim had been made effective, and whether an annexation of an island was good against other competing claims. Because both Canada (Great Britain prior to Canadian Confederation in 1867) and Russia had the largest claims in the region, most of these territorial disputes involved one of these states.

Canadian Arctic sovereignty

As is the case with most claims to sovereignty over polar areas, Canada's claim to sovereignty over the islands of the Canadian Arctic Archipelago is based on traditional legal grounds, that is, on a series of territorial claims and legislative acts over a period of time which, when combined, provide evidence of Canadian sovereignty as against the claims of other states. The basis for much of the Canadian claim to North America lies in various acts of discovery by English and French explorers as they travelled across the northern part of the continent and sailed through Arctic waters. They range from the initial voyage in 1497 by Sebastian Cabot to the northern coast of Labrador to the first crossing of the Northwest Passage in 1850-54 by McClure over both land and water. Most of these expeditions were 'voyages of discovery'. Not all were accompanied by the raising of the flag of the sponsoring sovereign. Nevertheless, as the great majority of the expeditions were British there was a substantial basis for sovereignty claims by Britain based upon discovery.

While Canada's basis of claim to much of the Arctic may rest upon acts of discovery (whether by British, French or Canadian explorers), these on their own are insufficient upon which to base title in international law.[33] As demonstrated in the *Island of Palmas Arbitration*, discovery on its own only confers an inchoate title upon the state making the discovery.[34] Further acts such as occupation and

32 No state has ever actively asserted a claim over the North Pole. It was a question, however, which some commentators considered: see A. R. Clute, 'The Ownership of the North Pole' (1927) 5 CanBR 19–26.

33 See D. P. O'Connell, *International Law* (vol. I) (London, 1970) 408–9.

34 *The Netherlands* v. *United States of America* (4 April 1928), 2 RIAA 829. See Sir Robert Jennings and Sir Arthur Watts, *Oppenheim's International Law* (9th, vol. I: Pts 2–4) (Harlow, UK, 1992) 688–90. See also the discussion in chapter 3.

administration are also required in order to solidify a title originally based on discovery. While France, Britain, the Canadian colonies and subsequently Canada (after Confederation in 1867) did engage in these activities, the Canadian claim in the Arctic also had other foundations.[35] Various treaties ceded first to Great Britain and then to Canada certain Arctic lands. In 1763, the Treaty of Paris ceded to Great Britain all of France's possessions in British North America with the exception of the islands of St Pierre and Miquelon.[36] The 1825 Boundary Treaty between Russia and Great Britain is also important. It establishes what is now the Canadian–United States boundary between Yukon and Alaska along 141°W. The Treaty provides that at the terminus of the land frontier the boundary extends as far as 'the Frozen Ocean'.[37]

Following Canadian Confederation in 1867 there was a desire to settle the legal status of all Canadian territory previously claimed by Great Britain. In 1875 an Order in Council was passed requesting the transfer by Great Britain to Canada of all the lands to the north of the Dominion. There was no doubt that the Parliament at Westminster did consider these lands to be British possessions and that it was competent to transfer sovereignty over them. Accordingly, an 1880 Order in Council provided for the transfer to Canada of 'all the British possessions on the American continent, not hitherto annexed to any colony'.[38] This proclamation included 'all British territories and possessions in North America, not already included within the Dominion of Canada, and all islands adjacent to any of such territories or possessions . . . with the exception of Newfoundland and its dependencies'.[39] Canada also took steps independent of Great Britain to complete its legal title over the Arctic lands. In 1869 it purchased from the Hudson's Bay Company the area known as Rupert's Land which in conjunction with the region known as the North-Western

[35] Ivan L. Head, 'Canadian Claims to Territorial Sovereignty in the Arctic Regions' (1963–64) 9 *McGill Law Journal* 200 at 211 noted: 'What it did not discover, the Canadian nation acquired by purchase and treaty.'

[36] Definitive Treaty of Peace between France, Great Britain and Spain, 42 ConTS 279.

[37] 1825 Convention between Great Britain and Russia Concerning the Limits of their Respective Possessions on the North-West Coast of America and the Navigation of the Pacific Ocean, 75 ConTS 95, Art. 3.

[38] *Canada Gazette* (9 October 1880).

[39] Adjacent Territories Order, 1880 (UK) (formerly 'Order of Her Majesty in Council admitting all British possessions and territories in North America and islands adjacent thereto into the Union', 31 July 1880). For a comment on this transfer see Head, 'Canadian Claims' at 212.

Territory subsequently became the 'Northwest Territory'.[40] While Canada was through these various acts gradually acquiring a stronger basis upon which eventually to assert sovereignty over vast areas of the North American Arctic, there was great uncertainty over the full extent of the potential claim. There were also threats to the 'Canadian Arctic' posed by the United States which had, throughout the nineteenth century, not formally recognised foreign claims in the North American Arctic, and whose whalers used Arctic waters and islands as if no foreign power had any title over them.[41] The Canadian government was so concerned over the extent of its Arctic claims and potential threats to them, that in 1905 it commissioned a confidential report outlining the potential extent of Canada's claims over the islands of the Arctic Archipelago.[42] The recommendation of the Chief Astronomer, W. F. King, was that Canada should make a greater effort to establish its authority in the far north.[43]

A more positive assertion of the potential extent of the Canadian claim was made in 1907 when Senator Pascal Poirier, in a speech to the Canadian Senate, recommended that Canada should make a declaration proclaiming possession of all the lands and islands lying between its northern coast and the Pole. As the basis for this assertion, Poirier argued that:

> in future partition, of northern lands, a country whose possession today goes up to the Arctic regions, will have a right, or should have a right, or has a right to all the lands that are to be found in the waters between a line extending from its eastern extremity north, and another line extending from the western extremity north. All the lands between the two lines up to the north pole should belong and do belong to the country whose territory abuts up there.[44]

[40] W. H. McConnell, *Commentary on the British North America Act* (Toronto, 1977) 28. The Northwest Territories are now the largest of the political units within the Canadian federation, and include all the islands of the Canadian Arctic Archipelago.

[41] See Shelagh D. Grant, *Sovereignty or Security?* (Vancouver, 1988) 7. W. Gillies Ross, 'Canadian Sovereignty in the Arctic: The Neptune Expedition of 1903–04' (1976) 29 *Arctic* 87–104 discusses the 'Neptune Expedition' to the eastern Arctic in an attempt more effectively to assert Canadian sovereignty and combat the increasing interest in the region being shown by American whalers.

[42] W. F. King, *Report upon the Title of Canada to the Islands North of the Mainland of Canada* (Ottawa, 1905).

[43] Grant, *Sovereignty or Security?* at 11. For a further review of Canada's Arctic claims in the period between Confederation and the 1930s, see Gordon W. Smith, *Territorial Sovereignty in the Canadian North: A Historical Outline of the Problem* (Ottawa, 1963); William R. Morrison, *Under the Flag: Canadian Sovereignty and the Native People in Northern Canada* (Ottawa, 1984).

[44] Canada, Senate, Debates, 271 (20 February 1907).

This speech is recognised as being the first formal suggestion by a Canadian that a 'sector approach' be relied upon in making claims to the Arctic region.[45]

Poirier's attitude towards Canada's Arctic sovereignty was apparently shared by the Canadian explorer, Captain J. E. Bernier, who took 'formal possession' of the whole Arctic Archipelago on 1 July 1909 by unveiling and depositing a plaque on Melville Island. The inscription on the plaque read:

> The Memorial is erected today to commemorate the taking possession for the Dominion of Canada of the whole Arctic Archipelago lying to the north of America from long. 60°W to 141°W up to the latitude of 90°N.[46]

However, despite the Poirier speech and Bernier's proclamation, there is no conclusive evidence of Canadian support for a sector claim in the Arctic. The truth is that since the Poirier speech considerable doubt has been cast over the validity of the sector theory by legal academics.[47] Public statements from Canadian officials have never adopted the very wide approach towards Canada's Arctic claims advocated by Poirier.[48] Nevertheless, the sector theory has been relied upon as one basis, but not the sole justification, for Canada initially to assert sovereignty over Arctic lands and adjacent waters.[49]

[45] Head, 'Canadian Claims' at 202–3 notes:

> An Arctic sector is deceptively simple, and is compounded of only two ingredients: a base line or arc described along the Arctic Circle through territory unquestionably within the jurisdiction of a temperate zone state, and sides defined by meridians of longitude extending from the North Pole south to the most easterly and westerly points on the Arctic Circle pierced by the state. Under the theory, nations possessing territory extending into the Arctic regions have a rightful claim to all territory – be it land, water, or ice – lying to their north. This claim springs from the geographical relationship of the claimant state to the claimed territory; the two areas must be contiguous along the Arctic Circle.

See also the discussion in chapter 3.

[46] J. E. Bernier, *Master Mariner and Arctic Explorer* (Ottawa, 1939) 128.

[47] See G. Smedal, *Acquisition of Sovereignty over Polar Areas* (Oslo, 1931) 54–76; Oscar Svarlien, 'The Legal Status of the Arctic' (1958) 52 ProcAmSocIL 136 at 142; Oscar Svarlien, 'The Sector Principle in Law and Practice' (1960) 10 *Polar Record* 248 at 260; O'Connell, *International Law* at 450; Donat Pharand, *Canada's Arctic Waters in International Law* (Cambridge, 1988) 1–88, who at 79 notes: 'the sector theory has not developed as a principle of customary international law, neither general nor regional, and cannot serve as a root of title for the acquisition of sovereignty'; Jennings and Watts, *Oppenheim's International Law* at 693.

[48] Head, 'Canadian Claims' at 202–10.

[49] *Ibid.* at 210. This is despite the fact that numerous maps seem to indicate a 'boundary' line running from the eastern and western extremities of the Canadian mainland north to the Pole: see Franckx, *Maritime Claims* at 91–2.

Canada's equivocation over reliance upon the sector theory did not result in an abandonment of its claims to the Arctic. Much effort was made at the beginning of the twentieth century to exercise effective administration of Arctic lands, despite the financial burdens this imposed upon the new country. Officers of the Royal Canadian Mounted Police were despatched to various outlying settlements and regions in efforts designed to confirm Canadian authority.[50] Various ministerial statements were also made concerning Canada's territorial claims towards the islands in the Archipelago and also over the waters between the islands and the Northwest Passage itself. While some of these statements are contradictory on the actual extent of the Canadian claim, there is no dispute that Canada claims title to the islands of the Archipelago.[51] In fact, one commentator has noted that by 1947 the Canadian claim with respect to the land territory of the Canadian Arctic had become so uncontentious that '. . . it could be assumed that Canada's title had been perfected to most of the arctic islands'.[52] However, given Canada's partial reliance upon the suspect sector theory, and in light of the international law of the sea concerning internal waters, territorial seas and navigation through straits, the same cannot be said concerning the apparent Canadian position with respect to the waters around the Archipelago or the Northwest Passage. The true status of these waters remains in doubt.

Russian Arctic sovereignty

Russia's Arctic claims have also been a matter of some controversy. Not only have there been some disputes over adjacent offshore islands which have become subject to Russian–Soviet claims but there has also been reliance upon the sector theory. The Soviet scholar Lakhtine has noted that Russian claims to the Arctic were asserted as far back as an 1821 *ukase* (an order or decree of the Tsar) over the waters of the Bering

50 See William R. Morrison, 'Canadian Sovereignty and the Inuit of the Central and Eastern Arctic' (1986) 10(1/2) *Etudes Inuit Studies* 245–59.

51 See R. S. Reid, 'The Canadian Claim to Sovereignty over the Waters of the Arctic' (1974) 12 CYIL 111 at 112–14; V. Kenneth Johnston, 'Canada's Title to the Arctic Islands' (1933) 14 *Canadian Historical Review* 24–41; Gordon W. Smith, 'Canada's Arctic Archipelago: 100 Years of Canadian Jurisdiction, Part II: Making the North Canadian' (1980) 17(2) *NorthNord* 10–17.

52 N. D. Bankes, 'Forty Years of Canadian Sovereignty Assertion in the Arctic, 1947–87' (1987) 40 *Arctic* 285 at 287. This does not mean that sovereignty was never a 'live' issue in the Arctic: see Nancy Fogelson, 'The Tip of the Iceberg: The United States and International Rivalry for the Arctic, 1900–25' (1985) 9 *Diplomatic History* 131–48.

Sea.[53] Subsequently, the boundary between British and Russian claims was demarcated along 141 °W. Until such time as the cession of Alaska to the United States this boundary was the eastern limit of Russia's Arctic claims. Even after the 1867 Convention ceding Alaska which established the Russian–United States boundary in the Bering Straits,[54] Russia's Arctic claims to the west of 169°W were respected.[55] Russian claims were also eventually asserted over discovered Arctic lands and islands which lay due north of continental Russia. This included the Kolgueff and Vaigatz Islands, Novaya Zemlya, Franz Joseph Land, Sverdroup Island, Ouedinenie Island, the Taymir Archipelago, Sannikoff Land, the New Siberian Islands, Henriette, Jeanette, the Bear Islands and Wrangel and Herald Islands.[56] By and large the assertion of sovereignty over many of these lands and islands was uncontroversial. Many of these lands had been discovered by Russian explorers, and Russia was the most adjacent Arctic state and in the best position to be able to assert administrative authority. Even in instances where sovereignty had previously been asserted over these lands by other powers, the inability effectively to occupy the land resulted in claims, such as that by the United States and Great Britain over Wrangel Island, eventually reverting to Russia.[57]

Despite Russia's ability effectively to assert a number of claims over Arctic lands, there is still evidence that reliance was placed upon the sector theory to assert even wider claims to other lands which remained to be discovered. The first indication of Russian reliance upon the sector theory came in 1916 when the Russian Minister for Foreign Affairs notified foreign governments of a claim to certain islands in the Arctic Ocean during which it was noted that such lands fell within a 'northern extension of the Siberian continental upland'.[58] A more positive act of reliance by the Soviet government upon the sector theory came in 1924 when it issued a Note specifically claiming eleven islands, including Wrangel Island, situated west of 169°W.[59]

[53] W. Lakhtine, 'Rights over the Arctic' (1930) 24 AJIL 703 at 707. [54] Note 28 above.

[55] Lakhtine, 'Rights over the Arctic' at 708; David Hunter Miller, 'Political Rights in the Arctic' (1925–1926) 4 *Foreign Affairs* 47 at 53–4.

[56] Lakhtine, 'Rights over the Arctic' at 707.

[57] T. E. M. McKitterick, 'The Validity of Territorial and other Claims in Polar Regions' (1939) 21(I & IV) (3rd Ser.) *Journal of Comparative Legislation and International Law* 89 at 92; Hunter Miller, 'Political Rights' at 53.

[58] Lakhtine, 'Rights over the Arctic' at 708; *cf.* Pharand, *Canada's Arctic Waters* at 64 who contests that Russia placed any reliance upon the sector theory at that time.

[59] Pharand, *Canada's Arctic Waters* at 64. Despite the Russian/Soviet assertion of sovereignty over Wrangel Island, some queries still remain over the validity of the

The principal assertion by the Soviet Union of a sector claim over northern lands came in 1926 when a decree of the Presidium of the Central Executive Committee of the USSR provided that:

> All lands and islands situated in the Arctic to the North, between the coastline of the Union of Soviet Socialist Republics and the North Pole, both already discovered and those which may be discovered in the future, which at the time of the publication of the present decree are not recognised by the Union of Soviet Socialist Republics as the territory of any foreign state, are [hereby] declared territory of the Union . . .[60]

This Soviet claim was to a very wide arc of the Arctic Ocean and effectively sought to encompass all land north of continental Russia. While this Decree may have had the effect of confirming previous Russian and Soviet claims, some commentators were of the view that these claims had not been perfected.[61]

Joyner has argued that the Soviet interpretation of the sector theory was based upon a radical modification of the traditional doctrine of discovery:

> The Soviet sector policy asserted in no uncertain terms that, regardless of the nationality of future explorers, sovereignty to any lands discovered within the compass of the declared sector of 'terrestrial gravitation' would belong to the Soviet Union. For all intents and purposes, then, the international legal doctrine of discovery was perforce rendered moot and inapplicable to lands in the Soviet Arctic.[62]

However, despite the initial legal uncertainty of Russian sector claims, over the course of time, and through its ability to support legislative decrees with positive assertions of sovereignty such as the construction of buildings, use of the islands by fishermen and regular visits by government vessels, throughout the twentieth century the Soviets were able to build up uncontestable claims to their northern Arctic lands.

claim: see Don Eric Salom, 'The United States' Claim to Wrangel Island: The Dormancy Should End' (1981) 11 CalWILJ 140–67.

[60] Reprinted in Manley O. Hudson (ed.), *Cases and Other Materials on International Law* (2nd) (St Paul, MN, 1936) 380. The specific area which fell within this claim was:

> between the meridian 32°4'34" longitude, East of Greenwich, passing over the Eastern side of the Bay of Vaida Cay by the triangulation mark on the Cape of Kekursk, and the meridian 168°49'30" longitude, West of Greenwich, passing over the middle of the strait between the Ratmanov and Kruzenshtern islands, of the group of Diomid islands in the Strait of Bering.

[61] See Smedal, *Acquisition of Sovereignty* at 70–2 in regard to the contested Soviet and Norwegian claims to Franz Joseph Land.

[62] Christopher C. Joyner, 'A Comparison of Soviet Arctic and Antarctic Policies' in Lawson W. Brigham (ed.), *The Soviet Maritime Arctic* (London, 1991) 284 at 286.

Svalbard

From the date of its discovery by Barents in 1596 and subsequent acts of exploration, both Denmark and Norway expressed interest in the Svalbard Archipelago. Norway continued to express interest in the islands after they were ceded to Sweden by the Treaty of Kiel in 1814. However, when in 1871 Russia contested whether the islands were subject to claim by other states, agreement was reached amongst the interested states that the islands should be treated as *terra nullius*.[63] The discovery of large coal deposits on the island of West Spitsbergen at the end of the nineteenth century renewed interest in the islands and raised the potential for disputes to occur over conflicting claims. Several international conferences were held prior to World War I in an effort to resolve the question,[64] but it was not till after the War with the assistance of the Versailles Peace Conference that a solution was found.[65] The result of this process was the adoption in 1920 of the Spitsbergen (Svalbard) Treaty.[66] The Treaty recognises that Norway is the territorial sovereign of the islands,[67] while also granting to all other Treaty parties rights of access and entry to the waters, fjords and ports of the islands and the ability to carry out mining, industrial and other commercial operations.[68] The effect of the Treaty was that while Norway was recognised as being the territorial sovereign, all states were guaranteed equal rights of access and economic rights.[69] Despite these terms, since the 1930s only Russia, along with Norway, has taken up the opportunity to engage in economic activities on the islands, though other nationals have visited to engage in scientific work.[70] While the Treaty effectively recognised Norwegian sovereignty over the islands, Norway has still sought effectively to assert its sovereignty by way of government and administrative acts in order to ensure that its Treaty-based sovereignty remains unchallenged.[71]

[63] Scott, 'Arctic Exploration' at 941.

[64] For a review of these Conferences and a discussion of the legal issues discussed therein, see Robert Lansing, 'A Unique International Problem' (1917) 11 AJIL 763–71.

[65] See Willy Ostreng, *Politics in High Latitudes* (London, 1977) 2–3; Robin Churchill and Geir Ulfstein, *Marine Management in Disputed Areas* (London, 1992) 25–6.

[66] Ostreng explains that 'Svalbard' is the collective name for the islands which make up the Archipelago, of which the largest island is Spitsbergen (formerly known as West Spitsbergen): *Politics in High Latitudes* at 1.

[67] Spitsbergen Treaty, Art. 2.

[68] Spitsbergen Treaty, Art. 3.

[69] Ostreng, *Politics in High Latitudes* at 26; Churchill and Ulfstein, *Marine Management* at 30–1.

[70] Ostreng, *Politics in High Latitudes* at 4.

Characteristics of Arctic maritime boundaries

A review of the various maritime boundaries which exist in the Arctic Ocean shows that there have been various impediments placed in the way of successful bilateral negotiation of these boundaries. Three factors can be identified as being responsible for these difficulties: sector claims, pre-existing boundary treaties and resource potential. Initially it is appropriate to consider these issues before briefly reviewing the existing maritime boundaries and disputes.

Sector claims

The sector theory represented for both Canada and Russia a basis upon which to assert claims to their northern lands. As noted, its status is controversial and many commentators question its validity.[72] Nevertheless, given the special circumstances which exist in the Arctic it provided a convenient starting point for the assertion of territorial claims which could, once asserted, be acted upon and solidified.[73] Though primarily applied to land areas, there has also been occasional reference to the sector theory in relation to maritime claims. This has occurred in two areas. First, it has been argued that waters which fall within the western and eastern limits of an Arctic state's sector are under the sovereignty or jurisdiction of that state. The influence over these waters can extend all the way to the North Pole. Second, it has been argued in bilateral maritime boundary delimitations that the maritime claims of a coastal state run from the terminus of a land boundary due north to the Pole. By relying upon this approach, Canada and Russia in particular have been able to assert that there is no scope for the application of other maritime boundary delimitation techniques in Arctic maritime boundary disputes.

[71] *Ibid.* at 28.

[72] See Smedal, *Acquisition of Sovereignty* at 60–4; McKitterick, 'Validity of Territorial Claims' at 95; O'Connell, *International Law* at 449–50.

[73] Bo Johnson Theutenberg, 'The Arctic Law of the Sea' (1983) 52 Nordic JIL 3 at 18 notes:

> It could very well be that the sector principle – in spite of its weak roots in international law – can still be useful as a fall-back position in present and future negotiations regarding the delimitation of national borderlines in the Arctic.

See also Svarlien, 'The Sector Principle' at 260 who notes:

> the conclusion must be that there exists no legal foundation in support of the 'sector principle' either in the Arctic or in the Antarctic. Yet we are tempted to suggest that in the Arctic, at least, the 'sector principle' of territorial claims, if confined to lands and islands within the respective sectors, is sufficiently in accord with the inevitable to make its tacit adoption highly probable.

Canada's position with respect to a maritime sector claim extending to the Pole is less strong than that over the Canadian Arctic Archipelago.[74] However, there is evidence of such a claim occasionally being made. For example, Canada's Ambassador to the United States, Lester Pearson, advocated in 1946 that a large part of the Arctic was Canadian, which included not only Canada's northern mainland and the islands, but also 'the frozen sea north of the mainland between the meridians of its east and west boundaries, extended to the North Pole'.[75] When Pearson subsequently entered Parliament he made a number of speeches in the House of Commons which also referred to the sector theory and implied that Canada's claim extended right to the North Pole.[76] Further evidence to suggest that Canada continues to rely upon the sector theory to assert maritime claims can be seen in the boundaries adopted in the Inuvialuit Final Agreement signed in 1984 between the Canadian government and the Inuvialuit peoples, in which the western boundary of the settlement claim extended into the Beaufort Sea as far north as 80°N along 141°W.[77] Canada thus does have some history of occasionally relying upon the sector theory to assert extensive maritime claims. However, these claims have never been actually proclaimed by decree or enforced. This practice seems to be consistent with Pharand's assessment that Canada has preferred to keep the sector theory 'in reserve' as a potential basis of claim to northern waters.[78]

In the case of Russia and the Soviet Union the sector theory has been relied upon to assert claims over those waters which now make up the Northern Sea Route and the Northeast Passage.[79] In combination with claims that these waters represent historic waters and closed seas, it has been possible over time to build a strong case that these waters are

[74] Franckx, *Maritime Claims* at 90 notes that the application of the sector theory to water 'is a rather farfetched construction to serve as a basis for a Canadian claim of sovereignty over its northern water expanses. Nevertheless, this theory seems to exert some mystical attraction as a fall-back position whenever the Canadian sovereignty claim over its northern waters had to be buttressed.'

[75] L. B. Pearson, 'Canada Looks "Down North"' (1945–1946) 24 *Foreign Affairs* 638 at 638–9.

[76] See Pharand, *Canada's Arctic Waters* at 56–8.

[77] The Western Arctic Claim – The Inuvialuit Final Agreement (1984), Annexes A and A-1. See Pharand, *Canada's Arctic Waters* at 62.

[78] D. Pharand, 'Canada's Arctic Jurisdiction in International Law' (1983) 7 DalLJ 315 at 324. Another commentator has argued that the Canadian position regarding the sector theory and maritime claims is 'unclear': see Susan B. Boyd, 'The Legal Status of the Arctic Sea Ice: A Comparative Study and a Proposal' (1984) 22 CYIL 98 at 107.

[79] See Taracouzio, *The Soviet Union* at 66.

not open to international navigation.[80] However, despite the views of some Soviet scholars such as Lakhtine, who asserted that the sovereignty of polar states should attach to the Arctic Ocean within their sectors of attraction,[81] there is nothing to suggest that any expansive claims to all the maritime areas, including ice, due north of the outer limits of the Russian territorial claim up to and converging at the North Pole, have ever been made by the Soviet Union or Russia. This is the view of Butler, who upon a review of Soviet practice since the making of the 1926 Decree,[82] concludes that there is nothing to imply a claim by the Soviets of a national frontier which extends over the waters of the Arctic Ocean up to the North Pole.[83] This is not to suggest, however, that the Soviets have not relied upon the sector theory in regard to bilateral maritime boundary delimitations. In their negotiations with Norway over the maritime boundary in the Barents Sea some reliance has been placed on a boundary founded on a sector claim.[84]

Pre-exisiting boundaries

There are two instances in the Arctic where maritime boundary delimitations have been affected by previously negotiated boundaries. The first is the maritime boundary between Russia and the United States in the Bering Sea through the Bering Straits into the Chukchi Sea. In the 1867 Convention which ceded Alaska to the United States,[85] Article 1 provided that Russia agreed to cede certain lands to the United States with the dividing line passing through designated points 'due north, without limitation, into the same Frozen Ocean'. The effect of this territorial delimitation was that when negotiations commenced over the delimitation of the continental shelf and EEZ boundary there was uncertainty whether the 1867 Convention boundary was intended, or could be interpreted, to apply to maritime claims which at the time it was drafted had no recognition in international law.[86] This continued to be an area of disagreement between the two states up until 1990 when agreement was reached upon a new

[80] W. E. Butler, *Northeast Arctic Passage* (Alphen aan den Rijn, 1978) 77.

[81] Lakhtine, 'Rights over the Arctic' at 713. [82] Note 60 above.

[83] Butler, *Northeast Arctic Passage* at 77. [84] Pharand, *Canada's Arctic Waters* at 66.

[85] Note 28 above. For a history of the implementation and issues surrounding this Treaty, see David Hunter Miller, *The Alaska Treaty* (Kingston, Ontario, 1981).

[86] See Susan J. Rolston and Ted L. McDorman, 'Maritime Boundary Making in the Arctic Regions' in Douglas M. Johnston and Phillip M. Saunders (eds.), *Ocean Boundary Making* (London, 1988) 16 at 46.

boundary delimitation.[87] While the new boundary is in fact based on the line established by the 1867 Convention, this is not because the parties determined that the 1867 line was also intended to serve as a maritime boundary but rather through convenience.[88]

In the case of the boundary between the United States and Canada in the Beaufort Sea, the original boundary treaty between Russia and Great Britain has proved an obstacle.[89] So far as it is relevant, the Treaty provides that:

> the line of demarcation shall follow the summit of the mountains situated parallel to the Coast, as far as the point of intersection of the 141st degree of West longitude . . . and, finally, from the said point of intersection, the said Meridian Line of the 141st degree, in its prolongation as far as the Frozen ocean.[90]

Canada has maintained that the Treaty can be extended from the land frontier into the Beaufort Sea and that as a result the boundary should be drawn north of the land boundary terminus along 141°W.[91] The United States has rejected this interpretation of the Treaty which – given that it had relied upon similar words found in the 1867 Convention ceding Alaska as a basis for the Bering Strait maritime boundary – has placed the United States in a difficult bargaining position.[92] This boundary dispute still remains unresolved.[93]

[87] 1990 Agreement between the United States of America and the Union of Soviet Socialist Republics on the Maritime Boundary, (1990) 29 ILM 941 (hereinafter Bering Sea Maritime Boundary Agreement). For a review of the negotiations between the Soviet Union and the United States over the interpretation of the 1867 Treaty see Camile M. Antinori, 'The Bering Sea: A Maritime Delimitation Dispute Between the United States and the Soviet Union' (1987) 18 ODIL 1–47.

[88] Alex Oude Elferink, 'The 1990 USSR–USA Maritime Boundary Agreement' (1991) 6 IJECL 41 at 43.

[89] 1928 Convention between Great Britain and Russia concerning the Limits of their Respective Possessions on the North-West Coast of America and the Navigation of the Pacific Ocean, 75 ConTS 95. This Treaty is relevant as it determined the territorial boundary between Russia and Great Britain in the region. This boundary, and the Treaty upon which it is based, still applies as a result of the cession of Alaska to the United States and Canada being the successor state to Great Britain.

[90] *Ibid.*, Art. 3.

[91] Rolston and McDorman, 'Maritime Boundary Making' at 48.

[92] Antinori, 'The Bering Sea' at 34.

[93] For an historical perspective on the interpretation of the provisions of these two treaties, see Hunter Miller, 'Political Rights' at 58–60. Despite the boundary remaining unresolved, Canada takes the attitude that it can offer oil and gas exploration rights in parts of the western Beaufort Sea: see 'Oil, Gas Rights Offered in Arctic', 5 January 1993, *The [Toronto] Globe and Mail*, B8.

Resource potential

A further dynamic which has been important in maritime boundary delimitations in the Arctic has been the resource potential of the area under dispute. Through the extension of maritime zones by successive revisions to the law of the sea in the second half of this century, coastal states have been able to gain greater sovereignty over living and non-living resources in their offshore zones. This has been especially important to those Arctic states which have resource-dependent economies. It has also opened up new areas for resource development. Many Arctic maritime areas which now fall within national jurisdiction potentially contain substantial reserves of oil and gas. This factor has been influential in negotiations over the Canada–United States boundary in the Beaufort Sea,[94] the Norway–Russia boundary in the Barents Sea,[95] the Iceland–Norway boundary around Jan Mayen in the Iceland Sea,[96] and more recently in the dispute before the International Court of Justice concerning delimitation of the area between Greenland and Jan Mayen.[97] In the case of fishery stocks, while many Arctic waters are not suitable for extensive fishing activities because of environmental conditions and the stock quality, nevertheless, at lower latitudes the fishery is relatively extensive.[98] As a result, EEZ rights are also an important issue in some maritime boundary delimitations.[99] Because of the importance of resources, Arctic states have been reluctant to determine maritime boundaries in the region without full account being taken of their various positions concerning access to marine resources. This explains why there have been widely divergent views taken by some states with respect to how their

[94] See Dawn Russell, 'International Ocean Boundary Issues and Management Arrangements' in David VanderZwaag (ed.), *Canadian Ocean Law and Policy* (Toronto, 1992) 463 at 494.

[95] Arnfinn Jorgensen-Dahl, 'The Soviet–Norwegian Maritime Disputes in the Arctic: Law and Politics' (1990) 21 ODIL 411 at 414–15.

[96] This boundary was eventually resolved by an Arbitration Commission: see 'The Agreement between Iceland and Norway of May 28, 1980, in Continental Shelf Area between Iceland and Jan Mayen' (1981) 20 ILM 797.

[97] *Case Concerning Maritime Delimitation in the Area Between Greenland and Jan Mayen (Denmark* v. *Norway)* Judgment [1993] ICJ Reports 38 at 71–2.

[98] See Bo Johnson Theutenberg, *The Evolution of the Law of the Sea* (Dublin, 1984) 58–60.

[99] This proved to be the case in the Bering Sea delimitation between the United States and the Soviet Union: see Rolston and McDorman, 'Maritime Boundary Making' at 46; in the Jan Mayen dispute between Iceland and Norway: *ibid.* at 34–7; and remains the case with the Barents Sea dispute between Norway and Russia: see Jorgensen-Dahl, 'The Soviet–Norwegian Maritime Disputes' at 415.

boundaries should be delimited, and also why joint development of disputed offshore resource zones has become a prospect in some instances.[100]

Arctic maritime boundaries

Canada–United States: Beaufort Sea

The maritime boundary in the Beaufort Sea between Canada and the United States has been the subject of ongoing negotiation. As noted above, Canada believes that the terms of the original 1825 boundary Treaty between Great Britain and Russia should be respected and favours a maritime boundary extending north along 141°W. The United States favours a boundary line based on equidistance which, if adopted, would lie considerably to the east of a line based on 141°W. Despite the major resource at stake in the Beaufort Sea region being non-renewable hydrocarbons which both sides are eager to develop, there does not seem to be any desire at present to rush into a negotiated settlement of the boundary or to have the matter resolved by arbitration or by the International Court of Justice.[101] Nevertheless, Canada and the United States have been able to cooperate in various measures designed to protect the marine environment of the region.[102]

United States–Russia: Bering Sea and Chukchi Sea

The United States–Russian maritime boundary dispute in the Bering and Chukchi Seas has many similarities to that in the Beaufort Sea. The primary issue in the delimitation concerned the boundary created by the 1867 Convention ceding Alaska, and whether it had any bearing upon the Beaufort Sea maritime boundary.[103] The matter was finally determined by an Agreement in 1990 which substantially adopted the 1867 Convention as the basis for the maritime boundary subject to

100 This has occurred in the so-called 'Grey Zone' in the Barents Sea between Norway and Russia: see Churchill and Ulfstein, *Maritime Management* at 111–14.

101 Russell, 'International Ocean Boundary Issues' at 496. For further discussion of this boundary dispute see Rolston and McDorman, 'Maritime Boundary Making' at 48–9; D. Pharand, 'The Legal Regime of the Arctic: Some Outstanding Issues' (1984) 39 IntJ 742 at 753–4; K. L. Lawson, 'Delimiting Continental Shelf Boundaries in the Arctic: The United States–Canada Beaufort Sea Boundary' (1981) 22 VaJIL 221–46; Donald R. Rothwell, *Maritime Boundaries and Resource Development: Options for the Beaufort Sea* (Calgary, 1988).

102 See Russell, 'International Ocean Boundary Issues' at 495–6.

103 Elferink, 'The 1990 USA–USSR Maritime Boundary Agreement' at 43.

some modification.[104] However, the boundary established between Russia and the United States by the 1867 Treaty was interpreted as not providing for a maritime boundary. Rather, it was concluded that the original boundary was intended only as a means to divide ceded Russian territory from islands which remained under Russian control.[105] Nevertheless, the original 1867 boundary was relied upon as a basis for the new maritime boundary in the Bering and Chukchi Seas. This extends not only to the territorial sea, where applicable, but also the continental shelf and EEZ. The Agreement also specifies that all geographic positions along the boundary are connected by geodetic lines, except where otherwise noted,[106] and provides for a more precise determination of the exact location of the geographical coordinates of the original 1867 boundary. In addition, it is also provided that irrespective of a maritime area lying within 200 nautical miles of one state, the other state is recognised as being fully entitled to exercise continental shelf and EEZ rights on the basis of such a zone falling on that state's side of the boundary line.[107]

Russia–Norway: Barents Sea

Norway and Russia share a maritime boundary in the Barents Sea which is offshore to where their joint land boundaries terminate on the Kola Peninsula. A small portion of the maritime boundary was the subject of negotiation and agreement in 1957 in the area of the Varangerfjord.[108] However, beyond this region out into the Barents Sea proper, negotiations are still continuing. The principal area of dispute is over the use of a median line as a basis for the boundary. Norway relies upon such a line, asserting that this approach is in conformity with the 1958 Geneva Convention on the Continental Shelf (Continen-

[104] Note 87 above; for a comment on this Agreement, and other cooperative arrangements between the United States and the former Soviet Union in the Bering Sea region, see David Shakespeare, 'Recent US–USSR Agreements Relating to the Bering Region' (Fall 1991) 5 *Arctic Research of the United States* 37–47.

[105] Elferink, 'The 1990 USA–USSR Maritime Boundary Agreement' at 43.

[106] Bering Sea Maritime Boundary Agreement, Art. 2(3).

[107] See Elferink, 'The 1990 USSR–USA Maritime Boundary Agreement' at 45–6; for further background see Rolston and McDorman, 'Maritime Boundary Making' at 46–8; Pharand, 'Legal Regime of the Arctic' at 754–7.

[108] 1957 Agreement between the Royal Norwegian Government and the Government of the Union of the Soviet Socialist Republics concerning the Sea Frontier between Norway and the USSR in the Varangerfjord, 312 UNTS 322; and 1957 Descriptive Protocol relating to the Sea Frontier between Norway and the Union of the Soviet Socialist Republics in the Varangerfjord, demarcated in 1957, 312 UNTS 326.

tal Shelf Convention).[109] Russia and the former Soviet Union have argued that a median-line boundary is inappropriate because the geographical circumstances of the area constitute 'special circumstances' and because the Soviet Decree of 1926 asserted that Soviet maritime boundaries were to be delimited along a sector based on a line running north along 168°49′30″W.[110] Negotiations have been taking place over this boundary since 1967 and little progress has been made, apart from agreement over the establishment of a temporary fisheries zone in a so-called 'Grey Zone'.[111] This Agreement, concluded in 1978, covers a 26,000 square mile area, of which 8,900 square miles are undisputed Norwegian continental shelf and 1,200 square miles are on the Russian side of the sector line.[112] Recent events would seem to indicate that both parties are happy with the arrangements reached through this interim agreement, and there is no indication that pressure exists from either side to reach a final delimitation agreement.[113]

Svalbard

The maritime boundary issues that arise in relation to the Norwegian-controlled Archipelago of Svalbard are different from other boundary delimitations which exist in the Arctic because of the special legal regime provided for the islands under the 1920 Spitsbergen (Svalbard) Treaty. As has been noted above, the Treaty recognised Norwegian sovereignty in the islands but also provided that other Treaty parties were entitled to exercise economic rights over the islands in conjunction with those enjoyed by Norway. The terms of the Treaty are somewhat uncertain in regard to maritime areas adjacent to the islands. Article I recognises Norwegian sovereignty over the islands but makes no reference to adjacent maritime areas. This should not, however, be taken to mean that the Treaty did not seek to deal with

[109] 1958 Convention on the Continental Shelf, 499 UNTS 311 (hereinafter Continental Shelf Convention).

[110] Rolston and McDorman, 'Maritime Boundary Making' at 42–4; Churchill and Ulfstein, *Maritime Management* at 63, 70–80.

[111] 1978 Agreement on an Interim Practical Agreement for Fishing in an Adjoining Area in the Barents Sea, done on 11 January 1978. It appears that an English version of the Agreement has not been published; see Churchill and Ulfstein, *Marine Management* at 162, n. 24 who note the Norwegian source as [1978] *Overenskomster med fremmede Stater* 436.

[112] Churchill and Ulfstein, *Marine Management* at 65–7.

[113] See *ibid.* at 89–90; Jorgensen-Dahl, 'The Soviet–Norwegian Maritime Disputes' at 414–15; Theutenberg, 'The Arctic Law of the Sea' at 25–7;

maritime issues, as both Articles 2 and 3 refer to Norwegian rights to control activities in the territorial waters of the islands, subject always to equal treatment between all Treaty parties. The questions which have arisen in regard to Svalbard's maritime boundaries are whether the islands have a continental shelf and EEZ and, if they do, whether the provisions of the Treaty concerning Norway's obligation to share resource sovereignty applies to maritime zones beyond the territorial sea.[114] In 1970 Norway established a four nautical mile territorial sea around the islands and claimed at the time, and still maintains, that the Treaty's provisions only apply to the territorial sea and not to maritime zones beyond that. Under the Norwegian interpretation of the Treaty then, Norway is entitled to uncontested sovereignty over the Svalbard continental shelf and EEZ.[115] This position is contested by Russia (and previously by the USSR), the United States and the United Kingdom, who all argue that the 1920 Treaty was intended to extend to all maritime zones which surround Svalbard.[116] This dispute is unresolved, though Norway has been sensitive to the claims made by other Treaty parties. In 1977 Norway proclaimed a 200 nautical mile non-discriminatory fishery conservation zone around Svalbard, which while being seen as a concession to the claims of other Treaty parties and a retreat from its claim to an EEZ, has not been accepted by either Soviet and now Russian fishermen who operate in the area.[117] The resolution of this dispute would seem to be closely connected with the Russian–Norwegian boundary in the Barents Sea, with both states anxious to ensure that their own national interests are protected by any agreed resolution.[118]

Norway–Iceland: Jan Mayen

Jan Mayen is a volcanic island in the Iceland Sea north of Iceland. Norway is the recognised territorial sovereign over the island which has been used as a base over centuries by hunters, fishermen and

[114] Jorgensen-Dahl, 'The Soviet–Norwegian Maritime Disputes' at 412.

[115] Rolston and McDorman, 'Maritime Boundary Making' at 40.

[116] This view has been supported in a recent detailed analysis by Churchill and Ulfstein, *Marine Management* at 48–9.

[117] *Ibid.* at 51, 115–20; Jorgensen-Dahl, 'The Soviet–Norwegian Maritime Disputes' at 413; Rolston and McDorman, 'Maritime Boundary Making' at 41.

[118] See Robin Churchill, 'The Soviet Union and Jurisdiction Disputes in Northern Waters' in Clive Archer (ed.), *The Soviet Union and Northern Waters* (London, 1988) 44 at 53–8; Uwe Jenisch, 'The Maritime Policies and Practices of The Soviet Union after UNCLOS III, With Special Reference to Northern Waters' in Clive Archer (ed.), *The Soviet Union and Northern Waters* (London, 1988) 62 at 65–72.

scientific expeditions. Following the declaration of continental shelf and EEZ claims by both Norway and Iceland it became necessary to determine a maritime boundary between Jan Mayen and Iceland. Negotiations commenced to resolve the boundary in 1980 and while these successfully reached a determination on the extent of the respective EEZ and Fisheries Zone claims, the question of a continental shelf boundary remained unresolved. Accordingly the matter was sent to a Conciliation Commission which reported back to the two governments in 1981.[119] Under the terms of the negotiated agreement and the Commission's report, Iceland, because of its economic dependence upon fishery resources, received its full entitlement to a 200 nautical mile EEZ. In the case of the continental shelf it was recommended that the boundary follow that of the EEZ excepting for an area of the shelf which had the greatest resource potential, where it was recommended that a joint development zone be created.[120]

Iceland–Denmark–Norway: Iceland Sea/Greenland

There has also been a need to settle several maritime boundaries in the offshore areas of Greenland between Iceland, Jan Mayen and Svalbard. Accordingly these boundaries involve negotiations between Denmark (Greenland) and Iceland, and Denmark (Greenland) and Norway (Jan Mayen and Svalbard). In the case of the Denmark Strait between Greenland and Iceland, overlapping 200 nautical mile EEZs have been proclaimed off both islands, with the consequence that there is the need for a delimitation. Denmark favours the use of a median line boundary in accordance with the provisions of the Continental Shelf Convention.[121] However, the boundary remains the subject of continuing negotiation.

In the case of the Denmark–Norway boundaries between Greenland (Denmark) and Jan Mayen and Greenland and Svalbard (Norway), Denmark has taken note of the concessions Norway was prepared to make to Iceland in the Iceland–Jan Mayen EEZ delimitation and argued that given its dependence on fisheries it too is entitled to a full 200 nautical mile fisheries claim. Norway had rejected this argument in the past arguing that historical and economic circumstances do not

[119] See the report of the Commission, at (1981) 20 ILM 797.

[120] For a review see Rolston and McDorman, 'Maritime Boundary Making' at 32–7; R. R. Churchill, 'Maritime Delimitation in the Jan Mayen Area' (1985) 9 *Marine Policy* 16–38; Willy Ostreng, 'Delimitation Arrangements in Arctic Seas' (1986) 10 *Marine Policy* 132 at 137–40.

[121] Continental Shelf Convention, Art. 6.

warrant similar concessions to Denmark as those made to Iceland.[122] In 1988 Denmark filed an application with the International Court of Justice instituting proceedings against Norway with respect to the maritime boundary between Greenland and Jan Mayen.[123] Each state made submissions regarding where the boundary should be drawn. Denmark argued that Greenland was entitled to a full 200 nautical mile fishery zone and continental shelf and that because Jan Mayen was an island it should not be regarded as entitled to generate zones of the same extent. Norway argued that a median line boundary should be adopted, consistent with the provisions of the 1958 Continental Shelf Convention to which both states were parties.

In handing down its judgment on this matter in 1993 the Court accepted the argument of neither state.[124] Instead, it ruled that the delimitation line was to lie between the median line and the 200-mile line drawn from eastern Greenland's baselines.[125] To ensure equitable access to fishery resources within that area, three zones were created. Zone 1 was divided evenly between each party, while Zones 2 and 3 were divided in such a fashion that Norway received approximately two-thirds of each area.[126] Despite the substantial differences in the population of Greenland and Jan Mayen,[127] and their political status in relation to Denmark and Norway respectively, the Court concluded that there was no need to take Jan Mayen's limited population or socio-economic factors into account in this instance.[128] The Court also rejected arguments that Norway's concessions in favour of Iceland in the delimitation of the boundary between Iceland and Jan Mayen represented a precedent for this particular case.[129]

[122] For discussion see Rolston and McDorman, 'Maritime Boundary Making' at 37–9. For a review of the maritime issues which exist around Svalbard and the significance of the Treaty of Spitsbergen, see Willy Ostreng, 'Soviet-Norwegian Relations in the Arctic' (1984) 39 IntJ 866 at 875–82.

[123] Application Instituting Proceedings filed in the Registry of the Court, 16 August 1988, Maritime Boundary in the Area between Greenland and Jan Mayen (Denmark and Norway), Danish Application (English text), p. 4 asking the court to decide 'in accordance with international law, where a single line of demarcation shall be drawn between Denmark's and Norway's fishing zones and continental shelf areas in the waters between Greenland and Jan Mayen'. For comment see David Freestone, 'Maritime Boundary in the Area Between Greenland and Jan Mayen (Denmark v. Norway)' (1989) 4 IJECL 67–70.

[124] Note 97 above. [125] *Ibid.* at 79. [126] *Ibid.* at 79–81.

[127] Greenland's total population was 55,000 (of which 6 per cent live in East Greenland), while Jan Mayen has no settled population and is inhabited by approximately twenty-five persons engaged in scientific work: *ibid.* at 46. [128] *Ibid.* at 74.

[129] *Ibid.* at 75–7.

Denmark–Canada: Davis Strait/Greenland

In 1973 Canada and Denmark reached agreement over the delimitation of the continental shelf between Greenland and Baffin and Ellesmere Islands through Davis Strait, Baffin Bay and Nares Strait.[130] The Agreement is significant in that it is the first Arctic maritime boundary delimitation that was agreed upon during the era of extended coastal state maritime zones. The boundary is approximately 1,500 miles in length and is principally based on an equidistance line with certain adjustments due to islands and the geographical configuration of the coast. There are two interesting aspects of the boundary. First, it does not apply to the maritime area surrounding Hans Island, an uninhabited island in Nares Strait which is jointly claimed by both Canada and Denmark. Second, the boundary only extends as far north as 82°13′ North with the consequence that the boundary in the Lincoln Sea remains unsettled. However, this sea is virtually frozen year round and its resource potential is not considered significant. A further interesting aspect of this boundary is that Article III of the Agreement provides that neither party will issue licences for the exploitation of minerals immediately adjacent to the boundary because of perceived inadequacies in the exact drawing of the boundary.[131]

Law of the sea

As has been noted above, any review of the Arctic legal regime very quickly becomes dominated by an analysis of the international law of the sea as it applies to the Arctic Ocean. Consideration will now be given to the law of the sea particularly looking at the extension of maritime zones, Arctic shipping, rights of passage through the Northwest Passage and the Northeast Passage, and marine pollution.[132]

Arctic baselines

The international law of baselines

Under the law of the sea coastal states are *prima facie* required to delimit their offshore maritime zones using the low-water mark along

[130] 1974 Agreement between the Government of Canada and the Government of the Kingdom of Denmark Relating to the Delimitation of the Continental Shelf between Greenland and Canada, [1974] CTS 9.

[131] See Rolston and McDorman, 'Maritime Boundary Making' at 28–32; Russell, 'International Ocean Boundary Issues' at 489–93.

[132] Other law of the sea issues which arise in the Arctic will be considered in chapter 7.

their coastline as a basepoint.[133] Determining the low-water mark around most Arctic coastlines is not a major problem. This is because most Arctic coastlines are ice-free for portions of the year and in instances where the coastline is ice-bound, such as some far northern islands of the Canadian Arctic Archipelago, the northern Greenland coast, and the Franz Joseph Archipelago, it is easy to distinguish between land- and sea-ice.[134] A low-water mark basepoint can be abandoned when a variety of geographic features in the immediate offshore area or the coastline itself have the effect of distorting the coastline so that the use of the low-water mark is no longer appropriate. Well-recognised examples of this are bays, river mouths and deltas, and low-tide elevations which are adjacent to the coastline.[135] In these instances, baselines are drawn along the coast, or connect offshore islands, so as to create a starting point for offshore maritime zones which is beyond the normal low-water mark.

This practice was first sanctioned in the *Anglo-Norwegian Fisheries Case*,[136] where the International Court of Justice recognised that in instances where the coastline of a coastal state is deeply indented or where there is a cluster of offshore fringing islands, baselines can be drawn in such a way so that the outer points of these geographic features may be connected.[137] However, by way of a caveat the Court noted that while the drawn baselines must be adapted to practical needs they 'must not depart to any appreciable extent from the general direction of the coast'.[138] This decision was recognised and adopted in the 1958 Geneva Convention on the Territorial Sea and Contiguous Zone (Territorial Sea Convention)[139] and similarly in

[133] 1958 Convention on the Territorial Sea and Contiguous Zone, 516 UNTS 205 (hereinafter TSCZ), Art. 3; UNCLOS, Art. 5.

[134] This is to be distinguished from the position in Antarctica where ice shelves are subject to calving, thereby constantly changing the outer limits of the 'low-water mark'. See further discussion on this topic in chapter 7.

[135] See UNCLOS, Arts. 5, 7, 10 and 13.

[136] *United Kingdom* v. *Norway* [1951] ICJ Reports 116 (hereinafter *Anglo-Norwegian Fisheries Case*).

[137] Factors which the Court relied upon in this finding were that there be a close link between the land and adjacent sea, and that economic interests in the adjacent sea area be evidenced by long usage. See the discussion in D. P. O'Connell, *The International Law of the Sea* (vol. I), I. A. Shearer (ed.) (Oxford, 1982) 204–6; Pharand, *Canada's Arctic Waters* at 135–8.

[138] *Anglo-Norwegian Fisheries Case*, at 133.

[139] TSCZ, Art. 4.

UNCLOS.[140] UNCLOS also provided that archipelagic baselines can be drawn so as to connect the islands of an archipelago.[141] However, these provisions do not apply to all geographic archipelagoes but only to 'a State constituted wholly by one or more archipelagoes and may include other islands'.[142]

A consequence of the drawing of baselines is that waters which fall landward of a baseline are considered to be 'internal waters' of the state over which complete sovereignty may be exercised. Not only then does the declaration of a baseline have the consequence of extending a coastal state's maritime jurisdiction further offshore, but it will also result in waters which may previously have been territorial waters, and accordingly subject to rights of passage, becoming internal waters of a state.

The issue of baselines in the Arctic is important because there exist a number of large offshore island groups north of the Canadian and Russian Arctic coastline. The impact of these provisions for Arctic states is that both Canada and Russia can, by relying upon principles of both customary international law and conventions, draw baselines around the outer limits of their offshore fringing islands. Through these actions, both states have extended their maritime jurisdiction and sovereignty in the Arctic.[143]

Canadian practice

Canada had up till 1964 relied upon traditional principles of maritime boundary delimitation with respect to the basepoints for its maritime zone. However, in that year the Territorial Sea and Fishing Zones Act[144] provided for the declaration of straight baselines. In response to this

[140] UNCLOS, Art. 7. As per the decision in the *Anglo-Norwegian Fisheries Case* UNCLOS, Art. 7(3) also provides that the baselines must not depart to an appreciable extent from the general direction of the coast, and that sea areas lying within the baselines must be sufficiently closely linked to the adjacent land so as to be subject to the regime of internal waters. It is also possible for economic interests to be taken into account under UNCLOS, Art. 7(5): for a discussion see O'Connell, *International Law of the Sea* at 206–18; R. R. Churchill and A. V. Lowe, *The Law of the Sea* (rev. ed.) (Manchester, 1988) 28–33.

[141] See UNCLOS, Pt IV, especially Art. 47 dealing with archipelagic baselines.

[142] UNCLOS, Art. 46. The effect of this definition is to exclude geographic archipelagoes which lie offshore a continental mainland such as the Canadian Arctic Archipelago and the Hawaiian Islands.

[143] Apart from the Norwegian claim to straight baselines along its outermost fringing islands, baseline claims by other Arctic states have not been controversial: see the discussion of practice by Norway, Denmark and the United States in Pharand, *Canada's Arctic Waters* at 147–52.

[144] Statutes of Canada, 1964, c. 22.

Act, two sets of straight baselines were promulgated: one in 1967 along the coasts of Labrador, Newfoundland and Nova Scotia; the other along the west coast of British Columbia.[145] Despite the precedent of the *Anglo-Norwegian Fisheries Case* and the urgings of various Canadian commentators, Canada did not declare any baselines around the outer limits of the Canadian Arctic Archipelago.[146] This position changed in 1985 when it was announced as a direct response to the voyage through the Northwest Passage by the USCGC *Polar Sea* that straight baselines would be proclaimed around the outer islands of the Canadian Arctic Archipelago.[147] This declaration, which took effect on 1 January 1986, had the effect of linking all the northernmost islands of the Archipelago, with the consequence that the waters of the Archipelago have now become internal waters of Canada.

There has been considerable academic debate over the validity of Canada's Arctic baselines.[148] However, as neither the Territorial Sea Convention nor UNCLOS provides precise limits for straight baselines, the only requirements that must be met are those convention-based rules noted above. Given these rules plus the authority of the *Anglo-Norwegian Fisheries Case*, it would seem that the Canadian claim to validity for the action taken is strong.[149] Unlike the rules in UNCLOS applying to archipelagic baselines, there are no limits on the length of baselines drawn from coastal states. Despite this, it is of interest to note that the baselines around the Canadian Arctic Archipelago are an average of 17 nautical miles with the longest being 99.5 nautical miles.[150] In comparison to the rules applying to archipelagic baselines the Canadian claim does not seem excessive. However, despite this conclusion, navigation regimes which were in existence prior to the proclamation of the baselines still have some standing under

[145] Pharand, *Canada's Arctic Waters* at 155; O'Connell, *International Law of the Sea* at 213–14.

[146] Reid, 'Canadian Claim' at 130–3; D. M. McRae, 'Arctic Waters and Canadian Sovereignty' (1983) 38 IntJ 476 at 482–9; Pharand, *Canada's Arctic Waters* at 330–2.

[147] Statement by the Minister for External Affairs, Joe Clark, Canada House of Commons Debates, vol. V, 10 September 1985, 6,464.

[148] See D. Pharand, 'Canada's Sovereignty over the Newly Enclosed Arctic Waters' (1987) 25 CYIL 325 at 328–35; J. B. McKinnon, 'Arctic Baselines: A Litore Usque Ad Litus' (1987) 66 CanBR 790 at 801–13.

[149] This view has been adopted by Pharand, 'Canada's Sovereignty' at 328–33; McKinnon, 'Arctic Baselines' at 809, 811; Mark Killas, 'The Legality of Canada's Claims to the Waters of the Arctic Archipelago' (1987) 19 Ottawa LR 95–136; *cf.* P. A. Kettuner, 'The Status of the Northwest Passage under International Law' (1990) 4 *Detroit College of Law Review* 929 at 986–9.

[150] Pharand, *Canada's Arctic Waters* at 162.

UNCLOS.[151] This is a matter of some importance in Canada because the baselines have enclosed the waters of the Northwest Passage.[152]

Russian practice

Russian practice with respect to Arctic baselines is founded on the law and policy of the former USSR. In 1971, Soviet legislation made provision for three types of basepoints: the lowest ebb tide, straight baselines joining appropriate points, and basepoints as established by international treaties.[153] Despite the existence of this legislation, no straight baselines were actually proclaimed until 1984.[154] In that year the USSR Council of Ministers approved geographic coordinates for the declaration of straight baselines along the Soviet coasts of the Pacific Ocean, Sea of Japan, Sea of Okhotsk and the Bering Sea, and in 1985 similar coordinates were approved for the Baltic and Black Seas and the northern Arctic Ocean.[155] The baselines, while generally consistent with the provisions found in UNCLOS, have been the object of protest by other states.[156]

With respect to those Soviet baselines which particularly affect the Arctic, baselines have been proclaimed around the offshore archipelagoes of Novaya Zemlya, Severnaya Zemlya and Novosibirskiye Ostrova. In the case of the first two, the baselines have also been drawn so as to link the islands with the adjacent mainland.[157] The consequence is that the waters of the straits between the islands and the mainland have now become internal waters and this is made clear in the Soviet Decree of 1985.[158] In this respect the Soviet practice mirrors that of Canada.[159] The lengths of the baselines linking the islands of the archipelagoes with the mainland vary from 31 to 60.1 miles.[160] The most northern of Russia's archipelagoes, Zemlya Frantsa Iosifa, also

151 See UNCLOS, Art. 8(2).

152 This matter is considered further at pp. 196–200 below.

153 W. E. Butler, 'New Soviet Legislation on Straight Baselines' (1971) 20 ICLQ 750–2.

154 W. E. Butler, 'The Legal Regime of the Soviet Arctic Marine Areas' in Lawson W. Brigham (ed.), *The Soviet Maritime Arctic* (London, 1991) 215 at 216–17.

155 *Ibid.* at 217; Franckx, *Maritime Claims* at 181–6.

156 Butler, 'The Legal Regime' at 218; D. Brubaker, 'International Law and Russian Arctic Waters' (1992) 12 *International Challenges* 97 at 102; both authors noted that these protests had not been published.

157 Pharand, *Canada's Arctic Waters* at 153; E. Franckx, 'Non-Soviet Shipping in the Northeast Passage, and the Legal Status of Proliv Vil'kitskogo' (1988) 24 *Polar Record* 269 at 274.

158 Pharand, *Canada's Arctic Waters* at 153; Franckx, *Maritime Claims* at 181.

159 Kolodkin and Volosov, 'The Legal Regime' at 167.

160 Pharand, *Canada's Arctic Waters* at 153; Franckx, *Maritime Claims* at 181–5.

known as Franz Joseph Land, is also a potential site for the drawing of straight baselines. However, it is too far distant from the mainland to be connected under the principles provided for in UNCLOS.[161] The practice of the former Soviet Union then with respect to the drawing of baselines around archipelagoes adjacent to its Arctic fronting mainland and connecting those baselines with the mainland has been to impact upon navigation rights in the straits between these islands and the mainland and as a result to raise concerns over the status of the Northeast Passage.[162] This matter will be considered in greater detail below.

Arctic shipping and rights of passage

Because of the ice-covered nature of much of the Arctic Ocean, issues concerning Arctic shipping relate particularly to the waters adjacent to continental coastlines which during certain times of the year are free from ice and are suitable for navigation. This does not mean that the ice-covered waters of the Arctic are completely unsuitable for navigation. It has long been thought that specially built ice-breakers would be capable of navigating through Arctic ice and that there is the potential for the development of a sea route crossing the Arctic Ocean. In 1977, the Soviet nuclear-powered ice-breaker *Arktika* proved the potential of ice-breakers when it became the first surface vessel to reach the geographic North Pole.[163] There has also been a long history of submarine navigation of Arctic waters in the post-World War II era with both the United States and the Soviet Union using Arctic waters as a region for the strategic deployment of nuclear-powered submarines.[164] However, the main focus here is the operational potential of traditional cargo-carrying commercial vessels in Arctic waters which means, if the northern reaches of the North Sea are excluded, the

[161] Because of the need to delimit a maritime boundary between Norway (Svalbard) and Russia in the Barents Sea, the baselines around this archipelago have yet to be drawn because of the potential impact they may have upon the eventual boundary that is negotiated: see Pharand, *Canada's Arctic Waters* at 153.

[162] For further analysis, see Franckx, *Maritime Claims* at 192–3.

[163] Butler, *Northern Arctic Passage* at 61. A similar voyage was repeated by the *Sibir'* in 1987: see I. Frolov, 'The 1987 Expedition of the Icebreaker *Sibir'* to the North Pole' in Lawson W. Brigham (ed.), *The Soviet Maritime Arctic* (London, 1991) 33–44.

[164] For general discussion of the strategic significance of Arctic waters see O. Tunander, *Cold Water Politics* (London, 1989); Osherenko and Young, *The Age of the Arctic* at 17–44. For a specific discussion on the deployment of submarines in the Arctic see W. H. Critchley, 'Polar Deployment of Soviet Submarines' (1984) 39 IntJ 828–65.

potential for commercial shipping to use either the Northwest Passage or the Northeast Passage.[165]

Before considering in detail the navigational issues which have arisen in both the Northwest and Northeast Passages, it is helpful to consider basic law of the sea provisions dealing with navigation rights. A review of the history of the law of the sea demonstrates a tension between the rights of coastal states progressively to assert more extensive offshore sovereignty and jurisdiction and the rights of maritime states to enjoy freedom of navigation. Maintaining the notion of *mare liberum* – the freedom of the seas – publicists such as Grotius contended that the oceans were not subject to national appropriation and that vessels enjoyed a complete and absolute freedom of the seas.[166] Throughout much of the twentieth century, however, the notion of the freedom of the seas has been eroded by the extension of coastal state sovereignty and jurisdiction. This has had a particular effect upon navigation rights in the territorial sea and straits. One area in which UNCLOS definitively determined the law of the sea was in regard to the breadth of the territorial sea. While prior to and during the negotiation of UNCLOS there had been a range of state practice supporting maritime zones from 3 to 200 nautical miles in breadth, the Convention determined that 12 nautical miles would become the confirmed standard[167] and by and large this has been adhered to. As the sovereignty of a coastal state extends to the territorial sea, foreign-flagged vessels have no right to enter that maritime zone except when exercising their right of innocent passage. Innocent passage has become a well-recognised limitation upon the sovereignty of a coastal state over its territorial sea and more detailed rules for its application were progressively implemented in the Territorial Sea Convention[168] and in UNCLOS.[169]

Straits have presented another particular problem because of their great significance as corridors through which international maritime traffic passes. Especially following the acceptance of a twelve nautical mile territorial sea, they have increasingly become enclosed by the territorial sea of adjacent coastal states. The importance of ensuring a navigation regime which allowed for the continuous passage of vessels

[165] Arctic waters have been used for other purposes, such as cruises by tourist vessels to the North Pole. This occurred in 1990 when the Soviet ice-breaker *Rossiya* took a party of tourists to the Pole: see Terence E. Armstrong, 'Tourists Visit the North Pole, 1990' (1991) 27 *Polar Record* 130.

[166] For a review of this debate see O'Connell, *International Law of the Sea* at 1–18.

[167] UNCLOS, Art. 3.

[168] TSCZ, Arts. 14–17.

[169] UNCLOS, Arts. 17–26.

through straits with the minimum of interference was recognised in Article 16(4) of the Territorial Sea Convention which provided that innocent passage of foreign vessels through 'straits which are used for international navigation' could not be suspended. This provision substantially adopted the ruling of the International Court of Justice in the *Corfu Channel Case*[170] where it was held that British warships had a right to peaceful navigation through the waters of the Corfu Channel during times of peace.[171] UNCLOS has taken the regime of passage through international straits a step further by providing for a special regime of transit passage in Part III. These provisions essentially allow international shipping to pass through straits with the minimum of interference provided that activities which may substantially impact upon the sovereign integrity and interests of the coastal state are not engaged in. The right of transit passage is to be enjoyed through 'straits which are used for international navigation between one part of the high seas or an exclusive economic zone and another part of the high seas or an exclusive economic zone'.[172] It is the status of the Northwest and Northeast Passages as 'straits used for international navigation' which has become pivotal in the debate as to whether foreign-flagged vessels have rights of passage through these waters. The matter will now be considered in some detail.

International straits in the Arctic

The central issues with respect to navigation through straits in the Arctic region are whether any of the straits can be considered 'international' – in the sense that term was used in the *Corfu Channel Case* – and to what extent the principal criterion is the volume of usage of the strait. As to the status of this criterion, Bruel argued in 1947 that the importance of the strait to international sea commerce was the decisive factor.[173] However, in the *Corfu Channel Case* the International Court of Justice adopted a different approach. The Court preferred to place importance upon the geographic qualities of the strait and was

[170] *United Kingdom* v. *Albania* [1949] ICJ Reports 3.

[171] *Ibid.* at 28, where it was stated:

> States in time of peace have a right to send their warships through straits used for international navigation between two parts of the high seas without the previous authorisation of a coastal State, provided that the passage is *innocent*. Unless otherwise prescribed in an international convention, there is no right for a coastal State to prohibit such passage through straits in time of peace.

[172] UNCLOS, Art. 37.

[173] E. Bruel, *International Straits* (vol. I) (Copenhagen, 1947) 42.

of the view that the amount of maritime traffic which had or was passing through the strait was only a subsidiary consideration. Nevertheless, the Court did refer to various figures on shipping movement through the strait and seemed to imply that if there were any requisite standard, it had been met in the case of the Corfu Channel.[174]

Unfortunately neither the text of the Territorial Sea Convention nor UNCLOS clarifies what this exact requirement is. Nandan and Anderson, both delegates at the Third United Nations Conference on the Law of the Sea, take the view that potential use is insufficient. They argue that there must be actual use, though it does not have to be 'regular or reach any predetermined level'.[175] Because efforts at the Conference to insert terms such as 'normally', 'customarily', or 'traditionally' into the text of 'straits used for international navigation' failed, they argue that any type of use may be relevant.[176] Tommy Koh, President of the Conference from 1981-82, agrees that potential use of a strait is not enough and that actual use is necessary.[177] Koh's argument is that because the UNCLOS provisions dealing with transit passage in international straits adopt the same interpretation of straits as used in the Territorial Sea Convention the consequence is that both a geographic and functional requirement must be met. However, because there is no clear definition of what the functional requirement is he believes that the approach used in the *Corfu Channel Case* still applies. Interpreting the decision as one in which the Court rejected the view that a certain volume of traffic was necessary, Koh argues that what UNCLOS requires is evidence 'that a strait is actually being used, the volume of such usage being irrelevant, for international navigation'.[178]

Pharand takes a different view of the functional requirement laid down in the *Corfu Channel Case* and has consistently argued that the Court required not only that a strait have a history of usage for

[174] [1949] ICJ Reports at 28–9.

[175] S. N. Nandan and D. H. Anderson, 'Straits Used for International Navigation: A Commentary on Part III of the United Nations Convention on the Law of the Sea 1982' (1989) 60 BYIL 159 at 169.

[176] *Ibid.* For a discussion of how this issue was dealt with at the Conference see also J. A. De Yturriaga, *Straits Used for International Navigation: A Spanish Perspective* (Dordrecht, 1991) 3–4.

[177] Tommy B. Koh, 'The Territorial Sea, Contiguous Zones, Straits and Archipelagoes Under the 1982 Convention on the Law of the Sea' (1987) 29 *Malaya Law Review* 163 at 178.

[178] *Ibid.* at 180.

international navigation, but also that the volume of the traffic should be important.[179] Consequently, while admitting that the Court did not give any exact indication as to the degree of use necessary,[180] Pharand has continually stated that the strait must be a 'useful route for international maritime traffic' at the very least.[181] For the purposes of applying this test, Pharand suggests that:

> The sufficiency of the use is determined mainly, but not exclusively, by reference to two factors: the number of ships using the strait and the number of flag states represented. Both of these figures should normally reach the order of magnitude shown to exist in the *Corfu Channel* case. There, the ships using the North Corfu Channel averaged 137 a month, during a twenty-one-month period, and represented seven flag states.[182]

Northwest Passage

As a shipping route, the Northwest Passage is in reality a series of connected passages through straits. From the east, it allows shipping to pass from the North Atlantic Ocean up Davis Strait between Canada and Greenland, through the Arctic Archipelago, to the Beaufort Sea and then to the Chukchi Sea and the Bering Strait into the North Pacific. Given the large number of islands which make up the Arctic Archipelago, there exist many potential shipping routes from east to west and west to east. The practical reality, however, is that because of the heavy ice which is found in these polar waters, and the shallow draught which exists in some of the straits, there are only a handful of viable combinations of straits and channels which can be used to make the complete crossing. According to Pharand, there are five possible routes, some with variations, which can be taken for the purpose of navigating the Passage.[183] Not all of these routes are suitable for all

[179] Pharand, 'Canada's Sovereignty' at 337; Pharand, *Canada's Arctic Waters* at 224.

[180] D. Pharand, 'The Northwest Passage in International Law' (1979) 17 CYIL 99 at 106–7.

[181] *Ibid.* at 107; Pharand, *Canada's Arctic Waters* at 224.

[182] Pharand, 'The Northwest Passage' at 107.

[183] Pharand, *Canada's Arctic Waters* at 187–201. The routes are as follows:

Route 1 From east to west runs through Davis Strait into Baffin Bay and then west into Lancaster Sound, Barrow Strait, Viscount Melville Sound, Prince of Wales Strait and then Amundsen Gulf. High seas corridors only exist in Lancaster Sound, Viscount Melville Sound and Amundsen Gulf.

Route 2 This route, commonly known as 'Parry Channel', substitutes McClure Strait for Prince of Wales Strait as described in Route 1. A high seas corridor exists through McClure Strait.

Route 3 This route follows Parry Channel till Barrow Strait where it heads south through Peel Sound, Franklin Strait, Larsen Sound, Victoria Strait,

vessels due to limitations caused by water depth and shoals. The polar conditions and presence of ice also impose severe limitations upon shipping so that even during the summer months some ice-breaking capacity will be required in order for a vessel to complete the passage.[184]

The status of the Northwest Passage had been relatively uncontroversial throughout much of this century. This was primarily due to the lack of interest shown in the use of the Passage as a navigation route across the top of the North American continent, plus the enormous difficulties associated with such navigation. It therefore came as something of a surprise when in 1969 Canada was faced with an unexpected foreign policy crisis that was seen directly to threaten its Arctic sovereignty. The catalyst for this crisis was the voyage by the *SS Manhattan* from the Beaufort Sea through the Northwest Passage to Davis Strait. The *Manhattan*, carrying a small cargo of oil, was intentionally sent through the Passage by its owners to demonstrate that an ice-breaking bulk carrier was capable of year-round sailings between Alaska and the east coast of the United States. The voyage was only the eleventh complete transit of the Northwest Passage, and the first since the end of World War II by a non-government vessel.[185] Though the voyage was innocent enough, it did have great implications in Canada due to the fact that the *Manhattan* passed through waters which were traditionally considered Canadian. Consequently, despite the fact that a representative of the Canadian Government was on board the tanker during the passage and that the Canadian Coast Guard vessel *J. A. Macdonald* accompanied the *Manhattan*,[186] the voyage created considerable public controversy in Canada.[187]

Queen Maud Gulf, Lease Strait, Coronation Gulf, Dolphin and Union Strait and finally Amundsen Gulf. Most of the route is through Canadian territorial sea.

Route 4 This is a variation of Route 3 in which vessels leave Lancaster Sound to pass to the east of Somerset Island through Prince Regent Inlet and then use Bellot Strait to rejoin Route 3 in Franklin Strait. A substantial high seas corridor only exists through Prince Regent Inlet.

Route 5 This route approaches Somerset Island through Hudson Strait, Foxe Basin, Fury and Hecla Strait and then through the Gulf of Boothia to Bellot Strait where it connects with Route 3. The only substantial areas of high seas in this route are in Foxe Basin and the Gulf of Boothia.

184 On the difficulties of navigation in the Passage see Pharand, 'The Northwest Passage' at 100–1.

185 For details of the voyage see T. C. Pullen, 'What Price Canadian Sovereignty?' (1987) 113(9) *Proceedings of the US Naval Institute* 66 at 69–71. 186 *Ibid.* at 71.

187 E. J. Dosman, *The National Interest: The Politics of Northern Development 1968–75* (Toronto,

Canada's difficulty in responding to the *Manhattan* voyage was that apart from the proclamation of a three-mile territorial sea around the islands of the Canadian Arctic Archipelago,[188] there had been no formal assertion of Canadian sovereignty over all the waters of the Passage or those surrounding the Archipelago.[189] The consequence was that, apart from where Canadian territorial waters overlapped in the narrow McClure Strait, the *Manhattan* was passing through high seas during its navigation of the Passage.[190] Despite statements by Prime Minister Trudeau and other government ministers that Canadian sovereignty over the Passage was unquestioned, there was no concrete response to the *Manhattan* voyage made by Canada.[191]

It was subsequently announced that the *Manhattan* would attempt a second crossing of the Northwest Passage in 1970.[192] This second voyage raised further public fears about the status of the Passage. The United States was perceived, rightly or wrongly, as ignoring Canadian sovereignty by these voyages through 'Canadian waters' and public pressure grew for the government to reaffirm Canada's Arctic sovereignty and take positive action to ensure that future voyages did not pose a threat to that sovereignty.[193] The Canadian response in 1970 involved three initiatives. The first was the enactment of the Arctic Waters Pollution Prevention Act,[194] which extended Canadian jurisdiction 100 nautical miles from the low-water mark so as to enforce certain pollution standards on vessels using Canada's Arctic waters. The Act applied to proclaimed 'Arctic waters' which extended 100 miles out into the Beaufort Sea and Arctic Ocean along the coastlines of the Yukon and Northwest Territories, including the islands of the

1975) 46–7. For more background on concerns relating to Canadian Arctic sovereignty in the late twentieth century see John Honderich, *Arctic Imperative: Is Canada Losing the North?* (Toronto, 1987); Nathaniel French Caldwell Jr, *Arctic Leverage: Canadian Sovereignty and Security* (New York, 1990).

188 Territorial Sea and Fishing Zones Act, SC 1964, c. 22.

189 See Bankes, 'Forty Years' at 285 where the distinction is made between territorial claims to the islands of the Arctic Archipelago, and claims to the waters within the Archipelago and navigation routes such as the Northwest Passage.

190 D. Pharand, *The Law of the Sea of the Arctic with Special Reference to Canada* (Ottawa, 1973) 57.

191 See Canada, House of Commons, Debates, Vol. VIII at 8,720 (15 May 1969).

192 The *Manhattan* was to be once again accompanied by the *J. A. Macdonald.*

193 Maxwell Cohen, 'The Arctic and the National Interest' (1970) 26 IntJ 52 at 67–8.

194 Arctic Waters Pollution Prevention Act, SC 1970, c. 47.

Arctic Archipelago.[195] Under this Act, pollution-control regulations, such as vessel construction standards, navigation and operation, would be imposed on all shipping passing through Canadian Arctic waters and failure to comply would result in passage by such vessels being prohibited.[196]

The second response was to extend the territorial sea from three to twelve nautical miles,[197] not only from the Canadian Arctic mainland but also the islands. This extension of the territorial sea resulted in a great deal of the Northwest Passage becoming enclosed within Canadian territorial sea so that any transit of the Passage would now see vessels coming more frequently under Canadian jurisdiction. The final step was to vary Canadian acceptance of the compulsory jurisdiction of the International Court of Justice in regard to matters dealing with Canada's jurisdiction in the Arctic.[198] The effect was to ensure that no challenge could be brought before the Court as to the validity in international law of the Arctic Waters Pollution Prevention Act without Canada accepting the Court's jurisdiction in the matter.[199]

In justifying its action, Canada relied upon the growing concern for ecological protection of the Arctic. It was argued that as international law had not at that time sufficiently developed measures to protect the area from the dangers of pollution it was appropriate for Canada to take unilateral action.[200] This approach was not, however, welcomed

[195] *Ibid.*, s. 3(2) defines 'Arctic waters' as being waters:

> adjacent to the mainland and islands of the Canadian Arctic within the area enclosed by the sixtieth parallel of the north latitude, the one hundred and forty-first meridian of longitude and a line measured seaward from the nearest Canadian land a distance of one hundred nautical miles.

[196] See Pharand, *The Law of the Sea* at 224–32; Reid, 'Canadian Claim' at 117–29.

[197] Act to amend the Territorial Sea and Fishing Zones Act, SC 1970, c. 48.

[198] Canadian Declaration Concerning the Compulsory Jurisdiction of the International Court of Justice, reprinted in (1970) 9 ILM 598.

[199] Mitchell Sharp, Canadian Minister for External Affairs, frankly admitted that Canada was 'not prepared to litigate with other states on vital issues concerning which the law is either inadequate, non-existent or irrelevant to the kind of situation Canada faces, as in the case of the Arctic', Canada, House of Commons, Debates, vol. VI at 5,952 (16 April 1970).

[200] P. E. Trudeau, 'Canadian Prime Minister's Remarks on the Proposed Legislation' (1970) 9 ILM 600 at 601 where it is noted:

> we're saying somebody has to preserve this area for mankind until international law develops. And we are prepared to help it develop by taking steps on our own and eventually, if there is a conference of nations concerned with the Arctic, we will of course be a very active member in such a conference and try to establish an international regime. But, in the meantime, we had to act now.

in the United States. The Department of State responded that: 'International law provides no basis for these proposed unilateral extensions of jurisdiction on the high seas, and the United States can neither accept nor acquiesce in the assertion of such jurisdiction.'[201] Particular concern was also raised as to the impact of these measures upon the freedom of navigation.[202]

Controversy arose again over the status of the Northwest Passage in 1985 when it was announced that the United States ice-breaker *Polar Sea* would sail through the Passage from east to west.[203] The United States informed Canada of the planned voyage, but did not seek official permission. Two Canadian Coast Guard captains accompanied the *Polar Sea* as 'invited observers'. However, no attempt was made by either Canada or the United States to interpret this as official 'permission' being granted for the voyage.[204] Despite calls for Canada to issue a formal protest over the voyage, the Canadian Minister for External Affairs, Joe Clark, stated that the voyage 'does not compromise in any way the sovereignty of Canada over our northern waters, or affect the quite legitimate differences of views that exist between Canada and the United States on that question'.[205]

Following a review of Canadian Arctic policy,[206] the Minister for External Affairs, Joe Clark, on 19 September 1985 made a comprehensive statement on Canadian Arctic sovereignty to Parliament. This became the most definitive statement to date on Canadian policy over

[201] J. A. Beesley and C. B. Bourne (eds.), 'Canadian Practice in International Law during 1970 as Reflected Mainly in Public Correspondence and Statements of the Department of External Affairs' (1971) 9 CYIL 288.

[202] *Ibid.* at 287–8. For further discussion on the development of Canada's response to the *Manhattan* see Reid, 'Canadian Claim' at 117–26; and for comment on the status of the Passage at this time W. C. Reinhard, 'International Law: Implications of the Opening of the Northwest Passage' (1970) 74 *Dickinson Law Review* 678; J. A. Beesley, 'Rights and Responsibilities of Arctic Coastal States: The Canadian View' (1971) 3 JMLC 1. For further evidence of Canadian practice following the *Manhattan* voyage, see: 'Canadian Practice in International Law during 1973 as Reflected Mainly in Public Correspondence and Statements of the Department of External Affairs' (1974) 12 CYIL 279; 'Canadian Practice in International Law during 1980 as Reflected Mainly in Public Correspondence and Statements of the Department of External Affairs' (1981) 19 CYIL 320 at 322.

[203] Pullen, 'What Price Canadian Sovereignty?' at 71.

[204] 'USA: Arctic Sovereignty' (June/July 1985) *International Canada* 1.

[205] Canada, House of Commons, Debates, vol. IV at 6,043 (20 June 1985).

[206] 'Canada to Launch Sovereignty Review', *The [Toronto] Globe and Mail*, 2 August 1985, 1. Further government committees have subsequently considered the question of Canadian Arctic sovereignty: see Report of the Special Joint Committee of the Senate and of the House of Commons on Canada's International Relations, *Independence and Internationalism* (1986) 127–35.

the waters of the Northwest Passage and the Arctic Archipelago. In the statement, it was noted that: 'The policy of the Government is to exercise full sovereignty in and on the waters of the Arctic Archipelago and this applies to the airspace above as well. We will accept no substitute.'[207] The statement included six major policy initiatives. They were:

(1) the establishment of straight baselines around the Canadian Arctic Archipelago, effective from 1 January 1986;
(2) the adoption of new legislation to enforce Canadian civil and criminal laws in the offshore areas enclosed by the straight baselines;
(3) talks with the United States on cooperation in Arctic waters on the basis of full respect for Canadian sovereignty;
(4) increased aircraft surveillance and naval activity in the eastern Arctic;
(5) the withdrawal of Canada's reservation to the International Court of Justice; and
(6) the construction of a Polar Class 8 ice-breaker to operate in the enclosed waters and a review of the other means available through which effective control could be exercised over Canadian Arctic waters.[208]

The effect of the Clark statement was for the first time to remove all doubts about Canada's intentions in the Arctic and to clarify Canada's legal position over the region.[209] By the proclamation of straight baselines around the Arctic Archipelago, Canada had declared all the waters that fell within the baselines 'internal waters' of Canada over which it now claimed complete sovereignty and jurisdiction. The measures which accompanied the proclamation of the baselines were also designed to ensure that the Canadian action was not hollow and that it would be supported by positive evidence of Canadian sovereignty and jurisdiction over the waters.

[207] Canada, House of Commons, Debates, vol. V at 6,463 (10 September 1985). For an analysis of this initiative in Canadian polar policy, see Rob Huebert, 'Polar Vision or Tunnel Vision: The Making of Canadian Arctic Waters Policy' (1995) 19 *Marine Policy* 343–63.

[208] *Ibid.* at 6,464; this statement also initiated a review of other aspects of Canada's Arctic policies: see G. Graham, 'An Arctic Foreign Policy for Canada' (March/April 1987) *International Perspectives* 11.

[209] However, as was noted by W. Harriet Critchley, 'The Arctic' (1987) 42 IntJ 769 at 774: 'the original cause for such action was official embarrassment over Canada's lack of capability to enforce its sovereignty in the face of even an oblique challenge by a close friend and ally.'

Any analysis of the Northwest Passage's status in regard to international navigation must begin with asking whether it is possible to equate the Passage with a single strait. The Northwest Passage is a series of connecting straits which when combined offer a variety of navigation routes through the Canadian Arctic Archipelago. This is unlike the situation that is covered by both customary international law and the Conventions, which provide only for a regime based on passage through an 'international strait' and not a series of straits. There is no evidence that much consideration has been given to this question in the past, though it should be noted that UNCLOS created new provisions dealing with navigation within the waters of an archipelagic state.[210] While there is no suggestion that this particular regime applies to the waters under consideration here,[211] there has been some debate over whether, for the purposes of implementing provisions respecting freedom of navigation through straits which connect areas of high seas or EEZ, the straits which make up such a navigation route through an archipelago should be looked at in isolation or as a whole.[212] Irrespective of which approach is taken here, the 'straits' which make up the Northwest Passage are certainly 'geographic straits' consistent with the way in which this term has been interpreted.[213] They also connect areas of high seas and EEZ.[214] The Northwest Passage under either of these approaches therefore meets the geographic requirement of an international strait, or series of straits, as found in the *Corfu Channel Case*, the Territorial Sea Convention and UNCLOS.[215]

As to the principal requirement, that the strait actually be used for

[210] See the regime of Archipelagic States adopted in UNCLOS, Pt IV.

[211] It was never intended that the provisions of Pt IV of UNCLOS apply in the case of offshore archipelagoes such as those of Canada and the United States (Hawaii): see UNCLOS, Art. 46.

[212] See K. L. Koh, *Straits in International Navigation* (London, 1982) 18.

[213] On the question of the geographic conception of a strait, see Bruel, *International Straits* at 17–20; De Yturriaga, *Straits Used for International Navigation* at 4–6.

[214] If one views the Passage as a series of interconnecting straits which are so substantially related as to form one long strait, then clearly the Passage connects the waters of the Beaufort Sea and the North Atlantic Ocean; if on the other hand the straits are viewed in isolation they connect isolated patches of high seas corridors, which in the case of the Viscount Melville Sound, Amundsen Gulf, the Gulf of Boothia and Foxe Basin are substantial bodies of water.

[215] This conclusion has also been reached by other commentators: see McKinnon, 'Arctic Baselines' at 816; Pharand, *Canada's Arctic Waters* at 223–4; also D. Pharand, 'Sovereignty in the Arctic: The International Legal Context', in Edgar J. Dosman (ed.), *Sovereignty and Security in the Arctic* (London, 1989) 145 at 153–4.

international navigation, it has already been noted that there has been considerable debate over the status of this requirement and how it is to be applied. Whether the criterion is fulfilled in the case of the Northwest Passage is another difficult question. If the functional test for passage through a strait is applied to the Northwest Passage it would not be possible to classify it as a 'strait used for international navigation' because of the low number of recorded transits.[216] However, because of the presence of ice which makes it physically impossible for most conventional shipping to use many of the straits in the Passage not only during the winter but also the summer, should a special polar standard be applied in the case of straits such as the Northwest Passage? Pharand has conceded that allowances should be made in such cases and that a 'brief history of transporting oil and gas by a few flag states' may be sufficient.[217] A similar view has been taken by Butler who favours a broad interpretation of the functional requirement in the case of the polar regions. He argues that not only will patterns of world commerce impact upon the usage of particular straits, but in the case of the polar regions:

> the very possibility of Arctic navigation is the direct consequence of impressive achievements in vessel design, icebreaking methods, greater knowledge of the polar environment, weather forecasting, human fortitude, and the like.[218]

Also relevant is the actual number of transits which have taken place,[219] and the percentage completed by non-Canadian flagged vessels.[220]

How should this functional criterion then be applied in the case of

[216] See Pharand, *Canada's Arctic Waters* at 202–14.

[217] Pharand, 'The Northwest Passage' at 114.

[218] Butler, *Northeast Arctic Passage* at 135.

[219] From the time of the very first transit of the Passage in 1903–6 by Amundsen until 1988 there had been fifty-six complete transits: see D. Pharand, 'Canada's Sovereignty over the Northwest Passage' (1989) 10 *Michigan Journal of International Law* 653, 676–8; *cf*. T. C. Pullen and C. Swithinbank, 'Transits of the Northwest Passage, 1906–1990' (1991) 27 *Polar Record* 365–7, who for the period 1906–90 noted fifty transits; however, it seems that this figure did not include return journeys by the same vessel during the same season; neither sets of figures include instances of submarine navigation of the Passage which, though strongly suspected, have not been documented. There have been no further published figures on transit through the Northwest Passage since those noted above.

[220] In the period 1903–88, Pullen and Swithinbank, 'Transits of the Northwest Passage' at 365–7 recorded twenty-three transits by foreign vessels of which fifteen were by United States-flagged vessels.

the Northwest Passage? Relying upon the actual degree of usage of the Northwest Passage since the first successful navigation, Pharand maintains that the Passage is not an international strait.[221] He argues that those who contend otherwise have confused potential use with actual use and that mere capacity is not what is required but rather actual use.[222] The few examples of crossings by foreign-flagged vessels are not considered by Pharand to alter this assessment, especially as he points out that none were made for commercial navigation.[223] Other Canadian-based commentators have also adopted a similar view.[224]

Irrespective of whether the customary international law recognised in the *Corfu Channel Case* or the provisions of the Convention on the Territorial Sea or UNCLOS apply, there is room for considerable difference of opinion on this question. Certainly the amount of traffic through the Northwest Passage is not comparable to that of the Corfu Channel, or of other commonly accepted international straits. However, different standards must apply in the polar regions,[225] with the consequence that when the presence of ice in the waters of the Passage and polar weather are taken into account, a lower volume of international navigation than normally required would be sufficient to establish the Passage as an international strait.[226]

Nonetheless, upon applying the functional criterion to the Northwest Passage one is struck by the very low number of transits that have occurred since it was first discovered. Most international navigation

[221] Pharand, 'Canada's Sovereignty' at 669–70; Pharand, *Canada's Arctic Waters* at 225; Pharand, 'The Northwest Passage' at 112–13.

[222] Pharand, *Canada's Arctic Waters* at 225; Pharand, 'The Northwest Passage' at 113.

[223] Pharand, *Canada's Arctic Waters* at 112–13.

[224] T. L. McDorman, 'In the Wake of the Polar Sea: Canadian Jurisdiction and the Northwest Passage' (1986) 10 *Marine Policy* 243 at 251, notes that: 'The amount of known traffic through the Northwest Passage has been insignificant'; McKinnon, 'Arctic Baselines' at 816 argues that: 'The Northwest Passage, however, does not meet the second, or functional criterion since it has not been sufficiently used for international navigation'; McRae 'Arctic Waters' at 488 argues that: 'The lack of use of the Northwest Passage for international shipping has prevented it from achieving the status of an international strait'; see also R. R. Roth, 'Sovereignty and Jurisdiction over Arctic Waters' (1990) 28 *Alberta Law Review* 845 at 864; Kettuner, 'The Status of the Northwest Passage' at 979.

[225] See *Legal Status of Eastern Greenland* (*Norway* v. *Denmark*) (1933) PCIJ Reports, Ser. A/B, No. 53, at 46; Pharand, 'The Northwest Passage' at 114.

[226] One commentator has even suggested that the functional criterion is so inexact as to be meaningless and that perhaps one foreign-flagged vessel per decade would suffice to evidence international navigation: see L. M. Alexander, 'Exceptions to the Transit Passage Regime: Straits with Routes of "Similar Convenience"' (1987) 18 ODIL 479 at 480, n. 3.

since 1945 has also been by government vessels, although there is no settled view as to whether navigation by commercial vessels is essential to constitute 'international navigation'. The Court in the *Corfu Channel Case* did take note of how often the British navy had used the channel. Accordingly, voyages by various United States Coast Guard vessels can be taken to represent evidence of international navigation through the Passage. Whether, taking into account the *Corfu Channel* test, the views of various commentators, and making allowance for polar conditions, there has been a sufficient number of transits by ships engaged in international navigation through the Passage to meet the functional criterion is difficult to determine. There is evidence of increasing usage of the Passage, with twenty-three transits, eight by non-Canadian-flagged vessels, having been recorded during the 1980s.[227] Nevertheless, without further judicial guidance on the question of international straits it is extremely difficult to determine conclusively whether the Passage is or is not an international strait.[228]

Northeast Passage

The Northeast Passage, rather than being a continuous passage between islands and a continental mainland, is in reality a sea route. It runs from the far northern reaches of the North Sea across the frozen waters of the Arctic Ocean north of Russia east to the Chukchi Sea and the Bering Straits from which access can be gained to the North Pacific Ocean. For a voyage being undertaken from Norway to Alaska, the jurisdictional issues only arise in relation to that portion which runs directly to the north of the Russian mainland or between the mainland and offshore islands, all of which are claimed by Russia. The Passage runs to the north of Russia through the Barents, Kara, Laptev, East Siberian and Chukchi Seas.[229] Butler has identified fourteen straits in the Passage which can be classified as connecting two areas of Arctic seas, of which only five could be considered to have high seas corridors following the declaration by the Soviet Union of a twelve nautical mile

[227] Pharand, 'Canada's Sovereignty' at 677–8; Pullen and Swithinbank, 'Transits of the Northwest Passage' also recorded twenty-three transits up till 1990, eleven by foreign-flagged vessels, five of which were United States flagged.

[228] For further consideration of this question see Donald R. Rothwell, 'The Canadian–US Northwest Passage Dispute: A Reassessment' (1993) 26 Cornell ILJ 331–72.

[229] For a description see Butler, *Northeast Arctic Passage* at 5–41. Passages through the straits connecting the Barents and Kara Seas, Kara and Laptev Seas, and the Laptev and East Siberian Seas particularly raise questions as to the extent of Russian jurisdiction over the waters of the straits.

territorial sea.[230] In addition, there are also forty-four other straits which exist within the various seas and in the vicinity of the Northeast Passage which vessels may have occasion to use. These straits are all very narrow with only one, the Gore Strait in the White Sea, having a minimum width in excess of twenty-four nautical miles.[231]

The Northern Sea Route (NSR) is a dedicated Russian (previously Soviet) sea route. It was developed by the Soviet government in the 1930s with the aim of providing safe navigation for Soviet vessels between the White Sea and Bering Strait.[232] With shipping lanes leading to and from mainland ports, the NSR operates along much of the same route as the Northeast Passage. The course of the NSR was recently defined in 1990 *Regulations for Navigation of the Seaways of the Northern Sea Route*. It is:

> the essential national transportation line of the USSR that is situated within its inland seas, territorial sea (territorial waters), or exclusive economic zone adjacent to the USSR Northern Coast and includes seaways suitable for leading ships in ice, the extreme points of which are limited in the west by the W(estern) entrances to the Novaya Zemlya Straits and the meridian running north through Mys Zhelaniya, and in the east (in the Bering Strait) by the parallel 66°N and the meridian 168°58′37″W.[233]

The importance of the NSR for Russia and the previous Soviet Union should not be underestimated. It played a vital role in developing an internal sea route along the northern coasts of Russia and Siberia so as to assist with the Soviet Union's economic restructuring before and after World War II. The route, which is some 5,610km in length, has been steadily improved and upgraded by various Soviet and Russian authorities.[234] There has throughout this time been a steady increase in the number of Soviet and Russian vessels using the NSR with the consequence that it is now one of the most significant commercial transport routes in Russia and the former Soviet republics.[235] To that end there has been a heavy investment in ice-breakers so as to engage

[230] *Ibid.* at 39; the minimum width of the Eterikan Strait was given as unknown.

[231] *Ibid.* at 40–1.

[232] D. A. Pharand, 'Innocent Passage in the Arctic' (1968) 6 CYIL 3 at 18.

[233] Section 1.2, reprinted in Franckx, *Maritime Claims*, Appendix 1, 315. For other descriptions of the route taken by the NSR see Pharand, 'Innocent Passage' at 22; Butler, *Northwest Arctic Passage* at 54–7; Willy Ostreng and Henning Simonsen, 'The Barents Region and the Northern Sea Route' (1992) 12(4) *International Challenges* 95 at 99.

[234] E. Franckx, 'New Developments in the North-east Passage' (1991) 6 IJECL 33 at 33.

[235] Pharand, 'Innocent Passage' at 22 where it was noted that in 1968, 300 vessels of the USSR carried 1,000,000 tons of cargo a year through the NSR; Franckx, 'New Developments' at 35.

in ice-clearing operations along the NSR and also to escort cargo vessels in times of heavy ice.[236] The NSR should not, however, be characterised as an internal Russian waterway. As the 1990 *Regulations* indicated, Soviet authorities considered that the NSR could extend out to the EEZ.[237] For the purposes of this study then, the NSR can be equated with the Northeast Passage.

The question of whether the Northeast Passage is a potential route for navigation by foreign-flagged vessels has been a matter of some controversy. Much of the Northeast Passage passes through considerable areas of high sea – that is areas of the sea which are beyond the twelve nautical mile territorial sea limit of the adjacent littoral state. As a consequence, traditional freedoms of high seas passage apply in much of the Northeast Passage. However, this position is clouded by the uncertainty which rests over whether the previous Soviet Union, and now Russian, claim that the various seas which make up the Northeast Passage are either 'closed seas' or internal waters. The doctrine of closed seas, the basis of which can be found in debates between Grotius and Selden over the freedom and appropriation of the seas, found support amongst various Imperial Russian and Soviet jurists. They expressed the view that bodies of waters such as the Black Sea were closed because of their geographical configuration and geopolitical significance for the Imperial Russian and Soviet state.[238] However, despite rather extensive claims to certain 'Russian seas' there is no evidence that such a claim was ever actively asserted officially by either the Russian or Soviet government.[239]

[236] Butler, *Northeast Arctic Passage* at 57–61. For discussion as to its use see L. Brigham, 'Plying the Northern Sea Route' (1991) 1(4) *Arctic Circle* 10–11; Terence Armstrong, 'The Northern Sea Route, 1990' (1991) 27 *Polar Record* 136–8; A. I. Arikainen, 'Management of the Northern Sea Route: Stages and Problems of Development' in Lawson W. Brigham (ed.), *The Soviet Maritime Arctic* (London, 1991) 140–57; Terence Armstrong, 'The Northern Sea Route, 1991' (1992) 28 *Polar Record* 239–40. Ostreng and Simonsen, 'The Barents Region' at 95 note that discussions took place in October 1992 in which the importance of the NSR was highlighted as a transportation route for the Barents region; see also 100–5 for their assessment of the potential for greater Western use of the NSR.

[237] Franckx, *Maritime Claims* at 190 considered that it was possible for the 1990 *Regulations* in fact to apply beyond the 200 nautical mile EEZ. For further consideration of the status of the NSR see Leonid Timtchenko, 'The Legal Status of the Northern Sea Route' (1994) 30 *Polar Record* 193–200.

[238] W. E. Butler, *The Soviet Union and the Law of the Sea* (Baltimore, 1971) 116.

[239] *Ibid.* at 119. However, it should be noted that it had been recommended that the White and Kara Seas be closed to foreign vessels by a special interdepartmental commission in 1906–7.

Another basis of Russian and Soviet jurisdiction over its adjacent Arctic waters which has been asserted is that much of the route comprising the Northeast Passage is comprised of 'internal waters'. The status of such a claim does not seem to have significant official backing. Nevertheless, there were numerous Soviet jurists who asserted that certain of the Arctic oceans were internal waters of the USSR.[240] Butler maintains that the development of such claims began to crystallise after 1947 when the Soviet definition of internal waters was significantly broadened to include 'seas fully encircled by the territory of a single state or seas whose shores were connected with another sea, both of which belong to the same state'.[241] By 1958-9 the jurist Meshera had further expanded on this classification to include as internal waters 'historic bays and seas of the USSR as determined by special economic, security, or other vital interests'.[242] Such a categorisation would have included the Kara, Laptev and East Siberian Seas. However, a 1960 statute on the state boundaries of the USSR did not give such a wide ambit to 'Soviet internal waters' and it can be concluded then that while there was theoretical support for such a claim there was no similar official support.[243] Soviet legislation has also recognised in the past that seas and straits which 'historically belonged' to the USSR could be classified as internal waters.[244] This claim will be given further attention in due course. More significant for current purposes, however, is the claim that since the 1984–85 proclamation of baselines around the Soviet coastline and adjacent islands, those straits of the Northeast Passage which are now enclosed by such baselines are internal waters within which neither the right of innocent passage nor transit passage exists.[245] To that end, it is now necessary to examine past Soviet and Russian practice concerning rights of innocent passage and the rights of foreign-flagged shipping to pass through straits.

There is an extensive and continuous history throughout this century of both Imperial Russia and the Soviet Union asserting offshore jurisdiction over the adjacent sea out to a twelve nautical

[240] For a recent comprehensive review of these writings, see Franckx, *Maritime Claims* at 152–5, 168–75.

[241] Butler, *The Soviet Union* at 104.

[242] *Ibid*. at 106.

[243] *Ibid*. at 106–7; Pharand, 'Innocent Passage' at 35–6.

[244] Butler, 'The Legal Regime of the Soviet Arctic' at 218.

[245] A. L. Kolodkin, 'Remarks – Legal Regimes of the Arctic' (1988) 82 ProcAmSocIL 315 at 316, 334.

mile limit.[246] The assertion of a twelve nautical mile territorial sea was affirmed in the 1982 Law on the USSR State Boundary which, given the acceptance of the twelve nautical mile limit at UNCLOS, was uncontroversial.[247] What has, however, been the subject of some controversy regarding the assertion of Soviet and Russian sovereignty and jurisdiction in the territorial sea has been the interpretation of the right of innocent passage. In 1960 the Soviet Union adopted a new law entitled Statute on the Protection of the State Border of the USSR in which innocent passage by merchant vessels was specifically protected in conformity with the provisions of the Territorial Sea Convention. However, this same right did not extend to foreign warships.[248] Rather, consent was required prior to navigation taking place.[249]

The Soviet attitude to navigation through its adjacent Arctic waters was highlighted during a number of incidents in the 1960s. As part of its programme to assert the freedom of the seas, including the freedom to engage in marine scientific research, the United States during the 1960s sent a number of its vessels into the waters of the Arctic Ocean north of the then USSR. A series of voyages were undertaken between 1962 and 1964 by United States Coast Guard and United States naval vessels, during which marine scientific research was conducted. By and large these voyages passed without incident.[250] The voyage of the USCGC *Northwind* in the summer of 1965 was of more interest to the Soviet Union. The United States announced that the vessel intended to pass from the Kara Sea into the Laptev Sea via the Vilkitsky Straits. Following strong diplomatic protests by the Soviet Union that the vessel would be entering Soviet territorial waters, the United States State Department instructed the *Northwind* to abandon its attempt on the straits.[251] A similar passage was attempted again in 1967 by two United States ice-breakers, the USCGC *Edisto* and the *Eastwind*. However, once again after strong diplomatic protests by the Soviet Union that any passage by these vessels through the Vilkitsky

[246] This state practice can be traced back to the 1909 Law on the Extension of Maritime Customs Zone which claimed a twelve nautical mile offshore jurisdiction for the purposes of customs control; for a review of this law and other state practice till 1960, see Pharand, 'Innocent Passage' at 28–30.

[247] Butler, 'The Legal Regime of the Soviet Arctic' at 216.

[248] Pharand, 'Innocent Passage' at 30–1; *cf.* TSCZ Arts. 14, 15, 16, 17 and 23.

[249] See Rules for Visits by Foreign Warships to Territorial Waters and Ports of the USSR, adopted 25 June 1960 and discussed in Pharand, 'Innocent Passage' at 32.

[250] Franckx, 'Non-Soviet Shipping' at 270.

[251] Pharand, 'Innocent Passage' 232 at 16; Franckx, 'Non-Soviet Shipping' at 270.

Straits would be a violation of Soviet frontiers which was only acceptable if permission was requested, the voyages were cancelled.[252] Since that time there has been little further attempt by the United States or any other state actively to assert a right of freedom of navigation for its ships through the Russian Arctic straits.

The current position then is that irrespective of some evidence for a Soviet and previous Imperial Russian claim that several of the Arctic seas adjacent to the mainland are closed seas or internal waters, there is no evidence of such a claim currently being pursued in the Barents, Kara, Laptev, East Siberian or Chukchi Seas. There is, however, continuing and consistent practice by previous Soviet administrations and by Russia that the straits which connect some of these waters are considered to be internal waters through which no right of innocent passage exists. With respect to the attempted crossing of the Vilkitsky Straits by United States vessels in the 1960s, prior to the enclosure of those waters by straight baselines, Pharand concluded that the only possible rationalisation for the attitude of the then Soviet Union towards these voyages was that the United States ice-breakers had been classified as warships.[253] Accordingly, under the then current Soviet law concerning navigation by foreign warships, prior permission was necessary before passage could take place. However, this practice would still have been contrary to the guarantee of the right of innocent passage through international straits provided by Article 16(4) of the Territorial Sea Convention.

When the status of these straits is considered in light of the provisions found in UNCLOS, the principal question is whether these straits can be considered 'international'. Pharand noted that by 1968 only three foreign vessels had ever traversed the NSR and concluded that with those exceptions it was doubtful whether any foreign ship had ever traversed the Vilkitsky Straits without a Soviet escort.[254] Irrespective of the foreign-flagged vessels under Soviet charter which have operated through the Vilkitsky and other straits in the NSR, it

[252] Pharand, 'Innocent Passage' at 16–17; Franckx, 'Non-Soviet Shipping' at 270–1. For an overview of these various attempted voyages through the Northeast Passage see Franckx, *Maritime Claims* at 146–50.

[253] Pharand, 'Innocent Passage' at 38.

[254] *Ibid*. at 40. The three voyages that were noted were the *Vega* (Sweden) 1878–79, *Maud* (Norway) 1918–19 and *Komet* (Germany) 1940. Terence Armstrong, 'Northern Sea Route Operations in the 1986–7 Season' in Lawson W. Brigham (ed.), *The Soviet Maritime Arctic* (London, 1991) 150–7 concluded that during the 1986–7 season 600 freight voyages were conducted along the NSR but only three complete transits (no mention was made whether these vessels were foreign-flagged).

must be conceded that the Northeast Passage has not been the subject of significant international navigation. Given the relative infrequency of foreign-flagged vessels passing through these straits, which seems even less frequent when compared to similar voyages through the Northwest Passage, it would seem to be difficult to classify any of the major straits in the Northeast Passage as 'international straits'. This is certainly the view adopted by recent Soviet publicists.[255]

Despite the view of the previous Soviet Union towards navigation of the Northeast Passage, there have from time to time been active efforts to encourage greater foreign shipping to use the Passage. The first attempt to this end was made in late 1966, when the advantages of the Northeast Passage were advertised as a viable alternate shipping route from Europe to Asia. However, this offer was never actively taken up by foreign shippers.[256] A more positive attempt to encourage foreign shippers to use the NSR and the Passage came in 1987 when then Secretary-General of the Communist Party, Mikhail Gorbachev, speaking in Murmansk, delivered a major policy statement with respect to the Arctic and northern affairs. In that statement, the final of the six initiatives noted that:

> across the Arctic runs the shortest sea route from Europe to the Far East, to the Pacific. I think that, depending on how the normalization of international relations goes, we could open the Northern Sea Route to foreign ships under our icebreaker escort.[257]

There has been little concrete evidence that foreign shippers have more actively begun to use the NSR and Northeast Passage since this statement. No doubt this has been partly due to concerns over the safety of the route. Despite assurances that Soviet ice-breakers would assist in safe passage, there have been instances when vessels have been lost in the ice even during the middle of the summer season.[258]

It should be noted that irrespective of these efforts to encourage greater use of the Passage and NSR, there has never been any suggestion that the Soviets or Russians have viewed these waters as being open to unrestricted passage by international vessels. It would

255 Kolodkin and Volosov, 'The Legal Regime of the Soviet Arctic' at 163.

256 Franckx, 'New Developments' at 37.

257 Translated from Pravda and reprinted in T. E. Armstrong, 'Soviet Proposals for the Arctic: A Policy Declaration by Mr Gorbachev' (1988) 24 *Polar Record* 68 at 69.

258 Franckx, 'New Developments' at 39. For a review of the events during the 1983 season, see William Barr and Edward A. Wilson, 'The Shipping Crisis in the Soviet Eastern Arctic at the Close of the 1983 Navigation Season' (1985) 38 *Arctic* 1–17.

seem then the legal status of the NSR as far as the Soviets and now the Russians are concerned is that it is a national transport route which is under full Russian control and jurisdiction.[259] The Northeast Passage, however, is distinct from the NSR as it begins and ends in high seas. In addition, there are various straits within the Passage that now fall within the Russian definition of internal waters. Irrespective of the proclamation of baselines which enclose these straits as internal waters, UNCLOS does provide that if the enclosed waters were not previously considered to be internal waters then a right of innocent passage remains.[260] This is similar to the position which exists in the Northwest Passage following the proclamation by Canada in 1986 of straight baselines. Accordingly more detailed consideration will now be given to whether the waters of both the Northwest and Northeast Passage can be classified as 'historic waters'.

Historic waters

Historic waters have a special status in the law of the sea. They allow a coastal state to claim exclusive jurisdiction over certain waters, akin to internal waters, on the grounds of long usage and prescription. The concept is especially well developed in the case of 'historic bays'.[261] However, the International Court of Justice in the *Anglo-Norwegian Fisheries Case* recognised a claim to 'historic waters' with respect to waters which fell between the Norwegian mainland and the *skjaergaard*.[262] The principle of historic waters has since been recognised in the Conventions.[263] Relying upon some of the same principles which have been applied to the acquisition of territory in international law, the doctrine of historic waters 'is conceptually unimpeachable, but ... the debate does have spurious overtones because there are so few examples where a national title has been validated exclusively by historic methods'.[264] The Convention rules also indicate that the

[259] Brubaker, 'International Law and Russian Arctic Waters' at 98.

[260] See UNCLOS, Arts. 8(2), 35(a).

[261] Jennings and Watts, *Oppenheim's International Law* at 630–1 where it is noted that three factors are relevant in determining historic bay status: (1) the claiming nation must have exercised authority over the area; (2) that exercise must have been continuous; and (3) foreign states must have acquiesced in the exercise of authority.

[262] *Anglo-Norwegian Fisheries Case*, [1951] ICJ Reports 116.

[263] TSCZ, Art. 7(6); UNCLOS, Art. 10(6).

[264] O'Connell, *International Law of the Sea* at 422. O'Connell lists the supposed elements of historic waters as being: (1) the control exercised over the waters must be sovereign jurisdiction and exclusive; (2) the effluxion of time; (3) the attitude of foreign states: *ibid.* at 427–35.

doctrine applies mostly to 'historic bays'.[265] Nevertheless, this has not stopped historic claims being made from time to time to other bodies of water. Another important aspect of claims over historic waters is that in some cases pre-existing navigation rights remain in place.[266]

In the case of the Northwest Passage, while it has occasionally been argued that Canada can justify its claim over the waters of the whole Archipelago on the basis of historic title, the considerable ambit and breadth of such a claim has dissuaded many commentators to the point where few are prepared to accept that any such claim would be legally upheld.[267] If Canada's claim cannot be supported on this basis, then what is the true effect of the 1986 baselines? Under both the Territorial Sea Convention and UNCLOS, previously existing rights of passage are preserved notwithstanding the proclamation of baselines which may convert previous high seas into internal waters.[268] In addition, UNCLOS clearly implies that transit passage through international straits can be enjoyed where the waters have only become 'internal' following the establishment of straight baselines under the Convention.

The central question then as to whether the Northwest Passage is a strait through which the right of transit passage exists is to determine what the status of the Passage was prior to the declaration of the 1986 baselines. This is recognised by various commentators who accept that if Canada's claim that transit passage cannot be exercised through the waters of the Archipelago is to succeed, it is first necessary to demonstrate that the waters of the Northwest Passage are not and have never been considered an international strait.[269] The waters of

[265] See TSCZ, Art. 7(2); UNCLOS, Art. 10(6). [266] See TSCZ, Art. 5(2); UNCLOS, Art. 8(2).

[267] Pharand, *Canada's Arctic Waters* at 125; Bankes, 'Forty Years' at 290; McKinnon, 'Arctic Baseline' at 800–1; Kettuner, 'The Status of the Northwest Passage' at 989; Roth, 'Sovereignty and Jurisdiction' at 859. This may not be the case, however, with all the waters of the Canadian Arctic: see Nigel Bankes, 'The Status of Hudson Bay' (1987) 15(3) *Northern Perspectives* 14–15.

[268] See TSCZ, Art. 5(2) under which rights of innocent passage recognised in Art. 16, including passage through international straits, remained in place despite the waters being converted into internal waters as a result of the baselines. UNCLOS, Art. 35(a) provides:

> Nothing in this Part affects:
>
> (a) any areas of internal waters within a strait, except where the establishment of a straight baseline in accordance with the method set forth in article 7 has the effect of enclosing as internal waters areas which had not previously been considered as such.

[269] Pharand, 'Canada's Sovereignty' at 335–42; McKinnon, 'Arctic Baselines' at 816–17; Kettuner, 'The Status of the Northwest Passage' at 982.

the Canadian Arctic Archipelago may therefore be properly classified as internal waters. But, if a pre-existing right of navigation did exist through the strait then foreign-flagged vessels are still entitled to claim a right of passage through the Northwest Passage.

The position with the Northeast Passage is very similar. Many Soviet and Russian jurists have throughout this century claimed that Arctic waters due north of the previous USSR and Russia were historic waters. While at times this classification has been confused with claims for 'closed seas', there is no denying that a strong view has been presented that not only are certain bays properly classified as historic but also that the various seas which make up the Russian Arctic waters can also be so classified.[270] Despite these claims of historic waters made by Russian and Soviet publicists there is little evidence to suggest that they have ever received any official sanction apart from the case of certain historic bays.[271] Therefore, while the position of the previous USSR and Russia over 'historic waters' in the Arctic has been reserved, there has been no official attempt to assert such a claim over the various seas which make up the Northeast Passage. The waters of the straits of the Northeast Passage can accordingly be classified as either territorial or internal, within which a right of either innocent or transit passage exists.

Marine pollution

To conclude this discussion of law of the sea issues in the Arctic, brief mention should also be made of marine pollution and multilateral efforts which have been taken to deal with this problem in the Arctic. To begin it should be noted that like most other oceans of the world, the Arctic is protected by the existing international legal regime dealing with marine pollution. To that end the major international conventions such as the 1973 International Convention for the Prevention of Pollution from Ships and its 1978 Protocol[272] and the 1972 Convention on the Prevention of Marine Pollution by Dumping of Wastes and other Matter[273] apply in Arctic waters. In addition the 1990 International Convention on Oil Pollution Preparedness, Response and Co-Operation provides a basis for stronger cooperative

[270] See Butler, *The Soviet Union and the Law of the Sea* at 107–15; Butler, *Northeast Arctic Passage* at 82–90; Franckx, *Maritime Claims* at 154–5, 171–5.

[271] Pharand, *Canada's Arctic Waters* at 107.

[272] 1973 Convention, (1973) 12 ILM 1,319; 1978 Protocol, (1978) 17 ILM 546.

[273] 1046 UNTS 120,

responses to marine pollution incidents such as wreck.[274] However, as was demonstrated in the *Exxon Valdez* incident, Arctic waters are particularly susceptible to the effects of marine pollution; a point strongly pressed at the Third United Nations Conference on the Law of the Sea by Canada. As a consequence, the Conference adopted Article 234 of UNCLOS which provides as follows:

> Coastal States have the right to adopt and enforce non-discriminatory laws and regulations for the prevention, reduction and control of marine pollution from vessels in ice-covered areas within the limits of the exclusive economic zone, where particularly severe climatic conditions and the presence of ice covering such areas for most of the year create obstructions or exceptional hazards to navigation, and pollution of the marine environment could cause major harm to or irreversible disturbance of the ecological balance. Such laws and regulations shall have due regard to navigation and the protection and preservation of the marine environment based on the best available scientific evidence.[275]

While the importance of Article 234 should not be overstated, it does give to some coastal states the ability unilaterally to implement much more stringent marine pollution provisions within their adjacent 200 nautical mile EEZ. It goes no further than that and so cannot be read as a provision conferring upon the Arctic states the ability to implement extensive marine pollution provisions for the entire Arctic Ocean. Nevertheless, Article 234 is significant in that it does recognise the special importance of ice-covered waters which are within the limits of national jurisdiction and that adjacent coastal states have a responsibility and interest to protect those waters.[276]

The full impact of Article 234 remains to be seen. When Canada

[274] (1991) 30 ILM 735.

[275] For more details on the background to Art. 234, see D. M. McRae and D. J. Goundrey, 'Environmental Jurisdiction in the Arctic Waters: The Extent of Article 234' (1982) 16 UBCLR 197 at 215–22.

[276] Art. 234 has been criticised because of its uncertain terms and the impact coastal state marine pollution legislation may have upon the freedom of navigation. See C. Lamson and D. VanderZwaag, 'Arctic Waters: Needs and Options for Canadian–American Cooperation' (1987) 18 ODIL 49 at 81, where the language of Art. 234 is described as 'a witch's brew, a caldron of legal uncertainty which could be stirred in favour of either the coastal or shipping state'. For a discussion of the broad and narrow interpretations that can be given to Art. 234 also see C. Lamson, 'Arctic Shipping, Marine Safety and Environmental Protection' (1987) 11 *Marine Policy* 3 at 4; Boyle, 'Legal Regimes of the Arctic' at 327–8; William E. Westermeyer and Vinod Goyal, 'Jurisdiction and Management of Arctic Marine Transportation' (1986) 39 *Arctic* 338 at 346–7.

enacted its Arctic Waters Pollution Prevention Act in 1970[277] there was much debate both within Canada and internationally as to the validity of the legislation.[278] Article 234 removes the uncertainty of this Canadian initiative and invites other Arctic states to implement similar legislation. However, the extent to which international navigation may be legitimately impacted upon by legislation based upon Article 234 remains unknown.[279] Certainly there are some grounds for Russia especially to argue that some of its laws regulating passage through the Northeast Passage, if grounded in environmental protection, have greater validity under Article 234 than they would previously have had.[280]

While Article 234 of UNCLOS may provide a basis for unilateral state action to protect the Arctic marine environment, other provisions in UNCLOS and developments in the law of the sea more generally may allow for greater cooperative action to be taken to protect the Arctic Ocean. One possibility is that the Arctic Ocean be classified as an 'enclosed' or 'semi-enclosed sea'. Under UNCLOS, Part IX makes reference to such seas, defining them to mean:

> a gulf, basin, or sea surrounded by two or more States and connected to another sea of the ocean by a narrow outlet or consisting entirely or primarily of the territorial sea and exclusive economic zones of two or more coastal states.[281]

The importance of such a classification is that the states bordering such seas are to cooperate either directly or through a regional organisation to protect and preserve the marine environment.[282] There is some debate as to whether the Arctic Ocean can be legitimately considered as either an enclosed or semi-enclosed sea. Some of the criteria are present but others are not.[283] Irrespective of this debate there can be no denying that the Arctic Ocean is a regional sea, and

[277] SC 1970, c. 47.

[278] O'Connell, *The International Law of the Sea* (vol. II.) at 1,022–4.

[279] UNCLOS, Art. 233 provides that some provisions in UNCLOS dealing with marine pollution do not affect the legal regime of straits; however, this exception does not include Art. 234.

[280] Franckx, *Maritime Claims* at 179, 235.

[281] UNCLOS, Art. 122.

[282] UNCLOS, Art. 123.

[283] Two issues in particular which raise concern with respect to the application of the definition found in Art. 122 are whether the Arctic is connected to another sea by a 'narrow outlet', and whether the Ocean is one that primarily consists of territorial sea and EEZ: see Harders, 'In Quest of an Arctic Legal Regime' at 295–6.

similar to other seas which have increasingly come under specific regional marine pollution regimes in recent years.[284]

Environmental protection

To conclude this review of Arctic legal issues, an overview will be given of legal mechanisms dealing with the protection of the Arctic environment.[285] To that end, emphasis will be given to both global multilateral regimes, which through their operation assist to protect the Arctic from the effects of transboundary pollution originating in other parts of the globe, and specific Arctic multilateral and bilateral initiatives which have been developed to deal with Arctic issues in particular. Detailed consideration of the Arctic Environmental Protection Strategy will be left till chapter 6 as part of a review of the push towards a comprehensive Arctic legal regime.

Global initiatives

The Arctic has become subject to an ever-increasing array of international legal instruments designed to protect the global environment. In 1991 the Arctic states identified twenty-six 'global conventions' which could impact upon the protection of the Arctic environment.[286] These instruments fell into four groupings: atmosphere, marine environment, wildlife and other.

Of the global legal instruments which seek to protect the atmosphere, five have been identified as having particular application in the Arctic. Three of these deal with nuclear and military materials,[287] which, given the strategic significance the Arctic has had since the commencement of the Cold War and the emphasis many Arctic states have placed on military security, are matters of considerable interest in the Arctic. The international concern expressed over the depletion

[284] Examples are the Baltic and Mediterranean. For further examples, see P. H. Sand, *Marine Environment Law in the United Nations Environment Programme* (London, 1988). See also the discussion in Douglas Brubaker, *Marine Pollution and International Law* (London, 1993) 276–448.

[285] More specific attention will be given to some of these initiatives in chapters 8 and 9 dealing with resource management and environmental protection.

[286] See 'List of Major International Instruments and Policy Declarations Pertaining to the Arctic Environment' (final version, as presented at the Officials and Ministerial Meeting of 10–14 June 1991 at Rovaniemi, Finland), 2–31.

[287] 1963 Treaty Banning Nuclear Weapon Tests in the Atmosphere, in Outer Space and Under Water, 480 UNTS 43; 1976 Convention on the Prohibition of Military or any other Hostile Use of Environmental Modification Techniques, (1977) 16 ILM 88; 1979 Convention on the Physical Protection of Nuclear Material, (1979) 18 ILM 1,422.

of the ozone layer, particularly over the polar regions, makes the principal legal instrument dealing with this problem significant for the Arctic.[288] The Arctic states have accordingly given strong support to the 1985 Vienna Convention for the Protection of the Ozone Layer[289] and its subsequent Protocols.[290]

Nearly all of the relevant international conventions dealing with the protection of the marine environment have some application in the Arctic. Most have already been considered above. There is also scope for both the 1958 Convention on the High Seas[291] and the Continental Shelf Convention[292] to play a role in protecting the Arctic marine environment. However, there is no evidence that either have been particularly influential in regulating Arctic state conduct.

Five conventions dealing with global protection of wildlife have been particularly identified as having application in the Arctic. Of these, perhaps the most important is the 1946 International Convention for the Regulation of Whaling.[293] The Convention, which created the International Whaling Commission (IWC), is of particular importance in Arctic waters because of the large numbers of whale species found in the region. It is also important to Arctic states because of the commercial significance of whaling to states such as Iceland and Norway, and the importance of whales to indigenous peoples throughout the region. During the last decade the IWC has imposed a moratorium on commercial whaling and this has created considerable tension between whaling parties and non-whaling parties to the Convention. This has raised the prospect of some whaling states withdrawing from the Convention and recommencing commercial whaling. Given these developments, unless Arctic states seek to prohibit whaling within their EEZs, it would seem that the scene is set for the resumption of commercial whaling in Arctic waters.[294] Other significant international conventions seeking to protect wildlife in

[288] See Anne Gallagher, 'The "New" Montreal Protocol and the Future of International Law for the Protection of the Global Environment' (1992) 14 *Houston Journal of International Law* 267 at 276–7.

[289] (1987) 26 ILM 1,541.

[290] 1987 Montreal Protocol on Substances that Deplete the Ozone Layer, as amended, (1987) 26 ILM 1,541.

[291] 450 UNTS 82, Arts. 24, 25.

[292] Continental Shelf Convention, Arts. 1, 5.

[293] 161 UNTS 74.

[294] For a comprehensive overview of the whaling regime created by the Convention and the operations of the IWC see Patricia Birnie, *International Regulation of Whaling* (vols. I and II) (New York, 1985).

the Arctic are the 1973 Convention on International Trade in Endangered Species of Wild Fauna and Flora[295] and the 1979 Convention on the Conservation of Migratory Species of Wild Animals.[296] There are also conventions dealing with the protection of natural and cultural heritage (under which some sites in the Arctic have been classified)[297] and also certain wetlands which are waterfowl habitat.[298]

There is also a group of conventions dealing with miscellaneous matters such as the transboundary movement of hazardous wastes[299] and cooperation and notification in case of nuclear accidents.[300] The 1989 Basle Convention controlling the transboundary movement of hazardous wastes is of special significance in the Arctic because of the amount of industrial waste generated in some areas such as Siberia and the Kola Peninsula, and the potential for such wastes to be transported through Arctic waters. All the Arctic states are signatories to the Convention which entered into force in 1992. Under the terms of the Convention a state intending to ship such wastes must notify not only the importing state but also states through which the waste shall transit.[301] Under certain circumstances, transboundary movement of the waste may he halted if permission is not forthcoming from exporting and transit states. This Convention could be of particular importance in controlling the movement of hazardous wastes by ship from Russia.

To conclude the discussion concerning global environmental conventions, reference should be made to the 1992 United Nations Conference on Environment and Development, which adopted two important Conventions. They are the Convention on Biological Diversity[302] and the Framework Convention on Climate Change.[303] It is important to acknowledge that what both of these Conventions seek to achieve is a more integrated framework within which states can deal with environmental issues of global significance. Their import-

[295] 993 UNTS 243. [296] (1980) 19 ILM 15.

[297] 1972 Convention Concerning the Protection of the World Cultural and Natural Heritage, (1972) 11 ILM 1,358.

[298] 1971 Convention on Wetlands of International Importance Especially as Waterfowl Habitat, 996 UNTS 245.

[299] 1989 Basle Convention on the Control of Transboundary Movements of Hazardous Wastes and their Disposal, (1989) 28 ILM 657 (hereafter Basle Convention).

[300] 1986 Convention on Early Notification of a Nuclear Accident, (1986) 25 ILM 1,370; 1986 Convention on Assistance in the Case of a Nuclear Accident or Radiological Emergency, (1986) 25 ILM 1,377. [301] Basle Convention, Arts. 4, 6.

[302] (1992) 31 ILM 818 (hereafter Biological Diversity).

[303] (1992) 31 ILM 849.

ance for the Arctic should not be underestimated, especially as the region has increasingly been seen as the centre of environmental impacts resulting from pollutants and actions taken in other parts of the hemisphere. Under the Convention on Biological Diversity, state parties are obliged to ensure *in situ* conservation,[304] *ex situ* conservation,[305] sustainable use,[306] and the development of impact assessment procedures.[307] The Climate Change Convention builds on the process already initiated by the 1985 Vienna Convention and later Montreal Protocol on the Ozone Layer. While only a framework instrument, it strengthens the existing international legal regime to halt climate change, the consequences of which have been most readily apparent in the polar regions.

Regional initiatives

The Arctic states have also entered into a number of agreements, protocols and conventions which have specific application to the Arctic and associated regions. Many of these instruments are purely bilateral and seek to ensure greater cooperation between Arctic states in specific areas of environmental concern. Of the thirty-two agreements which have been catalogued as having an environmental focus,[308] five deal with the protection of wildlife, six with marine pollution, seven with general environmental protection, nine with cooperation and notification in case of nuclear accident, and five with scientific cooperation and joint boundary agreements.[309]

There have also been a number of regional initiatives which the Arctic states have entered into at a multilateral level which have importance for the Arctic. These deal with a variety of issues from marine and transboundary pollution to species and wildlife protection. Only a few of these specifically apply to the Arctic as a region. Others, dealing with North America or Western Europe, also have an Arctic impact. It is not intended here to review all of these agreements.

[304] Biological Diversity, Art. 8. [305] Biological Diversity, Art. 9.

[306] Biological Diversity, Art. 10. [307] Biological Diversity, Art. 14.

[308] See note 286 above, 'List of Major International Instruments'. Some examples are the 1983 Agreement Between the Government of Canada and the Government of the Kingdom of Denmark for Cooperation Relating to the Marine Environment, [1983] CTS 19; 1987 Agreement Between the Government of Canada and the Government of the United States of America on the Conservation of the Porcupine Caribou Herd, [1987] CTS 31.

[309] For a general review of some of these bilateral agreements, see VanderZwaag, Donihee and Faegteborg, 'Towards Regional Ocean Management' at 15–21.

Some will be discussed in greater detail in later chapters. At this stage, three multilateral agreements will be briefly considered to illustrate the types of issues dealt with and how they specifically or generally apply in the Arctic.

1973 Polar Bear Agreement

Following an initial meeting in Fairbanks, Alaska, during 1965 between representatives of Canada, Denmark, Norway, the United States and the USSR to discuss concerns over the future of polar bears, and the assistance of the International Union for the Conservation of Nature and Natural Resources in drafting the terms of a suitable agreement, an Agreement on the Conservation of Polar Bears was signed by all five states in November 1973.[310] The Agreement entered into force in 1976. However, it was not till 1978 that all five states ratified it.[311] The Agreement has several objectives, the most important being to prohibit the taking of polar bears except as provided for under its terms.[312] These terms allow for limited taking of polar bears in cases of: *bona fide* scientific research, conservation purposes, preventing serious disturbance of the management of other living resources, and by indigenous people using traditional methods of hunting where polar bears have been subject to taking by traditional means.[313] The state parties to the Agreement are also under an obligation to take appropriate action to protect polar bear habitat with the population to be managed according to 'sound conservation practices based on the best available scientific data'.[314] National research programmes dealing with polar bears are also to be coordinated in order to achieve better conservation and management of the species.[315] Despite there being no central administrative body to oversee its implementation, the Agreement has been seen as a success.[316] The Agreement does not provide for much in the way of

[310] For a discussion on the negotiation of the Agreement see Ian Stirling, 'Research and Management of Polar Bears *Ursus Maritimus*' (1986) 23 *Polar Record* 167 at 167–9; Anne Fikkan, 'Polar Bears – Hot Topic in Cold Climate' (1990) 10(2) *International Challenges* 32–8; Anne Fikkan, Gail Osherenko and Alexander Arikainen, 'Polar Bears: The Importance of Simplicity' in Oran R. Young and Gail Osherenko (eds.), *Polar Politics* (Ithaca, NY, 1993) 96 at 96–124

[311] Simon Lyster, *International Wildlife Law* (Cambridge, 1985) 55.

[312] Polar Bear Agreement, Art. I.

[313] Polar Bear Agreement, Art. III.

[314] Polar Bear Agreement, Art. II.

[315] Polar Bear Agreement, Art. VII.

[316] Lyster, *International Wildlife Law* at 61.

cooperation between the Arctic states. Apart from occasional meetings to review the operation of the Agreement, the state parties have been left to develop their own individual policies.[317]

Transboundary pollution

A particular area of pollution concern in the Arctic has been the effects of long-range transboundary air pollution, the main source of which has been Western Europe and Russia.[318] The problem is actually visible in the Arctic as the pollution manifests itself in the form of so-called 'Arctic haze'.[319] To date, Arctic states have sought to deal with the problems of transboundary air pollution through participation in extra-regional regimes. The most important regime is that created by the 1979 Convention on Long-Range Transboundary Air Pollution[320] and its associated Protocols.[321] Though the Convention does not include any provisions which strictly regulate the emission of pollutants into the atmosphere, it has provided a cooperative forum in which states have been able to work together and treat the European air mass as a shared resource which requires coordinated pollution-control measures and common emission standards.[322] While the 1979 Convention and its Protocols will not completely solve the problem of transboundary air pollution in the Arctic, it does have a significant impact in controlling emissions from extra-regional sources and helps to alleviate the Arctic haze problem. Until the Arctic states adopt their own specific regional response to this issue, the 1979 Convention

317 For further details see Stirling, 'Research and Management' at 172–4.

318 Osherenko and Young, *The Age of the Arctic* at 122–5; B. Stonehouse (ed.), *Arctic Air Pollution* (Cambridge, 1986);

319 Marvin S. Soroos, 'The Odyssey of Arctic Haze: Toward a Global Atmospheric Regime' (1992) 34(10) *Environment* 6–11, 25–7; Jost Heintzenberg, 'Arctic Haze: Air Pollution in Polar Regions' (1989) 18 AMBIO 50–5.

320 (1979) 18 ILM 1,442.

321 1984 Protocol to the 1979 Convention on Long-Range Transboundary Air Pollution on Long-Term Financing of the Co-operative Programme for Monitoring and Evaluation of the Long-Range Transmission of Air Pollutants in Europe (EMEP), (1988) 27 ILM 701; 1985 Protocol to the 1979 Convention on Long-Range Transboundary Air Pollution on the Reduction of Sulphur Emissions or their Transboundary Fluxes by at least 30 per cent, (1988) 27 ILM 707; 1986 Protocol to the 1979 Convention on Long-Range Transboundary Air Pollution Concerning the Control of Emissions of Nitrogen Oxides or their Transboundary Fluxes, (1989) 28 ILM 212; 1991 Protocol to the 1979 Convention on Long-Range Transboundary Air Pollution Concerning the Control of Emissions of Volatile Organic Compounds or their Transboundary Fluxes, (1992) 31 ILM 568.

322 Patricia W. Birnie and Alan E. Boyle, *International Law and the Environment* (Oxford, 1992) 398.

represents a valuable regime in which they can participate in order to protect the Arctic environment.[323]

A recent development in this area of transboundary pollution is the 1991 Convention on Environmental Impact Assessment in a Transboundary Context[324] which is open to all members of the UN Economic Commission for Europe. The Convention seeks to put in place procedures in which activities that are likely to cause 'significant adverse transboundary impact' will be subjected to an environmental impact review.[325] Parties which may be affected by such polluting activities are required to be notified and consultations must be undertaken between the relevant states on measures to reduce or eliminate the potential transboundary impact.[326] While it is not yet possible to judge the success of the Convention, it has the potential to provide new measures which will protect Arctic states from transboundary environmental impact.

Oslo and Paris Conventions on Marine Pollution

Parts of the Arctic Ocean and associated seas have also benefited from conventions adopted by European states which deal with marine pollution. The 1972 Convention for the Prevention of Marine Pollution by Dumping from Ships and Aircraft (Oslo Convention)[327] and the 1974 Convention for the Prevention of Marine Pollution from Land-Based Sources (Paris Convention)[328] both applied to the waters of the north-east Atlantic and in particular to the Greenland Sea, Norwegian Sea, Barents Sea and the Arctic Ocean up to the North Pole in an arc north of 36°N between 42°W and 51°E. The Oslo Convention regulated the dumping of harmful substances into the seas by both ships and aircraft, while the Paris Convention sought to eliminate land-based pollution through the creation of various categories of pollutants some of which are strictly prohibited and others of which are subject to regulation. In 1992, states in the North Atlantic region negotiated a

[323] For a discussion of how the 1991 Arctic Environmental Protection Strategy seeks to deal with the issues of transboundary air pollution, see chapter 9. An analysis of the relationship between the problem of Arctic haze and the 1979 Convention regime is found in Marvin S. Soroos, 'Arctic Haze and Transboundary Air Pollution: Conditions Governing Success and Failure' in Oran R. Young and Gail Osherenko (eds.), *Polar Politics* (Ithaca, NY, 1993) 186–222.

[324] (1991) 30 ILM 733. [325] *Ibid.*, Arts. 4, 6.

[326] *Ibid.*, Art. 3 and Annex I which provides that a wide range of activities may be caught by this procedure, i.e. oil refineries, power stations, dams and reservoirs, pulp and paper manufacturing and major mining activities.

[327] 932 UNTS 3. [328] (1974) 13 ILM 352.

further convention in order to implement a more comprehensive approach towards combating marine pollution. The 1992 Convention for the Protection of the Marine Environment of the North-east Atlantic[329] is designed to supersede the Oslo and Paris Conventions by dealing with all possible sources of pollution of the marine environment. A number of the Arctic states have become parties.[330] While none of these Conventions deals with the whole Arctic region, they are important from the perspective of seeking to control marine pollution problems in one part of the Arctic which is heavily used for commercial navigation and also subject to considerable impact from land-based sources.

Conclusion

There are a number of issues around which international law converges in the Arctic. These include common questions of sovereignty over both terrestrial and maritime areas and rights of access over these areas. The law of the sea regime is another unifying force amongst the Arctic states. In every case, each Arctic state has a maritime outlook so that questions of resource exploitation, navigation rights and control of offshore maritime zones are governed by the law of the sea. UNCLOS also gave greater recognition to marine regions and the responsibility of states within such regions to implement measures for the protection of their own regional marine environment. It is, however, the emerging Arctic-wide concern for the protection of the Arctic environment which has, perhaps, recently proved to be the strongest catalyst for the development of closer multilateral relations amongst the Arctic states. It has forced them to work cooperatively to deal with regional issues which have an impact upon each individual Arctic state. However, despite the Polar Bear Agreement being an encouraging forerunner to these more recent developments, there has still been little attempt to develop any truly integrated Arctic legal regime to deal with the environment.

This chapter has demonstrated that there is an Arctic legal regime based on international law principles, custom and conventions. However, given the lack of substantial international cooperation amongst Arctic states, this regime is still in reality nothing more than

[329] (1993) 32 ILM 1,069.

[330] Denmark, Finland, Iceland, Norway, Sweden and the European Community, all participated in the negotiation of the Convention.

a wide-ranging series of international law measures with application to the Arctic region. Much remains to be done before a truly coordinated and coherent approach, specifically directed to regional issues, can be said to have emerged. There are examples of where such an approach has occasionally been adopted. The sector principle was first proposed in the Arctic; the Svalbard solution is a unique Arctic experiment to deal with sovereignty and resource management; Article 234 of UNCLOS was designed by Arctic states to meet their particular needs; and the 1973 Polar Bear Agreement was an ambitious attempt to protect wildlife and their habitat. Each of these initiatives has contributed to international law both regionally and globally. However, cooperative efforts have until recently tended to be centred on either bilateral arrangements or global multilateral initiatives. The 1990s has witnessed a major change in this approach and in chapter 6 emphasis will be placed upon the development of the Arctic Environmental Protection Strategy and whether this, in conjunction with other developments, can be seen as an indicator that a more comprehensive Arctic legal regime will begin to develop.

6 Initiatives for Arctic regional cooperation

Chapter 5 demonstrated that while it is possible to isolate various specific areas around which legal rules have developed to deal with Arctic issues, it is not possible to characterise the Arctic as having a comprehensive legal regime. This has very much been a consequence of how international law has evolved in the Arctic. International law as it has developed and applied in the region has no doubt responded to certain specific Arctic issues, but by and large the law which has been applied is general international law. Another reason why international law in the Arctic is neither integrated nor comprehensive is that regional multilateral cooperation has only been a recent development. This, more than any other reason, has hindered the development of the Arctic legal regime.

The lack of greater multilateral cooperation in the Arctic is curious. The region has always been seen as distinctive, one which because of its harsh climate and inaccessibility raises different political and legal issues from other more temperate regions.[1] While the common interest of adjacent states may have been a factor encouraging greater international cooperation, there are also a number of countervailing factors. Apart from Svalbard, there have been few major territorial

[1] These questions were the subject of much debate early in the century in both legal and social science literature. See e.g., James Brown Scott, 'Arctic Exploration and International Law' (1909) 3 AJIL 928–41; Thomas Willing Balch, 'The Arctic and Antarctic Regions and the Law of Nations' (1910) 4 AJIL 265–75; David Hunter Miller, 'Political Rights in the Arctic' (1925–26) 4 *Foreign Affairs* 47–60; A. R. Clute, 'The Ownership of the North Pole' (1927) 5 CanBR 19–26; Leonid Breitfuss, 'Territorial Division of the Arctic' (1928–9) 8 *Dalhousie Review* 456–69; W. Lakhtine, 'Rights over the Arctic' (1930) 24 AJIL 703–17; T. E. M. McKitterick, 'The Validity of Territorial and other Claims in Polar Regions' (1939) 21 (I & IV) (3rd Ser.) *Journal of Comparative Legislation and International Law* 89–97.

disputes which have required a regional response. The Arctic Ocean has long been accepted as being high seas by most states including Arctic states themselves. Though the claims occasionally made by Canadians and Russians to the lands and waters up to the North Pole were certainly seen as irregular, given that there were few Arctic lands which fell within these sectors which had not already been claimed by these two states, and that exploitation of the ice-covered Arctic Ocean was a remote possibility, no major dispute arose. The Cold War period resulted in the whole region being a potential frontline for any hostilities between the United States and the USSR. The development of nuclear-powered submarines which could cruise underneath the ice made the Arctic a major strategic theatre of the Cold War. The Cold War also saw some Arctic states, such as Canada, support one of the superpowers, while others, such as the Nordic states, sought to maintain neutrality. This created a situation not conducive to regional cooperation. During the Cold War many Arctic states were active in security organisations such as NATO and the Warsaw Pact. Finally, in more recent times the European Community and the Economic Commission for Europe have considered issues which have impacted upon the economies and environment of Arctic states. Because of the existence of these fora and the United Nations, Arctic states have not felt the need for a special institution to discuss Arctic affairs. In short, they have preferred that the region remain on the periphery of world affairs.

Despite these factors, Arctic states have gradually begun to engage in greater bilateral and multilateral initiatives. This process has been aided by the cooling of Cold War tensions between the United States and the former USSR, and the realisation that the Arctic environment is unique, fragile, particularly subject to transboundary pollution, and in urgent need of protection. Real developments towards greater cooperation amongst Arctic states first began in the 1970s. By the 1980s a number of initiatives towards regional cooperation and the need for specific responses to Arctic problems were being developed and this led some commentators to predict that the region was about to enter a period of intense regime formation.[2] For example, Young

[2] See Lincoln P. Bloomfield, 'The Arctic: Last Unmanaged Frontier' (1981–1982) 60 *Foreign Affairs* 87–105; J. Enno Harders, 'In Quest of an Arctic Legal Regime' (1987) 11 *Marine Policy* 285–98; Clive Archer, 'General Features of Political Development and Possibilities for Cooperation in the Arctic' (1988) 11(4) *Current Research on Peace and Violence* 137–45; Vladimir Golitsyn, 'The Arctic – On the Way to Regional Cooperation' (1989) 1 *Marine Policy Reports* 91–9; Alexei Yu Roginko, 'Arctic Environmental Cooperation: Prospects and Possibilities' (1989) 12 *Current Research on Peace and Violence* 133–43.

suggested that the world was entering the 'Age of the Arctic' during which the Arctic region would begin to play a dominant role in international affairs.[3] Whether the Arctic has achieved this status is doubtful. Nevertheless, the hopes that a period of greater regional cooperation was beginning have not been completely dashed. Two major developments occurred towards the end of the 1980s. The first was the proposal that the Arctic states negotiate a regime dealing with regional environmental protection. The second was a Canadian proposal that an 'Arctic Council' be formed. Both of these initiatives will be reviewed in this chapter, as will other discussions concerning greater Arctic cooperation. This will allow for an assessment of the future prospects for the region, and most importantly what the prospects are for the development of the Arctic legal regime.

Early proposals

The piecemeal discovery of Arctic lands early this century raised for legal commentators many interesting issues. What was the status of ice in international law? Was the Arctic ice subject to claims of territorial sovereignty? Was the North Pole itself subject to a national claim? Could states assert claims to Arctic sectors which included not only land but also frozen sea? These were questions that international law struggled to deal with.[4] In response to these problems, some commentators suggested that because of the unique characteristics of the Arctic region these legal and political issues should be dealt with by a specific international agreement. For example, McKitterick in 1939 suggested:

> In view of the increasing importance of Polar regions for scientific, aeronautical and perhaps strategic purposes, it is highly desirable that the present unsatisfactory position should be regulated by a general convention, or at least by a treaty between the states most closely interested.[5]

Because of the uncertainties associated with doctrines of territorial acquisition such as the sector theory, McKitterick argued that it would be appropriate for those lands which had not already been the subject

[3] Oran R. Young, 'The Age of the Arctic' (1985–1986) 61 *Foreign Policy* 160-79; Oran R. Young, *The Arctic in World Affairs* (Seattle, 1989); *cf.* Robert L. Friedheim, 'The Regime of the Arctic – Distributional or Integrative Bargaining?' (1988) 19 ODIL 493 at 499.

[4] As an example of how these issues remain of contemporary importance, see the discussion in Sir Robert Jennings and Sir Arthur Watts, *Oppenheim's International Law* (9th, vol. I: Pts 2–4) (Harlow, UK, 1992) 692–3.

[5] McKitterick, 'The Validity of Territorial and other Claims' at 97.

of definitive acts of acquisition to be governed by an international commission which 'would have power to further and regulate their development for the common benefit'.[6] It was also argued that 'the more remote islands in the North Polar area, together with the ice-cap, could well be regarded as the common possession of all states who have an interest in them'.[7]

Strong political support for Arctic cooperation can first be traced to United States Vice-President, Henry A. Wallace, who during the course of World War II proposed to both the Department of State and Congress that the United States should take the initiative to develop an international treaty for the region, one which would provide for cooperative efforts to promote transportation, communication and Arctic exploration.[8] These views were partly supported by President Roosevelt, who, sensing the growing strategic importance of the Arctic, argued in 1944 that the United States should place greater emphasis on Arctic affairs and the economic development of Alaska.[9] However, it was primarily Wallace who was responsible for promoting a greater awareness in the United States of the Arctic as an adjoining region and of the benefits to be gained from greater economic development and international cooperation there.[10]

The Cold War dashed immediate hopes for the implementation of Wallace's vision.[11] But there is evidence of a similar proposal being

[6] *Ibid.*

[7] *Ibid.* These views are similar to those associated with the common heritage concept, adopted later in the twentieth century for areas such as outer space, the moon, and the deep sea bed.

[8] Herman Pollack and Peter J. Anderson, 'United States Policy for the Arctic' (1973) 1(1) *Arctic Bulletin* 2 at 2; R. Tucker Scully, 'Arctic Policy: Opportunities and Perspectives' in Ira Dyer and Chryssostomos Chryssostomidis (eds.), *Arctic Technology and Policy* (Washington, 1984) 3 at 5.

[9] Samuel E. Fry, 'The Arctic and United States Foreign Policy, 1730-1990' (Fall 1990) 4 *Arctic Research of the United States* 31 at 38.

[10] See John Morton Blum (ed.), *The Price of Vision* (Boston, 1973) 35, where it is noted that in discussions with Soviet Foreign Minister Molotov, Wallace presented a view of the Arctic region which would involve a great mingling of peoples from America, Siberia, China and Mongolia where a new centre of civilisation could be formed. See also Fry 'The Arctic and United States Foreign Policy' at 38.

[11] United States President Eisenhower did propose in the 1950s that an 'Open Skies' regime apply between the United States and the USSR in an effort to assist with arms control agreements between the two Cold War nations. If implemented it would have had an Arctic focus since northern transpolar routes were the most likely for surprise attack; however, the proposal never received enthusiastic support from the Soviets: see David Cox and Tariq Rauf, *Security Co-operation in the Arctic* (Ottawa, 1989) 12–14. At one stage this initiative took the form of a proposal made by the United States to the

revived in the late 1960s. Following the successful implementation of the Antarctic Treaty, in which the United States had been instrumental, the idea of a 'Northlands Compact' emerged. The proposal, put forward by the United States, involved the negotiation of an agreement promoting cooperation in the fields of scientific research, northern economic development, environmental protection, health and medicine.[12] However, the proposal received little support from either Canada or the Soviet Union and was never formally raised at a ministerial level.[13] Another United States effort, a proposal for a multilateral conference to discuss matters relating to Arctic jurisdiction in the early 1970s, also failed.[14] Notwithstanding these setbacks, the United States continued its support of greater Arctic cooperation. A 1971 National Security Decision Memorandum stated that the United States 'will promote mutually beneficial international cooperation in the Arctic'. An Interagency Arctic Policy Group was established to review possible initiatives to that end.[15] But despite another National Security Decision Memorandum in 1973 which reaffirmed the President's desire for the United States to 'actively develop and

United Nations Security Council of a 'northern zone of international inspection against surprise attack' under which it was suggested that an international system of armament inspection be created in the Arctic under the auspices of the United Nations: see Robert D. Hayton, 'Polar Problems and International Law' (1958) 52 AJIL 746 at 750-3; 'The Arctic Zone of International Inspection Proposed in 1957 and 1958' (1960-61) 10 *Polar Record* 153–7. A modern version of this initiative based on satellite monitoring has also been proposed: see Walter A. Dorn, 'An International Monitoring Agency for the Arctic' (1989) 15(1) *Information North* (Newsletter of the Arctic Institute of North America) 1–4.

12 Tucker Scully, 'Arctic Policy' at 5.

13 *Ibid.* at 5–6, where Tucker Scully suggests that this was due to a lack of interest amongst the Arctic states and also the sporadic attention paid in the United States to the development of Arctic policy. This analysis is confirmed by a personal communication, Charles Myers, Office of Polar Studies, National Science Foundation, Washington, DC, 7 April 1993; *cf.* Trevor Lloyd, 'Research and the Circumpolar North: One Canadian Viewpoint' (address to the Nansen Institute, Oslo, Norway, 18 May 1981 – 'The Papers of Trevor Lloyd', National Archives of Canada, MG 30 B97, v. 46), who suggested that while the Canadian government was interested at that time in sponsoring an Antarctic-type agreement for the north polar region, the United States was known to have opposed such a proposal.

14 Erik Franckx, *Maritime Claims in the Arctic* (Dordrecht, 1993) 244. However, a private meeting sponsored by the Ditchley Foundation was held during May 1971 in the UK with participants from Canada, Denmark, Iceland, Norway, the United States and the UK attending.

15 Tucker Scully, 'Arctic Policy' at 5–6; William E. Westermeyer, 'United States Arctic Interests: Background for Policy' in William E. Westermeyer and Kurt M. Shusterich (eds.), *United States Arctic Interests* (New York, 1984) 1 at 14.

pursue programs for increasing bilateral and multilateral cooperation in the Arctic, particularly in the areas of scientific research, resource development, and environmental protection',[16] United States attempts to enhance Arctic regional cooperation were unsuccessful.[17]

Private initiatives were also launched. For example in 1946, Lester Pearson, who subsequently became Canadian Minister for External Affairs and eventually Prime Minister, sought to encourage amongst Canadians and most other Arctic states greater Arctic cooperation. He argued that:

> It is in Canada's interest, and in the general interest, that each northern nation should cooperate with every other in all Arctic problems . . . If the fullest use is to be made of the resources of the northern regions, there should be a pooling of scientific data and a coordination of research and experimentation. All the polar nations can learn from each other and thereby advance the knowledge and resources of mankind.[18]

Another strong Canadian supporter of greater Arctic cooperation was the geographer Trevor Lloyd.[19] For example, he argued in 1965 that scientific collaboration could be used as a basis for improving political relations in the region so that it would be possible for an Antarctic-type treaty to be adopted.[20] However, by 1981, after persisting with this

[16] National Security Decision Memorandum 202, as discussed in Westermeyer, 'United States Arctic Interests' at 14.

[17] In June 1983 National Security Decision Directive 90 was issued which sought to reaffirm the previous two directives of the 1970s. However, in this instance the government was required to advise how best United States activities in the Arctic could be coordinated with those of other Arctic states rather than calling for greater multilateral Arctic cooperation: see Westermeyer, 'United States Arctic Interests' at 14–15.

[18] L. B. Pearson, 'Canada Looks "Down North"' (1945–46) 24 *Foreign Affairs* 638 at 643.

[19] Lloyd worked with the Canadian Institute of International Affairs in the 1940s on a project designed to enhance greater Canadian knowledge of the 'Canadian North' and the potential for its economic development. In the process he also alerted Canadians to strategic issues concerning the North and the need for greater international cooperation amongst the Arctic states: see Trevor Lloyd, 'The New North' (1943) 1(8) *Canadian Affairs* 1–10; Trevor Lloyd, 'Canada's Last Frontier' (1943) 3(4) *Behind the Headlines* 1–30; Trevor Lloyd, 'Frontier of Destiny – The Canadian Arctic' (1946) 6(7) *Behind the Headlines* 1–16.

[20] Trevor Lloyd, 'International Scientific Cooperation in the Arctic' (notes prepared for Vice-Presidential Address, section on geology and geography, American Association for the Advancement of Science, Berkeley, California, 27 December 1965 – 'The papers of Trevor Lloyd', National Archives of Canada, MG 30 B97, v. 46, File 1); see also Trevor Lloyd, 'Some International Aspects of Arctic Canada' (1969–70) 25 IntJ 717 at 724–5.

call for nearly thirty years, Lloyd had become disheartened with the prospects for such cooperation and believed that existing political forces made any comparable Arctic agreement impossible.[21]

Growth in regional cooperation

Thus, although there has long been interest in greater multilateral cooperation amongst Arctic states, the reality is that for much of this century little progress has been made. In the last twenty years, however, there have been some important developments. Bilateral relationships did develop amongst Arctic states. Based on the military relationship in the North which had developed during World War II, Canada and the United States forged a very strong security relationship in the post-war era through their common concern over the need to protect the American Arctic from possible attack by the Soviet Union. Throughout the 1940s and 1950s the Canadian North was in some respects 'occupied' by American military personnel as various defence establishments were built and manned.[22] Multilateral regional cooperation was, however, slow to emerge. The 1973 Polar Bear Agreement[23] was one of the first indications that cooperation of this kind amongst the Arctic states was possible. Commentators believe that its success, however modest, paved the way for subsequent developments.[24]

Since the 1973 Polar Bear Agreement there has been a gradual increase in multilateral and bilateral cooperation between Arctic states.[25] Not surprisingly, cooperation in the field of scientific research

[21] Lloyd, 'Research and the Circumpolar North'.

[22] Through their common concern over continental security, Canada and the United States entered into a number of cooperative arrangements in the post-war era which still have ongoing application and importance for the national security of both states. See John Kirton, 'Beyond Bilateralism: United States-Canadian Cooperation in the Arctic' in William E. Westermeyer and Kurt M. Shusterich (eds.), *United States Arctic Interests* (New York, 1984) 295 at 297–300; David Lenaric and Robert Reford, 'Sovereignty versus Defence: The Arctic in Canadian–American Relations' in Edgar J. Dosman (ed.), *Sovereignty and Security in the Arctic* (London, 1989) 159–75.

[23] Agreement on the Conservation of Polar Bears, (1974) 13 ILM 13.

[24] Gail Osherenko and Oran R. Young, *The Age of the Arctic* (Cambridge, 1989) 241; Oran R. Young, 'Global Commons: The Arctic in World Affairs' (1990) 93(2) *Technology Review* 52 at 57; Clive Archer, 'Arctic Cooperation: A Nordic Model' (1990) 21(2) *Bulletin of Peace Proposals* 165 at 168.

[25] See US Arctic Research Commission, *Arctic Research in a Changing World* (Washington, 1991) 16–17 where it was noted that as at April 1990, 446 agreements, comprising various instruments such as protocols and conventions, dealing with Arctic research had been negotiated. The figure for the period 1970–9 was approximately 150 while the comparative figure for the period prior to 1939 was 30.

has featured prominently. Canada and the Soviet Union negotiated a series of agreements relating to scientific cooperation in the Arctic from the early 1970s[26] which have proved particularly successful.[27] These agreements began to have a particular focus on monitoring the Arctic environment, leading in 1989 to a specific Canada–USSR Agreement on Cooperation in the Arctic and the North which was subsequently renewed by a 1992 Agreement.[28] While the United States and the USSR had agreements on scientific cooperation dating from the period of detente in the early 1970s, these did not have any specific application in the Arctic. However, in 1988 a new five-year agreement was reached between the United States National Academy of Science and the USSR Academy on the area of joint Arctic research cooperation.[29]

One factor which assisted in the push for greater Arctic cooperation during this period was the role played by various non-governmental organisations. The most significant of these were the groups representing the indigenous peoples of the north. The Inuit Circumpolar Conference (ICC) is perhaps the most influential of these. Formed in 1977 by the Inuit of the United States, Canada and Denmark (Greenland), the ICC's mandate is to ensure that Inuit are consulted in the development of policies which affect their homeland and to make substantive contributions to the development of Arctic policy.[30] In furtherance of this policy the ICC has worked with the indigenous

[26] Many of these agreements are unpublished, but are referred to in a number of sources: see Walter Slipchenko, 'Canada–USSR Arctic Science Exchange Programme: An Historical Perspective of Arctic Cooperation' in Lawson W. Brigham (ed.), *The Soviet Maritime Arctic* (London, 1991) 235–57; Archer, 'Arctic Cooperation' at 167; Report of the Working Group of the National Capital Branch of the Canadian Institute of International Affairs, *The Arctic Environment and Canada's International Relations* (Ottawa, 1991) 51–3; Franckx, *Maritime Claims* at 254–7.

[27] Over 150 scientists from Canada and the USSR were involved in exchanges between 1984 and 1989: see Walter Slipchenko, 'International Arctic Cooperation: A Canadian Dream or a Necessity' in *The Arctic* (West Vancouver, 1989) 93 at 99. For a review of some of these initiatives, see Department of Indian and Northern Affairs (Canada), *Building International Relations in the Arctic* (Ottawa, 1991).

[28] Agreement between the Government of Canada and the Government of the Union of the Soviet Socialist Republics on Cooperation in the Arctic and the North, [1989] CTS 21. This Agreement has since been superseded by the Agreement between the Government of Canada and the Government of the Russian Federation on Cooperation in the Arctic and the North (with Annex), [1992] CTS 18.

[29] Archer, 'Arctic Cooperation' at 167.

[30] Frances Abele, 'Confronting "Harsh and Inescapable Facts"': Indigenous Peoples and the Militarisation of the Circumpolar Region' in Edgar J. Dosman (ed.), *Sovereignty and Security in the Arctic* (London, 1989) 176 at 187.

peoples of the Arctic which they represent, and taken a proactive role in urging Arctic states to develop greater cooperative measures on matters of importance to the Inuit. A focus has been cooperative measures to protect the Arctic environment.[31] Other indigenous peoples groups which have supported greater cooperation amongst the Arctic states include the Russian Small Peoples Federation and the Saami. Non-governmental organisations with an interest in disarmament, international cooperation and the Arctic were also active throughout the 1980s, especially in Canada where the Canadian Arctic Resources Committee and the Canadian Centre for Arms Control have been prominent.[32]

The Murmansk initiative

Much of the success in greater Arctic cooperation during the 1980s can be seen as a direct result of the change in political approach by the USSR towards its Arctic neighbours.[33] The most significant event during this era of *glasnost* and *perestroika* was the October 1987 speech by General Secretary Gorbachev in Murmansk. In the 'Murmansk speech' (as it became known) Gorbachev called for greater cooperation amongst the Arctic states. In indicating that the Soviet Union favoured the Arctic becoming a 'zone of peace', he suggested:

(a) that a nuclear-free zone be declared in northern Europe;
(b) that naval activity be limited in the seas adjacent to northern Europe;
(c) that peaceful cooperation be the basis for utilising the resources of the Arctic;

[31] See Inuit Circumpolar Conference, *Principles and Elements for a Comprehensive Arctic Policy* (Montreal, 1992); Inuit Circumpolar Conference, *Direct Involvement of the Arctic's Indigenous Peoples in the International Arctic Council* (Ottawa, 1992). For discussion on the impact of the ICC upon Arctic policy see Report of the Working Group of the National Capital Branch of the Canadian Institute of International Affairs, *The North and Canada's International Relations* (Ottawa, 1988) 47–8.

[32] See Cox and Rauf, *Security Co-operation* at 1–28; Report of the Working Group of the National Capital Branch of the Canadian Institute of International Affairs, *The North and Canada's International Relations* at 1–71. The Canadian Centre for Arms Control is now known as the Canadian Centre for Global Security. See also the reports of the Working Group on Arctic International Relations: e.g., Franklyn Griffiths and Oran R. Young (co-chairs), 'Sustainable Development and the Arctic' (Second Session, Ilulissat and Nuuk, Greenland, 20-4 April 1989) (1989–1) *Working Group on Arctic International Relations Reports and Papers.*

[33] See Gail Osherenko, 'Environmental Cooperation in the Arctic: Will the Soviets Participate?' (1989) 1 *International Environmental Affairs* 203–21.

(d) that scientific study of the Arctic has great significance for all mankind;
(e) that the countries of the north cooperate in matters of environmental protection;
(f) that the Northern Sea Route be opened by the Soviet Union to ice-breaker escorted passage.[34]

Following the Murmansk speech the USSR sought to implement aspects of Gorbachev's Arctic agenda. A State Commission for Arctic Affairs was established in the USSR, Arctic cooperation was actively discussed in December 1987 by Gorbachev and President Reagan in Washington, and the Soviet Union entered into a further round of cooperative scientific exchange agreements with the Scandinavian states.[35] However, it was recognised that the 'zone of peace' could not be created instantly. Rather, as noted by the Soviet Ambassador to Canada in 1989, the process:

includes parallel steps along the following directions: lowering the level of military confrontation in the region; building confidence between Subarctic and northern states; expanding cooperation in the field of Arctic natural resource development; conducting scientific research, including research aimed at keeping an ecological balance in the region; and ensuring the social and economic rights of the native population.[36]

A further development following the Murmansk initiative was the creation of the International Arctic Science Committee (IASC). A proposal for the formation of such a Committee had first been made in early 1987 and following the Gorbachev speech the groundwork was laid for its eventual establishment in 1990.[37] The creation of the IASC, which like the Scientific Committee on Antarctic Research is a non-governmental body, was an important initiative.[38] A major part of

[34] Reprinted in T. E. Armstrong, 'Soviet Proposals for the Arctic: A Policy Declaration by Mr Gorbachev' (1988) 24 *Polar Record* 68–9.

[35] See Young, *The Arctic in World Affairs* at 18–19; Archer, 'Arctic Cooperation' at 167. For further discussion of responses to the Murmansk speech, see Clive Archer, 'Western Responses to the Murmansk Initiative' (1989) 14 *Centrepiece* (Centre for Defence Studies, Aberdeen).

[36] Alexei A. Rodionov, 'Soviet Approaches to Security and Peaceful Cooperation in the Arctic: An Overview' in *The Arctic* (West Vancouver, 1989) 209 at 210. For a further analysis of the Murmansk speech see Ronald Purver, 'Arctic Security: The Murmansk Initiative and its Impact' (1988) 11(4) *Current Research on Peace and Violence* 147–58.

[37] Peter Gizewski, 'Arctic Security After the Thaw: A Post-Cold War Reassessment (Report of the Panel on Arctic Security)' (1993) 17 *Aurora Papers* (Canadian Centre for Global Security) 6.

[38] Archer, 'Arctic Cooperation' at 168–9 has argued that the IASC potentially represents a 'breakthrough in Arctic international organizations'. For a review of the

the Committee's work is the facilitation of greater cooperative efforts amongst Arctic scientists, especially those working in environmental science. The creation of the IASC was a further indicator that representatives from Arctic states were increasingly prepared to take a regional approach in dealing with areas of common interest.[39]

Arctic Environmental Protection Strategy

One of the most significant developments in multilateral arrangements in the Arctic in recent years was the adoption in 1991 of the Arctic Environmental Protection Strategy (AEPS).[40] The AEPS had been the subject of negotiation since 1989 and was the culmination of attempts led by Finland to produce greater multilateral cooperation amongst Arctic states for protection of the Arctic environment. Its acceptance by the eight Arctic states – Canada, Denmark, Finland, Iceland, Norway, Sweden, the USSR and the United States – represents a further step towards more substantive and integrated cooperation amongst Arctic states.

The genesis of the AEPS was a letter sent by Finland to the other seven Arctic states in January 1989 proposing a conference on the protection of the Arctic environment.[41] On 20 September 1989 the first Consultative Meeting on the Protection of the Arctic Environment was held in Rovaniemi, Finland. Prior to the meeting Finland prepared a working paper identifying the major environmental threats to the Arctic environment. Climate change, pollution of the marine environment and exploitation of the living and non-living resources were all identified.[42] Finland argued that the effective protection of the Arctic required greater intergovernmental cooperation, scientific research, and monitoring of the ecosystem. As to the legal form that any

development of the IASC and its founding articles, see Odd Rogne, 'The International Arctic Science Committee: From Conception to Birth' (Fall 1990) 4 *Arctic Research of the United States* 65–9.

[39] While the IASC is strictly a non-governmental body, most of the scientists who represent Arctic states are employed or directly funded by government agencies. For an assessment of the IASC, see Franckx, *Maritime Claims* at 258–61.

[40] (1991) 30 ILM 1624 (hereinafter AEPS). For a review see David D. Caron, 'Towards an Arctic Environmental Regime' (1993) 24 ODIL 377–92.

[41] 'Time Runs out in the Protection of the Arctic Environment', Press Release, Ministry for Foreign Affairs, Helsinki, Finland, 30 August 1989; for further detail see Esko Rajakoski, 'Multilateral Cooperation to Protect the Arctic Environment: The Finnish Initiative' in *The Arctic* (West Vancouver, 1989) 53–9.

[42] Rajakoski, 'Multilateral Cooperation' at 56–7.

instrument resulting from these discussions should take, it was suggested by one Finnish diplomat that the process 'could lead, for example, to a declaration, convention, or other multilateral arrangement exclusively dedicated to the protection of the environment of the Arctic'.[43]

The September 1989 Rovaniemi Meeting was partly designed to ascertain the level of support amongst Arctic states for more enhanced cooperative measures on the Arctic environment, and, if the support for this initiative was positive, to commence a process of determining the environmental and legal issues confronting the region. To that end, two working groups were established in order to: (1) review the state of the environment in the Arctic and the need for further action; and (2) consider the existing international legal instruments for the protection of the Arctic environment and the organisation of future cooperation.[44] The outcomes of this meeting were positive enough, with enough issues of common concern identified for a further meeting to be scheduled for Yellowknife, Canada in April 1990. Meanwhile, each participating state was requested to prepare reports on certain focal areas of the Arctic environment.

The Yellowknife Meeting saw for the first time reference made to the need for developing a 'strategy' to deal with the protection of the Arctic environment. The work of the two previously established working groups was continued, and an *ad hoc* group to develop the elements of a strategy for Arctic environmental protection was created.[45] It also became possible to identify various concerns amongst the participants over the need for action on certain environmental issues. It was agreed:

(a) that research and monitoring were fundamental to understanding environmental problems to enable appropriate solutions to be found;
(b) that action taken on a national, bilateral and multilateral basis would all be necessary to resolve Arctic environmental problems;
(c) that a programme of international ecological cooperation should be established for the Arctic;
(d) that an Arctic Sustainable Development Strategy would be a clear expression of commitment by Arctic states to the problem; and

[43] *Ibid.* at 58.

[44] 'Protection of the Arctic Environment', Report of the Consultative Meeting on the Protection of the Arctic Environment, Rovaniemi, 20–6 September 1989, 1 (hereinafter Rovaniemi 1).

[45] 'Protecting the Arctic Environment, Report of the Yellowknife Preparatory Meeting, Yellowknife, NWT, Canada, 18–23 April 1990, 1–2 (hereinafter Rovaniemi 2).

(e) that existing legal instruments may provide the basis for improved Arctic environmental protection through their strengthening and broader application.[46]

By the conclusion of the Yellowknife Meeting a draft document had been prepared which formed the basis for future discussions over the content of the AEPS.[47]

A third Preparatory Meeting was held in Kiruna, Sweden from 15–17 January 1991. On this occasion work proceeded somewhat differently to that of previous meetings with a working group established to deal with drafting the AEPS and another to deal with specific environmental issues.[48] As good progress was made on both these issues it was considered that the draft was well enough advanced to be presented for signature at a ministerial meeting later that year in Rovaniemi.[49]

The final meetings associated with the negotiation of the AEPS took place in Rovaniemi from 10–14 June 1991. Three days were dedicated to meetings amongst government officials so as to finalise both the AEPS draft and a 'Declaration on the Protection of the Arctic Environment'. To conclude, a ministerial-level Meeting was held on 13–14 June. Present as observers were representatives of Germany, Poland, the UK, the UN Economic Commission for Europe, the IASC, the ICC, the USSR Association of Small Peoples of the North and the Nordic Saami Council. All states attending the Conference and the observers were given an opportunity to address the Conference on the question of circumpolar environmental cooperation.[50] The AEPS and Declaration were formally adopted on 14 June. The Declaration takes the form of a statement of intention and support for the AEPS by the eight Arctic states, with many of the important features of the Strategy summarised and a commitment given to 'take steps towards its implementation and consider its future elaboration'.[51]

[46] *Ibid.* at 2–3.

[47] See *ibid.*, Annex II:10, 140-9. For a review of the initiative up to this meeting, and other cooperative efforts being taken by Arctic states towards greater environmental protection, see David D. Caron, 'Arctic – 1990: The Year in Review' (1990) 1 YIEL 181–5.

[48] 'Protecting the Arctic Environment', Report of the Kiruna Preparatory Meeting, 15–17 January 1991, 2–3 (hereinafter Rovaniemi 3).

[49] *Ibid.* at 3.

[50] 'Arctic Environmental Protection Meeting – Report', Rovaniemi, Finland, 10-14 June 1991); see the speeches reproduced at Appendix 3 of this document.

[51] 'Declaration on the Protection of the Arctic Environment', reprinted in *ibid.* at 151–4.

Principal AEPS provisions

The AEPS outlines existing Arctic environmental issues, the existing legal regime dealing with those issues, and proposes certain responses to the identified problems. In doing so, the eight Arctic states confirm their commitment to international cooperation so as 'to ensure the protection of the Arctic environment and its sustainable and equitable development, while protecting the cultures of indigenous peoples'.[52] The five objectives of the AEPS are:

(a) to protect the Arctic ecosystem including humans;
(b) to provide for the protection, enhancement and restoration of environmental quality and the sustainable utilisation of natural resources, including their use by local populations and indigenous peoples in the Arctic;
(c) to recognise and, to the extent possible, seek to accommodate the traditional and cultural needs, values and practices of the indigenous peoples as determined by themselves, related to the protection of the Arctic environment;
(d) to review regularly the state of the Arctic environment; and
(e) to identify, reduce and, as a final goal, eliminate pollution.[53]

The AEPS is also guided by various principles of implementation in which conservation, sustainable utilisation, the interdependence of ecosystem components, the interests of indigenous peoples and the transfer of appropriate technology are all to be taken into account.[54]

In response to the work done at the Preparatory Meetings, the AEPS identified six specific pollution issues requiring attention. 'State of the Environment' reports had been prepared on each of these issues so that all parties would have a similar basis of information upon which to judge their responses to these identified problems. The identified pollution problems were: persistent organic contaminants, oil pollution, heavy metals, noise, radioactivity and acidification.[55] In seeking to determine what response should individually and collectively be taken to these identified problems, the existing international legal regimes covering each pollutant are also identified. Only in the case of radioactivity was it considered that the existing legal regime adequately dealt with the identified pollution problem.[56]

In response to the inadequacy of most existing legal regimes to deal

[52] AEPS, Section 1, p. 2. [53] AEPS, Section 2, p. 4. [54] AEPS, Section 2.2, pp. 4–6.

[55] AEPS, Section 3, pp. 7–17. However, this does not represent a comprehensive listing of Arctic environmental problems: for more detail see Lassi Heininen (ed.), *Arctic Environmental Problems* (2nd) (Tampere, 1990). [56] AEPS, Section 4, pp. 18–23.

with these pollutants and the difficulties encountered hitherto by the Arctic states in unilaterally or cooperatively resolving these problems, an 'action plan' is prescribed for the Arctic environment. As noted in the AEPS:

> The eight Arctic countries agree to proceed cooperatively with the following action plan. These commitments will begin the process of addressing the serious environmental issues identified and assessed through the preparation of specific state of environment reports.[57]

To assist in this process, an 'Arctic Monitoring and Assessment Program' (AMAP) is established with a view to making further enquiries into the state of the Arctic environment, reviewing and coordinating existing national programmes within an international framework and making recommendations to reduce further risks to Arctic ecosystems.[58] AMAP has since been implemented through the establishment of an Arctic Monitoring and Assessment Task Force and a small secretariat established by the Norwegian government.

Other measures taken under the AEPS include: agreement to utilise the terms of the 1982 United Nations Convention on the Law of the Sea (UNCLOS)[59] to improve protection of the Arctic marine environment;[60] a commitment to improve emergency prevention, preparedness and response;[61] and cooperation on the conservation of Arctic flora and fauna.[62] In response to the establishment of AMAP and in recognition of the need for further continuing cooperation and discussion on Arctic environmental matters, regular meetings on the Arctic environment are to be held.[63] At such meetings it is provided that the further identification of measures to implement the Strategy, discussions on cooperation in new fields relevant to Arctic environmental protection, the making of recommendations to protect the Arctic environment and the improvement of existing Arctic environmental regimes will be considered.[64]

Implementation of AEPS

There has been considerable activity among the Arctic states in implementing AEPS programmes. The most substantial of these has been AMAP. An AMAP Task Force has been established and meets annually. Between sessions, Task Force activities are dealt with by a

[57] AEPS, Section 5, p. 24. [58] AEPS, Section 6, pp. 30-3. [59] (1982) 21 ILM 1,261.
[60] AEPS, Section 7, pp. 34–5. [61] AEPS, Section 8, pp. 36–8.
[62] AEPS, Section 9, pp. 39–43. [63] AEPS, Section 10, pp. 44–5.
[64] AEPS, Section 10, pp. 44–5.

board which is supported by a secretariat. Five AMAP sub-programmes have also been established with various states given the responsibility for managing progress. These programmes are: Atmospheric (Canada), Human Health (Denmark), Freshwater (Finland), Marine (Norway) and Terrestrial (Sweden).[65] In addition, in 1993 an updated 'state of the environment' report was prepared and recommendations were made with regard to areas of concern requiring immediate action.[66] The Conservation of Arctic Flora and Fauna (CAFF) Working Group has been operational since 1992 and a small secretariat has been established in Canada.[67] To date the Working Group has operated through designated CAFF agencies and national contacts in each Arctic state. The International Working Group of CAFF also meets annually, with the chairing of meetings rotating between the Arctic states. Smaller working groups within CAFF have also been established to deal with seabirds, biodiversity and circumpolar protected areas. In 1994, CAFF released a major report titled 'The State of Protected Areas in the Circumpolar Arctic 1994' which has become a baseline study for future initiatives.[68] The Working Group on Protection of the Arctic Marine Environment (PAME) has also been established and held its first meeting in 1994.[69] Action has also been taken to deal with other initiatives concerning emergency prevention, preparedness and response, while a task force has also been created to deal with sustainable development.

The first post-1991 ministerial meeting to review the AEPS was held in Nuuk, Greenland on 16 September 1993.[70] The meeting reviewed the progress made in implementing the AEPS and to that end reports

[65] See 'First Meeting of Arctic Monitoring and Assessment Task Force' (Spring 1992) 6 *Arctic Research of the United States* 121–2; Arctic Monitoring and Assessment Programme, *The Monitoring Programme for Arctic Monitoring and Assessment Programme, AMAP* (Oslo, July 1993).

[66] Arctic Monitoring and Assessment Task Force, 'Report to Ministers – Update on Issues of Concern to the Arctic Environment, Including Recommendations for Action' (September 1993) 8 at para. 7.2. For a review of the early implementation of AMAP see L.-O. Reiersen, 'Arctic Monitoring and Assessment Programme (AMAP) – A Presentation of the Process, Organization and the Programme' in E. Tikkanen *et al.* (eds.), *Symposium on the State of the Environment and Environmental Monitoring in Northern Fennoscandia and the Kola Peninsula* (Rovaniemi, 1992) 13–22.

[67] See *CAFF Newsletter* 1 (1) (1995).

[68] CAFF: Conservation of Arctic Flora and Fauna, *The State of Protected Areas in the Circumpolar Arctic 1994* (Habitat Conservation Report No. 1) (Trondheim, 1994).

[69] See Working Group on the Protection of the Arctic Marine Environment (PAME), *Report from the First Meeting* (Oslo, Norway, 3–5 May 1994).

[70] The meeting is formally known as the 'Second Ministerial Conference'; the 'First Ministerial Conference' was held at the formal signing of the AEPS in 1991.

were received from AMAP and the CAFF Working Group. Matters relating to the protection of the Arctic marine environment, emergency prevention, preparedness and response, and indigenous knowledge were also reviewed.[71] The meeting also resulted in a formal declaration: the Nuuk Declaration on Environment and Development in the Arctic.[72] In many respects the Declaration seeks to reaffirm the principles of cooperation embodied in the AEPS; however, there are also provisions which contemplate new initiatives. In particular the need for additional action or instruments dealing with the prevention of pollution to the Arctic marine environment is to be reviewed, while the need for effective domestic environmental legislation was recognised as being a prerequisite for protection of the environment.[73] Reference was also made to the need for effective application of existing legal instruments relevant to the protection of the Arctic environment, and to consideration being given to the development of regional instruments to implement such protection.[74]

With the AEPS only having been adopted in 1991, it is difficult to assess the actual impact that it has had at the domestic level in the Arctic states. This is partly due to no formal review of AEPS implementation yet having taken place, and also because each Arctic state has varying mechanisms in place to implement the AEPS. Canada has perhaps been the best placed to meet its domestic obligations under the Strategy. In 1991 the government announced $100m in funding to support Canadian Arctic environmental research and clean-up operations,[75] and also released an 'Arctic Environmental Strategy' for the Canadian Arctic.[76] Following the break-up of the USSR, Russia has faced substantial barriers in implementing its commitments under the AEPS.[77] This has directly raised the prospect of the Arctic states providing either bilateral or multilateral funding assistance to Russia

[71] AEPS, *Report of the Second Ministerial Conference* (Nuuk, Greenland, 16 September 1993) 7–16. [72] *Ibid.* at 3–6. [73] *Ibid.*, paras. 2 and 4. [74] *Ibid.*, paras. 10 and 11.

[75] Ross Howard, 'Arctic Protection Program Unveiled' 30 April 1991, *The [Toronto] Globe and Mail*, A4. For a review of this domestic initiative, and others taken by Canada prior to the AEPS, see Robert F. Keith, 'Canada's Arctic Environmental Strategy: Critique and Prospect' (1992) 8/9 *Northern Review* 83–113.

[76] See Department of Indian and Northern Affairs (Canada), *The Arctic Environmental Strategy* (Ottawa, 1991). For an example of how this initiative has been implemented, see Water Resources Division, Natural Resources and Environment Branch, Indian and Northern Affairs (Canada), *Arctic Environmental Strategy Water Program, Annual Report 1993–1994* (Ottawa, 1994).

[77] Arctic Monitoring and Assessment Task Force, 'Report to Ministers' at 9, para. 8.0 refers to the financial issues relating to the contribution from Russia.

so as to assist in Arctic clean-up operations and AEPS implementation.[78] With Sweden, Finland and Norway all vitally interested in the impact of pollution upon the Kara Peninsula and Barents Sea region such assistance may be the only solution. Whatever solution is adopted, however, it is clear that the financial obligations imposed upon states under the AEPS have become a matter of concern.

Legal aspects of the AEPS

Two important legal issues arise in regard to the AEPS: (1) its jurisdictional reach; and (2) its legal status and the extent of the obligations it creates for the parties. There is no definition of the 'Arctic' in the Strategy. All of the eight state parties have territory within the Arctic region,[79] but some have land territories in very temperate climates. Reference is made throughout the Strategy to both the Arctic ecosystem and Arctic environment, but there are no definitions of what these terms mean. It seems that a decision was made in the course of the negotiations not to include a definition of the 'Arctic'.[80] When this issue was raised it became obvious that there were a great variety of definitions and that this could have resulted in a stalemate. It was decided to leave the question undefined so that each member state could determine for itself exactly what the reach of the Strategy would be. Accordingly, it would seem that how far each state wishes to extend the operation of the Strategy is a domestic matter. For some states such as Canada, the United States, Denmark and Iceland this is a relatively simple matter because each has defined geographical and jurisdictional boundaries in the region. The situation in Finland, Norway, Russia and Sweden is a little different. It does not seem, however, that this has created any major difficulties in implementing the Strategy.[81]

[78] See Kevin D. O'Shea, 'Canadian Technical Assistance in Russia' in *A Northern Foreign Policy for Canada*, John M. Lamb (ed.) (Ottawa, 1994) 165–7.

[79] Iceland would be the only state excluded from the 'Arctic' if the boundary was determined on the basis of the Arctic Circle. However, as noted in chapter 2 this is not a commonly accepted boundary for the region. As the region is defined for the purposes of this study, only those states who are parties to the AEPS qualify as Arctic states.

[80] Personal communication, Garth E. Bangay, Director, Environment and Renewable Resources Directorate, Department of Indian and Northern Affairs, Ottawa, Canada (22 April 1993).

[81] See Arctic Monitoring and Assessment Programme, *The Monitoring Programme* at 5 where it is noted:

> For the AMAP process, the definition of the Arctic has been kept flexible. The

As for the legal status of the AEPS, a question arises as to whether it can be considered a treaty. Article 2 of the 1969 Vienna Convention on the Law of Treaties[82] defines a 'treaty' as:

> an international agreement concluded between States in written form and governed by international law, whether embodied in a single instrument or two or more related instruments and whatever its particular designation.

While the AEPS is in written form and concluded between states, there is doubt as to whether it was intended to be governed by international law.[83] There is nothing to indicate that the AEPS was subject to ratification by the parties, or that it was intended to be registered with the United Nations. Nonetheless, it is significant that in the 'Introduction' to the Strategy it is noted that: 'The implementation of the Strategy will be carried out through national legislation and in accordance with international law, including customary international law as reflected in the 1982 United Nations Convention on the Law of the Sea.'[84] While the AEPS acknowledges that it shall be implemented consistently with international law, the language which is used throughout is not such that legal rights and obligations are created or imposed upon the state parties.[85] Nevertheless, there are numerous instances where the state parties do make commitments to pursue various courses of action to protect the Arctic environment, and there is contemplation of joint cooperative action being taken to deal with the identified Arctic environmental problems.

> Arctic has been defined as a combination of either the area north of the Polar circle, or the area affected by permafrost. This means that in Scandinavia the Polar circle is used as the southern limit, while in Russia, Canada, USA and Greenland the southern limit will be at approximately 60 degrees North or even further south at the southern limit of permafrost.

[82] 1155 UNTS 331.

[83] That the instrument is called a 'Strategy' is not conclusive in a determination as to whether it is or is not a treaty: this follows from the general acceptance in the Vienna Convention and by many jurists that 'treaty' is a generic term which covers many types of international agreements between states in written form: see T. O. Elias, *The Modern Law of Treaties* (Dobbs Ferry, NY, 1974) 14.

[84] AEPS, Section 1, p. 3.

[85] Alexei Yu Roginko and Matthew J. LaMourie, 'Emerging Marine Environmental Protection Strategies for the Arctic' (1992) 16 *Marine Policy* 259 at 267, where the AEPS is described as not entailing 'legally binding obligations on the signatories'; Franckx, *Maritime Claims* at 247. Oscar Schachter, 'The Twilight Existence of Nonbinding International Agreements' (1977) 71 AJIL 296 at 297 notes that:

> Statements of general aims and broad declarations of principles are considered too indefinite to create enforceable obligations and therefore agreements which do not go beyond that should be presumed to be nonbinding.

While commentators on the law of treaties emphasise that a treaty may take many forms and be concluded under a great many differing circumstances,[86] it is also essential that the parties to the instrument intended to create international legal relations.[87] As has been noted by Rosenne:

> if the participants in that negotiation, for whatever reason, do not intend the arrangement which comes out of the negotiation, however formal that arrangement might look, to be an agreement covered by international law, it will not be a 'treaty' for the purposes of international law, whatever else it might be, and however much of a 'commitment' it might express.[88]

On balance, the AEPS may be more appropriately classified as being an example of 'soft law' in that it calls for the acquisition of more scientific data concerning the Arctic environment, the gradual implementation of additional legal instruments and the enhancement of multilateral cooperation amongst the Arctic states through existing and emerging legal mechanisms.[89] However, even if the AEPS is properly classified as an example of soft law, this does not mean an absence of legal rights and obligations for the parties to it,[90] but rather different consequences for the enforcement of those soft law rights and obligations.[91]

A close review of the AEPS does reveal in places an intention to rely upon existing legal instruments, the enhancement of others and the development of new legal mechanisms to deal with Arctic environmental problems. In short, the Strategy does not ignore legal mechanisms and indeed makes reference to their use to achieve its goals. As regards the Action Plan to deal with the problems of the Arctic environment, the state parties agree to take certain action and implement various measures to deal with these problems. In the case of Persistent Organic Contaminants, support is given for the further implementation of existing international instruments plus the ongo-

[86] Elias, *The Modern Law of Treaties* at 13; Jennings and Watts, *Oppenheim's International Law* at 1207–11; A. McNair, *The Law of Treaties* (Oxford, 1961) 5–34; I. A. Shearer, *Starke's International Law* (11th) (London, 1994) 397–401.

[87] Jennings and Watts, *Oppenheim's International Law* at 1202; McNair, *The Law of Treaties* at 4.

[88] Shabtai Rosenne, *Developments in the Law of Treaties 1945–1986* (Cambridge, 1989) 87.

[89] Caron, 'Towards an Arctic Environmental Regime' at 379; for a discussion of soft law see C. M. Chinkin, 'The Challenge of Soft Law: Development and Change in International Law' (1989) 38 ICLQ 850 at 851.

[90] Rosenne, *Developments* at 87; Schachter, 'The Twilight Existence' at 301–4.

[91] See Chinkin, 'The Challenge of Soft Law' at 865–6. For a further discussion of the effect of non-binding international instruments, see Anthony Aust, 'The Theory and Practice of Informal International Instruments' (1986) 35 ICLQ 787–812.

ing negotiations for the extension of the 1979 Convention on Long-Range Transboundary Air Pollution.[92] With respect to oil pollution, there is agreement to adhere to existing international standards and to work towards the strengthening of measures specifically dealing with the Arctic Ocean.[93] A similar commitment is given in regard to heavy metals pollution.[94] In the case of pollution caused by radioactivity, the AEPS identifies a need for further consideration being given to the development of more specific measures to deal with this problem within the existing international legal framework.[95]

Some of the strongest provisions in the AEPS concerning the taking of appropriate legal action to deal with the identified issues occur in those parts of the Strategy dealing with the protection of the Arctic marine environment and the protection of Arctic flora and fauna. In the case of the marine environment, particular emphasis is placed upon the taking of action through existing international organisations and UNCLOS. The state parties agree to apply the principles adopted in UNCLOS concerning the protection and preservation of the marine environment and further strengthen rules dealing with the Arctic, and also to review other international instruments connected with the protection of the marine environment in order to ascertain whether all the Arctic states should accede to such instruments.[96] In the case of conservation of Arctic flora and fauna a more detailed plan is proposed to deal with this issue. In particular, reference is made to an 'understanding' reached on the need to 'develop more effective laws, regulations and practices for the conservation of Arctic flora and fauna, their diversity, and their habitats in close cooperation with Arctic indigenous peoples'.[97]

The position of the AEPS parties seems to be that they do not believe that the Strategy imposes any legal obligations upon them.[98] Rather, they see the AEPS as a cooperative multilateral agreement which is designed to expose Arctic environmental problems, discuss how they can be best dealt with and then allow states to go away and deal with these matters on a domestic basis. At most, they see the AEPS as only

[92] AEPS, Section 5.1, pp. 24–5; (1979) 18 ILM 1,442. In 1994, a Protocol on Further Reduction of Sulphur Emissions, (1994) 33 ILM 1,540 was adopted with six of the Arctic states (Canada, Denmark, Finland, Norway, Russia, Sweden) original signatories. [93] AEPS, Section 5.2, p. 26. [94] AEPS, Section 5.3, p. 27.

[95] AEPS, Section 5.5, p. 28. [96] AEPS, Section 7, p. 34–5. [97] AEPS, Section 9.1.iv, p. 41.

[98] Bangay, note 80 above; personal communication with Dr Robert G. McRae, Deputy Director, Environment Division, Department of External Affairs, Ottawa, Canada (21 April 1993).

imposing 'soft' obligations. If these obligations had been put any higher it was likely that states such as the United States may have refused to sign. Nevertheless, the parties do seem to have committed themselves to working towards the more effective implementation of existing legal mechanisms, and developing others to deal with specific Arctic environmental problems. In this respect the AEPS resembles a framework legal instrument in which various measures to deal with problems of the Arctic environment are proposed. Some of these measures may have legal consequences while others may lead to the exchange of further information. Because of the uncertain nature of the obligations created by the AEPS it is difficult to predict how the Arctic states will individually or collectively go about implementing its terms. There is the potential for a wide variety of responses to be taken towards the AEPS and each may be consistent with the expectations of the original negotiators.

The Canadian proposal for an Arctic Council

Another recent Arctic proposal is that the eight Arctic states create an Arctic Council. This concept, which has been sponsored by Canada, originated outside of government and was supported by a number of prominent Canadian academics and non-governmental organisations throughout the 1970s and 1980s. Maxwell Cohen proposed in the early 1970s that Canada use its good offices to promote amongst the Arctic states 'an Arctic basin treaty' which would allow for the development of broad Arctic basin policies relating to maritime issues and environmental protection.[99] As has been noted above, proposals for Arctic international cooperation were not well received in the 1970s. However, the idea was revived in 1988 by both Donat Pharand[100] and a Working Group of the National Capital Branch of the Canadian Institute of International Affairs (CIIA).[101] In supporting the concept, the CIIA argued in a report titled 'The North and Canada's International Relations' that an 'Arctic

[99] Maxwell Cohen, 'The Arctic and the National Interest' (1970) 26 IntJ 52 at 79, 81; see Donat Pharand, 'The Case for an Arctic Region Council and a Treaty Proposal' (1992) 23 *Revue générale de droit* 163 at 166.

[100] See Donat Pharand, 'Remarks - Legal Regimes of the Arctic' (1988) 82 ProcAmSocIL 328 at 332.

[101] Report of a Working Group of the National Capital Branch of the Canadian Institute of International Affairs, *The North and Canada's International Relations* at 49–50, 58–9.

Basin Council' could deal with issues such as scientific and exploratory activities, problems of resource and economic development, conservation and the environment, indigenous peoples, the application of the law of the sea and the exchange of relevant information between the Antarctic Treaty parties.[102]

Political support for the proposal came in 1989 when Canadian Prime Minister, Brian Mulroney, while on a visit to Leningrad to conclude bilateral agreements with the Soviet Union concerning the Arctic, asked in the course of a speech to polar specialists: 'And why not a council of Arctic countries eventually coming into existence to coordinate and promote cooperation among them?'[103] The Canadian Minister for External Affairs, Joe Clark, subsequently developed the Canadian proposal further. Speaking in Ottawa in 1990, Clark stated:

> The Government believes that now is the time to move forward to establish that Arctic Council. Canada intends to propose an Arctic Council to the seven other Arctic Countries – Finland, Sweden, Norway, Iceland, Greenland, the United States and the Soviet Union. We will raise the proposal at a ministerial meeting in Finland next spring on environmental cooperation. Canada is willing to host a small secretariat for this Council and contribute to sustaining it from the outset.[104]

At the same time, Canadian non-governmental organisations were continuing to develop models for what form and role such a Council should take in Arctic affairs. In May 1991 a major report was released by the 'Arctic Council Panel'.[105] Titled 'To Establish an International Council: A Framework Report', this report sought to deal with a wide range of issues concerning the creation of an Arctic Council.[106] Describing the goals of the Council as being both procedural and substantive, it argued that:

[102] *Ibid.* at 58–9.

[103] Notes for an address by the Right Honourable Brian Mulroney, 24 November 1989, PMO Press (27 November 1989), 14:12, p. 6, cited in Pharand, 'The Case for an Arctic Region Council' at 167.

[104] Address by the Right Honourable Joe Clark, 'The Changing Soviet Union: Implications for Canada and the World' (28 November 1990), cited in Pharand, 'The Case for an Arctic Region Council' at 167.

[105] The Panel's work was supported by the Canadian Arctic Resources Committee, the ICC and the Canadian Centre for Arms Control and Disarmament.

[106] Arctic Council Panel (Franklin Griffiths and Rosemarie Kuptana, co-chairs), *To Establish an International Arctic Council* (Ottawa, 1991). The Arctic Council Panel was a private initiative formed under the 'Arctic Council Project' in which northerners and northern experts came together to study the feasibility of an Arctic Council.

The ultimate mandate of an Arctic Council should be to make the circumpolar region into a domain of enhanced civility – an area in which aboriginal peoples enjoy their full rights, and where national governments that speak for southern majorities accord progressively greater respect to the natural environment, to one another, and, in particular, to aboriginal peoples.[107]

In an effort to provide a framework for the Arctic Council debate, fourteen founding articles were proposed. These described the Council as 'a general-purpose inter-governmental institution established to encourage civility in arctic affairs by means of co-operation for the harmonious and equitable evolution of the region'.[108] Since the release of this Report other non-governmental organisations such as the CIIA and the Canadian Centre for Global Security have also strongly supported the Arctic Council proposal.[109]

Canada formally put the Arctic Council proposal to the other Arctic states at the 1991 Rovaniemi ministerial meeting convened to conclude the AEPS. The first formal meeting to discuss the proposal was held during May 1992 in Ottawa.[110] Since then, a number of meetings have taken place between the Arctic states in an effort to finalise the concept. The major questions which arise from the Arctic Council proposal are:

(a) which states and other entities will be eligible to become members of the Council?;
(b) over which area shall the Council's mandate extend?;
(c) what shall be the mandate of the Council?; and
(d) what institutional structure shall the Council take?

Each will be briefly discussed.

Membership

Since the Canadian proposal was initially made to the eight Arctic states (the Arctic Eight), there seems little doubt that it is intended that the existing eight Arctic states be founding members of the Council. The more difficult issues regarding membership are whether

[107] *Ibid.* at 2. [108] *Ibid.* at 28, Art. 1.

[109] Report of the Working Group of the National Capital Branch of the Canadian Institute of International Affairs, *The Arctic Environment* at 68–71, 76–7; Gizewski, 'Arctic Security' at 19; see also a special theme issue of the Canadian Arctic Resources Committee newsletter 'Northern Perspectives' – 'Arctic Council: Canada Prepares for a New Era in Circumpolar Relations' (Summer 1991) 19(2) *Northern Perspectives* 1–23.

[110] 'Arctic Nations Approve Council Framework Agreement' (Summer 1992) 2 (6) *CARC Members' Update* 2.

other states and governmental entities with interests in the Arctic will be able to join and what role, if any, will non-governmental organisations play. States outside the Arctic Eight which may be interested in becoming members of the Arctic Council would include Germany, Poland, Japan and the United Kingdom. All of these states currently have an interest, whether it be historic, economic or scientific, in Arctic affairs. The status conferred on these non-Arctic states would depend on the institutional structure of the Council. A similar issue exists in regard to the potential role of northern territorial governments such as Alaska, Yukon and Greenland, and regional governments such as Chukotski and Nunavik.[111] Some of these territorial governments are currently members of the 'Northern Forum' and it may be possible for this body to represent northern territorial and regional governments as an associate member or observer.[112]

One of the most important issues concerning the Council is the potential status or role of non-governmental organisations. This particularly relates to the interests of the indigenous peoples of the Arctic. Should indigenous people's organisations be accorded the same status as state representatives, be included on state governmental delegations which attend Council meetings, or be offered observer status? All the draft proposals emanating from Canada consider that indigenous peoples groups such as the ICC have a major role to play in the Council structure.[113] The Canadian approach is based on a respect for and understanding of the legitimate role that the indigenous peoples of the Arctic have to play in any local, national or international process which concerns the region in which they live. The Arctic Council Panel supported the ICC, or a similar representative organisation, having a full seat on the Arctic Council.[114] Given the role that

[111] Pharand, 'The Case for an Arctic Region Council' at 192.

[112] The Northern Forum is an international organisation comprising regional northern leaders and additional representatives from business, universities, special interest groups and the private sector. It was formed in 1991 to address a broad range of northern concerns (health care, education, transportation). Representatives from regional and territorial governments and councils from Canada, Russia, the USA, Finland, Norway, the People's Republic of China, Mongolia, Sweden and Korea have attended meetings of the forum: see Lisa Frostad, 'Northern Forum Update' (Fall 1991) 5 *Arctic Research of the United States* 60-1.

[113] Arctic Council Panel, *To Establish* at 2, where it is argued: 'an Arctic Council must provide for direct, full and meaningful participation by arctic aboriginal peoples in the work of the Council itself and in the international negotiating process that brings it into being', and at 29, Art. 12–13; see also generally Pharand, 'The Case for an Arctic Region Council'.

[114] Arctic Council Panel, *To Establish* at 19.

indigenous peoples played in the negotiation and current implementation of the AEPS, it is inconceivable that this group will not have some significant representation in the Council structure. The problem that arises with accommodating the interests of these peoples is whether other non-governmental organisations should also be accommodated in the Council structure. It could be argued, for example, that environmental groups also have a legitimate interest in an Arctic Council which seeks to deal with Arctic environmental issues. Given the political power of some environmental groups in countries such as Canada, Denmark and the United States there may be strong pressure on governments to allow such organisations to play an active role in the Council. This may result in some Arctic states adopting the view that the Council would become too cumbersome if all the potentially interested parties were to be represented in the Council. As a result a minimalist position may be taken on membership, with the Arctic Eight the only states allowed to participate.

Area of application

As already noted in chapter 2 there is no agreed definition of what comprises the Arctic region. While this was not a major issue in regard to the AEPS, the creation of an international organisation which seeks to deal with issues of a particular concern to the Arctic as a region does require a definition of the area over which it is to have jurisdiction. That the Arctic Council proposal has only been put to states with an Arctic Ocean outlook indicates that a minimum area of application is the Arctic Ocean region. The inclusion of states such as Denmark has not been seen as a suggestion that the Council's reach would extend to continental Europe or similarly to continental Russia or Canada. Early references were made to an 'Arctic Basin Council' which implied that the area of application would be limited to those areas directly related to the Arctic Ocean. However, Pharand has argued that this approach would be too limiting as such a definition could exclude Iceland, Finland and Sweden. His approach is rather to encompass the area north of 60° North and also to include the Aleutian Islands, Labrador and the northern area of Quebec known as 'Nunavik'.[115] This definition has the advantage of not relying on the Arctic Circle (a somewhat artificial polar border) and is more certain than the scientifically correct, but very irregular, treeline.[116] Pharand's definition includes

[115] Pharand, 'The Case for an Arctic Region Council' at 191.

[116] Other boundaries of the Arctic which are occasionally suggested are the 10° and 5°

all the land areas that front the Arctic Ocean and surrounding seas plus all the marine and terrestrial areas that could be said to be a part of the Arctic ecosystem.[117]

Mandate

The mandate of the Arctic Council to consider Arctic questions is potentially very sensitive because of ongoing strategic and defence issues which impact upon the region. It is therefore important to determine whether the Council would have open to it for consideration all issues which impact upon the Arctic region or rather have a limited mandate to deal with issues of civil cooperation. Another issue is what relationship the Council would have with the AEPS.

The Arctic Council Panel proposed that the Council be given an extremely wide mandate to consider and discuss 'any field of human endeavour with international implications'.[118] The Canadian Centre for Global Security also argued that the Council have a wide mandate, but did concede that:

> the principal focus of the Council's work will be in the civil sphere. This suggests that other bodies, notably NATO and the CSCE, may be called upon by the Arctic Council to play a part in the development of Arctic security co-operation.[119]

Pharand also supports the Council having a focus on civil matters and that it not expressly consider Arctic security and military questions except under the heading of promoting the use of the region 'exclusively for peaceful purposes'.[120] With the United States and Russia involved in the negotiations concerning the Council there will

isotherm; however, both these and the treeline boundary have the disadvantage that they may radically shift with climate change. See Figure 2 in chapter 2 and the discussion accompanying.

117 A related issue may be how far the Council would be expected to deal with issues which occur outside the area of application but have Arctic area impacts. This would be an issue in regard to marine, estuarine and air pollution.

118 Arctic Council Panel, *To Establish* at 28, Art. 5. While this would not extend to duplicating or subordinating existing international cooperation occurring in other circumpolar bodies there would be nothing to stop such bodies or organisations seeking to come under the umbrella of the Arctic Council: see Art. 6.

119 Gizewski, 'Arctic Security' at 19; the CSCE is the 'Conference on Security and Co-operation in Europe'.

120 Pharand, 'The Case for an Arctic Region Council' at 191. In addition Pharand listed the other major purposes of the Council as being the facilitation of regional cooperation, taking measures to protect the environment, promotion of scientific research, managing living resources, and furthering the social conditions of the region's indigenous peoples.

be some concern as to its mandate in this regard. Given the continuing military interests these two states have in the region even following the end of the Cold War it is envisaged that they will be particularly opposed to the creation of any regional organisation that may seek to consider as sensitive a question as Arctic military security.[121]

Institutional structure

The final question that relates to the Council is what form of institutional structure it shall have. Canada has already offered to provide a secretariat to support the work of the Council. What structure the Council will take is important because of the differing roles that may be accorded to the Council participants and the ability of various Council organs to discuss and make recommendations on a range of issues. The Arctic Council Panel canvassed four potential options for the Council's structure – a plenary, bicameral, compact and tripartite delegation structure. Each would recognise the primary role of the Arctic Eight. However, there are variations as to what role could be played by groups such as non-Arctic states, indigenous peoples and territorial governments.[122] A preference was stated for the proposed compact structure, which was seen as the one which would best allow for active representation and participation by Arctic indigenous peoples.[123] Pharand's favoured option is for a bicameral structure involving an Assembly and a Commission. The Assembly would be open to all parties and be available to hear discussion on all issues which fall within the Council's mandate. The Commission, which would comprise the Arctic Eight and four other elected non-permanent members, would decide on ways and means to implement measures recommended by the Assembly. It would decide issues by consensus, or on the vote of eight members.[124]

Prospects for the Arctic Council

The Arctic Council proposal has received varying degrees of support from Arctic states. Though Canada made the initial proposal for an Arctic Council, it took some time before it seriously sought support for the initiative.[125] Following a change of government in late 1993,

[121] This is essentially the view taken by the Canadian Centre for Global Security in its 1993 report assessing post-Cold War Arctic Security: see Gizewski, 'Arctic Security' at 1–7. [122] Arctic Council Panel, *To Establish* at 17–21.

[123] *Ibid.* at 21–2. [124] Pharand, 'The Case for an Arctic Region Council' at 192–3.

[125] This may have been due to the political difficulties which the Progressive Conservative government of Brian Mulroney and Kim Campbell faced during 1991–3:

Canada has more actively pursued support for the Arctic Council. In October 1994, Foreign Minister, Andre Ouellet, announced that Canada would create an 'Arctic Circumpolar Ambassador' to assist in the Arctic Council negotiations. At the time it was noted: 'The Arctic Council is the best forum in which to address issues of common concern to Arctic communities.'[126] Since that time an Ambassador has been appointed and Canada has hosted a number of additional meetings to discuss the Arctic Council proposal. While Russia has expressed support for the concept,[127] its own domestic difficulties have meant that full attention has not been given to international Arctic questions. The United States undertook a review of its Arctic policy following the election in 1992 of the Clinton Administration. After some substantial delay, the United States also expressed broad support for the Arctic Council.[128] All of the Scandinavian states are interested in the Arctic Council concept; however, they have not taken any political initiative to provide strong support for the proposal. While it has taken Canada some time to generate support for the Arctic Council, there are a number of indicators to suggest that the Arctic states are moving towards the adoption of an institution in which circumpolar Arctic affairs can be discussed. However, what form that institution will take remains uncertain.[129]

Models for an Arctic legal regime

The above review has considered the history of various initiatives for greater international cooperation in the Arctic. The more recent AEPS negotiations and the Canadian proposal for an Arctic Council are the most substantive attempts so far to implement Arctic-wide multilat-

see the discussion in Thomas S. Axworthy, 'Rallying around the North Pole' 13 November 1992, *The [Toronto] Globe and Mail*, A23.

126 Andre Ouellet, 'A Northern Foreign Policy for Canada' in John Lamb (ed.) *A Northern Foreign Policy for Canada* (Ottawa, 1994), 55 at 58.

127 At a meeting in Ottawa on 1 February 1992, Canadian Prime Minister Brian Mulroney and Russian Federation President Boris Yeltsin signed a 'Declaration of Friendship and Cooperation' in which the two states affirmed their support for 'the creation of an international Arctic Council to protect the Arctic, its peoples and resources, while fostering prosperity in the region through enhanced cooperation among circumpolar States': Pharand, 'The Case for an Arctic Region Council' at 168.

128 Ouellet, 'A Northern Foreign Policy' at 58.

129 For further consideration of the Arctic Council proposal, see Terry Fenge, 'An Arctic Treaty: With Teeth' (Spring 1993) *Arctic Circle* 12–13 detailing the case for an 'Arctic Environment Sustainable Development Treaty' in light of the AEPS and other developments.

eral cooperation across a range of issues. Before these initiatives are considered in the context of the prospects for greater international cooperation in the Arctic, attention will be given to various models which have been proposed as being suitable for the development of greater Arctic multilateral cooperation.

The AEPS and Arctic Council proposal represent a significant advance in the development towards a more comprehensive Arctic legal regime. However, neither of these initiatives have sought to deal with whether an overall legal framework is needed in the Arctic. This may be because such a framework is unnecessary and Arctic states are content to allow the Arctic legal regime to develop in a piecemeal fashion based upon a recognition that state sovereignty prevails. Nevertheless, both the AEPS and Arctic Council proposals indicate that Arctic states are interested in greater coordination of Arctic affairs. The legal regime too, would benefit from improved coordination.

A number of commentators have given some thought as to how it would be possible for the Arctic legal regime to be strengthened and upon what basis such a regime could be founded.[130] In considering this question in 1978, Feder envisaged that four main hurdles would exist to the implementation of an environmentally centred Arctic regime.[131] They were: resolution of existing claims into a new structure; adoption of environmental standards and administrative procedures; adoption of procedures for enforcement; and international acceptance. The adoption of adequate enforcement procedures was seen to be a major problem, which Feder foresaw as being particularly difficult in the Soviet sector of the Arctic. In this respect the break-up of the Soviet Union in 1991 and the emergence of Russia as the successor state may result in enforcement being a continuing problem in the Russian Arctic. Interestingly, Feder believed that the successful development of an Arctic regime would be difficult without the cooperation of non-Arctic states which are interested in the use of the Arctic.[132] He makes the important point that the effective protection of the Arctic environment cannot be achieved in isolation and that it would be necessary to ensure that appropriate relationships exist between any Arctic regime and non-Arctic organisations 'if decisions about world-

[130] There has been considerable discussion of this question in the literature with respect to security issues. See e.g., Ronald G. Purver, 'Arms Control Proposals for the Arctic: A Survey and Critique' in Kari Mottola (ed.), *The Arctic Challenge* (Boulder, CO, 1988) 183–219; Oran R. Young, *Arctic Politics* (Dartmouth, NH, 1992) 190-213.

[131] B. J. Feder, 'A Legal Regime for the Arctic' (1976–8) *Ecology Law Quarterly* 785–829.

[132] *Ibid.* at 825 where specific reference was made to the then West Germany and Japan.

wide development of arctic resources are to take into account the environmental pressures inherent in obtaining similar or substitute resources elsewhere'.[133]

Since the conclusion of UNCLOS many commentators have placed emphasis on its potential as a basis for the development of an Arctic legal regime. Most attention has been given to Articles 122 and 123 dealing with 'enclosed and semi-enclosed' seas.[134] Under the Convention, states which surround either of these types of seas are under an obligation to cooperate with each other in order to protect the marine environment. In the case of the Arctic Ocean there has been some debate over whether it can properly be classified under one of these categories. Yet, while the Article 122 definition of enclosed or semi-enclosed seas may be too narrow for the Arctic, McRae sees that the principle provided for in the Convention could still be applied. He has argued that 'it is the littoral states who are primarily affected by the use of those seas, and thus they should have the principal, if not exclusive, responsibility for management and control' so that this 'does provide some analogy for approaches to the management of arctic waters and in particular the management of arctic marine transportation'.[135] While it is possible to debate the effect of Article 123, the overall spirit of UNCLOS is to encourage regional cooperation to ensure the effective implementation of environmental protection measures for adjacent ocean areas. This is emphasised in Article 197 which seeks to ensure cooperation 'for the protection and preservation of the marine environment'.[136] Other provisions in the Convention can also be identified which when combined place a substantial responsibility upon coastal states to ensure adequate protection of the adjacent marine environment.[137] It can therefore be argued that

133 *Ibid.* at 827.

134 UNCLOS, Art. 122 provides that an 'enclosed or semi-enclosed sea' is:

> a gulf, basin or sea surrounded by two or more States and connected to another sea or the ocean by a narrow outlet or consisting entirely or primarily of the territorial seas and exclusive economic zones of two or more coastal States.

135 D. M. McRae, 'Management of Arctic Marine Transportation: A Canadian Perspective' (1986) 39 *Arctic* 350 at 354.

136 See H. Mils, 'Ocean Policy Making in the Canadian Arctic' in *National and Regional Interests in the North* (Ottawa, 1984) 506.

137 David L. VanderZwaag and Cynthia Lamson, 'Ocean Development and Management in the Arctic: Issues in American and Canadian Relations' (1986) 39 *Arctic* 327 at 329; *cf.* Franckx, *Maritime Claims* at 239–243 who concludes, upon a review of the provisions found in UNCLOS, that 'no firm legal obligation exists at present in international law which requires bordering states to cooperate with one another'.

UNCLOS may provide a framework within which to implement a certain type of regime to deal with maritime issues in the Arctic.[138]

Harders, in his review of the Arctic regime, identifies the possibility for two diametrically opposed structures to emerge in the Arctic: one based on unilateral state action within each state's adjacent maritime zones, beyond which high seas freedoms would apply; and the other based on a regional cooperative approach to maritime issues centred on a recognition that the Arctic should be considered a region *sui generis*.[139] Relying on principles of international environmental law, the growth in marine regionalism, and the obligations imposed upon coastal states by UNCLOS cooperatively to manage the marine environment, Harders argues that the Arctic states are under a legal obligation to ensure that the Arctic Ocean is appropriately managed.[140] This view is not, however, based on the assumption that the Arctic is a semi-enclosed sea. As Harders acknowledges:

> The open sea spaces of the Greenland Sea, the Norwegian Sea and the Bering Sea clearly contradict the status of the Arctic Ocean as semi-enclosed, both from the geographical and from the legal point of view.[141]

This does not, however, stop the Arctic being legitimately considered a marine region,[142] which creates legal obligations for the coastal states of the region to work together cooperatively to manage the marine environment under the terms of both UNCLOS and general principles of international environmental law which have recognised such a concept.[143] Harders' conclusion then, is that the Arctic states can build on developments in marine regionalism to develop an umbrella convention dealing with the Arctic marine environment, which,

[138] See Douglas Brubaker, *Marine Pollution and International Law* (London, 1993) 295–9.

[139] Harders, 'In Quest of an Arctic Legal Regime' at 288.

[140] *Ibid*. at 292.

[141] *Ibid*. at 295–6.

[142] *Ibid*., where it is noted:

> it is firmly established that the Arctic Ocean is a regional sea, and, though not being semi-enclosed, this lack of required geographical conditions is supplemented by the unique ice-infested environment and the circulation pattern in the polar area.

See also Aldo Chircop, 'Framework for a Regional Environmental Regime for the Arctic' in *Proceedings - Radioactivity and Environmental Security in the Oceans* (Woods Hole, MA, 1993) 535–40

[143] To that end, Harders places emphasis on the United Nations Environment Programme 'Regional Seas' action plan, see Harders, 'In Quest of an Arctic Legal Regime' at 292, 296.

through protocols covering various pollution sources, can form the basis for an Arctic accord.[144]

Writing at much the same time as when Finland commenced its push for the AEPS, Roginko argued that the time had arrived for the Arctic states to adopt an 'Arctic Action Plan'.[145] The Plan would be modelled on those which already exist in other regional seas such as the Baltic, or those which have been developed under the United Nations Environment Programme 'Regional Seas' plan.[146] Similarly to the proposals made by Harders, Roginko believes that by adopting the approach of implementing an umbrella convention followed by specific protocols dealing with particular issues an Arctic accord could be reached. Such an approach would not only protect the marine environment, but would also leave scope for the protection of coastal tundra areas, wildlife and possibly the Arctic atmosphere.[147] Roginko also argues that the Arctic states should submit a proposal to the International Maritime Organization for the Arctic to be classified as a 'special area' under the terms of the MARPOL regime.[148] By obtaining such a classification a more comprehensive legal regime for the protection of the Arctic marine environment would result because coastal states would still be able to rely upon the terms of Article 234 to implement strict marine pollution controls within their EEZs, while MARPOL would provide additional protection in high seas areas beyond national jurisdiction.[149] Roginko also argues that the Arctic states could pursue greater cooperation in dealing with transboundary air pollution. He suggests that by specifically dealing with the issue under the Arctic Action Plan, in addition to negotiating stronger

[144] *Ibid.* at 298. For a further review of these proposals by Harders, see J. Enno Harders, 'The Arctic Ocean: Environmental Protection and Circumpolar Co-operation - An Assessment and a Proposal for a Legal Regime' in *Energy Law '86* (New York, 1986) 493–532. For similar proposals along this theme, see Brubaker, *Marine Pollution* at 276–448.

[145] Roginko, 'Arctic Environmental Cooperation' at 136, the reasons for why there was a need for greater Arctic cooperation were given as being: (1) a greater international exchange of information on the polar ecosystem was required; (2) given the small pool of Arctic experts, international resource pooling had great benefits; (3) Arctic cooperation would lead to an increase in navigational safety; (4) it would demonstrate a commitment to the preservation of Arctic ecosystems; and (5) it would assist in the eventual creation of a zone of peace and international cooperation in the European North.

[146] *Ibid.*

[147] *Ibid.*

[148] *Ibid.* at 137.

[149] *Ibid.*

measures under the existing legal regime, both a regional and global approach could be adopted to deal with the special problems the Arctic is facing from this form of pollution.[150]

Archer is another commentator who has looked at possible models for Arctic cooperation but in doing so has not placed as much emphasis on the Arctic as a marine region as have Harders and Roginko. Archer is of the view that throughout the 1980s there emerged strong prospects for greater Arctic cooperation in the humanitarian area – such as search and rescue, scientific research and environmental matters.[151] Archer saw the model of 'Nordic cooperation' as a basis upon which Arctic-wide cooperation could be built.[152] The advantage of this approach is that rather than creating a formal international organisation, such a model would allow involvement by both governmental and non-governmental organisations and not have a rigid structure but be flexible enough to accommodate various interests and issues.[153] Meetings would be held amongst the Arctic states in which government representatives and also members of local Arctic councils and indigenous peoples such as the Saami councils would be present. With a small secretariat to coordinate the work of the body, issues such as environmental protection, needs of indigenous peoples, transportation and communication, and educational and

[150] *Ibid.* at 138, in which it is argued that such a regime would necessarily require the participation of Japan and the People's Republic of China. For a further discussion of some of these proposals see Roginko and LaMourie, 'Emerging Marine Environmental Protection Strategies'. More recently Roginko and colleagues have argued that the Arctic is a region in which the concept of 'international environmental security' could apply: see Anatoly Kolodkin, Natalia Mirovitskaya and Alexei Roginko, 'The Arctic: Arena for International Environmental Security?' (1993) 10 *Ocean Yearbook* 277–89, in which the concept of 'international environmental security' is defined at 278 as being:

> a state of international relations that provides for the preservation, rational use, renewal, and improvement of the environment, when interaction of all the members of the international community, and development of each of them, is not accompanied by an irreversible loss of natural resources and/or other changes in the biosphere harmful to the various forms of life. IES requires elaboration and adoption of a global strategy as well as of a concept of legal, political and economic actions.

See also Renat Perelet, 'Environmental Security and Governance Issues in the Arctic Ocean' in *Proceedings – Radioactivity and Environmental Security in the Oceans* (Woods Hole, MA, 1993) 595–601.

[151] Archer, 'General Features' at 140-2, it was, however, acknowledged that similar prospects may not have existed in the areas of economic development and military cooperation.

[152] Archer, 'Arctic Cooperation' at 171.

[153] *Ibid.* at 171–2.

cultural links could be considered. Proposals for action on certain issue areas would be made and recommendations would be forwarded for formal legislative or policy implementation by the Arctic governments.[154] Archer's view is that by adopting this type of approach greater sub-regional transborder cooperation would result across a wide spectrum of Arctic interests, not just at the formal level of government departments, so that a structure would be created upon which more lasting international organisations could be constructed.[155]

Future prospects for Arctic cooperation

This chapter has sought to review developments towards greater Arctic cooperation. Despite the evidence that there has been considerable interest in Arctic cooperation at both the government, academic and private level throughout much of the century, substantial progress has only been made in recent years. This has impacted upon the development of the Arctic legal regime. While the region has not been immune from the application of general principles and provisions of international law, it has primarily been through bilateral and multilateral treaties that international law has developed in the United Nations era. The gaps and problems in the Arctic legal regime have also been highlighted by a large number of commentators. Many have addressed the prospects for the further development of the regime. Emphasis has been placed on the law of the sea as providing the foundation for the further development of the legal regime. However, if the AEPS is any guide, it may well be that overall regional concerns about atmospheric, marine and terrestrial pollution will be the catalyst for such a development.

In the meantime, the Arctic legal regime remains incomplete. While international law has been able to resolve some issues in the region, many remain. Some, such as jurisdictional disputes over Arctic waters and environmental protection, have increasingly become of great importance to the Arctic states and various efforts have been made to resolve them. The 1988 Arctic Cooperation Agreement between Canada and the United States[156] is one initiative aimed at seeking to resolve

154 *Ibid.* at 172.
155 *Ibid.* at 173.
156 Agreement between the Government of Canada and the Government of the United States of America on Arctic Cooperation, [1988] CTS 29.

the jurisdictional problem. However, as noted in chapter 5, it has limited application and does not deal with the issue at the heart of the dispute – navigation in the Northwest Passage. The AEPS is also a major initiative aimed at dealing with the Arctic's environmental problems. However, its legal obligations are very weak and much will depend on the goodwill of the Arctic states if it is to succeed.

Nevertheless, these recent developments are a great encouragement.[157] They demonstrate that the Arctic states are increasingly prepared to enter into bilateral, multilateral and regional arrangements to deal with specific Arctic problems. Prior to the developments of the past twenty years Arctic states took a unilateral state-sovereignty approach to Arctic issues. International cooperation only occurred when there were major jurisdictional issues in need of resolution or when resource scarcity demanded management. With these exceptions, the major focus of Arctic international relations during this century has been concern over militarisation and national security. As a result, many opportunities were lost to adopt a regional response to specific Arctic issues. The jurisdictional disputes noted in chapter 5 largely emerged during this period. Apart from some unilateral initiatives, there were also few efforts made to control the effects of transboundary pollution in the region.

Gradually, attitudes towards cooperation have changed. The gradual move towards greater cooperation in the fields of science and the environment since the 1970s has demonstrated that the Arctic states are increasingly of the view that some Arctic issues can only be effectively dealt with by Arctic states. This is best exemplified by the AEPS. Despite numerous global fora dealing with pollution and environmental problems, plus a major global environmental conference that was scheduled for 1992, the Arctic states concluded in 1991 a specific Arctic environmental strategy. The AEPS is characterised by its specific responses to Arctic environmental problems, the commitments to implement Arctic-wide clean-up programmes, and the efforts to seek further protection for the region under existing international law and through new initiatives. The AEPS demonstrates that the Arctic states are beginning to see that the challenge of protecting and cleaning up their environment is a responsibility which they must share. To combat effectively this problem, only regional solutions are appropriate.

[157] See Gizewski, 'Arctic Security' at 6–7.

What the future holds for the region though is still uncertain. In 1988 Archer argued that:

> It seems more likely that cooperation in the Arctic, rather than being organised as a grand scheme, will grow in an incremental fashion in particular functional areas. Preconditions for meaningful cooperation are the continuation of the rapprochement between the two superpowers and the strengthening of the programme of perestroika (with the associated policy of glasnost) in the Soviet Union.[158]

While some of the political forces have changed since the late 1980s, there can be no denying that Archer's basic premise still holds. In the post-Cold War era there are still lingering security concerns over the Arctic which are potentially a major impediment to further Arctic cooperation. The cautious response of the United States to the AEPS and Arctic Council proposal demonstrates that it is not enthusiastic about some forms of multilateral Arctic cooperation.[159] The Russian position is also difficult because of the domestic instability it is experiencing and the potential financial burdens it may be placed under by Arctic regimes which seek to deal with environmental problems. With the two major powers in the Arctic region either unwilling or unable to give the political lead to Arctic cooperation, the responsibility falls to either Canada or the Scandinavian states to fill this void. Certainly if the speedy negotiation and implementation of the AEPS is taken as an indicator, there is significant support amongst the Arctic states for greater international cooperation. Whether they take the next step and form an Arctic Council remains to be seen.

158 Archer, 'General Features' at 143–4.

159 For an assessment of what may occur in the field of Arctic environmental cooperation post-Rovaniemi, see Olav Schram Stokke, 'Arctic Environmental Cooperation after Rovaniemi – What Now?' in Lise Lyck (ed.), *Nordic Arctic Research on Contemporary Arctic Problems* (Copenhagen, 1992) 221–34.

Part III

The impact of the polar regions

7 The polar regions and the law of the sea

Because both polar regions incorporate large areas of ocean, the law of the sea plays an important role in their respective legal regimes. The Arctic Ocean, largely frozen year round, dominates the Arctic region. In Antarctica, the Southern Ocean surrounds the Antarctic continent and is a natural ecological boundary between the region and more temperate northern areas. In the Arctic, it can be argued that it is the law of the sea which has provided the basis for the development of the legal regime in that region. In Antarctica, while not as prominent, the law of the sea raises some very difficult questions for the Antarctic Treaty System (ATS), many of which continue to be unanswered. In this chapter five specific law of the sea issues will be considered. Each issue is present in both regions, though not necessarily to the same extent or degree. The five are: ice-covered waters, polar baselines, maritime zones, high seas freedoms and marine environmental protection.[1] Each will be considered in turn with emphasis given to specific Antarctic and Arctic questions as necessary. Attention will principally be given to the provisions of the 1982 United Nations Convention on the Law of the Sea (UNCLOS);[2] however, reference shall also be given to the four 1958 Geneva Conventions on the Law of the Sea where appropriate.[3]

[1] This is not a comprehensive list of law of the sea issues in the polar regions. Others which could be considered are the status of icebergs and jurisdiction over them, the delimitation of maritime boundaries, jurisdiction over and management of fisheries, and marine scientific research. Some of these issues are considered in greater detail in other chapters of this work.

[2] (1982) 21 ILM 1261. While not all polar states are currently parties to UNCLOS, state practice would indicate that many of its provisions represent customary international law.

[3] The four Conventions: (1) Convention on the Continental Shelf, 499 UNTS 311

Ice-covered waters

A unique feature of the polar oceans is that for much of the year they are ice-covered.[4] The dominant presence of ice in the polar oceans raises for consideration questions concerning the status of ice not dealt with under general principles of international law or UNCLOS. One approach would be to argue that ice is best classified as *sui generis* because it does not easily fall into the category of either land or sea. The unusual status of ice is reflected in the legal regimes which apply to it.

Status of ice in international law

Because of the fundamental differences between various types of ice the accepted view is that its international law status changes depending on where the ice is located.[5] There is not much difficulty in classifying sheet ice or glacial ice as equivalent to *terra firma*. As it is located on land it should be treated no differently to other land formations.[6] The Antarctic ice sheet has been the subject of territorial claim and as shown by the establishment of some scientific bases in Antarctica is subject to occupation.[7] More difficulty exists in determining the legal status of shelf, fast and pack ice.[8] In all cases these forms

(hereinafter Continental Shelf Convention); (2) Convention on the Territorial Sea and Contiguous Zone, 516 UNTS 205 (hereinafter TSCZ); (3) Convention on the High Sea, 450 UNTS 82 (hereinafter High Seas Convention); and (4) Convention on Fishing and Conservation of the Living Resources of the High Seas, 559 UNTS 285 (hereinafter Geneva Fishing Convention).

[4] The characteristics and types of ice found in the polar regions were discussed in chapter 2.

[5] See generally on this question, F. Orrego Vicuna, *Antarctic Mineral Exploitation* (Cambridge, 1988) 159–62.

[6] *Cf.* C. C. Joyner, 'Ice-Covered Regions in International Law' (1991) 31 NatResJ 213 at 222 who argues that the Antarctic ice sheet is responsible for much of the legal uncertainty surrounding Antarctic territorial claims:

> The plain fact is that incredibly harsh climatic conditions caused by the thick ice mantle have rendered effective occupation of Antarctica through permanent settlement thus far impossible, a physical situation that gravely undercuts substantiation of any national claim of valid legal title to – and hence sovereign jurisdiction over – Antarctic territory, and Antarctic ice.

[7] Most scientific bases in Antarctica are in and around the 2 per cent of the continent which is ice-free; however, there are some notable exceptions such as the US Amundsen–Scott Base at the South Pole: see F. M. Auburn, *Antarctic Law and Politics* (London, 1982) xvi–xvii, xx for details on locations.

[8] The status of icebergs in international law also raises interesting questions. See Joyner, 'Ice-Covered Regions' at 231–7; Christopher C. Joyner, *Antarctica and the Law of the Sea* (Dordrecht, 1992) 201–8; G. J. Mangone, 'The Legal Status of Ice in International

of ice can be reasonably permanent and in the case of shelf and fast ice both are attached to land. Many commentators are of the view that shelf ice should be equated to land. This not only follows because it is attached to land, but because it exhibits similar physical and utilitarian qualities. Joyner argues:

shelf ice is several hundred feet thick, relatively immobile, generally impenetrable by ships, and characterized by areas of considerable dimension. An ice shelf is not open space: it is *glaçes firma*. Hence, the conclusion that ice shelves ought not to be designated high seas areas. Instead, ice shelves serve as the natural projection of land seaward, over which the natural boundary between a shelf and its land-based glacier is indistinguishable.[9]

Accordingly, it would seem appropriate for international law to approximate ice shelves to land and not water.[10]

Fast ice must, however, be classified as lying somewhere between shelf ice and water. This ice is formed by seawater and clings to the coastline on a seasonal basis. In some parts of both polar regions fast ice is permanent, while in other areas it is subject to seasonal variation. The question of the status of sea ice has been the subject of debate in Arctic states, especially in Canada and Russia where the ice has been appropriated for use by indigenous peoples and local authorities.[11] In an extensive review of the literature on this subject, Boyd concluded in 1984 that: 'The physical properties of fast ice provide a basis for the assimilation of fast ice to land territory in much the same way as do the physical properties of shelf ice.'[12] In 1970 a Canadian court considered the legal status of fast ice in *R.* v. *Tootalik*.[13] The issue before the court was whether a criminal offence which took place on fast ice was subject to the court's, and by implication

Law' in Rudiger Wolfrum (ed.), *Antarctic Challenge III* (Berlin, 1988) 371 at 382–4; T. R. Lindquist, 'The Iceberg Cometh? International Law Relating to Antarctic Iceberg Exploitation' (1977) 17 NatResJ 1–41.

9 Joyner, 'Ice-Covered Regions' at 226.

10 See also Mangone, 'The Legal Status of Ice' at 387. See also M. W. Mouton, 'The International Regime of the Polar Regions' (1962) III ReDC 175 at 197, who takes a more equivocal approach to the status of ice shelves in noting: 'In view of the objections against considering the floating part of the ice-shelves as land territory an indisputable answer is not self-evident.'

11 S. Boyd, 'The Legal Status of the Arctic Sea Ice: A Comparative Study and a Proposal' (1984) 22 CYIL 98 at 113 refers to Soviet practice in 1976 of using fast ice as a quay in certain waters close to shore so as to allow unloading of vessels without the use of boats.

12 *Ibid.* at 140.

13 *R.* v. *Tootalik* (1970) 71 Western Weekly Reports 435, reversed on other grounds in (1970) 74 Western Weekly Reports 740.

Canadian, jurisdiction.[14] The court held that it had jurisdiction over sea ice and the Eskimo concerned, Tootalik, was accordingly found guilty of the offence charged. Despite the fact that the ice in question was not permanent, the court held that ice has the 'attribute of land' and concluded that it had been part of the territory transferred from the Queen of England to the Dominion of Canada in 1870 and 1880.[15] It therefore seems that because of its semi-permanent nature, it is possible for fast ice to be equated in some respects with land. Whether, as the Canadian court determined, it is properly subject to legal claim, is another matter.

The final type of ice found on the sea which is relevant to this study is pack ice. In the Arctic especially, pack ice can have a permanent nature. Large areas of pack ice have been occupied for scientific research in both polar regions and these are known as 'ice islands'.[16] In one instance, the American courts were prepared to exercise jurisdiction in a case involving the murder of an American scientist stationed on an ice island in the Arctic Ocean.[17] Because of the very different nature of pack ice, as a creation of seawater and constantly floating on the ocean, it should be equated with the sea and be considered subject to a law of the sea regime.[18] There can be no question of this classification where pack ice is free from coastal areas and found on the high seas.[19] Perhaps more difficulty could be said to arise when pack ice and fast ice merge together during winter months to form impenetrable barriers around coastal areas. Nonetheless, while this ice may in some cases be relatively stable (as shown from the ability to

[14] The case concerned an Eskimo hunter who was charged with illegally hunting polar bears under the Game Ordinance, 1960 (Northwest Territories) (2nd Sess., c. 2).

[15] R. v. *Tootalik*, (1970) 71 WWR 435 at 443. See for a comment F. M. Auburn, 'International Law – Sea-Ice – Jurisdiction' (1970) 48 CanBR 776–82.

[16] T. Armstrong, B. Roberts and C. Swithinbank, *Illustrated Glossary of Snow and Ice* (2nd) (Cambridge, 1973) 23 define an 'ice island' as: 'A form of tabular berg found in the Arctic Ocean, with a thickness of 30 to 50m and from a few thousand square m to 500 square km in area. Ice islands often have an undulating surface, which gives them a ribbed appearance from the air.' For a discussion of the legal status of ice islands see D. Pharand, 'The Legal Status of Ice Shelves and Ice Islands in the Arctic' (1969) 10 *Les cahiers de droit* 461 at 467–75; D. Pharand, *The Law of the Sea of the Arctic with Special Reference to Canada* (Ottawa, 1973) 188–204; F. M. Auburn, 'International Law and Sea-Ice Jurisdiction in the Arctic Ocean' (1973) 22 ICLQ 552–7.

[17] *US* v. *Escamilla* 467 F.2d 341 (1972). For discussion see D. Pharand, 'State Jurisdiction over Ice Island T-3: The Escamilla Case' (1971) 24 *Arctic* 83–9; Pharand, *The Law of the Sea* at 199–204.

[18] See Boyd, 'The Legal Status' at 144; Mouton, 'The International Regime' at 207.

[19] Joyner, *Antarctica and the Law of the Sea* at 198.

construct scientific stations on large areas of pack ice), it essentially is only frozen seawater and in most cases will eventually return to that state.

Is ice subject to claim?

A further important question regarding ice is whether it can be subject to a territorial claim. Different considerations again apply for the three types of ice under review. In the case of ice shelves, most questions have arisen over their status in Antarctica. This occurs because ice shelves are expressly referred to, but are undefined, in Article VI of the Antarctic Treaty.[20] This is an important issue as most territorial claimants have ice shelves within their Antarctic sectors. Despite their uncertain status, none of the territorial claimants makes any express reference to ice shelves in their Antarctic claims.[21] This approach may indicate that the territorial claimants see no need to treat ice shelves located on land any differently from the land itself. As many legal commentators are prepared to equate ice shelves with land, or at least accord them a *sui generis* classification,[22] it would seem reasonable to conclude that ice shelves are subject to sovereign claims.[23]

[20] 402 UNTS 71.

[21] See the following assertions of claim: Argentina – 'Argentine Note to the International Bureau of the Universal Postal Union Asserting Argentine Jurisdiction over Antarctica and other Territories', 14 September 1927, reprinted in Bush (vol. I), 584–5; Australia – Australian Antarctic Territory Acceptance Act, 1933 (Australia), s. 2; Chile – 'Decree No. 1,747 Declaring the Limits of the Chilean Antarctic Territory', 6 November 1940, reprinted in Bush (vol. II), 310–12; France – 'Decree Defining the Limits of Adelie Land', 1 April 1938, reprinted in Bush (vol. II), 505–6; New Zealand – 'Order in Council Under the British Settlements Act, 1887 (50 & 51 Vict. c. 54) Providing for the Government of the Ross Dependency', 30 July 1923, reprinted in Bush (vol. III), 44–5; Norway – 'Royal Proclamation Defining the Area of Norwegian Sovereignty in Antarctica', 14 January 1939, reprinted in Bush (vol. III), 149; UK – 'Letters Patent Providing for the Government of the Falkland (Malvinas) Islands Dependencies', 21 July 1908, reprinted in Bush (vol. III), 251–4. The only claim which makes any reference to ice is that of Chile which refers to 'glaciers (pack-ice)', which Bush (vol. II), 312 argues makes Chile the only claimant to demonstrate a belief that frozen sea is susceptible to claim. See also the discussion in Auburn, *Antarctic Law* at 35.

[22] See Auburn, *Antarctic Law* at 35; Sir Arthur Watts, *International Law and the Antarctic Treaty System* (Cambridge, 1992) 115–18.

[23] Both Auburn and Boyd also come to this conclusion, see Auburn, *Antarctic Law* at 35; Boyd, 'The Legal Status' at 139. Joyner does not go so far but does state that: 'Notwithstanding that some shelf ice may move and float over water, it still exhibits qualities much more akin to land, and should be legally regarded as such': Joyner, 'Ice-Covered Regions' at 227.

In the case of fast ice, some commentators have argued that because of its semi-permanent nature it is susceptible to claim where it extends beyond land. This argument is especially relevant where sea ice plays an important part in the daily life of indigenous peoples in the Arctic. It is well documented, for example, that the Inuit regularly use fast ice for hunting and other economic and cultural activities.[24] As an Inuit commentator has noted:

> A persistent difficulty in any discussion of the legalities of offshore rights is the fact that in the Arctic the 'offshore' does not have any physical significance for most of the year. In practice, the real boundary is the shoreline; it is the line of contact between shore-fast ice and moving ice, the floe edge. During most of the year, this line of demarcation is the only boundary for land-based transportation. As such, it is often the boundary of an area of traditional Inuit occupancy and, for ecological and environmental considerations, it is the location of the most intense biological activity.[25]

These characteristics of fast ice again suggest that as with shelf ice, it should be considered subject to appropriation or sovereign claims like land, or be given a special *sui generis* classification in international law.[26] Apart from an Imperial Russian decree suggesting that the outer limits of fast ice be used for the delimitation of the territorial sea,[27] there is no evidence of any state asserting a claim to fast ice. Nonetheless, as the above discussion indicates some states have asserted jurisdiction over fast ice.[28] It has also been argued that the historic Inuit interest in fast ice supports claims to historic rights over sea ice or at least the waters on which they float.[29] It can therefore be

[24] See M. M. R. Freeman, 'Contemporary Inuit Exploitation of the Sea-Ice Environment' in *Sikumiut 'The People Who Use the Sea Ice'* (Ottawa, 1984) 73–96. For an analysis of Inuit interests in Arctic offshore claims based on their use of sea ice, see Peter Jull and Nigel Bankes, 'Inuit Interests in the Arctic Offshore' in J. M. Harrison and Ken Beauchamp (eds.), *Ocean Policy and Management in the Arctic* (Ottawa, 1984) 85–114.

[25] M. Denhez, 'Inuit Rights and Canadian Arctic Waters' in *Sikumiut 'The People Who Use the Sea Ice'* (Ottawa, 1984) 123 at 139.

[26] Boyd, 'The Legal Status' at 140. For a general review of the international law implications of the relationship between the Inuit and ice see David VanderZwaag and Donat Pharand, 'Inuit and the Ice: Implications for Canadian Arctic Waters' (1983) 21 CYIL 53–84.

[27] A 1911 Imperial Russian decree provided that the territorial sea was to be 'computed from the line of lowest ebb tide or from the edge of the stationary coastal ice', reprinted in Joyner, *Antarctica and the Law of the Sea* at 81. See also Erik Franckx, *Maritime Claims in the Arctic* (Dordrecht, 1993) 153–4 who describes the Imperial Russian/Soviet approach as the 'ice-is-land' theory.

[28] R. v. *Tootalik* (1970) 71 WWR 435.

[29] See D. Pharand, 'The Legal Status of the Waters of the Canadian Arctic Archipelago'

concluded that fast ice is most probably subject to some form of sovereignty claim but that it would most probably require a high degree of permanence and the record of some historic usage to support such a claim.

While pack ice also has a certain permanence, there are sound reasons for treating it differently to fast ice. Pack ice is found in the high seas and as such should be subject to traditional law of the sea principles. Though in some areas of the Arctic during the middle of winter, pack ice has the same sort of permanence associated with fast ice, it still remains in constant motion. During the summer it is subject to break-up with the result that open water will appear where ice was previously situated. Given these circumstances, the conclusion is inescapable that despite having some permanent qualities which allow scientific research to be conducted on ice islands, pack ice is not susceptible to claim and should be considered as part of the sea, and subject to the law of the sea regime.[30]

Ice shelves under the Antarctic Treaty

Any complete consideration of the status of the ice shelves requires some analysis of how they are treated under the Antarctic Treaty. Article VI expressly includes within the Treaty's area of application 'all ice shelves'. As this provision also refers to the high seas it can be assumed that the Treaty negotiators believed that there was a distinction between ice shelves and traditional maritime areas. Ice shelves are also referred to in various instruments negotiated under the Treaty. The 1964 Agreed Measures for the Conservation of Antarctic Fauna and Flora adopt the same area of application as the Treaty and expressly include within its area of application 'ice shelves' south of 60°S.[31] Ice shelves are also specifically referred to in the 1991 Madrid Protocol.[32] The effect of these various provisions is to regulate

in *Sikumiut 'The People Who Use the Sea Ice'* (1984) 97 at 115–19; and more generally D. Pharand, *Canada's Arctic Waters in International Law* (Cambridge, 1988) 113–25.

30 See Boyd, 'The Legal Status' at 144–6; Joyner, *Antarctica and the Law of the Sea* at 198.

31 See Agreed Measures, Art. I, reprinted in Bush (vol. I), 146–69; Art. VII(3) also makes express reference to ice shelves. The Convention for the Conservation of Antarctic Seals, (1972) 11 ILM 251 (hereinafter CCAS), did not seek specifically to regulate sealing activities on ice shelves as this was considered a subject dealt with by the Agreed Measures; however, Art. 5(7) of the Convention did seek to collect data on sealing activities which took place on floating sea ice. See also Bush (vol. I) 252.

32 Protocol on Environmental Protection to the Antarctic Treaty, (1991) 30 ILM 1,455; Annex II, Art. 4(1); Annex II, Art. 4(2); Annex III, Art. 4(2), Annex III, Art. 7; Annex IV, Art. 5(3); Annex III, Art. 6(1)(a).

activities which occur on ice shelves. Yet, all the Treaty provisions seek to do is assert jurisdiction over activities which take place on the ice shelves under the terms of the Treaty. There is no attempt actually to define their status.[33] The continued specific reference to ice shelves under Antarctic Treaty provisions in fact indicates that the Treaty parties believe that the ice falls into a special category, worthy of separate consideration, as distinct from simply being part of the continent or the surrounding high seas.[34]

Polar baselines

In both polar regions the declaration of baselines has been important from two perspectives. First, because of coastal fringing ice and continental ice-shelves, it is sometimes difficult to identify a low-water mark from which maritime zones can be delimited. This is particularly a problem in Antarctica where the continent is surrounded by pack ice during the winter. The second issue, which arises more particularly in the Arctic, is how baselines should be drawn where there are extensive groups of offshore islands fringing the mainland of a coastal state. If the practice allowed by the International Court of Justice in the *Anglo-Norwegian Fisheries Case*[35] is adopted, coastal states can expand their offshore jurisdiction by using the outer limits of their offshore islands as basepoints for their maritime zones. The drawing of baselines around offshore archipelagoes also has an impact upon navigation rights.

Ice-covered coastlines

Arctic practice

The determination of the low-water mark around Arctic coastlines does not present a major problem. This is because most Arctic coasts are free of ice for portions of the year and even in the case of those that are ice-bound, such as the far northern islands of the Canadian Arctic Archipelago, the northern Greenland coast and the Franz Joseph

[33] Orrego Vicuna, *Antarctic Mineral Exploitation* at 160 has argued that: 'If one were to derive a general rule within the Antarctic system, it might be said that the stable ice formations, such as the large barriers, tend to be assimilated to the land regime.'

[34] *Cf.* Watts, *International Law* at 118 who argues the various provisions adopted by the ATS 'appear to place ice shelves in a non-high seas, and thus in a more territorial category'.

[35] *Anglo-Norwegian Fisheries Case (United Kingdom* v. *Iceland)*, [1951] ICJ Reports 116.

Archipelago, it is possible easily to distinguish between land and sea ice. It appears that Imperial Russia has been the only state to declare baselines from the ice edge along its Arctic coast.[36] With there being few ice shelves in the Arctic the determination of a low-water mark from which to delimit maritime boundaries has not been a major problem. As a result, there has been no extensive debate over whether fringing coastal ice could be used as basepoints for Arctic maritime zones.

Antarctic ice shelves

As a consequence of the presence of ice around the Antarctic continent for much of the year, and especially because of the number of ice shelves which exist, determining traditional 'low-water mark' baselines in Antarctica is very difficult. The unique nature of this problem has attracted a number of solutions from a variety of commentators. One popular view is that ice shelves can only be equated with land, with the result that basepoints can be determined from the outer edge of the ice.[37] There has been some consideration given to adopting Antarctic baselines from the outer limits of the ice shelves. A 1926 report by a British Imperial Conference Committee recognised that an exception to the low-water mark rule for determining the limit of territorial waters could be made in the case of 'ice-barriers which are to all intents and purposes a permanent extension of the land proper'.[38] However, these recommendations were never actively implemented.[39] In his recent consideration of this issue, Joyner proposed one of two solutions. The first relied upon the contours of the sub-glacial continental landmass as the standard baseline.[40] However, if such a scientific approach is adopted the question must also be raised as to whether the landmass beneath the ice would extend further into the ocean if the weight of the ice pressing down upon it were actually or theoretically

[36] Note 27 above; also see Joyner, *Antarctica and the Law of the Sea* at 80–1.

[37] Such a view appears to be taken by Van der Essen when he indicates that the low-water mark cannot be located anywhere but the outward face of the ice shelves 'which are the seaward prolongation of the Antarctic continent': A. Van der Essen, 'The Application of the Law of the Sea to the Antarctic Continent' in F. Orrego Vicuna (ed.), *Antarctic Resources Policy* (Cambridge, 1983) 231 at 234. See also Emilio J. Sahurie, *The International Law of Antarctica* (New Haven, CT, 1992) 553; Mangone, 'The Legal Status of Ice' at 387.

[38] Bush (vol. II), 103.

[39] For a comment see Orrego Vicuna, *Antarctic Mineral Exploitation* at 161; J. R. V. Prescott, 'Boundaries in Antarctica' in Stuart Harris (ed.), *Australia's Antarctic Policy Options*, (Canberra, 1984) 83 at 93–4.

[40] Joyner, *Antarctica and the Law of the Sea* at 84–5.

removed.[41] Accepting that this first approach may be inequitable to those coastal states which possess substantial ice shelves, Joyner also advanced the more popular view that the outer limits of both the ice shelves and the circumpolar ice pack are suitable for designation as basepoints.[42] Other commentators have suggested that a compromise to the above suggestions may be to determine a baseline by relying upon the ice shelf's extent at a known date plus an arbitrary distance,[43] or based on the average extent of the ice shelf.[44]

No matter which approach is taken towards the delimitation of Antarctic baselines complications will arise.[45] Any maritime zones which are delimited from ice shelf basepoints would constantly change as the ice shelves advance and retreat as a result of calving.[46] The adoption of a fixed point on an ice shelf has the advantage of certainty, but would result in the denial of surface navigational freedoms within the territorial sea if the shelf extended beyond that point. By ignoring the ice shelf and instead drawing baselines from a geological low-water mark some Antarctic claimants would also be substantially disadvantaged because their maritime zones would be either partly or completely covered by ice shelves which extend beyond the basepoints. One solution to this problem may be found in UNCLOS where Article 7(2) deals with the drawing of straight baselines in certain circumstances. It provides that where the coastline is highly unstable, basepoints:

> may be selected along the furthest seaward extent of the low-water line and, notwithstanding subsequent regression of the low-water line, the straight baselines shall remain effective until changed by the coastal State in accordance with this Convention.[47]

However, while there can be no denying that Antarctic coastlines are highly unstable, it is doubtful whether Article 7(2) was designed to deal with the situation where through an ice shelf calving the

[41] Watts, *International Law* at 143.

[42] Joyner, *International Law* at 85, stating that this is the 'loose constructionist view'.

[43] Auburn, *Antarctic Law* at 36–7.

[44] Emil A. Zuccaro, 'Iceberg Appropriation and the Antarctic's Gordian Knot' (1979) 9 CalWILJ 405 at 419. Boyd prefers a combination of both proposals for the Arctic: see Boyd, 'The Legal Status' at 139. For a further review of the various options see Prescott, 'Boundaries in Antarctica' at 94–6.

[45] D. P. O'Connell, *The International Law of the Sea* (vol. I), I. A. Shearer (ed.), (Oxford, 1982) 197–8.

[46] Auburn, *Antarctic Law* at 36; Watts, *International Law* at 144.

[47] Mangone favours the adoption of this approach, see Mangone, 'The Legal Status of Ice' at 380.

'furthest seaward extent' of the low-water line can in a matter of seconds retreat by a considerable distance from where it was previously.[48] If then this provision was to be relied upon, it would be necessary for Antarctic coastal states to ensure that their claims were not excessive and that changes in the baseline were made when ice shelves were in regression.[49]

Application in Antarctica

There is little evidence that any of the Antarctic territorial claimants have given much consideration to either baselines or basepoints around their Antarctic coastlines.[50] In 1927 the British Foreign Office relied on the report of the 1926 British Imperial Conference Committee in advising New Zealand that the territorial sea for the Ross Dependency should be determined from the edge of the Ross Ice Shelf.[51] There is no evidence though that the UK ever adopted this approach towards its Antarctic maritime claim. Under Australian law, any declared baselines are not to be inconsistent with the provisions of UNCLOS.[52] While there is scope under Australian legislation for baselines to be proclaimed, and this has occurred in the case of the Australian mainland,[53] no baselines have yet been proclaimed around the AAT. Despite Australia extending its territorial sea adjacent to the AAT in 1990 from three to twelve nautical miles,[54] it is still uncertain from which point along the AAT coastline the territorial sea is delimited.[55]

48 Antarctic icebergs can be of tremendous size and when the calving of an ice shelf occurs there is the potential for the coastline to retreat by a great distance. Joyner notes that icebergs can be from a few hundred metres to more than 100 kilometres in length: Joyner, *Antarctica and the Law of the Sea* at 15. UNCLOS, Art. 7(2) was designed to deal with unstable delta areas, such as the Ganges Delta. For comment see O'Connell (vol. I), *The International Law of the Sea* at 211.

49 Watts, *International Law* at 145; *cf.* Joyner, *Antarctica and the Law of the Sea* at 86.

50 See the discussion in Stuart Kaye and Donald R. Rothwell, 'Australia's Antarctic Maritime Claims and Boundaries' (1995) 26 ODIL 195 at 204–5.

51 This advice was given in regard to the operation of the Ross Dependency Whaling Regulations: see 'Foreign Office Opinion on the Territorial Scope of the Ross Dependency Whaling Regulations', 15 March 1927, reprinted in Bush, vol. III, 56–7.

52 Seas and Submerged Lands Act 1973 (Australia), s. 7.

53 New baselines were proclaimed in 1983, *Commonwealth of Australia Gazette*, No. S29 (9 February 1983) 4–8.

54 *Commonwealth of Australia Gazette*, No. S 297 (13 November 1990), reprinted in (1992) 13 AYIL 278.

55 See the response by an Australian government minister to a question in Parliament concerning Australia's position with regard to the 'ice mass' adjacent to the AAT: Bush (vol. II), 199–200; Kaye and Rothwell, 'Australia's Antarctic Maritime Claims' at 205–6.

This brief review of Antarctic practice regarding baselines demonstrates the need for a more definite approach to be taken to the problem of determining baselines along ice-covered coastlines. As Joyner has noted:

> In sum, the ice shelves around Antarctica do not neatly lend themselves to treatment either as land or sea. International law consequently must adapt and adopt new tenets for setting baselines for offshore maritime zones that comply with these circumpolar geophysical realities.[56]

Fringing islands

In the case of the offshore islands which fringe Antarctica, there has been little consideration given to drawing baselines so as to connect them to the continental mainland. It would be difficult to justify such baselines on the basis of either general principles, such as those in the Conventions codifying the principles of the *Anglo-Norwegian Fisheries Case*, or on the grounds that the islands are 'legal archipelagoes'. While it could be argued that some Antarctic island groups such as the South Shetland, South Orkney and South Sandwich Islands do have archipelagic characteristics, they do not meet the criteria established by UNCLOS allowing 'archipelagic baselines' to be drawn around the outer limits of such island groups.[57] Under the Convention, only an 'archipelagic state' is entitled to draw such baselines, and only then where the state is comprised of one or more island groups which form an 'intrinsic geographical, economic and political entity'.[58] Given this limitation, it is impossible for any of the above-mentioned island groups to be enclosed by archipelagic baselines or linked to the continent by such baselines.[59] The declaration of any baselines around offshore islands in Antarctica within the area of 60°S would also raise for consideration the question of whether there was an attempt to assert a new claim in breach of Article IV(2) of the Antarctic Treaty.[60]

Baselines have been proclaimed around the outer limits of the islands of the Canadian Arctic Archipelago and also the islands which

[56] Joyner, *Antarctica and the Law of the Sea* at 87.

[57] UNCLOS, Art. 47. Orrego Vicuna, *Antarctic Mineral Exploitation* at 161.

[58] UNCLOS, Art. 46.

[59] This is not to suggest that some areas within the Antarctic region may not in the future claim archipelagic status. If the Falkland Islands were ever to achieve a measure of self-determination from the UK, they could seek to claim archipelagic status.

[60] Under UNCLOS, Art. 8, waters enclosed by baselines become 'internal waters' of the coastal state over which the coastal state has extensive sovereign rights, while Art. 49 extends to archipelagic states extensive sovereign rights over waters enclosed within archipelagic baselines.

fringe the Russian Arctic coastline. Both claims have a number of similarities. First, they treat as internal, waters previously considered to be either territorial sea or high sea. This represents an extension of sovereignty. Second, both sets of baseline declarations have had an impact upon navigation rights. The baseline declarations enclose waters of the Northwest and Northeast Passage, which in both instances are the most extensive and significant navigation routes in the Arctic. As a result, large areas of internal waters have been created through which no guaranteed rights of navigation exist.[61] As the exercise of navigation rights in the Arctic is made difficult due to climatic conditions and ice, the imposition of further limitations upon navigation imposes another restriction.

Neither the Canadian nor Russian baseline declarations have been completely accepted. In the case of Canada's baseline declaration, there has been considerable discussion over its impact upon navigation through the Northwest Passage. While commentators such as Pharand see the Canadian action as justifiable,[62] others are less approving.[63] It seems unlikely that the Canadian action will be challenged, especially following the 1988 Agreement on Arctic Cooperation with the United States.[64] Russian policy concerning its Arctic baselines has many similarities with the Canadian position.[65] The 1985 baseline declarations, while supported by Russian and Soviet commentators,[66] are contested by others.[67] Franckx in particular has

[61] See UNCLOS, Art. 8(2) which provides that certain navigational freedoms remain in place after waters become internal waters if those waters previously were the waters of an international strait.

[62] See especially Pharand, *Canada's Arctic Waters* at 187–257. See also J. Bruce McKinnon, 'Arctic Baselines: A Litore Usque Ad Litus' (1987) 66 CanBR 790 at 817 who notes:

> Canada's straight baselines in the Arctic are valid under customary international law, but not for the reason publicly relied upon by the government. Foreign ships do not have a right of innocent passage through the waters of the Arctic archipelago. Canada is therefore able to take any steps it wishes in order to regulate or prohibit activity in these waters.

[63] Franckx, *Maritime Claims* at 101–7. Also see Donald R. Rothwell, 'The Canadian – US Northwest Passage Dispute: A Reassessment' (1993) 26 Cornell ILJ 331 at 359–60.

[64] Agreement between the Government of Canada and the Government of the United States of America on Arctic Cooperation, [1988] CTS 29.

[65] For a comparison of the claims and a consideration of their interrelationship, see Franckx, *Maritime Claims* at 234–8, noting at 236 the 'similarity and almost simultaneity of these claims'.

[66] See as an example A. L. Kolodkin and M. E. Volosov, 'The Legal Regime of the Soviet Arctic: Major Issues' (1990) 14 *Marine Policy* 158 at 163.

[67] See generally Douglas Brubaker, 'International Law and Russian Arctic Waters' (1992) 12 *International Challenges* 97–106.

noted that the Russian claim is surrounded by 'uncertainties'.[68] However, despite past efforts to challenge Soviet restrictions on the freedom of navigation through Arctic waters, no similar challenges are likely to occur over the recent baseline declarations.

In these circumstances, it seems that both the Canadian and Russian baseline claims in the Arctic, despite being surrounded by various legal uncertainties, are being accepted by the international community as a *fait accompli*. These Arctic baseline claims demonstrate some of the difficulties in applying the law of the sea to polar waters. In both instances the baseline claims can have substantial impacts upon the freedom of navigation. With navigation in Arctic waters already difficult, the imposition of additional navigational burdens upon international shipping is a considerable restriction on the freedom of navigation. It also results in placing large areas of Arctic waters under national jurisdiction.

Maritime zones

Throughout much of this century there has been a gradual process of creeping jurisdiction over waters previously considered high seas. The extension of the territorial sea from three to twelve nautical miles,[69] the recognition of a continental shelf regime in customary international law[70] and also in the Conventions of 1958 and 1982,[71] and the acceptance of 200 nautical mile exclusive economic zones (EEZ)[72] illustrate this trend.[73] As a result, areas of the world's oceans that were previously considered high seas have been continually shrinking. Because of the physical differences of the two polar regions the effects of 'creeping jurisdiction' in the law of the sea has had distinctive impacts. In the Arctic, the consequence is that the Arctic Ocean, surrounded as it is by continental and island landmasses, has slowly become enclosed by littoral state maritime claims. In the Southern Ocean, because of the uncertain sovereignty status of the territorial

[68] Franckx, *Maritime Claims* at 192–3.

[69] UNCLOS, Art. 3.

[70] See 1945 Truman Declaration on the Continental Shelf, reprinted in M. M. Whiteman, *Digest of International Law* (vol. IV) (Washington, 1963) 756; *North Sea Continental Shelf Cases (Federal Republic of Germany* v. *Denmark, Federal Republic of Germany* v. *The Netherlands)* [1969] ICJ Reports 3.

[71] Continental Shelf Convention; UNCLOS, Art. 76.

[72] See UNCLOS, Art. 55.

[73] See B. Kwiatkowska, 'Creeping Jurisdiction Beyond 200 Miles in the Light of the 1982 Law of the Sea Convention and State Practice' (1991) 22 ODIL 153–87.

claimants, questions arise as to whether maritime claims can even be asserted under the terms of the Antarctic Treaty. The result of these distinctive consequences of extended maritime jurisdiction in the polar regions has been to create further uncertainty over the extent of the law of the sea regime.

The need for a coastal state

Only coastal states may assert maritime claims.[74] It is therefore necessary to determine whether any state has a valid claim over a coastal area before it is eligible to assert a maritime claim. While this is not a contentious issue in the Arctic, it is a major area of concern in Antarctica. Article IV of the Antarctic Treaty dominates any discussion on the ability of the territorial claimants to assert maritime claims. Given the uncertain status in international law of the validity of the Antarctic claims, a threshold question is whether there exist any states in Antarctica whose territorial claims are recognised so as to allow them to assert a maritime claim.[75] This question can only be answered by a long historical review of each of the territorial claims, which is beyond the scope of this work.[76] It is appropriate, however, to consider whether the Antarctic Treaty's provisions allow for the assertion of Antarctic maritime claims. In the lead-up to the negotiation of the Treaty in 1959 the resolution of disputes over the status of Antarctic territorial claims was considered one of the pivotal issues. The provisions of Article IV(1) of the Treaty were considered the answer to this problem. Article IV(2) also prohibits the making of any additional or new sovereignty claims while the Treaty is in force.[77] How Article IV(2) is interpreted can have a significant impact upon the ability of Antarctic territorial claimants to assert maritime claims.[78] The attitude of Australia towards the declaration of an Australian Fishing Zone (AFZ) offshore the Australian Antarctic Territory (AAT) illustrates the type of problems which territorial claimants face. When Australia

74 See UNCLOS, Arts. 1 and 56.

75 This question is considered in some detail by Joyner, *Antarctica and the Law of the Sea* at 41–67; see also Ulrich Nussbaum, 'Legal Status of Antarctic Off-Shore Areas' (1993) 6 *ASOLPO Paper* 1 at 2–12.

76 For an analysis of some of these questions see Auburn, *Antarctic Law* at 5–47; G. Triggs, *International Law and Australian Sovereignty in Antarctica* (Sydney, 1986) 1–96.

77 There has been considerable debate over the effect and impact of Art. IV: see the discussion in chapter 3. As to whether new maritime claims can be made while the Treaty is in force see Bush (vol. I), 60–3.

78 Orrego Vicuna, *Antarctic Mineral Exploitation* at 130–3.

first proclaimed an AFZ in 1979,[79] it specifically included the waters of Australia's external territories. However, a little over one month later, a new proclamation was made which excepted the waters around the AAT.[80] The effect of this action was to exempt foreign vessels from the reach of Australian law so that the waters of the AAT beyond the territorial sea remained open to foreign fishing. Australian nationals and vessels were, however, still caught by the reach of Australian law because even though the waters were not part of the Australian fishing zone they were still 'proclaimed waters' under Australian law.[81] Australia's actions in this instance indicate how sensitive some of the Antarctic territorial claimants have been to the questions that may arise from the active assertion of offshore maritime sovereignty and jurisdiction.

Territorial sea

Territorial sea claims have been actively asserted in both polar regions. In the Arctic the claims range from three to twelve nautical miles consistent with current international law.[82] In most cases, Arctic states have gradually extended their territorial sea jurisdiction though Denmark still claims only a three nautical mile territorial sea around Greenland while Finland and Norway claim only four nautical mile territorial seas.[83] In Antarctica there has been variable practice concerning territorial sea claims. In some instances claims have been made in conjunction with territorial claims.[84] In other instances, separate proclamations have been made over territorial sea zones.[85] In

79 *Commonwealth of Australia Gazette*, No. S189 (26 September 1979), reprinted in Bush (vol. II), 202–3.

80 *Commonwealth of Australia Gazette*, No. S225 (2 November 1979), reprinted in Bush (vol. II), 208–9.

81 See Fisheries Act 1952 (Australia); and discussion in Bush (vol. II), at 205, 209; Brian R. Opeskin and Donald R. Rothwell, 'Australia's Territorial Sea: International and Federal Implications of its Extension to 12 Miles' (1991) 22 ODIL 395 at 402.

82 The claims of the various Arctic states are as follows: Canada – 12, Denmark – 3, Finland – 4, Iceland – 12, Norway – 4, Russia -12, Sweden – 12, USA – 12, see Judith Fenwick, *International Profiles of Marine Scientific Research* (Woods Hole, MA, 1992) 186–93.

83 For a discussion see Kolodkin and Volosov, 'The Legal Regime of the Soviet Arctic' at 161.

84 See the claims of Argentina and Chile referred to at note 21 above; also Norway – 'Royal Proclamation Defining the Area of Norwegian Sovereignty in Antarctica', 14 December 1939, reprinted in Bush (vol. III), 149; UK – 'British Note to Chile Providing Information Sought Concerning British Claims to Certain Territory', 23 May 1914, reprinted in Bush (vol. II), 304–5.

85 See the Australian practice noted at note 54 above; and France – 'Law No. 66–400

the case of New Zealand's territorial sea off the Ross Dependency it seems that there was no formal proclamation as such but rather a gradual recognition that through the application of previous UK legislation a territorial sea did indeed exist.[86] Despite this variable practice, the limitations on claims in Article IV(2) of the Treaty cannot be interpreted as inhibiting territorial claimants from asserting territorial sea claims.[87] This follows because the territorial sea is considered an inherent right of coastal states[88] recognised in customary international law and conventions prior to the entry into force of the Antarctic Treaty.[89] A more difficult question arises over whether territorial sea claims can be enlarged without breaching Article IV(2). If customary international law now recognises that coastal states are entitled to a twelve nautical mile territorial sea it could be argued that the enlargement of an Antarctic territorial sea claim from three to twelve nautical miles is not an enlargement for the purposes of Article IV(2) of the Treaty, but merely an act adopting a current coastal state entitlement recognised by international law. Nevertheless, it must be

Concerning Marine Fishing and the Exploitation of the Produce of the Sea in French Southern and Antarctic Lands', 18 June 1966, reprinted in Bush (vol. II), 551–5, and 'Order No. 5 Promulgating Legislation Concerning the Delimitation of the French Territorial Sea', 13 January 1972, reprinted in Bush (vol. II), 579–80.

86 See note 51 above; also 'Parliamentary Statement Concerning Jurisdiction over the Territorial Sea of the Ross Dependency', 23 September 1977, reprinted in Bush (vol. III), 97.

87 As Antarctic Treaty, Art. IV(2) refers to claims to 'territorial sovereignty' and not 'maritime sovereignty', the question arises whether it has any application in the case of claims over offshore maritime zones. It can be inferred that as the intent of Art. IV was to preclude the assertion of new sovereignty claims, or the enlargement of existing ones for the duration of the Treaty, and that the Treaty applies to the area south of 60°S, it was intended that the Teaty not only apply to the Antarctic continent and ice shelves, but also maritime areas. As such the Art. IV(2) limitation extends to maritime claims as well as to claims made to the Antarctic continent and offshore islands.

88 UNCLOS, Art. 2(1) provides as follows:

> The sovereignty of a coastal state extends, beyond its land territory and internal waters and, in the case of an archipelagic State, its archipelagic waters, to an adjacent belt of sea, described as the territorial sea.

89 See the extensive discussion in O'Connell (vol. I), *The International Law of the Sea* at 60–169; R. R. Churchill and A. V. Lowe, *The Law of the Sea* (rev. ed.) (Manchester, 1988) 59–63; TSCZ, Art. 1. Despite the acceptance in international law of the territorial sea, UNCLOS was the first global convention which recognised a twelve nautical mile territorial sea. The international recognition of a twelve nautical mile territorial sea raises the issue of whether the extension of a previously asserted territorial sea claim from three to twelve nautical miles, as Australia did in 1990, represented an extension of a claim for the purposes of Art. IV(2): see Opeskin and Rothwell, 'Australia's Territorial Sea' at 402.

conceded that the enlargement of a pre-existing claim to a territorial sea offshore Antarctica will result in the assertion of sovereignty over a greater maritime area.[90] This may explain why some Antarctic claimants seek to assert more extensive maritime claims but do not enforce them against foreign nationals.[91] By adopting this approach they can be seen as asserting sovereignty in Antarctica but not offending other Treaty parties.

Continental shelf

Continental shelf claims have also been actively asserted in both polar regions. All Arctic states have asserted claims to their adjacent continental shelf but the limits are variable.[92] This no doubt reflects the changes in the potential outer limits of continental shelf claims which were adopted by UNCLOS.[93] Continental shelf claims have also been asserted by the Antarctic claimants in the Southern Ocean; however, the practice has again been variable. Both Australia and Chile made claims to the continental shelf adjacent to their Antarctic claims prior to the entry into force of the Antarctic Treaty.[94] In 1966 Argentina claimed sovereignty over its adjacent Antarctic continental shelf out to the edge of the 200 mile limit or the limit of exploitation.[95] No other claimant has asserted a continental shelf claim, though France has asserted claims with respect to the adjacent continental

[90] Opeskin and Rothwell, 'Australia's Territorial Sea' at 402.

[91] For a review of the position in the AAT, see James Crawford and Donald R. Rothwell, 'Legal Issues Confronting Australia's Antarctica' (1992) 13 AYIL 53 at 79–85.

[92] Canada – 200 miles or edge of the continental margin, Denmark – 200 miles or depth of exploitation, Finland – 200 miles or depth of exploitation, Iceland – 200 miles or edge of the continental margin, Norway – 200 miles plus the natural prolongation, Russia – 200 miles or depth of exploitation, Sweden – 200 miles or depth of exploitation, USA – proclaimed but no specific limit set: see Fenwick, *International Profiles*. In regard to Svalbard, some uncertainty has existed over whether, under the 1920 Treaty Concerning the Archipelago of Spitsbergen (Svalbard), 2 LNTS 8, Norway can claim maritime zones beyond the territorial sea: see R. R. Churchill, 'The Maritime Zones of Spitsbergen' in W. E. Butler (ed.), *The Law of the Sea and International Shipping* (New York, 1985) 189 at 193–5; Robin Churchill and Geir Ulfstein, *Marine Management in Disputed Areas* (London, 1992) 38–40.

[93] See the definition of the continental shelf under UNCLOS, Art. 76; *cf.* Continental Shelf Convention, Art. 1.

[94] See for Australia, *Commonwealth of Australia Gazette*, No. 56 of 1953 (11 September 1953) at 1, col. 1, reprinted in Bush (vol. II), 172–3; for Chile, 'Presidential Declaration over Continental Shelf and Seas Adjacent to the Coasts', 23 June 1947, discussed in Bush (vol. II), 448–9. For further discussion of the Australian claim, see Kaye and Rothwell, 'Australia's Antarctic Maritime Claims' at 207–8.

[95] 'Law No. 17.094', 29 December 1966, Bush (vol. II), 72.

shelves of its sub-Antarctic islands.[96] The validity of Antarctic continental shelf claims, whether asserted prior to or after the entry into force of the Antarctic Treaty, raises similar issues to the validity of territorial sea claims. Coastal state rights to a continental shelf had been recognised under both customary international law and convention prior to 1961.[97] While the outer limits of the continental shelf were extended by UNCLOS, the extent of coastal state rights to a continental shelf did not change. The law of the sea recognises that coastal states have inherent sovereign rights over a continental shelf which need not be actively proclaimed. As such, it can be argued that an Antarctic continental shelf claim is an inherent right of every claimant and does not represent the assertion of a new claim.[98] Consequently under the terms of the Antarctic Treaty it would seem that coastal states are entitled to assert continental shelf claims in Antarctica. However, as in the case of the territorial sea, an issue can arise over whether the enlargement of a previously asserted continental shelf claim in order to meet the new standards set by UNCLOS breaches the terms of Article IV(2).[99]

[96] See 'Order No. 10 Promulgating Decrees No. 71–360 and No. 71–361 of 6 May 1971 Concerning the Continental Shelf', 9 June 1971, reprinted in Bush (vol. II), 572–3 and discussion at 580–1.

[97] Continental Shelf Convention; Churchill and Lowe, *The Law of the Sea* at 121–7; O'Connell (vol. I), *The International Law of the Sea* at 475–6. In the *North Sea Continental Shelf Cases (Federal Republic of Germany* v. *Denmark, Federal Republic of Germany* v. *The Netherlands)* [1969] ICJ Reports 3 at 31 the court noted:

> What confers the *ipso jure* title which international law attributes to the coastal State in respect of its continental shelf, is the fact that the submarine areas concerned may be deemed to be actually part of the territory over which the coastal State already has dominion – in the sense that, although covered by water, they are a prolongation or continuation of that territory, an extension of it under the sea.

Also see Orrego Vicuna, *Antarctic Mineral Exploitation* at 156.

[98] UNCLOS, Art. 77(1) provides:

> The coastal state exercises over the continental shelf sovereign rights for the purpose of exploring it and exploiting its natural resources.

A number of commentators are of the view that the assertion of a continental shelf claim is not in conflict with Art. IV(2): see Patricia Birnie, 'The Effect of Article VI of the Antarctic Treaty on Scientific Research', in Rudiger Wolfrum (ed.), *Antarctic Challenge III* (Berlin, 1988) 105 at 116; G. D. Triggs, 'The Antarctic Treaty System: Some Jurisdictional Problems' in G. D. Triggs (ed.), *The Antarctic Treaty Regime* (Cambridge, 1987) 88 at 90; Auburn, *Antarctic Law* at 136; Nussbaum, 'Legal Status' at 13–15.

[99] See Crawford and Rothwell, 'Legal Status' at 81. For a consideration of how the new limits of the continental shelf would be applied in Antarctica see Joyner, *Antarctica and the Law of the Sea* at 126–7.

EEZ

EEZ or equivalent claims have also been asserted in the Arctic.[100] As a result of these claims there has been a need to delimit a number of maritime boundaries.[101] In Antarctica, EEZ or fisheries zones have only been claimed by Argentina, Australia and Chile.[102] However, varying practices have been adopted by the claimant states towards their mainland claims and those of offshore and sub-Antarctic islands.[103] In 1994 Australia converted its AFZ claim offshore the AAT to an EEZ.[104] This was consistent with an Australian approach to take full advantage of the range of maritime zones available to a coastal state under UNCLOS. However, as was the case with the legislative regime Australia applied previously to the AFZ, the legal regime of the EEZ is ambiguous. Under Australian law, only Australian nationals and their vessels are subject to a fisheries regime in the EEZ.[105] Australian law also prohibits any whaling activities in the EEZ; however, this is subject to Australia's international law obligations.[106] It can be concluded therefore that while Australia has proclaimed an EEZ offshore the AAT, it has not yet implemented a legislative regime that seeks to enforce Australia's

[100] The types of Arctic claims are: Canada – 200 mile Fisheries Zone, Denmark – 200 mile Fisheries Zone, Finland – 12 mile Fisheries Zone, Iceland – 200 mile EEZ, Norway – 200 mile EEZ, Sweden – 200 mile Fisheries Zone, Russia – 200 mile EEZ, USA – 200 mile EEZ, see Fenwick: *International Profiles*. For further discussion also see Kolodkin and Volosov, 'The Legal Regime of the Soviet Arctic' at 162–3.

[101] See the discussion in chapter 5.

[102] See Argentina, note 95 above, Law No. 17,094 (29 November 1966), Law No. 17,500 (25 October 1967), Law No. 20,136 (5 February 1973), discussed in Bush (vol. II), 72; Australia – notes 79 and 80 above; Chile – note 94 above. Chile has also indicated its desire to extend further its offshore claims to encompass an 'El Mar Presencial' or 'Presencial Sea': see Jane Gilliland Dalton, 'The Chilean Mar Presencial: A Harmless Concept or a Dangerous Precedent?' (1993) 8(3) *International Journal of Marine and Coastal Law* 397–418.

[103] Australia, France and South Africa have all made EEZ/Fisheries claims around their Antarctic and sub-Antarctic islands: see Joyner, *Antarctica and the Law of the Sea* at 88. In 1993 the UK declared by proclamation a 200 nautical mile maritime zone around South Georgia and the South Sandwich Islands. In a statement accompanying the proclamation, it was explained that the measures were taken to strengthen conservation and management of marine resources and to supplement the Convention on the Conservation of Antarctic Marine Living Resources, (1980) 19 ILM 837 (hereinafter CCAMLR): see United Nations, Report of the Secretary General, *Law of the Sea* (UN Doc. A/48/527: 10 November 1993) 10–11, para. 24.

[104] *Commonwealth of Australia Gazette*, No S290 (29 July 1994); for comment see I. A. Shearer, 'Australia's New Maritime Zones' (1995) 69 *Australian Law Journal* 26 at 27.

[105] See Fisheries Management Act 1991 (Australia).

[106] See Whale Protection Act 1980 (Australia).

rights over the EEZ against foreign nationals or their vessels.[107] The Australian position concerning its Antarctic EEZ demonstrates the difficulties that claimants face in making such claims consistently with Article IV(2) of the Antarctic Treaty. This follows because the EEZ concept was not recognised in international law prior to 1961,[108] and unlike the territorial sea or continental shelf it is not recognised as an inherent sovereign right of a coastal state.[109] It follows that EEZ claims must be proclaimed if they are to be asserted.[110] Under these circumstances, the conclusion seems inescapable that the declaration of an EEZ in Antarctica seeking to assert territorial sovereignty and jurisdiction is either an enlargement of an existing claim or assertion of a new claim and thereby infringes Article IV(2).[111] On these grounds, the effect of the Australian approach of asserting an EEZ but not giving the claim any real legal content still remains doubtful.

Deep sea bed

One of the major developments in the law of the sea during the past twenty years has been the development of a regime for the deep sea

[107] For a review of the Australian position see Kaye and Rothwell, 'Australia's Antarctic Maritime Claims' at 209–11.

[108] The earliest point in time at which the concept could be said to have been recognised in customary international law was in the 1970s during the early stages of negotiations at the Third United Nations Conference on the Law of the Sea: see David Joseph Attard, *The Exclusive Economic Zone in International Law* (Oxford, 1987) 30–1; O'Connell (vol. I), *The International Law of the Sea* at 553–8 (reviewing state practice up till the commencement of the Third UN Conference on the Law of the Sea).

[109] See UNCLOS, Art. 56. See the discussion in Attard, *The Exclusive Economic Zone* at 54–61; O'Connell (vol. I), *The International Law of the Sea* at 571–2; Barbara Kwiatkowska, *The 200 Mile Exclusive Economic Zone in the New Law of the Sea* (Dordrecht, 1989) 7–9.

[110] Attard, *The Exclusive Economic Zone* at 56 notes: 'A review of the relevant State practice demonstrates that the large majority of EEZ claimants consider an express proclamation necessary for the existence of EEZ rights'; Ralph L. Harry, 'The Antarctic Regime and the Law of the Sea Convention: An Australian View' (1981) 21 VaJIL 727 at 733; *cf.* Triggs, *International Law and Australian Sovereignty* at 160.

[111] Crawford and Rothwell, 'Legal Issues' at 81; Churchill and Lowe, *The Law of the Sea* at 136. For further discussion on EEZ claims in Antarctica see Christopher C. Joyner, 'The Exclusive Economic Zone and Antarctica' (1981) 21 VaJIL 691–725; Christopher C. Joyner, 'The Exclusive Economic Zone and Antarctica: The Dilemmas of Non-Sovereign Jurisdiction' (1988) 19 ODIL 469–91; Francisco Orrego Vicuna, 'The Application of the Law of the Sea and the Exclusive Economic Zone to the Antarctic Continent' in Francisco Orrego Vicuna (ed.), *Antarctic Resources Policy* (Cambridge, 1983) 243–51.

bed. This regime is found in Part XI of UNCLOS.[112] Notwithstanding some amendments made to that Part of UNCLOS prior to its entry into force,[113] there has been a gradual movement towards the recognition of a regime for the deep sea bed based upon resource sharing and common heritage concepts. In the polar regions, this raises jurisdictional issues as to where areas within national jurisdiction end and where the deep sea bed commences.

Where does the Area begin?[114]

Arctic Ocean

Irrespective of whether it would be possible to engage in deep sea bed mining in the Arctic, is the Arctic deep sea bed potentially subject to the UNCLOS Part XI regime? Basic law of the sea principles would suggest that those areas of the Arctic Ocean beyond the limits of national jurisdiction are part of the 'Area' as defined in UNCLOS and fall within the reach of the International Seabed Authority (ISA). A determination of what is the Area in the Arctic is also made simpler because all Arctic states have made either continental shelf or EEZ claims. As a result the 'Area' in the Arctic Ocean is that part of the seabed which is beyond the limits of existing continental shelf or EEZ claims. The only possible alternative is that the Arctic states have established some special regime over the circumpolar Arctic Ocean so that it remains subject to Arctic state jurisdiction and hence beyond the reach of the ISA. This argument will be considered further below.

Southern Ocean

Any consideration as to whether parts of the Southern Ocean could be classified as part of the 'Area' under UNCLOS raises several difficult issues.[115] First, because only three Antarctic claimants have actually asserted continental shelf claims, the question arises whether for the purposes of determining the area beyond the limits of national

[112] For a review see Churchill and Lowe, *The Law of the Sea* at 177–201.

[113] See Agreement Relating to the Implementation of Part XI of the United Nations Convention on the Law of the Sea of 10 December 1982, (1994) 33 ILM 1309.

[114] UNCLOS, Art. 1(1) provides that the 'Area' is the seabed and ocean floor and subsoil thereof, beyond the limits of national jurisdiction. Under the new law of the sea the 'Area', therefore, is that region of the seabed which is beyond the outer limits of continental shelf or EEZ claims. Art. 137 confers upon the International Seabed Authority the right to manage the resources of the Area.

[115] See generally on this question Joyner, *Antarctica and the Law of the Sea* at 127–31.

jurisdiction in the Southern Ocean account is to be taken of potential maritime zones or only those which have actually been asserted. An issue here is whether territorial claimants who failed to assert offshore claims prior to the entry into force of the Antarctic Treaty are now precluded from doing so under Article IV(2)[116] or whether rights to a continental shelf are inherent in every coastal state.[117] Given the uncertainty surrounding this issue, it is difficult to determine conclusively what the outer limits of national maritime jurisdiction are in Antarctica. A second issue is whether the ISA would have authority over the seabed offshore the unclaimed sector. As there is no territorial claimant no maritime zones have been proclaimed offshore this sector. As a result, it could be argued that the ISA would be entitled to exploit the seabed up to the edge of the low-water mark of the Antarctic unclaimed sector.[118]

The third, and perhaps most substantial, question is whether Part XI of UNCLOS can even be said to apply in Antarctica.[119] The question of Antarctica was expressly excluded during the negotiation of UNCLOS, which, given the tentative discussions then taking place between the Antarctic Treaty parties over the implementation of a mining regime in Antarctica, can be seen as significant. It is therefore helpful to reconsider the provisions of the 1988 Convention on the Regulation of Antarctic Mineral Resource Activities (CRAMRA).[120] Article 5 adopted the same area of application as the Antarctic Treaty. It specified that 'Antarctic mineral resource activities which take place on the continent of Antarctica and all Antarctic islands, including all ice shelves, south of 60° South latitude and in the seabed and subsoil of adjacent

[116] The view that Antarctic territory cannot generate maritime zones in addition to those existing at the time of the commencement of the Antarctic Treaty appears to have been taken by the USSR: see Bush (vol. I), 260; and by New Zealand in respect of a potential EEZ claim for the Ross Dependency: see Bush (vol. III), 96. The United States also has adopted this view and takes the stance that the high seas extend right to the edge of the coastline, see B. H. Oxman, 'Antarctica and the New Law of the Sea' (1982) 19 Cornell IJL 211 at 228. See also M. J. Peterson, 'Antarctic Implications of the New Law of the Sea' (1986) 16 ODIL 137 at 153; Francisco Orrego Vicuna and Maria Teresa Infante, 'Le droit de la mer dans l'Antarctique'(1980) 84 *Revue générale du droit international public* 340 at 344–6.

[117] See the discussion at pp. 278–9 above.

[118] For discussion on this question see Joyner, *Antarctica and the Law of the Sea* at 89–91.

[119] See the discussion in Maria Teresa Infante, 'The Continental Shelf of Antarctica: Legal Implications for a Regime on Minerals Resources' in Francisco Orrego Vicuna (ed.), *Antarctic Resources Policy* (Cambridge, 1983) 253 at 259–60; S. Muller, 'The Impact of UNCLOS III on the Antarctic Regime' in Rudiger Wolfrum (ed.), *Antarctic Challenge* (Berlin, 1984) 169 at 175–6.

[120] (1988) 27 ILM 868 (hereinafter CRAMRA).

offshore areas up to the deep seabed' were regulated by the Convention.[121] However, for the purposes of CRAMRA, the 'deep seabed' was defined as the seabed and subsoil beyond the geographic extent of the continental shelf.[122] This suggested that even though some territorial claimants have not asserted continental shelf claims offshore Antarctica, it was intended that CRAMRA would apply within those areas as if such claims had been asserted.[123] Not only did CRAMRA seek to exercise a form of 'collective jurisdiction' over all potential continental shelf areas within the Antarctic Treaty area, but there was also an inference that its provisions concerning limitations on environmental impact as a result of mining activities also applied beyond the continental shelf to the deep sea bed.[124] The CRAMRA regime therefore implied that irrespective of UNCLOS, the Antarctic Treaty parties sought to exercise some jurisdiction over mining activities in the Southern Ocean. The Protocol also affects seabed mining because all minerals activities are prohibited under Article 7. Unlike CRAMRA, the Protocol applies to the same area as the Treaty. This implies that the Protocol's area of application includes both the continental shelf and deep sea bed up to 60°S. It follows that by adopting the same area of application as the Antarctic Treaty, the Protocol seeks to regulate all mineral resource activities that may take place in the deep sea bed within the Antarctic Treaty area.[125] Irrespective of what constitutes the 'Area' in the Southern Ocean, the Protocol is an indicator that the Antarctic Treaty parties do not believe there is any scope for the

[121] CRAMRA, Art. 5(2).

[122] CRAMRA, Art. 5(3), defining the continental shelf in accordance with international law.

[123] This presumably applied also to the unclaimed sector.

[124] See CRAMRA, Art. 5(4) providing:

> Nothing in this Article shall be construed as limiting the application of other Articles of this Convention in so far as they relate to possible impacts outside the area . . . including impacts on dependent or on associated ecosystems.

See also discussion in R. Wolfrum, *The Convention on the Regulation of Antarctic Mineral Resource Activities* (Berlin, 1991) 31–4; P. Gautier, 'The Maritime Area of the Antarctic and the New Law of the Sea' in J. Verhoeven, P. Sands and M. Bruce (eds.), *The Antarctic Environment and International Law* (London, 1992) 121 at 132.

[125] *Cf.* Bush (Bin I), Pt AT90A, 54, who argues that the Protocol is not as explicit on this point as it could be. He contrasts the provisions of Art. 7 of the Protocol with a draft New Zealand proposal which provided:

> Mineral resource activities shall be prohibited on the continent of Antarctica and on all Antarctic islands, including all ice shelves, south of 60° South latitude, and in the seabed and subsoil of adjacent offshore areas up to the deep seabed.

application of the UNCLOS deep sea bed minerals regime in Antarctic waters.[126]

High seas freedoms

One of the consequences of the extension of coastal state maritime zones has been a shrinking of high seas areas. There has also been a consequential impact upon traditional freedoms of navigation. This has occurred in a number of ways. The adoption of baselines around the outer fringes of coastal states has enclosed waters previously considered territorial. The extension of traditional maritime zones such as the territorial sea and the development of new zones such as the EEZ have also imposed limitations on navigation. The gradual expansion of marine pollution provisions and limitations upon freedoms of high seas fishing have also substantially derogated from previously exercised high seas rights. While these consequences for high seas freedoms have been experienced in all waters, they have had a special impact in the polar regions. A brief review will first be undertaken of the international high seas regime before considering a specific polar issue.

The new UNCLOS regime

The high seas were traditionally considered to be those ocean areas which were not included in either the territorial sea or internal waters of coastal states.[127] As indicated above, the high seas under UNCLOS have been substantially altered. Article 86 of UNCLOS provides that the high seas are 'all parts of the sea that are not included in the exclusive economic zone, in the territorial sea or in the internal waters of a State, or in the archipelagic waters of an archipelagic State'. However, this provision must be read in conjunction with Article 58. The result is that the high seas freedoms of navigation and overflight and the laying of submarine cables may be exercised within the EEZ provided they do not conflict with coastal state EEZ rights.[128] While many traditional high seas freedoms remain in place under UNCLOS,[129] new obligations have been created regarding the duty to

[126] Watts, *International Law* at 159–62; Triggs, *International Law and Australian Sovereignty* at 225–6. For a further analysis of these issues see Donald R. Rothwell, 'A Maritime Analysis of Conflicting International Law Regimes in Antarctica and the Southern Ocean' (1994) 15 AYIL 155 at 165–8. [127] See High Seas Convention, Art. 1.

[128] As a result the traditional high seas freedom of fishing is subject to the jurisdiction of the relevant coastal state within that state's EEZ.

[129] See Churchill and Lowe, *The Law of the Sea* at 166–8.

conserve and manage the living resources of the high seas.[130] This has an important consequence for areas of the polar oceans beyond the reach of coastal state jurisdiction over marine living resources.

Other international controls

Other controls which exist over the exercise of traditional navigational freedoms on the high seas are contained in a variety of international instruments. Those dealing with marine pollution and the transportation of hazardous materials are discussed in detail below.[131] Of the remainder, the 1946 International Convention for the Regulation of Whaling[132] is particularly important because of the large numbers of whales which frequent polar waters and the historical interest of many polar states in whaling. The Convention, which has been signed by most whaling nations and the principal parties to the Antarctic Treaty, creates a regulatory regime for the catching of whales in all the world's oceans. Administered by the International Whaling Commission (IWC), Convention parties can, through the IWC forum, set catch quotas, designate protected species and regulate whaling methods. While the Convention seeks to prevent the overexploitation of whales it could not be claimed that it is protectionist. Rather it seeks to ensure sustainable whaling.[133]

The Convention has an extremely wide application. Article 2(1) provides:

> This Convention applies to factory ships, land stations, and whale catchers under the jurisdiction of the Contracting Governments and to all waters in which whaling is prosecuted by such factory ships, land stations, and whale catchers.

Consequently, Article 2(1) has allowed the IWC to regulate all whaling activity on the high seas, including the Arctic and Southern Oceans. Given the serious depletion of whale stocks that had occurred before the Convention's entry into force, the IWC has always sought to monitor closely and regulate any whaling activities taking place in the Southern Ocean. To that end the provisions of the Schedule to the Convention have played a significant role.[134] The Schedule has been subject to a number of major amendments and revisions at the annual meetings of the IWC. The most important was a 1982 amendment

130 UNCLOS, Arts. 116–20. 131 See pp. 293–300 below.

132 161 UNTS 74 (hereinafter Whaling Convention).

133 See Simon Lyster, *International Wildlife Law* (Cambridge, 1985) 19–20.

134 Whaling Convention, Art. V provides the IWC with this power.

which prohibited all commercial whaling from the 1985/86 season in Antarctica and elsewhere from 1986.[135]

In regard to the waters of the Southern Ocean, while whaling has been substantially regulated and even prohibited in recent years, 'scientific whaling' still occurs for research purposes. This has been the subject of controversy as claims have been made that Japanese whalers have used this as a loophole to engage in commercial whaling in disguise.[136] The issue has caused some concern for Antarctic territorial claimants as Japanese vessels have engaged in whaling offshore the continent within some Fishing Zones.[137] A specific response to the concerns over the future management of whales in the Southern Ocean was a 1992 proposal by France that a 'whale sanctuary' be established in the Southern Ocean.[138] After considerable debate amongst IWC members, a revised version of this proposal was accepted by the IWC at its forty-sixth Annual Meeting in 1994 in Mexico. The 'Southern Ocean Sanctuary' applies south of 40° S, except in the Indian Ocean where it meets the southern boundary of the already existing Indian Ocean Sanctuary at 55° S, and an area in the western Pacific immediately to the north of the Antarctic Peninsula where the boundary is set at 60° S.[139] The Sanctuary only applies to commercial whaling and this still leaves open the prospect that scientific whaling will continue in the Southern Ocean.[140]

Who controls polar waters?

While traditional law of the sea principles suggest that polar waters beyond the limits of national jurisdiction are high seas, a contrary view is that the polar states individually or collectively are able to assert jurisdiction over polar waters. Rather than the polar waters

135 See Whaling Convention, Schedule, para. 10(e), reprinted in Patricia Birnie (ed.), *International Regulation of Whaling* (vol. II) (New York, 1985) 714; and for comment see Lyster, *International Wildlife Law* at 19, 25–7.

136 See Sara L. Ellis, 'Japanese Whaling in the Antarctic: Science or Subterfuge?' (1988) 31(2) *Oceanus* 68–9.

137 James Shevlin, 'Japanese Whaling Activity Observed near Davis Station' (1992) 69 *ANARE News* 18–19.

138 'A Southern Ocean Whale Sanctuary Proposed by the Government of France to the 44th Annual Meeting of the IWC' (IWC/44/19).

139 'Proposal for a Widely-Accepted Southern Ocean Sanctuary' (IWC/46/53) (25 May 1994).

140 Japan has indicated that it intends to continue taking whales for scientific purposes in the Southern Ocean: see 'Japan May Continue Whale Hunt', 28–9 May 1994, *The Weekend Australian*, 9.

being subject to the international law of the sea regime, they could on this view be subject to specialised legal regimes created by the polar states. Different considerations apply to this question in both polar regions.

The Arctic Lake and sector theory

With the extension of coastal state jurisdiction in the Arctic, the area beyond the reach of national jurisdiction has been continually shrinking. This has had the effect of enclosing the central core of the Arctic Ocean as high seas.[141] Yet the Arctic predominantly remains an area in which high seas freedoms can be exercised. Both the EEZ and continental shelf are the only zones conferring resource sovereignty. While the EEZ may have some consequential impacts upon navigation rights, these impacts are not so substantive as to prohibit such navigation. However, while it may be true that much of the Arctic Ocean is open to high seas navigation, the reality is that because access to the high seas portions of the Arctic is so difficult only vessels from the Arctic states frequent the area on any regular basis.[142]

While traditional law of the sea principles suggest that the Arctic is predominantly a high seas area beyond the limits of national jurisdiction, this assumes that the Arctic Ocean is not capable of falling under the sovereignty and jurisdictional reach of Arctic states. Such an approach conflicts with theories that have been advocated by some Soviet scholars.[143] The two most significant of these theories are the 'Arctic Lake' and sector theory.

The Soviet scholar Lakhtine was a strong supporter of the 'Arctic Lake' theory. The basis of his argument was that the whole Arctic Ocean was capable of falling under the region of attraction of the adjacent Arctic states. In regard to the high seas regime, he noted:

> When taking into account, however, the peculiarities of the Arctic Ocean, and the legal status of the adjacent territories and ice, we are obliged to conclude

[141] This has been described as the 'Arctic Mediterranean' by B. Johnson Theutenberg, 'The Arctic Law of the Sea' (1983) 52 Nordic JIL 3 at 3. See also Uwe Jenisch, 'The Arctic Ocean and the New Law of the Sea' (1984) 35 *Aussen Politik* 199 at 216.

[142] For example, no non-Soviet/Russian vessel has in recent times passed through the Northeast Passage without using the Vilkitsky Strait, as access north of Severnaya Zemlya is extremely difficult, even in high summer. See Erik Franckx, 'Non-Soviet Shipping in the Northeast Passage, and the Legal Status of Proliv Vil'kitskogo' (1988) 24 *Polar Record* 269–76; William E. Butler, *Northeast Arctic Passage* (Alphen aan den Rijn, 1978) 54.

[143] For a review see Franckx, *Maritime Claims* at 152–5, 168–75.

that the doctrine of the high seas, if applied to the Arctic Ocean, is quite unsatisfactory. Sovereignty should attach to the Polar States over the Arctic Ocean within their sectors of attraction.[144]

The basis of the 'Arctic Lake' theory was that because the Arctic Ocean was encircled by the Asian–European continent and North America, the Arctic states had a special interest in the Ocean and accordingly should be entitled to assert their own sovereignty and jurisdiction over the Ocean either on an individual or multilateral basis.[145]

The sector theory builds on the 'Arctic Lake' approach which has been advocated by various Russian scholars and occasionally advanced by the Canadian government. The sector theory argues that polar states should be able to claim sovereignty over all lands and water falling within the limits of a polar sector which are delimited from the eastern and western limits of continental territorial claims and run directly to the Pole.[146] It has been suggested that both Canada and Russia have relied upon the sector theory in Arctic maritime boundary delimitations. For Canada, in the case of the Beaufort Sea boundary with the US,[147] and for Russia, the Barents Sea boundary with Norway.[148] Despite their strong support for the sector theory throughout the twentieth century, one Western commentator has recently suggested that Soviet scholars are now moving away from it.[149] Nevertheless, in combination the 'Arctic Lake' and sector theory go some way to providing a basis for potentially sweeping claims being made to those areas of the Arctic currently beyond the limits of national jurisdiction. This approach can be seen in the writings of a number of Western commentators who have put forward an argument that the Arctic Ocean is either capable of unilateral coastal state jurisdiction and management,[150] or should be considered *sui generis* so that the Arctic states be given control over a variety of high seas

144 W. Lakhtine, 'Rights over the Arctic' (1930) 24 AJIL 703 at 713.

145 For a consideration of the views of other Russian and Soviet scholars (whose works are primarily published in Russian) see Franckx, *Maritime Claims* at 154–5.

146 The sector theory is discussed in greater detail in chapter 5.

147 See Donald R. Rothwell, *Maritime Boundaries and Resource Development* (Calgary, 1988) 34; D. Russell, 'International Ocean Boundary Issues and Management Arrangements', in D. VanderZwaag (ed.), *Canadian Ocean Law and Policy* (Toronto, 1992) 463 at 494.

148 Arnfinn Jorgensen-Dahl, 'The Soviet–Norwegian Maritime Disputes in the Arctic: Law and Politics' (1990) 21 ODIL 411–29.

149 See Franckx, *Maritime Claims* at 170.

150 D. M. McRae, 'Management of Arctic Marine Transportation: A Canadian Perspective' (1986) 39 *Arctic* 350 at 354–5.

activities.[151] These views have also been supported by potential claims that the Arctic Ocean is a semi-enclosed sea under Article 123 of UNCLOS, thereby conferring a special obligation upon Arctic states to cooperate to protect the marine environment.[152]

Whether Arctic states will adopt a unilateral approach to such claims, or join together to make a multilateral claim remains to be seen. Nevertheless, the question remains whether the Arctic Ocean is really high seas for the purposes of the law of the sea. Not only is it a sea virtually enclosed by landmasses to the south, but it is also unique in that it is covered by ice for much of the year, thereby making it impossible for vessels engaged in normal modes of navigation to exercise high seas freedoms. Can the concept of the high seas be adequately applied to an area in which navigational freedoms are more easily exercised under water than on the surface?[153] While the high seas are an area traditionally associated with the freedom of navigation, the Conventions have recognised that high seas freedoms extend to a wide variety of activities.[154] Apart from the freedom of overflight,[155] however, most high seas rights involve the use of vessels. As already noted, with much of the Arctic Ocean permanently ice-covered it is very difficult for all but specially designed ice-breaking vessels to navigate through the Arctic Ocean.[156] Therefore, with the

[151] J. Enno Harders, 'The Arctic Ocean: Environmental Protection and Circumpolar Cooperation – An Assessment and a Proposal for a Legal Regime' in *Energy Law '86* (New York, 1986) 493 at 503.

[152] For a review of writers discussing this view see Franckx, *Maritime Claims* at 240–3.

[153] Bo Johnson Theutenberg, *The Evolution of the Law of the Sea* (Dublin, 1984) 34. This is not to suggest that traditional navigation through the Arctic Ocean does not take place: there has in fact been a recent upsurge in the number of vessels which have visited the North Pole: see Frank S. Todd, R. K. Headland and Norman Lasca, 'Animals at the North Pole' (1992) 28 *Polar Record* 321 at 321 where it is noted that seven vessels have visited the North Pole since 1977.

[154] High Seas Convention, Art. 2 lists as certain 'freedoms, and others which are recognized by the general principles of international law', the freedom of navigation, freedom of fishing, freedom to lay submarine cables and pipelines and the freedom of overflight; UNCLOS, Art. 87 lists the freedoms as being navigation, overflight, to lay submarine cables and pipelines, to construct artificial islands and other installations, to fish, and scientific research. Churchill and Lowe, *The Law of the Sea* at 166 note:

> Precisely because States cannot in principle control foreign shipping on the high seas, so that users remain at liberty to do as they please apart from a few restrictive rules, and because new ocean technology is constantly developing, the freedoms of the high seas cannot be exhaustively listed.

[155] This freedom is extensively exercised over the Arctic Ocean: many commercial airliners use the circumpolar route between North America and Europe, and Asia and North America; Theutenberg, *Evolution* at 34.

[156] Even specially designed ice-breakers can experience difficulties in parts of the Arctic

exception of the freedom of overflight, and underwater navigation by submarines, there is very little actual exercise of traditional high seas navigation rights in the Arctic. The Arctic Ocean then does not possess traditional high seas characteristics,[157] and this inevitably raises for consideration whether areas traditionally considered high seas should be subject to another regime.[158] While the 'Arctic Lake' and sector theories may present alternative jurisdictional bases to the high seas regime, they have never been widely accepted and their validity is questionable. Another, more realistic approach may be to consider that areas beyond national jurisdiction in the Arctic Ocean fall within the regional sphere of influence of the Arctic states. Such an approach, especially if considered from the perspective of marine regionalism and the obligations on adjacent coastal states to cooperate collectively to protect distinctive marine regions,[159] may present a viable management approach for the Arctic Ocean. The Arctic Environmental Protection Strategy (AEPS)[160] and Arctic Council proposal may be influential in the Arctic states eventually adopting an all-encompassing regional approach for the Arctic Ocean.[161]

The ATS and high seas freedom of navigation

To date, the actions of the Antarctic territorial claimants have had little impact upon the traditional freedoms of navigation in the

Ocean: see Ivan Frolov, 'The 1987 Expedition of the Icebreaker *Sibir*' to the North Pole' in Lawson W. Brigham (ed.), *The Soviet Maritime Arctic* (London, 1991) 33 at 34–7.

157 Theutenberg, *Evolution* at 34 argues that another characteristic of high seas is the 'presence of sea traffic in any form'.

158 There are a number of authors who put a contrary view and see no difficulty in the Arctic Ocean being considered part of the high seas for the purposes of the law of the sea regime: see Jenisch, 'The Arctic Ocean' at 216; Pharand, *The Law of the Sea* at 150 who reviews those scholars who favour this approach; also see Donat Pharand, 'The Legal Status of the Arctic Regions' (1979) II ReDC 53 at 84.

159 See UNCLOS, Arts. 123, 194, 197.

160 (1991) 30 ILM 1,624 (hereinafter AEPS).

161 In furtherance of principles established by UNCLOS, Douglas Brubaker, *Marine Pollution and International Law* (London, 1993) 294–305 proposes a 'regional Arctic Convention' dealing with protection of the marine environment and prevention and control of marine pollution within territorial sea, EEZ and high seas areas of the Arctic Ocean; in addition Protocols dealing with Arctic oil rigs, counter-pollution, vessel-source pollution, dumping, land-based pollution, and liability are considered at 309–452. For further consideration on various law of the sea management options for the Arctic Ocean, see chapter 5; also see David VanderZwaag, John Donihee and Mads Faegteborg, 'Towards Regional Ocean Management in the Arctic: From Co-existence to Cooperation' (1988) 37 *UNB Law Journal* 1–33.

Southern Ocean.[162] This is a consequence of the variable practice adopted by the territorial claimants towards territorial sea and EEZ claims and their ability to enforce those claims against foreign-flagged vessels. Thus there is very little Antarctic 'coastal state' regulation which has impacted upon the traditional freedoms of navigation as recognised in the right of innocent passage and high seas freedoms through the EEZ. The more important question that arises in regard to the Antarctic legal regime generally, and the Southern Ocean in particular is whether the measures adopted under the terms of the Treaty and its associated Conventions can be applied so as to limit navigational freedoms.

This is not so much a question which directly arises from the application of the Treaty. The Treaty's terms are vague as to its application to non-parties, and under Article VI traditional high seas rights remain unaffected. The issue does, however, directly arise in regard to the marine living resources of the Southern Ocean. Both the 1972 Convention for the Conservation of Antarctic Seals (CCAS) and the 1980 Convention on the Conservation of Antarctic Marine Living Resources (CCAMLR) sought to impose conservation regimes upon the Treaty parties in regard to specific marine resources. Implementing CCAS did not prove to be a problem because seals were mostly harvested on the continent or on Antarctic and sub-Antarctic islands.[163] Sealing in Antarctic waters had substantially decreased by the time the Convention was implemented. CCAMLR, however, raises very fundamental questions as to whether a regional fishing regime, which substantially limits the traditional high seas freedom of fishing, can be applied and enforced against non-parties in an area that is high seas.[164] CCAMLR does not seek to impose legal obligations upon non-parties, and the only reference to the potential for the activities of such parties to conflict with the CCAMLR regime is found in Article X, which provides that infringing states may have their activities drawn to their attention by the CCAMLR Commission.[165] The greatest concern

[162] Antarctic Treaty, Art. VI guarantees the preservation of high seas freedoms within the Treaty Area. This is also a consequence of the Southern Ocean not being a carrier of large volumes of commercial sea traffic with the Drake Passage between Cape Horn and the Antarctic Peninsula the only major sea route through the Ocean.

[163] Other forms of sealing in Antarctica had previously been regulated under the 1964 Agreed Measures: see chapter 4.

[164] Sahurie, *International Law* at 546–9.

[165] CCAMLR, Art. XXII also imposes obligations upon the state parties to the Convention to ensure, consistently with the provisions of the United Nations Charter, that no other state engages in activities contrary to the terms of the Convention.

over activities by non-CCAMLR parties in the Southern Ocean has been with the activities of Taiwanese fishermen, though in recent years there have also been sightings of fishermen from Belize and Lithuania.[166] Whether the CCAMLR regime applies to such non-Convention parties raises the question of whether the Southern Ocean and Antarctica is covered by an objective regime based upon the ATS. If this is not the case, it is difficult to see how, even with the high seas conservation measures recognised in UNCLOS, states from outside the Antarctic region may not engage in fishing activities throughout the Southern Ocean.

Marine environmental protection

The protection of the marine environment has increasingly become an important issue in the polar regions. This development has coincided with global concern not only over protection of the marine environment, but also through concerns expressed by polar states over the condition of the marine environment in the Arctic and Southern Oceans. Three approaches can be taken in considering measures for the protection of the polar marine environment. They are: the UNCLOS regime; specific marine pollution instruments adopted under international law; and specific measures adopted by the polar states. Each will be reviewed in turn.

UNCLOS

Not only was UNCLOS a most important instrument from the perspective of clarifying coastal state rights over adjacent maritime areas, it also contained some very important provisions dealing with the protection of the marine environment. These provisions are found in Part XII of the Convention, titled 'Protection and Preservation of the Marine Environment'.[167] Article 192 sets the general theme for this Part of the Convention by providing: 'States have the obligation to protect and preserve the marine environment.' In turn, Article 194

166 See Commission for the Conservation of Antarctic Marine Living Resources, Report of the Tenth Meeting of the Commission (21 October–1 November 1991, Hobart, Australia) paras. 11.1–11.2; Commission for the Conservation of Antarctic Marine Living Resources, Report of the Thirteenth Meeting of the Commission (26 October–4 November 1994, Hobart, Australia) para. 3.11 and Annex 5, para. 1.33.

167 For a review of UNCLOS provisions dealing with environmental management, see M. L. O'Connell and E. Gold, 'The Modern Law of the Sea: Framework for the Protection and Preservation of the Marine Environment' (1991) 23 Case WRJIL 83–105.

outlines some of the measures which states can take to prevent, reduce and control pollution of the marine environment.[168] In seeking to achieve this goal, UNCLOS places emphasis on greater global and regional cooperation.[169] It seeks to deal with pollution from a number of sources. These include land-based sources,[170] seabed activities,[171] dumping at sea,[172] vessel-source pollution[173] and atmospheric pollution.[174] While the Convention's marine pollution provisions do not go any further than existing marine pollution measures they are important because for the first time principles which had developed in various international marine pollution conventions since the 1950s are codified. Part XII therefore assists to recognise certain principles of state responsibility towards the marine environment and confirms more extensive coastal state jurisdiction so as to regulate polluting activities.[175] Its provisions can also be interpreted as providing a basis for greater regional cooperation by polar states to deal with problems of marine pollution and the protection of the marine environment.[176]

From the perspective of the polar regions, the most important provision in UNCLOS is Article 234. It is considered by most commentators, and apparently was assumed by its negotiators, only to apply to the Arctic.[177] It provides multilateral recognition of the special features of the Arctic Ocean and the interests of the adjacent coastal states in protecting the marine environment. However, while Article 234 represents a significant advance in multilateral recognition of the need for marine environmental protection in the Arctic, its importance should not be overstated. It does provide coastal states with the ability to implement laws and regulations for the 'prevention, reduction and control of marine pollution from vessels in ice-covered areas within the limits of the exclusive economic zone'. It cannot, however,

[168] This Article has been described as the 'core operative stipulation', see Christopher C. Joyner, 'The Southern Ocean and Marine Pollution: Problems and Prospects' (1985) 17 Case WRJIL 165 at 179.

[169] See UNCLOS, Arts. 197–201. [170] UNCLOS, Art. 207. [171] UNCLOS, Arts. 208, 209.

[172] UNCLOS, Art. 210. [173] UNCLOS, Art. 211. [174] UNCLOS, Art. 212.

[175] See Joyner, 'The Southern Ocean' at 180; Joyner, *Antarctica and the Law of the Sea* at 156–60; John Lawrence Hargrove and Nancy J. Kellner, 'The International Legal Regime of the Arctic' in Ira Dyer and Chryssostomos Chryssostomidis (eds.), *Arctic Technology and Policy* (Washington, 1984) 47 at 51–2; Harders, 'The Arctic Ocean' at 509.

[176] See Brubaker, *Marine Pollution* at 295–9.

[177] Art. 234 is reproduced in chapter 5, p. 210, where the negotiation of the provision during the Third United Nations Conference on the Law of the Sea is also discussed.

be read as a provision conferring upon states the ability to implement extensive marine pollution provisions for all polar waters. Any provisions adopted under Article 234 must be 'non-discriminatory' and have due regard for navigation. Provisions adopted in reliance on Article 234 cannot then impose such high construction standards on vessels which seek to navigate through such waters that the effect is to limit severely navigational freedoms.

Setting aside the threshold issue of whether there exist any 'coastal states' in Antarctica, the assessment that Article 234 does not apply in the Southern Ocean is based on the view that the Third United Nations Conference on the Law of the Sea excluded Antarctica from consideration.[178] While this may have been the view adopted during the Conference negotiations,[179] there is nothing in UNCLOS to suggest that it has a limited area of application. Certainly the Southern Ocean meets the physical characteristics of an ice-covered area.[180] It is therefore suggested that the potential does exist for the Antarctic territorial claimants to rely upon Article 234 to assert more extensive offshore jurisdiction in the Southern Ocean.[181] To date, none has taken such an approach.

Other global conventions

Of the specific global marine pollution regimes, the 1973 International Convention for the Prevention of Pollution from Ships and its 1978 Protocol (MARPOL 73/78),[182] and the 1972 London Dumping Convention (LDC)[183] apply in both the Arctic and Southern Oceans.[184] However, while these Conventions are generally considered to have been successful in combating vessel-sourced oil pollution, dumping and other forms of vessel-sourced discharges which occur at sea, neither deal with any of the specialised pollution problems which can

[178] Auburn, *Antarctic Law* at 126. See also Watts, *International Law* at 163; Van der Essen, 'The Application of the Law of the Sea' at 242.

[179] See Auburn, *Antarctic Law* at 126; Peterson, 'Antarctic Implications' at 138, 165.

[180] Further consideration will be given to the scope of UNCLOS, Art. 234 at pp. 297–8 below.

[181] See the discussion on this question in Gautier, 'The Maritime Area' at 134.

[182] 1973 Convention – (1973) 12 ILM 1,319; 1978 Protocol – (1978) 17 ILM 546.

[183] Convention on the Prevention of Marine Pollution by Dumping of Wastes and other Matter, 1046 UNTS 120.

[184] For a discussion concerning the application of these regimes in the Southern Ocean see Joyner, *Antarctica and the Law of the Sea* at 149–56; and in the Arctic see C. Lamson, 'Arctic Shipping, Marine Safety and Environmental Protection' (1987) 11 *Marine Policy* 3 at 3–6.

arise in polar waters.[185] This was highlighted by the fact that it was only in 1991 that the Southern Ocean was declared a 'special area' under MARPOL. This had the effect that all operational discharges were absolutely prohibited from vessels except under cases of extreme peril.[186] A further amendment was proposed in 1992 so that the Southern Ocean south of 60°S would also be included as a Special Area under Annex II.[187] No similar special provisions have been adopted for the Arctic Ocean.[188] With this exception, the major conventions dealing with vessel-source pollution do not take into account the navigational and operational difficulties which vessels can experience in polar waters, or recognise that the polar marine environment is particularly susceptible to damage from pollution. The 1989 Basle Convention on the Transboundary Movement of Hazardous Wastes and their Disposal is another convention of global application.[189] This Convention may have particular significance in the Arctic, especially in regard to the maritime shipment of such wastes from Russia. However, only one provision specifically applies to polar waters. Under Article 4(6) the parties agree not to allow the export of hazardous wastes or other wastes for disposal within the area covered by the Antarctic Treaty.

Specific polar initiatives

Arctic

Concern over Arctic marine pollution has been growing for some time and a number of significant unilateral and multilateral initiatives have been taken to deal with the issue. In the late 1960s Canada took the view that existing international norms were inadequate to protect

[185] Chapter 5 considered how these Conventions applied in the Arctic. For a critique concerning their application in Arctic waters see Brubaker, *Marine Pollution* at 234–8, 244–54.

[186] See IMO Doc. 30/24; Antarctic Treaty Special Consultative Meeting Doc. XI ATSCM/2/Info.2 of 22 April 1991. For further discussion, see Joyner, *Antarctica and the Law of the Sea* at 155–6.

[187] See IMO Doc. MEPC 33/20. Add.1 – Resolution MEPC.57 (33) adopted on 30 October 1992 (Designation of the Antarctic Area as a Special Area and Lists of Liquid Substances in Annex II).

[188] For discussion on this point see Alexei Yu Roginko and Matthew J. LaMourie, 'Emerging Marine Environmental Protection Strategies for the Arctic' (1992) 16 *Marine Policy* 259 at 269. Unlike the Southern Ocean, however, the Arctic is covered under certain regional marine environment conventions: see Harders, 'The Arctic Ocean' at 512–16.

[189] (1989) 28 ILM 657.

the Arctic marine environment and in 1970 unilaterally implemented the Arctic Waters Pollution Prevention Act.[190] The Canadian initiative applied to all 'Arctic waters . . . in a liquid or frozen state' adjacent to the mainland and Canadian islands to an outer distance of 100 nautical miles.[191] Within such waters, provisions were implemented dealing with the control of wastes from a wide variety of sources including pollution from land-based and ship-based sources. In response to the possibility that the United States would challenge the validity of Canada's assertion of such extensive offshore jurisdiction in the International Court of Justice, Canada also withdrew its acceptance of the Court's compulsory jurisdiction to deal with such matters.[192]

The adoption of Article 234 in UNCLOS was seen as an endorsement of the Canadian action in 1970.[193] As already noted, the full impact of Article 234 remains to be seen. Nevertheless, Article 234 does provide the Arctic states with stronger powers to implement more extensive jurisdiction over foreign-flagged vessels within certain Arctic waters. The effect of Article 234 then will be to validate already existing marine environmental protection legislation and provide justification for some stronger measures. Russia especially can argue that some of its laws regulating passage through both the Northeast Passage and Northern Sea Route can, if grounded in environmental protection, have greater validity under Article 234 than may previously have been the case. In its 1984 Edict on the Economic Zone of the USSR, the Soviet Union sought to implement marine protection measures for its waters consistent with the terms of Article 234[194] and

190 Arctic Waters Pollution Prevention Act, Statutes of Canada 1969–70, c. 47; see J. A. Beesley, 'Rights and Responsibilities of Arctic Coastal States: The Canadian View' (1971) 3 JMLC 1–12; R. Michael M'Gonigle, 'Unilateralism and International Law: The Arctic Waters Pollution Prevention Act' (1976) 34 *University of Toronto Faculty of Law Review* 180–98; Pharand, *The Law of the Sea* at 224–44.

191 Arctic Waters Pollution Prevention Act, Statutes of Canada 1969–70, c. 47, s. 3(1), 3(2).

192 Canada subsequently withdrew its reservation to the Court's jurisdiction in 1985 when it was announced that new baselines would be proclaimed around the limits of the Canadian Arctic Archipelago; see Rothwell, 'The Canadian–US Northwest Passage Dispute' at 344.

193 See generally D. M. McRae, 'The Negotiation of Article 234' in F. Griffiths (ed.), *The Politics of the Northwest Passage* (Kingston, Ontario, 1987) 98 at 112–14.

194 See the discussion in Erik Franckx, 'Nature Protection in the Arctic: Recent Soviet Legislation' (1992) 41 ICLQ 366 at 376–7, 380–1; Franckx, *Maritime Claims* at 178–80. For further discussion on the Soviet position see Anatoly L. Kolodkin, 'Remarks – Legal Regimes of the Arctic' (1988) 82 ProcAmSocIL 315–18.

this was subsequently reaffirmed by a 1990 Decree of the USSR Council of Ministers.[195]

Despite the ability of Article 234 to confer upon Arctic states greater jurisdictional control over marine environmental protection, concerns have continued to be expressed over the lack of a comprehensive regime.[196] The AEPS recognises the unsatisfactory state of marine protection measures in the Arctic.[197] As a result the AEPS encourages the Arctic states to initiate stricter standards for the transportation of oil in Arctic waters under the framework of the International Maritime Organization.[198] The AEPS also calls upon the Arctic states unilaterally and as a regional group to implement various measures to ensure stricter marine pollution standards in Arctic waters, although it is too early to determine whether there has been much progress towards this goal.[199]

Antarctica

Apart from the global marine pollution regimes already noted, there has been no attempt to implement an individual marine pollution regime in the Southern Ocean. Nevertheless, the Antarctic Treaty parties have increasingly become concerned over marine pollution issues and have adopted a variety of Recommendations to deal with

[195] See Franckx, 'Nature Protection' at 377, 381–3; Franckx, *Maritime Claims* at 188–189. This decree is reprinted in Erik Franckx, 'Nature Protection in the Arctic: A New Soviet Legislative Initiative' (1991) 6 IJECL 377 at 379–83. Franckx has subsequently cast doubt over whether this was a proper implementation of the terms of Art. 234: see Franckx, *Maritime Claims* at 192–3.

[196] See Roginko and LaMourie, 'Emerging Marine Environmental Protection Strategies' at 259–76; Harders, 'The Arctic Ocean' at 493–532; Brubaker, *Marine Pollution* at 259. Marine transportation safety has been a particular issue of concern, as has the need for increased cooperation between the US and Canada on shipping issues in the American Arctic: see McRae, 'Management of Arctic Marine Transportation' at 357–8; Lamson, 'Artic Shipping' at 13–15; William E. Westermeyer and Vinod Goyal, 'Jurisdiction and Management of Arctic Marine Transportation' (1986) 39 *Arctic* 338–49; Cynthia Lamson and David VanderZwaag, 'Arctic Waters: Needs and Options for Canadian–American Cooperation' (1987) 18 ODIL 49–99; Oran R. Young, 'Arctic Shipping: An American Perspective' in Franklyn Griffiths (ed.), *The Politics of the Northwest Passage* (Kingston, Ontario, 1987) 115–33.

[197] AEPS, para. 4.2 details the then existing international instruments which dealt with oil pollution in the Arctic.

[198] AEPS, para. 4.2.

[199] AEPS, para. 5.2 provides *inter alia* that the Arctic states will monitor the Arctic environment for hydrocarbons under the Arctic Monitoring and Assessment Program, establish a reporting system for discharges and spills, and in international fora take joint action to strengthen further the international recognition of the sensitive character of the ice-covered parts of the Arctic Ocean.

the problem.[200] The most significant initiative to date is Annex IV of the Madrid Protocol dealing with the 'Prevention of Marine Pollution'. Annex IV makes applicable within the Treaty area provisions similar to those in MARPOL. In particular the following polluting activities are prohibited: the discharge of oil except in cases permitted under Annex I of MARPOL,[201] the discharge into the sea of noxious liquid substances,[202] the disposal of garbage at sea[203] and the discharge into the sea of sewage.[204] While the adoption of these measures under the Protocol is a positive step, it would be inaccurate to argue that they are an improvement on the MARPOL regime. As noted by one commentator: 'While attempts were made to repeat here the phraseology of the MARPOL annexes, the language necessarily diverges. This is generally because the present annex encompasses in one relatively short annex what is dealt with in five lengthy annexes under MARPOL.'[205] Few attempts are made in Annex IV to go beyond the reach of the MARPOL provisions. Where there is an exception to the MARPOL regime, as in the case of Article 9(1) which imposes obligations upon parties to ensure that vessels supporting its Antarctic operations are equipped with adequate retention capacity, the overriding impact of Article 14 providing that nothing in the Annex is to derogate from rights and obligations under MARPOL seems to defeat the effort.[206]

Annex IV also suffers because of inherent problems in the Protocol itself and the Treaty regime. First, any measures adopted under the ATS regime are necessarily limited by the Treaty's jurisdictional reach. Article VI provides that the terms of the Treaty apply only south of 60° S, and stipulates that nothing in the Treaty is to interfere with the exercise of high seas rights within that area.[207] As a result, it can be argued that any measures which the Antarctic Treaty parties adopt must give due recognition to high seas navigational freedoms. In regard to marine pollution, the question which arises from Article VI

200 See for example the following Recommendations adopted to deal with marine pollution issues: Recommendations IX-6, X-7, XI-2. For a review see Joyner, *Antarctica and the Law of the Sea* at 161–72.

201 Protocol, Annex IV, Art. 3.

202 Protocol, Annex IV, Art. 4.

203 Protocol, Annex IV, Art. 5.

204 Protocol, Annex IV, Art. 6.

205 Bush (Bin I), Pt AT91C, at 129.

206 Bush (Bin I), Pt AT91C at 129; see also Francesco Francioni, 'The Madrid Protocol on the Protection of the Antarctic Environment' (1993) 28 TexILJ 47 at 72. For another review of Annex IV see Joyner, *Antarctica and the Law of the Sea* at 172–4.

207 In particular, Art. VI provides that nothing 'shall prejudice or in any way affect the rights, or the exercise of the rights, of any State under international law with regard to the high seas within the area'. For a discussion of the interpretation of Art. VI of the Treaty, see Auburn, *Antarctic Law* at 130–6; Bush (vol. I), 66–70.

is whether the high seas freedoms which existed at the time of the Antarctic Treaty's entry into force are the standard which must be maintained, or rather the current international law standards as regulated by UNCLOS and the global marine pollution regimes. The application of the Treaty against third parties is also a matter of some concern for any effective marine pollution regime.[208] Finally, the area of application of the Protocol is the same as that of the Antarctic Treaty. Irrespective of the debate over whether the Protocol should apply further north of this limit under the provisions protecting 'dependent and associated ecosystems', there are strong grounds for arguing that the application of any marine pollution regime in the Southern Ocean should at the very least extend as far north as the limits of CCAMLR.[209] The ambiguity on this matter remains to be resolved as the Antarctic Treaty parties have yet to implement the Protocol.

Conclusion

In five areas of the law of the sea, considerable difficulties occur in applying existing international law rules to polar waters. This situation exists primarily because the legal rules which have developed have failed to take into account polar conditions. This is evident from a review of the four 1958 Geneva Conventions on the Law of the Sea and UNCLOS. Only one provision in these five conventions specifically addresses a polar law of the sea problem. Given the importance of maritime areas in the polar regions the lack of general international law rules or conventions dealing with polar law of the sea problems represents a major failing of international law.

These problems in applying traditional law of the sea principles in the polar regions are best exemplified when the legal position of ice is considered. Given that mariners have had to deal with the perils of ice ever since they took to northern and southern waters, it is interesting to reflect that neither general international law nor the law of the sea deals in any detail with various forms of ice. Despite three law of the sea conferences in the latter part of this century, there is only one Convention provision which deals with ice. Even then there is some

[208] See Triggs, *International Law and Australian Sovereignty* at 140–50; Auburn, *Antarctic Law* at 118; Watts, *International Law* at 184.

[209] The northern limit of CCAMLR is considered to be the 'Antarctic convergence'. For further discussion see Bush (Bin 1), Pt AT91C, 3.

debate over whether Article 234 applies to both the Arctic and Antarctic. As a result, the status of ice in international law is still unresolved. In Antarctica this is important because of the great ice shelves which fringe the continent and make it impossible in many areas to determine properly a low-water mark for maritime boundaries. In the Arctic, the fast ice which clings to the shoreline for much of the year is used by indigenous peoples for a variety of activities. During the winter this ice, in combination with pack ice, forms an ice bridge between islands. Arctic fast ice is therefore more akin to *terra firma* than sea, but the law of the sea does not provide any distinctive solution to the status of this type of ice.

Problems have also arisen in applying other aspects of the law of the sea to the polar regions. The creation of new maritime zones has raised problems in Antarctica due to the limitations imposed by Article IV of the Antarctic Treaty. In the Arctic, new maritime claims have had the effect of enclosing the Arctic Ocean. While this may have confirmed its high seas status, it may also give added impetus to claims by the Arctic states to treat the Arctic Ocean as a large regional sea over which they should exercise primary jurisdiction. Finally, global marine pollution provisions have also proven to be inadequate for the special conditions which exist in the polar regions. Apart from Article 234, there has been no specific attempt to deal with the potential consequences of polar marine pollution. Increasingly, the polar states are dealing with this issue on a regional basis and there are signs that they may implement much stricter measures than those which apply generally either in the EEZ or on the high seas. This response is indicative of increasing regional responses by polar states to law of the sea issues. This has especially been evident in the Arctic, where concerns over the protection and current state of the marine environment have resulted in increasing bilateral and multilateral cooperation. It is still the belief of some commentators that the best prospects for a more integrated Arctic legal regime result from concerns over the state of the Arctic Ocean and adjacent maritime areas.[210] In Antarctica, the Treaty parties are taking an increasing interest in the Southern Ocean. Not only have there been efforts to regulate marine living resource management but the Madrid Protocol also seeks to control marine pollution.

This chapter has demonstrated that many traditional law of the sea principles found in the international conventions encounter great

210 See generally Roginko and LaMourie, 'Emerging Marine Environmental Protection Strategies' at 265–76; Erik Franckx, *Maritime Claims* at 239–70.

difficulty when applied in the polar regions. This suggests that the best approach to adopt in dealing with polar law of the sea issues is a *sui generis* one.[211] By viewing the polar regions as *sui generis* it will be possible to adopt a more distinctive approach towards law of the sea problems in which specific measures can be developed to deal with polar problems. Polar states have already adopted such an approach at various times. The sector and Arctic Lake approach are particular responses to how maritime areas in the Arctic should be managed. More recently, there has been an emphasis on adopting a specific regional approach to the management of Arctic marine environmental issues involving not only areas within national jurisdiction but extending over the whole Arctic Ocean. The AEPS process may result in such proposals becoming operative. In the Southern Ocean there are major jurisdictional problems caused by the limitations imposed by the Antarctic Treaty upon 'coastal states'. However, increasingly the territorial claimants in conjunction with the other Treaty parties are adopting more comprehensive measures for the Southern Ocean. The rejection of continental shelf and seabed mining is an example. The approach indicates that in the view of the ATCPs, the Southern Ocean should be considered differently from other ocean areas. The effort under the Protocol also to implement tougher marine pollution measures is a further indication of this approach. These various polar responses to law of the sea problems are not only examples of the need to view such legal issues as *sui generis*, but also are examples of alternative responses to law of the sea problems which could be applied elsewhere. They represent a contribution to the development of international law and demonstrate the unique character of international law in the polar regions.

[211] For a further consideration of these issues see Donald R. Rothwell and Stuart Kaye, 'Law of the Sea and the Polar Regions: Reconsidering the Traditional Norms' (1994) 18 *Marine Policy* 41–58.

8 The polar regions and resource management

The polar regions share the common feature of being resource-rich. This applies in respect of both living and non-living resources. In the case of Antarctica, reports from Cook's 1772–5 circumnavigation of the continent of plentiful marine life[1] were the catalyst for commercial interest being shown in sealing. Debate over whether Antarctica's mineral resources should be subject to exploitation has more recently dominated discussions over Antarctic resource exploitation. In the case of the Arctic, living resources such as bears, fish, seals, caribou and reindeer have long been the basis of native subsistence economies. In many instances these resources have also been commercially exploited. The Arctic too is rich in non-renewable resources, with extensive exploitation having occurred across Russia and Siberia, while oil and gas fields exist in Alaska and in offshore areas such as the Barents and Beaufort Seas.

One feature of the exploitation of Antarctic resources is that they have been used 'extractively'. Holdgate explains that 'the ecological systems have not been managed with the aim of producing a desired product at maximum yield, but cropped at rates that have often been determined more by external economic pressures than by the productivity of the system'.[2] The relative lack of interest in sealing in the late twentieth century is a good example of this phenomenon. In both polar regions the market for seal products has drastically fallen since 1970 and apart from a subsistence hunt in the Arctic there is virtually no interest in commercial sealing. This contrasts vividly with the boom the industry experienced in the nineteenth century.

1 Deborah Shapley, *The Seventh Continent* (Washington, 1985) 7.

2 Martin W. Holdgate, 'The Use and Abuse of Polar Environmental Resources' (1984) 22 *Polar Record* 25 at 30.

A feature of how both polar regions have dealt with resource issues is that there has increasingly been an attempt to adopt a precautionary approach.[3] This is best illustrated by the adoption of the Convention on the Conservation of Antarctic Marine Living Resources (CCAMLR)[4] in the 1980s, prior to the exploitation of krill reaching a critical stage for the Antarctic ecosystem. This approach towards the management of polar living and non-living resources may be a product of the regions. As Holdgate has noted, 'the uncertainties are greater in the polar regions and the rate of recovery of their ecosystems, once damaged, may be very much slower'.[5] Certainly this was a factor behind the negotiation of the Convention on the Regulation of Antarctic Mineral Resource Activities (CRAMRA)[6] during the 1980s.

The resource management regimes which have been adopted in the polar regions are important examples of how resources can be responsibly managed. This is not to suggest that sustainable development has been the goal,[7] but rather that throughout the later part of the twentieth century polar resources have been managed in an effort to achieve some balance between economic interests and environmental protection. In some instances, such as the debate over whether to implement CRAMRA or adopt a comprehensive Antarctic environmental protection regime, environmental protection has won out

[3] A definition of the 'precautionary approach' can be found in the 1990 Bergen ECE Ministerial Declaration on Sustainable Development (15 May 1990), reprinted in Harold Hohmann (ed.), *Basic Documents in International Environmental Law* (vol. I) (Graham and Trotman: London, 1992) 558, where it provides:

> Environmental measures must anticipate, prevent and attack the causes of environmental degradation. Where there are threats of serious or irreversible damage, lack of full scientific certainty should not be used as a reason for postponing measures to prevent environment degradation.

[4] (1980) 19 ILM 841 (hereinafter CCAMLR).

[5] Holdgate, 'Use and Abuse' at 40.

[6] (1988) 27 ILM 868.

[7] The concept of 'sustainable development' has been subject to a wide range of definitions; however, Principles 2, 3 and 4 of the 1992 Rio Declaration on Environment and Development, (1992) 31 ILM 874 refer to some of the basic elements understood to be a part of the concept, especially Principle 3 which provides: 'The right to development must be fulfilled so as to equitably meet developmental and environmental needs of present and future generations.' On how sustainable development as a concept could be applied to the Arctic see Franklyn Griffiths and Oran R. Young, 'Sustainable Development and the Arctic' 1989–91 *Working Group on Arctic International Relations Reports and Papers* 1–25; Oran R. Young, *Arctic Politics* (Dartmouth, NH, 1992) 214–28.

over economic interests. However, in the case of Arctic mineral resource exploitation, economic interests have so far dominated.

A further dynamic in the management of resources in the Arctic is the need to make allowances for resource harvesting by indigenous peoples. This issue has risen in prominence because of demands by indigenous peoples that they play a greater role in resource management decisions. The Inuit Circumpolar Conference (ICC) is the most vocal and influential of these groups in the Arctic. In their 1992 document, 'Principles and Elements for a Comprehensive Arctic Policy', reference is made to the development and implementation of policy for both renewable and non-renewable resources. The ICC advocate that an 'ecosystem management' approach be adopted for entire ecosystems.[8] They argue that:

> Renewable resources must be managed and protected in a manner that maintains ecological balance, respects Inuit resource rights, and sustains the renewable resource needs of Inuit, both now and in the future.[9]

The need to recognise Inuit rights to participate in renewable resource management is also noted. Where such resources are shared with others, cooperative and joint management arrangements must be entered into at the regional, national or international level.[10] Similar principles are articulated with respect to Inuit rights over non-renewable resources. Within their traditional territories, Inuit claim the right to possession, ownership and control of surface and subsurface resources.[11] However, it is recognised that because of the finite nature of these resources they must be subject to 'responsible management, conservation, and rational exploitation'.[12] The exploitation of resources in the Arctic will inevitably raise issues of balancing development needs against the rights of native and indigenous peoples. These rights, which are increasingly being recognised in

[8] Inuit Circumpolar Conference, *Principles and Elements for a Comprehensive Arctic Policy* (Montreal, 1992) 43, para. 2.

[9] *Ibid.* at 43, para. 1.

[10] *Ibid.* at 43–4, para. 5.

[11] *Ibid.* at 48, para. 1.

[12] *Ibid.* at 48, para. 4. See also Declaration of the Arctic Indigenous Leaders' Summit, 'Statement on Subsistence, the Traditional and Direct Dependence on Renewable Resources', reproduced in Mads Faegteborg (ed.), *Towards an International Indigenous Arctic Policy* (Copenhagen, 1993) 36–7.

international law,[13] can already be found in some Arctic resource management regimes.

This chapter will assess resource management in the polar regions from the perspective of living and non-living resources.[14] In the case of living resources, the analysis will be divided between marine and terrestrial resources. Each polar region will be separately considered in each section.

Management of polar living resources

Marine living resources

Convention on the Conservation of Antarctic Marine Living Resources

The most comprehensive management mechanism which exists in the polar regions for any resource is the 1980 Convention on the Conservation of Antarctic Marine Living Resources (CCAMLR). The Convention was adopted as a result of concerns which developed during the 1970s that unregulated exploitation of fishery stocks in the Southern Ocean could develop into a major commercial activity.[15] Given what had occurred with unregulated whaling in the nineteenth and early twentieth centuries there was a desire to deal with resource management issues before major problems arose.[16] CCAMLR represents an

[13] See e.g., 1966 International Covenant on Civil and Political Rights, 999 UNTS 171, Art. 1; 1992 Rio Declaration on Environment and Development, (1992) 31 ILM 874, Principle 22 provides:

> Indigenous people and their communities, and other local communities, have a vital role in environmental management and development because of their knowledge and traditional practices. States should recognize and duly support their identity, culture and interests and enable their effective participation in the achievement of sustainable development.

For a further discussion of indigenous people's perspectives on Arctic resource management, see International Work Group for Indigenous Affairs, *Arctic Environment* (Copenhagen, 1991).

[14] Resources are for these purposes defined as any living or non-living material or substance subject to exploitation. Living resources in the polar regions include fish, krill, whales, penguins, seals, polar bears and caribou. Non-living resources include all forms of hard minerals, oil and gas, and icebergs.

[15] For some background on the negotiations leading to CCAMLR, see Matthew Howard, 'The Convention on the Conservation of Antarctic Marine Living Resources: A Five-Year Review' (1989) 38 ICLQ 104 at 108–12.

[16] David M. Edwards and John A. Heap, 'Convention on the Conservation of Antarctic Marine Living Resources: A Commentary' (1981) 20 *Polar Record* 353 at 354.

attempt to adopt the 'precautionary approach' to resource management in the Antarctic.[17] This approach is encapsulated in Article II which sets down a series of objectives for Antarctic marine living resource conservation. These objectives outline the 'ecosystem approach' to resource management.[18] For the purposes of the Convention this approach can be summarised as involving adherence to conservation principles which allow for the rational use of existing resources providing that:

(a) harvested populations do not fall below a level which ensures their stable recruitment;
(b) the ecological relationship between harvested and non-harvested dependent species is maintained; and
(c) irreversible changes in the marine ecosystem are prevented or minimised.

Unlike some of the other institutions established under the Antarctic Treaty System (ATS), CCAMLR is supported by a permanent Commission administered by a small secretariat in Hobart, Australia. The Commission's functions are wide-ranging. Its primary aim is to 'give effect to the objectives and principles set out in Article II'.[19] Perhaps the most important role it has is the adoption of Conservation Measures to manage Antarctic marine living resource harvesting. The Commission makes its decisions by consensus,[20] and is assisted by a Scientific Committee which acts as a consultative body to the Commission.[21] The Scientific Committee reviews data concerning Southern Ocean marine living resources, but does not have the ability to conduct its own research.[22] In this respect, both the operation of the Commission and the Scientific Committee is dependent on the annual provision of statistical, biological and other data by Commission members.[23] Membership of both the Commission and

[17] This is recognised in the Preamble to CCAMLR, which provided as follows:

> Recognising the importance of safeguarding the environment and protecting the integrity of the ecosystem of the seas surrounding Antarctica . . .
>
> Noting the concentration of marine living resources found in Antarctic waters and the increased interest in the possibilities offered by the ultilization of these resources as a source of protein

[18] Edwards and Heap, 'Convention' at 255.

[19] CCAMLR, Art. IX (1).

[20] CCAMLR, Art. XII(1).

[21] CCAMLR, Art. XIV.

[22] CCAMLR, Art. XV.

[23] CCAMLR, Art. XX.

the Scientific Committee is open to original contracting parties and other parties which engage in research and harvesting activities in the Convention area.[24]

Following the speedy entry into force of CCAMLR in 1982 there were high hopes that it would be able to deal with the emerging problem of Antarctic marine living resource management and rectify those difficulties which had been identified following years of unregulated access to the resource.[25] However, these expectations were not met, due to a combination of institutional and political problems.[26] One immediate problem, identified at the First Meeting of the Commission, was the consensus decision-making structure.[27] This approach had been adopted because of its success at Antarctic Treaty meetings. However, even before the first meeting of the Commission it was recognised that this decision-making procedure had the potential to impact upon the strength of the Conservation Measures adopted.[28] This has since been reflected in practice, with the ability of a single state to 'veto' any consensus, impairing the Commission's ability to adopt strict measures affecting fishing states.[29] Another problem was the lack of adequate data upon which the Scientific Committee or the Commission could assess how an ecosystem approach to resource management could be best implemented.[30] Much of the data initially

[24] CCAMLR, Arts. VII, XIV.

[25] Rainer Lagoni, 'Convention on the Conservation of Marine Living Resources: A Model for the Use of a Common Good' in Rudiger Wolfrum (ed.), *Antarctic Challenge* (Berlin, 1984) 93 at 98; Fernando Zegers, 'The Canberra Convention: Objectives and Political Aspects of its Negotiation' in Francisco Orrego Vicuna (ed.), *Antarctic Resources Policy* (Cambridge, 1983) 149–56; Simon Lyster, *International Wildlife Law* (Cambridge, 1985) 176; Robert J. Hofman, 'The Convention on the Conservation of Antarctic Marine Living Resources' in Lewis M. Alexander and Lynne Carter Hanson (eds.), *Antarctic Politics and Marine Resources* (Kingston, RI, 1984) 113 at 122; *cf.* Edwards and Heap, 'Convention' at 362.

[26] See generally Takesi Nagata, 'The Implementation of the Convention on the Conservation of Antarctic Marine Living Resources: Needs and Problems' in Francisco Orrego Vicuna (ed.), *Antarctic Resources Policy* (Cambridge, 1983) 119–37.

[27] Because of the debate as to how the Commission should distinguish between making decisions on matters of substance and procedure, Rules of Procedure were not agreed upon at the first meeting of the Commission: see Howard, 'Convention' at 117–20.

[28] Edwards and Heap, 'Convention' at 358.

[29] Lagoni, 'Convention' at 100; Jean-Pierre Puissochet, 'CCAMLR – A Critical Assessment' in Arnfinn Jorgensen-Dahl and Willy Ostreng (eds.), *The Antarctic Treaty System in World Politics* (London, 1991) 70 at 75.

[30] Howard, 'Convention' at 124–8; J. A. Gulland, 'The Management Regime for Living Resources' in Christopher C. Joyner and Sudhir K. Chopra (eds.), *The Antarctic Legal Regime* (Dordrecht, 1988) 219 at 232.

used was provided by commercial sources and proved to be inadequate. As a result, it was very difficult to implement sensitive management of harvesting activities until scientifically based judgments could be made.[31] It therefore became vital for the success or otherwise of CCAMLR that the parties supply information to the Commission and Scientific Committee on a regular basis.[32] A further area of difficulty which emerged early on was that the Convention did not adequately determine the nature of the relationship between the Commission and the Scientific Committee.[33] The distinction between the two could be characterised as that between a political decision-making body and an independent body of expert advisers. The problem in this instance was, as Edwards and Heap noted as far back as 1981: 'The need is to establish a relationship between the advisers and the executive in a manner in which, while sycophancy is avoided, the degree of independence will not be such as to allow the Commission to disregard the advice of the Scientific Committee.'[34] Various Working Groups have been established under the Scientific Committee which provide current data and advice to the Commission at its annual meetings.[35] However, this has resulted in tension over whether the opinions of the Scientific Committee should be accepted and implemented by the CCAMLR Commission or whether it remains able to make its own independent judgments.[36]

As CCAMLR has now been operative since 1982, it is possible to assess in some detail how it has managed Antarctic marine living

[31] Stephen Nicol, 'CCAMLR and its Approaches to Management of the Krill Fishery' (1991) 27 *Polar Record* 229 at 235. For details on catch data see Bo Fernholm and Goran T. Rudback, 'Marine Resource Management for the Antarctic' (1989) 18(1) AMBIO 68 at 69.

[32] Howard, 'Convention' at 122 who described information as being 'vital to the success or failure of the Convention'.

[33] Francisco Orrego Vicuna, 'The Effectiveness of the Decision-Making Machinery of CCAMLR: An Assessment' in Arnfinn Jorgensen-Dahl and Willy Ostreng (eds.), *The Antarctic Treaty System in World Politics* (London, 1991) 25 at 30 who notes that: 'The manner in which these institutional arrangements worked out in practice during the early period of the implementation of CCAMLR was disastrous.'

[34] Edwards and Heap, 'Convention' at 357.

[35] Howard, 'Convention' at 120. These meetings are usually held in late October or early November, by which time catch data from the previous season has been collated. This also allows for new Conservation Measures adopted at Commission meetings to apply during the forthcoming season, though remaining non-binding until 180 days after states have been notified of their content: CCAMLR, Art. IX(6).

[36] Puissochet, 'CCAMLR' at 73–4.

resources.[37] The first point to be made is that many of the initial institutional problems in the relations between the Commission and the Scientific Committee seem to have been resolved and that the consensus decision-making mechanism is now operating more effectively.[38] This is partly demonstrated by the considerable increase in the number of Conservation Measures adopted by the Commission at its recent Meetings.[39] A review of the Conservation Measures that have been adopted demonstrates an attempt to manage a wide range of issues. There has been a considerable focus on management of fish stocks in and around South Georgia with a number of Conservation Measures actually seeking to prohibit certain fishing activities in that area.[40] There has also been an emphasis on seasonal limitations on catches.[41] Additional measures have been taken to deal with the regulation of mesh size, limitation of by-catch, limitation of sea-bird mortality, the impact of marine debris upon living resources, requirements for the consideration of a new fishery, and improved catch-reporting systems. This experience demonstrates that over time the strength and ambit of Conservation Measures have continually been expanded and strengthened.[42] It is also a reflection of the improvement in data collection, and generally of the greater understanding that now exists with respect to Antarctic marine living resource stocks and ecosystem management.[43]

[37] Karl-Hermann Kock, 'Fishing and Conservation in Southern Waters' (1994) 30 *Polar Record* 3 at 10 argues that any consideration of the performance of CCAMLR needs to take into account that: large-scale exploitation and depletion of many fish stocks preceded CCAMLR; the krill catch is still low compared with the species' potential yield; CCAMLR's approach to regulating the various kinds of fisheries is evolving towards a precautionary management regime; CCAMLR is not a convention the sole purpose of which is to regulate fishing, but is rather an ecosystem convention; and the means to enforce conservation measures are weak.

[38] Orrego Vicuna, 'Effectiveness' at 28; Puissochet, 'CCAMLR' at 73.

[39] In recent years, there has been an increase in the number of Conservation Measures adopted: 1991 – fourteen Conservation Measures; 1992 – nineteen Conservation Measures; 1993 – fourteen Conservation Measures; 1994 – thirteen Conservation Measures.

[40] See Conservation Measure 3/IV; D. G. M. Miller, 'Exploitation of Antarctic Marine Living Resources: A Brief History and a Possible Approach to Managing the Krill Fishery' (1991) 10 *South African Journal of Marine Science* 321 at 330.

[41] Because of the seasonal operation of some Conservation Measures, many expire after a certain duration: see Conservation Measures 44/XI, 49/XI, 50/XI, 53/XI, 55/XI, 56/XI, 57/XI, 58/XI, 60/XI, 66/XII, 67/XII, 68/XII, 69/XII, 70/XII, 71/XII, 74/XII.

[42] John A. Heap, 'Has CCAMLR Worked? Management Policies and Ecological Needs' in Arnfinn Jorgensen-Dahl and Willy Ostreng (eds.), *The Antarctic Treaty System in World Politics* (London, 1991) 43 at 49–50.

[43] Orrego Vicuna, 'Effectiveness' at 35.

Despite the considerable emphasis placed upon the need to manage krill when CCAMLR was negotiated, there was a substantial delay before Conservation Measures were finally adopted to deal with the fishery.[44] Although krill were discussed both formally and informally within the Commission and the Scientific Committee throughout the first eight years of the Convention's operation,[45] the CCAMLR Commission's failure to deal formally with krill until 1991 has been subject to criticism.[46] To date most of the emphasis in regulating the krill fishery has been in the South Atlantic where the current overall limit has been set at 1.5 million tonnes.[47] In 1992 a Conservation Measure was also adopted for the krill fishery in the South Indian Ocean.[48] If the total catch in any season within certain subareas exceeds 620,000 tonnes, then the Commission, on the advice of the Scientific Committee, can apply other precautionary catch limits for krill to other subareas.[49] One difficulty which has been encountered in adopting an ecosystem approach in the management of the resource is that scientists still have an incomplete understanding of krill.[50] In addition to krill, the Commission has in recent years also dealt with a small but developing crab fishery in waters around South Georgia and Shag Rocks.[51]

Any analysis of CCAMLR inevitably focuses on its innovative efforts to adopt an ecosystem approach to resource management. This represented not only a major step forward for the ATS but also for resource management regimes generally.[52] However, it resulted in two difficulties. The first was how to implement adequately such an

44 See Nicol, 'CCAMLR'.

45 *Ibid.* at 230–4; J. P. Croxall, I. Everson and D. G. M. Miller, 'Management of the Antarctic Krill Fishery' (1992) 28 *Polar Record* 64–6.

46 Conservation Measures 32/X, 45/XI. Stephen Nicol, 'Management of the Krill Fishery: Was CCAMLR Slow to Act?' (1992) 28 *Polar Record* 155–7; *cf.* R. R. Makarov *et al.*, 'A Current Assessment of the Antarctic Krill Fishery' (1994) 18 *Polar Geography and Geology* 76–94 who argue that the total area of the krill fishery can be expanded.

47 Conservation Measure 32/X. Due to the absence of firm scientific advice on how to divide the potential yield and precautionary catch limit, the Commission at its Thirteenth Meeting decided this Conservation Measure should remain in force: Commission for the Conservation of Antarctic Marine Living Resources, *Report of the Thirteenth Meeting of the Commission* (Hobart, 26 October–4 November 1994) 25 at para. 8.5.

48 The limit was set at 390,000 tonnes in Conservation Measure 45/XI.

49 Commission for the Conservation of Antarctic Marine Living Resources, *Report of the Thirteenth Meeting of the Commission* at 26, para. 8.7.

50 See Stephen Nicol and William de la Mare, 'Ecosystem Management and the Antarctic Krill' (1993) 81(1) *American Scientist* 36 at 38–44.

51 Kock, 'Fishing and Conservation' at 6; see Conservation Measure 79/XIII.

52 Howard, 'Convention' at 113; Lagoni, 'Convention' at 98.

approach.[53] While Article II broadly defines the ecosystem approach to Antarctic marine living resource management, it failed to lay down a procedure for its implementation. This has not only created difficulties for the Commission but also raised debates amongst scientists as to how best this goal could be achieved.[54] Nevertheless, this approach towards resource management distinguishes CCAMLR from other similar institutions in that it creates what Watts has described as 'almost wholly an international institutional resource management regime'.[55] Article II stipulates the objectives to be met in Antarctic marine living resource management and then places the responsibility for determining how best to meet this objective upon the Commission and Scientific Committee. Because the Convention relies upon estimates of the harvesting impact upon a fishery and the ecosystem, successful implementation of such a management system requires a continual flow of data to the Scientific Committee plus accurate analysis of that data.[56] The lack of accurate data can result in poor management decisions being made, as occurred with fin fish in the early 1980s.[57] While this problem has gradually been rectified, it is still an issue of concern. For example, in 1992 the Scientific Committee noted that difficulties were being encountered in obtaining appropriate information on the catching capacity of certain vessels and that this was impacting upon the ability to make assessments on the future development of the fishery.[58] More recently, concern has also been expressed over the failure of member states to provide environmental monitoring data or advise the Scientific Committee of intended fishing plans.[59] The institutional division between the Commission

[53] Howard, 'Convention' at 115.

[54] See Douglas S. Butterworth, 'Antarctic Marine Ecosystem Management' (1986) 23 *Polar Record* 37–47; Marinelle Basson and John R. Beddington, 'CCAMLR: The Practical Implications of an Eco-System Approach' in Arnfinn Jorgensen-Dahl and Willy Ostreng (eds.), *The Antarctic Treaty System in World Politics* (London, 1991) 54–69. The adoption of appropriate resource management mechanisms for krill still seems to be a matter of debate between the Commission and the Scientific Committee: see Commission for the Conservation of Antarctic Marine Living Resources, *Report of the Eleventh Meeting of the Commission* (Hobart, Australia, 26 October–6 November 1992) para. 4.12.

[55] Arthur Watts, *International Law and the Antarctic Treaty System* (Cambridge, 1992) 219.

[56] Nicol and de la Mare, 'Ecosystem Management' at 45–7, where this approach is described as 'feedback management'.

[57] J. A. Heap, 'Current and Future Problems Arising from Activities in the Antarctic' in Gillian D. Triggs (ed.), *The Antarctic Treaty Regime* (Cambridge, 1987) 201 at 205.

[58] Commission for the Conservation of Antarctic Marine Living Resources, *Report of the Eleventh Meeting of the Commission* at para. 4.8–4.10.

[59] Commission for the Conservation of Antarctic Marine Living Resources, *Report of the*

and the Scientific Committee has also created tension, especially with some concern that science could be subverted for political means to ensure that certain Conservation Measures were or were not adopted.[60] However, the initial difficulties seem to have disappeared and the signs are that an effective working relationship has now been created between the two institutions. This has not necessarily resolved all internal problems within the Commission. There is still a need for harvesting states and conserving states to cooperate if effective decisions are to be made.[61] A further difficulty with CCAMLR is its relatively weak enforcement mechanisms.[62] Aside from the question of whether the Convention can be enforced against third parties, there has been some delay in implementing the inspection procedures provided for under Article XXIV. While these procedures were improved at both the 1991 and 1992 Meetings of the Commission their effectiveness remains to be assessed.[63]

To summarise, CCAMLR represented a major breakthrough in marine living resource management when it was adopted. It may have been inevitable that because of its innovative nature, problems were initially encountered in implementing its provisions. This is especially the case given that the 'ecosystem approach' requires accurate data on the ecosystem being managed, and that in the early stages of the Convention's operation scientific data on marine life in the Southern Ocean was limited. There does not seem, however, to have been any major depletion of the krill stock, and there are no current concerns over the potential of overfishing in the Southern Ocean resulting in

Thirteenth Meeting of the Commission at para. 3.12; Commission for the Conservation of Antarctic Marine Living Resources, *Report of the Twelfth Meeting of the Commission* (Hobart, Australia, 25 October–5 November 1993) para. 4.5.

60 Heap, 'Current and Future Problems' at 205; Howard, 'Convention' at 117.

61 Miller, 'Exploitation' at 335; see also John Wells, *Antarctic Resources* (Canberra, 1991) 8.

62 Gulland, 'The Management Regime' at 236.

63 See 'Report of the Meeting of the Standing Committee on Observation and Inspection', reprinted in Commission for the Conservation of Antarctic Marine Living Resources, *Report of the Eleventh Meeting of the Commission* at Annex 5, 89–93. See Puissochet, 'CCAMLR' at 75–6, who argues that even if the inspection procedures established by CCAMLR were fully complied with they would still fail to ensure independent monitoring of harvesting activities by state parties. At the 1992 Meeting of the Commission procedures allowing for a 'Scheme of International Scientific Observation' were agreed upon. This scheme is designed to supplement the existing inspection procedures established under CCAMLR: see Commission for the Conservation of Antarctic Marine Living Resources, *Report of the Eleventh Meeting of the Commission* at paras. 6.6–6.12; Commission for the Conservation of Antarctic Marine Living Resources, *Report of the Twelth Meeting of the Commission* at Annex 5.

substantial damage to the Antarctic ecosystem. From this perspective CCAMLR seems to have been a success.

Arctic fisheries

Arctic fishery resources are more diverse than those in the Southern Ocean, but, because of climatic conditions and the stock type, not as commercially exploitable.[64] There is a substantial subsistence hunt which takes place across much of the Arctic and this has raised issues in cases where the fishery is shared, such as along the Alaska–Yukon border where anadromous stocks exist,[65] and how the interests of indigenous peoples are to be accounted for in fisheries management.[66] Generally, there has been no real effort at multilateral management of Arctic fisheries.[67] However, there are examples of bilateral management schemes.[68] Some of these have been by way of formal interna-

[64] David VanderZwaag, 'Canadian Marine Resource Development in the Arctic' in Clive Archer and David Scrivener (eds.), *Northern Waters* (London, 1986) 125 at 131.

[65] For a discussion of the resource, see John J. Burns, 'Living Resources' in William E. Westermeyer and Kurt M. Shusterich (eds.), *United States Arctic Interests* (New York, 1984) 75 at 89–91.

[66] Robert F. Keith *et al.*, 'Arctic Fisheries: New Approaches for Troubled Waters' (1987) 15 (4) *Northern Perspectives* 1–5.

[67] The North-east Atlantic Fisheries Commission created in 1959 was one initiative designed to deal with an area that crosses into the Arctic: however, the Commission was never particularly effective; see Robin Churchill and Geir Ulfstein, *Marine Management in Disputed Areas* (London, 1992) 91–2. In a separate development, and partly in response to concerns over the International Whaling Commission, the North Atlantic Marine Mammal Commission (NAMMCO) was formed in 1992. NAMMCO seeks further cooperation in research, conservation and management of marine mammals in the North Atlantic and has a particular interest in whales. At present Iceland, Norway and Greenland and the Faroe Islands (the home governments of both signed) are members. In the early stages of NAMMCO's operation, emphasis has been placed upon the work of a scientific committee investigating the state of stocks and management procedures: see North Atlantic Marine Mammal Commission, *Report of the Third Meeting of the Council* (Reykjavik, Iceland, 1–2 July 1993); David D. Caron, 'The International Whaling Commission and the North Atlantic Marine Mammal Commission: The Institutional Risks of Coercion in Consensual Structures' (1995) 89 AJIL 154–74. It has been suggested that the north-east Atlantic and Barents Sea region is suitable for further multilateral resource management initiatives due to the need for multispecies management initiatives to be implemented: see Per Ove Eikeland, 'Distributional Aspects of Multispecies Management' (1993) 17 *Marine Policy* 256–71.

[68] See e.g., 1953 Convention between the United States of America and Canada for the Preservation of the Halibut Fishery of the Northern Pacific Ocean and Bering Sea, 222 UNTS 77. Art. I(2) established the area of application as being the territorial waters and high seas off the western coasts of the US and Canada including both the south and western coasts of Canada. This Convention represented a continuation of earlier agreements concluded in 1923, 1930 and 1937 on the halibut fishery, all of which were overseen by the 'International Pacific Halibut Commission'.

tional agreement and others through cooperative inter-government arrangements, or through regional management organisations.[69] Two particular examples of Arctic fisheries management will be considered.

Bering Sea

As a result of the extension by both the US and USSR in 1976 of their fishery conservation zones to 200 miles, the maritime areas of both states overlapped in the Bering Strait and Sea region. This precipitated the negotiation in 1988 of an Agreement on Mutual Fisheries Relations.[70] The Agreement sought to implement general principles regarding management of shared fishery resources in the Bering and Chukchi Sea region,[71] cooperation on fishery scientific research,[72] and trade.[73] An Intergovernmental Consultative Committee was also established to deal with cooperation in the management and conservation of anadromous fish in the North Pacific and groundfish in the Bering Sea.[74] In addition, a Bering Sea Fisheries Advisory Body was created to advise on issues relating to the co-management of pollock stocks in the Bering Sea.[75] There have also been industry initiatives to manage other Bering Sea fisheries.[76]

Following the declaration by both the USA and USSR of EEZs in the

[69] There have also been ongoing disputes over access to certain fisheries in internationally disputed areas. This is especially the case in and around Svalbard where the then USSR was engaged in a dispute with Norway over terms of access to fisheries within the Svalbard EEZ/Fishing Zone: see David Scrivener, 'Soviet Fisheries and Offshore Exploitation in the Barents Sea' in Clive Archer (ed.), *The Soviet Union and Northern Waters* (London, 1988) 76 at 79–80; Robin Churchill and Geir Ulfstein, *Marine Management*; David Scrivener, 'Resources and Environment in Norwegian–Soviet Relations in the Arctic' (paper presented at the BISA Annual Conference, Swansea, 1992) 5.

[70] Agreement between the Government of the United States of America and the Government of the Union of Soviet Socialist Republics on Mutual Fisheries Relations, TIAS 11442 (hereinafter US–USSR Fisheries Agreement). See also David Shakespeare, 'Recent US–USSR Agreements Relating to the Bering Region' (Fall 1991) 5 *Arctic Research of the United States* 37 at 39.

[71] US–USSR Fisheries Agreement, Arts. III–VII.

[72] US–USSR Fisheries Agreement, Art. IX.

[73] US–USSR Fisheries Agreement, Art. X.

[74] US–USSR Fisheries Agreement, Art. XIV.

[75] Shakespeare, 'Recent US–USSR Agreements' at 39.

[76] Jeffrey L. Canfield, 'Recent Developments in Bering Sea Fisheries Conservation and Management' (1993) 24 ODIL 257–89; Olav Schram Stokke, 'The Northern Environment: Is Cooperation Coming?' (1990) 512 *Annals of the American Academy of Political and Social Science* 58 at 63–4.

Bering Sea, many states began fishing in the central high seas area of the Bering Sea known as the 'Doughnut Hole'. This development, when combined with increased catches of pollock stocks in the late 1980s, resulted in the collapse of the fishery in 1992. In response to this dramatic development, the states concerned agreed to a moratorium on pollock fishing in the region while an agreed-upon resource management mechanism was adopted. This eventually resulted in the adoption in 1994 of the Convention on the Conservation and Management of Pollock Resources in the central Bering Sea.[77] The Convention applies to the high seas area of the Central Bering Sea beyond the limits of the USA and Russian EEZ claims.[78] The aim of the Convention is to establish a regime for 'conservation, management and optimum utilization of the pollock resources' but also to 'restore and maintain the pollock resources at levels which will permit their maximum sustainable yield'.[79] The operation of the Convention is achieved through an Annual Conference of Parties, and a Scientific and Technical Committee.[80] The primary functions of the Conference of Parties is to establish an allowable harvest level for pollock, and an individual national quota for each party.[81] In addition, the Conference of Parties may adopt other conservation and management measures for pollock within the Convention area, consider terms and conditions for trial fishing operations of pollock within the Convention area, and also discuss cooperative enforcement measures.[82] The Convention relies upon flag-state enforcement, and creates mechanisms for a system of observation and inspection.[83] Third states are also dealt with under the Convention, with the Parties agreeing to bring to the attention of the third states any fishing operations within the Convention area that may affect the Convention's objectives. If the activities of third states are considered to 'affect adversely' the attainment of Convention objectives, then 'the Parties shall take measures, individually or collectively, which are consistent with international law, and which they deem necessary and appropriate, to deter such operations'.[84] The Convention was signed by the People's Republic of China, Japan, the Republic of Korea, Poland, Russia and the USA, but will not enter into force until ratified by at least four states including Russia and the USA. Other states who wish to conduct

[77] (1994) 34 ILM 67; hereafter Bering Sea Convention.
[78] Bering Sea Convention, Art. I. [79] Bering Sea Convention, Art. II.
[80] Bering Sea Convention, Art. III. [81] Bering Sea Convention, Art. IV.
[82] *Ibid.* [83] Bering Sea Convention, Art. XI. [84] Bering Sea Convention, Art. XII.

pollock fishing within the Convention area may also be invited to become parties.[85] The Convention is a most important initiative for high seas fishing within an Arctic subregion. While it has yet to enter into force, it represents a useful model for resource management in situations where both Arctic states and states from beyond the region seek to exploit a single resource within a high seas area.[86]

Norway – USSR cooperation in the Barents Sea[87]

There has been a history of cooperative fisheries management between Norway and the USSR/Russia in the Barents Sea. This has occurred despite a dispute over the maritime boundary in the region. Three fisheries agreements have been concluded. In 1975 the Mixed Soviet–Norwegian Fishery Commission was concluded. This provides an annual forum for quota negotiations and other fishery management issues.[88] In 1976 a fisheries treaty was entered into on the basis of 200 nautical mile EEZ/fisheries zones.[89] This agreement secured for the two countries' fishing rights in each others' waters.[90] The final agreement was the 1978 Grey Zone agreement.[91] This agreement relates directly to the disputed maritime boundary area and provides for access by fishermen of both countries to the disputed area known as the 'Grey Zone'.[92] While these agreements have allowed for quota determina-

[85] Bering Sea Convention, Art. XVI.

[86] For comment on the Convention see Stuart Kaye, 'Legal Approaches to Polar Fisheries Regimes: A Comparative Analysis of the Convention for the Conservation of Antarctic Marine Living Resources and the Bering Sea Doughnut Hole Convention' (1995) 26 CalWILJ 75–112; William V. Dunlap, 'Bering Sea: The Donut Hole Agreement' (1995) 10 *International Journal of Marine and Coastal Law* 114–35.

[87] For an overview, see Churchill and Ulfstein, *Marine Management* at 91–114; Alf Hakon Hoel, 'The Barents Sea: Fisheries Resources for Europe and Russia' in Olav Schram Stokke and Ola Tunander (eds.), *The Barents Region* (London, 1994) 115–30.

[88] Brit Floistad and Olav Schram Stokke, 'Common Concerns – National Interests: Norway, the Soviet Union and the Barents Sea Fisheries' (1989) 9(2) *International Challenges* 23 at 24.

[89] Agreement between the Government of the Kingdom of Norway and the Government of the Union of the Soviet Socialist Republics on Mutual Fishing Relations, reprinted in Robin Churchill, Myron Nordquist and S. Houston Lay (eds.), *New Directions in the Law of the Sea* (vol. V) (Dobbs Ferry, NY, 1977) 348.

[90] Floistad and Stokke, 'Common Concerns' at 25.

[91] 1978 Agreement on an Interim Practical Arrangement for Fishing in an Adjoining Area in the Barents Sea between Norway and the USSR; it appears that an English version of the Agreement has not been published: Churchill and Ulfstein, *Marine Management* at 162, n. 24, who note the Norwegian source as [1978] Overenskomster med fremmede Stater 436.

[92] See the discussion in chapter 5. Also see Floistad and Stokke, 'Common Concerns' at 25; Stokke, 'The Northern Environment' at 64; Scrivener 'Soviet Fisheries' at 76–9.

tions for each species to be made, it has not resulted in an equal sharing of all stocks. An equal sharing of Arctic cod and haddock does exist, but the capelin stock is divided 60/40 in favour of Norway.[93] The distribution of other fishery stocks is subject to negotiation and annual determination, and the quotas for some stocks can vary from year to year. Stokke and Hoel have noted that a pattern has emerged from these negotiations with Norway receiving higher quotas of high-value stocks such as cod and shrimp while the USSR and now Russia has received higher quotas of blue whiting, redfish, squid and herring.[94] However, because of the varying prices for the different species, it seems that there is an unequal exchange of the fishery between the two countries in favour of Russia.[95] A further result of these agreements is that the two countries have retained more than 90 per cent of the fishery quota for themselves, with the balance going to European Community fishermen.[96] There has also been a long history of cooperative research on the shared Norwegian–Soviet fisheries which has allowed for more informed management of the Barents Sea fish stocks.[97]

The above review of management arrangements for Arctic fisheries demonstrates that while these are not as sophisticated as the CCAMLR regime, they can nevertheless be judged a success. As Stokke notes: 'There is no reason to expect broader membership of these regimes, but conditions are favourable for increased coordination of management in the Bering Sea and, to a lesser extent, exploitation in the Barents Sea.'[98]

Seals

Sealing has been a popular industry in both polar regions. Sealing in the Southern Ocean and on sub-Antarctic islands began in the early nineteenth century. In the Arctic there has also been a substantial history of commercial and subsistence sealing. Large commercial sealing industries once existed along the US west coast, up along the Canadian west coast and into Alaska. A sealing industry has also existed throughout both eastern and western Russia especially in the Barents Sea and Northern Pacific/Bering Sea region.[99]

[93] Floistad and Stokke, 'Common Concerns' at 25.

[94] Olav Schram Stokke and Alf Hakon Hoel, 'Fisheries Management in the Barents Region: Safeguards and Swaps' (1992) 12(4) *International Challenges* 69 at 71.

[95] *Ibid.* at 71–3. [96] *Ibid.* at 69. [97] Floistad and Stokke, 'Common Concerns' at 26.

[98] Stokke, 'The Northern Environment' at 65.

[99] See generally Burns, 'Living Resources' at 83–5; L. A. Popov, 'On the Rational Exploitation, Management and Protection of Marine Mammal Resources in Arctic

Antarctic sealing

A considerable degree of unregulated Antarctic sealing took place in the nineteenth century. The sealers were mostly from America, Britain, Canada and South America. The consequences were devastating with fur seal populations on certain islands completely eliminated. Britain did take some action to regulate sealing in the late nineteenth century when Ordinances were proclaimed to regulate sealing activities in and around the Falkland Island Dependencies.[100] These measures were continuously updated throughout the twentieth century and still apply to waters north of 60° S.[101] It seems, however, that the enforcement of these measures was variable.[102]

Following the entry into force of the Antarctic Treaty,[103] the need to protect seals was first raised at ATCM I (1961). Recommendation I-VIII encouraged the Treaty parties to implement measures to conserve the living resources of the Treaty area.[104] More particular action was taken to combat sealing activities in the 1964 Agreed Measures.[105] Article VI provided that certain mammals could be listed as 'Specially Protected Species' and that permits could only be issued for their taking providing there was a 'compelling scientific purpose'. However, the Agreed Measures had certain limitations which meant that they could never truly regulate all sealing activities in Antarctica. First, the area of application was the same as the Antarctic Treaty, and reference was made to high seas rights not being prejudiced.[106] As a result, the

Waters of the USSR' in V. M. Kotlyakov and V. E. Sokolov (eds.), *Arctic Research* (Moscow, 1990), Pt 2, 233–40.

100 See Seal Fishery Ordinance, 1881, reprinted in Bush (vol. III), 226–7. The Preamble to the Ordinance provided:

> WHEREAS the seal fishery of these islands, which was at one time a source of profit and advantage to the colonists, has been exhausted by indiscriminate and wasteful fishing, and it is desirable to revive and protect this industry by the establishment of a close time, during which it shall be unlawful to kill or capture seals within the limits of this Colony and its dependencies.

101 See Seal Fishery (Consolidation) Ordinance, 1921, reprinted in Bush (vol. III), 268–73 and commentary therein.

102 See Bush (vol. III), 227 noting with respect to the existing ordinances and law that: 'Sealing at the time was, in any case, scarcely controlled.'

103 402 UNTS 71.

104 Particular mention was made in para. 3 of Recommendation I-VIII that the use of helicopters and explosives be limited so as not to disturb seal colonies. This was also the first Recommendation dealing with the protection of fauna and flora.

105 Recommendation III-VIII, reprinted in Bush (vol. I), 146; *Handbook* (Pt 2) 2,048.

106 Agreed Measures, Art. I.

Agreed Measures only sought to apply to seals found on the continent, ice shelves and islands within the Treaty area. This meant that sealing activities conducted at sea or on pack ice were exempt.[107] The second limitation was that only two species of seal were listed as 'Specially Protected Species': fur seals and Ross seals.[108] As a result, these provisions of the Agreed Measures provided only minimal protection for seals in Antarctica.

The limitations in the Agreed Measures with respect to sealing were quickly realised when a 1964 sealing expedition revived concerns that full-scale commercial sealing could recommence.[109] Various interim Recommendations were adopted by the ATCPs until such time as a special Conference could be convened to discuss a Convention.[110] The Conference on the Conservation of Antarctic Seals convened in 1972 and resulted in the adoption of the Convention for the Conservation of Antarctic Seals (CCAS).[111] CCAS was the first substantive attempt by the ATCPs at resource management in the Antarctic Treaty area. While it would be incorrect to say that it became a prototype for subsequent efforts to regulate marine living resources and mineral resources, it did provide the Treaty parties with experience in the regulation of a resource activity, and its institutional implications.

A number of CCAS provisions are worthy of note. First, it applied to the 'seas' south of 60°S.[112] As such, it did not overlap with the jurisdictional reach of the Agreed Measures. Second, CCAS sought to protect a greater range of seal species than the Agreed Measures.[113] Third, certain standards were established for the harvesting of seals

[107] One response to this was the adoption of Recommendation III-XI (1964) which sought to implement voluntary regulation of pelagic sealing on pack ice. The extent of the voluntary obligation was outlined in para. 3, which provided that governments were requested 'that when ships of their nationality engage in pelagic sealing or the taking of fauna on pack ice south of 60° South Latitude, each government voluntarily regulate these activities to ensure the survival of any species being taken and to ensure that the natural ecological system is not seriously disturbed'.

[108] Agreed Measures, Annex A.

[109] Watts, *International Law* at 212.

[110] See Recommendations IV-21 'Interim Guide Lines for the Voluntary Regulation of Antarctic Pelagic Sealing'; V-7 'Concerning the Proposals of SCAR for the Revision of the Interim Guide Lines for the Voluntary Regulation of Antarctic Pelagic Sealing'. A draft Convention had been considered by the Treaty parties at ATCM V (1968): see Recommendation V-8 'Examination of Draft Convention for the Regulation of Antarctic Pelagic Sealing'.

[111] (1972) 11 ILM 251 (hereinafter CCAS).

[112] CCAS, Art. 1(1).

[113] CCAS, Art. 1(2) provides for the protection of the southern elephant seal, leopard seal, Weddell seal, crabeater seal, Ross seal and southern fur seal.

under Article 3, but these were left unspecified in the Convention so that flexible measures could be implemented under an Annex.[114] Fourthly, the Convention provided for the exchange of information concerning sealing activities and for the Scientific Committee on Antarctic Research (SCAR) to provide scientific advice on permissible catch limits.[115] Not only was this a recognition of the importance of SCAR within the growing ATS, but also that to manage effectively a living resource the Treaty parties needed scientific data upon which judgments could be made about the impact of harvesting upon the 'total stocks of such species or on the ecological system in any particular locality'.[116] Finally, management measures for the resource were provided for under the Annex. Catch limits were set for three species of seal, with closed seasons also established.[117] To protect further these species from indiscriminate sealing, zones were created within which sealing was closed during certain seasons, and certain seal reserves were created within which seals were totally protected.[118] Ross seals, Southern elephant seals and certain species of fur seals were totally protected under the Annex.[119]

Since the Convention first entered into force in 1978 it has had a relatively uncontroversial period of operation.[120] This has undoubtedly been a result of the lack of interest in commercial sealing activities. Nevertheless, a 1988 review of the Convention did highlight some issues concerning the Convention's operation.[121] While there was no evidence before the meeting of any commercial sealing having taken place since the Convention's entry into force, between 1964–85 a total of 10,142 seals were reported as having been captured or killed under the special permit system established under the Agreed Measures or CCAS.[122] In advice tendered by SCAR to the meeting, this take was

[114] CCAS, Art. 4, also provided that special permits could be issued for the killing of seals in certain non-commercial circumstances.

[115] CCAS, Art. 5.

[116] CCAS, Art. 5(4).

[117] CCAS, paras. 1, 2, 3, Annex.

[118] CCAS, paras. 4, 5, Annex.

[119] CCAS, para. 1, Annex.

[120] For a review of CCAS and measures taken under the ATS to regulate sealing see Eugenio A. Genest, *La Convencion para la Conservacion de las Focas Antarticas y el Sistema del Tratado Antartico* (Buenos Aires, 1991).

[121] See 'Report of the 1988 Meeting to Review the Operation of the Convention for the Conservation of Antarctic Seals' reprinted in Bush (Bin I), Bk AT5, 4–11 (hereinafter CCAS Report). For a discussion of this meeting see Anne Marchal, 'Convention for the Conservation of Antarctic Seals: 1988 Review of Operations' (1989) 25 *Polar Record* 142–3.

[122] CCAS Report, at para. 11.

considered low and not one that would have any significant adverse impact on seal populations.[123] The meeting also noted that during the 1986/87 austral summer two Soviet vessels had engaged in sealing operations as part of a research programme.[124] While some fears existed over whether this activity indicated that commercial sealing was about to recommence, it was concluded on the basis of a report of this operation that commercial sealing was not foreseeable within the next five to ten years. Delegates to the meeting confirmed this by indicating that they did not foresee their own countries engaging in commercial sealing in the foreseeable future.[125] Despite the relative lack of interest in sealing, the parties to CCAS did demonstrate that they remained concerned to ensure that no permanent damage to seal species occurred through unchecked sealing activities. To that end it was noted that SCAR had a special role under the Convention to report any increase in sealing activities or potential concerns over seal stocks. The Report thus concluded 'if the Convention is to operate in a predictive rather than a reactive manner, it would be essential to receive reports, not only when such effects had been clearly demonstrated to be occurring, but when there was a significant probability that they might be occurring, or could occur in the near future'.[126]

CCAS has been praised as the first instance in which a legal framework was created for the management of a resource prior to any commercial exploitation of the resource occurring.[127] In this respect CCAS can be said to represent the 'precautionary principle' at work. While these assessments are correct in the post-Antarctic Treaty context, they disregard the uncontrolled exploitation of seals which occurred in the nineteenth century. Nevertheless, the Convention has contributed to effective management of seals in the Southern Ocean. CCAS places any potential commercial exploiter on notice that not

[123] *Ibid.* This does raise the question, however, of when scientific sealing could be considered to be commercial sealing, a matter which CCAS does not adequately distinguish between; see also para. 20.

[124] Knowles Kerry, 'Terrestrial Flora and Fauna of the AAT', in John Handmer and Martijn Wilder (eds.), *Towards a Conservation Strategy for the Australian Antarctic Territory* (Canberra, 1993) 53 at 62 notes that the Soviet harvest was of approximately 4,500 seals.

[125] CCAS Report at para. 14.

[126] *Ibid.* at para. 26.

[127] Watts, *International Law* at 212–13; J. A. Gulland, 'The Antarctic Treaty System as a Resource Management Mechanism' in Gillian D. Triggs (ed.), *The Antarctic Treaty Regime* (Cambridge, 1987) 116 at 120. See also the review in Lyster, *International Wildlife Law* at 48–51.

only does the Convention place catch limits on certain seal species, but also that once commercial sealing commences any party may request a meeting to consider the establishment of further measures to ensure an 'effective system of control' of sealing activities.[128] Perhaps the one major flaw in the regulation of sealing in Antarctica and the Southern Ocean is that because of the different approaches of the 1964 Agreed Measures and CCAS, two management regimes were created. This result seems primarily due to concerns in 1964 that the Treaty parties could not regulate any activities which took place on the high seas, including sea ice or pack ice. Likewise, when CCAS was negotiated there was a belief that by adopting a Convention separate from the Antarctic Treaty, it was possible to regulate 'high seas' sealing south of 60°S.[129] As a result certain seals in Antarctica fall under different management regimes depending on where they are at the time. In this respect, Bush has argued that 'it clearly cannot be an optimum solution to subject seals to different regimes determined on the basis of arbitrary jurisdictional rules'.[130] Despite this problem, the regulation of all forms of sealing in Antarctica has not posed a major problem since the entry into force of the Antarctic Treaty. It should however be noted that because of the lack of interest in commercial sealing CCAS has never really been tested since its entry into force.

Arctic sealing

Resource management of seals in the Arctic has also been a major issue of regional concern with a number of bilateral agreements having been reached as far back as the nineteenth century. More recently, Norway and the then USSR concluded an Agreement on Measures to Regulate Sealing and to Protect Seal Stocks in the Northeastern Part of the Atlantic Ocean in 1957,[131] while Canada and Norway reached a similar agreement in 1971.[132]

[128] CCAS, Art. 6.

[129] This explains why CCAS was negotiated at a specially convened conference outside the Treaty system, unlike the meetings convened for the negotiation of CCAMLR and CRAMRA which were classified as Special Antarctic Treaty Meetings.

[130] W. M. Bush, 'The Antarctic Treaty System: A Framework for Evolution' in R. A. Herr, H. R. Hall and M. G. Haward (eds.), *Antarctica's Future* (Hobart, 1990) 119 at 132.

[131] Agreement between the Government of Norway and the Government of the Union of Soviet Socialist Republics on Measures Regulating the Catch and Conserving Stocks of Seals in the Northeastern Part of the Atlantic Ocean, 309 UNTS 269.

[132] Agreement between the Government of Canada and the Government of Norway on Sealing and Conservation of the Seal Stocks in the Northwest Atlantic, [1971] CTS 49. See the discussion in Lyster, *International Wildlife Law* at 51–4.

The area of the Arctic which has historically been subject to the most intensive sealing activities and also regulation has been the Bering Sea. Commercial hunting in the region began in the eighteenth century, with a Russian company responsible for harvesting more than 2.5 million seals in a sixty-year period up till 1860.[133] Following the 1867 cession of Alaska to the United States, American sealers also became active. This development, in conjunction with both Canadian and Japanese sealers who engaged in pelagic sealing, and the Russians who still enjoyed good sealing on the Siberian coasts of the Bering region, saw the region rapidly develop as a major centre for the sealing industry. However, this also resulted in major disputes over resource management and resource rights.[134] The United States was particularly concerned over pelagic sealing. It argued that American seal herds were under threat because of excessive pelagic sealing by foreign vessels.[135] Some bilateral agreements were entered into in an effort to resolve these matters;[136] however, problems still remained and in 1891 the United States and Great Britain (Canada) agreed to submit their dispute over access to and management of American seal stocks to arbitration. In the *Behring Sea Fur Seals Arbitration* the United States was unsuccessful in having its claim to resource rights over seal stocks beyond the territorial sea recognised.[137] However, this decision was a catalyst to further negotiation towards a settlement to the dispute. More bilateral agreements were entered into,[138] until finally in 1911 a multilateral Convention was agreed upon between the United States, Great Britain (Canada), Russia and Japan.[139]

[133] Natalia S. Mirovitskaya, Margaret Clark and Ronald G. Purver, 'North Pacific Fur Seals: Regime Formation as a Means of Resolving Conflict' in Oran R. Young and Gail Osherenko (eds.), *Polar Politics* (Ithaca, NY, 1993) 22 at 23. [134] See *ibid.* at 24–8.

[135] For background to and an assessment of the subsequent dispute between the US and other sealing nations in the region, see James Thomas Gay, *American Fur Seal Diplomacy* (New York, 1987) 1–134.

[136] See Exchange of Notes between Great Britain and Russia for the Protection of Russian Sealing Interests in the North Pacific during the Year 1893, (1893) 178 ConTS 451.

[137] *Behring Sea Arbitration Award between Great Britain and the United States Given at Paris, 15 August 1893*, 179 ConTS 97. For detailed background on the arbitration and the decision see John Bassett Moore, *History and Digest of International Arbitrations to which the United States has been a Party*, (vol. I) (Washington, 1898) 755–961. For discussion of the arbitration ruling see Patricia W. Birnie and Alan E. Boyle, *International Law and the Environment* (Oxford, 1992) 493–4; Mirovitskaya, Clark and Purver, 'North Pacific Fur Seals' at 29–30.

[138] See Treaty between Great Britain and the United States for the Protection of Fur Seals, (1911) 213 ConTS 73.

[139] Convention between Great Britain, Japan, Russia and the United States respecting

The major effect of the Convention for the Preservation and Protection of Fur Seals was to prohibit pelagic sealing in the waters of the North Pacific Ocean north of 30°N including the Bering, Kamchatka, Okhotsk and Japan Seas.[140] A ban was also placed on the importation of any seal skins from certain seal species taken within the Convention's area of application.[141] Importantly for a resource management agreement of the time, the Convention did not apply to Indians, Ainos, Aleuts or other aboriginals living along the coast of the Convention area.[142] Article IV of the Convention particularly limited the application of this exemption to instances where the indigenous peoples:

> carry on pelagic sealing in canoes not transported by or used in connection with other vessels, and propelled entirely by oars, paddles, or sails, and manned by not more than five persons each, in the way hitherto practiced and without the use of firearms; provided that such aborigines are not in the employment of other persons or under contract to deliver the skins to any person.

In return for the prohibition on pelagic sealing, the Convention sought to provide compensation to those states which previously engaged in pelagic sealing and which had no areas in which substantial land-based harvesting could occur. Both Canada and Japan were particularly affected by the prohibition on pelagic sealing and the US and Russia, whose sealing activities were mostly conducted on land and within territorial seas, were required to pay compensation to Canada and Japan. Payments were to be made by the US to Japan and Canada in return for the taking of seals on the Pribilof Islands in the eastern Bering Sea,[143] while Russia was required to make similar payments in regard to sealing operations on the Commander Islands in the western Bering Sea.[144] Obligations were also placed upon Canada and Japan to make payments to the other Convention parties in regard to harvesting operations conducted on their respective

Measures for the Preservation and Protection of Fur Seals in the North Pacific Ocean, 214 ConTS 80 (hereinafter Fur Seal Convention).

140 Fur Seal Convention, Art. I. Art. IX defined pelagic sealing as being 'the killing, capturing or pursuing in any manner whatsoever of fur seals at sea'.

141 Fur Seal Convention, Art. III.

142 Fur Seal Convention, Art. IV.

143 Fur Seal Convention, Art. X. Art. XI also established a complicated mechanism for the advance payment of monies to Great Britain and Japan in regard to sealing on these islands.

144 Fur Seal Convention, Art. XII.

shorelines.[145] The Convention was to remain in force for fifteen years and thereafter remain operative until one party asked for termination.[146] In October 1940, Japan gave notice of its intention to withdraw and the Convention subsequently terminated in 1941.[147]

In 1957 the same four parties to the 1911 Convention negotiated the Interim Convention on the Conservation of North Pacific Fur Seals.[148] The Convention, which was subject to amendment by various subsequent Protocols,[149] contained essentially the same obligations as the 1911 Convention, with one exception.[150] This was a provision for the establishment of the 'North Pacific Fur Seal Commission'.[151] The main duties of the Commission were to coordinate research programmes into both the maximum sustainable productivity of fur seal resources, and the relationship between fur seals and other marine living resources, and make recommendations to the parties on the basis of these findings.[152] The Convention continued to recognise the rights of indigenous peoples to engage in pelagic sealing and acknowledged that recommendations of the Commission regarding commercial sealing should take note of the subsistence needs of these peoples.[153] The Convention continued to operate in its various forms till 1984 when the US failed to ratify a Protocol which would have extended its operation for a further four years.[154] Since that

[145] Fur Seal Convention, Arts. XIII, XIV. For a review of the Convention's provisions see Mirovitskaya, Clark and Purver, 'North Pacific Fur Seals' 32–4.

[146] Fur Seal Convention, Art. XVI.

[147] Mirovitskaya, Clark and Purver, 'North Pacific Fur Seals' at 34; Lyster, *International Wildlife Law* at 41; Oran R. Young, *The Arctic in World Affairs* (Seattle, 1989) 16–17.

[148] 314 UNTS 105 (hereinafter 1957 Interim Convention). In 1942, Canada and the United States had entered into a provisional agreement on this matter: Canada–USA Exchange of Notes Constituting a Provisional Agreement Relating to Fur Seals, 26 UNTS 363. For discussion, see Birnie and Boyle, *International Law* at 495–6.

[149] These Protocols were: 1963 Protocol Amending the Interim Convention, 494 UNTS 303; 1969 Agreement Extending the Interim Convention, TIAS 6,774; 1976 Protocol Amending the Interim Convention, TIAS 8,368; 1980 Protocol Amending the Interim Convention, TIAS 10,020.

[150] While the 1957 Interim Convention continued the prohibition on pelagic sealing generally, it did allow some such sealing to occur for research purposes under Art. II(3)(b); however, in practice the limit set by this provision was never reached: see Lyster, *International Wildlife Law* at 43.

[151] 1957 Interim Convention, Art. V.

[152] 1957 Interim Convention, Arts. II, V.

[153] 1957 Interim Convention, Arts. VII, V(2)(d).

[154] Gail Osherenko and Oran R. Young, 'The Formation of International Regimes: Hypotheses and Cases' in Oran R. Young and Gail Osherenko (eds.), *Polar Politics* (Ithaca, NY, 1993) 1 at 5 note: 'The regime finally collapsed in 1984, when the United States Senate, influenced by lobbying on the part of antiharvesting organizations

time domestic management regimes for fur seals have been implemented.[155]

The 1911 Convention 'characterized by unique environmental factors, relatively simple government regulations, and an absence of new entrants, not only functioned satisfactorily for all of the participants but also resulted in the restoration of both the Asian and the American northern fur seal herds'.[156] The subsequent North Pacific Fur Seal Commission had a less successful period of operation and as a result of political concerns over the continued harvesting of fur seals raised by wildlife groups the 1957 Interim Convention was eventually not renewed. Nevertheless, the management of fur seals in the Bering Sea region represents an important example of not only cooperation amongst Arctic states, but also of resource management in which some innovative techniques were pioneered at the beginning of the century.

Terrestrial resources

Polar bears

Polar bear management in the Arctic is regulated by the 1973 Agreement on the Conservation of Polar Bears.[157] The Agreement has as members all Arctic states which have polar bear populations.[158] Though polar bears are of secondary importance to northern subsistence hunters,[159] the Agreement eventuated because of concerns during the 1960s over the unprecedented increases in the number of

opposed to arrangements sanctioning any consumptive use of wild animals, refused to extend it, even with modifications.'

155 V. A. Vladimirov, 'Present State of Northern Fur Seal Populations in the USSR and the Problems of their Rational Exploitation' (English translation of the original Russian) in L. A. Popov (ed.), *Research Papers on Marine Mammals of the North Pacific, 1989–1990* (Moscow, 1991) 112–40.

156 Mirovitskaya, Clark and Purver, 'North Pacific Fur Seals' at 35. See also Oran R. Young, *Natural Resources and the State* (Berkeley, CA, 1981) 47–84, who at 49 characterised the fur seal regime created by successive conventions throughout the twentieth century as one which treated 'all northern fur seal herds as common property at the international level coupled with a set of provisions allocating managerial authority over individual herds to the government of the state on whose territory the hauling grounds of a herd are located'.

157 (1974) 13 ILM 13 (hereinafter Polar Bear Agreement). For a detailed assessment on the background to the Agreement and its negotiation, see Anne Fikkan, Gail Osherenko and Alexander Arikainen, 'Polar Bears: The Importance of Simplicity' in Oran R. Young and Gail Osherenko (eds.), *Polar Politics* (Ithaca, NY, 1993) 96–151.

158 Those being Canada, Denmark (Greenland), Norway (Svalbard), Russia and the US.

159 Burns, 'Living Resources' at 85.

polar bears reported killed. This may have been a result of the growing value of bear hides or the increase in mechanised transportation across the snow and ice facilitating better hunting.[160] From this perspective the Agreement was initiated and implemented due to environmental concerns but it also seeks to implement resource management mechanisms. Article III of the Agreement allows for the taking of polar bears under certain specified circumstances including by local people using traditional methods in accordance with the laws of that state party. The use of aircraft and large motorised vessels in the taking of polar bears is prohibited by the Agreement.[161] The Agreement also contains a provision which imposes obligations upon state parties to protect the ecosystems of polar bears and to manage polar bear populations in accordance with 'sound conservation practices based on the best available scientific data'.[162] To assist in this process, the parties are to undertake research programmes relating to the conservation and management of polar bears.[163] The results of this research have been exchanged through an International Union for Conservation of Nature and Natural Resources (IUCN) Polar Bear Specialist Group forum.[164] The Agreement does not have any enforcement mechanism other than requiring the state parties to take appropriate measures to implement the Agreement's terms.[165] Provision is made for a Consultative Meeting to occur between the parties to determine whether further protection should be given to polar bears.[166] One such meeting did occur in 1981 to ensure the continuation of the Agreement after the initial five-year period.[167]

[160] Ian Stirling, 'Research and Management of Polar Bears *Ursus Maritimus*' (1986) 23 *Polar Record* 167 at 168–9.

[161] Polar Bear Agreement, Art. IV; this provision applies 'except where the application of such prohibition would be inconsistent with domestic laws'. This is a curious exception and its effect is to give little weight to the prohibition which the Agreement seeks to enforce.

[162] Polar Bear Agreement, Art. II. [163] Polar Bear Agreement, Art. VII.

[164] Research on polar bears has been extensive, as evidenced in the reports of the following meetings: Oystein Wiig, Erik W. Born and Gerald W. Garner, *Polar Bears* (Proceedings of the Eleventh Working Meeting of the IUCN/SSC Polar Bear Specialist Group, 25–27 January 1993, Copenhagen, Denmark) (Gland, Switzerland, 1995); Steven C. Amstrup and Oystein Wiig (eds.), *Polar Bears* (Proceedings of the Tenth Working Meeting of the IUCN/SSC Polar Bear Specialist Group, 25–9 October 1988, Sochi, USSR) (Gland, Switzerland, 1991).

[165] Polar Bear Agreement, Art. VIII.

[166] Polar Bear Agreement, Art. IX.

[167] Malcolm J. Forster and Ralph U. Osterwoldt, 'Nature Conservation and Terrestrial Living Resources' in Peter H. Sand (ed.), *The Effectiveness of International Environmental Agreements* (Cambridge, 1992) 59 at 88.

The Agreement has resulted in a decline in the numbers of polar bears being hunted to below 800 per annum.[168] It provides each party with considerable latitude to set its own catch limits on the basis of its own internal laws. Despite the potential for this freedom to be abused, the various state parties have expressed no concerns over how the Agreement has operated. Lyster notes that in practice very few polar bears are taken, even under the exceptions allowed for in Article III. Of all the state parties, the largest subsistence hunt occurs in Canada which has accounted for up to 75 per cent of polar bears killed annually.[169] Each state has also taken varying measures to provide greater protection for polar bears in certain areas. In Canada, for example, a Polar Bear National Park was established along the coast of Hudson Bay while the Northeast Greenland National Park protects a large area of polar bear habitat.[170] The Agreement has also facilitated transborder management schemes amongst some of the Arctic states. Communities in the Southern Beaufort Sea area of the US and Canada concluded in 1988 a management agreement for polar bears in the area which sought to preserve 'a healthy viable population' of polar bears while also allowing for management on a sustainable yield basis.[171] 'Management Agreements' have also been negotiated in Canada between local communities so as to ensure that harvesting of polar bears from within local populations is sustainable.[172] The Agreement's failure strictly to define circumstances in which polar bears may be taken has resulted in some anomalies. Reports have been published of polar bears being shot because they are deemed to pose a threat to personnel on offshore drilling sites in the Eastern Beaufort

[168] Pal Prestrud and Ian Stirling, 'The International Polar Bear Agreement and the Current Status of Polar Bear Conservation' (1994) 20(3) *Aquatic Mammals* 113 at 116–17 noting that between 1965–70 the annual harvest reached between 1,400–1,600 per annum.

[169] Lyster, *International Wildlife Law* at 58–9 where it is also noted that in the former USSR and Norway the taking of polar bears has been prohibited since 1955 and 1973 respectively.

[170] *Ibid.* at 60; Stirling, 'Research and Management' at 171–2; David VanderZwaag, John Donihee and Mads Faegteborg, 'Towards Regional Ocean Management in the Arctic: From Co-existence to Cooperation' (1988) 37 *UNB Law Journal* 1 at 16.

[171] Management Agreement for Polar Bears in the Southern Beaufort Sea, Agreement between Inuvialuit Game Council of Inuvik, NWT, Canada and the North Slope Borough Fish and Game Management Committee, Barrow, Alaska, USA, 29 January 1988, Art. II. For a review also see Henry P. Huntington, *Wildlife Management and Subsistence Hunting in Alaska* (London, 1992) 130–3.

[172] Prestrud and Stirling, 'The International Polar Bear Agreement' at 116.

Sea.[173] While the numbers killed have not been substantial, this practice seems difficult to justify under the terms of the Agreement.[174] A further anomaly is the practice in Canada where native residents, who have a subsistence quota allocated to various communities, sell off part of the quota to non-resident hunters.[175] When ratifying the Agreement in 1974, Canada indicated its intention to permit a so-called 'token sports hunt'.[176] This allowed the local people in an Inuit or Indian settlement to sell a polar bear permit to a non-Inuit or non-Indian hunter, provided that the hunt was conducted under the guidance of a native hunter by using a dog team. Despite the Canadian Declaration, and its apparent acceptance by the other parties, this interpretation of the Article III provisions allowing for local people to use traditional methods to take bears does not seem to be in the spirit of the Agreement.[177]

Caribou

A significant living resource in Alaska and Canada are the large caribou herds which extend from Alaska across into northern Quebec and Labrador. For some time the caribou have been subject to management on the basis of individual herds and during the past twenty years concern has been expressed about the impact of industrial growth and Arctic pollution upon these herds.[178] A number of

[173] Ian Stirling, 'Attraction of Polar Bears *Ursus Maritimus* to Off-shore Drilling Sites in the Eastern Beaufort Sea' (1988) 24 *Polar Record* 1 at 7.

[174] *Ibid.* where Stirling notes that whenever possible the bears have been shot by Inuk and included under the native quota.

[175] See Commentary to the Polar Bear Management in the Southern Beaufort Sea Agreement (note 171 above) at 5 where it is noted that: 'Since the International Agreement permits the hunting of polar bears by local people using traditional means, Canada requires that dog teams be used for transportation in the guided hunts.'

[176] Canadian Declaration upon Ratification of the Agreement on the Conservation of Polar Bears, [1976] CTS 24.

[177] For a more detailed assessment of the Canadian management of polar bears see W. Calvert *et al.*, 'Polar Bear Management in Canada 1988–92' in Oystein Wiig, Erik W. Born and Gerald W. Garner (eds.), *Polar Bears* (Proceedings of the Eleventh Working Meeting of the IUCN/SSC Polar Bear Specialist Group, 25–7 January 1993, Copenhagen, Denmark) (Gland, Switzerland, 1995) 61–79. Suggestions have also been made that the US Marine Mammal Protection Act, 1972 does not meet the provisions of the Agreement: see Huntington, *Wildlife Management* at 53. For a recent assessment of the Agreement, see Prestrud and Stirling, 'The International Polar Bear Agreement'.

[178] Burns, 'Living Resources' at 86–7; Jerome F. Sheldon, 'Oil Versus Caribou in the Arctic: The Great Debate' (1988) 24 *Polar Record* 95–100. For a review of caribou

management schemes have been implemented across Canada and the US to ensure the sustainability of the herds while allowing for a subsistence take by indigenous peoples. In many cases these management schemes involve both federal and state or provincial governments plus the local communities.[179] In the early 1980s initiatives were set in place for management arrangements for caribou to be formalised,[180] and this precipitated the 1985 Porcupine Caribou Management Agreement being reached between the government of Canada with the governments of the Yukon Territory, Northwest Territories and various Canadian indigenous peoples' organisations.[181] The most significant development in caribou management occurred in 1987 when Canada and the US signed an Agreement on the Conservation of the Porcupine Caribou Herd.[182] This Agreement seeks to conserve the Porcupine Caribou herd and its habitat through international cooperation and coordination while also ensuring opportunities for customary and traditional uses of the herd by communities in Alaska, the Yukon and Northwest Territories.[183] The Porcupine Caribou managed by the Agreement are those migratory barren ground caribou found north of 64°30′N and north of the Yukon River which share common and traditional calving and post-calving aggregation grounds in parts of Alaska and the Yukon and which migrate within Alaska, Yukon and the Northwest Territories.[184] An International Porcupine Caribou Board is established to make recommendations to ensure that the herd, its habitat and the interests of the

management policies and how, between 1950–60, subsistence harvesting was reconciled with rational management, see Peter Clancy, *Native Hunters and the State* (Kingston, Ontario, 1987).

179 See Charles Andersen and Judy Rowell, 'Joint Management Inaction – George River Caribou Herd' (1991) 11 (Special Issue 7) *Rangifer* 67–72; Donald C. Thomas and James Schaefer, 'Wildlife Co-management Defined: The Beverly and Kaminuriak Caribou Management Board' (1991) 11 (Special Issue 7) *Rangifer* 73–89; Gail Osherenko, 'Wildlife Management in the North American Arctic: The Case for Co-Management' in Milton M. R. Freeman and Ludwig N. Carbyn (eds.), *Traditional Knowledge and Renewable Resource Management in Northern Regions* (Edmonton, 1988) 92 at 95–8.

180 See N. D. Bankes, 'A Migratory Cariboo Convention' (1980) 18 CYIL 285–300.

181 The Council for Yukon Indians, the Inuvialuit Game Council, the Dene Nation and the Metis Association of the Northwest Territories. See Huntington, *Wildlife Management* at 135.

182 Agreement between the Government of Canada and the Government of the United States of America on the Conservation of the Porcupine Caribou Herd, [1987] CTS 31 (hereinafter 1987 Caribou Agreement).

183 1987 Caribou Agreement, Art. 2. Art. 3(h) prohibits the commercial sale of meat from the herd.

184 1987 Caribou Agreement, Art. 1.

users of the herd are respected when consideration is given to proposed activities within the range of the herd. When activities in one country may affect the status of the herd in the other the Agreement calls for the two states to consult. Activities which may interfere with the cross-border migration of the herd are to be avoided or minimised.[185] The Agreement also establishes a procedure allowing for the Board to recommend overall harvest quotas for each country.[186] This domestic quota is then shared between various user groups on the basis of determinations made by domestic bodies constituted by a majority of native users.[187]

Management of polar non-living resources

Antarctica

When the Antarctic Treaty was negotiated there was no consideration given to the question of mining being carried out on the continent or in the Southern Ocean. There were a number of reasons for this. First, the Treaty negotiations were dominated by concerns over the resolution of sovereignty. If the possible exploitation of minerals had been discussed there was the potential for the consensus over the Article IV sovereignty solution to break down. Second, Antarctica's resource potential at the time was unknown and while scientists had discovered a wide range of minerals throughout the continent, none were then thought to have much commercial potential. Third, up till that time there had been very little mineral exploration in the Southern Ocean and this in conjunction with the relative worldwide abundance of oil and gas reserves meant that little interest was shown in Antarctica's non-renewable resource potential. As a result, it comes as no surprise that the Antarctic Treaty made no reference at all to minerals and that the only provision in the Treaty dealing with resource management was the reference in Article IX(1)(f) to living resources.

A change in attitude began to occur during the 1970s. In 1973 the research vessel *Glomar Challenger* discovered ethane and methane gas in the Ross Sea area and this raised expectations that commercially

185 1987 Caribou Agreement, Arts. 3, 4.

186 1987 Caribou Agreement, Art. 4(d).

187 See Robert F. Keith, 'Arctic Borderlands: Environment and Development Issues in Canadian–American Relations' (1991) 2 *Northern Notes* 27 at 33–4; Huntington, *Wildlife Management* at 135–6.

recoverable reserves could exist in the Southern Ocean.[188] There had also been, in the period since the Treaty was negotiated, a substantial development in mining technology which had been applied in the Arctic and which made mining operations in Antarctica more feasible. The final factor which saw commercial mining become a possibility was the global concern which existed in the 1970s over the scarcity of energy resources and the need to find alternate sources, especially given the political instability which then existed in the Middle East oil fields. As a result of these developments the exploitation of Antarctic mineral resources became an agenda item for the ATCPs.

Pre-1988

The first formal proposal for the negotiation of an Antarctic minerals regime was made at ATCM VI (1970) and Recommendations were actually adopted at both ATCM VII (1972) and VIII (1975).[189] In both instances the approach was to encourage the further study of the impact of mineral resource activity upon the Antarctic environment. This demonstrated that even at this early stage in the debate the ATCPs realised that mining would raise important environmental issues. ATCM IX (1977) saw the issue dealt with in more substance with a Working Group of Experts on the Exploration and Exploitation of Antarctic Minerals convened. A report was submitted to the plenary session of the meeting and this resulted in Recommendation IX-I.[190] This Recommendation took account of previous work done on the impact of mineral resource activities upon the Antarctic environment and called for continued research on the issue and eventual negotiation of a regime for Antarctic mineral resources. Significantly, this Recommendation also sought to regulate mineral resource activities on an interim basis. It provided that the ATCPs:

> urge their nationals and other States to refrain from all exploration and exploitation of Antarctic mineral resources while making progress towards the timely adoption of an agreed regime concerning Antarctic mineral resource activities. They will thus endeavour to ensure that, pending the

188 See the discussion of Antarctica's mineral resource potential in chapter 2.

189 See Recommendations VII-6 and VIII-14.

190 The Working Group had before it a report of the SCAR Group of Specialists entitled 'A Preliminary Assessment of the Environmental Impact of Mineral Exploration/Exploitation in Antarctica'. Another Working Group on the Legal and Political Aspects of Mineral Resources also met during this meeting: see Bush (vol. I), 339.

timely adoption of agreed solutions pertaining to exploration and exploitation of mineral resources, no activity shall be conducted to explore or exploit such resources. They will keep these matters under continuing examination.

Minerals were again considered at the next ATCM where Recommendation X-1 was adopted. It called for further consultations on the question between the ATCPs and noted that any agreed regime should include: means to assess the impact of resource activities upon the Antarctic environment; means to determine whether resource activities were acceptable; and means for 'governing the ecological, technological, political, legal, and economic aspects of those activities in cases where they would be determined acceptable'.[191] Finally in 1981, Recommendation XI-1 was adopted which set the guidelines for the future negotiation of a minerals regime. It provided that a minerals regime should be concluded as a matter of urgency via a Special Consultative Meeting which would base its work on previous Recommendations on the issue and five additional principles. These were:

(a) that the ATCPs should continue to play an active and responsible role in dealing with the question of Antarctic mineral resources;
(b) that the Treaty be maintained in its entirety;
(c) that the protection of the environment and its dependent ecosystems be a basic consideration;
(d) that in dealing with this question the ATCPs should not prejudice the interests of all mankind in Antarctica; and
(e) that the provisions of Article IV of the Treaty not be affected by the regime.[192]

The first session of Special ATCM IV on Antarctic Mineral Resources was held in Wellington in June 1982 and a further eleven sessions were held till the negotiations were concluded in June 1988. The result of these negotiations, the 1988 Convention on the Regulation of Antarctic Mineral Resource Activities (CRAMRA) was, however, scarcely finalised, before another debate commenced over whether mining should even be allowed in Antarctica. In conjunction with the push for greater environmental protection in Antarctica, this in a political

[191] Recommendation X-1, para. 4.

[192] For a discussion of the importance of these Recommendations and the early debates concerning the negotiation of a minerals regime see Gillian D. Triggs, 'Negotiation of a Minerals Regime' in Gillian D. Triggs (ed.), *The Antarctic Treaty Regime* (Cambridge, 1987) 182–95; C. D. Beeby, 'An Overview of the Problems which should be Addressed in the Preparation of a Regime Governing the Mineral Resources of Antarctica' in Francisco Orrego Vicuna (ed.), *Antarctic Resources Policy* (Cambridge, 1983) 191–8.

sense ended any opportunity for CRAMRA to enter into force. It is now an abandoned instrument.

CRAMRA

While CRAMRA has now been overtaken by other events, it remains an important attempt at resource management and deserves special consideration.[193] Initially it should be noted that CRAMRA sought to regulate prospecting, exploration and development of Antarctic mineral resources. It did not extend to any scientific research activities conducted under Article III of the Antarctic Treaty.[194] 'Mineral resources' were defined to include all non-living natural non-renewable resources and included fossil fuels and metallic and non-metallic minerals but not ice.[195] Article 2 established objectives and general principles for the Convention and reiterates many of the provisions regarding the conduct of such activities provided for in Antarctic Treaty Recommendations adopted prior to the mineral negotiations commencing. Emphasis is placed on the special responsibility of the parties to protect the Antarctic environment.[196] Perhaps one of the most important provisions in the Convention as far as the conduct of resource activities is concerned is Article 4. It imposes a strict obligation upon the parties to ensure that before mining takes place adequate information exists to enable judgments to be made about the impact of such activities.[197] It also required an assessment of the possible impacts upon the environment by the proposed activity in order to determine whether it would cause: significant adverse effects on air and water quality; significant changes in the environment, or

[193] For reviews of CRAMRA see Watts, *International Law* at 221–48; US Office of Technology and Assessment, *Polar Prospects* (Washington, 1989); United Kingdom, Foreign and Commonwealth Office, *Convention on the Regulation of Antarctic Mineral Resource Activities* (London, 1989); Peter J. Beck, 'Convention on the Regulation of Antarctic Mineral Resource Activities: A Major Addition to the Antarctic Treaty System' (1989) 25 *Polar Record* 19–32; Christopher C. Joyner, 'CRAMRA: The Ugly Duckling of the Antarctic Treaty System' in Arnfinn Jorgensen-Dahl and Willy Ostreng (eds.), *The Antarctic Treaty System in World Politics* (London, 1991) 161–85; Francis Auburn, 'Convention on the Regulation of Antarctic Mineral Resource Activities' (1990) 51 *Antarctic Research Series* 259–71; R. Tucker Scully and Lee A. Kimball, 'Antarctica: Is There Life After Minerals?' (1989) 13 *Marine Policy* 87–98; Francesco Francioni, 'Resource Sharing in Antarctica: For Whose Benefit?' (1990) 1 *European Journal of International Law* 258–68; Rudiger Wolfrum, *The Convention on the Regulation of Antarctic Mineral Resource Activities* (Berlin, 1991).

[194] CRAMRA, Art. 1(7).

[195] CRAMRA, Art. 1(6). On the question of why CRAMRA excluded ice see Watts, *International Law* at 250.

[196] CRAMRA, Art. 2(3).

[197] CRAMRA, Art. 4(1).

populations of species of fauna and flora; further jeopardy to endangered or threatened species; or degradation of, or substantial risk to, areas of special significance.[198] Article 4 further provides that no resource activities shall take place until it is judged that adequate technology and procedures exist to ensure safe operations and compliance with the Convention's standards, that a capacity exists to monitor the environment and ecosystem so as to identify any adverse effects of such activity, and that there exists the capacity to respond effectively to accidents which may have an environmental effect.

CRAMRA created four institutional bodies to implement and monitor its provisions. The principal body was the Antarctic Mineral Resources Commission, comprised of original parties to the Convention and others which demonstrated a substantial scientific research interest or were sponsoring mineral resource activities.[199] Under the terms of CRAMRA, the Commission's functions were numerous. The most important were: to facilitate the collection and exchange of information upon which judgments could be made regarding resource activities; to identify areas for possible exploration and development, and those in which resource activities were prohibited or restricted; to adopt measures for the protection of the environment and promotion of safe and effective exploration and development techniques; and to adopt measures dealing with prospecting.[200] Commission decisions on matters of substance were to be by a three-quarters majority.[201] An Antarctic Mineral Resources Regulatory Committee was also to be established for each area identified by the Commission for exploration.[202] This Committee was to have had a membership of only ten, which was to include the state or states which claimed sovereignty over the area in question, together with the US and the former USSR.[203] Each Regulatory Committee would have wide-ranging functions concerning the issuing of exploration and development permits and the monitoring of exploration and development activities.[204] A Scientific, Technical and Environmental Advisory Committee would also have been established with membership open to all Convention parties.[205] The Advisory Committee was to provide the Commission and Regulatory Committees with advice on scientific, technical and environmental aspects of resource activities.[206] Provi-

[198] CRAMRA, Art. 4(2).
[199] CRAMRA, Art. 18.
[200] CRAMRA, Art. 21.
[201] CRAMRA, Art. 22.
[202] CRAMRA, Art. 29.
[203] CRAMRA, Art. 29(2).
[204] CRAMRA, Art. 31.
[205] CRAMRA, Art. 23.
[206] CRAMRA, Art. 26.

sion existed in the Convention for these views to be taken account of, though there was no requirement that they be acted upon.[207] The final institutional body to be created by CRAMRA was a 'Special Meeting of Parties'.[208] This body, which was open to all parties to the Convention, would have convened to consider the identification of areas for possible exploration and development. It was required to report back to the Commission twenty days after convening.[209]

The processes regulating the conduct of mineral resource activities are found in Chapters III, IV and V of the Convention dealing respectively with prospecting, exploration and development. At each stage in the application process for a permit to engage in any one of these activities the various bodies established in CRAMRA would be involved in the decision-making process. Perhaps the most rigorous process was to occur at the exploration stage where the applying state would have been required to submit a detailed notification of the activity proposed and an assessment of its impact under the objects of the Convention.[210] Reports were to be received from both the Advisory Committee and Special Meeting of Parties before the Commission would initially consider the application.[211] A Regulatory Committee would have been convened for the identified area in question with the purpose of adopting general requirements for the exploration and development of the area in question.[212] Following this process, it would have been open to a state party to lodge with the Regulatory Committee an application for an 'exploration permit'. This would have been considered by the Regulatory Committee,[213] and a detailed Management Scheme for the area in question approved before any exploration permit was issued.[214] The Commission was given authority to review decisions by the Regulatory Committee to issue an exploration permit and also the terms of a management scheme.[215] From this outline it can be seen that obtaining an exploration permit was the most difficult stage for a state and its operator to pass through before mining could commence. CRAMRA also sought to deal with response action in case of environmental damage and operator liability as a consequence of such damage.[216] The provision dealing with operator liability was deliberately left incomplete; it being

[207] See CRAMRA, Arts. 41, 43, 45, 54. [208] CRAMRA, Art. 28.
[209] CRAMRA, Arts. 28(1), 40. [210] CRAMRA, Art. 39.
[211] CRAMRA, Arts. 40, 41. [212] CRAMRA, Art. 43.
[213] CRAMRA, Arts. 44, 45. [214] CRAMRA, Arts. 45, 46, 47.
[215] CRAMRA, Art. 49. [216] CRAMRA, Art. 8.

intended that further liability provisions would be elaborated by a Protocol to the Convention.[217]

A thorough assessment of CRAMRA would require considerable understanding of the political nature of the document and the compromises which occurred during its negotiation in order to reach a consensus on the final text.[218] Such a review is not appropriate here, but assessing CRAMRA from the perspective of a resource management instrument raises two alternative approaches. One is to argue that CRAMRA was a resource management instrument designed to allow mining to take place in Antarctica. The other is to argue that CRAMRA was an environmental protection instrument which only allowed mining after rigorous environmental standards had been met.[219] The detailed environmental standards and objectives of the Convention plus the various stages through which applications for permits to engage in resource activities were to proceed, certainly support the view that CRAMRA did not make a judgment that mining was acceptable or would inevitably take place. Rather, it has been argued that CRAMRA was an 'assessment regime' which constituted 'a mechanism for assessing the possible impact on the environment of Antarctic mineral resource activities, determining whether they are acceptable and, if so, regulating them in detail'.[220] From this perspective, CRAMRA sought to implement a total ban on mining activities till such time as a state, and the operator it was sponsoring, were able to demonstrate adequately that all CRAMRA's environmental protection standards had been and would be met during the course of mineral

[217] See Recommendation XV-2 adopted at ATCM XV (1989) which envisaged the negotiation of such a Protocol. The debate over the adoption of the Madrid Protocol in 1989–91 saw this initiative overtaken. The provisions of Art. 8 are discussed in more detail in chapter 9.

[218] See Rolf Trolle Andersen, 'Negotiating a New Regime: How CRAMRA Came into Existence' in Arnfinn Jorgensen-Dahl and Willy Ostreng (eds.), *The Antarctic Treaty System in World Politics* (London, 1991) 94–109.

[219] These differing approaches are reflected in the opposing views of Heap and Brown: see John Heap, 'The Political Case for the Minerals Convention' in Grahame Cook (ed.), *The Future of Antarctica* (Manchester, 1990) 44–52; Alan D. Brown, 'The Design of CRAMRA: How Appropriate for the Protection of the Environment?' in Arnfinn Jorgensen-Dahl and Willy Ostreng (eds.), *The Antarctic Treaty System in World Politics* (London, 1991) 110–19.

[220] Christopher Beeby, 'The Convention on the Regulation of Antarctic Mineral Resource Activities and Its Future' in R. A. Herr, H. R. Hall and M. G. Haward (eds.), *Antarctica's Future* (Hobart, 1990) 47 at 49. This was not a view necessarily shared by environmentalists: see Kelly Rigg, 'Environmentalists' Perspectives on the Protection of Antarctica' in Grahame Cook (ed.), *The Future of Antarctica* (Manchester, 1990) 68–80.

activities. CRAMRA therefore reversed the CCAMLR presumption that resource exploitation would occur, to one where a total prohibition existed until such time as CRAMRA's institutional bodies decided to lift it.[221] Some commentators have even argued that because CRAMRA's institutional mechanism for approving resource activities was so strict, a ban on minerals activities had in effect been created.[222] In this regard, the standard established under Article 4 that no resource activities would take place until such time as 'informed judgments' could be made about their possible environmental impacts is important.[223]

In the final analysis, it would be incorrect to characterise CRAMRA as an instrument which prohibited Antarctic minerals resource activities. It was negotiated on the premise that there was a need to regulate such activities in Antarctica. In the process it created very demanding environmental standards for any state seeking to engage in such activities. How it would have functioned in practice is, and always was, uncertain. It must be accepted, however, that if the strict environmental guidelines contained in the Convention were followed by the Commission, it would have been difficult not only for political reasons, but also because of the management mechanisms established, for mining activities beyond the prospecting stage to have ever taken place. From this perspective it can be said that CRAMRA was unique for a mining regime but given the environmentally sensitive area over which it sought to regulate mining activities such standards were essential.

Madrid Protocol

The 1991 Madrid Protocol to the Antarctic Treaty was not designed as a supplement to CRAMRA but rather as an alternative instrument. It

[221] Beeby, 'Convention' at 56; I. D. Hendry, 'How Much Environmental Protection in the 1988 Wellington Convention?' in Joe Verhoeven, Philippe Sands and Maxwell Bruce (eds.), *The Antarctic Environment and International Law* (London, 1992) 63 at 64; Lee A. Kimball, *Southern Exposure* (Washington, DC, 1990) 16; Francisco Orrego Vicuna, *The Protection of the Antarctic Environment* (Lysaker, Norway, 1992) 18.

[222] Trolle Andersen, 'Negotiating a New Regime' at 107; see also Lee A. Kimball, 'CRAMRA and other Environmental Regimes in the ATS: How Well does it Fit?' in Arnfinn Jorgensen-Dahl and Willy Ostreng (eds.), *The Antarctic Treaty System in World Politics* (London, 1991) 133 at 134 where it is noted: 'I would argue that for those of us who oppose minerals development in Antarctica, CRAMRA provides a very solid basis to prevent it.'

[223] Kimball, *Southern Exposure* at 16; Hendry, 'How Much Environmental Protection' at 64.

establishes a total prohibition on mineral resource activity in Antarctica. The only exception to this is where scientific research is being conducted.[224] Three issues arise over the Protocol's prohibition on mining. The first is what regime applies till such time as the Protocol enters into force. The Protocol requires the ratification of all the Consultative Parties which participated in its negotiation.[225] To date only sixteen of the required twenty-six ATCPs have ratified,[226] and it may be some time before the Protocol enters into force. In the Final Act of Special ATCM XI which negotiated the Protocol it was agreed that 'pending entry into force of the Protocol, which would take place as soon as possible, current constraints on Antarctic mineral resource activity should continue'.[227] This represents the third exhortation by the ATCPs to continue in force a *de facto* moratorium on mining until such time as a mining regime legally takes effect.[228] Given the abandonment of CRAMRA, the current regime dealing with mineral resource activities in Antarctica till such time as the Protocol enters into force would seem to be found in the terms of the Final Act of Special ATCM XI. However, even that provision is based on the entry into force of the Protocol 'as soon as possible'. If substantial delays occur in the entry into force of the Protocol, then what regime applies? In this regard, it is important to recall the terms of Recommendation IX-1. It provided that 'pending the timely adoption of agreed solutions pertaining to exploration and exploitation of mineral resources, no activity shall be conducted to explore or exploit such resources'.[229] Given the length of time taken to negotiate first CRAMRA and now the

[224] Protocol, Art. 7. However, any such scientific research will be regulated under the Protocol's environmental impact assessment procedures. [225] Protocol, Art. 23.

[226] As of ATCM XIX, the states which had ratified the Protocol were Argentina, Australia, Chile, China, Ecuador, France, Germany, Italy, Netherlands, New Zealand, Norway, Peru, Spain, Sweden, the UK and Uruguay.

[227] Final Act of the Eleventh Antarctic Treaty Special Consultative Meeting, reprinted in (1991) 30 ILM 1,460 at 1,461; also Bush (Bin II), Part AT91D, 1.

[228] The first occurred with Recommendation IX-1 (1977), while the second is found in the Final Act of Special ATCM IV which drew up CRAMRA, reprinted in *Handbook* (Pt 1) 201, where it was noted:

> The Meeting also considered the question of continuing the restraint of Antarctic mineral resource activities agreed to in Recommendation IX-1 for the interim period before the entry into force of the Convention. Taking into account Recommendation IX-1 and the adoption by the Meeting of the Convention on the Regulation of Antarctic Mineral Resource Activities, the Meeting agreed that all States represented at the Meeting would urge their nationals and other States to refrain from Antarctic mineral resource activities as defined in the Convention pending its timely entry into force.

[229] Recommendation IX-1, para. 8.

Protocol, it could well be argued that there has been no 'timely adoption of agreed solutions' so that the moratorium proposed by this Recommendation no longer stands. In these circumstances, the current mineral resource regime in Antarctica does seem very much dependent upon the timely entry into force of the Protocol.

A second point to note is that Article 7 of the Protocol does not extend to the mining of ice.[230] Once again this interpretation is to be found in the Final Act of Special ATCM XI. However, this does not imply that ice harvesting is unregulated as the other provisions of the Protocol are considered to apply to any such activity. Under these circumstances an environmental impact assessment would have to take place before such an activity could occur.[231] The final point to note is that even if the Protocol does enter into force, the prohibition on mining imposed by Article 7 may be subject to amendment or review.[232] Two methods apply for modification or amendment. The first adopts the same procedure found in Article XII(1) of the Antarctic Treaty requiring unanimous agreement of all the parties.[233] The other adopts a review conference mechanism which may be convened fifty years after entry into force of the Protocol.[234] In this event, special provision is made for any renunciation of the Protocol's mining prohibition. Before any change to the mining prohibition can occur, there must be 'in force a binding legal regime on Antarctic mineral resource activities that includes an agreed means for determining whether, and, if so, under what conditions, any such activities would be acceptable'.[235] This provision seems to imply that a resource management mechanism similar to CRAMRA may be required before any mineral activities could occur in Antarctica if the Protocol's mining prohibition was one day lifted.

[230] Iceberg and ice harvesting is considered to be a potentially viable economic activity in Antarctica: see P. Schwerdtfeger, 'Antarctic Icebergs as Potential Sources of Water and Energy' in Rudiger Wolfrum (ed.), *Antarctic Challenge II* (Berlin, 1986) 377–89. For a consideration of some of the legal issues see Donald R. Rothwell and Stuart Kaye, 'Law of the Sea and the Polar Regions: Reconsidering the Traditional Norms' (1994) 18 *Marine Policy* 41 at 55–7; James E. Carroll, 'Of Icebergs, Oil Wells and Treaties: Hydrocarbon Exploitation Offshore Antarctica' (1983) 19 Stanford JIL 207–27; T. R. Lindquist, 'The Iceberg Cometh? International Law Relating to Antarctic Iceberg Exploitation' (1977) 17 NatResJ 1–41.

[231] Final Act; see also the discussion in Bush (Bin II), Part AT91D at 4.

[232] See Protocol, Art. 25. [233] Protocol, Art. 25(1). [234] Protocol, Art. 25(2).

[235] Protocol, Art. 25(5)(a). For a discussion of these provisions, see S. K. N. Blay, 'New Trends in the Protection of the Antarctic Environment: The 1991 Madrid Protocol' (1992) 86 AJIL 377 at 394–7; Bush (Bin I), Part AT91C, 68–76.

Arctic

There are few examples of cooperative management of Arctic non-living resources between Arctic states. This partly is a consequence of the Arctic being a region where sovereignty is by and large settled in many areas where these resources are to be found. However, in those areas where sovereignty and jurisdictional disputes do exist, such as in maritime areas, cooperative agreements are still uncommon. This is partly a result of states not perceiving their interests as being severely disadvantaged by these disputed areas remaining undeveloped. Many other Arctic regions are subject to uncontested mineral resource development so access to the disputed areas is not presently seen as vital. The high cost of Arctic minerals development also demands that there be secure resource development infrastructure and political and legal certainty. Nevertheless, in many border areas this has been difficult to guarantee. Perhaps the best example of this situation is the disputed boundary area between Canada and the US in the Beaufort Sea. Notwithstanding the tremendous resource potential of the region, both parties have to date been content to allow resource development on either side of the disputed area without actively engaging in negotiations to settle the boundary. Further, despite the precedents for joint development zones and the long history of cooperation between Canada and the US there seems no immediate prospect of this boundary and resource dispute being settled.[236] While the future remains uncertain for increased bilateral cooperation on Arctic non-living resource management,[237] there are some examples of where joint management of resources has occurred and others where commercial joint ventures have been encouraged.[238] In addition, the 1920 Treaty concerning the Archipelago of Spitsbergen (Svalbard)[239] remains an interesting example of Arctic non-living resource management.

[236] Dawn Russell, 'International Ocean Boundary Issues and Management Arrangements' in David VanderZwaag (ed.), *Canadian Ocean Law and Policy* (Toronto, 1992) 463 at 496. This has not deterred the Canadian government from offering for bid oil and gas exploration rights in the area: see 'Oil, Gas Rights Offered in Arctic', 5 January 1993, *The [Toronto] Globe and Mail*, B8.

[237] Stokke, 'The Northern Environment' at 65–6.

[238] See W. E. Butler, 'Joint Ventures and the Soviet Arctic' (1990) 14 *Marine Policy* 169 at 175–6.

[239] 2 LNTS 8 (hereinafter Spitsbergen Treaty).

The Canada–Denmark boundary

The Canada–Denmark continental shelf boundary between Baffin and Ellesmere Islands and Greenland was negotiated in 1973 and entered into force in 1974.[240] An important feature of the Agreement is its cooperative provisions designed to facilitate bilateral resource management if transborder resources are discovered. Article III limits the parties from issuing exploitation licences for areas adjacent to the boundary. If such resources are discovered, then Article V becomes operative. It provides:

> If any single geological petroleum structure or field, or any single geological structure or field of any other mineral deposit, including sand and gravel, extends across the dividing line and the part of such structure or field which is situated on one side of the dividing line is exploitable, wholly or in part, from the other side of the dividing line, the Parties shall seek to reach an agreement as to the exploitation of such structure or field.

To date there have been no resources discovered which require the operation of Article V, though there have been some encouraging results from exploration conducted along the western Greenland continental shelf.[241]

The Jan Mayen development zone

As a result of a maritime boundary delimitation dispute between Norway and Iceland over the maritime area adjacent to Jan Mayen, in 1980 a Conciliation Commission was convened. In making its decision in 1981, the Commission recommended that Norway and Iceland should work towards the establishment of a joint development zone in the disputed area between Jan Mayen and Iceland.[242] These Recommendations were subsequently adopted by both states and agreement was reached on cooperation on exploration and exploitation of the petroleum resources of an area of the continental shelf. The cooperation takes the form of joint venture contracts, unless other arrange-

240 Agreement between the Government of Canada and the Government of the Kingdom of Denmark Relating to the Delimitation of the Continental Shelf between Greenland and Canada, [1974] CTS 9.

241 Russell, 'International Ocean Boundary Issues' at 490–2.

242 Continental Shelf Area Between Iceland and Jan Mayen (Jan Mayen Continental Shelf) (Report and Recommendations to the Governments of Iceland and Norway), 19–20 May 1981, (1981) 20 ILM 797. See also Willy Ostreng, 'Delimitation Arrangements in Arctic Seas: Cases of Precedence or Securing of Strategic/Economic Interests' (1986) 10 *Marine Policy* 132 at 139.

ments are agreed upon. In each area of the joint development area the laws of each state respectively apply. If any resource area extends beyond the area of joint development, it remains wholly under the joint management regime. If, however, a resource area extends into the Iceland EEZ then it becomes subject to Icelandic law.[243]

Svalbard

One area of the Arctic which does exemplify an international resource management approach is Svalbard. Under the 1920 Spitsbergen (Svalbard) Treaty, Norwegian sovereignty is fully recognised.[244] However, the other parties are also entitled to engage in various activities on the islands of the Archipelago, including resource exploitation.[245] Throughout much of the century Norway and the USSR have engaged in extensive coal-mining operations throughout the islands. Under the Treaty, Norway may only impose a maximum 1 per cent royalty on minerals which are exported from the island, on the proviso that such imposts do not exceed what is necessary to provide government-financed facilities for the residents of the islands.[246] This provision is very favourable to mining interests. As the islands have no native inhabitants and are only populated by a small and scattered mining community, this results in any charges Norway may impose being very low.[247] To date, most of the mining activity conducted in Svalbard has been by Norwegian and Soviet/Russian nationals and companies.[248] Under the Treaty, Norway is required to establish mining regulations and accordingly a 'Mining Code' was adopted by a Norwegian Royal Decree in 1925.[249]

The provisions of the Mining Code have been relatively uncontroversial as they apply to the islands; however, there is some uncertainty as to whether the Treaty and the Mining Code were intended to apply in offshore areas. The Treaty is silent on this question. Article 2 does extend the Treaty's provisions to 'territorial waters' and subsequent

243 Ostreng, 'Delimitation Arrangements' at 139.

244 Spitsbergen Treaty, Art. 1.

245 Spitsbergen Treaty, Art. 3.

246 Spitsbergen Treaty, Art. 8; Ostreng, 'Delimitation Arrangements' at 150.

247 See the population data for 1923–75 reprinted in Willy Ostreng, *Politics in High Latitudes* (London, 1977) 4.

248 *Ibid.* at 5–7. Since the 1960s oil companies from other states, including Norway, have been exploring for oil in Svalbard, but to date there have been no commercial finds: Churchill and Ulfstein, *Marine Management* at 7.

249 Churchill and Ulfstein, *Marine Management* at 31.

state practice supports the application of the Mining Code also in those waters.[250] The more controversial issue has been whether Norway can claim a continental shelf/EEZ maritime zone offshore the islands, and if they can whether the Treaty also intended other Treaty parties also to have resource rights in that area. Norway has taken the view that the Treaty was not intended to extend beyond the territorial sea of the Archipelago and adjacent islands and as a result there is no limitation on Norway proclaiming and enforcing an EEZ/Fisheries Zone plus a continental shelf.[251] The former USSR took a different position to that of Norway, and it is suspected that other parties to the Treaty also favour a more liberal interpretation which would allow them access to resources within Svalbard's maritime zones.[252] To date this disagreement has not advanced any further because no serious exploration for offshore minerals has occurred and it seems probable that the matter will rest until such time as minerals are discovered in sufficient quantities to encourage settlement of this issue.[253]

Conclusion

As in many regions throughout the world, resource management in the polar regions has been characterised by the need to balance economic growth with environmental and resource sustainability. In some instances economic interests have prevailed, such as in the case of whaling and sealing in the nineteenth century. The twentieth century has, however, resulted in a more enlightened attitude towards polar resource management with the result that there has been an increasing emphasis on protection of the environment, respect for the rights of indigenous peoples, and resource sustainability. With the exception of Arctic non-living resource development, these have been defining characteristics of all resource development in the polar regions from the 1911 Arctic Fur Seal Treaty through to CCAMLR. In

[250] *Ibid.* at 36–8.

[251] Scrivener, 'Resources and Environment', at 7–8; Robin Churchill, 'The Soviet Union and Jurisdictional Disputes in Northern Waters' in Clive Archer (ed.), *The Soviet Union and Northern Waters* (London, 1988) 44 at 54. Access to the fisheries areas adjacent to Svalbard is currently more economically important than access to the continental shelf: see Scrivener, 'Resources and Environment', at 7.

[252] Churchill, 'The Soviet Union' at 56.

[253] Scrivener, 'Resources and Environment', at 8. Churchill and Ulfstein, *Marine Management* at 40–52 contend that the Treaty was intended to apply beyond the territorial sea, that other parties are entitled to access to resources found in those areas, and that the current Mining Code also applies to the continental shelf.

some instances, such as Antarctic mineral resources, complete prohibitions have been imposed in order to protect the environment. The polar regions then provide examples throughout the past 200 years of the whole range of resource management options, from completely unmanaged resource exploitation to complete prohibition.

A number of common themes emerge from this review. One is the need to engage in pre-emptive resource management in order not only to preserve the resource but also to protect the dependent environment. The disastrous consequences of unregulated sealing and whaling in the nineteenth century demonstrated the folly of allowing unmanaged exploitation to occur. One result of this has been that the polar states are very conscious of the environmental impact of such unregulated activity and have taken steps to ensure that it does not occur again. CCAMLR presents the best example of the pre-emptive approach. Krill was identified as potentially being a major commercial resource and the ATCPs took steps to regulate its exploitation, prior to serious impacts upon the resource. The same attitude was adopted with the growing unregulated exploitation of polar bears during the late 1960s.

To implement effective management regimes for living resources, the polar regions especially demonstrate the importance of management decisions being based on sound scientific data. This was initially recognised as far back as the 1911 Fur Seals Convention and has continued through to CCAMLR. From this perspective, CCAMLR represents one of the most advanced resource management mechanisms of this type. CCAMLR, however, also demonstrates that if a management system is developed around the need for scientific data then the quality of the data being relied upon becomes vital. Obtaining this data can be very difficult unless all parties to the management regime are cooperative. Further problems can arise when the data is commercially sensitive.

There has also increasingly been an attempt to implement the ecosystem approach in resource management. CCAMLR also represents the best example of this approach. How intensely an ecosystem approach is adopted will often depend upon the resource. In the case of CCAMLR, with krill being seen as the primary resource in need of protection, a very sophisticated ecosystem approach was required because of the pivotal role krill play in the Antarctic food chain. A similar approach does not necessarily apply to polar bears which are at the top of their particular food chain. Implementing an ecosystem approach in an international management regime, based on an international legal instrument, also poses great difficulties. Here the CCAMLR experience demonstrates the benefits of seeking to lay down in international law terms only the principles upon which the regime is to be based and then allowing the parties to refine how these principles are to be implemented through appropriate institutions. In conjunction with the ecosystem approach has been a growing awareness in the Arctic especially that resource management mechanisms cannot be developed without recognising the rights of indigenous peoples. In this respect, the Arctic agreements concerning fur seals, polar bears and caribou all reflect this reality. The increasing political role of indigenous peoples' organisations in the development of Arctic resource management policy ensures that this will be a continuing feature of Arctic resource management.

The polar regions, perhaps more than any others, reflect the diversity of resource management interests which are currently at play.[254] Some advocate that more extensive development of polar resources should take place,[255] while others favour a more environmentally centred approach to resource development.[256] Sustainable development is also a concept which is being discussed, especially in the Arctic where there is a large indigenous and settled population in an area subject to industrial and resource development.[257] As shown in the debate in the Antarctic over whether to proceed with CRAMRA or adopt an absolute prohibition on mining, doubts also exist over whether resource activities should even take place. The conflict between increased resource development and enhanced environmental protection is presently creating new challenges for polar resource management. In a simple sense this can be seen as a debate between industry and conservationists. This debate has, however, become more intense in recent years and attracted groups with more diverse interests. In both polar regions the development–environment debate has the potential to create the greatest tension in future years. While Antarctic mineral resource activity may have been prohibited under

[254] For a discussion of various approaches see Gail Osherenko, 'Human/Nature Relations in the Arctic: Changing Perspectives' (1992) 28 *Polar Record* 277–84.

[255] M. C. W. Pinto, 'Authority to Manage Fisheries and Mineral Resources of the Southern Ocean: Objectives of Management' in T. A. Clingan (ed.), *The Law of the Sea* (Honolulu, 1988) 343–65.

[256] M. W. Holdgate, 'Regulated Development and Conservation of Antarctic Resources' in Gillian D. Triggs (ed.), *The Antarctic Treaty Regime* (Cambridge, 1987) 128–42.

[257] Griffiths and Young, 'Sustainable Development'; Young, *Arctic Politics* at 214–28.

the Madrid Protocol, there is no guarantee that the consensus which existed amongst the ATCPs at the time of the Protocol's negotiation will remain in place. Political and other pressures may eventually force the ATCPs to reconsider the prohibition.[258] Similarly in the Arctic, it is foreseeable that without a multilateral management mechanism such as the ATS, states will increasingly come under collective and individual pressure to decide whether resources are more freely exploited or be preserved for indigenous peoples by way of rigorous management.[259]

The polar regions provide important examples of the difficulties encountered in resource management, but also the potential effectiveness of international law in regulating resource exploitation. While this may be simple to achieve where a regulatory void previously existed, the polar regimes discussed above demonstrate that in nearly all instances serious efforts have been made to implement sophisticated resource management mechanisms. In total, they represent an important feature of the polar regions' contribution to international law.

[258] Wells, *Antarctic Resources* at 19.

[259] In this regard, see Young's proposal for the establishment of an 'Arctic Resources Council', *Arctic Politics* at 118–24.

9 The polar regions and international environmental law

Through the twentieth century, and particularly since the 1938 and 1941 decisions in the *Trail Smelter Arbitration* between Canada and the US,[1] there has been a steady growth in international law focusing on environmental problems.[2] During this time new principles have emerged concerning state responsibility for protection of the environment, cooperation between states to deal with environmental problems, and the need for an 'ecosystem' approach towards environmental protection. Together with an increased global consciousness about the need to protect the environment,[3] these legal developments have placed high on the international agenda state responsibility for protecting the local, regional and global environment. As a result states have become increasingly concerned about meeting their international obligations in this area.[4] There is also an increased

[1] *Trail Smelter Arbitration*–Decision (16 April 1938) (1939) 33 AJIL 182; (11 March 1941) (1941) 35 AJIL 684.

[2] Patricia W. Birnie and Alan E. Boyle, *International Law and the Environment* (Oxford, 1992) 10. In work conducted in preparation for the 1992 United Nations Conference on Environment and Development (UNCED), the UNCED Preparatory Committee surveyed a total of 124 multilateral environmental instruments, all of which had been adopted this century and 97 of which had been adopted since 1970: see Peter H. Sand (ed.), *The Effectiveness of International Environmental Agreements* (Cambridge, 1992).

[3] See for example: International Union for Conservation of Nature and Natural Resources, *World Conservation Strategy* (Gland, Switzerland, 1980); World Charter for Nature, UNGA Res. 37/7 (9 November 1982), reprinted in (1983) 22 ILM 455; World Commission on Environment and Development, *Our Common Future* (Oxford, 1987); 1989 Hague Declaration on the Environment, reprinted in (1989) 28 ILM 1308.

[4] An example of the concern of some states in meeting their obligations under international law to protect the environment is the nomination by Australia of various sites under the 'World Heritage List' created by the 1972 UNESCO Convention Concerning the Protection of the World Cultural and Natural Heritage, 1037 UNTS 151. As a result of these nominations and subsequent protection of the designated

willingness amongst states to assert claims for environmental damage.[5] It can now be said, therefore, that international environmental law has emerged as a distinct field of international law.[6]

There are many facets to international environmental law. Recently much attention has been given to the area of state responsibility for environmental damage.[7] One of the continuing problems of international law in general and international environmental law in particular has been the enforcement of liability provisions dealing with wrongful acts having environmentally injurious consequences.[8] Yet, it is recognised that more effort needs to be directed towards protection rather than after-the-event legal consequences. As Kiss notes, 'it is unanimously recognised that the best way to protect the environment is to prevent damage instead of trying to restore what has been spoiled or lost'.[9] It is in this area that the polar regions have made a significant contribution to the development of international environmental law. In Antarctica especially there has been an attempt to implement the 'precautionary principle' in environmental management.[10] There are also several instances in the Arctic where this approach has been adopted to deal with certain resources.

The polar regions also demonstrate the effectiveness of utilising

sites, a number of disputes occurred in Australia between the federal and state governments over both constitutional issues and the extent of Australia's obligations under the Conventions to protect these areas: see Ben Boer, 'World Heritage Disputes in Australia' (1992) 7 *Journal of Environmental Law and Litigation* 247–79.

5 This is exemplified by the increasing number of cases which have come before the International Court of Justice which raise environmental issues, and also the Court's recent decision to create a separate Chamber dealing with environmental disputes: see 'Chamber for Environmental Matters' (1993) 23(6) *Environmental Policy and Law* 243.

6 *Cf.* the discussion in Birnie and Boyle, *International Law* at 1.

7 See the collection of essays in Francesco Francioni and Tullio Scovazzi (eds.), *International Responsibility for Environmental Harm* (London, 1991).

8 This debate is reflected in the International Law Commission's Draft Articles on State Responsibility: see (1980) II (Pt Two) YBILC 30; (1986) II (Pt Two) YBILC 38; Birnie and Boyle, *International Law* at 139–41, 149; Gunther Handl, 'Territorial Sovereignty and the Problem of Transnational Pollution' (1975) 69 AJIL 50–78. Also see the International Law Commission's reports on 'International Liability for Injurious Consequences Arising out of Acts not Prohibited by International Law', note 56 below.

9 Alexandre Kiss, 'Present Limits to the Enforcement of State Responsibility for Environmental Damage' in Francesco Francioni and Tullio Scovazzi (eds.), *International Responsibility for Environmental Harm* (London, 1991) 3 at 12.

10 See the discussion of this issue in chapter 8 and at pp. 365–9 below; also see Laura Pineschi, 'The Antarctic Treaty System and General Rules of International Environmental Law' in Francesco Francioni and Tullio Scovazzi (eds.), *International Law for Antarctica* (Milan, 1987) 187 at 203–7.

regional management mechanisms in dealing with environmental issues. While many global legal instruments apply to the polar regions, there are few examples of these instruments having a significant impact upon the polar environment.[11] The Arctic states have recently demonstrated their own belief in the virtue of regional management of environmental problems by adopting the 1991 Arctic Environmental Protection Strategy (AEPS).[12] While the AEPS can only be said to impose 'soft law' obligations, it does seek to build upon existing international environmental law standards and create new ones for the Arctic states. The Antarctic Treaty System (ATS) has also placed emphasis upon the protection of the environment. From the 1964 Agreed Measures on the Protection of Fauna and Flora[13] to the more recent 1991 Protocol on Environmental Protection to the Antarctic Treaty (hereinafter Protocol),[14] the ATS has evolved into a very complex regime dealing with Antarctic environmental protection. Commentators are increasingly of the view that the ATS represents a model for international environmental law.[15]

The environmental protection mechanisms which have been adopted in the polar regions are important examples of international law at work.[16] They also further demonstrate how the polar regions have

[11] A significant exception is the 1946 International Convention for the Regulation of Whaling, 161 UNTS 74.

[12] Reprinted in (1991) 30 ILM 1,624 (hereinafter AEPS).

[13] Reprinted in Bush (vol. I), 146; *Handbook* (Pt 2), 2048. For a review of this and other measures taken to protect the Antarctic environment up till 1989, see W. N. Bonner, 'International Agreements and the Conservation of Antarctic Systems' in K. R. Kerry and G. Hampel (eds.), *Antarctic Ecosystems* (Berlin, 1990) 386–91.

[14] (1991) 30 ILM 1455 (hereinafter Protocol).

[15] See Philippe Sands, 'The Antarctic Treaty Regime: A Model for International Environmental Law?' in Joe Verhoeven, Philippe Sands, Maxwell Bruce (eds.), *The Antarctic Environment and International Law* (London, 1992) 53–61; Boleslaw Adam Boczek, 'The Protection of the Antarctic Ecosystem: A Study in International Environmental Law' (1983) 13 ODIL 347–425.

[16] For a comprehensive treatment of how various principles of international environmental law have been applied in Antarctica, see Pineschi, 'The Antarctic Treaty System' where it is noted at 243 that:

> The Consultative Parties, which claim a 'primary responsibility' for the protection of the Antarctic environment . . . on the whole may be considered to have concretely applied general environmental rules in Antarctica, and given them a specific content.

With respect to the application of these principles in the Arctic see Louis Rey, 'The Impact of Human and Industrial Activities on the Arctic Environment: Legal Considerations and International Liabilities' (paper presented at Arctic Atmospheric Pollution Conference, Scott Polar Research Institute, Cambridge, 2–5 September 1985).

made contributions to the development of international law. This chapter will focus upon these issues. It will begin with a review of the development of international environmental law throughout this century.

International environmental law

The development of international environmental law

As noted, there has been a gradual development of international environmental law throughout the century. In the last twenty-five years, however, there has been a considerable acceleration in that process.[17] Two factors have been responsible for these developments: an increase in major environmental incidents which have had trans-boundary impact,[18] and the increased attention given to the problem at major international (particularly United Nations) fora. The first major international conference which addressed environmental problems from a global perspective was the 1972 United Nations Conference on the Human Environment (Stockholm Conference). This Conference is often credited with crystallising a number of important environmental principles and also providing the foundation for subsequent international law developments.

The Stockholm Conference also recognised some developments which had already occurred in international law relating to the environment. Of these earlier developments, the *Trail Smelter Arbitration* was the first and most important. It concerned action brought by the United States for air pollution caused by a Canadian smelter in British Columbia. It was alleged that emissions from the smelter were drifting across the border so as to cause harm to land and other interests in the United States state of Washington. One of the difficulties the Arbitral Tribunal faced in deciding the case was the lack of comprehensive international law principles on this question. However, a decision was able to be reached by relying on general principles of international

[17] Geoffrey Palmer, 'New Ways to Make International Environmental Law' (1992) 86 AJIL 259 at 262.

[18] The *Torrey Canyon* tanker disaster in 1967 is credited with being the catalyst for the development of a number of International Maritime Organization conventions dealing with marine pollution, intervention in the case of maritime incidents, and liability; likewise the 1986 accident at the Chernobyl nuclear power plant in the USSR resulted in a number of international instruments, see Alan E. Boyle, 'Chernobyl and the Development of International Environmental Law' in W. E. Butler (ed.), *Perestroika and International Law* (Dordrecht, 1990) 203–19.

law, and also domestic principles of United States law as applied with respect to the rights of states in the American federation.[19] It was held that no state had the right to use or permit the use of its territory such that emissions cause injury in or to the territory of another state or the properties or persons therein.[20] Canada was therefore held responsible for the past and future conduct of the Trail Smelter, irrespective of whether it was a state-owned enterprise.[21] The Tribunal also emphasised the importance of the states working together to eliminate transfrontier environmental problems.[22]

The *Trail Smelter* decision substantially advanced principles of state responsibility in regard to transfrontier pollution but uncertainty existed as to how far these principles could extend. The principle of state responsibility for injurious acts caused to another state was further developed in the *Corfu Channel Case*.[23] In that decision, the International Court of Justice had to determine whether Albania was responsible for damage caused to British naval vessels by mines in the Corfu Channel, despite not being actually aware of the mines' existence. The Court adopted the principle that every state had an obligation 'not to allow knowingly its territory to be used for acts contrary to the rights of other states'.[24] While the judgment did not suggest what the rights of states might be in cases of environmental damage, it did confirm the principle of state responsibility for injurious acts which occur within territory under state control.[25] As a result of this decision, the potential now existed for the principle of *Trail Smelter* to be extended beyond air pollution to a wide variety of injurious acts.[26]

[19] (1941) 35 AJIL 698, 713 and 714, where decisions of the United States Supreme Court were referred to.

[20] *Ibid.* at 716 where the Tribunal noted:

> under the principles of international law, as well as the law of the United States, no State has the right to use or permit the use of its territory in such a manner as to cause injury by fumes in or to the territory of another or the properties or persons therein, when the case is of serious consequence and the injury is established by clear and convincing evidence.

[21] *Ibid.* at 717.

[22] *Ibid.* at 734. See the discussion in Alexandre Kiss and Dinah Shelton, *International Environmental Law* (London, 1991) 122–5.

[23] *Corfu Channel Case* (*UK* v. *Albania*) [1949] ICJ Reports 3.

[24] [1949] ICJ Reports 22.

[25] Birnie and Boyle, *International Law* at 90.

[26] A further decision which confirmed the obligation in international law upon a state to not engage in acts which harmed the environment of another state came in the *Lake Lanoux Arbitration* (*France* v. *Spain*) (1957) 12 RIAA 281; for an English translation see (1959) 53 AJIL 156–71. See the discussion in Kiss and Shelton, *International Environmental Law* at 126.

These decisions dealt with damage to the environment which had already occurred or which might occur at some time in the future. They did not address the issue of what responsibility existed upon states to protect the environment.[27] The principle that states were under an obligation to protect the environment in order to minimise the risk of environmental damage had begun to appear, however, in various international treaties. The 1946 International Convention for the Regulation of Whaling[28] sought for the first time to create a management regime in which whale stocks would be closely monitored and decisions regarding allowable catch levels would be based on scientific data. The 1954 International Convention for the Prevention of Pollution of the Sea by Oil (OILPOL)[29] also sought to implement a management mechanism for international shipping that sought to minimise the risk of oil pollution rather than merely to deal with liability for damage caused. The 1958 Geneva Conventions on the Law of the Sea also contained provisions seeking to protect the marine environment, especially in regard to the prevention of marine pollution and the need to implement conservation principles for living resources of the high seas.[30]

Through a combination of various decisions by tribunals and courts, plus bilateral and multilateral conventions, certain international law principles applicable to the environment slowly began to emerge.[31] However, these developments were disparate and as international concern began to rise over environmental issues it became obvious that a global conference was needed to discuss matters relating to the present state and future of the human environment. The result was the 1972 Stockholm Conference,[32] which agreed upon the 'Stockholm Declaration on the Human Environment'.[33] The Declaration included a set of guiding principles for the future direction of activities which impact upon the environment, especially economic development, and the need for states to take more coor-

[27] For comment see Riccardo Pisillo-Mazzeschi, 'Forms of International Responsibility for Environmental Harm' in Francesco Francioni and Tullio Scovazzi (eds.), *International Responsibility for Environmental Harm* (London, 1991) 15 at 31.

[28] Note 11 above. [29] 327 UNTS 3.

[30] See Convention on the High Seas, 450 UNTS 82, Arts. 24, 25; Convention on Fishing and Conservation of the Living Resources of the High Seas, 559 UNTS 285, Art. 2.

[31] For a review of the development of the law up till that time, see Lynton Keith Caldwell, *International Environmental Policy* (Durham, NC, 1984) 19–48.

[32] The Conference was convened pursuant to UNGA Res. 2398 (XXIII) (3 December 1968).

[33] Stockholm Declaration on the Human Environment (16 June 1972), UN Doc. A/Conf.48/14/ and Corr. 1, reprinted in (1972) 11 ILM 1416.

dinated action to deal with existing and emerging problems. Some provisions in the Stockholm Declaration were important for the development of international law. Principle 21 provided:

> States have, in accordance with the Charter of the United Nations and the principles of international law, the sovereign right to exploit their own resources pursuant to their own environmental policies, and the responsibility to ensure that activities within their jurisdiction or control do not cause damage to the environment of other States or of areas beyond the limits of national jurisdiction.

The significance of this statement is that states had for the first time agreed that there was a universal notion of state responsibility for any environmental damage or harm not only to other states but also for areas beyond national jurisdiction. Though not yet accepted in treaty form, the Stockholm Declaration became a basis for the development of customary international law on this question of state responsibility.

In addition to Principle 21, Principle 22 expressly referred to international law in providing that states were to cooperate together to develop further principles regarding liability and compensation for victims of pollution and other environmental damage. This Principle endorsed the *Trail Smelter* decision but also recognised that in the thirty years since its decision there had been little comprehensive development of the international law of state responsibility.[34] While the Stockholm Declaration was not an attempt to create legally binding principles regarding environment and development, the subsequent continued reference to Principle 21 in various fora and international instruments has seen it now commonly accepted as representing customary international law.[35] One result of the Stock-

[34] While no specific principles in the Stockholm Declaration referred to the Arctic or Antarctic, some dealt with issues of importance to the polar regions. Principle 4 provided that 'Man has a special responsibility to safeguard and wisely manage the heritage of wildlife and its habitat', while Principle 7 provided that states were to take all possible steps to prevent pollution of the seas.

[35] Birnie and Boyle, *International Law* at 46, and at 90 where it is noted:

> the totality of the provision, including its emphatic reference to responsibility for environmental damage, was regarded by many states present at the Stockholm Conference, and subsequently by the UN General Assembly, as reflecting customary international law.

For examples of subsequent conventions adopting Principle 21 see 1972 Convention on the Prevention of Marine Pollution by Dumping of Wastes and other Matter, 1046 UNTS 120, Art. 1; 1982 United Nations Convention on the Law of the Sea, (1982) 21 ILM 1,261, Arts. 192, 193; 1989 Basle Convention on the Control of Transboundary Movements of Hazardous Wastes and their Disposal, (1989) 28 ILM 657, Preamble.

holm Conference was that a large number of international fora increasingly became dominated by questions of environmental protection. As a result, international law dealing with the protection of the environment expanded considerably.[36]

While there have been a great many international law conventions and agreements dealing with the environment since the 1972 Stockholm Conference, most developments have tended to be in response to specific sectoral problems such as marine and air pollution, and wildlife and habitat protection. Little effort has been made to implement a comprehensive approach such as that taken in relation to the law of the sea by the 1982 United Nations Convention on the Law of the Sea (UNCLOS).[37] Despite the lack of emphasis in the United Nations Charter on protection of the environment,[38] the United Nations has attempted to keep environmental issues at the forefront of its agenda. To that end, to celebrate the twentieth anniversary of the Stockholm Conference, it was decided in 1989 to convene a Conference on Environment and Development (UNCED) for 1992.[39] The purpose of the Conference was to devise various strategies to allow for the integration of environment and development by taking account of current global conditions and those of the future.[40]

UNCED did not achieve all of its initial goals.[41] Nevertheless, there were some important achievements. Conventions dealing with biological diversity[42] and climate change[43] were agreed upon. 'Agenda 21'

[36] See generally Birnie and Boyle, *International Law* at 39–53; Kiss and Shelton, *International Environmental Law* at 41–54; Caldwell, *International Environmental Policy* at 49–81. [37] Note 35 above.

[38] For a critique of the United Nations' lack of institutional structure and capability to deal comprehensively with environmental issues, see Palmer, 'New Ways' at 261, 279.

[39] UNGA Res. 44/228 (22 December 1989).

[40] Peter H. Sand, 'Preparing for Brazil 1992 – Environmental Legal Issues' in *Contemporary International Law Issues* (Dordrecht, 1992) 28 at 28 noted that in 1991, UNCED was expected to produce six categories of outcomes: (1) an agreed statement of environment and development principles to govern the conduct of nations and people ('the Earth Charter'); (2) an agreed programme of work by the international community addressing major environment and development priorities for the period 1993–2000, and leading to the twenty-first century ('Agenda 21'); (3) agreement on financial resources required for implementing the programme; (4) agreement on access to environmentally sound technologies for developing countries; (5) agreement on measures to strengthen and supplement existing international institutional processes; and (6) specific legal instruments on climate change and biodiversity.

[41] For example, the so-called 'Earth Charter' was not adopted nor was a specific legal instrument dealing with forests.

[42] 1992 Convention on Biological Diversity, (1992) 31 ILM 818.

[43] 1992 Framework Convention on Climate Change, (1992) 31 ILM 849. While this

was also adopted.[44] This document is intended to represent 'an agreed programme of work by the international community addressing major environment and development priorities for the initial period 1993–2000 and leading into the twenty-first century'.[45] Agenda 21 adopts a broad range of responses to existing and emerging environmental problems, setting out a range of important environmental initiatives for the global community. Some of these are intended to build upon existing legal regimes and others to develop new ones.[46] Similarly to the Stockholm Conference, UNCED also adopted a Declaration.[47] The 'Rio Declaration' reinforces some of the principles from Stockholm,[48] but also recognises principles which have emerged subsequently[49] and adopts new principles to deal with emerging and future issues.[50] Principle 13 of the Rio Declaration places particular importance upon the role of international law in developing mechanisms for liability and compensation.[51]

While the achievements of the Stockholm and UNCED Conferences have been impressive and there has been a considerable growth in international legal instruments dealing with a variety of issues confronting the environment, problems still remain for international environmental law. Identified weaknesses include the proliferation of soft law instruments, the lack of comprehensive coverage, and problems with implementation and enforcement.[52]

Convention was formally adopted prior to UNCED it was first opened for signature at the Conference and had been negotiated as part of the UNCED process.

[44] See *Agenda 21* (New York, 1993).

[45] Marlene Jahnke, 'UNCED: Rio Conference on Environment and Development' (1992) 22(4) *Environmental Policy and Law* 204 at 208.

[46] While Agenda 21 does not specifically address the polar regions, if its programmes are implemented they will have a polar impact. Chapter 17, dealing with the protection of the oceans and rational development of living resources may be particularly important.

[47] The Rio Declaration on Environment and Development, UN Doc. A/CONF.151/5/Rev.1 (13 June 1992), reprinted in (1992) 31 ILM 874 (hereinafter Rio Declaration).

[48] See Rio Declaration, Principle 2.

[49] Rio Declaration, Principle 15 recognises the 'precautionary approach', while Principle 17 recognises the value of 'Environmental impact assessment'.

[50] This is reflected in the number of principles which refer to the need for sustainable development: see Rio Declaration, Principles 1, 4, 8, 21, 22, 27.

[51] Rio Declaration, Principle 13 provides in part:

> States shall also cooperate in an expeditious and more determined manner to develop further international law regarding liability and compensation for adverse effects of environmental damage caused by activities within their jurisdiction or control to areas beyond their jurisdiction.

[52] Birnie and Boyle, *International Law* at 542.

There can be no denying that environmental law is dominated by soft law instruments and that a trend has developed against the adoption of 'hard law' obligations.[53] Nevertheless, the reliance on soft law has allowed a greater number of states to commit themselves to a wide range of environmentally focused conventions and declarations.[54] Through use of soft law instruments the law has also been able to develop rapidly since Stockholm and respond to issues more quickly than it would through traditional legal instruments.[55]

It must also be accepted that the lack of a comprehensive set of legal rules (general principles or custom) does represent a problem for international environmental law. International environmental law is rooted in general principles of state responsibility, an approach continued in the work of the International Law Commission in its reports on 'International Liability for Injurious Consequences Arising out of Acts not Prohibited by International Law'.[56] As a result, it has been difficult for international environmental law to forge a distinctive jurisprudence. However, through widespread state practice and adoption of many legal instruments it has now become possible to discern some basic international environmental law principles. These are by no means comprehensive. Nevertheless, the adoption of the Convention on Biological Diversity may serve as an indication that states are now beginning to move away from a specific sectoral-dominated approach to a broader ecosystem approach which recognises the inter-relationship of environmental issues.

Finally, while implementation and enforcement have been a problem, there are encouraging signs that states are beginning to take their international obligations more seriously. The rapid entry into force of the 1987 Montreal Protocol on Substances that Deplete the Ozone Layer[57] and its successful implementation,[58] plus the speedy entry into force of both the 1992 Convention on Biological Diversity

[53] Artemy Saguirian, 'Preparing for Brazil 1992–Environmental Legal Issues' in *Contemporary International Law Issues* (Dordrecht, 1992) 37 at 38.

[54] Gunther Handl, 'Environmental Security and Global Change: The Challenge to International Law' (1990) 1 YIEL 3 at 7–8; Peter H. Sand, 'International Cooperation: The Environmental Experience' in Jessica Tuchman Matthews (ed.), *Preserving the Global Environment* (New York, 1991) 236 at 252–4.

[55] Palmer, 'New Ways' at 269; Sand, 'International Cooperation' at 240–1.

[56] See Second Report by Robert Q. Quentin-Baxter, Special Rapporteur, (1981) II (Pt One) YBILC 103 and subsequent reports by the same Rapporteur: (1982) II (Pt One) YBILC 51, (1983) II (Pt One) 201; (1984) II (Pt One) 155; in addition see Second Report by Julio Barboza, Special Rapporteur, (1986) II (Pt One) YBILC 145.

[57] (1987) 26 ILM 1,541.

[58] Birnie and Boyle, *International Law* at 410–11.

and 1992 Framework Convention on Climate Change are indicators of this trend. Nevertheless, the true test of the effectiveness of some of these international instruments will be determined on the basis of state compliance and a reversal of global and regional environmental impacts.

Perhaps the critics of international environmental law have too high an expectation. States are naturally reluctant to agree to new laws which limit their ability to exploit resources and impose substantial economic burdens with respect to pollution control and environmental monitoring.[59] Despite these limitations, the achievements noted above, which have primarily occurred in the twenty-year period between Stockholm and Rio, are substantial. As Birnie and Boyle note:

> Although evaluation of the precise character of existing customary rules, and even more so of general principles of law from which it is permissible to draw inferences, is not without difficulty . . . there is today rather more evidence for the existence of customary rules . . . than sceptics have in the past suggested. Certainly, there is no doubt that the content of customary international environmental law today is much less modest than was true in 1972.[60]

Principles of international environmental law

It is now possible to identify several core principles of international environmental law. These principles are found in a variety of traditional international law sources.[61] The principles are:

(a) the obligation of all states to conserve the environment and its natural resources;
(b) the need for states to assess potential, and monitor actual environmental impact;
(c) the need for international cooperation to conserve the environment both within and beyond areas of national jurisdiction.[62]

This list is not exhaustive. It may well be possible to identify other principles which are in a state of development, or which have particular application for specific environmental problems.[63] The purpose here, however, is to provide a general overview.

[59] P. W. Birnie, 'Legal Techniques of Settling Disputes: The "Soft Settlement" Approach' in W. E. Butler (ed.), *Perestroika and International Law* (Dordrecht, 1990) 177 at 185.

[60] Birnie and Boyle, *International Law* at 544. [61] *Ibid.* at 9–26.

[62] Kiss and Shelton, *International Environmental Law* at 145–54.

[63] For a more comprehensive review see Birnie and Boyle, *International Law* at 82–214; Ranee Khooshie Lal Panjabi, 'From Stockholm to Rio: A Comparison of the Declaratory Principles of International Environmental Law' (1993) 21 *Denver Journal of International Law and Policy* 215–87.

The first principle has been recognised in numerous international instruments since the Stockholm Conference. Perhaps the most significant of these, given the number of participating states, was UNCLOS.[64] As a result of these provisions, it can be said that throughout international law it generally is now recognised that states have an obligation to prevent environmental harm.[65] Having developed from the decision in the *Trail Smelter* case, the result is that states are not under a negative obligation to refrain from damaging the environment, but a positive obligation to protect it.[66] One manifestation of this obligation is the 'precautionary principle' or the 'precautionary approach'.[67] While this approach has now found expression in a large number of international instruments,[68] its scope is still indefinite. The most recent statement of the principle can be found in Principle 15 of the Rio Declaration. It provides that: 'In order to protect the environment, the precautionary approach shall be widely applied by States according to their capabilities. Where there are threats of serious or irreversible damage, lack of full scientific certainty shall not be used as a reason for postponing cost-effective measures to prevent environmental degradation.' Despite the attempt in Principle 15 to ensure that reliance upon the precautionary principle is not avoided in certain instances, no real attempt was made to define the concept. As a result, despite the developments in this area the potential exists for varying standards to exist.[69] Perhaps the most important issue is the degree of foreseeability. Are states under an obligation to protect the environment from all risks, whether they are foreseeable or not, or is there a common law standard of foreseeability

[64] See UNCLOS, Part XII – Protection and Preservation of the Marine Environment. An example is Art. 192, which provides: 'States have the obligation to protect and preserve the marine environment'; also see Art. 194(2).

[65] Birnie and Boyle, *International Law* at 98–9.

[66] Pisillo-Mazzeschi, 'Forms of International Responsibility' at 35.

[67] Birnie and Boyle, *International Law* at 95; Handl, 'Environmental Security' at 20–4.

[68] See the instruments listed in David Freestone, 'The Precautionary Principle' in Robin Churchill and David Freestone (eds.), *International Law and Global Climate Change* (London, 1991) 21–39.

[69] Handl, 'Environmental Security' at 23 lists three notions which underlie the principle: (1) the application of the principle is not limited to transboundary risks of harm but reaches environmentally sensitive activities generally; (2) restraint is advocated not only in the face of present and clear danger but because of the limited knowledge of ecological implications of human activities; and (3) the principle implies a broad systemic approach to global environmental management in which the 'react and correct' model must be complemented by 'forecast and prevent'.

applied?[70] Kiss and Shelton argue that 'there is a duty to impose a regulatory regime on activities which could harm the environment of other states or areas outside the limits of their jurisdiction'.[71] Birnie and Boyle characterise this obligation as primarily one of 'diligent prevention and control'.[72] While there remains debate over how the concept is to be implemented, it is clear that as part of the obligation upon states to prevent harm, a state is under an obligation to control an activity when the environmental consequences of that activity are unknown.

Secondly, there is a duty to monitor the environment and to assess the risk of potential transboundary environmental damage from proposed or existing activities. States need to be aware of the state of the environment and the potential that their activities may have for environmental damage. This is especially the case with new activities which may not be considered environmentally harmful when first initiated.[73] To a degree these principles have developed from municipal law where environmental impact assessments began to be recognised as part of environmental and planning law in the 1960s.[74] Initiatives developed through the United Nations Environmental Programme (UNEP) have also seen environmental monitoring and prior impact assessment become essential features of international environmental risk management.[75] A recent convention implementing this principle is the 1991 Convention on Environmental Impact Assessment in a Transboundary Context negotiated under the auspices of the UN Economic Commission for Europe.[76]

The third general principle of international environmental law, the need for greater international cooperation to deal with environmen-

[70] See UNCLOS, Art. 206 which provides in part:

> Where States have reasonable grounds for believing that planned activities under their jurisdiction or control may cause substantial pollution of or significant and harmful changes to the marine environment ...

[71] Kiss and Shelton, *International Environmental Law* at 129–30.

[72] Birnie and Boyle, *International Law* at 95. How far this obligation extends will depend on the circumstances of the actual case. The ICJ stressed the importance of actual knowledge on the part of Albania in the *Corfu Channel Case* [1949] ICJ Reports 22. However, the International Law Commission has emphasised 'foreseeability' rather than actual foresight: see Birnie and Boyle, *International Law* at 96.

[73] An example of such an activity which may not have been considered environmentally harmful when it first developed was air transportation by jet aircraft.

[74] See Kiss and Shelton, *International Environmental Law* at 147.

[75] Birnie and Boyle, *International Law* at 104–5. See also UNCLOS, Art. 204.

[76] (1991) 30 ILM 800 (hereinafter Espoo Convention).

tal problems both within and beyond areas of national jurisdiction, also has its roots in the *Trail Smelter* decision and Principle 21 of the Stockholm Declaration.[77] The United Nations has played an important role in implementing this principle. Through bodies such as UNEP it has facilitated and sponsored a great number of international conferences dealing with a range of specific, regional and global environmental problems.[78] This principle has found expression in a number of bilateral and multilateral conventions dealing with issues ranging from marine pollution[79] to nuclear accidents.[80] It has also been recognised in regard to the law of the sea, which encourages a regional response to dealing with problems afflicting the marine environment.[81]

The polar regions and the development of international environmental law

Management of specific issue areas

In the past, states tended to adopt an issue-by-issue approach towards environmental protection in the polar regions rather than seeking to protect the total environment. This reflected international environmental law where a sectoral attitude was adopted to environmental issues without much consideration for the global environment. Recently, there has been a change in this attitude. Partly influenced by the 1972 Stockholm Conference, there has been a gradual recognition that environmental issues cannot easily be separated and singled out. The UNCED Conference and instruments such as the Convention on Biological Diversity demonstrate vividly this fundamental change in attitude towards environmental protection. Parallel with these global developments, there has also been a change in attitude towards environmental protection in the polar regions. Both the Protocol and

[77] Birnie and Boyle, *International Law* at 102–4. The *Lake Lanoux* decision, (1957) 12 RIAA 281, was also influential in the development of this principle.

[78] See e.g., UNEP Principles of Conduct in the Field of the Environment for the Guidance of States in the Conservation and Harmonious Utilization of Natural Resources Shared by Two or More States, (1978) 17 ILM 1,097. See Birnie and Boyle, *International Law* at 102–3.

[79] See UNCLOS, Art. 197; 1983 Agreement Between the Government of Canada and the Government of the Kingdom of Denmark for Cooperation Relating to the Marine Environment, [1983] CTS 19, Art. IV.

[80] See 1986 Convention on Early Notification of a Nuclear Accident, (1986) 25 ILM 1,370.

[81] UNCLOS, Arts. 123, 197.

the AEPS illustrate this change. These two initiatives will be considered in some detail below, but first there will be a review of the issue-specific measures which have been adopted.

Antarctic fauna and flora

Despite the fact that the only provision in the Antarctic Treaty[82] dealing with the protection of the environment is Article IX(1)(f), concern was soon expressed at initial ATCMs over the need to develop appropriate measures to protect certain aspects of the Antarctic environment.[83] This initiative eventually resulted in the adoption in 1964 of the Agreed Measures for the Conservation of Antarctic Fauna and Flora.[84] The Agreed Measures have been described as 'one of the most comprehensive and successful international instruments for wildlife conservation on land that has yet been negotiated'.[85] While this view is not shared by all commentators,[86] the Agreed Measures represented the first attempt by the ATCPs at adopting what Heap and Holdgate have termed 'an exercise in forethought'.[87] That is, the Agreed Measures were formulated prior to Antarctic fauna and flora being under any serious threat. They made general provision for the protection of Antarctic fauna such as native mammals and birds.[88] Certain acts which were considered to constitute harmful interference were absolutely prohibited, except in certain cases of extreme emergency.[89] To augment these provisions, 'Specially Protected Areas' were created under Article VIII in order to 'preserve their unique natural ecological system'.

The Agreed Measures became the model for an extensive system of Antarctic protected areas, developed by way of additional recommendations. Since 1964, in addition to Specially Protected Areas, there have also been created Sites of Special Scientific Interest, Historic Sites and Monuments, Specially Reserved Areas and Multiple-Use Planning

[82] 402 UNTS 71.
[83] See Recommendations I-VIII, II-II.
[84] Recommendation III-VIII.
[85] Brian Roberts, 'International Co-Operation for Antarctic Development: The Test for the Antarctic Treaty' (1978) 19 *Polar Record* 107 at 109.
[86] M. W. Holdgate, 'Regulated Development and Conservation of Antarctic Resources' in Gillian D. Triggs (ed.), *The Antarctic Treaty Regime* (Cambridge, 1987) 128 at 133.
[87] John A. Heap and Martin W. Holdgate, 'The Antarctic Treaty System as an Environmental Mechanism – An Approach to Environmental Issues', in *Antarctic Treaty System* (Washington, 1986) 195 at 203.
[88] Agreed Measures, Arts. VI, VII.
[89] Agreed Measures, Arts. V, VI, VII.

Areas.[90] This expanded system of protected areas has considerably extended the reach of the original Agreed Measures but has been consistent with the original approach. In the Preamble to the 1964 Agreed Measures, the ATCPs declared Antarctica to be a 'Special Conservation Area', the first time such a status had been given to a whole continent.[91] The Agreed Measures and protected area system have remained faithful to this designation. They also demonstrate that even as early as 1964 the ATCPs had begun to adopt an 'assumed responsibility for the Antarctic environment'.[92] The Agreed Measures have not, however, been without problems. First, because they are based upon a Recommendation, their legal status remains uncertain.[93] Second, partly because they took the form of a Recommendation, there was a considerable delay in their adoption and a great variation in their implementation by the ATCPs.[94] Third, there have also been a number of breaches documented which apparently have gone unsanctioned.[95] Nevertheless, the Agreed Measures were an ambitious attempt by the ATCPs to protect initially certain aspects of the Antarctic environment. Through the adoption of subsequent measures dealing with tourism, waste disposal, marine pollution and environmental impact assessment the Agreed Measures and additional Recommendations have over time been expanded to cover a wide range of activities which seek to protect the Antarctic environment.[96] Some of the problems which have been encountered with the status of the Agreed Measures and additional provisions will be overcome by the Protocol which will have the effect of superseding many of these provisions.[97]

[90] See the discussion in chapter 4 of these designated Protected Areas, and for a review of the system see R. I. Lewis Smith *et al.* (eds.), *Developing the Antarctic Protected Area System* (Switzerland, 1994).

[91] F. M. Auburn, *Antarctic Law and Politics* (London, 1982) 268.

[92] Gillian D. Triggs, *International Law and Australian Sovereignty in Antarctica* (Sydney, 1986) 182.

[93] W. M. Bush, 'The Antarctic Treaty System: A Framework for Evolution' in R. A. Herr, H. R. Hall and M. G. Haward (eds.), *Antarctica's Future* (Hobart, 1990) 119 at 128.

[94] Auburn, *Antarctic Law* at 272.

[95] The best example of this was the decision by France during the 1980s to build an airstrip at their Pointe Geologie base in Adelie Land: see Pineschi, 'The Antarctic Treaty System' at 202–3. Also see Auburn, *Antarctic Law* at 277 for other breaches of the Agreed Measures.

[96] See for discussion Sir Arthur Watts, *International Law and the Antarctic Treaty System* (Cambridge, 1992) 260–1; Boleslaw A. Boczek, 'Specially Protected Areas as an Instrument for the Conservation of the Antarctic Nature' in Rudiger Wolfrum (ed.), *Antarctic Challenge II* (Berlin, 1986) 65–101.

[97] See Antarctic Treaty, *Final Report of the Seventeenth Antarctic Treaty Consultative Meeting*

Antarctic marine living resources

The two most important instruments developed to deal with Antarctic marine living resources have been the 1972 Convention on the Conservation of Antarctic Seals (CCAS)[98] and the 1980 Convention on the Conservation of Antarctic Marine Living Resources (CCAMLR).[99] Both are important examples of the precautionary principle at work.[100]

In the case of CCAS, there was little prospect at the time that the regulation of Antarctic sealing was first considered by the ATCPs during the 1960s that commercial sealing was about to recommence in Antarctica.[101] Not only was there little prospect of sealing recommencing as a major industry, but CCAS was also established by a majority of states which had no intention of participating in sealing activities.[102] Despite sealing not being a current or foreseeable activity, and although the viability of seals as a species was not under threat from such an activity, CCAS set very conservative annual catch limits, established closed seasons and prohibited the harvesting of certain species.[103] This was partly due to a lack of adequate scientific knowledge about both the size of the stock and the dynamics of the species.[104] Recognising that this lack of information would make management of the resource very difficult, CCAS also introduced mechanisms whereby the Scientific Committee on Antarctic Research (SCAR) would provide scientific advice to the parties.[105] The parties to the Convention were not only required to exchange information between themselves regarding reported catches and implementation, but also to pass this data on to SCAR which was invited to make reports so as to alert the parties to any 'significantly harmful effect on the total stocks of such species or on the ecological system in any particular locality' as a result of harvesting.[106] By adopting this approach, the

(Venice, 11–20 November 1992), 24, para. 54 (superseded Recommendations) and 37, para. 97 (impact of Protocol).

98 (1972) 11 ILM 251.

99 (1980) 19 ILM 841.

100 Heap and Holdgate, 'The Antarctic Treaty System' at 203.

101 This was despite the main target species for any potential sealing industry, crabeater seals, at that time having an estimated worldwide population of between 20 and 50 million: see Holdgate, 'Regulated Development' at 135.

102 Auburn, *Antarctic Law* at 210.

103 Holdgate, 'Regulated Development' at 135.

104 *Ibid.*

105 CCAS, Art. 5.

106 CCAS, Art. 5(4). See the discussion in Bush, 'The Antarctic Treaty System' at 130.

CCAS parties ensured that SCAR operated as a *de facto* scientific committee for the Convention. Because of the independence of SCAR as an international non-governmental scientific organisation, it was well placed to provide this advice.

CCAMLR substantially advanced the CCAS approach. No intensive fishing activities were being undertaken in the Southern Ocean at the time it was negotiated. It was also negotiated by a group of states which at that time had no substantial interest in, or intention to engage in, fishing activities.[107] The most important aspect of CCAMLR, however, is its attempt to implement an ecosystem approach to resource management. This broke new ground not only in Antarctic environmental protection but also globally in that the Antarctic ecosystem was treated as a whole, rather than individually assessing the state of specific resource stocks.[108] It has already been noted that while the ecosystem approach has been universally applauded, there have been difficulties in its implementation.[109] Some commentators are still of the view that it is difficult to combine an ecosystem approach, which seeks to protect the environment, with provisions dealing with harvesting of certain resources.[110] However, this view seems to assume that CCAMLR was an environmental protection Convention. This is not the case. CCAMLR was based on the assumption that harvesting would take place. As a result, what it seeks to do is ensure that sustainable harvesting can take place without doing irreparable damage to the resource stock and those other species which may depend upon it. Holdgate has described this as considering the 'ecological consequence' of harvesting.[111] This is defined as an approach which specifies:

> principles of conservation which include the prevention of decrease in the size of any harvested population to levels below those which ensure its stable recruitment, the maintenance of the ecological relationships between the harvested, dependent and related populations of Antarctic marine species, the restoration of depleted populations, and the prevention of changes or minimisation of the risk of changes in the marine ecosystem which are not potentially reversible over two or three decades.[112]

[107] David M. Edwards and John A. Heap, 'Convention on the Conservation of Antarctic Marine Living Resources: A Commentary' (1981) 20 *Polar Record* 353 at 359.

[108] Watts, *International Law* at 262. [109] See chapter 8.

[110] See Emilio J. Sahurie, *The International Law of Antarctica* (New Haven, CT, 1992) 527.

[111] Holdgate, 'Regulated Development' at 136.

[112] *Ibid.* at 136–7.

Not only does CCAMLR adopt an ecosystem approach but it also makes the protection of the environment an obligation of the CCAMLR parties. This is provided for in Article V(1) which refers to 'the special obligations and responsibilities of the Antarctic Treaty Consultative Parties for the protection and preservation of the environment of the Antarctic Treaty area'. This statement, in conjunction with the Preamble to the Convention,[113] firmly evidences the importance CCAMLR places upon conservation and protection of the environment.[114] Further emphasis upon the protection of the environment is found in Article IX outlining the functions of the Commission for the Conservation of Antarctic Marine Living Resources. Its primary task is the conservation of Antarctic marine living resources.[115] CCAMLR is then the prime operational example of the importance placed within the ATS on environmental protection. This is not to suggest that it has been a complete success. It has quickly been discovered that the success of an ecosystem approach depends very much on the quality of species and catch data. Without this information it is impossible to make effective resource management recommendations that ensure the continued viability of the resource and the dependent ecosystem.[116] Yet, even despite its problems of implementation, CCAMLR remains a unique instrument which is a model for similar living resource regimes.

Antarctic mineral resource activities

While the 1988 Convention on the Regulation of Antarctic Mineral Resource Activities (CRAMRA) has now been effectively superseded by the adoption of the Protocol, it remains a significant instrument because it demonstrates not only the commitment of the ATCPs to environmental protection but also the implementation of such standards. CRAMRA was an environmentally centred mining Convention. Despite being negotiated on the premise that mineral resource activities were a possibility in Antarctica, its emphasis was more on

[113] See Preamble where it is noted:

> Recognising the prime responsibilities of the Antarctic Treaty Consultative Parties for the protection and preservation of the Antarctic environment and, in particular, their responsibilities under Article IX, paragraph 1(f) of the Antarctic Treaty in respect of the preservation and conservation of living resources in Antarctica ...

[114] See Watts, *International Law* at 263. [115] CCAMLR, Art. II.

[116] J. P. Croxall, I. Everson and D. G. M. Miller, 'Management of the Antarctic Krill Fishery' (1992) 28 *Polar Record* 64 at 65; see also the discussion in chapter 8.

ensuring that mining activities had minimal environmental impact than encouraging mass exploitation of Antarctic mineral resources. Watts has even gone so far as to suggest that CRAMRA contains 'remarkably strong environmental protection provisions, probably stronger than any other provisions of that kind in any other multilateral treaty'.[117] As a result, CRAMRA demands a separate, albeit brief, review.

The Convention recognised the importance associated with the protection of the Antarctic environment in its Preamble. It referred to the 'unique ecological, scientific and wilderness value of Antarctica and the importance of Antarctica to the global environment' and the possibility that mineral resource activities could adversely affect the Antarctic environment. Article 2 of the Convention reaffirmed this approach by noting that a key objective of the Convention was to assess the 'possible impact on the environment of Antarctic mineral resource activities'. The special responsibility of the ATCPs with respect to the Antarctic environment was also reaffirmed in Article 2. The principles upon which all mineral resource activities were to be judged were also environmentally centred. Article 4 stated that such activities would not take place unless it was judged that there would not be certain adverse impacts on the 'Antarctic environment and on dependent and on associated ecosystems'.[118] If mineral resource activities were to take place, then the Antarctic Minerals Resource Commission was obliged to adopt 'Measures for the protection of the Antarctic environment and dependent and associated ecosystems and for the promotion of safe and effective exploration and development techniques'.[119] Provision also existed for exploration and development applications to be rejected, or resource activity management schemes to be modified if certain environmental standards were not met. In addition there was to be constant monitoring of mineral resource activities to ensure adverse environmental impacts were not occurring.[120]

While it is now only possible to speculate as to how CRAMRA may have operated, there is sufficient evidence scattered throughout the

[117] Watts, *International Law* at 264. See also Bush, 'The Antarctic Treaty System' at 146.

[118] CRAMRA, Art. 4(2).

[119] CRAMRA, Art. 21(1)(c).

[120] See S. K. N. Blay, 'New Trends in the Protection of the Antarctic Environment: The 1991 Madrid Protocol' (1992) 86 AJIL 377 at 383; Watts, *International Law* at 268–73.

Convention to suggest that there was a very strong intention to ensure that strict environmental standards were applied to a whole range of mineral resource activities.[121] It is acknowledged that the effectiveness of the environmental protection standards of the Convention would very much have depended on their interpretation by the various institutions created by CRAMRA. To that end, the failure to define more precisely, or to give further guidance on, what 'significant adverse effects' or 'significant changes' in the environment were, represented an omission.[122] Nevertheless, CRAMRA did represent another example of the ATCPs adopting the precautionary approach to an activity which may have occurred in Antarctica and which would have had significant environmental effects.[123] When this is combined with its strict environmental protection standards, CRAMRA was certainly a unique initiative.

Protection of the Arctic environment

The protection of the Arctic environment has primarily been considered an issue falling within the national jurisdiction of individual Arctic states.[124] To that end a large number of unilateral initiatives have been taken. Many of these have been consistent with the ability of a state to administer its own sovereign territory and are hence uncontroversial. Some, however, have impacted upon the rights of other states, raising questions as to their validity under international law. In addition, as noted in chapter 5, the Arctic has been impacted upon by a large number of global conventions dealing with environmental protection. There have, by comparison, been few examples of a regional approach towards protection of the Arctic environment. However, when attempted, such regional approaches have been a success.

121 An example here is that prospecting (which is similar in many respects to some scientific research conducted in Antarctica) could have been halted if there was a concern that it would have a detrimental environmental impact: see CRAMRA Arts. 21(1)(e)(ii), 37, 38; also see Blay, 'New Trends' at 383.

122 Blay, 'New Trends' at 382–3.

123 William Bush, 'The 1988 Wellington Convention: How Much Environmental Protection?' in Joe Verhoeven, Philippe Sands and Maxwell Bruce (eds.), *The Antarctic Environment and International Law* (London, 1992) 69 at 71.

124 For a Canadian perspective, see Robert Page, 'Environmental Protection in the Canadian North' (June 1984) *International Business Lawyer* 253–60. For a review of Soviet initiatives, see Erik Franckx, 'Nature Protection in the Arctic: Recent Soviet Legislation' (1992) 41 ICLQ 366–86.

Unilateral initiatives

The best example of a unilateral initiative to protect the Arctic remains Canada's Arctic Waters Pollution Prevention Act.[125] This initiative was taken in response to the 1969–70 voyage through the Northwest Passage by the United States tanker SS *Manhattan*.[126] The intent of the 1970 Act was to confer broad powers of control over shipping within Canadian Arctic waters. 'Arctic waters' were defined to include waters in either a 'frozen or a liquid state',[127] that were adjacent to the mainland and islands of the Canadian Arctic within an area enclosed by 60°N, 141°W and a line measured 100 miles seaward from the nearest Canadian land.[128] The intent behind this extended jurisdiction was to enforce pollution control regulations on all shipping passing through such Arctic waters. Under the Act, standards could be prescribed for vessel construction, navigation and operation. Failure to comply with the standards would result in passage by such vessels being prohibited.[129] The deposit of 'waste' in Arctic waters was also prohibited. 'Waste' was widely defined so as to include any substance that would degrade or alter the waters to an extent that is detrimental to their use by 'man or by any animal, fish or plant that is useful to man'.[130] In addition to these provisions dealing with pollution control, shipping safety control zones were created within which certain standards for hull and fuel tank construction, navigational aids, manning of ships, pilotage, ice-breaker assistance and maximum quantity of cargo were established.[131] Strict liability standards were also imposed for the deposit of any waste.[132]

[125] Statutes of Canada 1969–70, c. 47. R. Michael M'Gonigle, 'Unilateralism and International Law: The Arctic Waters Pollution Prevention Act' (1976) 34 *University of Toronto Faculty of Law Review* 180 at 181 described the initiative as 'the most significant unilateral action on the international marine environment ever undertaken'.

[126] Donat Pharand, 'Oil Pollution Control in the Canadian Arctic' (1971) 7 TexILJ 45 at 47–8; J. A. Beesley, 'Rights and Responsibilities of Arctic Coastal States: The Canadian View' (1971) 3 JMLC 1–12.

[127] Arctic Waters Pollution Prevention Act, Section 3(2).

[128] Section 3(1). The eastern limits were set as being a line of equidistance in waters between Canadian Arctic islands and Greenland: this was necessary because at that time Canada had not delimited the maritime boundary in Davis Strait with Denmark.

[129] See Donat Pharand, *The Law of the Sea of the Arctic with Special Reference to Canada* (Ottawa, 1973) 224–32; Robert S. Reid, 'The Canadian Claim to Sovereignty over the Waters of the Arctic' (1974) 12 CYIL 111 at 117–29.

[130] Section 2(1). For analysis see Pharand, *The Law of the Sea* at 226–7.

[131] Section 12(1). See Pharand, *The Law of the Sea* at 229–31.

Given that enforcement of pollution standards by coastal states upon foreign-flagged vessels had up till this time only been accepted within internal waters and the territorial sea, asserting such jurisdiction 100 miles offshore was a very extensive claim which exceeded existing conventions and customary international law. In justifying the measures taken, Canada sought to rely upon the growing concern for ecological protection of the Arctic. It argued that as international law had not sufficiently developed measures to protect the area from the dangers of pollution, it was appropriate for Canada to take unilateral action. Prime Minister Trudeau asserted at the time that 'we're saying somebody has to preserve this area for mankind until the international law develops. And we are prepared to help it develop by taking steps on our own.'[133] Similarly the Minister for External Affairs, Mitchell Sharp, referred to the 'gap' which existed in international environmental law and how the Canadian action sought to overcome this deficiency.[134]

The Canadian legislation was considered radical at the time.[135] Not only was it an attempt by a coastal state to extend its jurisdiction beyond the territorial sea, but the basis for this extension was protection of the marine environment.[136] The legislation was directed primarily towards United States-flagged vessels which, following the success of the *Manhattan* voyages, may have been encouraged to use the Northwest Passage and Canadian Arctic waters. The USA reacted unfavourably to Canada's initiatives. Concern was expressed over not only the limitations the Canadian action would have on the freedom

[132] Sections 6 and 7. See Pharand, *The Law of the Sea* at 227–9. See generally M'Gonigle, 'Unilateralism' at 188–9; Cynthia Lamson, 'Arctic Shipping, Marine safety and Environmental Protection' (1987) 11 *Marine Policy* 3 at 7.

[133] P. E. Trudeau, 'Canadian Prime Minister's Remarks on the Proposed Legislation' (1970) 9 ILM 600 at 601.

[134] Canada, House of Commons, Debates, vol. 6 at 5,951 (16 April 1970) where it was stated:

> We are determined to discharge our own responsibility for the protection of our territory. We are equally determined to act as pioneers in pushing back the frontiers of international law so that the laissez-faire regime of the high seas will no longer prevent effective action to deal with a pollution threat of such a magnitude that even the vast seas and oceans of the world may not be able to absorb, dissolve or wash away the discharges deliberately or accidentally poured into them.

[135] For discussion of the response by the United States see Pharand, *The Law of the Sea* at 234–6; Lamson, 'Arctic Shipping' at 7.

[136] See D. M. McRae, 'The Negotiation of Article 234' in Franklyn Griffiths (ed.), *The Politics of the Northwest Passage* (Kingston, Ontario, 1987) 98 at 101 who called the Canadian response 'as radical as it was novel'.

of the high seas but also over the unilateral declaration of maritime jurisdiction.[137] As if to acknowledge that the action taken may not be universally approved, Canada varied its acceptance of the compulsory jurisdiction of the International Court of Justice.[138] This ensured that the new Canadian measures could not be challenged before the Court.[139]

The subsequent efforts by Canada, partly in conjunction with the USA and USSR, at the Third United Nations Conference on the Law of the Sea in arguing for and eventually having accepted Article 234 of UNCLOS proved to be a vindication of the Canadian position concerning protection of Arctic waters.[140] Since that time other Arctic states, especially the USSR,[141] have taken advantage of Article 234 to implement legislation dealing with the protection of the Arctic marine environment. One difficulty with Article 234 is that it does not create a comprehensive list of measures which may be taken to protect the marine environment. Rather, it only refers to such measures dealing with the 'prevention, reduction and control of marine pollution' with the only limitation, apart from geographic, being that navigation

[137] See 'US Statement on Canada's Proposed Legislation' reprinted in (vol. I), Robin Churchill, Myron Nordquist and S. Houston Lay (eds.), *New Directions in the Law of the Sea* (Dobbs Ferry, NY, 1973) 211. On the position of the USSR concerning this action, see W. J. Dehner, 'Creeping Jurisdiction in the Arctic: Has the Soviet Union Joined Canada?' (1972) 13 *Harvard International Law Journal* 271.

[138] 'Canadian Declaration Concerning the Compulsory Jurisdiction of the International Court of Justice', reprinted in (1970) 9 ILM 598 (hereinafter Canadian Declaration); McRae, 'The Negotiation of Article 234' at 101. Previously, Canada had accepted the jurisdiction of the International Court through a continuation of its original acceptance of the jurisdiction of the Permanent Court of International Justice under a procedure allowed by Article 36(5) of the Statute of the International Court of Justice.

[139] Canadian Declaration, note 138 above at 599, lodged under Article 36(2) of the Statute of the International Court of Justice, provided an exception to the acceptance of the Court's jurisdiction in cases concerning:

> disputes arising out of or concerning jurisdiction or rights claimed or exercised by Canada in respect of the conservation, management or exploitation of the living resources of the sea, or in respect of the prevention or control of pollution or contamination of the marine environment in marine areas adjacent to the coast of Canada.

Mitchell Sharp, Canadian Minister for External Affairs, frankly admitted that Canada was 'not prepared to litigate with other states on vital issues concerning which the law is either inadequate, non-existent or irrelevant to the kind of situation Canada faces, as in the case of the Arctic', Canada, House of Commons, Debates, vol. VI at 5,952 (16 April 1970).

[140] See generally McRae, 'The Negotiation of Article 234' at 98–114.

[141] Franckx, 'Nature Protection . . . Recent Soviet Legislation' at 376.

rights must be respected. This uncertainty is illustrated by the ambit of the legislation enacted by the USSR in reliance on Article 234. These initiatives can be traced back to the 1984 Edict on the Economic Zone, which provided in part:

The competent Soviet organs can determine, in a manner established by the USSR legislation, rules for the prevention, reduction and control of pollution of the marine environment... and can enforce these rules ... where pollution of the marine environment could cause major harm to the ecological balance or disturb it irreversibly.[142]

Another edict was also promulgated in 1984, described by Franckx as a 'full-fledged edict' based on Article 234 conferring special rights with respect to ice-covered areas within the EEZ.[143] However, the most significant Soviet initiative was the June 1990 Decree of the Council of Ministers of the USSR.[144] This Decree conferred powers to establish specially protected marine areas, provided for the management and control of marine pollution and dumping from vessels, and dealt with insurance and liability provisions relating to environmental damage. The Decree made particular reference throughout to the protection of ice-covered marine areas. The 1990 Decree substantially clarified the USSR position regarding protection of the Soviet Arctic and indicated that establishing and implementing environmental protection standards had received a high priority.[145]

Another example of unilateral protection of the Arctic environment occurs with the designation of national parks, reserves and other protected areas by individual states.[146] Sites have been protected

[142] Reprinted in Erik Franckx, 'Nature Protection in the Arctic: A New Soviet Legislative Initiative' (1991) 6 IJECL 377 at 377. For further analysis see Erik Franckx, *Maritime Claims in the Arctic* (Dordrecht, 1993) 178–9.

[143] Franckx *Maritime Claims* at 179, Franckx, 'Nature Protection . . . Recent Soviet Legislation' at 376. For a general discussion on this question see Alexei Yu Roginko, 'Environmental Protection in the Soviet Arctic Seas' in Lawson W. Brigham (ed.), *The Soviet Maritime Arctic* (London, 1991) 63 at 74–6.

[144] Reprinted in Franckx 'Nature Protection . . . New Soviet Initiative', at 379–83.

[145] For an analysis see Franckx, 'Nature Protection . . . Recent Soviet Legislation' at 383–6. The Russian position on domestic initiatives to deal with Arctic marine environmental protection is uncertain: see Franckx, *Maritime Claims* at 196–7.

[146] For a discussion of individual state initiatives see Terry Fenge, 'Parks and Protected Areas in the North: Completing the Agenda' (1994) 22(2–3) *Northern Perspectives* 1–2; Jim Baker, 'Protecting an Arctic Refuge: A Summer of Decision for the ANWR' (Summer 1993) *Arctic Circle* 16–21; A. E. Volkov and J. de Korte, 'Protected Nature Areas in the Russian Arctic' (1994) 30 *Polar Record* 299–310; Pekka Salminen, 'Finland's Experiences with its Wilderness Act in an Arctic Regional Context' in *Strategies for Protecting Arctic Wilderness* (Trondheim, 1994) 35–40.

within the Arctic since the beginning of the twentieth century; however, it has only been since 1960 that there has been a substantial increase in both the number of sites and total area subject to protection. In a 1994 survey conducted by the Conservation of Arctic Flora and Fauna Working Group under the AEPS, 280 areas were identified as being subject to protection within the Arctic with a total coverage of 2.079 million km^2.[147] The result of this extensive designation of protected areas within the Arctic is that approximately 14 per cent of Arctic land area is subject to some form of protected status.[148] The protected areas range from very large national parks, such as the Greenland National Park, approximately 70 million hectares in size, to small bird sanctuaries on Svalbard.[149] All of the identified sites are primarily subject to regulation and control by state authorities. However, other areas were identified which have been protected under international agreements or programmes. These include the 1972 Convention Concerning the Protection of the World Cultural and Natural Heritage,[150] the 1971 Convention on Wetlands of International Importance Especially as Waterfowl Habitat,[151] and the UNESCO Biosphere Reserve system.[152] Sites under each of these Conventions and programmes are scattered throughout the Arctic region. One interesting example of cooperation in this area has occurred with Kluane National Park (Canada/Yukon) and Wrangell–St Elias National Park and Preserve (USA/Alaska) which adjoin in southwest Yukon and the northern Alaskan Panhandle area. In 1980 both sites were jointly accepted as World Heritage sites under the Convention Concerning the Protection of the World Cultural and Natural Heritage and the 'Kluane–Wrangell–St Elias World Heritage Site' is now cooperatively managed by both states.[153]

[147] Conservation of Arctic Fauna and Flora, *The State of Protected Areas in the Circumpolar Arctic 1994* (Trondheim, 1994) 36 (hereafter CAFF Report). For an earlier study see Zbigniew Karpowicz and Jeremy Harrison, 'Circumpolar Protected Areas' in J. G. Nelson, Roger Needham and Linda Norton (eds.), *Arctic Heritage* (Ottawa, 1987) 179–214. [148] CAFF Report at 36.

[149] Karpowicz and Harrison, 'Circumpolar Protected Areas' at 181.

[150] Note 4 above.

[151] 996 UNTS 245, as amended in 1983 and 1987. Thirty-seven sites are identified in the CAFF Report at 48.

[152] CAFF Report, at 49 identifies six sites.

[153] Harold Eidsvik, 'Under Joint Responsibility: The Kluane–Wrangell–St Elias World Heritage Site' (1983) 12 (3/4) AMBIO 191–6. It has also been proposed that another international park be created between Alaska and the Yukon in the north slope area, see J. Dunn, 'Entire North Slope Should Be a Park, Conference Told Re. North Yukon National Park', 10 May 1990, *Whitehorse Star* 1.

Global agreements

With respect to global international agreements specifically directed towards the protection of the environment, a great many have some application in the Arctic region.[154] While these agreements have been helpful in combating some Arctic environmental problems, such as long-range transboundary air pollution[155] and more recently the depletion of the ozone layer,[156] none has had a specific Arctic focus. As a result, within the framework of these initiatives it has not been possible to address adequately the unique problems which the Arctic faces in regard to environmental impact from pollution and other activities.[157] Even within UNCLOS, which has substantial provisions dealing with the protection of the marine environment, only one provision specifically deals with ice-covered waters. There are also examples of some extra-regional agreements which touch upon the Arctic region. The 1974 Nordic Convention on the Protection of the Environment[158] and more recently the 1991 Convention on Environmental Impact Assessment in a Transboundary Context[159] which is open to members of the UN Economic Commission for Europe are noteworthy developments. This latter Convention seeks to put in place procedures under which activities that are likely to cause 'significant adverse transboundary impact' will be subjected to an environmental impact process.[160] Parties which may be affected by such polluting activities are required to be notified and consultations must be undertaken between the relevant states on measures to reduce or eliminate the potential transboundary impact.[161] The Convention has the potential to provide new measures which will

[154] See chapter 5.

[155] See 1979 Convention on Long-Range Transboundary Air Pollution, (1979) 18 ILM 1442.

[156] 1985 Vienna Convention for the Protection of the Ozone Layer, (1987) 26 ILM 1529; as amended by the 1987 Montreal Protocol on Substances that Deplete the Ozone Layer, (1987) 26 ILM 1541.

[157] The MARPOL 73/78 regime created by the 1973 International Convention for the Prevention of Pollution from Ships, (1973) 12 ILM 1319, as amended by the 1978 Protocol, (1978) 17 ILM 546 is a good example of this predicament as the Arctic Ocean has not been designated a 'Special Area' within which operating discharges from vessels are completely prohibited.

[158] 1092 UNTS 279

[159] Note 76 above. [160] Espoo Convention, Arts. 3, 5.

[161] As per Espoo Convention, Art. 3 and Annex I a wide range of activities may be caught by this procedure, e.g. oil refineries, power stations, dams and reservoirs, pulp and paper manufacturing, major mining activities.

protect Arctic states from transboundary environmental impact; however, as it is a recent initiative it remains too early to judge its success.[162]

Regional initiatives

Aside from these multilateral treaties which apply globally, there are also some specific agreements negotiated by the Arctic states which have sought to protect parts of the Arctic environment. The 1911 Convention for the Preservation and Protection of Fur Seals is one of the earliest examples of such a multilateral agreement.[163] The Convention sought to prohibit pelagic sealing in the waters of the North Pacific Ocean including the Bering, Kamchatka, Okhotsk and Japan Seas.[164] This was one of the first attempts by states to prohibit resource exploitation in areas beyond national jurisdiction where resources were traditionally considered *res communis* and high seas freedoms applied. While land-based sealing was permitted, the state parties were encouraged to apply limitations on the number of seals taken in order to 'protect and preserve the seal herd or to increase its number'.[165] If seal stocks fell below predetermined levels in certain areas, then apart from an allowance for subsistence sealing by indigenous peoples, commercial sealing activities were to cease.[166] The subsequent 1957 Interim Convention on the Conservation of North Pacific Fur Seals sought to build on the conservation principles of the 1911 Convention.[167] While seeking to ensure maximum sustainable productivity of the seal stocks, emphasis was placed upon scientific research into the seal populations and the impact of sealing upon their viability.[168] In addition, a North Pacific Fur Seal Commission was established to oversee the implementation and operation of the Convention and to ensure that sustainable harvesting of the

[162] See for a discussion of the Espoo Convention, Alexandre C. Kiss and Parvez Hassan, 'General Environmental Concerns' in Peter H. Sand (ed.), *The Effectiveness of International Environmental Agreements* (Cambridge, 1992) 28 at 50–3.

[163] 1911 Convention between Great Britain, Japan, Russia and the United States respecting Measures for the Preservation and Protection of Fur Seals in the North Pacific Ocean, 214 ConTS 80 (hereinafter 1911 Fur Seal Convention). See also the discussion in chapter 8.

[164] 1911 Fur Seal Convention, Art. I; Art. IX defined pelagic sealing to be 'the killing, capturing, or pursuing in any manner whatsoever of fur seals at sea'.

[165] 1911 Fur Seal Convention, Arts. X, XIII.

[166] 1911 Fur Seal Convention, Arts. XI, XII, XIII.

[167] 314 UNTS 105 (hereinafter 1957 Interim Convention).

[168] 1957 Interim Convention, Art. II.

resource took place.[169] The Commission was under a duty to recommend measures to the parties regarding seasonal sealing activities, based on the study of scientific data and which sought to achieve the objectives of the Convention. The fur seal regime which developed around these various conventions throughout much of this century not only had a resource management focus, but as illustrated also sought to implement some important conservation principles.

An early example of an environmentally centred bilateral convention is the 1916 Convention for the Protection of Migratory Birds between Canada and the USA.[170] The purpose of this Convention is to conserve and manage the harvest of ducks, geese and other game birds and to protect migratory non-game birds. The protection of these birds is important because of their migratory patterns across many states. They are also a major element of the Arctic ecosystem during spring and summer. The 1916 Convention has been described as a 'pioneering document'.[171] It prohibits the hunting of non-game and insectivorous birds while establishing a closed season for other types of game birds. While the Convention has been considered a particular success there is currently pressure upon the states to consider amendment in order to allow for a subsistence take of certain birds and also hunting out of season.[172]

The 1973 Agreement on the Conservation of Polar Bears is a modern example of a multilateral environmental protection agreement entered into by the Arctic States.[173] The Agreement has both resource management and environmental protection characteristics. The Agreement primarily prohibits the taking of polar bears except under certain conditions.[174] In addition, the state parties are placed under obligations to protect polar bear habitat. Article II provides that each party:

[169] 1957 Interim Convention, Art. V.

[170] 1916 Convention between Great Britain and the United States for the Protection of Migratory Birds, 221 ConTS 408.

[171] M. W. Wagner and J. G. Thompson, 'The Migratory Birds Convention: Its History and the Need for an Amendment' (1993) 21(2) *Northern Perspectives* 2 at 2.

[172] See *ibid.* at 2–6; Nigel Bankes and Lindsay Staples, *Canadian-US Relations in the Arctic Borderlands* (Ottawa, 1991) 17–19. The Convention is also supported by the 1986 North American Waterfowl Management Plan.

[173] 1973 Agreement on the Conservation of Polar Bears, (1974) 13 ILM 13 (hereinafter Polar Bear Agreement). For a more detailed assessment on the background to the Agreement, see chapter 8.

[174] Polar Bear Agreement, Art. I. For the purposes of the Agreement, 'taking' is defined to include 'hunting, killing and capturing': Art. I(2).

> shall take appropriate action to protect the ecosystem of which polar bears are a part, with special attention to habitat components such as denning and feeding sites and migration patterns, and shall manage polar bear populations in accordance with sound conservation practices based on the best available scientific advice.

This provision has potentially a wide area of application given that polar bears are spread throughout the Arctic and are known to roam across large tracts of country. Some state parties have created protected areas for polar bears;[175] however given the nature of polar bears permanent sanctuaries may be inadequate.[176] While the Agreement thus places an emphasis on individual state action, the effective implementation of measures to protect polar bears requires joint efforts especially between neighbouring states such as Canada and the USA.[177] The Agreement also does not deal with emerging threats to polar bears such as pollution of the Arctic environment, the impact of industrial and tourism development, and climate change.[178]

The Polar Bear Agreement allows for the taking of polar bears in defined circumstances. These include taking polar bears: in the pursuit of scientific and conservation purposes; where it is necessary to prevent serious disturbance of the management of other living resources; and by local people using traditional methods.[179] To ensure that exploitation of these exceptions does not occur, parties remain bound by the principles of Article II and also Article IV, which prohibits the use of aircraft or large motorised vessels for the purpose of taking polar bears. In practice the number of polar bears killed under Article III is low, with Canada recording the highest numbers.[180]

[175] Simon Lyster, *International Wildlife Law* (Cambridge, 1985) 60 who refers to initiatives in Greenland, Canada and Russia.

[176] *Ibid.*

[177] Polar Bear Agreement, Art. IX places an obligation upon the parties to continue to consult with one another in order to give further protection to polar bears.

[178] Pal Prestrud and Ian Stirling, 'The International Polar Bear Agreement and the Current Status of Polar Bear Conservation' (1994) 20(3) *Aquatic Mammals* 113 at 118–20; Ian Stirling and Andrew E. Derocher, 'Possible Impacts of Climate Warming on Polar Bears' (1993) 46 *Arctic* 240–5.

[179] Polar Bear Agreement, Art. III.

[180] Prestrud and Stirling, 'The International Polar Bear Agreement' at 114–16; W. Calvert *et al.*, 'Polar Bear Management in Canada 1988–92' in Oystein Wiig, Erik W. Born and Gerald W. Garner (eds.), *Polar Bears* (Proceedings of the Eleventh Working Meeting of the IUCN/SSC Polar Bear Specialist Group, 25–7 January 1993, Copenhagen, Denmark) (Gland, Switzerland, 1995) 61 at 75 where the most recent data on current total kill of polar bears in Canada was put at between 624 and 666 out of an estimated stock of 12,670.

To support management of polar bear populations, the Agreement also provides for the parties to conduct national research programmes which particularly deal with conservation and management of the species.[181]

Finally, note should be made of the 1987 Canada–USA Agreement on the Conservation of the Porcupine Caribou Herd.[182] The Agreement is solely directed towards the management of those caribou which migrate between the USA and Canada in areas of Alaska, the Yukon and Northwest Territories.[183] Its objective is to conserve the herd and its habitat so as to allow for the continuation of customary and traditional uses of the herd by peoples in both the USA and Canada.[184] To that end, an International Porcupine Caribou Board is established to make recommendations for the management of the herd. The Board particularly seeks input from local communities, users of the herd and scientists in making its recommendations.[185] The commercial sale of porcupine caribou meat is also prohibited.[186]

Initiatives for the comprehensive protection of the polar environment

Protocol on Environmental Protection to the Antarctic Treaty

The Protocol has a vast scope with the potential to impact upon all human activities in Antarctica and in the Southern Ocean.[187] The objective of the Protocol is found in Article 2 which provides that: 'The Parties commit themselves to the comprehensive protection of the Antarctic environment and dependent and associated ecosystems and

181 Polar Bear Agreement, Art. VII.

182 1987 Agreement Between the Government of Canada and the Government of the United States of America on the Conservation of the Porcupine Caribou Herd, [1987] CTS 31 (hereinafter 1987 Caribou Agreement).

183 1987 Caribou Agreement, Art. 1.

184 1987 Caribou Agreement, Art. 2. Art. 2(b) specifies how the user groups in each state are defined.

185 1987 Caribou Agreement, Art. 4.

186 1987 Caribou Agreement, Art. 3(h). For review, see Bankes and Staples, *Canadian–US Relations* at 20–1.

187 It was not intended, however, that the Protocol would impact upon activities regulated under either CCAS or CCAMLR: see Final Act of the Eleventh Antarctic Special Consultative Meeting, reprinted in (1991) 30 ILM 1,460 at 1,460 where it is noted that:

> The Meeting noted that nothing in the Protocol shall derogate from the rights and obligations of parties under the Convention on the Conservation of Antarctic Marine Living Resources, the Convention for the Conservation of Antarctic Seals and the International Convention for the Regulation of Whaling.

hereby designate Antarctica as a natural reserve devoted to peace and science.' This provision, which reflects the heart of the Australian–French proposal for Antarctica to be declared a 'nature reserve-land of science',[188] introduces for the first time the notion that Antarctica is a 'nature reserve'.[189] Little interpretation is given of what this concept means other than in Article 3 which lays down certain environmental principles for the conduct of activities in Antarctica. Watts has suggested that given this phrase has no common international use, it is perhaps best to justify it in political terms.[190] While this is a credible explanation given the political background to the negotiation of the Protocol, the designation of a whole continent as a 'nature reserve' is without precedent.[191] Despite the intent that the Protocol not modify or amend the Antarctic Treaty,[192] the designation of Antarctica as a nature reserve places a greater responsibility upon the Antarctic Treaty parties to maintain, protect and preserve the Antarctic environment.[193] It is arguable whether the Treaty in its original form created such an obligation.

Article 3(1) establishes the principal basis upon which all future activities in Antarctica are to be conducted. It provides that in the planning and conduct of all activities in Antarctica, fundamental consideration shall be given to 'the protection of the Antarctic

[188] Blay, 'New Trends' at 387; Catherine Redgwell, 'Environmental Protection in Antarctica: The 1991 Protocol' (1994) 43 ICLQ 599 at 606.

[189] It is important to distinguish the Australian–French proposal from the Antarctic 'World Park' concept which was favoured by a number of environmental groups in the 1980s. While the Australian–French proposal placed considerable emphasis on protecting the Antarctic environment, it also envisaged that current activities such as scientific research and tourism would continue. For discussion, see Donald R. Rothwell, 'A World Park for Antarctica? Foundations, Developments and the Future' (1990) 3 *ASOLPO Paper*. For an analysis of the relationship between the world park concept and the Protocol see Christopher C. Joyner, 'The 1991 Madrid Environmental Protocol: Rethinking the World Park Status for Antarctica' (1992) 1(3) *Review of European Community and International Environmental Law* 328 at 334–6.

[190] Watts, *International Law* at 277; *cf.* Redgwell, 'Environmental Protection' at 606.

[191] While the 1964 Agreed Measures designated 'the Treaty area as a Special Conservation Area', because this designation was only found in the Preamble of the Agreed Measures, which itself only forms part of a Recommendation, this designation does not have as much import as that found in a provision of the Protocol.

[192] Protocol, Art. 4. See also Blay, 'New Trends' at 388 regarding the Protocol supplementing the Antarctic Treaty and the significance of this.

[193] See Francisco Francioni, 'The Madrid Protocol on the Protection of the Antarctic Environment' (1993) 28 TexILJ 47 at 61 where it is suggested that the designation has 'a legal influence on the terms of the Madrid Protocol and the Annexes which concern limiting the various freedoms of use'.

environment and dependent and associated ecosystems and the intrinsic value of Antarctica, including its wilderness and aesthetic values and its value as an area for the conduct of scientific research'. Importantly, while the Protocol seeks to protect the Antarctic's 'environment and dependent and associated ecosystems' it neither seeks to define what this may mean nor does it have an area of operation extending beyond the Antarctic Treaty area.[194] As a result some uncertainty exists over what exactly the Protocol seeks to protect and whether in protecting dependent or associated ecosystems its provisions extend north of the Antarctic Treaty area to the Antarctic convergence and the zone covered by CCAMLR or even further north.

Article 3(1) is to be implemented by a series of principles laid down in Article 3(2). These are:

> (a) that activities are to be planned and conducted so as to limit adverse impacts on the environment;
> (b) that activities which are undertaken shall be based on prior assessments of their potential impact and of their value for scientific research; and
> (c) that monitoring shall take place of ongoing activities to allow for assessment of their impact and to facilitate early detection of possible unforeseen effects.[195]

The principles in Article 3 are wide-ranging. They have the potential, if strictly implemented, to impact upon all activities undertaken in Antarctica and the Southern Ocean from the simplest biological research project on Antarctic lichen to the construction of new scientific bases. The result is that for the first time a uniform standard for the assessment of all human activity has been created by the Treaty parties which will have the effect of overriding fragmentary Recommendations dealing with this topic and a variety of national standards which had been established.[196]

The means to implement the provisions of Articles 2 and 3 of the Protocol are found in Article 8 which establishes a rigorous Environ-

[194] Protocol, Art. 1.

[195] For comment on how the provisions of Art. 3 mirror similar provisions found in CRAMRA, see Watts, *International Law* at 278; Blay, 'New Trends' at 389; Joyner, 'The 1991 Madrid Environmental Conference' at 331; *cf.* Redgwell, 'Environmental Protection' at 607–8.

[196] Blay, 'New Trends' at 389.

mental Impact Assessment (EIA) procedure.[197] In conjunction with the more detailed operational provisions found in Annex I, the effect of the EIA process is that all proposed activities in Antarctica, whether they be a new activity or the alteration of an existing use, will be identified as having one of three types of environmental impact.[198] Under the terms of Annex I, an activity will only be allowed to proceed automatically if, in accordance with procedures established by each party, the activity will have less than a minor or transitory impact.[199] If the proposed activity potentially has a greater impact, then an initial environmental evaluation and possibly a comprehensive environmental evaluation will have to take place. At each stage of this process the EIA required is more detailed with greater review mechanisms established so that other interested parties may comment.

The operation of the EIA process will be overseen and in some instances administered by the Committee for Environmental Protection established under Article 11 of the Protocol.[200] The Committee, which is open to all parties to the Protocol,[201] has an overall monitoring role in relation to the implementation and operation of the terms of the Protocol. It also has the responsibility to provide advice and formulate Recommendations for consideration at ATCMs in connection with the operation of the Protocol and its Annexes.[202]

In addition to Annex I, the Protocol has three further original Annexes while another was added at ATCM XVI (1991). Annex II deals with the conservation of Antarctic fauna and flora and is in many

[197] The EIA procedures established under the Protocol will build upon procedures which have recently been adopted to deal with environmental monitoring on human impact on the Antarctic environment: see Recommendation XV-5 (1989), *Final Report of the Sixteenth Antarctic Treaty Consultative Meeting* (Bonn, 7–18 October 1991) 17–18, paras. 62–6; *Final Report of the Seventeenth Antarctic Treaty Consultative Meeting* at 29–33, paras. 72–85.

[198] Protocol, Art. 8(1) provides for categorisations on the basis of:
(a) less than a minor or transitory impact;
(b) a minor or transitory impact;
(c) more than a minor or transitory impact.

[199] Protocol, Annex I, Art. 1.

[200] See for discussion Watts, *International Law* at 281–4; Blay, 'New Trends' at 390–2; Redgwell, 'Environmental Protection' at 611–12; Francioni, 'The Madrid Protocol' at 62–6; Sander van Bennekom, 'A New Regime to Protect the Antarctic Environment' (1992) 5 *Leiden Journal of International Law* 33 at 45–6.

[201] Protocol, Art. 11(2). Observer status is open to Contracting Parties to the Antarctic Treaty who are not a party to the Protocol.

[202] For preliminary discussion on the implementation of the Protocol's EIA procedures, see *Final Report of the Seventeenth Antarctic Treaty Consultative Meeting* at 33–4, paras. 86–9.

respects a restatement of the provisions of the 1964 Agreed Measures.[203] Perhaps the most important consequence of Annex II is not only that it will supersede the original Agreed Measures but also that the measures dealing with the protection of fauna and flora now have much greater legal force. This follows from the somewhat uncertain status of Antarctic Treaty Recommendations by which the Agreed Measures were implemented.[204]

Annex III deals with waste disposal and management, a problem which had been given increasing attention by the ATCPs throughout the 1980s.[205] The Annex seeks to establish a comprehensive scheme for the removal of waste from Antarctica,[206] the incineration of waste,[207] disposal of waste on land and at sea,[208] and waste management planning.[209] While these provisions represent an improvement on previous measures, there are anomalies such as the constant use throughout of the term 'maximum extent practicable' as a waste disposal standard.[210]

Annex IV deals with the prevention of marine pollution and seeks to implement standards similar to those which are found in the MARPOL 73/78 Convention.[211] Provisions deal with the discharge of oil,[212] noxious liquid substances,[213] garbage[214] and sewage.[215] The application of this Annex extends to each party to the Protocol, ships that fly their flags, and ships which are engaged in or supporting their Antarctic operations.[216] However, Article 11 of this Annex allows for a significant exception: its provisions do not apply to warships and other ships 'owned or operated by a State and used, for the time being,

[203] Blay, 'New Trends' at 392; van Bennekom, 'A New Regime' at 44–5; Redgwell, 'Environmental Protection' at 622.

[204] Watts, *International Law* at 285.

[205] See for a discussion of some of the problems concerning Antarctic waste management, James N. Barnes, Peter J. Lipperman and Kelly Rigg, 'Waste Management in Antarctica' in Rudiger Wolfrum (ed.), *Antarctic Challenge III* (1988) 491–529.

[206] Protocol, Art. 2. [207] Protocol, Annex III, Art. 3.

[208] Protocol, Annex III, Arts. 4, 5. [209] Protocol, Annex III, Art. 8.

[210] See as an example Protocol, Annex III, Art. 4(2), which provide: 'Sewage, domestic liquid wastes and other liquid wastes . . . shall, to the maximum extent practicable, not be disposed of . . .' For comment, see Blay, 'New Trends' at 392–4; Joyner, 'The 1991 Madrid Environmental Protocol' at 333.

[211] See the discussion in chapter 7. Also see Christopher C. Joyner, *Antarctica and the Law of the Sea* (Dordrecht, 1992) 174.

[212] Protocol, Annex IV, Art. 3. [213] Protocol, Annex IV, Art. 4.

[214] Protocol, Annex IV, Art. 5. [215] Protocol, Annex IV, Art. 6.

[216] Protocol, Annex IV, Art. 2.

only on government non-commercial service'. As a result, a great many vessels which visit Antarctic waters on behalf of national expeditions in order to resupply scientific bases or to conduct scientific research in the Southern Ocean are exempt from these provisions.[217] The Annex also includes a provision dealing with the need to ensure that vessels are fitted with adequate waste-retention capacity and that ports are equipped with reception facilities for such vessels.[218] Article 12 of this Annex also deals with the need to develop more comprehensive emergency preparedness and response procedures for marine pollution incidents. This is especially important after the grounding of the *Bahia Paraiso* in 1989.[219]

The final Annex to the Protocol, Annex V, was added at ATCM XVI (1991) shortly after the Protocol was concluded.[220] This Annex deals with the Antarctic Protected Area system and seeks to reorganise the previously existing system of area management under a single Annex. Two types of special areas are provided for: Antarctic Specially Protected Areas and Antarctic Specially Managed Areas. Antarctic Specially Protected Areas can be designated in order to protect any area, including a marine area, which has 'outstanding environmental, scientific, historic, aesthetic or wilderness values'.[221] Areas which meet certain criteria are eligible for designation under this category, in addition to those areas that were previously designated as either

[217] Blay, 'New Trends' at 394 comments that: 'This exclusion significantly undermines the annex.' See also Joyner, 'The 1991 Madrid Environmental Protocol' at 334; Redgwell, 'Environmental Protection' at 217.

[218] Protocol, Annex IV, Art. 9.

[219] The *Bahia Paraiso* was an Argentine supply vessel which in January 1989 grounded and eventually sank in waters near Palmer Station (USA) on the Antarctic Peninsula. Eighty-one tourists were on board the vessel at the time. A United States rescue operation was mounted from the base in conjunction with Argentine authorities and other vessels in the area. While no lives were lost, the environmental damage to the coastline and marine life in the area was extensive. See Marcia Barinaga and David Lindley, 'Wrecked Ship Causes Damage to Antarctic Ecosystem' (1989) 337 (6207: 9 February) *Nature* 495; 'Argentine Ship Sinks Near Palmer Station' (1989) 24 (2) *Antarctic Journal of the United States* 3–7; Polly A. Penhale, 'Research Team Focuses on Environmental Impact of Oil Spill' (1989) 24(2) *Antarctic Journal of the United States* 9–12.

[220] Protocol, Art. 9 provided that additional Annexes could be adopted under the procedure provided for under Art. IX of the Antarctic Treaty. As a result, additional Annexes can be adopted through the Recommendation process at ATCMs.

[221] Protocol, Annex V, Art. 3. For a discussion of the protected area system created by Annex V see Colin M. Harris, 'Standardisation of Zones Within Specially Protected and Managed Areas under the Antarctic Environmental Protocol' (1994) 30 *Polar Record* 283–6.

Specially Protected Areas or Sites of Special Scientific Interest.[222] Entry into these areas is by permit only.[223] Antarctic Specially Managed Areas are areas of the continent, including marine areas, where permissible activities have and are being conducted. Such areas will probably have been subject to heavy use resulting from interest in their scientific research potential or as a tourism destination. In order 'to assist in the planning and co-ordination of activities, avoid possible conflicts, improve co-operation between Parties or minimise environmental impacts'[224] these sites can be designated as Specially Managed Areas. Entry into these sites is restricted to persons holding a permit.[225] Before any site can be designated under either of these categories it is necessary for a Management Plan for the area to be submitted to an ATCM for approval. Management Plans are to include not only full details on the area, but also a clear description of the conditions under which permits for entry may be issued and codes of conduct for the use of the area.[226] The Committee on Environmental Protection will play a significant role in assessing areas that have been put forward for designation under this Annex and also review the adequacy of Management Plans.[227] Despite the Protocol not yet having entered into force, a number of ATCPs have already begun to revise their Management Plans for Antarctic protected areas and comply with the terms of Annex V.[228]

The Protocol has been described as being the 'most pervasive and far-reaching legislative step that has ever been taken within the Antarctic Treaty system'.[229] Given that previous instruments adopted by the ATS have taken a sectoral approach towards environmental protection this description is warranted. However, it cannot be said that the Protocol represents the very best efforts of the ATCPs to protect the Antarctic environment. Some commentators have been

[222] Protocol, Annex V, Art. 3(2), 3(3).
[223] Protocol, Annex V, Art. 3(4).
[224] Protocol, Annex V, Art. 4(1).
[225] Protocol, Annex V, Art. 4(3).
[226] Protocol, Annex V, Art. 5(3). The development of Antarctic management plans had been a matter of some debate throughout the 1980s: see P. L. Keage, P. R. Hay and J. A. Russell, 'Improving Antarctic Management Plans' (1989) 25 *Polar Record* 309–14.
[227] Protocol, Annex V, Art. 6. For discussion of the relationship between Annex V and the previous Protected Area System see Lewis Smith *et al.*, *Developing the Antarctic Protected Area System*.
[228] Harris, 'Standardisation' at 283.
[229] John A. Heap, 'Environmental Issues and Future Prospects of the Antarctic Regime' in Dalchong Kim *et al.* (eds.), *Maritime Issues in the 1990s* (Seoul, 1992) 43 at 52.

critical of it.[230] There are a number of gaps in its provisions,[231] no doubt partly a consequence of the political compromises made during its speedy negotiation.[232] Nevertheless, from an international environmental law perspective, it reflects existing standards and principles plus those which had already applied in Antarctica, but in addition introduces new elements.[233] The most significant of these is the EIA procedure. While this is a major advance for the ATS there will no doubt be difficulties in implementing the process, given the potentially varying standards which each state may apply, and the absence in some instances of details in the Protocol as to how its standards are to be implemented.[234] In addition, implementation of the Protocol will eventually depend on domestic legal initiatives by the ATCPs and this process can also result in widely varying responses.[235] Certain states will also find it difficult to prepare Comprehensive Environmental Evaluations under Annex I because of their lack of experience in dealing with the Antarctic environment.[236] As a result of the economic burden which the EIA process will impose on certain states there is also the potential for literal compliance to suffer.[237] Nevertheless, despite these potential difficulties the Protocol is a significant advance on the previous standards which applied in Antarctica. It seeks to impact not only upon existing 'traditional' uses of the

[230] See Redgwell, 'Environmental Protection' at 633–4; Jorn-Axel Kammerer, 'The Protocol on Environmental Protection to the Antarctic Treaty' (1992) 45 *Law & State* 68–80; Elaine F. Foreman, 'Protecting the Antarctic Environment: Will a Protocol be Enough?' (1992) 7 *American University Journal of International Law and Policy* 843–79.

[231] For this author's comments, see Donald R. Rothwell, 'Environmental Regulation of the Southern Ocean' in James Crawford and Donald R. Rothwell (eds.), *The Law of the Sea in the Asian Pacific Region* (Dordrecht, 1995) 93–118.

[232] See generally, Francioni, 'The Madrid Protocol' at 48–55.

[233] *Ibid.* at 59.

[234] For a specific analysis of how the Protocol's EIA process may be implemented see David Lyons, 'Environmental Impact Assessment in Antarctica under the Protocol on Environmental Protection' (1993) 29 *Polar Record* 111–20. For a general review of the difficulties associated with implementing an EIA process in Antarctica and the polar regions see W. Nigel Bonner, 'Environmental Assessment in the Antarctic' (1989) 18 (1) AMBIO 83–9; Michael A. Champ *et al.*, 'The Roles of Monitoring and Research in Polar Environments: A Perspective' (1992) 25 *Marine Pollution Bulletin* 220–6.

[235] For a discussion of some of the political issues confronting the USA in implementing the Protocol see Robert M. Anderson, 'Leading International Efforts to Improve Environmental Controls in Antarctica While Navigating National Politics' (1994) 6 *Georgetown International Environmental Law Review* 303–51.

[236] This may also have the consequence of disadvantaging states which are seeking to conduct scientific research in Antarctica for the first time as a means eventually to gain ATCP status: see Heap, 'Environmental Issues' at 53.

[237] Watts, *International Law* at 284.

continent, such as scientific research and the building of scientific research stations, but also upon new or emerging activities such as tourism.

Arctic Environmental Protection Strategy

The most comprehensive attempt to implement an Arctic-wide regime dealing with the protection of the Arctic environment has been the 1991 Arctic Environmental Protection Strategy (AEPS).[238] The AEPS, which has all eight Arctic states as parties, is an ambitious document which seeks to identify existing Arctic environmental problems, how they should be dealt with and how emerging problems should be jointly controlled. Negotiated over a two-year period between 1989 and 1991, it is still in the process of being implemented. However, initial indications are that all eight parties are seriously committed to its implementation and, where appropriate, extension so as to deal with emerging issues.[239]

The AEPS recognises: the importance of the Arctic environment to the peoples of the region, especially indigenous inhabitants; that the environment has global importance and influence, but is also influenced by factors from outside the region; and that there exists a need to provide greater protection for Arctic ecosystems.[240] The principal objectives include: protecting the Arctic ecosystem; enhancing and restoring environmental quality; recognising and accommodating the traditional interests of indigenous peoples; identifying and eliminating pollution; and monitoring the state of the Arctic environment.[241]

Six major Arctic environmental problems were identified in the AEPS as being in need of immediate response action: persistent organic contaminants, oil pollution, heavy metals, noise, radioactivity and acidification. The problems associated with each of these are detailed in the AEPS along with global and regional legal regimes which exist for each.[242] Through this process several gaps in the existing regulatory regimes were identified as requiring a response,

[238] Reprinted in (1991) 30 ILM 1,624. See also the discussion in chapter 6.

[239] See 'Nuuk Declaration on Environment and Development in the Arctic', reprinted in *Report of the Second Ministerial Conference* (1993, 16 September, Nuuk, Greenland).

[240] Introduction, AEPS, where it is stated:

> The Arctic countries are committed to international cooperation to ensure the protection of the Arctic environment and its sustainable and equitable development, while protecting the cultures of indigenous peoples.

[241] AEPS, Section 2.1. These objectives are also supported by a series of principles: see AEPS, Section 2.2.

[242] AEPS, Sections 3, 4.

and these actions are detailed as part of an 'action plan' which the eight Arctic countries agree to proceed with cooperatively.[243] All six identified environmental problems have specific response actions detailed for them. Generally these actions include additional monitoring of pollutants, the strict implementation of existing international agreements, domestic action to reduce emission of pollutants, the taking of joint action in relevant international fora so as to assist in the adoption of agreements which further protect the Arctic environment, and action designed to increase knowledge of the environmental impacts of the identified pollutants.[244] This process is assisted by the 'Arctic Monitoring and Assessment Program' (AMAP) which is designed to encourage further the monitoring of Arctic environmental problems by facilitating and coordinating further research.[245] The primary objective is 'the measurement of the levels of anthropogenic pollutants and the assessment of their effects in relevant component parts of the Arctic environment' with initial focus being given to persistent organic contaminants and selected heavy metals and radionuclides.[246] Initially, AMAP has a brief of working with already existing national and international programmes dealing with these problems; however, there remains scope at the periodic review meetings of the AEPS for new programmes under AMAP to be approved.[247] In addition to AMAP, other programmes have been established under the AEPS,[248] the most active of which has been the Conservation of Arctic Flora and Fauna (CAFF) Working Group. In 1994, CAFF released 'The State of Protected Areas in the Circumpolar Arctic' report.[249] This represents the most extensive inventory to date of protected areas within the Arctic and provides the foundation for more extensive analysis of both individual state responses and collective regional responses to Arctic environmental protection.[250]

While the AEPS represents a significant step forward for the Arctic states not only with respect to Arctic-wide multilateral cooperation

[243] AEPS, Section 5. [244] See generally AEPS, Sections 5.1–5.6.

[245] AEPS, Section 6. [246] AEPS, Section 6.

[247] AEPS, Section 10. See also *Report of the Second Ministerial Conference*, note 239 above at 7–11 in which recommendations were made regarding the taking of urgent measures concerning contaminants, according acidification priority pollutant status, and the taking of new measures to deal with radioactive pollution.

[248] For more details see the discussion in chapter 6.

[249] Note 147 above.

[250] For an analysis of the work of CAFF, see Jan-Peter Huberth Hansen, 'The State of Habitat Protection in the Arctic' in *Strategies for Protecting Arctic Wilderness* (Trondheim, 1994) 13–20.

but also for environmental protection, it has received mixed reviews. Some commentators believe that because it does not impose any legally binding obligations it is only a basis for the development of future legal obligations dealing with Arctic environmental protection.[251] Stokke has been particularly critical of the outcome of the Rovaniemi negotiating process, calling the AEPS 'a shallow and quite unambitious regime'.[252] He sees the AEPS as basically doing nothing more than establishing a regime to deal with environmental monitoring, something which the Arctic states had already implemented on either a bilateral or individual state basis. The failure to implement a more rigorous institutional structure and regulative elements is also seen as a failing.[253]

Despite this criticism, the AEPS does represent a first step in a process which may lead to more intensive cooperation on protection of the Arctic environment and it certainly leaves open the prospect of legal measures being agreed upon at some time in the future.[254] In the meantime, the AEPS will greatly assist in adopting mechanisms for the protection of the Arctic environment where previously none existed or were being implemented on a state-by-state basis with little regional coordination. The preparatory work leading up to the conclusion of the Strategy was pivotal in the identification of six pressing environmental problems. As a result, there is now a much greater regional awareness about these problems. The AEPS emphasises the need for greater cooperation to combat these common problems, especially with respect to research and the sharing of information. While little emphasis is placed on the development of legal means at the international level to deal with these problems, all states are placed under obligations to adopt stricter domestic standards in conformity with existing international standards. From this perspective the AEPS seeks to work within existing international fora and mechanisms for the protection of the Arctic environment. If this proves to be difficult, the way is now open for specific Arctic environmental protection mechanisms to be implemented.

[251] Alexei Yu Roginko and Matthew J. LaMourie, 'Emerging Marine Environmental Protection Strategies for the Arctic' (1992) 16 *Marine Policy* 259 at 267.

[252] See Olav Schram Stokke, 'Arctic Environmental Cooperation after Rovaniemi' in Lise Lyck (ed.), *Nordic Arctic Research on Contemporary Arctic Problems* (Copenhagen, 1992) 221 at 225.

[253] *Ibid.* at 225–6; see also Olav Schram Stokke, 'Western Environmental Interests in the Arctic' (1991–92) 21 *Centre Piece* 1 at 16–25.

[254] Franckx, *Maritime Claims* at 247.

Despite the implementation of the AEPS and its initial successes, there remain a series of continuing challenges for the Arctic states in dealing with environmental problems. To date the concept of sustainable development has not been given detailed consideration. There is currently an AEPS Task Force addressing this issue and it will no doubt be confronted by many of the same problems which face the implementation of sustainable development principles in other parts of the world. In the Arctic, however, the challenge will be greater because of the need to engage in environmental clean-up at the same time as implementing sustainability.[255] There are also the interests of the Arctic's indigenous peoples to consider.[256] Much work therefore remains to be done by the Arctic states in dealing with their existing and developing environmental problems.

Liability for environmental damage

While international law has steadily developed throughout the twentieth century, and recently there has been a greater emphasis on legal measures concerning environmental protection, principles concerning liability for environmental damage have lagged behind. There are many areas in international environmental law where inadequate liability regimes exist with the result that too often it is difficult to make the 'polluter pay'.[257] One of the special problems in this area is applying principles of liability to areas beyond national jurisdiction. If environmental damage occurs in areas under national jurisdiction then normal domestic standards will be applied as a result of that damage. Another possibility, as demonstrated in the *Trail Smelter* case, is that international environmental law may have developed standards of liability for states. However, this is not necessarily the case where environmental damage occurs in areas beyond national jurisdiction such as the high seas. Antarctica presents a good example of this problem. Because of the constraints imposed by Articles IV and VIII of the Antarctic Treaty, many territorial claimants have failed to develop comprehensive measures to protect the environment of their

[255] Terry Fenge, 'Environmental Clean-up and Sustainable Development in the Circumpolar Arctic' (1993–1994) 21(4) *Northern Perspectives* 1–3.

[256] Chester Reimer, 'Moving Towards Co-operation: Inuit Circumpolar Policies and the Arctic Environmental Protection Strategy' (1993–1994) 21 (4) *Northern Perspectives* 22–6.

[257] See Birnie and Boyle, *International Law* at 264 and more generally 264–73. In regard to liability by private actors for transnational environmental damage, see Gunther Handl, 'State Liability for Accidental Transnational Environmental Damage by Private Persons' (1980) 74 AJIL 525–65.

claimed areas. In conjunction with the general non-recognition of the territorial claims, there is little scope for claimant states to bring an action claiming liability for Antarctic environmental damage.[258] This dilemma is well demonstrated by the *Bahia Paraiso* incident. In 1989 the *Bahia Paraiso*, an Argentine vessel, grounded off the Antarctic coastline and caused extensive environmental damage to the coastline and marine environment.[259] As noted by Charney, this incident exposed the dilemmas facing Antarctica:

> With the grounding of the *Bahia Paraiso*, no State territory or property, or that of its nationals, has suffered a particular injury; the continent of Antarctica is considered by most states to be outside of the sovereignty of any State. If no State or a national of a State has suffered a particular injury as a result of the spill, may no State possess standing to seek a remedy? If the injury requirement is a firm one, from which no derogation is permitted, the injury to Antarctica might go unremedied.[260]

These questions have recently been addressed in both CRAMRA and the Protocol. They go some way to indicating how more effective standards of liability for environmental damage may be implemented and also where international environmental law may be heading.

CRAMRA and strict liability

It is generally accepted by many commentators that one of the most attractive features of CRAMRA was its attempt to deal with liability for environmental damage to Antarctica as a result of mineral resource activities.[261] Many commentators believe that it may be relied upon as

[258] See Martijn Wilder, *Liability on Ice* (Canberra, 1993) 4–13, noting at 13 that:

> At present there exist limited avenues for the resolution of liability disputes other than party negotiation as provided for under Article XI of the Antarctic Treaty and Article 18 of the Protocol, or through the broad obligations imposed by international law. As to the liability of non-ATP States and private operators, recourse for pursuing liability is extremely limited.

See also Arthur D. Watts, 'Liability for Activities in Antarctica – Who Pays the Bill to Whom?' in Rudiger Wolfrum (ed.), *Antarctic Challenge II* (Berlin, 1986) 147–61.

[259] See note 219 above.

[260] Jonathan I. Charney, 'Third State Remedies for Environmental Damage to the World's Common Spaces' in Francesco Francioni and Tullio Scovazzi (eds.), *International Responsibility for Environmental Harm* (London, 1991) 149 at 150.

[261] For reviews see Henry C. Burmester, 'Liability for Damage from Antarctic Mineral Resource Activities' (1989) 29 VaJIL 621–60; Rudiger Wolfrum, *The Convention on the Regulation of Antarctic Mineral Resource Activities* (Berlin, 1991) 62–9; Watts, *International Law* at 196–203.

a model in international environmental law.[262] Article 8 provided for liability in a number of circumstances. Strict liability was imposed upon a mineral resource operator in circumstances where damage occurred 'to the Antarctic environment or dependent or associated ecosystems arising from its Antarctic mineral resource activities'.[263] This immediately raises the question of what constitutes 'damage' to the environment. CRAMRA defined damage as 'any impact on the living or non-living components of that environment or those ecosystems, including harm to atmospheric, marine or terrestrial life, beyond that which is negligible or which has been assessed and judged to be acceptable pursuant to this Convention'.[264] As such, liability could extend not only to the immediate Antarctic environment but also to associated ecosystems, an especially important feature given the extent of the Antarctic marine ecosystem north of 60° S. However, because CRAMRA was a Convention based on regulated mining it was inevitable that some form of 'damage' to the environment would occur once a mining activity commenced. As a result, the Convention recognised that once a minerals activity had been sanctioned, sufficient account had already been taken of the consequential environmental impacts of that activity. It would therefore have been acceptable if dust from a mining operation settled upon a lichen colony because this presumably would have been anticipated when the mining permit had been applied for and granted. Damage to the same lichen colony as a result of the escape of fuel would not, however, have been accepted and strict liability would have been imposed for such damage.[265] Compared to other provisions dealing with liability in international environmental law, CRAMRA's concept of 'damage' was much wider.[266] Beyond this provision, strict liability also existed in case of loss or impairment to an established use,[267] loss of or damage to property of a third party or the loss of life or personal injury of a third party,[268] and the reimbursement of costs as a result of any response action taken as a consequence of the damage.[269] In instances where the damage occurred as a result of an omission on the part of a sponsoring state, then that state would also have been liable under the terms of

[262] See van Bennekom, 'A New Regime' at 48–9; C. W. Pinto, 'A Proposal' in Joe Verhoeven, Philippe Sands and Maxwell Bruce (eds.), *The Antarctic Environment and International Law* (London, 1992) 165 at 167.

[263] CRAMRA, Art. 8(2)(a). [264] CRAMRA, Art. 1(15).

[265] See other examples and the discussion in Burmester, 'Liability for Damage' at 637–40. [266] *Ibid.* at 634.

[267] CRAMRA, Art. 8(2)(b). [268] CRAMRA, Art. 8(2)(c). [269] CRAMRA, Art. 8(2)(d).

international law to the extent that the liability was not satisfied by the operator.[270]

The notion of strict liability was not defined in CRAMRA, but it is generally understood as having required fault to be established on the part of the operator.[271] Despite the imposition of this rigorous standard, certain exceptions were recognised. An exception existed in the case where the damage resulted from a natural disaster 'of an exceptional character which could not reasonably have been foreseen',[272] or in the case of armed conflict or acts of terrorism.[273] In the case of loss of life, personal injury, or the loss of or damage to property other than that provided for under Article 8, an operator was open to being held liable under any other applicable laws.[274] There was also provision made for where the damage had been contributed to by the party claiming the loss.[275] Importantly, despite the far-reaching terms of Article 8 of CRAMRA, it was acknowledged at the time of its negotiation that a need would exist for further provisions to be implemented dealing with liability. As such, Article 8(7) made provision for the negotiation of a Protocol which would further develop the Convention's liability provisions.[276] Until such time as this envisaged Protocol had entered into force, no applications for an exploration or development permit could be made.[277] Finally, to ensure the smooth implementation of these liability standards, CRAMRA also provided that each party was to ensure that recourse was available in its national courts for adjudicating liability claims pursuant to the terms of Article 8.[278]

Burmester has argued that CRAMRA's liability provisions demonstrate 'the particular circumstances of the Antarctic where the environment is acknowledged to be of prime importance, as opposed

[270] CRAMRA, Art. 8(3)(a).

[271] Watts, *International Law* at 196.

[272] CRAMRA, Art. 8(4)(a).

[273] CRAMRA, Art. 8(4)(b). See Burmester, 'Liability for Damage' at 642–4.

[274] CRAMRA, Art. 8(5).

[275] CRAMRA, Art. 8(6).

[276] For discussion see Rudiger Wolfrum, 'The Unfinished Task: CRAMRA and the Question of Liability' in Arnfinn Jorgensen-Dahl and Willy Ostreng (eds.), *The Antarctic Treaty System in World Politics* (London, 1991) 120–32. A meeting was held in 1990 to consider the negotiation of this Protocol; however, as this took place at the first Vina del Mar meeting of Special ATCM XI which eventually negotiated the 1991 Madrid Protocol, little progress was made: see 'Report to the XVIth Antarctic Treaty Consultative Meeting on the Meeting held Pursuant to Recommendation XV-2', reprinted in *Final Report of the Sixteenth Antarctic Treaty Consultative Meeting* at 256.

[277] CRAMRA, Art. 8(9).

[278] CRAMRA, Art. 8(10). See Burmester, 'Liability for Damage' at 645–7.

to the usual homocentric view of the world manifested in other conventions'.[279] This is because CRAMRA's liability provisions are triggered by damage to the environment, not damage to individuals or their personal property. From this perspective, CRAMRA's liability provisions are further evidence of the precautionary principle at work. As Wolfrum has noted, these provisions 'are based upon the belief that the Antarctic environment is best served if the necessary precautionary measures are taken or – when these have failed – the restoration of the Antarctic environment to the *status quo ante* is pursued'.[280]

The liability provisions of the Protocol

The rejection of the CRAMRA mining regime between 1989–91 and subsequent adoption of the Protocol has meant that CRAMRA's strict liability provisions will now not enter into force.[281] While the ATCPs had the opportunity to adopt CRAMRA's strict liability provisions in the Protocol, this was not the approach taken. This was partly a consequence of the belief that there was no longer the need for such a strict liability regime once the potentially devastating effects of minerals activities had been removed. There was also a concern that as the Protocol impacted upon so many activities in Antarctica the adoption of such a liability regime could impose very substantial burdens upon states. The result was that Article 16 of the Protocol merely accepts that there is the need to develop appropriate rules dealing with liability for environmental damage and that such rules should eventually be adopted by way of an Annex to the Protocol.[282] The commitment of the ATCPs to develop this Annex was confirmed in the Final Act of Special ATCM XI which negotiated the Protocol.[283]

Since that time there has been some progress towards the development of a Protocol liability regime; however, it is uncertain when such

[279] Burmester, 'Liability for Damage' at 635.

[280] Wolfrum, *The Convention* at 63.

[281] See generally Wilder, *Liability on Ice* at 14–22.

[282] Protocol, Art. 16 provides:

> Consistent with the objectives of this Protocol for the comprehensive protection of the Antarctic environment and dependent and associated ecosystems, the Parties undertake to elaborate rules and procedures relating to liability for damage arising from activities taking place in the Antarctic Treaty area and covered by this Protocol. These rules and procedures shall be included in one or more Annexes to be adopted in accordance with Article 9(2).

[283] Final Act of the Eleventh Antarctic Treaty Special Consultative Meeting, reprinted in (1991) 30 ILM 1,460–1.

a regime will be finalised. The issue has been discussed at ATCMs since 1991 and a meeting of legal experts has been convened to provide detailed advice on the elaboration of rules and procedures relating to liability.[284] The first meeting of legal experts took place in November 1993 with Germany acting as host.[285] A 'Draft Annex on Liability' has been prepared as an outcome from these meetings.[286] Notwithstanding the final form of the Protocol 'Liability Annex', it will differ from that developed for CRAMRA. This is because the nature of the activities for which states will be prepared to accept liability under the Protocol will be much different than those under CRAMRA.[287] As van Bennekom has noted, the harsh Antarctic environment will inevitably result in accidents and environmental damage without the intervention of human fault or negligence.[288] Nevertheless, there are enough examples of numerous items of equipment left over from scientific expeditions and research stations causing significant environmental impact to suggest that a strong liability regime under the Protocol would act as a further incentive for the ATCPs and other parties active in Antarctica to keep the continent clean.

Regional management of environmental issues

Antarctic Treaty System

The Antarctic Treaty was not designed as an instrument to protect the environment. A reading of the Treaty quickly confirms this. The only specific reference in the Treaty to the environment is in Article IX(1)

[284] See *Final Report of the Seventeenth Antarctic Treaty Consultative Meeting* at 20–1, paras. 37–40, where the Meeting noted at para. 38 '. . . that work on the elaboration of such rules and procedures could begin at an early stage and acknowledged the importance of developing a liability regime as being significant for the comprehensive protection of the Antarctic environment and its dependent and associated ecosystems'.

[285] See 'Liability Annex to the Protocol on Environmental Protection to the Antarctic Treaty' (submitted by Germany) XVIII ATCM/WP 2 (10 April 1994), 8 where it was noted by Professor Rudiger Wolfrum, Chair of the Meeting of Legal Experts: 'In trying to draft such a new Annex several features will have to be taken into account. One of the most important ones . . . is that this new Annex has to be fully integrated into the existing Antarctic Treaty regime including the Protocol and its Annexes. It is essential that all aspects of the existing Antarctic Treaty regime are fully taken into account and that we do not try to reduplicate what has already been regulated in the Antarctic Treaty, in CCAMLR or in the Protocol.'

[286] See *Final Report of the Nineteenth Antarctic Treaty Consultative Meeting* (Seoul, 8–19 May 1995) 12–13, paras. 48–50.

[287] Van Bennekom, 'A New Regime' at 48–50.

[288] Van Bennekom, *ibid.* at 49.

where in referring to matters that may be considered at Consultative Meetings, mention is made of 'preservation and conservation of living resources'. No reference is made to preserving Antarctica's unique marine and terrestrial environment. Rather the emphasis throughout the Treaty is on the setting aside of sovereignty questions, the demilitarisation of the continent, and ensuring that peaceful scientific research can continue. However, one distinguished commentator has noted that while the Treaty does not expressly state that it seeks to protect the overall Antarctic environment, its fundamental provisions are important if that goal is to be met. Heap argues that it is self-evident that: 'At the most basic level of agreement, there can be no protection of the Antarctic environment unless the peace of Antarctica is maintained.'[289] From this perspective then, the Antarctic Treaty has proved an effective instrument for the protection of the Antarctic environment.

Apart from the basic provisions in the Antarctic Treaty, the ATS has also developed a sophisticated range of mechanisms to regulate the Antarctic environment. Heap and Holdgate have identified two distinct approaches adopted by the ATS towards environmental questions. The first is an attempt to define principles that should govern the protection of the environment from the impact of present or future activities. The second is to identify and guard against particular activities which could have a deleterious effect on the environment. They note that: 'The first approach is general and essentially non-specific; the second is activity specific. Both are precautionary in their approach.'[290] Both of these approaches have been justifiable because in a sense the ATS had to deal with pre-existing activities in Antarctica, such as scientific research and scientific bases, and also contemplated activities such as mining. In both instances it has been successful. First, because an incremental approach has been adopted towards imposing stricter environmental protection standards. The best example here is with respect to the siting and building of new scientific bases. Originally this activity went largely unregulated, but it has gradually become more regulated until now under the terms of the Protocol a very detailed EIA process will have to be undertaken before such a building project can commence. Second, a stricter approach was called for as occurred with CCAS, CCAMLR and CRAMRA. Mechanisms were developed in these instruments to regulate activ-

[289] Heap, 'Environmental Issues' at 44.

[290] Heap and Holdgate, 'The Antarctic Treaty System' at 200–1.

ities that had the potential to cause substantial environmental impact prior to the activity having such an impact.

The success of the ATS in adopting a variety of measures for the protection of the Antarctic environment demonstrates the advantages of a regional approach towards international environmental protection. While some could argue that this has been forced upon the ATCPs because of unresolved sovereignty issues, there remains nothing to stop individual claimants and other states from adopting their own conservation policies for Antarctica consistently with the terms of the Treaty. Some states have in fact adopted this course of action. The United States has for some time sought to control the environmental impact of its activities and of its nationals in Antarctica,[291] while Australia is completing a 'Conservation Strategy' for the Australian Antarctic Territory which aims not only to give effect to the Protocol but also implement additional environmental protection measures.[292] Despite this scope for both claimant states and others which have a presence on the continent to implement their own 'domestic' environmental protection laws,[293] the ATCPs have preferred to implement regional environmental protection mechanisms through the ATS. The Antarctic Treaty assisted in this process by forcing states to cooperate and placing limitations on their own exercise of sovereignty. From that perspective the Treaty has acted as a catalyst for environmental protection.[294] The need for consensus amongst the ATCPs to develop mechanisms for resource development (as demonstrated with the abandonment of CRAMRA) has also assisted in the environmental protection process. In effect, the institutional and procedural structure of the ATS has assisted in the development of increasingly more

[291] Generally see Anderson, 'Leading International Efforts'; with respect to the application of the United States' National Environmental Policy Act, 1969 see the decision in *Environmental Defense Fund, Inc v. Massey* (1993) 986 F.2d 528 and discussion in David A. Wirth, 'Environment – Extraterritorial Effects of Activities of Federal Agencies – Waste Disposal in Antarctica – National Environmental Policy Act of 1969' (1993) 87 AJIL 626–35; in regard to the operation of the United States' Antarctic Conservation Act, 1978 see 'NSF Issues Final Regulations for Antarctic Conservation Act' (1989) 24(1) *Antarctic Journal of the United States* 1–3.

[292] See John Handmer and Martijn Wilder, 'Australia and Environmental Management in Antarctica' (1994) 1 *Australian Journal of Environmental Management* 175–91; and the papers in John Handmer and Martijn Wilder (eds.), *Towards a Conservation Strategy for the Australian Antarctic Territory* (Canberra, 1993).

[293] Such legislation is acceptable under the jurisdictional reach of Antarctic Treaty, Art. VIII.

[294] J. A. Gulland, 'The Antarctic Treaty System as a Resource Management Mechanism' in Gillian D. Triggs (ed.), *The Antarctic Treaty Regime* (Cambridge, 1987) 116 at 122–3.

complex Antarctic environmental protection mechanisms.[295] In some respects it would seem that it has been simpler for the ATCPs to retain the *status quo* than seek to implement substantial changes to the ATS; however, this fails to acknowledge the substantial advances in environmental protection achieved through both CCAMLR and the Protocol. From all these perspectives then, the ATS has proved very effective in protecting the Antarctic environment and demonstrates the advantages in adopting a regional approach to environmental protection.

Arctic environmental cooperation

The recent developments in the Arctic also demonstrate the virtue of adopting cooperative approaches towards environmental protection. For much of this century the Arctic has not been considered a distinctive region either by the Arctic states themselves or by others. As a result there have been very few examples of agreements dealing with the Arctic as such on any subject, let alone protection of the environment. On the other hand those agreements which have sought to protect the Arctic environment from a regional perspective have been a success. Both the 1911 Fur Seal Convention and the 1973 Polar Bear Agreement aptly demonstrated that when the Arctic states joined together they were capable of negotiating effective environmental protection instruments. However, one of the difficulties with environmental protection in the Arctic has been that to date the incentives for regional cooperation have not been great. With sovereignty relatively resolved, states tended to view environmental problems as their own and not shared with Arctic neighbours. The political insecurity in the Arctic during the height of the Cold War, which saw the region heavily militarised, also did not assist in engendering regional cooperation. As a result, those initiatives which did occur were primarily bilateral.

The 1980s saw enhanced prospects for multilateral cooperation in the Arctic. Growing concerns over the state of the environment were a major catalyst in this development. An increasing realisation that the Arctic was being affected by pollution from industrial areas to the south, that isolated areas of industrial development had led to severe environmental degradation, and the existence of better political relations between the Arctic states meant that by the end of the 1980s the prospects were good for more enhanced regional cooperation.[296]

[295] Sands, 'The Antarctic Treaty Regime' at 56–60.

[296] Arkady Kudrya, 'A Growing Arctic Evironmental Agenda' (July/August 1991) 1(2) *Arctic Circle* 10–11.

In short, a large number of environmental issues existed throughout the Arctic which could only be effectively dealt with through greater bilateral and multilateral Arctic cooperation.[297] Building on these developments, a number of commentators have also suggested that greater Arctic-wide cooperation can be developed around a regime based on the law of the sea and maritime law dealing with Arctic shipping and marine pollution problems.[298] In total, there now exist a number of incentives for multilateral Arctic environmental cooperation. Roginko and LaMourie have identified these as being:

(a) the need to cooperate to avoid losses to shared ecosystems;
(b) that sharing information regarding the protection of the Arctic environment will prevent duplication of expensive research programmes;
(c) the relative lack of expertise on Arctic environmental problems suggests greater expediency in the sharing of resources; and
(d) the development of greater cooperative mechanisms will demonstrate the importance attached to the protection of the Arctic environment and its ecosystem by the Arctic states.[299]

Given this background it is not surprising that the AEPS emerged. While it cannot be characterised as an environmental treaty for the Arctic,[300] the AEPS does represent a significant regional initiative. It demonstrates the virtue of adopting a cooperative approach to regional environmental problems which are in need of specific regional responses. The AEPS displays many of these features: the need

[297] This point had been increasingly stressed by a number of commentators: see Roginko and LaMourie, 'Emerging Marine Environmental Protection Strategies' at 265–6; David L. VanderZwaag and Cynthia Lamson, 'Ocean Development and Management in the Arctic: Issues in American and Canadian Relations' (1986) 39 *Arctic* 327–37; J. Enno Harders, 'The Arctic Ocean: Environmental Protection and Circumpolar Co-operation: Proposal for a Legal Regime' in *Energy Law '86* (New York, 1986) 493–532.

[298] Roginko and LaMourie, 'Emerging Marine Environmental Protection Strategies' at 268–70; J. Enno Harders, 'In Quest of an Arctic Legal Regime' (1987) 11 *Marine Policy* 285–98; VanderZwaag and Lamson, 'Ocean Development' at 334–6; D. VanderZwaag and C. Lamson, 'Shipping and Marine Environmental Protection in the Arctic: Present Approaches and Future Options' in J. G. Nelson, Roger Needham and Linda Norton (eds.), *Arctic Heritage* (Ottawa, 1987) 425 at 441–3.

[299] Roginko and LaMourie, 'Emerging Marine Environmental Protection Strategies' at 266.

[300] At one stage in the negotiating process for the AEPS this was apparently the aim of the Canadian government: see Memorandum from the Legal Bureau, Department of External Affairs (13 March 1990), reprinted in Edward G. Lee (ed.), 'Canadian Practice in International Law at the Department of External Affairs in 1989–90' (1990) 28 CYIL 472 at 502.

for cooperative response action; sharing of information on common problems; and the desire for uniform rules and regulations to be implemented. It does not provide for any international legal action to be taken to deal with Arctic environmental problems, but there is the real prospect that this could eventually occur, especially if efforts at the international level to raise the profile of the Arctic as a distinct region in need of special protection fail. This initiative demonstrates that, to a degree, the Arctic states have begun to reject global environmental protection regimes and instead have realised that if Arctic environmental protection is to be ensured then a regional approach will be more effective.

The polar regions and their impact on international environmental law

Despite the considerable emphasis which has been placed upon resource management in the polar regions, polar environmental protection now seems to head the agenda for polar states. In Antarctica there has been a gradual movement towards greater environmental protection. The decision to reject CRAMRA and opt instead for a Protocol seeking to implement comprehensive environmental protection provisions perhaps represents a watershed in the management of the continent and the Southern Ocean.[301] Not only has the result been that 'the Antarctic environment is probably the best protected of all continents',[302] but also that the ATCPs now have a much stronger legal obligation to protect Antarctica than originally was envisaged in the Antarctic Treaty. With respect to the Arctic, there now seems to be a recognition amongst the Arctic states that urgent attention needs to be given to Arctic environmental protection. To date, resource management and development has been given priority. However, the growing realisation that global environmental initiatives are on their own inadequate, plus the increasing political strength of Arctic

[301] Not all states have indicated satisfaction with the 1991 Protocol. At the 1991 session of the United Nations, a number of UN member states expressed concern over the terms of the Protocol and the environmental management approach being adopted towards Antarctica by the ATCPs: see Peter J. Beck, 'The 1991 UN Session: The Environmental Protocol Fails to Satisfy the Antarctic Treaty System's Critics' (1992) 28 *Polar Record* 307–14.

[302] Peter J. Beck, 'Managing the Last Great Wilderness: Antarctica Today' (paper presented at British International Studies Association Conference, University of Wales, Swansea, December 1992) 12.

indigenous peoples who are concerned about the future of their environment,[303] has seen these external factors influence the Arctic states to take greater action themselves. In this regard, it is significant that the AEPS is the first cooperative arrangement involving all the Arctic states.

The polar regions through the actions of the polar states have made several contributions to international environmental law during the past thirty years.[304] In a general sense there has been a contribution to the broad principle that the environment needs to be preserved and protected. This is the foundation principle upon which both the Protocol and the AEPS are based. However, even before these recent initiatives the polar regions were contributing to the development of this principle. As far back as 1911 some of the Arctic states sought to preserve and protect stocks of fur seals through the Fur Seal Convention, while both the Agreed Measures, CCAS and CCAMLR also had this expressed intention in Antarctica. More importantly, the polar regions have made significant contributions to the development of the precautionary principle in international environmental law. The Fur Seal Convention, CCAS, the Polar Bear Agreement, CCAMLR and CRAMRA are all examples of the precautionary principle at work. In some instances this approach was applied to such an extent that legal mechanisms to control activities were negotiated prior to those activities even being a commercial possibility. In the case of CRAMRA, all Antarctic mineral resource activities were completely prohibited until it was demonstrated that they could be conducted without causing unacceptable harm. The subsequent permanent prohibition imposed by the Protocol represents a more extreme application of the principle.

Environmental impact assessment and environmental monitoring are also aspects of international environmental law to which the polar regions have contributed. The experience in both regions shows that if certain activities are to be allowed, then the environment can only be

[303] See Inuit Circumpolar Conference, *Principles and Elements for a Comprehensive Arctic Policy* (Montreal, 1992) 31–76. For an assessment of the relationship between environmental issues and interests of indigenous peoples in Russia see Alexei Yu Roginko, 'Environmental Issues in the Soviet Arctic and the Fate of Northern Natives' in John Massey Stewart (ed.), *The Soviet Environment* (Cambridge, 1992) 213–22.

[304] Lee Kimball, 'Environmental Law and Policy in Antarctica' in Philippe Sands (ed.), *Greening International Law* (1993) 122 at 123 has commented that: 'Antarctica has, in many ways, served as a microcosm for the evolution of environmental law and policy.'

effectively protected if knowledge exists about their potential environmental impact. For such an assessment to be made it is also necessary that substantial knowledge exists about the environment. The outstanding example of this approach is CCAMLR and its 'ecosystem' approach to Antarctic marine living resource management, supported by an institutional structure in which a Scientific Committee has a pivotal role. The development of environmental impact assessment procedures for land-based activities has only recently been adopted in Antarctica, but the Protocol has embraced it to such an extent that once it enters into force any activity undertaken in Antarctica will need to be assessed through some form of EIA process.[305] The importance placed upon the sharing of information gained about the environment between the parties to various environmental protection regimes is another feature of the polar regions. The AEPS with its 'Arctic Monitoring and Assessment Program' is the most advanced example of this type of process, with a secretariat having been established to administer it. In Antarctica, however, the sharing of information was made a requirement under the Antarctic Treaty and this has been perpetuated in later instruments under the ATS.[306]

Another important contribution made by the polar regions, and perhaps their most important, has been the success of adopting a regional approach to dealing with environmental problems.[307] A number of factors have contributed to this, not the least political and sovereignty-related concerns. However, irrespective of the motives involved, both the ATS and the AEPS demonstrate the advantages in adopting a regional approach to solving and dealing with environmental problems. These advantages have of course long been realised.[308] But encouraging cooperation amongst states to implement such measures is not easy. Gaining agreement amongst the ATCPs to adopt a common approach to environmental issues has been a long process.[309] However, the ATS has provided a forum in which the

[305] On the relationship between these provisions of the Protocol and international environmental law, see Francioni, 'The Madrid Protocol' at 59–61.

[306] See Sands, 'The Antarctic Treaty Regime' at 57–8.

[307] In some instances this approach has been taken to such an extent that some global mechanisms have been rejected by the polar states. For a discussion of some of the difficulties which have existed between the United Nations Environment Programme and the ATS, see Sveneld Evteev, 'Antarctica and its Place in the Contemporary Environmental Movement' in Arnfinn Jorgensen-Dahl and Willy Ostreng (eds.), *The Antarctic Treaty System in World Politics* (London, 1991) 147–52.

[308] Sand, 'International Cooperation' at 246–8.

[309] This is best demonstrated by the fact that the 'World Park' concept was first

ATCPs have been able to discuss environmental problems and work towards solutions to problems which have been far more effective than any measures the international community as a whole may have been able to apply. In the Arctic, increased regional cooperation to protect the Arctic environment is slowly coming after a realisation that global mechanisms were inadequate. The Arctic Ocean has always been the focus for potential efforts to protect the Arctic, and in conjunction with the move towards greater marine regionalism adopted in UNCLOS, it has been anticipated that the Arctic states would eventually move towards greater multilateral cooperation to protect the region.[310] That the AEPS takes an even wider approach towards regional cooperation on Arctic environmental problems is further indication that a regional approach, not just one which is issue-specific, is favoured by states when it comes to dealing with the environment.

Finally, the polar regions are also examples of how international environmental law standards may be developed through both hard and soft law approaches. The benefits of soft law options for environmental protection have been recognised for some time, in that they allow states to adopt broader 'aspirational' measures than they would do under hard law mechanisms. This was the approach which eventually won favour with the Arctic states. Other important considerations also apply here such as the costs involved in implementing environmental protection and assessment regimes. In Antarctica a different approach was adopted due to the framework provided by the Antarctic Treaty. While there has been some reliance upon various Recommendations adopted at ATCMs to protect the Antarctic environment, the most substantial mechanisms have been either additional conventions or additions to the Treaty.

Despite the many examples of how the polar regions have developed and implemented principles of international environmental law, problems do still exist in implementing mechanisms to protect the polar environments. The enforcement of a variety of measures dealing with the protection of the environment presents real problems in the ATS not only with regard to parties to the System but also for third parties.[311] In parts of the Arctic some regions have not been subject to

discussed at ATCM VII (1972) and that it took till 1991 before a comprehensive approach to Antarctic environmental protection was adopted.

[310] Harders, 'In Quest of an Arctic Legal Regime' at 295–8.

[311] *Cf.* Sands, 'The Antarctic Treaty Regime' at 60.

any form of environmental regulation. In the Kara Peninsula region and other parts of the Russian north substantial environmental damage has occurred.[312] The polar states have also been unable to deal effectively with transboundary environmental problems which have affected their regions; the best example of this is the depletion of the ozone layer. Hence, while the polar states have taken active measures to protect their local environments, their record is not spotless. Nevertheless, they have made important contributions to the development of international environmental law. Their impact is such that many of the common principles applied in the polar regions are now looked upon as being the existing or emerging international standard.

[312] See the discussion in chapter 2; for a discussion of the problems being experienced in Siberia, see Armin Rosencranz and Antony Scott, 'Siberia, Environmentalism, and Problems of Environmental Protection' (1991) 14 *Hastings International and Comparative Law Quarterly* 929–47.

10 Regime theory, the polar regions and international law

In chapter 1 international relations regime theory was discussed and the characteristics of regimes were noted. It was asserted that regimes are principles, norms, rules and decision-making procedures around which actor expectations converge in a given issue area.[1] For the regime to form, the issue area must be one that is understood and sufficiently politicised. This causes states and other international actors to perceive that their interests will be enhanced by coming to a formal agreement, understanding or loose arrangement with others as to how the issue area is to be regulated, organised, perceived, or understood by the participants. Once the necessary conditions exist for regime formation, various approaches can be taken. Though not mutually exclusive, three different methods of regime formation were identified: the contractarian approach, the evolutionary approach and the piecemeal approach. Once the regime is in existence, various factors can impact upon its success. The structure of the regime, importance of certain actors, strength of the issue area and willingness of actors to continue to participate are all important. Regimes will also eventually face pressure to change and it is at this stage that the regime is most vulnerable. Responses can range from regime disintegration, to modification allowing for new issue areas to be dealt with. It is possible for regimes which seemingly are solid and have substantial support suddenly to collapse due to changes in the issue area and actor perceptions.

In this chapter, international relations regime theory will be applied to gain a fuller appreciation of international cooperation and

[1] S. Krasner, 'Structural Causes and Regime Consequences: Regimes as Intervening Variables' in Stephen D. Krasner (ed.), *International Regimes* (Ithaca, NY, 1983) 1 at 2.

how international law has developed in the polar regions. To begin, consideration will be given as to why it is helpful to study regimes.

Why study regimes?

It was argued in chapter 1 that despite regime theory having been ignored by international law,[2] there are potential benefits in undertaking a regime analysis of international law developments. However, the mere existence of this theory is not a justification on its own as to why it should be given further consideration. To that end, it is important to assess whether regime theory provides any basis for a greater understanding of the international system. This question has been addressed by the regime theorists.[3]

Haggard and Simmons note that regime theory seeks to explain state behaviour in two ways. First, that because regimes alter the situation or setting in which states interact, cooperation is more likely.[4] Regime dynamics, therefore, offer a greater incentive for states to cooperate and with less cost than in other forms of international cooperation. Second, regimes can have a persuasive effect upon states and can alter state interests or preferences.[5] Regimes can so impact upon state behaviour that some states are persuaded to alter radically their domestic or international policies. The result is that the regime creates homogeneous state behaviour within the given issue area. From this perspective, regimes offer an explanation of why international cooperation occurs and is sustained. Keohane argues that regimes are important because they offer some very practical attractions to international actors:

> Far from being threats to governments, they permit governments to attain objectives that would otherwise be unattainable. They do so in part by facilitating intergovernmental agreements. Regimes facilitate agreements by raising the anticipated costs of violating others' property rights, by altering

[2] *Cf.* Anne-Marie Slaughter-Burley, 'International Law and International Relations Theory: A Dual Agenda' (1993) 87 AJIL 205–39.

[3] See e.g., Peter M. Haas, 'Do Regimes Matter? Epistemic Communities and Mediterranean Pollution Control' (1989) 43 IntOrg 377–403; John S. Duffield, 'International Regimes and Alliance Behaviour: Explaining NATO Conventional Force Levels' (1992) 46 IntOrg 819 at 820 where it is argued that regimes do matter because they provide 'a convincing demonstration of their importance for explaining state behaviour and international outcomes'.

[4] Stephan Haggard and Beth A. Simmons, 'Theories of International Regimes' (1987) 41 IntOrg 491 at 513.

[5] *Ibid.* at 514.

transaction costs through the clustering of issues, and by providing reliable information to members. Regimes are relatively efficient institutions, compared with the alternatives of having a myriad of unrelated agreements, since their principles, rules and institutions create linkages among issues that give actors incentives to reach mutually beneficial agreements.[6]

Regimes thus offer to states and international actors the security of certainty in a world that is otherwise anarchic. Through the rules they impose on their members they offer the opportunity for common objectives within issue areas to be met, without imposing the political and other costs which are sometimes associated with unilateral or bilateral initiatives. Moreover, the interaction which occurs as the participants work towards the regime's common goals also assists in the process of enforcement.

A regime theory analysis also has the potential to provide for a better understanding as to how international law operates.[7] First, regime theory offers the prospect of understanding why some forms of international law are created and how that law may, and does, function. This can assist in understanding why some regimes create new forms of international law which would have been unacceptable in a non-regime setting.[8] Second, regime theory may also allow for a more confident analysis of which legal mechanisms will be employed to deal with certain international issues. Third, regime theory can also offer some explanation as to how states react when confronted with new developments.[9] As Krasner has noted: 'Regimes offer one way to account for the persistence of behaviour and outcomes even though basic causal factors associated with political power have changed.'[10]

[6] Robert O. Keohane, *After Hegemony* (Princeton, NJ, 1984) 97.

[7] For an extensive discussion of these issues see Oran R. Young, *International Governance* (Ithaca, NY, 1994) chapter 8, 'Governance Systems and International Legal Regimes'; Slaughter-Burley, 'International Law'; 'International Law and International Relations Theory: Building Bridges' (1992) 86 ProcAmSocIL 167–87.

[8] The development of so-called 'framework conventions' is an example. In these instances conventions outlining broad principles and objectives are negotiated in anticipation of more specific international instruments being negotiated subsequently: see 1992 United Nations Framework Convention on Climate Change, (1992) 31 ILM 849.

[9] See M. J. Peterson, *Managing the Frozen South* (Berkeley, CA, 1988) 206, who notes that regimes can result in greater certainty and '[c]ontent can thus be predicted through a knowledge of what proposed principles, norms, rules, and procedures appeal to the group of states most likely to forge such a coalition'.

[10] Stephen D. Krasner, 'Regimes and the Limits of Realism: Regimes as Autonomous Variables' in Stephen D. Krasner (ed.), *International Regimes* (Ithaca, NY, 1983) 355 at 358.

Fourth, regime theory can offer some explanations as to why in some instances international law fails or is ignored. Finally, regime dynamics can also influence the states which are members of the regime to such a degree that states will adhere to rules in a regime which they would reject as being unacceptable in similar situations.[11] All of these factors are very important attributes of regime theory when international law is so dominated by volatile state actors who are subject to a wide range of influences.

Regime theory, therefore, offers an explanation for the dynamics associated with a certain form of international cooperation. This is important for international lawyers, because international regimes are often regulated by some form of international law. More often than not, they are centred around an international instrument such as a treaty.[12] Regime theory allows for a greater understanding of how that law is created, functions and evolves during the life of the regime. While such an analysis is dominated by regime dynamics and the role of the participants, it offers the opportunity to gain a broader understanding of international law than that currently afforded by strict legal analyses. As international law increasingly evolves by way of treaties which seek to deal with specific issues or create regional or global management mechanisms, new regimes are being created. Regime theory also allows for some understanding as to why international law develops in these situations and why it is subject to pressures to change. As both the Arctic and Antarctic are examples of international regimes in which international law plays an important role, regime theory therefore provides the opportunity to assess how that law has evolved, functions and may be impacted upon in the future.

[11] See 1982 United Nations Convention on the Law of the Sea, (1982) 21 ILM 1,261, Part IV recognising 'Archipelagic States'. This section of the Convention provides for a compromise between the interests of archipelagic states such as Indonesia and the Philippines who sought to have their status as archipelagic states recognised, and the interests of maritime nations who wished to maintain the freedom of navigation through the waters of an archipelago: see R. R. Churchill and A. V. Lowe, *The Law of the Sea* (rev. ed., Manchester, 1988) 98–100.

[12] Oran R. Young and Gail Osherenko, 'International Regime Formation: Findings, Research Priorities, and Applications' in Oran R. Young and Gail Osherenko (eds.), *Polar Politics* (Ithaca, NY, 1993) 223 at 225 who note after a study of individual Arctic regimes:

> In every case, however, the process of regime formation centered on efforts to negotiate the terms of a package of mutually acceptable provisions to be set forth in a constitutional contract. We are now convinced that this pattern of negotiation eventuating in one or more explicit agreements constitutes the normal process of regime formation in international society.

Antarctica and regime theory

Antarctic regime creation

Four factors can be pinpointed as being influential in the creation of the Antarctic regime: the need to resolve sovereignty disputes, national security, the military and nuclear threat, and a desire to continue scientific cooperation. First, resolution of sovereignty was a concern for the territorial claimants and other states with a major stake in Antarctic affairs. Though all of the seven territorial claims had been asserted by 1959, there was no mutual recognition of those claims and one sector remained unclaimed. The claims of Argentina, Chile and the UK to the Antarctic Peninsula overlapped. The two Cold War superpowers, the United States and the USSR, both had substantial historical and scientific interests in Antarctica but had not asserted a claim. Given these uncertainties the speedy creation of a regime which sought to resolve the sovereignty issue was important if Antarctica was to remain free of territorial disputes. Closely related to concerns over sovereignty were national security issues. An outbreak of hostilities in Antarctica would have been seen as an important threat to Argentina, Australia, Chile and New Zealand, especially if the dispute involved the United States and the USSR. There was also a fear that while Antarctic relations between the two superpowers may have been cordial, Cold War tension from others parts of the globe could always spill over in the Antarctic. The UK was also concerned that any unfavourable resolution to its territorial claims on the Antarctic Peninsula could rebound to its detriment on its dispute with Argentina over the Falkland Islands.[13]

Another factor which was directly related to those of sovereignty and national security was the fear that Antarctica would become a militarised continent and the location for nuclear weapons. With the Southern Ocean rim being relatively distant from the main theatres of the Cold War this again was a major concern for the four southern hemisphere territorial claimants. Any regime which sought both to demilitarise and denuclearise Antarctica was to be encouraged, especially as it seemed that both the United States and the USSR intended to maintain a substantial presence on the continent. Finally, the fourth factor which encouraged regime creation was science. While the early expeditions to Antarctica at the beginning of the

[13] See generally F. M. Auburn, *Antarctic Law and Politics* (London, 1982) 48–83.

twentieth century primarily sought to explore and discover new regions in Antarctica, there was also a substantial scientific component to these expeditions. Once the exploratory period of Antarctic history had passed science took over as the major activity, a fact highlighted by the International Geophysical Year (IGY). International scientists were keen to continue cooperation in the post-IGY years. The International Council of Scientific Unions, a non-governmental body of international scientists, was particularly keen to pursue and intensify the cooperation that had been achieved during the IGY.[14] They had seen that common goals in science allowed political barriers to be broken down and were concerned that following the IGY politics would intervene and make Antarctic scientific cooperation impossible. Rather, they wished the cooperation of the IGY to remain so that Antarctic science would continue to benefit all mankind.[15]

Antarctic regime formation and operation

The above four factors were influential in creating the necessary solidity in the issue area to attract the original parties to the Treaty. Irrespective of their various Antarctic interests each party had something to gain from becoming a member of the new regime. In the case of the territorial claimants they were able to benefit from a regime which offered some stability to their territorial claims[16] and assured them that the continent would be used for peaceful purposes without the threat of a military buildup or the presence of nuclear weapons.[17] Other parties, such as Belgium, Japan and South Africa, were able to continue to conduct their scientific research programmes on the continent secure in the knowledge that scientific cooperation was guaranteed by the Treaty.[18]

Since the Antarctic regime became operational in 1961 there has been some change in Antarctic issue areas and the priority that is accorded to the original four. Sovereignty and national security are still matters of importance. The 1982 Falklands War between Argentina and the UK was a reminder of how sensitive sovereignty issues can

[14] See Lucius Caflisch, 'The Interaction of Science and Politics in the Field of International Relations: The Case of Antarctica' (1992) 28 *Polar Record* 159 at 161.

[15] See generally on the important role of Antarctic science in regime formation, Willy Ostreng, 'Polar Science and Politics: Close Twins or Opposite Poles in International Cooperation?' in Steinar Andresen and Willy Ostreng (eds.), *International Resource Management* (London, 1989) 88 at 90–9.

[16] 1959 Antarctic Treaty, 402 UNTS 71 (hereafter Antarctic Treaty), Art. IV.

[17] Antarctic Treaty, Arts. I, V.

[18] Antarctic Treaty, Arts. II, III.

become. However, while most of the territorial claimants, with the possible exception of Norway, continue actively to 'assert' their sovereignty claims in ways consistent with the Treaty, the longevity of the regime has itself helped to dispel some of the threats that may have existed in the 1950s. Rather, it could be argued that as was demonstrated during the 1980s United Nations debate over the future of Antarctica, many of the territorial claimants and original Treaty parties are more concerned with Antarctic Treaty security than national security.[19] That Antarctica has remained demilitarised and denuclearised has been a major factor in providing for continued regime stability. In the 1990s it is not, however, as major an issue as it once was. The considerable thawing in relations amongst the superpowers throughout the 1980s and the negotiation of several disarmament treaties during the intervening thirty years has meant that military and nuclear weapons issues are no longer as significant. Scientific research in Antarctica, however, still remains a very high priority for the regime. With only a few exceptions all of the original parties conduct extensive scientific research on the continent, while bidding Consultative Parties are still required to meet certain standards of scientific interest before their applications are considered. The recent concerns over global warming, depletion of the ozone layer and the general state of the Antarctic environment have if anything helped to raise Antarctic science to an even higher profile so that both international scientific cooperation and the importance of the activity remain at a very high level.

Given then that some of the factors initially responsible for creating an Antarctic issue area have altered, are there any new issues which have arisen and which now impact upon the regime? Resource management and protection of the environment fall into this category. Neither were considered in any detail at the time of regime creation and the ATS has subsequently grappled with how they should be addressed. A review of the agenda items of ATCMs during the past twenty years demonstrates the dominance of resource management and environmental protection issues. While the Antarctic Treaty was short on detailed provisions dealing with these issues, Article IX(1)(f) did contemplate recommendations dealing with the 'preservation and conservation of living resources in Antarctica'. To that end the Consultative Parties adopted the 1964 Agreed Measures on Antarctic

[19] See M. Hayashi, 'The Antarctica Question in the United Nations' (1986) 19 Cornell ILJ 275–90.

Fauna and Flora by way of Recommendation.[20] Subsequently, the 1972 Convention for the Conservation of Antarctic Seals[21] and the 1980 Convention on the Conservation of Antarctic Marine Living Resources[22] plus numerous other Recommendations have been adopted dealing with the protection of the Antarctic terrestrial and marine environment.[23] The 1991 Protocol on Environmental Protection to the Antarctic Treaty[24] is the latest example of these provisions and demonstrates the level of priority which the regime has now given to environmental protection.

Regime change: the debate over a minerals regime

The change in emphasis in the Antarctic issue area to resource and environmental management in the 1980s resulted in greater pressures upon the regime.[25] As a result of these pressures the Antarctic regime had to face and eventually undergo considerable change. Theorists such as Young argue that the vital issue for any regime during this process is determining just how many of the central elements of the regime can be displaced before it faces possible fragmentation.[26] The challenge for the Antarctic regime in dealing with resource and environmental management was that it created substantial divisions amongst the Treaty parties and also exposed the regime to external criticisms from non-Treaty parties and increasingly influential non-governmental organisations. It also exposed a weakness in the regime because neither the effective protection of the Antarctic environment nor comprehensive regulation of renewable or non-renewable resources had been properly dealt with during the period of regime formation.

When concerns were raised in the early 1970s about the potential for mining activities being carried on in Antarctica, the Treaty parties responded in 1977 by adopting a moratorium on the exploration and exploitation of Antarctic mineral resources.[27] This response did not create any great tension amongst the parties because there were no commercial pressures to engage in mining on the continent at that

[20] Recommendation III-VIII, reprinted in *Handbook* (Pt 2), 2048.
[21] (1972) 11 ILM 251. [22] (1980) 19 ILM 841.
[23] Of the 204 Recommendations adopted by the ATCPs at ATCMs between 1961 and 1994, 118 (58 per cent) have dealt with environmental and resource management issues: see the discussion in chapter 4. [24] (1991) 30 ILM 1,455.
[25] Peterson, *Managing the Frozen South* at 145–6.
[26] Oran R. Young, *International Cooperation* (Ithaca, NY, 1989) 97.
[27] See Recommendation IX-1; and earlier Recommendations VII-6, VIII-14.

time. The Treaty parties subsequently decided at ATCM XI (1981) that a Special ATCM should be convened to negotiate a legal instrument dealing with Antarctic minerals.[28] After six years of negotiation between 1982 and 1988, the Convention on the Regulation of Antarctic Mineral Resource Activities (CRAMRA) was finally concluded in 1988 and opened for signature in November of that year.[29] However, immediately upon the conclusion of CRAMRA doubts began to surface amongst some Treaty parties over the credibility of an Antarctic minerals regime.[30] External pressures were also placed upon the regime. Through a combination of concern over the lack of comprehensive environmental protection measures in Antarctica and the possibility that following the implementation of CRAMRA substantial environmental damage could occur as a result of minerals activity, influential non-governmental organisations began to question the credibility of the regime to manage Antarctica in an environmentally sensitive way.[31] When Australia and France announced in May 1989 that they would not sign CRAMRA, but instead would campaign for the implementation of a comprehensive environmental protection instrument, it seemed that the Antarctic regime was heading for a major crisis.

The Australian and French rejection of CRAMRA cast doubt over whether the Convention would ever enter into force.[32] It also raised questions as to how pro-mining states such as the UK and the United States would respond to such developments. Following the Australia–French proposal for a comprehensive environmental protection regime in Antarctica, ATCM XV (1989) adopted a Recommendation calling for a special ATCM to consider 'the further elaboration, maintenance and effective implementation of a comprehensive system for the protection of the Antarctic environment and its dependent

[28] Recommendation XI-1.

[29] (1988) 27 ILM 868.

[30] S. K. N. Blay and B. M. Tsamenyi, 'Australia and the Convention on the Regulation of Antarctic Mineral Resource Activities (CRAMRA)' (1990) 26 *Polar Record* 195 at 197, 200 regarding concerns raised in Australia.

[31] Groups such as Greenpeace International and the Antarctic and Southern Ocean Coalition were very prominent in this debate. See P. S. Bogart, 'Environmental Threats in Antarctica' (1988) 31(2) *Oceanus* 104–7; G. Mosley, 'World Park for Antarctica' (1989) 17(5) *Habitat Australia* 4–7; B. S. Manheim, *On Thin Ice* (Washington, 1988).

[32] On the question of whether CRAMRA could enter into force after this action, see S. K. N. Blay and B. M. Tsamenyi, 'The Convention on the Regulation of Antarctic Mineral Resource Activities (CRAMRA): Can a Claimant Veto it?' (1989) 1 *ASOLPO Paper*.

and associated ecosystems'.[33] The same meeting also adopted a Recommendation which contemplated the eventual entry into force of CRAMRA![34] In late 1989 the regime was therefore seeking to deal with two initiatives, one to implement a negotiated minerals convention, the other to develop new mechanisms to protect the Antarctic environment. That the goals of both were incompatible did not seem to raise major concerns.

The first session of the Special ATCM XI was held from 19 November to 6 December 1990, at Vina del Mar, Chile. Australia and France presented to the meeting formal proposals for the creation of a new Antarctic environmental protection regime. While there was support for the implementation of greater environmental protection mechanisms in Antarctica, the major area of disagreement remained whether such new environmental protection measures would also result in a prohibition of commercial mining activities and the abandonment of CRAMRA.[35] Without resolving this question, a Draft Protocol on Environmental Protection was agreed upon as a working document for a second session in 1991.[36] The second session of Special ATCM XI convened in April 1991 at Madrid saw a major breakthrough in the negotiations when the coalition of pro-mining states split. When Germany announced that it was prepared to support a permanent ban on mining activities, and Japan also suddenly changed its position, pressure was placed on the remaining pro-mining states to abandon the minerals regime. The decision by Australia and France to abandon their position on the need for a permanent mining ban and instead agree to a fifty-year prohibition on mining activities was the final catalyst in breaking the deadlock.[37]

Antarctica after regime change

When the Antarctic regime of 1961 is compared to the current regime it can be seen that while the basic principles of the regime remain in place, there has been a substantial change in the issue areas around which the regime currently converges. The period between negoti-

[33] Recommendation XV-1. [34] Recommendation XV-2.

[35] See Peter J. Beck, 'Antarctica, Vina del Mar and the 1990 UN debate' (1991) 27 *Polar Record* 211–16.

[36] 'Antarctic Treaty: Comprehensive Protection for Antarctica' (1991) 21(1) *Environmental Policy and Law* 11–13, where the Draft Protocol is reprinted at 30–4.

[37] For a tentative regime theory analysis of the debate between the merits of CRAMRA and the need for greater Antarctic environmental protection, see Lorraine M. Elliott, *Continuity and Change in Cooperative International Regimes* (Canberra, 1991).

ation and entry into force of the Protocol is the final stage of this process. Once implemented this phase of regime change will be complete. Its impact is considerable. The Protocol supersedes the operation of the 1964 Agreed Measures and created such a conflict with CRAMRA that the Convention has now been abandoned. The Protocol also introduces a radical change to the way in which all human activities in Antarctica are conducted by requiring environmental impact assessments before new activities will be approved. These changes will be very substantial and the real test for whether regime change has succeeded will come with how the Protocol is implemented and accepted.

With the Protocol not yet in force it is difficult to assess how the regime has coped with changes it will bring about. But, it is possible to assess how the regime coped with the debate for change. Given that over a period of time there is bound to be some entrenchment of views on various fundamental regime issues, the debate between CRAMRA and the Protocol was surprisingly brief and harmonious. It only took from May 1989, when Australia and France announced that they would not sign CRAMRA, till October 1991 for CRAMRA to be rejected and the Protocol adopted. During that period there was one regularly scheduled ATCM, which recommended a process that resulted in four sessions of a Special ATCM being held specifically to discuss the Australian–French proposal.[38] The debate also demonstrated that while differing views amongst the Treaty parties were tolerated, some of the most powerful members were still influenced by the previous cohesive nature of the regime to abandon their pro-mining position in favour of consensus. When regime members were tested on their support for the regime, they chose to adopt a less favourable position to that which they had previously advocated, rather than rejecting the regime completely.[39] The Protocol experience also demonstrates how a fundamental change in the priority of issue areas and the emergence of new ones can result in regime change. While it is argued, however,

[38] The final October 1991 meeting held in Madrid was actually a signing ceremony for the Protocol.

[39] See Peterson, *Managing the Frozen South* at 174 who when commenting on this question prior to the height of the CRAMRA/Protocol debate noted:

> The breadth of the shared or parallel interests among participating governments also explains why they have been able to agree on amending the regime rather than replacing or terminating the regime. Termination is not regarded as desirable; it would produce massive confusion and trigger an all-out scramble for territory.

that the changes brought about by the Protocol will be significant, they are not radical because the four basic principles upon which the regime was founded still remain in place.

The future of the Antarctic regime

The future of the Antarctic regime depends on the response to the Protocol and how it deals with emerging environmental issues. Initially, this will be determined by the ratification of the Protocol by all of the twenty-six Consultative Parties which in October 1991 participated in the Protocol's final adoption at Madrid.[40] The next stage in the acceptance process will be the degree of support that it is given by the regime parties. Various levels of commitment will be imposed upon states depending on their Antarctic activities. Territorial claimants and other states which conduct scientific research activities on the continent will have the greatest responsibility in implementing terms of the Protocol. States such as Japan, which by Antarctic standards engage in extensive maritime activities, will also be bound by those provisions of the Protocol dealing with marine pollution prevention. States which support the activities of corporations that are engaged in Antarctic tourist operations will also have obligations to ensure that these activities meet the standards imposed by the Protocol.

While the implementation of the Protocol will create new internal pressures for the Antarctic regime, once the Protocol has entered into force it can be assumed that there is a level of commitment towards its implementation by all the Consultative Parties. The regime may also face other pressures for change in the future. These may result from the increasing interest in the Antarctic and Southern Ocean as a tourist destination. Some provisions of the Protocol will impact upon these developments.[41] However, there are still some activities related to tourism which remain unregulated and this may cause pressure for action to be taken.[42] A more likely source for change may come from the

[40] Protocol, Art. 23.

[41] See Protocol, Annex I regarding the requirement that an Environmental Impact Assessment be conducted for proposed human activities in Antarctica, and Annex III regarding waste disposal and waste management.

[42] At ATCM XVII (1992) some consideration was given to the proposal made at ATCM XVI (1991) for an Annex to be added to the Protocol dealing with Antarctic tourism activities; however, it was decided that such an Annex was not presently required: see *Final Report of the Seventeenth Antarctic Treaty Consultative Meeting* (Venice, 11–20 November 1992) 40–2, paras. 108–14. For discussion see Peter J. Beck, 'Managing Antarctic Tourism: A Front-Burner Issue' (1994) 21 *Annals of Tourism Research* 375–86.

pressure to make use of the world's diminishing resources. With both the renewable and non-renewable resources of the Antarctic and Southern Ocean region currently subject to strict regulation, the possibility exists that pressure may be exerted by third parties or even current Treaty parties to engage in some form of resource exploitation which is beyond the current imposed limits.[43] With the Protocol's prohibition on Antarctic mining activities only in place for fifty years, in the long term this will be an issue which will once again need to be addressed. Other issues which may in the future create pressure for regime change are those dealing with the membership structure of the Antarctic Treaty, involvement of non-governmental organisations in the regime, and the questioning of the legitimacy of the regime by non-regime states which wish to gain access to the region. How the Antarctic regime deals with any of these issues if they arise remains to be seen. The regime's first major encounter with regime change has, however, on initial indicators been a success.

The Arctic and regime theory

Creation of Arctic issue areas

The review in chapters 5 and 6 of the Arctic as a region and the legal mechanisms which are in place demonstrated that Arctic cooperation has been very slow in coming. This has partly been due to a failure by states to identify regional issue areas around which they can cooperatively converge and also because of the international and regional politics at play. A number of factors can be identified as being responsible for this. One could be termed the lack of a common 'Arctic outlook'. In this sense, the Arctic can be characterised as a region in which all the states which have a significant presence and interest have a greater concern with southern rather than northern issues. While there is a significant degree of interaction between the Arctic states on various issues, until very recently these relationships have been dominated by issues which have little to do with the region.[44] Nevertheless, relationships amongst Arctic states focused on 'southern' issues have impacted on the handling of northern

[43] The Japanese interest in whaling activities in the Southern Ocean is an example of the potential of this problem.

[44] Franklyn Griffiths, 'Introduction: The Arctic as an International Political Region' in Kari Mottola (ed.), *The Arctic Challenge* (Boulder, CO, 1988) 1 at 2.

questions.[45] There has also been a tendency for most Arctic states, with the exception of the Scandinavian states, to see little positive gain in engaging in bilateral or multilateral cooperation in order to administer and deal with Arctic issues. Each state has preferred to deal with Arctic issues individually.[46] Only where there have been serious unresolved issues,[47] or common strategic and military concerns, has cooperation been forthcoming.[48] The 1920 Treaty concerning the Archipelago of Spitsbergen (Svalbard) is a good example of such an instance.[49] Because of the potential for the unresolved sovereignty of the Archipelago to create serious disruptions in previously friendly relations, states were prepared to cooperate. This case demonstrates that when forced to come together to resolve an issue, the Arctic states can work cooperatively and adopt functional solutions. The post-World War II era also saw the strategic significance of the Arctic present major difficulties for Arctic cooperation. As a result of the development of nuclear weapons and modern missile technology, the Arctic was seen as a potential Cold War battleground.[50] The development of nuclear-powered submarines further added to the strategic significance of the region because of their ability to navigate under the Arctic ice for long periods without detection while maintaining the capacity to launch their weapons within striking range.[51]

While the above factors have to date worked against Arctic regime creation, as discussed in chapter 6 there are signs of the development

[45] The best example here is the relations between the United States and the USSR during the Cold War which had the result of making the Arctic a potential Cold War theatre.

[46] A good example of this was Canada's 1970 declaration of the Arctic Waters Pollution Prevention Act in which Canada essentially sought to go against the prevailing view of coastal state sovereignty and jurisdiction in an effort to protect its Arctic marine environment. See the discussion in chapter 9.

[47] The 1988 Agreement between the Government of Canada and the Government of the United States of America on Arctic Cooperation, [1988] CTS 29, is an example of where two Arctic states have sought to deal with differences of opinion. However, as noted in chapter 5, this Agreement failed to deal with all navigation issues in the Northwest Passage.

[48] Canada and the United States developed a very strong military relationship during World War II and in the Cold War era because of their concerns over the potential for a military strike by the USSR over the Arctic.

[49] 2 LNTS 8.

[50] For a Cold War assessment of the strategic significance of the Canadian Arctic, see R. J. Sutherland, 'The Strategic Significance of the Canadian Arctic' in R. St J. MacDonald (ed.), *The Arctic Frontier* (Toronto, 1966) 256–78. For a modern assessment, see Michael MccGwire, 'Strategic Interests in the Arctic Ocean', in Edgar J. Dosman (ed.), *Sovereignty and Security in the Arctic* (1989) 24–40.

[51] Oran R. Young, 'The Age of the Arctic' (1985–6) 61 *Foreign Policy* 160 at 161–5.

of significant issue areas around which an Arctic regime may be formed. While issue areas have existed throughout the region in the past there are only a few examples of instances where multilateral cooperation was forthcoming. Even in the successful instances of Arctic regime creation, such as the 1973 Polar Bear Agreement,[52] the issue area has been very specific and one in which participation involved little cost. In taking a broader view of the prospects for Arctic regime formation, Osherenko and Young identified in 1988 four potential issue areas around which Arctic regimes could form: Arctic arms control, industry and commerce, culture and science, and environmental cooperation.[53] In emphasising the importance of 'transboundary crises' in regime formation,[54] they were of the view at that time that the best prospects for regime formation were environmental cooperation resulting from environmental 'crises'. This has proved to be an accurate prediction with the 1991 Arctic Environmental Protection Strategy (AEPS)[55] directly resulting from concerns over the state of the Arctic environment. However, the late 1980s also saw a rush of other developments which indicate that other issue areas have begun to achieve the necessary salience around which a regime may form. The growth in scientific cooperation is one of these developments. Increased scientific cooperation in the Arctic during the past twenty years eventually led to the creation of the International Arctic Science Committee (IASC). While this is a most encouraging development, it also has other consequences. The scientists who attend IASC meetings come from government agencies or are engaged in government-funded research. As such, through the increased cooperation that will be achieved amongst the Arctic scientific community via the IASC, the potential exists for the scientists to influence other Arctic policy-makers about the virtues of greater Arctic cooperation. Another important development is the Canadian proposal for an Arctic Council. That Canada was even prepared to make this proposal at this time is an encouraging sign that there may be sufficient convergence of various Arctic issues for there to be positive gains from the creation of such a body. Issue areas such as environmental protection, cultural interaction, transboundary

[52] (1974) 13 ILM 13.

[53] Gail Osherenko and Oran R. Young, *The Age of the Arctic* (Cambridge, 1989) 244–68.

[54] *Ibid.* at 262–3; Oran R. Young, '"Arctic Waters": The Politics of Regime Formation' (1987) 18 ODIL 101 at 105.

[55] (1991) 30 ILM 1,624 (hereafter AEPS).

transportation and scientific research can all be identified as part of this process. There has, then, since the late 1980s, been a rapid emergence of issue areas around which an Arctic regime may form. This has been enhanced by a lessening of tension between the United States and Russia and a realisation that the time had come when there was a significant need for Arctic states to cooperate on environmental protection.

Prospects for Arctic regime creation

When assessing regime characteristics, the Arctic presents a contrast to Antarctica. In Antarctica there is a treaty which has provided a focus for the creation of an increasingly complex regime. In the Arctic there has been no central focus provided by a regional treaty or through common, integrated policies adopted by the Arctic states. Rather the current Arctic regime is disparate and comprised of a series of very specific regimes dealing with narrow issue areas.[56] Nevertheless, there has been continuing interest in the creation of a more integrated regime for the whole Arctic region. In the past there have been few positive signs that the creation of such a regime was imminent; however, since the 1970s positive indicators have emerged to indicate that Arctic states are capable of engaging in meaningful cooperation which could lead to regime creation.[57] This does not mean that in this new era of enhanced Arctic international relations the negotiation of a more comprehensive Arctic legal regime will be simple. Many issues remain to be resolved. Two of the most important are what form the regime will take and how will Arctic military and security issues be resolved.

In considering prospects for regime creation in the Arctic, Oran Young has consistently argued that it is inappropriate to consider whether an Antarctic-type treaty will be negotiated in the Arctic.[58]

[56] See e.g., the study of five separate regimes in the Arctic discussed in Oran R. Young and Gail Osherenko (eds.), *Polar Politics* (Ithaca, NY, 1993).

[57] For example, see Vladimir Golitsyn, 'The Arctic – On the Way to Regional Cooperation' (1989) 1 *Marine Policy Reports* 91 at 95–6; *cf.* Griffiths, 'Introduction: The Arctic' at 7 who noted in 1988 that:

> Multilateral interaction among the Arctic states, although increasing in frequency and scope as mentioned above, does not yet appear to be substantial.

[58] Young, 'Arctic Waters' at 102–3; Osherenko and Young, *The Age of the Arctic* at 242–4, where at 244 it is argued that 'simplistic comparisons between the Arctic and the Antarctic do more to confuse the analysis of prospects for international cooperation in the Arctic region than to shed light on this topic'. See also Lincoln P. Bloomfield, 'The Arctic: Last Unmanaged Frontier' (1981–82) 60 *Foreign Affairs* 87 at 103–4.

Instead, he has suggested that the Arctic is a region in which cooperative agreements should be tailored 'to the conditions prevailing in geographically distinct regions or functionally defined issue areas rather than imposing a single model of cooperation regardless of the circumstances at hand'.[59] The best prospects for regime creation in the Arctic in the view of Osherenko and Young arise through the potential for 'functionally specific arrangements' to be negotiated.[60] Because of the increasing prominence given to a variety of regional issues in the past decade, in their view the prospects for regime creation around these single regional issues are more promising than for an all-encompassing Arctic regime.[61] This analysis may go some way to understanding why so much attention has been given to the potential for the law of the sea to be the basis for an Arctic regime,[62] while proposals for broad regional institutions such as the Arctic Council have been resisted.

Because of the recent strategic importance of the Arctic and concerns expressed over the militarisation of the region there have been proposals for the region to be demilitarised, or alternatively, for arms-control mechanisms to adopted.[63] While this has been identified as an issue area around which regime formation could occur, many commentators are pessimistic over the prospects of this occurring.[64] It has always been acknowledged, however, that the environment may be the catalyst around which a regime would form. While it is still early in the AEPS process, the signs are certainly encouraging that this has become an important issue area around which the Arctic states are prepared to converge and cooperate.

However, this author has argued that there are some benefits in considering how certain Antarctic issues were dealt with to determine how similar Arctic issues may also be resolved: see Donald R. Rothwell, 'Polar Lessons for an Arctic Regime' (1994) 29 *Cooperation and Conflict* 55–76.

59 Oran R. Young, *The Arctic in World Affairs* (Seattle, 1989) 13–14.

60 Osherenko and Young, *The Age of the Arctic* at 268. 61 *Ibid.*

62 Barnaby J. Feder, 'A Legal Regime for the Arctic' (1976–8) *Ecology Law Quarterly* 785–829; J. Enno Harders, 'In Quest of an Arctic Legal Regime' (1987) 11 *Marine Policy* 285–98; Alexei Yu Roginko and Matthew J. LaMourie, 'Emerging Marine Environmental Protection Strategies for the Arctic' (1992) 16 *Marine Policy* 259–76; Douglas Brubaker, *Marine Pollution and International Law* (London, 1993) 294–432 who proposes an Arctic Convention plus additional Protocols based on the provisions of UNCLOS, Part XII.

63 See David Cox and Tariq Rauf, *Security Co-operation in the Arctic* (Ottawa, 1989).

64 Elizabeth Young, 'The Arctic: Prospects for an International Regime' in R. B. Byers and Michael Slack (eds.), *Strategy and the Arctic* (Toronto, 1986) 105 at 107–8; Osherenko and Young, *The Age of the Arctic* at 243.

Whether steps towards the creation of a comprehensive Arctic regime will occur is at present uncertain. While the signs are positive, a number of important issues will need resolution before a regime can form. One important impediment to regime formation may be sovereignty. While there are no territorial disputes in the Arctic, the disputes over maritime zones are important because of the potential resources states may gain access to following a favourable maritime boundary settlement. Jurisdictional disputes over the Northwest and Northeast Passages also present impediments to greater cooperation on transportation issues.[65] Unresolved sovereignty questions over the offshore are also matters of concern for indigenous peoples in the region in areas such as the Beaufort Sea, where sea ice has allowed native hunting to take place irrespective of political boundaries. Any Arctic regime that does not seek to solve these outstanding sovereignty and jurisdictional questions will face difficulties.[66] With the gradual political mobilisation of Arctic indigenous peoples, and the recognition which is now given to their legitimate interest in environmental and resource management,[67] an Arctic regime will need to accommodate their interests if it is to attain legitimacy. Dealing with non-state actors such as the Inuit Circumpolar Conference will present a challenge to the Arctic states. However, their commitment to the inclusion of indigenous peoples in the AEPS process does indicate that they are prepared to take into account the views of these peoples.[68] It will also be important for some Arctic states to take a lead in regime formation. While the salience of an issue area often brings states together, there will always be a need for one state to take the initiative to begin the consultation process. In the case of the AEPS Finland took this role, while Canada has led the way on the Arctic Council proposal. That the United States, the major political power in the region, has not taken an active role is curious. This may stem from the fact that of all the Arctic states the United States has the most

[65] Erik Franckx, *Maritime Claims in the Arctic* (Dordrecht, 1993) 297–307 argues that recent initiatives towards greater cooperation amongst Arctic states are conducive to solving some of the jurisdictional issues in both the Northeast and Northwest Passages.

[66] Robert L. Friedheim, 'The Regime of the Arctic – Distributional or Integrative Bargaining?' (1988) 19 ODIL 493 at 504.

[67] See 1992 Rio Declaration on Environment and Development, (1992) 31 ILM 874, Principle 22.

[68] See AEPS, 1,668, para. 10. Canada has also indicated that it favours the inclusion of Arctic indigenous peoples in negotiations concerning the 'Arctic Council': Dr Robert G. McRae, Deputy Director, Environment Division, Department of External Affairs (Canada) (personal communication, 21 April 1993).

tenuous connection with the region and often sees Arctic issues in terms of Alaskan state politics.[69] However, given the Cold War rivalry between the United States and the former USSR and the still simmering strategic tensions between the United States and Russia in the Arctic, there may be advantages for middle-power Arctic states to take the lead in suggesting regime creation. The recent initiatives by Finland and Canada are perhaps testimony to this function of power politics and a characteristic of regime formation.[70]

Regime theory and the polar regions

This chapter has sought to demonstrate the values of a regime analysis of international law in the polar regions. While unique polar conditions have primarily been responsible for the development of the polar legal regimes, the dynamics of the polar regimes have also contributed to the development of many specific polar responses to international law issues. Because this process is dominated by geopolitics, regime analysis allows for an enhanced understanding of international law in the polar regions. As Donnelly has argued, by considering:

> norms, decision-making procedures, and their political context as parts of a more comprehensive structure, regime analysis is particularly conducive to capturing the insights of realism, idealism, and legalism, while avoiding their one-sidedness. Furthermore, it requires us to combine them into a single coherent package.[71]

The recent process of regime change in Antarctica gives some insights into the forces which are at play within a regime and how carefully negotiated international legal instruments can suddenly be abandoned. This has been primarily due to the emergence of a new issue area around which the regime members have chosen to converge. The gradual emergence of the environment as an Antarctic issue area was partially obscured due to the consensus approach adopted amongst the parties in dealing with that issue. There was never any question prior to CRAMRA of any environmental measures

[69] Young, 'Arctic Waters' at 105 has noted that: 'Americans . . . are in the habit of not thinking about Arctic issues at all.'

[70] Osherenko and Young, *The Age of the Arctic* at 241–2.

[71] Jack Donnelly, 'International Human Rights: A Regime Analysis' (1986) 40 IntOrg 599 at 640. Kenneth W. Abbott, 'Elements of Joint Discipline' (1992) 86 ProcAmSocIL 167 at 169 also notes in this regard that: 'IR (international relations) theory shows, moreover, that legal arrangements are only one of many ways by which states structure cooperation.'

implemented under the regime substantially impacting upon the national interest of any party.[72] However, through a change in both domestic and international policies towards environmental protection this perception changed, with the result that CRAMRA could suddenly be overturned and with seemingly little hesitation the Protocol was adopted.

In the case of the Arctic, there is some evidence to suggest that states are interested in participating in a process which may lead to the eventual creation of a comprehensive regional regime. Despite international lawyers calling for the creation of an 'Arctic legal regime' ever since the 1970s, there has been little understanding of the dynamics at play amongst the Arctic states and the impediments which have existed for such a regime. Without an issue area around which Arctic states were willing to converge, the prospects for an international regime were dim. The changes in the late 1980s brought about by an increased awareness of transnational environmental issues in the Arctic, the reduction in tension following the close of the Cold War, and initiatives such as Gorbachev's Murmansk speech calling for greater cooperation amongst Arctic states,[73] have all assisted in bringing regime creation much closer to reality. As a result the conditions have been created where initiatives such as the AEPS, and possibly the Arctic Council, may succeed in creating an Arctic regime which will spawn more extensive international legal instruments to deal with specific Arctic issues.

The value of regime theory in expanding understanding of how international law evolves and operates is demonstrated by comparing a legal and regime analysis of the recent upheaval in the ATS.[74] International lawyers would most likely see the debate purely in terms of which are the most appropriate legal rules for Antarctica. Should rules be adopted to regulate Antarctic mining activities? Should an outright prohibition be implemented or rather an intricate regulatory

[72] This is based on the assumption that such measures were effective. During the 1980s considerable attention was placed on the decision by France to build an airstrip in the vicinity of a penguin colony. Consequently the question was raised as to why the Consultative Parties to the Treaty allowed such an activity to occur when it appeared to be in breach of the regime's existing environmental provisions: see C. C. Joyner, 'Protection of the Antarctic Environment: Rethinking the Problems and Prospects' (1986) 19 Cornell ILJ 259 at 268–70.

[73] See the discussion in chapter 6.

[74] The difference in approaches between regime theorists and international lawyers towards analysing international norms and institutions is developed further by Slaughter-Burley, 'International Law' at 220.

mechanism which allows some mining within strict guidelines (CRAMRA)? Similarly, the environmental debate can be seen in the same light. Should the existing legal rules which have been devised (Recommendations and Agreed Measures) be amended so as to become more effective, or rather should a new set of comprehensive legal measures be devised to regulate the protection of the complete Antarctic environment (Protocol)? Such a simplistic analysis does not get us very far in understanding the dynamics of these various debates, or allow us with much certainty to predict the outcome. Here a rule-driven international legal analysis does not allow much scope for an understanding of what is happening to a complex series of international law rules which have built up around the Antarctic Treaty and which regulate the affairs of a whole continent and its adjacent ocean area.

Regime analysis on the other hand views these problems in a different light.[75] Regime theorists would argue that the Antarctic regime, and by implication the Antarctic Treaty, were negotiated around the principal issues of sovereignty, demilitarisation, national security and science. The effectiveness of the regime to cope with the debate between mining and greater environmental protection was hampered by the impact of a substantial change in the issue area. With the environment having entered the regime as an issue and the post-Cold War era seeing a displacement of a demilitarised and denuclearised Antarctica as a pivotal issue, the regime is facing major change. With this shift in the issues, there has also occurred a shift in the power balances within the regime. The Antarctic hegemon, the United States, is discovering that it no longer holds as much sway in the regime as it once did. Middle powers such as Australia and France have instead taken the lead with the result that the United States has been forced either to accept regime change or abandon the regime. A regime analysis would also probably suggest that unless the regime dynamics suddenly shift back towards the hegemon, which on current indications is most unlikely, in the future the Antarctic regime will be more environmentally centred with science also a major issue. Previous concerns over sovereignty, militarisation and national security will remain, but will be seen as relatively minor and with little influence compared to the new concerns.

The difference in these analyses is considerable and serves as a

[75] For a comprehensive regime analysis of the ATS undertaken in 1988 see Peterson, *Managing the Frozen South* at 193–223.

reminder that if international lawyers wish to gain a greater understanding of what occurs in the legal system they study, then there is some value to be gained from crossing disciplinary boundaries.[76] This is not to suggest that regime theory offers an explanation for all occurrences in the international system. There are limits to how much it can explain. For international lawyers though, it does offer one way in which a greater understanding can be gained of systems controlled by international law. This is particularly the case with the two polar regions.

[76] Slaughter-Burley, 'International Law' at 205.

Part IV

Conclusion

11 The polar regions and their relationship with international law

This work has sought to explore the legal regimes of the polar regions and the impact they have had on certain areas of international law. In addition, an international relations analysis was undertaken in order to understand better some of the recent developments which have taken place in the polar regions and the international law responses to those developments. The study has been based on the premise that the Arctic and Antarctic are separate but similar regions, which, through a combination of geography, environment and political factors, have certain common elements which make them distinctive from other regions[1] and which require specific responses to international legal issues.[2] In this final chapter, these issues will be further explored. The relationship of the polar regions with international law will briefly be reviewed. The issues raised in previous chapters relating to the law of the sea, resource management, environmental protection and regimes will be highlighted. Conclusions will then be drawn on the influence of the polar regions upon the development of international law. Some comments will be made about the status of the polar regions in the international legal system and what that experience demonstrates for international law and international legal order generally.

1 In regard to the Arctic, see Trevor Lloyd, 'Frontier of Destiny – The Canadian Arctic' (1946) 6(7) *Behind the Headlines* 1–16; Gail Osherenko and Oran R. Young, *The Age of the Arctic* (Cambridge, 1989). With respect to Antarctica, this point is well made in the report of the World Commission on Environment and Development, *Our Common Future* (Oxford, 1987) 279–86.

2 Franklyn Griffiths, 'Introduction: The Arctic as an International Political Region' in Kari Mottola (ed.), *The Arctic Challenge* (Boulder, CO, 1988) 1 at 2.

Polar responses to international law

It has been emphasised throughout this study that from the perspective of international law, the polar regions are unique because of the difficulties they present in the application of traditional concepts and principles of international law. In the case of Antarctica, these difficulties primarily relate to the rules about the acquisition of territorial sovereignty, and in the case of the Arctic, those of the law of the sea. The result has been that distinctive responses have been developed to these problems. This has primarily been a consequence of the polar environment. The polar climate makes it very difficult for humans to establish a permanent presence there. Those that have, such as the Inuit, have lived a subsistence lifestyle controlled by their environment and the availability of food. While some settlements in the Arctic have now developed into traditional villages and towns, they have only done so because of the availability of food and certain services from the south.[3] In Antarctica, where there is no indigenous population, human settlements in the form of scientific bases are totally dependent on outside resources and assistance. As a result of these factors, it has been difficult for states to assert one of their fundamental rights under international law – state sovereignty.[4] This factor, more than any other, demonstrates the difficulties for the application of certain principles of international law in the polar regions. It also lies at the root of many subsequent initiatives to develop alternative approaches to polar legal problems.[5]

The other factor which has influenced the development of distinctive responses to polar legal issues has been the fragile nature of polar ecosystems. The impact of unregulated resource development in the polar regions was vividly demonstrated during the nineteenth century when extensive sealing and whaling activities occurred in the Arctic and Antarctic. Fortunately, polar states have been able to learn from that experience and have had a second chance to regulate

[3] Osherenko and Young, *The Age of the Arctic* at 56–60 describe this development in some parts of the Arctic as 'internal colonialism' in instances where isolated mining communities develop far from major settled areas and are dependent on the 'south' for basic supplies.

[4] John Kish, *The Law of International Spaces* (Leiden, 1973) at 117 argued that:

> The physical nature of Antarctica precludes, however, the concept of territorial sovereignty. Natural conditions in Antarctica do not admit of the exercise of permanent and effective control over Antarctica.

[5] Roberto E. Guyer, 'Antarctica's Role in International Relations' in Francisco Orrego Vicuna (ed.), *Antarctic Resources Policy* (Cambridge, 1983) 267 at 267.

resource exploitation so as to guard against further environmental impact. Not only has this occurred in the case of sealing, whaling and other marine living resources, but increasingly attention has also been given to the need to protect polar marine and terrestrial areas generally. This has resulted in the development of a number of specific polar responses which remain distinctive from those adopted in the wider international legal system.

These distinctive polar legal responses have not been due to the inapplicability of either general or specific principles of international law to the polar regions. As has been demonstrated throughout this study there is ample scope for the application of both general and specific international law in these regions.[6] The majority of territorial claims in the polar regions were originally asserted on the basis of traditional notions of territorial acquisition. The dominant legal regime dealing with marine pollution is that created by general principles in conventions such as the 1982 United Nations Convention on the Law of the Sea (UNCLOS)[7] as well as by the more specific provisions found in instruments such as the 1973/78 International Convention for the Prevention of Pollution from Ships.[8] Several of these global regimes, such as the law of the sea (both custom and treaty-based) and the regulation of international whaling, have had an important influence in the polar regions. However, there have been difficulties in applying some of these broad universal provisions of international law in both polar regions. There are also few examples of global international conventions making specific reference to the polar regions and seeking to deal with polar issues.[9] It has partly been a result of this experience, that the polar states have increasingly adopted their own specific response to international law issues.

The polar responses to these problems have primarily been concerned with sovereignty, resource management, environmental pro-

[6] In regard to Antarctica, see Jonathan I. Charney, 'The Antarctic System and Customary International Law' in Francesco Francioni and Tullio Scovazzi (eds.), *International Law for Antarctica* (Milan, 1987) 55–99. With respect to the Arctic, see 1991 Arctic Environmental Protection Strategy, (1991) 30 ILM 1,624, Pt 4 at 1,644–9 detailing existing international mechanisms for the protection of the Arctic.

[7] (1982) 21 ILM 1,261 (hereinafter UNCLOS).

[8] (1973) 12 ILM 1,319, as amended by 1978 Protocol, (1978) 17 ILM 546.

[9] One exception to this is UNCLOS, Art. 234. However, the fact that there is only one specific provision in a convention as large as UNCLOS which deals with the polar regions is further indication of how global legal regimes ignore polar issues.

tection and furthering regional cooperation. In the case of sovereignty, Article IV of the Antarctic Treaty[10] is indicative of the need for special solutions to be developed for polar problems.[11] Without Article IV, the Antarctic Treaty would not have eventuated and it is probable that the Treaty would not have continued for as long as it has if not for its success in dealing with the sovereignty issue.[12] Given the tension associated with sovereignty questions when the Treaty was negotiated, Article IV can also be characterised as a dispute-resolution mechanism. While it did not seek to settle permanently questions concerning Antarctic sovereignty, its effect has been to set aside successfully the issue for the Treaty's duration. The continued acceptance by the Treaty parties of the basic tenets of Article IV is demonstrated by their perpetuation of its terms in subsequent Antarctic Treaty System (ATS) instruments.[13]

In the Arctic there have been similar experiences dealing with sovereignty. The declaration of 'sector claims', despite not having any substantial legal foundation, is an example of how Arctic states developed and applied distinctive polar solutions to problems not encountered in other regions. The 1920 Spitsbergen (Svalbard) Treaty is another example.[14] While the Treaty nominally recognised Norwegian sovereignty, it provided equal economic access for all parties to the Archipelago's resources. This resolution went to the heart of the dispute over Svalbard's status – resource rights. Despite the potential for further disagreement, the Treaty has been a success. In another context, the 1988 Arctic Cooperation Agreement between Canada and the United States over the use of the Northwest Passage represents another attempt to set aside a sovereignty dispute.[15] These examples demonstrate that similarly to the Antarctic Treaty parties, Arctic

[10] 402 UNTS 71.

[11] For a discussion of the problems encountered in Antarctica in applying traditional principles concerning the acquisition of territory, the assertion of sovereignty and Article IV, see Donald W. Greig, 'Sovereignty, Territory and the International Lawyer's Dilemma' (1988) 26 *Osgoode Hall Law Review* 127 at 163–9.

[12] For a discussion of this aspect of the Treaty and how it successfully resolved a major conflict amongst the Treaty parties, see Arthur D. Watts, 'The Antarctic Treaty as a Conflict Resolution Mechanism' in *Antarctic Treaty System* (Washington, 1986) 65–75.

[13] See 1980 Convention on the Conservation of Antarctic Marine Living Resources, (1980) 19 ILM 841 (hereinafter CCAMLR), Art. IV; 1988 Convention on the Regulation of Antarctic Mineral Resource Activities, (1988) 27 ILM 868 (hereinafter CRAMRA), Art. 9.

[14] 1920 Treaty concerning the Archipelago of Spitsbergen (Svalbard), 2 LNTS 8.

[15] Agreement between the Government of Canada and the Government of the United States of America on Arctic Cooperation, [1988] CTS 29.

states have also been prepared to adopt imaginative solutions to sovereignty problems.

In the case of resource management, the earliest initiative was the 1911 Convention for the Preservation and Protection of Fur Seals in the North Pacific Ocean.[16] In this instance, Arctic states recognised the need to regulate resource exploitation in order to preserve the resource and lessen environmental impact. This initiative was so successful that it was continued in various forms up till the 1980s. A similar approach occurred with the 1972 Convention for the Conservation of Antarctic Seals (CCAS),[17] despite there being no firm prospects for commercial sealing recommencing in Antarctica at the time of its negotiation. The ecosystem approach has also been adopted in a number of polar responses to resource management issues. The 1973 Agreement on the Conservation of Polar Bears,[18] recognised for the first time in Arctic wildlife management that unless the protection of habitat was also taken into account in management decisions, species protection would be incomplete. The 1980 Convention on the Conservation of Antarctic Marine Living Resources (CCAMLR)[19] is the best example of this approach. It was understood that because of the nature of the food chain in the Southern Ocean marine environment, substantial harvesting of fish or krill resources would have an impact upon the whole ecosystem. In implementing this approach, CCAMLR placed emphasis on the need for scientific knowledge of the ecosystem so that management decisions could be made with an understanding of the potential environmental impact. This concentration on specific resource and environmental issues has recently shifted to deal with broader regional problems. The 1991 Protocol on Environmental Protection to the Antarctic Treaty (Protocol),[20] while partly a political response to the rejection of the 1988 Convention on the Regulation of Antarctic Mineral Resource Activities (CRAMRA),[21] is an acknowledgment by the Antarctic Treaty parties that a need existed to take a more comprehensive approach towards Antarctic environmental protection. The Arctic Environmental Protection Strategy (AEPS)[22] represents a particular Arctic response to the challenge of dealing with regional environmental problems. Without an existing legal instrument through which to be implemented, the AEPS will primarily rely on

[16] (1911) 214 ConTS 80. [17] (1972) 11 ILM 251 (hereinafter CCAS).

[18] (1974) 13 ILM 13. [19] Note 13 above.

[20] (1991) 30 ILM 1,455 (hereinafter Protocol). [21] Note 13 above.

[22] Note 6 above.

individual state initiatives, regional cooperation and goodwill to be successfully implemented. Despite these potential problems with its implementation, the AEPS is another example of the importance the polar states have attached to dealing with environmental issues through the adoption of specific regional responses.

Finally, the polar regions demonstrate the advantages of a regional approach to common issues. Globally, the ATS is perhaps the best developed and most sophisticated regional response to international law problems.[23] While it could be argued that the ATS was forced upon the Antarctic states, the way it has developed from the original Treaty to a complex network of additional Recommendations and legal instruments shows the confidence the Treaty parties have had in the ability of the ATS to deal with the region. The success of the ATS in Antarctic and Southern Ocean management has also been reflected in the fact that Antarctic issues have not been substantially debated at major international law-making conferences such as the Third UN Conference on the Law of the Sea and the 1992 UN Conference on Environment and Development.[24] While the Arctic has been slower in adopting a regional approach, partly due to political factors at play in the region up till the 1980s, there is evidence of increasing impetus for the adoption of regional cooperative mechanisms. The AEPS is the prime example of this; however, there was also encouraging evidence throughout the 1980s of greater bilateral cooperation amongst Arctic states. The Arctic Council proposal represents the present culmination of a push towards greater Arctic-wide multilateral cooperation.

Polar issues and international law

Law of the sea

In five areas of the law of the sea, considerable difficulties exist in applying existing international rules to polar waters. These are: the special characteristics of ice-covered waters, the determination of baselines, maritime zones, high seas freedoms, and marine environmental protection. These difficulties are primarily a result of the polar

[23] While the European Community is increasingly becoming more integrated through the development of 'European Community law', its development was not founded on the need to resolve international law issues, but rather on a desire to develop an integrated European economy based on trade and other common measures.

[24] This is not to suggest that the legitimacy of the ATS has not been questioned at other UN fora: see pp. 453–5 below.

environment and geography, and because legal rules developed globally fail to take account of the special circumstances of the polar regions. This is evident from a review of the four 1958 Geneva Conventions on the Law of the Sea and UNCLOS. Only one provision in these five conventions, Article 234 of UNCLOS, specifically addresses polar law of the sea problems, and even then there is a debate over whether it can apply to both the Arctic and Antarctic.

The status of ice in international law highlights these issues. Despite being a significant factor in maritime activities and impacting upon a range of areas dealt with by traditional and conventional notions of the law of the sea, there have been no attempts to deal with the status of ice or the problems it raises.[25] The ATS has partly responded to this by making express reference to ice shelves and pack ice in a number of instruments.[26] However, problems still remain with respect to the drawing of baselines around ice-covered coastlines, whether sea and fast ice is subject to claim, and the rights of indigenous peoples over ice-covered waters. The inadequacy of the law of the sea in dealing with the extent of the deep sea-bed regime has also been considered in the ATS with efforts made in both CRAMRA and the Protocol to assert jurisdiction over potential seabed mining activities. Finally, with the exception of Article 234, international law has given little substantive recognition to the special problems faced in dealing with marine pollution in the polar seas. In this area the polar states have been particularly active, with initiatives ranging from Canada's 1970 unilateral extension of jurisdiction in the Arctic to those more recently taken under the Protocol and AEPS.

Resource management

Throughout much of the twentieth century resource management in the polar regions has been characterised by a sustainable development approach. This contrasts with unregulated resource exploitation which took place in the nineteenth century. Despite this heritage, the polar regions have generally been able successfully to implement resource management techniques for living resources which have been both distinctive and far reaching. Commencing with the 1911 Fur Seals Convention, and extending through to CCAMLR, polar states have sought to ensure that resource exploitation has been based on

[25] Even in the case of UNCLOS, Art. 234, ice is primarily used as a descriptor for the area within which certain provisions may apply.

[26] See Antarctic Treaty, Art. VI; CCAS, Art. 5.

principles of conservation which increasingly have taken a wider ecosystem approach.

Three characteristics are evident in the resource management approaches adopted in the polar regions. One has been a desire to adopt pre-emptive resource management regimes in order to ensure unregulated exploitation of resources does not occur to the detriment of the resource and environment. Both the 1911 Fur Seals Convention and CCAS are examples of international instruments adopted to regulate activities which in the nineteenth century devastated seal stocks. CCAMLR, CRAMRA and the Protocol are other examples. A second characteristic has been a realisation that successful resource management demands an ecosystem approach, especially in areas where the ecosystem is particularly vulnerable to excessive exploitation. CCAMLR is the outstanding example here. Finally, environmentally sensitive resource management also requires stock data on which to base resource management decisions. Emphasis has been placed on the collection, analysis and implementation of management decisions based on such data. In the case of the CCAMLR Scientific Committee, such a process has been institutionalised.

Environment

Throughout the twentieth century the polar states, and international law in the polar regions, have increasingly adopted an environmental focus. From the 1911 Fur Seals Convention through to both the Protocol and AEPS, a variety of specific polar initiatives have been taken dealing with environmental protection and conservation. In many instances, these initiatives have been considered radical at the time, but have gradually been accepted as legitimate responses to environmental issues. There has been an increasing dedication to preservation and conservation of the environment. Initially, the approach taken was a sectoral one in which individual species such as seals and polar bears were singled out for protection. However, as demonstrated in CCAMLR, the Protocol and the AEPS, a broader ecosystem approach is now being adopted. A number of important initiatives have been taken in implementing such an approach. The jurisdictional reach of legal measures has not been determined by relying on legal definitions of a region, but, as in the case of CCAMLR, scientific definitions of what constitutes the relevant ecosystem have been adopted. A variety of measures have been put in place seeking to control environmental impact. These range from CCAMLR's Conservation Measures regulating harvesting of certain marine living resources, to the Protocol's environmental impact assessment procedures. Protected areas have also been designated under global international conventions and regional initiatives.

Perhaps the best example of how environmentally focused the polar regions have become is the Protocol to the Antarctic Treaty. The Protocol was adopted only after the Antarctic Treaty parties had spent much of the previous ten years debating the need for, and eventually negotiating, a regime for Antarctic minerals activities. Despite this effort, this initiative was abandoned in favour of the Protocol which adopted far-reaching measures for the protection of Antarctica. Not only does the Protocol designate Antarctica as a natural reserve, it also implements provisions which will consider every existing and future activity conducted in Antarctica from the perspective of potential environmental impact.

Polar regimes

This study has also emphasised the advantages of international cooperation in dealing with regional issues. While both polar regions are examples of this approach, they have relied upon different processes to enhance regional cooperation. Antarctica has also been more advanced than the Arctic in these developments. Why these differing approaches occurred cannot be explained solely on the basis of a legal analysis. Because of the different approaches which have been taken, there are major differences in how the legal regime of each region is structured. In chapter 10 the ability of regime theory to explain some of these developments was considered. As both polar regions constitute political regimes, adopting a regime analysis of what has occurred to these regimes during this century allows for a greater understanding of why international cooperation develops, why legal mechanisms are created and how variations may occur in both. This approach provides a valuable contribution to a better understanding of how international law is created, implemented and enforced and its role in world order.

A regime approach is particularly helpful when considering recent events in the polar regions. Why was CRAMRA abandoned and the Protocol adopted? International law cannot give a complete explanation of the reasons. However, a regime analysis of these events demonstrates that the Antarctic regime was undergoing a process of regime change at a time when new issue areas were dominating. In the Arctic, despite interest by international lawyers in the need for a comprehensive Arctic legal regime, there have been few real initiatives towards that end. However, in recent years there has been increased evidence of Arctic cooperation and indications that a new Arctic regime is in the process of being formed. Already, the AEPS is one outcome of this process, and if an Arctic Council is also formed, this will have further implications for international law. Regime analysis suggests that these events are due to a change of the political alignments amongst Arctic states and also to the emergence of a major issue area: the environment. Both these explanations provide additional insights into how international law is created by states through treaties, and why it continues to evolve or in some cases is abandoned. Given the complexities of the polar legal regimes, these are important insights from an international law perspective.

The polar regions and international law

Within the polar regions, a variety of approaches have been taken to deal with polar issues. These approaches have impacted upon the application of some traditional areas of international law and also led to a greater understanding of how some areas of international law evolve and operate. This is not to suggest that the solutions to all problems which exist in the polar regions can be applied equally to other similar issue areas. Even within the polar context, it has often been noted that the Antarctic Treaty could not readily be applied in the Arctic.[27] Nevertheless, the legal regimes of the polar regions may provide important models for other regions and states dealing with similar issues.[28] The contributions from the polar regions to the development of international law will now be discussed under a number of common headings.

[27] Osherenko and Young, *The Age of the Arctic* at 242–4. See also Erik Franckx, 'Environmental Protection: An Arctic–Antarctic Comparison' in Joe Verhoeven, Philippe Sands and Maxwell Bruce (eds.), *The Antarctic Environment and International Law* (London, 1992) 109–19. This is not to suggest that the Arctic cannot learn certain lessons from the Antarctic experience: see Donald R. Rothwell, 'Polar Lessons for an Arctic Regime' (1994) 29 *Cooperation and Conflict* 55–76.

[28] As an example of this approach, see Olav Schram Stokke, 'The Relevance of the Antarctic Treaty System as a Model for International Cooperation' in Arnfinn Jorgensen-Dahl and Willy Ostreng (eds.), *The Antarctic Treaty System in World Politics* (London, 1991) 357–71.

International cooperation

The most significant contribution of the polar regions to international law is that they demonstrate the importance of international cooperation. In an era of the United Nations, increased global interdependence and greater multilateral cooperation, this may not seem to be such a significant achievement. However, in light of the political climate which previously existed in the Arctic and Antarctic, the degree of international cooperation which exists today is remarkable. Prior to 1959 great political tension existed in Antarctica due to conflicting and uncertain territorial claims and the presence of the United States and the then USSR, both engaged in Cold War jostling which could have resulted in nuclear war.[29] In the Arctic, Cold War tensions were even more acute as both superpowers faced off against each other across the Arctic Ocean. The 'North' was seen by many as the frontline of any Cold War hostilities and the presence of military bases and naval patrols throughout the region served to heighten the security fears of many Arctic states.[30] From these regions developed the Antarctic Treaty, one of the most successful multilateral treaties of our time, and Arctic cooperation to a level where serious discussions are now occurring over the need for an Arctic Council.

In Antarctica, it has been argued that the Treaty 'made the difference between a continent of rivalry and conflict and one of peace and cooperation'.[31] Given the potential for conflict in Antarctica prior to the Treaty, and the current high level of international cooperation which now exists there, this assertion cannot be challenged. The Treaty was successfully able to demilitarise Antarctica, to declare that the continent was to be used for peaceful purposes, to emphasise the importance of continuing scientific cooperation, to prohibit the use of nuclear weapons, and to put an end to tensions over sovereignty.[32]

[29] Watts, 'The Antarctic Treaty' at 65.

[30] Osherenko and Young, *The Age of the Arctic* at 17 where it is noted: 'The Arctic has possessed an irreducible strategic significance throughout the postwar era.' For further discussion of the militarisation and strategic significance of the Arctic see Oran R. Young, *Arctic Politics* (Dartmouth, NH, 1992) 190–213; Michael MccGwire, 'Strategic Interests in the Arctic' in Edgar J. Dosman (ed.), *Sovereignty and Security in the Arctic* (London, 1989) 24–40.

[31] Francisco Orrego Vicuna, 'Antarctic Conflict and International Cooperation' in *Antarctic Treaty System* (Washington, 1986) 55 at 61; see also Watts, 'The Antarctic Treaty' at 65–75.

[32] World Commission on Environment and Development, *Our Common Future* at 282 commented that: 'This is a foundation on which humanity must build.' See also

These are significant results given the national interests involved. However, the ATS has continued to evolve since 1961. The sophisticated network of Treaty Recommendations, Conventions and finally the Protocol has allowed the ATS to deal with an increasingly wide range of Antarctic issues, and at each stage the institutional structure has expanded.[33] The number of parties to the ATS has also steadily grown during this time, with many of the acceding states not having any history of a long-standing interest in Antarctic affairs.

In the Arctic, international cooperation has gradually developed throughout the twentieth century. The 1911 Fur Seals Convention was an initial indicator that Arctic states were capable of cooperating in matters of common interest, as was the 1920 Spitsbergen (Svalbard) Treaty. However, there were no further non-military multilateral cooperative efforts amongst the Arctic states till the 1973 Polar Bear Agreement. Because of this interval in Arctic cooperation, the 1973 Agreement is considered symbolic.[34] Since its conclusion, there has been increased evidence of cooperation amongst Arctic states at both the bilateral and multilateral level. This cooperation has been centred on areas of resource management and environmental protection. Starting with President Gorbachev's Murmansk speech greater efforts have been made to broaden the scope of Arctic international cooperation. The results to date include the AEPS and the International Arctic Science Committee, with an Arctic Council still a possibility. Arctic states have gradually grown to realise that many of the issues confronting their region can only be adequately dealt with through international cooperation,[35] especially issues such as transboundary pollution and resource management. While the Arctic Council proposal still has an uncertain future, there remains sufficient momentum

Brian Roberts, 'International Co-operation for Antarctic Development: The Test for the Antarctic Treaty' (1978) 19 *Polar Record* 107 at 108–10; Sergei N. Karev, 'Cooperative Momentum? The Antarctic Treaty System and the Prevention of Conflict' in Arnfinn Jorgensen-Dahl and Willy Ostreng (eds.), *The Antarctic Treaty System in World Politics* (London, 1991) 372–7.

33 Philippe Sands, 'The Antarctic Treaty Regime: A Model for International Environmental Law?' in Joe Verhoeven, Philippe Sands and Maxwell Bruce (eds.), *The Antarctic Environment and International Law* (London, 1992) 53 at 56–7.

34 Gail Osherenko and Oran R. Young, 'The Formation of International Regimes: Hypotheses and Cases' in Oran R. Young and Gail Osherenko (eds.), *Polar Politics* (Ithaca, NY, 1993) 1 at 7 note that the Polar Bear Agreement 'stands as testimony to the feasibility of cooperation involving both of the superpowers and several lesser powers with regard to Arctic issues of mutual concern'.

35 Griffiths, 'Introduction: The Arctic' at 2.

on other issues of common concern to suggest that Arctic cooperation will continue to grow and develop.

When international relations regime theory is applied to the polar regions, it is possible to gain a greater understanding of why international cooperation has occurred. In Antarctica, despite disagreements over the status of sovereignty claims plus Cold War rivalry between the superpowers, a number of issue areas emerged which provided the impetus for states to enter into the Antarctic Treaty. In the Arctic, there is evidence that with the ending of the Cold War and a realisation that Arctic environmental problems are the concern of all Arctic states, strong prospects exist for a comprehensive Arctic regime. In both instances, these forms of international cooperation are important examples of how international law can form the basis for a regime which results in peaceful and cooperative management of areas both within and beyond areas of national jurisdiction. From this perspective, the polar regimes are a contrast to other multilateral regional arrangements which predominantly concentrate on security and economic and trade issues.

By adopting a regime approach it is also possible to gain a better insight into the processes at play during the creation and negotiation of international instruments, their subsequent amendment and variation, and even eventual failure. Two distinct benefits of a regime analysis of the polar regions can be identified. First, it allows for a better understanding of the developments in the polar regions which have impacted upon international law. In the case of regime formation, despite encouraging signs that a comprehensive Arctic regime is on the verge of being formed, regime analysis suggests that there will be a need for a hegemon or a group of states to play a pivotal role in encouraging and sponsoring that process.[36] In regard to regime change, recent events in Antarctica provide an interesting study of how political developments can impact upon international law. The sudden rejection of CRAMRA and adoption of the Protocol, a legal instrument with a fundamentally different focus, caught many legal commentators by surprise. Regime theory provides some of the answers to this radical shift in policy. Second, these case studies starkly demonstrate how certain international actors can have a substantial influence upon the emergence, implementation and adherence to international law. Third, they also demonstrate, es-

[36] Franklyn Griffiths, 'Challenge and Leadership in the Arctic' in Edgar J. Dosman (ed.), *Sovereignty and Security in the Arctic* (London, 1989) 211 at 222–7.

pecially in the case of Antarctica, how regime dynamics can impact upon participants and influence whether certain forms of international law are adopted or rejected. These are important insights and provide a better understanding of how international law has developed and been applied.

A regional approach

Regional responses to shared problems have a number of advantages. They often result in more specialised, sophisticated and usually effective legal regimes. Because national interests are usually more immediately at stake, regional regimes often engender greater support amongst participants than wide-ranging international regimes. The Arctic and Antarctic regimes demonstrate the advantages of adopting a common regional approach. By adopting such an approach, the parties to the ATS, and more recently the Arctic states, have dispensed with a reliance upon unilateral state-sponsored initiatives.[37] There has also been a recognition that global initiatives taken by the international community may not always be relevant or specific enough to deal with certain polar issues.[38] A consequence of the rejection of these approaches and adoption of regional responses has been the development of distinctive legal regimes which are more attuned to the shared legal issues of the region.

The ATS today represents one of the best examples of a regional approach in international law. Unlike other regions or groupings of states, Antarctica is an area dominated by international law, with municipal law having little influence.[39] While the regional approach adopted in Antarctica has been criticised as ignoring the interests of

[37] An example of one Arctic state which has begun to change its policies in this regard is Canada, which at one time adopted a unilateral approach in dealing with Arctic marine pollution but now as a member of the AEPS is adopting a more cooperative regional approach.

[38] One example are the initiatives in both polar regions to develop distinctive marine pollution regimes, despite the unquestioned application of the current global regime to both regions. For a discussion of the position in the Arctic, see Douglas Brubaker, *Marine Pollution and International Law* (London, 1993).

[39] A number of studies exist dealing with the application of municipal law in Antarctica; however, in all cases these laws are very much determined by the dynamics of the ATS. For a review of the municipal laws implemented by Australia, see Gillian D. Triggs, *International Law and Australian Sovereignty in Antarctica* (Sydney, 1986) 241–68; James Crawford and Donald R. Rothwell, 'Issues Confronting Australia's Antarctica' (1992) 13 AYIL 53 at 73–88; Australia, House of Representatives, Standing Committee on Legal and Constitutional Affairs, *Australian Law in Antarctica* (Canberra, 1992).

other states that may have legitimate interests in the region and its future, membership of the ATS is open to all states. Likewise in the Arctic, a regional approach has increasingly been adopted. In the case of the 1911 Fur Seals Convention, the four states directly involved in the harvesting of fur seals in the Bering Sea region reached agreement on future management practices. The 1920 Spitsbergen (Svalbard) Treaty is a further example dealing with broader regional issues. The Treaty sought to resolve a simmering issue that had the potential to result in regional conflict over sovereign and resource rights. The solution agreed to involved both Arctic and other interested states. It is interesting to note that the Treaty not only had as parties those states most closely concerned with the future status of the Archipelago (Norway and Russia) but also involved Arctic states and others geographically removed from the area (Japan and the USA). As the Arctic states have begun to realise that the region is both ecologically and politically linked, there have been increased regional efforts to deal with Arctic-wide issues. While commentators have devoted much attention to whether 'marine regionalism' can be applied in the Arctic,[40] there is increasing evidence that this legal concept has been overtaken by initiatives relating to the need to protect the complete Arctic environment.[41] In the Arctic and Antarctic, the success of regional initiatives has highlighted the inadequacies of adopting a state-centred or global international law approach to dealing with some polar issues.

Polar sovereignty

One of the consequences of participation by states in treaties and international organisations is the diminution of sovereign rights. In most instances these limitations placed upon state sovereignty are accepted because of the gains which are perceived to exist through participation in the legal regime. In one sense the polar legal regimes have had this impact upon the parties. Both polar regimes place

[40] See J. Enno Harders, 'In Quest of an Arctic Legal Regime' (1987) 11 *Marine Policy* 285–98; Alexei Yu Roginko and Matthew J. LaMourie, 'Emerging Marine Environmental Protection Strategies for the Arctic' (1992) 16 *Marine Policy* 259–76.

[41] One outgrowth of this has been the development of the concept of 'international environmental security': see Anatoly Kolodkin, Natalia Mirovitskaya and Alexei Roginko, 'The Arctic: Arena for International Environmental Security?' (1993) 10 *Ocean Yearbook* 277–89; Renet Perelet, 'Environmental Security and Governance Issues in the Arctic Ocean' in *Proceedings – Radioactivity and Environmental Security in the Oceans* (Woods Hole, MA, 1993) 595–601.

limitations upon the ability of states to harvest certain resources which otherwise would be within their accepted sovereign rights. The increased emphasis on environmental protection has also created limitations on the exercise of certain incidents of state sovereignty that may have a detrimental environmental impact. Accordingly, even Antarctic territorial claimants will now be required to undertake an environmental impact assessment if they propose to develop new, or even modify existing, scientific research facilities.[42] The AEPS also requires Arctic states to limit those activities within their control which have a continuing impact upon the Arctic environment.[43] The polar regions provide a model for reassessing traditional notions of state sovereignty.[44] They are at the forefront in an era in which increasing concern for the global environment is resulting in new forms of international environmental law that place further limitations on state sovereignty. This is perhaps best illustrated by the 1991 decision of the ATCPs to abandon CRAMRA and instead adopt the Protocol with its mining prohibition. Not only does this decision represent an extreme application of the precautionary approach, but it also represents a considerable limitation on the sovereign rights of the territorial claimants in ways never contemplated when the Antarctic Treaty was negotiated. This Antarctic model of placing a limitation upon one of the fundamental incidents of state sovereignty, is to be contrasted with other global regimes which facilitate resource exploitation within and beyond areas of national jurisdiction.

The polar legal regimes have also adopted distinctive solutions to questions of sovereignty. The characteristics of Antarctic sovereignty post-1961 have been subject to much comment. Not only did Article IV allow for the implementation of the ATS but it has proved to be the foundation upon which the whole ATS is based. Its provisions have been repeated in later Antarctic Treaty instruments and all ATS parties are sensitive to what it has achieved and the continuing importance of its role. The effect of Article IV has been to allow the territorial claimants, whose claims would in most instances have been susceptible to challenge from other potential claimants in 1959, to participate in a legal regime based on joint management and shared jurisdiction without fear that their claims are threatened. Non-claimants, especially those such as the United States and the then

[42] Protocol, Art. 8. [43] AEPS, para. 5.1–5.6.

[44] See the discussion in Greig, 'Sovereignty' at 127–75.

USSR, were also able to accept the Treaty in the knowledge that the claims they could have made in 1959 were not jeopardised and would not be affected by their participation in the Treaty. Through diffusing the potential for continuing conflict between claimants and potential claimants, Article IV also allowed other states to participate in Antarctic affairs in the knowledge that their presence on the continent would not raise political concerns.

From this perspective, Article IV of the Treaty is the fundamental basis on which the whole Antarctic legal regime rests. It limits the ability of the territorial claimants to assert their full sovereign rights and allows other states to engage freely in Antarctic activities irrespective of the existence of territorial claimants. In many respects, sovereignty does not exist in Antarctica. It has effectively become a non-issue, though not to the extent that the claimant states have been willing to give up their territorial claims.[45] A further example of how Antarctic sovereignty differs from the norm is that there is little territorial jurisdiction exercised in Antarctica. Instead, Article VIII of the Treaty recognises jurisdiction based on nationality.[46] The unusual, and sometimes baffling, attitude adopted by the territorial claimants towards Antarctic maritime claims illustrates the impact this provision has on the exercise of jurisdiction in Antarctica.[47] Yet, territorial jurisdiction is the primary basis for the exercise of jurisdiction in international law.[48] It is also a characteristic of a sovereign state. Combined with the provisions of Article IV, Article VIII is a further illustration of how the Antarctic Treaty has contributed to a reassessment of traditional notions of international law.

In the Arctic, there are also important examples of where differing approaches have been taken towards sovereignty. In at least two instances, Arctic maritime claims are based on sectors. Irrespective of the debate which exists over the validity of sector claims, and the

[45] There has been much evidence since 1961 of the seven territorial claimants engaging in activities which, under normal circumstances, would help to solidify their territorial claims. These activities range from the issuing of postage stamps, to visits by political leaders, and the proclamation of municipal laws. See F. M. Auburn, *Antarctic Law and Politics* (London, 1982) 108–9.

[46] For comment on how this operates in practice, see Sir Arthur Watts, *International Law and the Antarctic Treaty System* (Cambridge, 1992) chapter 7, esp. 186–7.

[47] See the discussion concerning Australia's maritime claims in Stuart Kaye and Donald R. Rothwell, 'Australia's Antarctic Maritime Claims and Boundaries' (1995) 26 ODIL 195–226.

[48] Sir Robert Jennings and Sir Arthur Watts, *Oppenheim's International Law* (9th, vol. I, Pt 1) (Harlow, 1992) 458.

degree of official support they have received,[49] the fact remains that maritime claims based on Arctic sectors still exist. While it is unlikely that claims solely based on such a foundation would be accepted today, this should not overshadow the fact that claims based on sectors have played an important role in efforts to assert Arctic sovereignty. They may also become important if Arctic states ever seek in the future to assert spheres of influence over the Arctic Ocean. The 1920 Spitsbergen (Svalbard) Treaty also adopts an interesting approach towards sovereignty. While Norwegian sovereignty over the Archipelago is recognised, it also recognises the rights of other Treaty parties to resources. As a result, an essential aspect of Norwegian sovereignty is missing and instead all it possesses is jurisdiction without full resource benefits.[50] Limitations on sovereign rights have also been imposed in other areas of the Arctic in the case of joint development of maritime resources.[51] Finally, despite Canada's best efforts to assert fully its sovereignty over the Northwest Passage, the 1988 Arctic Cooperation Agreement is another example of the redefinition of sovereignty in the Arctic.[52]

Environmental priority

The polar regimes have also placed increasing emphasis on the need to protect the environment. This originally developed through a concern over resource management, but is now practised in order to protect the whole ecosystem. In this general area, the polar regions provide a number of lessons for the application of international law. Excessive resource exploitation of polar marine living resources in the nineteenth century demonstrated the problems created by the failure of states either individually or collectively to regulate a resource-based industry. Fortunately this lesson had been learnt by the time the 1911 Fur Seals Convention was negotiated. This effort at polar cooperation not only represented a genuine resource management initiative but also sought to take into account the rights of indigenous peoples to a subsistence harvest and the need for adequate scientific knowledge of stocks if effective resource management decisions were to be made.

[49] Erik Franckx, *Maritime Claims in the Arctic* (Dordrecht, 1993) 237.

[50] Norway is in the unique position of having limited sovereign rights in regard to its Antarctic and Arctic (Svalbard) claims.

[51] Examples are the Barents Sea 'Grey Zone' between Norway and Russia and the Jan Mayen Development Zone between Norway and Iceland: see the discussion in chapter 5.

[52] Note 15 above.

This example paved the way for a number of later polar initiatives which are now considered to be important global models.[53]

A number of polar environmental initiatives represent the precautionary principle at work. Those regimes dealing with polar bears, Antarctic seals, Antarctic marine living resources and Antarctic minerals are all examples.[54] A variety of approaches have been adopted as to how best to regulate resource exploitation while maintaining the ecosystem. In some instances (Antarctic seals), a prohibition is placed on the exploitation of certain species. In the case of Antarctic marine living resources controlled exploitation is allowed, subject to the ability of the CCAMLR Commission not only to set catch limits for some regions but also to close those regions. The most extreme example of a precautionary approach to resource management occurred with Antarctic mineral resources. At an early stage a moratorium was placed on minerals activity so as to allow for a regime to be negotiated.[55] During the CRAMRA negotiation process it was accepted that while mining activity may be an appropriate Antarctic activity, because of the nature of the environment it would only be acceptable in cases of minimal environmental risk. Finally, the Protocol was adopted (which overrode the terms of CRAMRA). By placing a continuing prohibition on Antarctic mineral activities, it seeks to regulate completely a potentially damaging activity even before it commenced.

In instances where development and exploitation have been deemed acceptable in the polar regions, emphasis has increasingly been placed upon the need to adopt an ecosystem approach. Single species, marine living resources, defined areas, and complete regions have become subject to an ecosystem approach.[56] The 1964 Agreed Measures on the Protection of Fauna and Flora[57] developed a protected area system for Antarctica which emphasised not only the environmental importance

[53] See Sands, 'The Antarctic Treaty Regime' at 53–61; Natalia S. Mirovitskaya, Margaret Clark and Ronald G. Purver, 'North Pacific Fur Seals: Regime Formation as a Means of Resolving Conflict' in Oran R. Young and Gail Osherenko (eds.), *Polar Politics* (Ithaca, NY, 1993) 22 at 22–5.

[54] For a review of the Antarctic initiatives, see John A. Heap and Martin W. Holdgate, 'The Antarctic Treaty System as an Environmental Mechanism – An Approach to Environmental Issues' in *Antarctic Treaty System* (Washington, 1986) 195 at 206–7.

[55] Recommendation IX-1 (1977).

[56] For an example of how a defined area can be designated and managed, see Per Ove Eikeland, 'Distributional Aspects of Multispecies Management' (1993) 17 *Marine Policy* 256–71.

[57] Recommendation III-VIII, reprinted in Bush (vol. I), 146; *Handbook* (Pt 2), 2,048.

of certain regions but also areas of scientific and historic importance. In the case of polar bears, habitat as well as the species were subject to protection. In CCAMLR, the marine living environment of the Southern Ocean became the subject of extensive study in order to assess the impact of the harvesting of krill. The Protocol seeks to assess impact upon the 'Antarctic environment and dependent and associated ecosystems' before a wide variety of activities will be allowed.[58] For the ecosystem approach to be successfully implemented, polar experience has also shown the importance of having institutional mechanisms which provide independent scientific advice on the state of the ecosystem, and which have the ability to implement environmental impact assessment procedures that understand the special nature of polar environments.[59]

As demonstrated, there are numerous examples of these mechanisms at work in the polar regions. In most instances they have improved upon previous standards and set new ones to be matched in other areas of environmental management.[60] International law has provided the framework within which all of these mechanisms operate. In some instances, the legal instruments have even articulated the precautionary principle and ecosystem approach. No other regions in the world have adopted legal frameworks that provide for such environmental priority.

Distinctive solutions to regional problems

This work has sought to emphasise how a variety of legal responses have been adopted in the polar regions which in many instances were outside existing norms at the time, but have since become accepted as the standard. From this perspective, the polar regions demonstrate the importance of states seeking to devise new methods of dealing with international problems rather than relying upon traditional notions. As has also been stressed, the unique character of the polar environment and its history of development have undoubtedly contributed to some of the legal problems that have been faced and also some of the solutions which have been devised. The importance of these approaches is that in some instances existing norms and principles of international

[58] Protocol, Art. 3.

[59] W. Nigel Bonner, 'Environmental Impact Assessment in the Antarctic' (1989) 18(1) AMBIO 83–9.

[60] Sands, 'The Antarctic Treaty Regime' at 55 notes that the CCAMLR ecosystem approach was subsequently matched in regimes dealing with ozone depletion, climate change, forests and biological diversity.

law found in both custom and treaties have been ignored in favour of a distinctive *sui generis* approach to polar legal problems.[61] The ATS is perhaps the most advanced example of this approach. There is nothing comparable to the legal regime which applies in Antarctica. It is the only continent managed predominantly by international law. While the Arctic legal regime is not as developed as that in Antarctica, there has still been a history of adopting distinctive approaches to legal and regional problems. The 1911 Fur Seals Convention, 1920 Spitsbergen (Svalbard) Treaty and 1973 Polar Bear Agreement are all examples of initiatives which were significant for their time. Even the approach taken with the AEPS is different. After considering state of the environment reports, priority environmental problems were identified as being in need of immediate action by Arctic states.

The polar regions also demonstrate the advantages of employing a combination of mechanisms to achieve goals through international law.[62] The primary approach has been through the use of treaties which in some instances have created institutions to support their implementation. In the case of the Antarctic Treaty, a foundation was laid for the subsequent creation of a whole legal regime based on the fundamental principles of the Treaty. While not directly negotiated under the Treaty framework, both CCAS and CCAMLR adopted the same fundamental principles of the Treaty. The Protocol adopts another approach. In the main body of the instrument, basic principles regarding the protection of the Antarctic environment are laid out. Supporting Annexes then allow the Protocol's provisions to be applied in certain specific areas. The option for additional Annexes to be added when needed also allows the Protocol to be expanded so as to meet new challenges.[63] There has also been a reliance upon soft law instruments of which the AEPS is an example. While not imposing legal obligations upon the Arctic states it does commit them to a plan

61 For comments regarding the application of such an approach towards the law of the sea in the polar regions see Harders, 'In Quest of an Arctic Legal Regime' at 288; Donald R. Rothwell and Stuart Kaye, 'Law of the Sea and the Polar Regions: Reconsidering the Traditional Norms' (1994) 18 *Marine Policy* 41 at 57–8.

62 Such an approach is increasingly being urged with respect to international law responses to environmental problems: see Geoffrey Palmer, 'New Ways to Make International Environmental Law' (1992) 86 AJIL 259–83.

63 In this regard, there has been discussion over the need for an Annex dealing with tourism. See Recommendation XVI-13 (Tourism and Non-Governmental Activities in the Antarctic Treaty Area), and *Final Report of the Seventeenth Antarctic Treaty Consultative Meeting* (Venice, 11–20 November 1992) Item 13, 'Tourism and Non-Governmental Activities in the Antarctic Treaty Area', 40–2, paras. 108–14.

of action in regard to Arctic environmental protection. In the Arctic Monitoring and Assessment Program, an institution has been created to oversee the progress being made in meeting these goals. The Antarctic Treaty also adopted a mechanism whereby Recommendations could be adopted at Treaty meetings. While this is nothing extraordinary, the provisions contained in Article IX of the Treaty for the formal adoption of Recommendations by states, and the subsequent efforts by some states to implement Recommendations by way of domestic legislation, indicate that some Antarctic Treaty Recommendations are considered legally binding by Treaty parties. Under CCAMLR, Conservation Measures, which become binding on the parties, are also adopted. There is also some scope under the AEPS for the parties to adopt resolutions furthering its implementation. By relying on these various mechanisms, the polar legal regimes have considerable flexibility to deal with new and emerging problems. This is an important attribute in regions which are particularly sensitive to environmental impact.

The validity of the polar regimes

It has not been the intention of this work to subject the polar legal regimes to critical analysis. Consequently, little consideration has been given to either their political or legal validity. Major works do exist on the political and legal status of each region.[64] Some have been very critical of the regimes and the management methods and legal responses that have been adopted.[65] However, the validity or otherwise of the polar regimes can not detract from their contributions to international law. Despite the critics, the polar regimes do exist and there is no indication that either politically or legally they are about to disintegrate. Nevertheless, the validity of the polar regimes in the international legal and political system is important and some brief consideration needs to be given to the issues.

[64] In regard to Antarctica, see Philip W. Quigg, *A Pole Apart* (New York, 1983); M. J. Peterson, *Managing the Frozen South* (Berkeley, CA, 1988); Vladimir Golitsyn, 'Reflections on the Legality of the ATS' in Arnfinn Jorgensen-Dahl and Willy Ostreng (eds.), *The Antarctic Treaty System in World Politics* (London, 1991) 343–53; Emilio J. Sahurie, *The International Law of Antarctica* (New Haven, 1992). The primary study dealing with the Arctic is Osherenko and Young, *The Age of the Arctic*; see also Oran R. Young, *Arctic Politics* (Dartmouth, NH, 1992).

[65] See e.g., C. W. Pinto, 'A Proposal' in Joe Verhoeven, Philippe Sands and Maxwell Bruce (eds.), *The Antarctic Environment and International Law* (London, 1992) 165–9.

The political legitimacy of the polar regimes

The ATS is based on the premise that twelve states (seven claimant states plus five others) had the ability to negotiate a treaty for a whole continent and region. Through the expansion of the number of Treaty parties, this premise concerning the management of Antarctica still holds. While there is no similar number of participating state parties to either CCAS or CCAMLR, the intention remains for the ATS to create a legal regime which with very few exceptions manages all Antarctic affairs. By and large this situation was accepted until the early 1980s when states from outside the System began to question whether the ATS was the best form of management for Antarctica, whether it was a legitimate regime, and whether alternatives to the ATS were more appropriate.[66] This matter was placed on the UN agenda in 1982. It resulted in the UN Secretary-General conducting an investigation into the 'Question of Antarctica'[67] and the ATCPs undertaking a spirited defence of the ATS at both the UN and in other fora.[68] The UN debate over Antarctica had its roots in concerns by developing countries that the ATS operated as a 'club' into which non-parties were unable to gain admission. It was pointed out that for a state to accede to the Treaty was not enough. Real power lay with ATCPs. However, to become an ATCP under Article IX(2) required a substantial scientific and financial commitment. Concerns were also expressed over whether the ATCPs had the right to negotiate a minerals regime for Antarctica which sought to exclude non-parties from the process. The result of this

[66] Peter Beck, *The International Politics of Antarctica* (London, 1986) 148. Malaysia played a dominant role in bringing this matter before, and debating the question at, the United Nations. For a review of the Malaysian position see Rajmah Hussain, 'The Antarctic: Common Heritage of Mankind?' in Joe Verhoeven, Philippe Sands and Maxwell Bruce (eds.), *The Antarctic Environment and International Law* (London, 1992) 89–92.

[67] United Nations, Report of the Secretary-General: Study Requested under General Assembly Resolution 38/77, *Question of Antarctica* (UN Doc. A/39/583, 31 October 1984).

[68] See Richard A. Woolcott, 'The Interaction Between the Antarctic Treaty System and the United Nations System' in *Antarctic Treaty System* (Washington, 1986) 375–90. For a comprehensive review of the annual UN discussions concerning Antarctica see the numerous articles by Beck in *Polar Record*, e.g., Peter J. Beck, 'The United Nations and Antarctica' (1984) 22 *Polar Record* 137–44; Peter J. Beck, 'The United Nations' Study on Antarctica, 1984' (1985) 22 *Polar Record* 499–504; Peter J. Beck, 'The 1991 UN Session: The Environmental Protocol Fails to Satisfy the Antarctic Treaty System's Critics' (1992) 28 *Polar Record* 307–14. See also Moritaka Hayashi, 'The Antarctica Question in the United Nations' (1986) 19 Cornell ILJ 275–90; Gillian D. Triggs, 'The United Nations in Antarctica? A Watching Brief' in Gillian D. Triggs (ed.), *The Antarctic Treaty Regime* (Cambridge, 1987) 229–33.

debate was considerable analysis of whether Antarctica was a part of the common heritage of mankind,[69] or whether other forms of management such as UN trusteeship or 'internationalisation' would be appropriate.[70] However, with the rejection of CRAMRA and adoption of the Protocol, the debate over the legitimacy of the ATS, while still an issue,[71] has lost momentum.[72]

In the Arctic, greater debate has existed over the need for greater international cooperation than the actual form that cooperation should take.[73] This is due to the regime being primarily based on state-centred notions of sovereignty with few successful attempts at either bilateral or multilateral cooperation until the 1970s. There has been some discussion as to whether the Arctic is also a region to which the common heritage of mankind concept could apply;[74] however, this debate has never had the same intensity as that in Antarctica. This is due to territorial claims in the Arctic being unquestioned and explains why most Arctic common heritage debates centre on the future of the Arctic Ocean. Nevertheless, if the Arctic legal regime does continue to

[69] There have been many detailed studies on this question: see e.g., Francesco Francioni, 'Antarctica and the Common Heritage of Mankind' in Francesco Francioni and Tullio Scovazzi (eds.), *International Law for Antarctica* (Milan, 1987) 101–36; Sudhir K. Chopra, 'Antarctica as a Commons Regime: A Conceptual Framework for Cooperation and Coexistence' in Christopher C. Joyner and Sudhir K. Chopra (eds.), *The Antarctic Legal Regime* (Dordrecht, 1988) 163–86; Zou Keyuan, 'The Common Heritage of Mankind and the Antarctic Treaty System' (1991) 38 *Netherlands International Law Review* 173–98; Eric Suy, 'Antarctica: Common Heritage of Mankind?' in Joe Verhoeven, Philippe Sands and Maxwell Bruce (eds.), *The Antarctic Environment and International Law* (London, 1992) 93–6; Michael T. Kyriak, 'The Future of the Antarctic Treaty System: An Examination and Evaluation of the "Common Heritage" and "World Park" Proposals for an Alternative Antarctic Regime' (1992) 7 *Auckland University Law Review* 105–26; Triggs, *International Law and Australian Sovereignty* at 277–311.

[70] Benedetto Conforti, 'Territorial Claims in Antarctica: A Modern Way to Deal with an Old Problem' (1986) 19 Cornell ILJ 249–58; J. R. Rowland, 'Whither Antarctica? Alternative Strategies' in Gillian D. Triggs (ed.), *The Antarctic Treaty Regime* (Cambridge, 1987) 218–26.

[71] Arnfinn Jorgensen-Dahl, 'The Legitimacy of the ATS' in Arnfinn Jorgensen-Dahl and Willy Ostreng (eds.), *The Antarctic Treaty System in World Politics* (London, 1991) 287–98.

[72] See Peter J. Beck, 'The United Nations and Antarctica, 1992: Still Searching for that Elusive Convergence of View' (1993) 29 *Polar Record* 313–20.

[73] See e.g., Lincoln P. Bloomfield, 'The Arctic: Last Unmanaged Frontier' (1981–82) 60 *Foreign Affairs* 87–105; Clive Archer, 'General Features of Political Development and Possibilities for Cooperation in the Arctic' (1988) 11(4) *Current Research on Peace and Violence* 137–45; Gail Osherenko, 'Environmental Cooperation in the Arctic: Will the Soviets Participate?' (1989) 1 *International Environmental Affairs* 203–21.

[74] Louis Rey, 'The Arctic: Mankind's Unique Heritage and Common Responsibility' (1987) 19 *Arctic and Alpine Research* 345–50.

develop at the pace which it has, there is scope for questions to be raised over its legitimacy.[75]

In some respects, the increasing emphasis placed upon protection of the polar environments is assisting to enhance the legitimacy of the polar regimes. In the case of Antarctica, the greatest challenge to the legitimacy of the ATS came during the 1980s when the ATCPs were in the midst of negotiating the minerals regime. If implemented, the regime would not only have reinforced the sovereign interests of the seven territorial claimants, but also the rights of the other ATS parties to enjoy the benefits of resource exploitation. With the adoption in 1991 of the Protocol, the UN debate over Antarctica lost momentum. This action allowed the ATCPs to regain the initiative in the debate over legitimacy and also demonstrate to the world the benefits of ATS management of Antarctica. By prohibiting mining in Antarctica and establishing strict environmental guidelines for all activities carried out on the continent, the ATCPs have created a precedent for environmental management that will be difficult to duplicate elsewhere. Likewise, in the Arctic there has been an increased emphasis upon environmental protection. The Arctic states have not only sought to rely upon existing global norms of environmental protection, but have also sought to develop specific responses to Arctic problems. While it is true that parts of the Arctic have been subject to very extensive resource development, the Arctic states are now realising the need for sustainable development. By implementing these developing global environmental norms within areas of national jurisdiction, the Arctic states are increasing their political legitimacy and their capacity to manage comprehensively the whole Arctic environment.

Polar regimes and non-parties

One of the major issues facing the polar regimes is the ability to enforce their legal mechanisms against third parties. This does not so much reflect upon the legitimacy of the polar regimes, but rather their ability to ensure that third parties respect the legal regimes which are in place. With the polar legal regimes increasingly imposing limitations upon the conduct of resource exploitation, navigation rights,

[75] This issue has already arisen in the context of proposals for an Arctic Council in regard to the involvement of indigenous peoples, non-Arctic states and non-governmental organisations: see the discussion in chapter 6.

high seas freedoms and access to polar lands these are important issues.

Whether the ATS applies to non-parties has been the subject of much debate.[76] It is also a question of growing importance following the efforts of CCAMLR to regulate harvesting of marine living resources on the 'high seas' of the Southern Ocean, and the Protocol's prohibition on mining activities and provisions dealing with environmental protection. The main argument in regard to the application of the Treaty against non-parties is whether the Treaty intends to bind non-parties. This raises issues concerning the law of treaties. While third states are not bound by treaties to which they are not a party,[77] an exception does exist when the treaty expressly contemplates this possibility and the third state has consented.[78] The Antarctic Treaty is unclear as to whether it is intended to apply to third states. The Preamble refers to 'the interest of all mankind' that Antarctica be continually used for peaceful purposes and not become subject to international discord. Article X also obliges Treaty parties to ensure that 'no one engages in any activity in Antarctica contrary to the principles or purposes of the present Treaty'.[79] The Treaty also anticipates that nationals of non-parties may engage in activities in Antarctica.[80] From time to time the Treaty parties have also considered the activities in Antarctica of non-parties.[81] However, there has not yet been an instance when the Treaty has actually been applied to a non-party, though non-parties active or interested in Antarctic affairs are urged to accede to the Treaty.[82] Even if it is possible to argue that the Treaty was intended to apply to third states, there are no examples of third states having expressly accepted the Antarctic Treaty other than those which have

[76] See e.g., Bush (vol. I), 99–103; Auburn, *Antarctic Law* at 115–29; Francisco Orrego Vicuna, *Antarctic Mineral Exploration* (Cambridge, 1988), 423–47; Anna Wyrozumska, '*Erga Tertios* Effect of the Antarctic Treaty' (1993) 6 *ASOLPO Paper* 25–49.

[77] 1969 Convention on the Law of Treaties, 1155 UNTS 331 (hereinafter VCLT), Art. 34.

[78] VCLT, Arts. 35, 36. See generally on the issue of third states and treaties, Christine Chinkin, *Third Parties in International Law* (Oxford, 1993) 25–144.

[79] For discussion see Bush (vol. I), 99–103; Stefan Brunner, 'Article 10 of the Antarctic Treaty Revisited' in Francesco Francioni and Tullio Scovazzi (eds.), *International Law for Antarctica* (Milan, 1987) 27–51.

[80] See Antarctic Treaty, Art. VIII(1).

[81] See Recommendation VIII-8 and the discussion in Bush (vol. I), 99, *Handbook* (Pt 1), 149.

[82] Recommendation VIII-8. Pakistan, a non-party, has recently engaged in scientific research in Antarctica. It is understood that, through diplomatic channels, Pakistan has been urged to accede to the Treaty; however, there are no indications that such a course of action will be taken in the immediate future.

acceded. It is therefore difficult to argue that on the basis of the law of treaties, the Antarctic Treaty can apply to third states.

An additional argument for the application of both the Antarctic Treaty and the ATS to non-parties concerns the characterisation of the ATS as an objective regime which applies *erga omnes* against the whole world.[83] The difficulty with this argument is the uncertainty which surrounds the concept of objective regimes.[84] Some of the characteristics of an objective regime are: an intention on the part of the original Treaty parties to establish a regime valid for all states; that the regime has a sufficiently precise object; that there is a general international interest in the objective regime governing that object; and general acceptance by the international community of that objective quality.[85] The main difficulty in arguing that the ATS is an objective regime is the attitude of non-parties. Not only have states outside the ATS expressly failed to acknowledge its legitimacy, but beginning with the UN debates in 1982 they have criticised and questioned its legitimacy.[86] The difficulties with this argument are confirmed by the views of a large number of commentators who do not accept that the ATS is an objective regime.[87]

The final argument which exists for the application of the ATS against other states is that the Treaty has become a part of customary international law.[88] While the law of treaties does contemplate the provisions of a treaty becoming customary international law and binding third states,[89] this is also a difficult argument to make with respect to the Antarctic Treaty. The Treaty only has regional application and does not intend to apply globally to all states or to territories beyond the Treaty's limits. While the state practice of the Treaty parties may have been consistent enough to create regional customary

[83] Bruno Simma, 'The Antarctic Treaty as a Treaty Providing for an "Objective Regime"' (1986) 19 Cornell ILJ 189–209.

[84] This uncertainty was heightened following the International Law Commission's decision not directly to address the issue when preparing a draft Convention on the Law of Treaties: see Patricia Birnie, 'The Antarctic Regime and Third States' in Rudiger Wolfrum (ed.), *Antarctic Challenge II* (Berlin, 1986) 239 at 243–5; Simma, 'The Antarctic Treaty' at 192–7; Triggs, *International Law and Australian Sovereignty* at 145.

[85] Watts, *International Law* at 296.

[86] Chinkin, *Third Parties* at 83.

[87] Triggs, *International Law and Australian Sovereignty* at 150; Birnie, 'The Antarctic Regime' at 261; Auburn, *Antarctic Law* at 117; Watts, *International Law* at 296–8; *cf.* Orrego Vicuna, *Antarctic Mineral Exploitation* at 432–4.

[88] Simma, 'The Antarctic Treaty' at 202–8; Triggs, *International Law and Australian Sovereignty* at 147–50; Birnie, 'The Antarctic Regime' at 242–3.

[89] VCLT, Art. 38.

obligations binding upon them, the position for non-parties is different. Apart from mutual recognition granted by some other Treaty parties, Antarctic territorial claims have not been expressly recognised by non-parties. Those third states which have engaged in activities in the region, have not expressly recognised the legally binding nature of the ATS. The United Nations debates and suggestions by some states that the Antarctic Treaty be replaced by another form of international management further indicate a lack of consistent state practice and belief that the Treaty is legally binding. Given the weakness then of these arguments, it is difficult to assert that either the Antarctic Treaty itself or the ATS binds third states.[90]

There has not yet been much debate over whether the Arctic legal regime applies against third parties. This reflects the different realities of the Arctic where much of the region falls either within the sovereignty or maritime jurisdiction of the eight Arctic states. If the Arctic states do seek to assert more active jurisdiction, either individually or collectively, over those parts of the Arctic Ocean which are currently beyond the limits of national jurisdiction then the issue of enforcement against third states will arise. This particularly may become an issue with any efforts to halt the effects of transboundary pollution in the Arctic, the majority of such pollution currently being extra-regional.

Polar regions, international cooperation and international law

While the polar legal regimes can be subject to criticism because of their inability to accommodate certain interests or to enforce their provisions against both parties and non-parties, no viable alternatives currently exist to replace the regimes which are in place. Despite the discussion over the applicability of the common heritage of mankind concept, there is no example of an operating regime based on common heritage that has been tested. Both common heritage and other management options also ignore the fact that territorial sovereignty has been asserted in the polar regions and that it is unlikely that claimant states would relinquish their claims even in the face of UN-sponsored initiatives.

[90] *Cf.* Watts, *International Law* at 298 who suggests with reference to Arts. I and V that an '"objective" quality might attach to a part of the Antarctic Treaty regime even if not to all of it'.

Without the ATS there was a strong possibility that Antarctica could have become the scene of territorial conflict. It would have been impossible to conduct scientific research at the level which has been achieved without international cooperation. Likewise, there was scope for unregulated resource development to occur which could have had an irreparable environmental impact. At this level of achievement, the ATS must be considered successful. However, even at a higher level, from the perspective of managing a whole continent and region, the ATS must be considered a success. Richard Falk has commented that: 'The governance of Antarctica . . . is the closest thing to a "world order miracle" that the world has known.'[91] The miracle is that it has been possible to create and develop a legal regime over the course of thirty years which continues to operate to the satisfaction of the Treaty parties. This is an unusual record in international law. It is also unusual in that the Treaty and the ATS are firmly based on international law principles in which the parties place considerable confidence.

Slowly, a similar approach is also emerging in the Arctic. While it has been able to survive without a highly developed legal regime for much of this century, the push for a more integrated regime during the past twenty years reflects an understanding on the part of the Arctic states that their region can benefit from multilateral cooperation in attempting to deal with transboundary problems. Individually, states are unable to meet the challenges posed in protecting the Arctic environment. Cooperative efforts through a legal regime provides them with the ability to make collective and united responses. This demonstrates that it is possible, even in regions of great strategic importance, to develop successfully multilateral cooperative mechanisms through international law. This remains the most important lesson provided by the Arctic and Antarctic.

[91] Richard Falk, 'The Antarctic Treaty System: Are There Viable Alternatives?' in Arnfinn Jorgensen-Dahl and Willy Ostreng (eds.), *The Antarctic Treaty System in World Politics* (London, 1991) 399 at 399.

Bibliography

BOOKS AND EDITED COLLECTIONS

Alexander, Lewis M. and Hanson, Lynne Carter (eds.) *Antarctic Politics and Marine Resources: Critical Choices for the 1980s*. Centre for Ocean Management Studies, University of Rhode Island: Kingston, RI. 1984

Amstrup, Steven C. and Wiig, Oystein (eds.). *Polar Bears*: Proceedings of the Tenth Working Meeting of the IUCN/SSC Polar Bear Specialist Group 25–9 October 1988, Sochi, USSR (Occasional Papers of the IUCN Species Survival Commision (SSC) No. 7) IUCN: Gland, Switzerland. 1991

Andresen, Steinar and Ostreng, Willy (eds.), *International Resource Management: The Role of Science and Politics*. Belhaven Press: London. 1989

Antarctic Treaty System: An Assessment. National Academy Press: Washington. 1986

Archer, Clive (ed.). *The Soviet Union and Northern Waters*. Routledge: London. 1988

Archer, Clive and Scrivener, David (eds.). *Northern Waters: Security and Resource Issues*. Croom Helm: London. 1986

Arctic Council Panel (Franklyn Griffiths and Rosemarie Kuptana, co-chairs). *To Establish an International Arctic Council: A Framework Report*. Canadian Arctic Resources Committee: Ottawa. 1991

Armstrong, Terence, Roberts, Brian and Swithinbank, Charles. *Illustrated Glossary of Snow and Ice* (2nd). Scott Polar Research Institute: Cambridge. 1973

Attard, David Joseph. *The Exclusive Economic Zone in International Law*. Clarendon Press: Oxford. 1987

Auburn, F. M. *Antarctic Law and Politics*. C. Hurst & Co.: London. 1982

The Ross Dependency. Martinus Nijhoff: The Hague. 1972

Bankes, Nigel and Staples, Lindsay. *Canadian–US Relations in the Arctic Borderlands*. Canadian Arctic Resources Committee: Ottawa. 1991

Beck, Peter. *The International Politics of Antarctica.* Croom Helm: London. 1986

Benninghoff, W. S. and Bonner, W. N. *Man's Impact on the Antarctic Environment: A Procedure for Evaluating Impacts from Scientific and Logistic Activities.* Scientific Committee on Antarctic Research: Cambridge. 1985

Bernier, J. E. *Master Mariner and Arctic Explorer.* Le Droit: Ottawa. 1939

Bernier, Pierre. *The Arctic Grail: The Quest for the Northwest Passage and the North Pole 1818–1909.* Penguin: New York. 1988

Birnie, Patricia W. *International Regulation of Whaling* (2 vols.). Oceana: New York. 1985

Birnie, Patricia W. and Boyle, Alan E. *International Law and the Environment.* Clarendon Press: Oxford. 1992

Blake, Gerald (ed.). *Maritime Boundaries and Ocean Resources.* Croom Helm: London. 1987

Blum, John Morton (ed.). *The Price of Vision: The Diary of Henry A. Wallace 1942–1946.* Houghton Mifflin: Boston. 1973

Boggs, S. W. *The Polar Regions: Geographical and Historical Data for Consideration in a Study of Claims to Sovereignty in the Arctic and Antarctic Regions.* William S. Hein: Buffalo, NY. 1990 (1933 reprint)

Brigham, Lawson W. (ed.) *The Soviet Maritime Arctic.* Belhaven Press: London.

Brownlie, I. *Principles of Public International Law.* 4th. Clarendon: Oxford. 1990

Brubaker, Douglas. *Marine Pollution and International Law.* Belhaven Press: London. 1993

Bruel, E. *International Straits* (vol. I). Nyt nordisk Forlag: Copenhagen. 1947

Bush, W. M. *Antarctica and International Law: A Collection of Inter-State and National Documents* (4 vols. and binder). Oceana: London. Vol I/II – 1982; Vol III/IV – 1988; Binder – 1990

Butler, William E. *Northeast Arctic Passage.* Sijthoff & Noordhoff: Alphen aan den Rijn. 1978

The Soviet Union and the Law of the Sea. Johns Hopkins Press: Baltimore. 1971

Perestroika and International Law. Martinus Nijhoff: Dordrecht. 1990

The Law of the Sea and International Shipping: Anglo-Soviet Post-UNCLOS Perspectives. Oceana: New York. 1985

Byers, R. B. and Slack, Michael (eds.). *Strategy and the Arctic.* Canadian Institute of Strategic Studies: Toronto. 1986

Caldwell, Lynton Keith. *International Environmental Policy.* Duke University Press: Durham, NC. 1984

Caldwell, Nathaniel French, Jr. *Arctic Leverage: Canadian Sovereignty and Security.* Praeger: New York. 1990

Canadian Institute of International Affairs. *The Arctic Environment and Canada's International Relations* (The Report of a Working Group of the

National Capital Branch) Canadian Arctic Resources Committee: Ottawa. 1991

The North and Canada's International Relations (The Report of a Working Group of the National Capital Branch) Canadian Arctic Resources Committee: Ottawa. 1988

Challenges of a Changing World. Fridtjof Nansen Institute: Lysaker. 1991

Charney, Jonathan I. (ed.). *The New Nationalism and the Use of Common Spaces: Issues in Marine Pollution and the Exploitation of Antarctica*. Allanheld, Osmun: Totowa, NJ. 1982

Chinkin, Christine. *Third Parties in International Law*. Clarendon Press: Oxford. 1993

Christie, E. W. Hunter. *The Antarctic Problem*. George Allen & Unwin: London. 1951

Churchill, R. R. and Lowe, A. V. *The Law of the Sea* (rev. ed.). Manchester University Press: Manchester. 1988

Churchill, Robin and Ulfstein, Geir. *Marine Management in Disputed Areas*. Routledge: London. 1992

Churchill, Robin and Freestone, David (eds.). *International Law and Global Climate Change*. Graham & Trotman: London. 1991

Churchill, Robin, Nordquist, Myron and Lay, S. Houston (eds.). *New Directions in the Law of the Sea*. vol. V. Oceana: Dobbs Ferry, NY. 1977

Clancy, Peter. *Native Hunters and the State: The 'Caribou Crisis', in the Northwest Territories*. (Queen's University, Department of Political Studies Programme of Studies in National and International Development) Queen's University: Kingston, Ontario. 1987

Clingan, T. A. (ed.). *The Law of the Sea: What Lies Ahead?* Law of the Sea Institute: Honolulu. 1988

Contemporary International Law Issues: Sharing Pan-European and American Perspectives. Martinus Nijhoff: Dordrecht. 1992

Cook, Grahame (ed.). *The Future of Antarctica: Exploitation Versus Preservation*. Manchester University Press: Manchester. 1990

Cox, David and Rauf, Tariq. *Security Co-operation in the Arctic: A Canadian Response to Murmansk*. Canadian Centre for Arms Control and Disarmament: Ottawa. 1989

Crawford, James and Rothwell, Donald R. (eds.). *The Law of the Sea in the Asian Pacific Region*. Martinus Nijhoff: Dordrecht. 1995

Crossley, Louise. *Explore Antarctica*. Cambridge University Press: Cambridge. 1995

De Yturriaga, Jose A. *Straits Used for International Navigation: A Spanish Perspective*. Martinus Nijhoff: Dordrecht. 1991

Dellenbrant, Jan Ake and Olsson, Mats-Olav (eds.). *The Barents Region: Security and Economic Development in the European North*. Cerum: Umea, Sweden. 1994

Dosman, Edgar J. *The National Interest: The Politics of Northern Development 1968–75*. McClelland and Stewart: Toronto. 1975

Dosman, Edgar J. (ed.). *Sovereignty and Security in the Arctic.* Routledge: London. 1989

Dyer, Ira and Chryssostomidis, Chryssostomos (eds.). *Arctic Technology and Policy.* Hemisphere Publishing Corporation: Washington. 1984

Elias, T. O. *The Modern Law of Treaties.* Oceana: Dobbs Ferry, NY. 1974

Elliott, Lorraine M. *Continuity and Change in Cooperative International Regimes: The Politics of the Recent Environmental Debate in Antarctica* (Working Paper 1991/3) Department of International Relations, Australian National University: Canberra. 1991

Energy Law '86. Matthew Bender: New York. 1986

Environmental Defense Fund. *Securing Environmental Protection in Antarctica.* Environmental Defense Fund: Washington. 1989

Faegteborg, Mads (ed.). *Towards an International Indigenous Arctic Policy.* Arctic Infomation's Forlag: Copenhagen. 1993

Feld, Werner J., Jordan, Robert S. and Hurwitz, Leon. *International Organisations – A Comparative Approach.* Praeger: New York. 1983

Fenwick, Judith. *International Profiles of Marine Scientific Research.* Woods Hole Oceanographic Institute: Woods Hole, MA. 1992

Flegg, Jim, Hosking, Eric and Hosking, David. *Poles Apart.* Pelham Books: London. 1990

Fox, Robert. *Antarctica and the South Atlantic: Discovery, Development and Dispute.* British Broadcasting Corporation: London. 1985

Francioni, Francesco and Scovazzi, Tullio (eds.). *International Law for Antarctica.* Giuffre Editore: Milan. 1987

International Responsibility for Environmental Harm. Graham & Trotman: London. 1991

Franckx, Erik. *Maritime Claims in the Arctic: Canadian and Russian Perspectives.* Martinus Nijhoff: Dordrecht. 1993

Freeman, Milton M. R. and Carbyn, Ludwig N. (eds.). *Traditional Knowledge and Renewable Resource Management in Northern Regions.* Boreal Institute for Northern Studies: Edmonton. 1988

Gay, James Thomas. *American Fur Seal Diplomacy.* Peter Lang: New York. 1987

Genest, Eugenio A. *La Convencion para la Conservacion de las Focas Antarticas y el Sistema del Tratado Antartico.* Instituto Antartico Argentino: Buenos Aires. 1991

Gon, O. and Heemstra, P. C. (eds.). *Fishes of the Southern Ocean.* J. L. B. Smith Institute of Ichthyology: Grahamstown, South Africa. 1990

Grant, Shelagh D. *Sovereignty or Security? Government Policy in the Canadian North 1936–1950.* University of British Columbia Press: Vancouver. 1988

Griffiths, Franklyn (ed.). *The Politics of the Northwest Passage.* McGill–Queen's University Press: Kingston, Ontario. 1987

Hackworth, Green Haywood. *Digest of International Law* (vol. I). United States Government Printing Office: Washington. 1940

Hamzah, B. A. (ed.). *Antarctica in International Affairs.* Institute for Strategic and International Studies: Kuala Lumpur. 1987

Handmer, John (ed.). *Antarctica: Policies and Policy Development.* Centre for Resource and Environmental Studies, Australian National University: Canberra. 1989

Handmer, John and Wilder, Martijn (eds.). *Towards a Conservation Strategy for the Australian Antarctic Territory.* Centre for Resource and Environmental Studies, Australian National University: Canberra. 1993

Harris, Stuart (ed.). *Australia's Antarctic Policy Options.* Centre for Resource and Environmental Studies, Australian National University: Canberra. 1984

Harrison, J. M. and Beauchamp, Ken (eds.). *Ocean Policy and Management in the Arctic.* Canadian Arctic Resources Committee: Ottawa. 1984

Heininen, Lassi (ed.). *Arctic Environmental Problems* (2nd). Tampere Peace Institute: Tampere. 1990

Herr, R. A., Hall, H. R. and Haward, M. G. (eds.). *Antarctica's Future: Continuity or Change?* Tasmanian Government Printing Office: Hobart. 1990

Honderich, John. *Arctic Imperative: Is Canada Losing the North?* University of Toronto Press: Toronto. 1987

Hudson, Manley O. *Cases and Materials on International Law* (2nd). West: St Paul, MN. 1936

Hunter Miller, David. *The Alaska Treaty.* Limestone Press: Kingston, Ontario. 1981

Huntington, Henry P. *Wildlife Management and Subsistence Hunting in Alaska.* Belhaven Press: London. 1992

Hurrell, Andrew and Kingsbury, Benedict (eds.). *The International Politics of the Environment.* Clarendon Press: Oxford. 1992

International Union for the Conservation of Nature and Natural Resources (IUCN). *A Strategy for Antarctic Conservation.* IUCN: Gland, Switzerland. 1991

World Conservation Strategy: Living Resource Conservation for Sustainable Development. IUCN: Gland, Switzerland. 1980

International Work Group for Indigenous Affairs. *Arctic Environment: Indigenous Perspectives.* (IWGIA Document 69) International Work Group for Indigenous Affairs: Copenhagen. 1991

Inuit Circumpolar Conference. *Direct Involvement of the Arctic's Indigenous Peoples in the International Arctic Council.* Inuit Circumpolar Conference: Ottawa. 1992

Principles and Elements for a Comprehensive Arctic Policy. Centre for Northern Studies and Research (McGill University): Montreal. 1992

Jennings, Sir Robert and Watts, Sir Arthur. *Oppenheim's International Law* (9th, vol. I). Longman: Harlow, Essex. 1992

Jessup, Philip C. and Taubenfeld, Howard J. *Controls for Outer Space and the Antarctic Analogy.* Columbia University Press: New York. 1959

Johnston, Douglas M. (ed.). *Arctic Ocean Issues in the 1980s*. Law of the Sea Institute, University of Hawaii: Honolulu. 1982

Johnston, Douglas M. and Saunders, Phillip M. (eds.). *Ocean Boundary Making: Regional Issues and Developments*. Croom Helm: London. 1988

Jorgensen-Dahl, Arnfinn and Ostreng, Willy (eds.). *The Antarctic Treaty System in World Politics*. Macmillan: London. 1991

Joyner, Christopher C. *Antarctica and the Law of the Sea*. Martinus Nijhoff: Dordrecht. 1992

Joyner, Christopher C. and Chopra, Sudhir K. (eds.). *The Antarctic Legal Regime*. Martinus Nijhoff: Dordrecht. 1988

Jussila, Heikki, Persson, Lors Olaf and Wiberg, Ulf (eds.). *Shifts in Systems at the Top of Europe*. FORA: Stockholm. 1993

Keage, P. L. *Antarctic Protected Areas: Future Options*. University of Tasmania (Environmental Studies Occasional Paper No. 19): Hobart. 1986

Keohane, Robert O. *After Hegemony: Cooperation and Discord in the World Political Economy*. Princeton University Press: Princeton, NJ. 1984

Keohane, Robert O. and Nye, Joseph S. *Power and Interdependence: World Politics in Transition*. Little, Brown and Co.: Boston. 1977

Kerry, K. R. and Hempel, G. (eds.). *Antarctic Ecosystems: Ecological Change and Conservation*. Springer-Verlag: Berlin. 1990

Kim, Dalchong *et al.* (eds.). *Maritime Issues in the 1990s: Antarctica, Law of the Sea and Marine Environment*. Institute of East and West Studies, Yonsei University: Seoul. 1992

Kimball, Lee A. *Southern Exposure: Deciding Antarctica's Future*. World Resources Institute: Washington. 1990

Special Report on the Antarctic Minerals Convention. World Resources Institute: Washington. 1988

King, W. F. *Report Upon the Title of Canada to the Islands North of the Mainland of Canada*. Department of the Interior (Canada): Ottawa. 1905

Kish, John. *The Law of International Spaces*. A. W. Sijthoff: Leiden. 1973

Kiss, Alexandre and Shelton, Dinah. *International Environmental Law*. Graham & Trotman: London. 1991

Koh, K. L. *Straits in International Navigation*. Oceana: London. 1982

Kotlyakov, V. M. and Sokolov, V. E. (eds.). *Arctic Research Advances and Prospects* (Pt 2). Nauka: Moscow. 1990

Krasner, Stephen D. (ed.). *International Regimes*. Cornell University Press: Ithaca, NY. 1983

Kwiatkowska, Barbara. *The 200 Mile Exclusive Economic Zone in the New Law of the Sea*. Dordrecht: Martinus Nijhoff. 1989

Lamb, John M. (ed.). *Proceedings of a Conference on 'A Northern Foreign Policy for Canada'*. Canadian Polar Commission and Canadian Centre for Global Security: Ottawa. 1994

Lewis Smith, R. I., Walton, D. W. H. and Dingwall, P. R. (eds.). *Developing the Antarctic Protected Area System*. IUCN: Gland, Switzerland. 1994

Lovering, J. F. and Prescott, J. R. V. *Last of Lands . . . Antarctica*. Melbourne

University Press: Carlton, Victoria. 1979
Lyck, Lise (ed.). *Nordic Arctic Research on Contemporary Arctic Problems.* Nordic Arctic Research Forum: Copenhagen. 1992
Lyster, Simon. *International Wildlife Law.* Grotius Publications: Cambridge. 1985
Macdonald, R. St. J. (ed.). *The Arctic Frontier.* University of Toronto Press: Toronto. 1966
Manheim, Bruce. *On Thin Ice: The Failure of the National Science Foundation to Protect Antarctica.* Environmental Defense Fund: Washington. 1988
Marine Resources Project (University of Manchester). *Marine Resources of the Polar Regions: Scientific and Technological Priorities.* University of Manchester: Manchester. 1986
Massey Stewart, John (ed.). *The Soviet Environment: Problems, Policies and Politics.* Cambridge University Press: Cambridge. 1992
Matthews, Jessica Tuchman (ed.). *Preserving the Global Environment.* W. W. Norton & Co.: New York. 1991
Mawson, Douglas. *The Home of the Blizzard: Being the Story of the Australasian Antarctic Expedition, 1911–1914* (2 vols.). Greenwood Press: New York. 1915 (repr. 1969)
McConnell, W. H. *Commentary on the British North America Act.* Macmillan: Toronto. 1977
McNair, A. *The Law of Treaties.* Clarendon Press: Oxford. 1961
McRae, D. and Munro, G. (eds.). *Canadian Oceans Policy: National Strategies and the New Law of the Sea.* University of British Columbia Press: Vancouver. 1989
Moore, John Bassett. *History and Digest of International Arbitrations to which the United States has been a Party* (vol. I). Government Printing Office (US): Washington. 1898
Morrison, William R. *Under the Flag: Canadian Sovereignty and Native People in Northern Canada.* Research Branch, Department of Indian and Northern Affairs (Canada): Ottawa. 1984
Mosley, Geoff. *Antarctica: Our Last Great Wilderness.* Australian Conservation Foundation: Hawthorn, Victoria. 1986
Mottola, Kari (ed.). *The Arctic Challenge: Nordic and Canadian Approaches to Security and Cooperation in an Emerging International Region.* Westview: Boulder, CO. 1988
National and Regional Interests in the North: Third Workshop on People, Resources, and the Environment North of 60°. Canadian Arctic Resources Committee: Ottawa. 1984
Nelson, J. G., Needham, Roger and Norton, Linda (eds.). *Arctic Heritage: Proceedings of a Symposium.* Association of Canadian Universities for Northern Studies: Ottawa. 1987
O'Connell, D. P. *International Law* 2nd (2 vols.). Stevens & Son: London. 1970
The International Law of the Sea (vol. I), I. A. Shearer (ed.). Clarendon Press: Oxford. 1982

O'Connell, D. P. (ed.). *International Law in Australia.* Law Book Company: Sydney. 1966

Orrego Vicuna, Francisco. *Antarctic Mineral Exploitation.* Cambridge University Press: Cambridge. 1988

The Protection of the Antarctic Environment. Fridtjof Nansen Institute (International Antarctic Regime Project No. 5): Lysaker, Norway. 1992

Orrego Vicuna, Francisco (ed.). *Antarctic Resources Policy: Scientific, Legal and Political Issues.* Cambridge University Press: Cambridge. 1983

Osherenko, Gail and Young, Oran R. *The Age of the Arctic.* Cambridge University Press: Cambridge. 1989

Ostreng, Willy. *Politics in High Latitudes: The Svalbard Archipelago.* C. Hurst & Co.: London. 1977

Peterson, M. J. *Managing the Frozen South.* University of California Press: Berkeley, CA. 1988

Pharand, Donat. *Canada's Arctic Waters in International Law.* Cambridge University Press: Cambridge. 1988

The Law of the Sea of the Arctic wtih Special Reference to Canada. University of Ottawa Press: Ottawa. 1973

The Northwest Passage Arctic Straits. Martinus Nijhoff: Dordrecht. 1984

Popov, L. A. (ed.). *Research Papers on Marine Mammals of the North Pacific, 1989–1990.* Vniro: Moscow. 1991

Quigg, Philip W. *A Pole Apart.* McGraw-Hill: New York. 1983

Radioactivity and Environmental Security in the Oceans: New Research and Policy Priorities in the Arctic and North Atlantic (Proceedings). Woods Hole Oceanographic Institute: Woods Hole, MA. 1993

Rey, Louis (ed.). *The Arctic Ocean.* Macmillan Press: London. 1982

Ritberger, Volker (ed.). *International Regimes in East–West Politics.* Pinter Publishers: London. 1990

Rosenau, James N. and Tromp, Hylke (eds.). *Interdependence and Conflict in World Politics.* Avebury: Aldershot, UK. 1989

Rosenne, Shabtai. *Developments in the Law of Treaties, 1945–1986.* Cambridge University Press: Cambridge. 1989

Rothwell, D. R. *Maritime Boundaries and Resource Development: Options for the Beaufort Sea.* Canadian Institute of Resources Law: Calgary. 1988

Sahurie, Emilio J. *The International Law of Antarctica.* New Haven Press: New Haven, CT. 1992

Sand, Peter H. *Marine Environment Law in the United Nations Environment Programme.* Tycooly Publishing: London. 1988

Sand, Peter H. (ed.). *The Effectiveness of International Environmental Agreements: A Survey of Existing Legal Instruments.* Grotius Publications: Cambridge. 1992

Sands, Philippe (ed.). *Greening International Law.* Earthscan Publications: London. 1993

Schatz, Gerald S. (ed.). *Science, Technology and Sovereignty in the Polar Regions.*

Lexington Books: Lexington, MA. 1974
Scientific Committee on Antarctic Research. *Man's Impact on the Antarctic Environment.* Scientific Committee on Antarctic Research: Cambridge. 1985
The Role of Antarctica in Global Climate Change. Scientific Committee on Antarctic Research: Cambridge. 1989
Shapley, Deborah. *The Seventh Continent.* Resources for the Future, Inc.: Washington. 1985
Shearer, I. A. *Starke's International Law.* 11th. Butterworths: London. 1994
Sikumiut 'The People Who Use the Sea Ice'. Canadian Arctic Resources Committee: Ottawa. 1984
Smedal, Gustav. *Acquisition of Sovereignty over Polar Areas.* I Kommisjon Hos Jacob Dybwad: Oslo. 1931
Smith, Gordon W. *Territorial Sovereignty in the Canadian North: A Historical Outline of the Problem.* Northern Co-ordination Research Centre, Department of Northern Affairs and Natural Resources (Canada): Ottawa. 1963
Stirling, Ian. *Polar Bears.* University of Michigan Press: Ann Arbor. 1988
Stokke, Olav Schram and Tunander, Ola (eds.). *The Barents Region: Cooperation in Arctic Europe.* Sage Publications: London. 1994
Stonehouse, Bernard. *North Pole South Pole.* McGraw-Hill Ryerson: Toronto. 1990
Polar Ecology. Blackie: Glasgow. 1989
Arctic Air Pollution. Cambridge University Press: Cambridge. 1986
Strategies for Protecting Arctic Wilderness (proceedings from a symposium at the 5th World Wilderness Congress, Tromso, 1993) Directorate for Nature Management (Norway): Trondheim. 1994
Sugden, David. *Arctic and Antarctic.* Basil Blackwell: Oxford. 1982
Taracouzio, T. A. *The Soviet Union and International Law.* Macmillan: New York. 1935 (repr. 1972)
The Arctic: Choices for Peace and Security. Gordon Soules Book Publishers: West Vancouver. 1989
Theutenberg, Bo Johnson. *The Evolution of the Law of the Sea.* Tycooly International Publishing: Dublin. 1984
Tikkanen, E. *et al.* (eds.). *Symposium on the State of the Environment and Environmental Monitoring in Northern Fennoscandia and the Kola Peninsula.* Arctic Centre, University of Lapland: Rovaniemi. 1992
Triggs, Gillian D. *International Law and Australian Sovereignty in Antarctica.* Legal Books: Sydney. 1986
The Antarctic Treaty Regime: Law, Environment and Resources. Cambridge University Press: Cambridge. 1987
Tunander, Ola. *Cold Water Politics.* Sage Publications: London. 1989
VanderZwaag, David (ed.). *Canada Ocean Law and Policy.* Butterworths: Toronto. 1992
VanderZwaag, David L. and Lamson, Cynthia (eds.). *The Challenge of Arctic*

Shipping: Science, Environmental Assessment, and Human Values. McGill–Queen's University Press: Montreal. 1990

Verhoeven, Joe, Sands, Philippe and Bruce, Maxwell (eds.). *The Antarctic Environment and International Law.* Graham & Trotman: London. 1992

Watts, Sir Arthur. *International Law and the Antarctic Treaty System.* Grotius Publications: Cambridge. 1992

Wells, John. *Antarctic Resources: A Dichotomy of Interest.* Australian National University (Strategic and Defence Studies Centre Working Paper No. 242): Canberra. 1991

Westermeyer, William E. and Shusterich, Kurt M. (eds.). *United States Arctic Interests: The 1980s and 1990s.* Springer-Verlag: New York. 1984

Whiteman, M. M. *Digest of International Law* (vol. IV). US Department of State: Washington. 1963

Wiig, Oystein, Born, Erik W. and Garner, Gerald W. (eds.). *Polar Bears.* Proceedings of the Eleventh Working Meeting of the IUCN/SSC Polar Bear Specialist Group 25–7 January 1993, Copenhagen, Denmark (Occasional Papers of the IUCN Species Survival Commission (SSC) No. 10) IUCN: Gland, Switzerland. 1995

Wilder, Martijn. *Liability on Ice: Environmental Damage and the Antarctic Madrid Protocol.* Centre for Resource and Environmental Studies (Working Paper 1993/3): Canberra. 1993

Wolfrum, Rudiger. *The Convention on the Regulation of Antarctic Mineral Resource Activities.* Springer-Verlag: Berlin. 1991

Antarctic Challenge. Duncker & Humblot: Berlin. 1984

Antarctic Challenge II. Duncker & Humblot: Berlin. 1986

Antarctic Challenge III. Duncker & Humblot: Berlin. 1988

Wonders, William C. (ed.). *The Arctic Circle: Aspects of the North from the Circumpolar Nations.* Longman Canada: Don Mills, Ontario. 1976

Working Group on Arctic International Relations (Franklyn Griffiths and Oran R. Young, Co-chairs) 'Protecting the Arctic's Environment' (Third Session, Moscow and Murmansk, USSR, 22–7 January 1990) *Reports and Papers* (1990–1)

'Sustainable Development and the Arctic' (Second Session, Ililissat and Nuuk, Greenland, 20–4 April 1989) *Reports and Papers* (1989–1)

World Commission on Environment and Development. *Our Common Future.* Oxford University Press: Oxford. 1987

Young, Oran R. *Arctic Politics.* University of New England Press: Dartmouth, NH. 1992

International Cooperation: Building Regimes for Natural Resources and the Environment. Cornell University Press: Ithaca, NY. 1989

International Governance: Protecting the Environment in a Stateless Society. Cornell University Press: Ithaca, NY. 1994

Natural Resources and the State. University of California Press: Berkeley, CA. 1981

The Arctic in World Affairs. University of Washington: Seattle. 1989

Young, Oran R. and Osherenko, Gail (eds.). *Polar Politics*. Cornell University Press: Ithaca, NY. 1993

JOURNAL ARTICLES AND CONFERENCE PAPERS

'Antarctic Treaty: Comprehensive Protection for Antarctica' (1991) 21(1) *Environmental Policy and Law* 11–13

'Antarctica – A Continent of Harmony?' (1980) 51(2) *Australian Foreign Affairs Record* 4–12

'Arctic Council: Canada Prepares for a New Era in Circumpolar Relations' (Summer 1991) 19(2) *Northern Perspectives* 1–23

'Arctic Council Discussions Update' (1993) 2(1) *Circumpolar Notes* 1

'Arctic Nations Approve Council Framework Agreement' (Summer 1992) 2(6) *CARC Members' Update* 2

'Arctic Pollution: How Much Is Too Much?' (1990) 18(3) *Northern Perspectives* 1–8

'Argentine Ship Sinks Near Palmer Station' (1989) 24(2) *Antarctic Journal of the United States* 3–7

'Chamber for Environmental Matters' (1993) 23(6) *Environmental Policy and Law* 243

'First Meeting of Arctic Monitoring and Assessment Task Force' (Spring 1992) 6 *Arctic Research of the United States* 121–2

'International Law and International Relations Theory: Building Regimes' (1992) 86 ProcAmSocIL 167–87

'Legal Problems and the Political Situation in the Polar Areas' (1958) 52 ProcAmSocIL 145–74

'Legal Regimes of the Arctic' (1988) 82 ProcAmSocIl 315–34

'NSF Issues Final Regulations for Antarctic Conservation Act' (1989) 24(1) *Antarctic Journal of the United States* 1–3

'Soviet Nuclear Legacy' (1993) 26(10) *Marine Pollution Bulletin* 536

'The Arctic Zone of International Inspection Proposed in 1957 and 1958' (1960–61) 10 *Polar Record* 153–7

'The Future of the Antarctic Regime: New Directions' (1991) 85 ProcAmSocIL 461–82

'USA: Arctic Sovereignty' (June/July 1985) *International Canada* 1

Abbott, Kenneth W. 'Elements of a Joint Discipline' (1992) 86 ProcAmSocIL 167–72

'Modern International Relations Theory: A Prospectus for International Lawyers' (1989) 14 *Yale Journal of International Law* 335–411

Alexander, Frank C. 'Legal Aspects: Exploitation of Antarctic Resources' (1978–1979) 33 U Miami LR 371–423

Alexander, Lewis M. 'Exceptions to the Transit Passage Regime: Straits with Routes of "Similar Convenience"' (1987) 18 ODIL 479–91

'Regional Arrangements in the Oceans' (1977) 71 AJIL 84–109

Andersen, Charles and Rowell, Judy. 'Joint Management Inaction – George River Caribou Herd' (1991) 11 (Special Issue 7) *Rangifer* 67–72

Anderson, D. H. 'Legal Implications of the Entry into Force of the UN Convention on the Law of the Sea' (1995) 44 ICLQ 313–26

Anderson, Robert M. 'Leading International Efforts to Improve Environmental Controls in Antarctica While Navigating National Politics' (1994) 6 *Georgetown International Environmental Law Review* 303–51

Antinori, Camile. 'The Bering Sea: A Maritime Delimitation Dispute Between the United States and the Soviet Union' (1987) 18 ODIL 1–47

Archer, Clive. 'Arctic Cooperation: A Nordic Model' (1990) 21(2) *Bulletin of Peace Proposals* 165–74

'General Features of Political Development and Possibilities for Cooperation in the Arctic' (1988) 11(4) *Current Research on Peace and Violence* 137–45

'Western Responses to the Murmansk Initiative' (1989) 14 *Centrepiece* (Centre for Defence Studies, Aberdeen)

Armstrong, T. E. 'Soviet Proposals for the Arctic: A Policy Declaration by Mr Gorbachev' (1988) 24 *Polar Record* 68–9

'The Northern Sea Route, 1990' (1991) 27 *Polar Record* 136–8

'The Northern Sea Route, 1991' (1992) 28 *Polar Record* 239–40

'Tourists Visit the North Pole, 1990' (1991) 27 *Polar Record* 130

Auburn, F. M. 'Aspects of the Antarctic Treaty System' (1988) 26 *Archiv Des Völkerrechts* 203–15

'Consultative Status under the Antarctic Treaty' (1979) 28 ICLQ 514–22

'International Law – Sea-Ice – Jurisdiction' (1970) 48 CanBR 776–82

'Convention on the Regulation of Antarctic Mineral Resource Activities' (1990) 51 *Antarctic Research Series* 259–71

'International Law and Sea-Ice Jurisdiction in the Arctic Ocean' (1973) 22 ICLQ 552–7

'The Antarctic Environment' (1981) *Year Book of World Affairs* 248–65

Aust, Anthony. 'The Theory and Practice of Informal International Instruments' (1986) 35 ICLQ 787–812

Baker, Jim. 'Protecting an Arctic Refuge: A Summer of Decision for the ANWR' (Summer 1993) *Arctic Circle* 16–21

Balch, Thomas Willing. 'The Arctic and Antarctic Regions and the Law of Nations' (1910) 4 AJIL 265–75

Bankes, N. D. 'A Migratory Cariboo Convention' (1980) 18 CYIL 285–300

'Environmental Protection in Antarctica: A Comment on the Convention on the Conservation of Antarctic Marine Living Resources' (1981) 19 CYIL 303–19

'Forty Years of Canadian Sovereignty Assertion in the Arctic, 1948–87' (1987) 40 *Arctic* 285–91

'The Status of Hudson Bay' (1987) 15(3) *Northern Perspectives* 14–15

Barinaga, Marcia and Lindley, David. 'Wrecked Ship Causes Damage to Antarctic Ecosystem' (1989) 337 (6207: 9 February) *Nature* 495

Barr, William and Wilson, Edward A. 'The Shipping Crisis in the Soviet

Eastern Arctic at the Close of the 1983 Navigation Season' (1985) 38 *Arctic* 1–17

Barsh, Russel Lawrence. 'Demilitarizing the Arctic as an Exercise of Indigenous Self-Determination' (1985) 54 Nordic JIL 208–17

Beck, Peter J. 'Another Sterile Annual Ritual? The United Nations and Antarctica 1987' (1988) 24 *Polar Record* 207–12

'Antarctica, Vina del Mar and the 1990 UN Debate' (1991) *Polar Record* 211–16

'Convention on the Regulation of Antarctic Mineral Resource Activities: A Major Addition to the Antarctic Treaty System' (1989) 25 *Polar Record* 19–32

'Entering the Age of Polar Regions: The Arctic and Antarctic are No Longer Poles Apart' (1989) 18(1) *AMBIO* 92–4

'Managing Antarctic Tourism: A Front-Burner Issue' (1994) 21 *Annals of Tourism Research* 375–86

'Managing the Last Great Wilderness: Antarctica Today' (paper presented at the British International Studies Association Conference, University of Wales, Swansea, December 1992)

'Preparatory Meetings for the Antarctic Treaty 1958–59' (1985) 22 *Polar Record* 653–64

'The 1991 UN Session: The Environmental Protocol Fails to Satisfy the Antarctic Treaty System's Critics' (1992) 28 *Polar Record* 307–14

'The United Nations and Antarctica' (1984) 22 *Polar Record* 137-44

'The United Nations and Antarctica, 1992: Still Searching for the Elusive Convergence of View' (1993) 29 *Polar Record* 313–20

'The United Nations and Antarctica 1993: Continuing Controversy about the UN's Role in Antarctica' (1994) 30 *Polar Record* 257–64

'The United Nations' Study on Antarctica, 1984' (1985) 22 *Polar Record* 499–504

Begley, Sharon, Shenitz, Bruce and Underhill, William. 'Ice Cubes for Penguins' (4 April 1995) 116 (5964) *The Bulletin* 64

Berkman, Paul Arthur 'The Antarctic Marine Ecosystem and Humankind' (1992) 6 *Reviews in Aquatic Science* 295–333

Besley, J. A. 'Rights and Responsibilities of Arctic Coastal States: The Canadian View' (1971) 3 JMLC 1–12

Blay, S. K. N. 'New Trends in the Protection of the Antarctic Environment: The 1991 Madrid Protocol' (1992) 86 AJIL 377–99

Blay, S. K. N. and Tsamenyi, B. M. 'Australia and the Convention on the Regulation of Antarctic Mineral Resource Activities (CRAMRA)' (1990) 26 *Polar Record* 195–202

'The Convention on the Regulation of Antarctic Mineral Resource Activities (CRAMRA): Can a Claimant Veto It?' (1989) 1 *ASOLPO Paper*

Blay, S. K. N., Piotrowicz, R. W. and Tsamenyi, B. M. 'Antarctica after 1991: The Legal and Policy Options' (1989) 2 *ASOLPO Paper*

Bloomfield, Lincoln P. 'The Arctic: Last Unmanaged Frontier' (1981–82) 60

Foreign Affairs 87–105
Boczek, Boleslaw A. 'The Protection of the Antarctic Ecosystem: A Study in International Environmental Law' (1983) 13 ODIL 347–425
'The Soviet Union and the Antarctic Regime' (1984) 78 AJIL 834–58
Boer, Ben. 'World Heritage Disputes in Australia' (1992) 7 *Journal of Environmental Law and Litigation* 247–79
Bogart, P. S. 'Environmental Threats in Antarctica' (1988) 31(2) *Oceanus* 104–7
Bonner, W. Nigel. 'Environmental Assessment in the Antarctic' (1989) 18(1) AMBIO 83–9
Boyd, Susan B. 'The Legal Status of the Arctic Sea Ice: A Comparative Study and a Proposal' (1984) 22 CYIL 98–152
Boyle, Alan E. 'Remarks – Legal Regimes of the Arctic' (1988) 82 ProcAmSocIL 315–34
Breitfuss, Leonid. 'Territorial Division of the Arctic' (1928–9) 8 *Dalhousie Review* 456–69
Brigham, Lawson W. 'Arctic Icebreakers: US, Canadian, and Soviet' (1986) 29(1) *Oceanus* 47–58
'Plying the Northern Sea Route: Challenges and Opportunities of a New Era of the Soviet Arctic' (1991) 4(1) *Arctic Circle* 10–11
Brubaker, Douglas. 'International Law and Russian Arctic Waters' (1992) 12 *International Challenges* 97–106
Burmester, Henry C. 'Liability for Damage from Antarctic Mineral Resource Activities' (1989) 29 VaJIL 621–60
Bush, William M. 'The Future of the Antarctic Regime: New Directions' (1991) 85 ProcAmSocIL 470–5
Butler, W. E. 'Joint Ventures and the Soviet Arctic' (1990) 14 *Marine Policy* 169–76
'New Soviet Legislation on Straight Baselines' (1971) 20 ICLQ 750–2
Butterworth, Douglas S. 'Antarctic Marine Ecosystem Management' (1986) 23 *Polar Record* 37–47
Caflisch, Lucius. 'The Interaction of Science and Politics in the Field of International Relations: The Case of Antarctica' (1992) 28 *Polar Record* 159–62
Canfield, Jeffrey L. 'Recent Developments in Bering Sea Fisheries Conservation and Management' (1993) 24 ODIL 257–89
Caron, David D. 'Arctic – 1990: The Year in Review' (1990) 1 YIEL 181–5
'The International Whaling Commission and the North Atlantic Marine Mammal Commission: The Institutional Risks of Coercion in Consensual Structures' (1995) 89 AJIL 154–74
'Toward an Arctic Environmental Regime' (1993) 24 ODIL 377–92
Carroll, James E. 'Of Icebergs, Oil Wells, and Treaties: Hydrocarbon Exploitation Offshore Antarctica' (1983) 19 Stanford JIL 207–27
Champ, Michael A. *et al.* 'The Roles of Monitoring and Research in Polar Environments: A Perspective' (1992) 25 *Marine Pollution Bulletin* 220–6

Chinkin, C. M. 'The Challenge of Soft Law: Development and Change in International Law' (1989) 38 ICLQ 850–66

Churchill, R. R. 'Maritime Delimitation in the Jan Mayen Area' (1985) 9 *Marine Policy* 16–38

Clute, A. R. 'The Ownership of the North Pole' (1927) 5 CanBR 19–26

Cohen, Maxwell. 'The Arctic and the National Interest' (1970) 26 IntJ 52–81

Conforti, Benedetto. 'Territorial Claims in Antarctica: A Modern Way to Deal With an Old Problem' (1986) 19 Cornell ILJ 249–58

Crawford, James and Rothwell, Donald R. 'Legal Issues Confronting Australia's Antarctica' (1992) 13 AYIL 53–88

Critcheley, W. Harriet. 'Polar Deployment of Soviet Submarines' (1984) 39 IntJ 828–65

'The Arctic' (1987) 42 IntJ 769–88

Croxall, J. P., Everson, I. and Miller, D. G. M. 'Management of the Antarctic Krill Fishery' (1992) 28 *Polar Record* 64–6

Dalton, Jane Gilliland. 'The Chilean Mar Presencial: A Harmless Concept or a Dangerous Precedent?' (1993) 8(3) *International Journal of Marine and Coastal Law* 397–418

De La Barra, Oscar Pinochet. 'Reminiscences of the 1959 Antarctic Treaty Conference' (1992) 27(2) *Antarctic Journal of the United States* 9–11

Dehner, W. Joseph. 'Creeping Jurisdiction in the Arctic: Has the Soviet Union Joined Canada?' (1972) 13 *Harvard International Law Journal* 271–88

Donnelly, Jack. 'International Human Rights: A Regime Analysis' (1986) 40 IntOrg 599–642

Dorn, Walter A. 'An International Monitoring Agency for the Arctic' (1989) 15(1) *Information North* (newsletter of the Arctic Institute of North America) 1–4

Dryzek, John S., Clark, Margaret L. and McKenzie, Garry. 'Subject and System in International Interaction' (1989) 43 IntOrg 475–503

Duffield, John S. 'International Regimes and Alliance Behaviour: Explaining NATO Conventional Force Levels' (1992) 46 IntOrg 819–55

Dunlap, William V. 'Bering Sea: The Donut Hole Agreement' (1995) 10 *International Journal of Marine and Coastal Law* 114–35

Edwards, David M. and Heap, John A. 'Convention on the Conservation of Antartic Marine Living Resources: A Commentary' (1981) 20 *Polar Record* 353–62

Eidsvik, Harold. 'Under Joint Responsibility: The Kluane–Wrangell–St Elias World Heritage Site' (1983) 12(3/4) AMBIO 191–6

Eikeland, Per Ove. 'Distributional Aspects of Multispecies Management: The Barents Sea Large Marine Ecosystem' (1993) 17 *Marine Policy* 256–71

Elferink, Alex Oude. 'The 1990 USSR–USA Maritime Boundary Agreement' (1991) 6 IJECL 41–52

Ellis, Sara L. 'Japanese Whaling in the Antarctic: Science or Subterfuge?' (1988) 31(2) *Oceanus* 68–9

Elzinga, Aant and Bohlin, Ingemar. 'The Politics of Science in Polar Regions' (1989) 18(1) AMBIO 71–6

Everson, Inigo. 'Antarctic Fisheries' (1978) 19 *Polar Record* 233–51

Feder, Barnaby J. 'A Legal Regime for the Arctic' (1976–8) *Ecology Law Quarterly* 785–829

Fenge, Terry. 'An Arctic Treaty: With Teeth' (Spring 1993) *Arctic Circle* 12–13

'Environmental Clean-up and Sustainable Development in the Circumpolar Arctic' (1993–1994) 21(4) *Northern Perspectives* 1–3

'Parks and Protected Areas in the North: Completing the Agenda' (1994) 22(2–3) *Northern Perspectives* 1–2

Fernholm, Bo and Rudback, Goran T. 'Marine Resource Management for the Antarctic' (1989) 18(1) AMBIO 68–70

Fikkan, Ann. 'Polar Bears – Hot Topic in Cold Climate' (1990) 10(2) *International Challenges* 32–8

Floistad, Brit and Stokke, Olav Schram. 'Common Concerns – National Interests: Norway, the Soviet Union and the Barents Sea Fisheries' (1989) 9(2) *International Challenges* 23–30

Fogelson, Nancy. 'The Tip of the Iceberg: The United States and International Rivalry for the Arctic, 1900–25' (1985) 9 *Diplomatic History* 131–48

Foreman, Elaine F. 'Protecting the Antarctic Environment: Will a Protocol Be Enough?' (1992) 7 *American University Journal of International Law and Policy* 843–79

Fotinov, Vadim. 'United Northern Emirates: The Future of the Former Soviet North?' (1991) 2(3) *Arctic Circle* 10–11

Francioni, Francesco. 'Resource Sharing in Antarctica: For Whose Benefit?' (1990) 1 *European Journal of International Law* 258–68

'The Madrid Protocol on the Protection of the Antarctic Environment' (1993) 28 TexILJ 47–72

Franckx, Erik. 'Nature Protection in the Arctic: A New Soviet Legislative Initiative' (1991) 6 IJECL 377–83

'Nature Protection in the Arctic: Recent Soviet Legislation' (1992) 41 ICLQ 366–86

'New Developments in the Northeast Passage' (1991) 6 IJECL 33–40

'Non-Soviet Shipping in the Northeast Passage, and the Legal Status of Proliv Vil'kitskogo' (1988) 24 *Polar Record* 269–76

Freestone, David. 'Maritime Boundary in the Area Between Greenland and Jan Mayen (Denmark v. Norway)' (1989) 4 IJECL 67–70

Friedheim, Robert L. 'The Regime of the Arctic – Distributional or Integrative Bargaining?' (1988) 19 ODIL 493–510

Frostad, Lisa. 'Northern Forum Update' (Fall 1991) 5 *Arctic Research of the United States* 60–1

Fry, Samuel E. 'The Arctic and United States Foreign Policy, 1730–1990' (Fall 1990) 4 *Arctic Research of the United States* 31–47

Gallagher, Anne. 'The "New" Montreal Protocol and the Future of International Law for the Protection of the Global Environment' (1992) 14 *Houston Journal of International Law* 267–361

Gambell, Ray. 'Bowhead Whales and Alaskan Eskimos: A Problem of Survival' (1983) 21 *Polar Record* 467–73

Gardam, Judith G. 'Management Regimes for Antarctic Marine Living Resources – An Australian Perspective' (1985) 15 MULR 279–312

Gillies Ross, W. 'Canadian Sovereignty in the Arctic: The Neptune Expedition of 1903–04' (1976) 29 *Arctic* 87–104

Gizewski, Peter. 'Arctic Security After the Thaw: A Post-Cold War Reassessment (Report of the Panel on Arctic Security)' (1993) 17 *Aurora Papers* (Canadian Centre for Global Security)

Goldie, L. F. E. 'International Relations in Antarctica' (1958) 30 *Australian Quarterly* 7–29

Golitsyn, Vladimir. 'The Arctic – On the Way to Regional Cooperation' (1989) 1 *Marine Policy Reports* 91–9

Graham, G. 'An Arctic Foreign Policy for Canada' (March/April 1987) *International Perspectives* 11–14

Greig, D. W. 'Sovereignty and the Falkland Islands Crisis' (1983) 8 AYIL 20–70

'Sovereignty, Territory and the International Lawyer's Dilemma' (1988) 26 *Osgoode Hall Law Review* 127–75

'Territorial Sovereignty and the Status of Antarctica' (1978) 33 *Australian Outlook* 117–29

Haas, Ernst B. 'On Systems and International Regimes' (1974–75) 27 *World Politics* 147-74

'Regime Decay: Conflict Management and International Organizations, 1945–1981' (1983) 37 IntOrg 189–256

'Why Collaborate? Issue-Linkage and International Regimes' (1979–1980) 32 *World Politics* 357–405

Haas, Peter M. 'Do Regimes Matter? Epistemic Communities and Mediterranean Pollution Control' (1989) 43 IntOrg 377–403

Hagelin, Lena and Bogart, Paul, 'A Call for a World Park Antarctica' (1989) 18(1) AMBIO 95–6

Haggard, Stephan and Simmons, Beth A. 'Theories of International Regimes' (1987) 41 IntOrg 491–517

Handl, Gunther. 'Environmental Security and Global Challenge: The Challenge to International Law' (1990) 1 YIEL 3–33

'State Liability for Accidental Transnational Environmental Damage by Private Persons' (1980) 74 AJIL 525–65

'Territorial Sovereignty and the Problem of Transnational Pollution' (1975) 69 AJIL 50–78

Handmer, John and Wilder, Martijn. 'Australia and Environmental

Management in Antarctica' (1994) 1 *Australian Journal of Environmental Management* 175–91

Hanessian, J. 'Antarctica: Current National Interests and Legal Realities' (1958) 52 ProcAmSocIL 145–74

'The Antarctic Treaty 1959' (1960) 9 ICLQ 436–80

'The Antarctic Treaty Consultative Meetings – Form and Procedure' (1971) 5 *Cooperation and Conflict* 183–99

Harders, J. Enno. 'In Quest of an Arctic Legal Regime: Marine Regionalism – A Concept of International Law Evaluated' (1987) 11 *Marine Policy* 285–98

Harhoff, Frederik. 'Constitutional and International Legal Aspects of Aboriginal Peoples' (1988) 3 Nordic JIL 289–94

'Standardisation of Zones Within Specially Protected and Managed Areas under the Antarctic Environmental Protocol' (1994) 30 *Polar Record* 283–6

Harry, Ralph L. 'The Antarctic Regime and the Law of the Sea Convention: An Australian View' (1981) 21 VaJIL 727–44

Hawke, R. J. 'Government Plan for the Environment' (1989) 60 *Australian Foreign Affairs and Trade* 333–8

Hayashi, M. 'The Antarctica Question in the United Nations' (1986) 19 Cornell ILJ 275–90

Hayton, Robert D. 'Polar Problems and International Law' (1958) 52 AJIL 746-65

'The "American" Antarctic' (1956) 50 AJIL 583–610

'The Antarctic Settlement of 1959' (1960) 54 AJIL 349–71

Head, Ivan L. 'Canadian Claims to Territorial Sovereignty in the Arctic Regions' (1963–64) 9 *McGill Law Journal* 200–26

Heintzenberg, Jost. 'Arctic Haze: Air Pollution in Polar Regions' (1989) 18 *AMBIO* 50–5

Holdgate, Martin W. 'The Use and Abuse of Polar Environmental Resources' (1984) 22 *Polar Record* 25–48

Honderich, J. 'Canada–US Agreement on the Northwest Passage: Compromise or Cop-out?' (1988) 14(4) *Information North* (Newsletter of the Arctic Institute of North America) 1–4

Hong, Sungmin *et al.* 'Greenland Ice Evidence of Hemispheric Lead Pollution Two Millennia Ago by Greek and Roman Civilizations' (1994) 265 (5180) *Science* 1,841–3

Howard, Matthew. 'The Convention on the Conservation of Antarctic Marine Living Resources: A Five-Year Review' (1989) 38 ICLQ 104–49

Huebert, Rob. 'Polar Vision or Tunnel Vision: The Making of Canadian Arctic Waters Policy' (1995) 19 *Marine Policy* 343–63

Hunter Miller, David. 'Political Rights in the Arctic' (1925–26) 4 *Foreign Affairs* 47–60

Hyde, Charles Cheney. 'Acquisition of Sovereignty over Polar Areas' (1933–34) 19 *Iowa Law Review* 286–94

Innusuk, Rhoda. 'The Circumpolar Challenge' (1988) 3 Nordic JIL 348–52

Jahnke, Marlene, 'UNCED: Rio Conference on Environment and Development' (1992) 22(4) *Environment Policy and Law* 204–25

Jenisch, Uwe. 'The Arctic Ocean and the New Law of the Sea' (1984) 35 *Aussen Politik* 199–217

Jessup, Philip C. 'Sovereignty in Antarctica' (1947) 41 AJIL 117–19

Johnston, V. Kenneth. 'Canada's Title to the Arctic Islands' (1933) 14 *Canadian Historical Review* 24–41

Jones, Peter. 'Russia's Nuclear Dumping Legacy' (1993) 26(5) *Marine Pollution Bulletin* 231–2

Jorgensen-Dahl, Arnfinn. 'The Soviet–Norwegian Maritime Disputes in the Arctic: Law and Politics' (1990) 21 ODIL 411–29

Joyner, Christopher C. 'Ice-Covered Regions in International Law' (1991) 31 NatResJ 213–42

'Protection of the Antarctic Environment: Rethinking the Problems and Prospects' (1986) 19 Cornell ILJ 259–73

'The 1991 Madrid Environmental Protocol: Rethinking the World Park Status for Antarctica' (1992) 1(3) *Review of European Community and International Environmental Law* 328–39

'The Evolving Antarctic Minerals Regime' (1988) 19 ODIL 73–95

'The Exclusive Economic Zone and Antarctica' (1981) 21 VaJIL 691–725

'The Exclusive Economic Zone and Antarctica: The Dilemmas of Non-Sovereign Jurisdiction' (1988) 19 ODIL 469–91

'The Future of the Antarctic Regime: New Directions' (1991) 85 ProcAmSocIL 464–70

'The Southern Ocean and Marine Pollution: Problems and Prospects' (1985) 17 Case WRJIL 165–94

Kammerer, Jorn-Axel. 'The Protocol on Environmental Protection to the Antarctic Treaty' (1992) 45 *Law & State* 68–80

Kaye, Stuart. 'Legal Approaches to Polar Fisheries Regimes: A Comparative Analysis of the Convention for the Conservation of Antarctic Marine Living Resources and the Bering Sea Doughnut Hole Convention' (1995) 26 CalWILJ 75–112

Kaye, Stuart and Rothwell, Donald R. 'Australia's Antarctic Maritime Claims and Boundaries' (1995) 26 ODIL 195–226

'Australian Law in Antarctica' (1993) 29 *Polar Record* 215–18

Keage, P. L., Hay, P. R. and Russell, J. A. 'Improving Antarctic Management Plans' (1989) 25 *Polar Record* 309–14

Keith, Robert F. 'Arctic Borderlands: Environment and Development Issues in Canadian American Relations' (November 1991) 2 *Northern Notes* 27–51

'Canada's Arctic Environmental Strategy: Critique and Prospect' (1992) 8/9 *Northern Review* 38–113

Keith, Robert F. *et al.* 'Arctic Fisheries: New Approaches for Troubled Waters' (1987) 15(4) *Northern Perspectives* 1–5

Keohane, Robert O. 'International Institutions: Two Approaches' (1988) 32 *International Studies Quarterly* 379–96

Kettuner, P. A. 'The Status of the Northwest Passage under International Law' (1990) 4 *Detroit College of Law Review* 929–95

Keyunan, Zou: 'The Common Heritage of Mankind and the Antarctic Treaty System' (1991) 38 *Netherlands International Law Review* 173–98

Killas, Mark. 'The Legality of Canada's Claims to the Waters of the Arctic Archipelago' (1987) 19 Ottawa LR 95–136

Kimball, Lee A. 'Antarctica: The Challenges That Lie Ahead' (1989) 18 AMBIO 77–82

'Special Report on the Antarctic Minerals Convention' (1990) 51 *Antarctic Research Series* 273–310

'Whither Antarctica?' (1985) 11(3) *International Studies Notes* 16–21

Kock, Karl-Hermann. 'Fishing and Conservation in Southern Waters' (1994) 30 *Polar Record* 3–22

Koh, Tommy B. 'The Territorial Sea, Contiguous Zones, Straits and Archipelagoes under the 1982 Convention on the Law of the Sea' (1987) 29 *Malaya Law Review* 163–99

Kolodkin, Anatoly L. 'Remarks – Legal Regimes of the Arctic' (1988) 82 ProcAmSocIL 315–34

Kolodkin, A. L. and Volosov, M. E. 'The Legal Regime of the Soviet Arctic: Major Issues' (1990) 14 *Marine Policy* 158–68

Kolodkin, Anatoly, Mirovitskaya, Natalia and Roginko, Alexei. 'The Arctic: Arena for International Environmental Security?' (1993) 10 *Ocean Yearbook* 277–89

Krasner, S. 'The Toyko Round: Pluralistic Interests and Prospects for Stability in the Global Trading System' (1979) 23 *International Studies Quarterly* 491–531

Kratochwil, Friedrich and Ruggie, John Gerard. 'International Organization: A State of the Art on an Art of the State' (1986) 40 IntOrg 753–75

Kudrya, Arkady. 'A Growing Arctic Environmental Agenda' (July/August 1991) 1(2) *Arctic Circle* 10–11

Kusumaatmadja, M. 'The Concept of the Indonesian Archipelago' (1982) 10 *The Indonesian Quarterly* 12–26

Kwiatkowska, Barbara. 'Creeping Jurisdiction Beyond 200 Miles in the Light of the 1982 Law of the Sea Convention and State Practice' (1991) 2 ODIL 153–87

Kyriak, Michael T. 'The Future of the Antarctic Treaty System: An Examination and Evaluation of the "Common Heritage" and "World Park" Proposals for an Alternative Antarctic Regime' (1992) 7 *Auckland University Law Review* 105–26

Lakhtine, W. 'Rights over the Arctic' (1930) 24 AJIL 703–17

Lamson, Cynthia. 'Arctic Shipping, Marine Safety and Environmental Protection' (1987) 11 *Marine Policy* 3–15

Lamson, Cynthia and VanderZwaag, David. 'Arctic Waters: Needs and Options for Canadian-American Cooperation' (1987) 18 ODIL 49–99

Lansing, Robert. 'A Unique International Problem' (1917) 11 AJIL 763–71

Lawson, K. L. 'Delimiting Continental Shelf Boundaries in the Arctic: The United States–Canada Beaufort Sea Boundary' (1981) 22 VaJIL 221–46

Lee, Edward G. (compiler). 'Canadian Practice in International Law at the Department of External Affairs in 1989–90' (1990) 28 CYIL 472–588

Lindquist, T. R. 'The Iceberg Cometh? International Law Relating to Antarctic Iceberg Exploitation' (1977) 17 NatResJ 1–41

Lloyd, Trevor. 'Canada's Last Frontier' (1943) 3(4) *Behind the Headlines* 1–30

'Frontier of Destiny – The Canadian Arctic' (1946) 6(7) *Behind the Headlines* 1–16

'International Scientific Cooperation in the Arctic' (notes prepared for Vice-Presidential address, section on geology and geography, American Association for the Advancement of Science, Berkeley, California, 27 December 1965 – 'The Papers of Trevor Lloyd', National Archives of Canada, MG 30 B97, v. 46, File 1)

'Research and the Circumpolar North: One Canadian Viewpoint' (address to the Nansen Institute, Oslo, Norway, 18 May 1981 – 'The Papers of Trevor Lloyd', National Archives of Canada, MG 30 B97, v. 46)

'Some International Aspects of Arctic Canada' (1969–1970) 25 IntJ 717–25

'The New North' (1943) 1(8) *Canadian Affairs* 1–10

Luton, Gary. 'Strategic Issues in the Arctic Region' (1986) 6 *Ocean Yearbook* 399–416

Lyons, David. 'Environmental Impact Assessment in Antarctica under the Protocol on Environmental Protection' (1993) 29 *Polar Record* 111–20

M'Gonigle, R. Michael. 'Unilateralism and International Law: The Arctic Water Pollution Prevention Act' (1976) 34 *University of Toronto Faculty of Law Review* 180–98

MacLachlan, L. J. 'Comprehensive Aboriginal Claims in the NWT' (1992) 18(1) *Information North* 1–7

Makarov, R. R. *et al.* 'A Current Assessment of the Antarctic Krill Fishery' (1994) 18 *Polar Geography and Geology* 76–94

Marchal, Anne. 'Convention for the Conservation of Antarctic Seals: 1988 Review of Operations' (1989) 25 *Polar Record* 142–3

Maxwell, J. Barrie and Barrie, Leonard A. 'Atmospheric and Climatic Change in the Arctic and Antarctic' (1989) 18 *AMBIO* 42–9

McDorman, Ted L. 'In the Wake of the Polar Sea: Canadian Jurisdiction and the Northwest Passage' (1986) 10 *Marine Policy* 243-57

McKinnon, J. Bruce. 'Arctic Baselines: A Litore Usque Ad Litus' (1987) 66 CanBR 790–817

McKitterick, T. E. M. 'The Validity of Territorial and other Claims in Polar Regions' (1939) 21(I & IV) (3rd Ser.) *Journal of Comparative Legislation and*

International Law 89–97

McRae, D. M. 'Arctic Waters and Canadian Sovereignty' (1983) 38 IntJ 476–92

'Management of Arctic Marine Transportation: A Canadian Perspective' (1986) 39 *Arctic* 350–9

McRae, D. M. and Goundrey, D. J. 'Environmental Jurisdiction in the Arctic Waters: The Extent of Article 234' (1982) 16 UBCLR 197–228

Miles, P. and Wright, N. J. R. 'An Outline of Mineral Extraction in the Arctic' (1978) 19 *Polar Record* 11–38

Miller, D. G. M. 'Exploitation of Antarctic Marine Living Resources: A Brief History and a Possible Approach to Managing the Krill Fishery' (1991) 10 *South African Journal of Marine Science* 321–39

Miller, David Hunter. 'Political Rights in the Arctic' (1925–1926) 4 *Foreign Affairs* 47–60

Mokrousova, Z. I. *et al.* 'Environmental Pollution and Radiation Circumstances in the Russian Federation in November of 1992' (1993) No. 2 *Russian Meteorology and Hydrology* 99–100

Morrison, William R. 'Canadian Sovereignty and the Inuit of the Central and Eastern Arctic' (1986) 10(1/2) *Etudes Inuit Studies* 245–59

Mosley, Geoff. 'World Park for Antarctica' (1989) 17(5) *Habitat Australia* 4–7

Mouton, M. W. 'The International Regime of the Polar Regions' (1962) III ReDC 175–284

Nandan, S. N. and Anderson, D. H. 'Straits Used for International Navigation: A Commentary on Part III of the United Nations Convention on the Law of the Sea 1982' (1989) 60 BYIL 159–203

Nicol, Stephen. 'CCAMLR and its Approaches to Management of the Krill Fishery' (1991) 27 *Polar Record* 229–36

'Management of the Krill Fishery: Was CCAMLR Slow to Act?' (1992) 28 *Polar Record* 155–7

'No Agreement Yet on Krill Fishery' (December 1990) 64 *ANARE News* 6

Nicol, Stephen and De La Mare, William. 'Ecosystem Management and the Antarctic Krill' (1993) 81(1) *American Scientist* 36–47

Nussbaum, Ulrich. 'Legal Status of Antarctic Off-Shore Areas' (1993) 6 *ASOLPO Paper* 1–23

O'Connell, M. L. and Gold, E. 'The Modern Law of the Sea: Framework for the Protection and Preservation of the Marine Environment' (1991) 23 Case WRJIL 83–105

Opeskin, Brian R. and Rothwell, Donald R. 'Australia's Territorial Sea: International and Federal Implications of its Extension to 12 Miles' (1991) 22 ODIL 395–431

Orrego Vicuna, Francisco and Infante, Maria Teresa. 'Le droit de la mer dans l'Antarctique' (1980) 84 *Revue générale du droit international public* 340–50

Osherenko, Gail. 'Environmental Cooperation in the Arctic: Will the Soviets Participate?' (1989) 1 *International Environmental Affairs* 203–21

'Human/Nature Relations in the Arctic: Changing Perspectives' (1992) 28 *Polar Record* 277–84

Ostreng, Willy. 'Delimitation Arrangements in Arctic Seas: Cases of Precedence or Securing of Strategic/Economic Interests' (1986) 10 *Marine Policy* 132–54

'Soviet–Norwegian Relations in the Arctic' (1984) 39 IntJ 866–87

Ostreng, Willy and Simonsen, Henning. 'The Barents Region and the Northern Sea Route' (1992) 12(4) *International Challenges* 95–105

Ovanesyants, A. M. *et al.* 'Natural Environment Pollution from Oil and Gas Production and Refinery Industry' (1991) No. 8 *Soviet Meteorology and Hydrology* 96–7

Oxman, B. H. 'Antarctica and the New Law of the Sea' (1986) 19 Cornell ILJ 211–47

Page, Robert. 'Environmental Protection in the Canadian North' (June 1984) *International Business Lawyer* 253–60

Pain, Stephanie and Kleiner, Kurt. 'Frustrated West Watches as Arctic Oil Spill Grows' 5 November 1994, No. 1950, *New Scientist* 8

Palmer, Geoffrey. 'New Ways to Make International Environmental Law' (1992) 86 AJIL 259–83

Panjabi, Ranee Khooshie Lal. 'From Stockholm to Rio: A Comparison of the Declaratory Principles of International Environmental Law' (1993) 21 *Denver Journal of International Law and Policy* 215–87

Pannatier, Serge. 'Acquisition of Consultative Status under the Antarctic Treaty' (1994) 30 *Polar Record* 123–9

Parriott, Todd Jay. 'Territorial Claims in Antarctica: Will the United States Be Left Out in the Cold?' (1986) 22 Stanford JIL 67–121

Pearson, L. B. 'Canada Looks "Down North"' (1945–1946) 24 *Foreign Affairs* 638–47

Penhale, Polly A. 'Research Team Focuses on Environment Impact of Oil Spill' (1989) 24(2) *Antarctic Journal of the United States* 9–12

Peterson, M. J. 'Antarctic Implications of the New Law of the Sea' (1986) 16 ODIL 137–81

Pharand, Donat. 'Canada's Arctic Jurisdiction in International Law' (1983) 7 DalLJ 315–42

'Canada's Sovereignty over the Newly Enclosed Arctic Waters' (1987) 25 CYIL 325–43

'Canada's Sovereignty over the Northwest Passage' (1989) 10 *Michigan Journal of International Law* 653–78

'Innocent Passage in the Arctic' (1968) 6 CYIL 3–60

'Oil Pollution Control in the Canadian Arctic' (1971) 7 TexILJ 45–72

'Remarks – Legal Regimes of the Arctic' (1988) 82 ProcAmSocIL 328–32

'State Jurisdiction over Ice Island T-3: The Escamilla Case' (1971) 24 *Arctic* 83–9

'The Case for an Arctic Region Council and a Treaty Proposal' (1992) 23 *Revue générale de droit* 163–95

'The Legal Regime of the Arctic: Some Outstanding Issues' (1984) 39 IntJ 742–99
'The Legal Status of Ice Shelves and Ice Islands in the Arctic' (1969) 10 *Les cahiers de droit* 461–75
'The Legal Status of the Arctic Regions' (1979) II ReDC 53–115
'The Northwest Passage in International Law' (1979) 17 CYIL 99–133
Pollack, Herman and Anderson, Peter J. 'United States Policy for the Arctic' (1973) 1(1) *Arctic Bulletin* 2–3
Prestrud, Pal and Stirling, Ian. 'The International Polar Bear Agreement and the Current Status of Polar Bear Conservation' (1994) 20(3) *Aquatic Mammals* 113–24
Pullen, Thomas C. 'What Price Canadian Sovereignty?' (1987) 113(9) *Proceedings of the US Naval Institute* 66–72
Pullen, T. C. and Swithinbank, C. 'Transits of the Northwest Passage, 1906–1990' (1991) 27 *Polar Record* 365–7
Purver, Ronald. 'Arctic Security: The Murmansk Initiative and its Impact' (1988) 11(4) *Current Research on Peace and Violence* 147–58
'Security and Arms Control at the Poles' (1984) 39 IntJ 888–910
Redgwell, Catherine. 'Environmental Protection in Antarctica: The 1991 Protocol' (1994) 43 ICLQ 599–634
Reeves, J. S. 'Antarctic Sectors' (1939) 33 AJIL 519–21
Reid, Robert S. 'The Canadian Claim to Sovereignty over the Waters of the Arctic' (1974) 12 CYIL 111–36
Reimer, Chester. 'Moving Towards Co-operation: Inuit Circumpolar Policies and the Arctic Environmental Protection Strategy' (1993–1994) 21(4) *Northern Perspectives* 22–6
Reinhard, W. C. 'International Law: Implications of the Opening of the Northwest Passage' (1970) 74 *Dickenson Law Review* 678–90
Rey, Louis. 'The Arctic: Mankind's Unique Heritage and Common Responsibility' (1987) 19 *Arctic and Alpine Research* 345–50
'The Impact of Human and Industrial Activities on the Arctic Environment: Legal Considerations and International Liabilities' (paper presented at Arctic Atmospheric Pollution Conference, Scott Polar Research Institute, Cambridge, 2–5 September 1985)
Rich, Roland. 'A Minerals Regime for Antarctica' (1982) 31 ICLQ 709–25
Richardson, Ivor L. M. 'New Zealand's Claims in the Antarctic' (1957) 33 *New Zealand Law Journal* 38–42
Ries, Tomas. 'The Nordic Region and Post-Soviet Radioactive Pollution' (September 1993) 5(9) *Jane's Intelligence Review* 398–400
Riewe, Rick. 'The Demise of the Great White North: Environmental Impacts on the Circumpolar Aboriginal Peoples' (December 1992) 18(4) *Information North* 1–7
Roberts, Brian. 'International Co-Operation for Antarctic Development: The Test for the Antarctic Treaty' (1978) 19 *Polar Record* 107–20
Robertson, Gordon. 'Nunavut and the International Arctic' (May–June

1987) 15(2) *Northern Perspectives* 9
Robinson, Nicholas A. 'Universal and National Trends in International Environmental Law' (1993) 23(3/4) *Environmental Policy and Law* 148–54
Roginko, Alexei Yu. 'Arctic Environmental Cooperation: Prospects and Possibilities' (1989) 12 *Current Research on Peace and Violence* 133–43
Roginko, Alexei Yu and LaMourie, Matthew J. 'Emerging Marine Environmental Protection Strategies for the Arctic' (1992) 16 *Marine Policy* 259–76
Rogne, Odd. 'The International Arctic Science Committee: From Conception to Birth' (Fall 1990) 4 *Arctic Research of the United States* 65–9
Rosencranz, Armin and Scott, Antony. 'Siberia, Environmentalism, and Problems of Environmental Protection' (1991) 14 *Hastings International and Comparative Law Quarterly* 929–47
Roth, R. R. 'Sovereignty and Jurisdiction over Arctic Waters' (1990) 28 *Alberta Law Review* 845–72
Rothwell, Donald R. 'A Maritime Analysis of Conflicting International Law Regimes in Antarctica and the Southern Ocean' (1994) 15 AYIL 155–81
'A World Park for Antarctica? Foundations, Developments and Future' (1990) 3 *ASOLPO Paper*
'International Law and the Protection of the Arctic Environment' (1995) 44 ICLQ 280–312
'Polar Lessons for an Arctic Regime' (1994) 29 *Cooperation and Conflict* 55–76
'The Canadian–US Northwest Passage Dispute: A Reassessment' (1993) 26 Cornell ILJ 331–72
'The Madrid Protocol and its Relationship with the Antarctic Treaty System' (1992) 5 *ASOLPO Paper*
Rothwell, Donald R. and Kaye, Stuart. 'Law of the Sea and the Polar Regions: Reconsidering the Traditional Norms' (1994) 18 *Marine Policy* 41–58
Ruggie, J. C. 'International Responses to Technology: Concepts and Trends' (1975) 29 IntOrg 557–83
Sagers, Matthew J. 'Oil Spill in Russian Arctic' (1994) 18 *Polar Geography and Geology* 95–105
Salom, Don Eric. 'The United States Claim to Wrangel Island: The Dormancy Should End' (1981) 11 CalWILJ 140–67
Schachter, Oscar. 'The Twilight Existence of Nonbinding International Agreements' (1977) 71 AJIL 296–304
Scott, James Brown. 'Arctic Exploration and International Law' (1909) 3 AJIL 928–41
Scrivener, David. 'Resources and Environment in Norwegian–Soviet Relations in the Arctic' (paper presented to the BISA Annual Conference, 14–16 December 1992, Swansea)
Shakespeare, David. 'Recent US–USSR Agreements Relating to the Bering

Region' (Fall 1991) 5 *Arctic Research of the United States* 37–47

Shearer, I. A. 'Australia's New Maritime Zones' (1995) 69 *Australian Law Journal* 26–9

Sheldon, Jerome F. 'Oil Versus Caribou in the Arctic: The Great Debate' (1988) 24 *Polar Record* 95–100

Shevlin, James. 'Japanese Whaling Activity Observed near Davis Station' (1992) 69 *ANARE News* 18–19

Shusterich, Kurt M. 'The Antarctic Treaty System: History, Substance, and Speculation' (1984) 39 IntJ 800–27

Simma, Bruno. 'The Antarctic Treaty as a Treaty Providing for an "Objective Regime"' (1986) 19 Cornell ILJ 189–209

Slaughter, Anne-Marie. 'Book Review: *Regime Theory and International Relations*' (1995) 89 AJIL 454–6

Slaughter-Burley, Anne-Marie. 'International Law and International Relations Theory: A Dual Agenda' (1993) 87 AJIL 205–39

Smith, Gordon W. 'Canada's Arctic Archipelago: 100 Years of Canadian Jurisdiction, Part I: The Transfer' (1980) 17(1) *NorthNord* 10–15

'Canada's Arctic Archipelago: 100 years of Canadian Jurisdiction, Part II: Making the North Canadian' (1980) 17(2) *NorthNord* 10–17

Soroos, Marvin S. 'The Odyssey of Arctic Haze: Toward a Global Atmospheric Regime' (1992) 34(10) *Environment* 6–11, 25–7

Stirling, Ian. 'Attraction of Polar Bears *Ursus Maritimus* to Off-shore Drilling Sites in the Eastern Beaufort Sea' (1988) 24 *Polar Record* 1–8

'Research and Management of Polar Bears *Ursus Maritimus*' (1986) 23 *Polar Record* 167–76

Stirling, Ian and Calvert, Wendy. 'Environmental Threats to Marine Mammals in the Canadian Arctic' (1983) 21 *Polar Record* 433–49

Stirling, Ian and Derocher, Andrew E. 'Possible Impacts of Climate Warming on Polar Bears' (1993) 46 *Arctic* 240–5

Stokke, Olav Schram. 'The Northern Environment: Is Cooperation Coming?' (November 1990) 512 *Annals of the American Academy of Political and Social Science* 58–68

'Western Environmental Interests in the Arctic' (1991–92) 21 *Centre Piece* 1–42

Stokke, Olav Schram and Hoel, Alf Hakon. 'Fisheries Management in the Barents Region: Safeguards and Swaps' (1992) 12(4) *International Challenges* 69–80

Sullivan, W. 'The International Geophysical Year' (1959) 521 *International Conciliation* 259–336

Svarlien, Oscar. 'The Legal Status of the Arctic' (1958) 52 ProcAmSocIL 136–44

'The Sector Principle in Law and Practice' (1960) 10 *Polar Record* 248–63

Swithinbank, C., McClain, P. and Little, P. 'Drift Tracks of Antarctic Icebergs' (1977) 18 *Polar Record* 495–501

Talboys, B. E. 'New Zealand and the Antarctic Treaty' (1978) 28(3/4) *New*

Zealand Foreign Affairs Review 29-35

Tennberg, Monica. 'The Rovaniemi Process and New International Actors' (paper presented at the First International Congress of Arctic Social Sciences, Université Laval, Ste-Foy, Quebec, Canada, 28–31 October 1992)

Theutenberg, Bo Johnson. 'The Arctic Law of the Sea' (1983) 52 Nordic JIL 3–39

Thomas, Donald C. and Schaefer, James. 'Wildlife Co-management Defined: The Beverly and Kaminuriak Caribou Management Board' (1991) 11 (Special Issue 7) *Rangifer* 73–89

Timtchenko, Leonid. 'The Legal Status of the Northern Sea Route' (1994) 30 *Polar Record* 193-200

Todd, Frank S., Headland, R. K. and Lasca, Norman. 'Animals at the North Pole' (1992) 28 *Polar Record* 321–2

Toma, Peter A. 'Soviet Attitude Towards the Acquisition of Territorial Sovereignty in the Antarctic' (1956) 50 AJIL 611-26

Triggs, Gillian D. 'A Minerals Regime for Antarctica: Compromise or Conflict?' (1984) *Australian Mining and Petroleum Law Association Yearbook* 525–54

'Australan Sovereignty in Antarctica: Part II' (1982) 13 MULR 302–33

'The Antarctic Treaty Regime: A Workable Compromise or a "Purgatory of Ambiguity"' (1985) 17 Case WRJIL 195–228

Tucker Scully, R. 'The Eleventh Antarctic Treaty Special Consultative Meeting' (1991) 11(1) *International Challenges* 77–90

Tucker Scully, R. and Kimball, Lee A. 'Antarctic: Is There Life After Minerals?' (1989) 13 *Marine Policy* 87–98

Underdal, Arild. 'The Concept of Regime "Effectiveness"' (1992) 27 *Cooperation and Conflict* 227–40

Van Bennekom, Sander. 'A New Regime to Protect the Antarctic Environment' (1992) 5 *Leiden Journal of International Law* 33–52

VanderZwaag, David L. and Lamson, Cynthia. 'Ocean Development and Management in the Arctic: Issues in American and Canadian Relations' (1986) 39 *Arctic* 327–37

VanderZwaag, David and Pharand, Donat. 'Inuit and the Ice: Implications for Canadian Arctic Waters' (1983) 21 CYIL 53–84

VanderZwaag, David, Donihee, John and Faegteborg, Mads. 'Towards Regional Ocean Management in the Arctic: From Co-existence to Cooperation' (1988) 37 *UNB Law Journal* 1–33

Volkov, A. E. and de Korte, J. 'Protected Nature Areas in the Russian Arctic' (1994) 30 *Polar Record* 299–310

Wagner, M. W. and Thompson, J. G. 'The Migratory Birds Convention: Its History and the Need for an Amendment' (1993) 21(2) *Northern Perspectives* 2–5

Waldock, C. H. D. 'Disputed Sovereignty in the Falkland Islands Dependencies' (1948) 25 BYIL 311–53

Watts, A. D. 'The Convention on the Regulation of Antarctic Mineral Resource Activities, 1988' (1990) 39 ICLQ 169–82

Westermeyer, William E. and Goyal, Vinod. 'Jurisdiction and Management of Arctic Marine Transportation' (1986) 39 *Arctic* 338–49

Wirth, David A. 'Environment – Extraterritorial Effects of Activities of Federal Agencies – Waste Disposal in Antarctica – National Environmental Policy Act of 1969' (1993) 87 AJIL 626–35

Wrenn, Sue C. 'First Inuit Circumpolar Conference, 1977' (1978) 19 *Polar Record* 64–6

Wyrozumska, Anna. '*Erga Tertios* Effect of the Antarctic Treaty' (1993) 6 *ASOLPO Paper* 25–49

Young, Euan C. 'Ecology and Conservation of the Polar Regions' (1989) 18(1) AMBIO 23–33

Young, Oran R. '"Arctic Waters": The Politics of Regime Formation' (1987) 18 ODIL 101–14

'Global Commons: The Arctic in World Affairs' (1990) 93(2) *Technology Review* 52–61

'International Regimes: Problems of Concept Formation' (1979–1980) 32 *World Politics* 331–56

'International Regimes: Toward a New Theory of Institutions' (1986) 39 *World Politics* 104–22

'Political Leadership and Regime Formation: On the Development of Institutions in International Society' (1991) 45 IntOrg 281–308

'The Age of the Arctic' (1985–86) 61 *Foreign Policy* 160–79

'The Age of the Arctic' (1986) 29(1) *Oceanus* 9–17

'The Politics of International Regime Formation: Managing Natural Resources and the Environment' (1989) 43 IntOrg 349–75

Zacher, Mark W. 'Toward a Theory of International Regimes' (1990) 44(1) *Journal of International Affairs* 139–57

Zacher, Mark W. and McConnell, James G. 'Down to the Sea with Stakes: The Evolving Law of the Sea and the Future of the Deep Seabed Regime' (1990) 21 ODIL 71–103

Zuccaro, Emil A. 'Iceberg Appropriation and the Antarctic's Gordian Knot' (1979) 9 CalWILJ 405–29

DOCUMENTS

AEPS, Arctic Monitoring and Assessment Programme. *The Monitoring Programme for Arctic Monitoring and Assessment Programme, AMAP* (AMAP Report 93:3) Arctic Monitoring and Assessment Programme: Oslo. 1993

Report to Ministers – Update on Issues of Concern to the Arctic Environment, Including Recommendations for Action. Arctic Monitoring and Assessment Programme: Oslo. 1993

AEPS, Conservation of Arctic Flora and Fauna. *Report of the Working Group 1992–1993.* 1993

The State of Protected Areas in the Circumpolar Arctic 1994 (Habitat Conservation Report No. 1) Directorate for Nature Management (Norway): Trondheim. 1994

AEPS, Working Group on the Protection of the Arctic Marine Environment (PAME). *Report from the First Meeting* (Oslo, Norway, 3–5 May 1994)

AEPS. 'List of Major International Instruments and Policy Declarations Pertaining to the Arctic Environment' (final version, as presented at the Officials and Ministerial Meeting, 10–14 June 1991, Rovaniemi, Finland)

'Arctic Environmental Protection Meeting – Report' (Rovaniemi, Finland, 10–14 June 1991) Department of External Affairs and International Trade: Ottawa. 1991

'Protecting the Arctic Environment' (Report of the Yellowknife Preparatory Meeting, Yellowknife, NWT, Canada, 18–23 April 1990)

'Protecting the Arctic Environment' (Report of the Kiruna Preparatory Meeting, 15–17 January 1991)

'Protection of the Arctic Environment' (Report of the Consultative Meeting on the Protection of the Arctic Environment, Rovaniemi, 20–6 September 1989)

'Report of the Second Ministerial Conference' (Nuuk, Greenland, 16 September 1993)

Antarctic Treaty. *Final Report of the Fourteenth Antarctic Treaty Consultative Meeting* (Rio de Janeiro, 5–16 October 1987)

Final Report of the Fifteenth Antarctic Treaty Consultative Meeting (Paris, 9–20 October 1989)

Final Report of the Sixteenth Antarctic Treaty Consultative Meeting (Bonn, 7–18 October 1991)

Final Report of the Seventeenth Antarctic Treaty Consultative Meeting (Venice, 11–20 November 1992)

Final Report of the Eighteenth Antarctic Treaty Consultative Meeting (Kyoto, 11–22 April 1994)

Draft Final Report of the Nineteenth Antarctic Treaty Consultative Meeting (Seoul, 8–19 May 1995) (XIX ATCM/Working Paper 35: 19 May 1995)

Australia, House of Representatives, Standing Committee on Environment, Recreation and the Arts. *Tourism in Antarctica.* Australian Government Publishing Service: Canberra. 1989

Australia, House of Representatives, Standing Committee on Legal and Constitutional Affairs. *Australian Law in Antarctica.* Australian Government Publishing Service: Canberra. 1992

Australia, Senate, Standing Committee on Natural Resources. *The Natural Resources of the Australian Antarctic Territory.* Australian Government Publishing Service: Canberra. 1985

Canada, Department of Foreign Affairs and International Trade. *International Instruments Arctic Marine Pollution Prevention (Preliminary*

Draft). Department of Foreign Affairs and International Trade: Ottawa. 1994

Canada, Department of Indian and Northern Affairs. *Building International Relations in the Arctic: 25 Years of Canada–USSR Cooperation.* Department of Indian and Northern Affairs: Ottawa. 1991

The Arctic Environmental Strategy: An Action Plan. Department of Indian and Northern Affairs: Ottawa. 1991

The Western Arctic Claim: The Inuvialuit Final Agreement. Department of Indian and Northern Affairs: Ottawa. 1984

Canada, Report of the Special Joint Committee of the Senate and of the House of Commons on Canada's International Relations. *Independence and Internationalism.* Queen's Printer: Ottawa. 1986

Canada, Water Resources Division, Natural Resources and Environmental Branch, Indian and Northern Affairs. *Arctic Environmental Strategy Water Program, Annual Report 1993–1994.* Department of Indian and Northern Affairs: Ottawa. 1994

Commission for the Conservation of Antarctic Marine Living Resources. *Report of the Ninth Meeting of the Commission.* (Hobart, Australia, 22 October–2 November 1990)

Report of the Tenth Meeting of the Commission. (Hobart, Australia, 21 October–1 November 1991)

Report of the Eleventh Meeting of the Commission. (Hobart, Australia, 26 October–6 November 1992)

Report of the Twelfth Meeting of the Commission. (Hobart, Australia, 25 October–5 November 1993)

Report of the Thirteenth Meeting of the Commission (Hobart, Australia, 26 October–4 November 1994)

Schedule of Conservation Measures in Force 1992/93

International Arctic Science Committee. *Founding Articles for an International Arctic Science Committee.* International Arctic Science Committee: Ottawa. 1990

International Whaling Commission. 'A Southern Ocean Whale Sanctuary Proposed by the Government of France to the 44th Annual Meeting of the IWC' (IWC/44/19)

'Proposal for a Widely Accepted Southern Ocean Sanctuary' (IWC/46/53) 25 (May 1994)

North Atlantic Marine Mammal Commission. *Report of the Third Meeting of the Council* (Reykjavik, Iceland, 1–2 July 1993)

United Kingdom, Foreign and Commonwealth Office. *Convention on the Regulation of Antarctic Mineral Resource Activities: Article-by-Article Commentary Prepared by Members of the UK Delegation.* Foreign and Commonwealth Office: London. 1989

United Nations Conference on Environment and Development. *Agenda 21: Programme of Action for Sustainable Development.* UN Department of Public Information: New York. 1993

United Nations. Report of the Secretary-General: Study Requested Under General Assembly Resolution 38/77. *Question of Antarctica.* UN Doc. A/39/583: 31 October 1984

United Nations. Report of the Secretary-General. *Law of the Sea.* UN Doc. A/48/527: 10 November 1993

United States, Department of State. *Handbook of the Antarctic Treaty System* (8th/2 vols.) US Department of State: Washington. 1994.

United States of America, National Science Foundation. *Final Supplemental Environmental Impact Statement for the US Antarctic Program.* National Science Foundation: Washington. 1991

United States of America, Office of Technology and Assessment. *Polar Prospects: A Minerals Treaty for Antarctica.* US Congress, Office of Technology and Assessment: Washington. 1989.

United States of America, US Arctic Research Commission. *Arctic Research in a Changing World.* US Arctic Research Commission: Washington. 1991.

NEWSPAPERS

Australian. 24 April 1991, 5 July 1991

Canberra Times. 24 June 1991

Sydney Morning Herald. 21 June 1989, 30 September 1989, 12 December 1990, 1 May 1991, 15 June 1991, 20 June 1991, 5 July 1991, 30 June 1995

The [Toronto] Globe and Mail. 2 August 1985, 30 April 1991, 13 November 1992, 5 January 1993

The Ottawa Citizen. 26 August 1994

The Weekend Australian. 28–9 April 1995

Toronto Star. 10 May 1992

Washington Post. 11 October 1988

Whitehorse Star. 10 May 1990

Index

BOOKS IN THE SERIES

1 **Principles of the institutional law of international organizations**
C. F. Amerasinghe

2 **Fragmentation and the international relations of Micro-states**
Jorri Duursma

3 **The polar regions and the development of international law**
Donald R. Rothwell